This is dedicated to my beautiful wife Jennifer without who's help, support, and Love the book would never have been published.
My Love, My Co-writer and my Soul Mate.

Hartley Weston

Shadows on the Wind

Hartley A. Weston

Order this book online at www.trafford.com
or email orders@trafford.com

Most Trafford titles are also available at major online book retailers.

Note for Librarians: A cataloguing record for this book is available from Library
and Archives Canada at www.collectionscanada.ca/amicus/index-e.html

Printed in Victoria, BC, Canada.

ISBN: 978-1-4269-0189-8

*Our mission is to efficiently provide the world's finest, most comprehensive book publishing
service, enabling every author to experience success. To find out how to publish your book, your
way, and have it available worldwide, visit us online at www.trafford.com*

Trafford rev. 4/27/2010

 www.trafford.com

North America & international
toll-free: 1 888 232 4444 (USA & Canada)
phone: 250 383 6864 ♦ fax: 812 355 4082

Contents

End Of Innocence

MY INITIAL FORAY INTO COLORFULL world of "Bush Pilots" began innocently enough being born and raised in a small northern mining town next to the lake that abounded with a large and diversified collection of aircraft of the era both summer and winter coming and going in an endless stream at all hours.

Perhaps that auspicious beginning led the way to my eventually becoming a bush pilot, as it turned out a long and rewarding career that spanned a total of thirty six years, and what a diverse life style it offered, a virtual kaleidoscope of unparalleled adventure that included travel through out the realm of the Canadian north that few are familiar with including the high arctic regions where seemingly normal situations could all too easily end up as a threat to one's well being.

In time as I became accepted as one of them, it was learned the fraternity of bush pilots to be very tight knit whose members on the average largely tended toward being notoriously close mouthed while varying greatly in personality and individual traits, tending to-ward keeping their innermost thoughts and emotions to themselves.

How ever the individual reader perceives the following stories, that is strictly left up to them, my having kept a daily log of my flying experiences worthy of note through out the years the reader is warned that more than a few unusual experiences will appear to transcend the boundaries of reality, in some cases appearing to be so audacious that some may find as being difficult to accept as the truth and not the work of fiction or the results of a fertile imagination.

The following stories follow no special sequence or order being chosen at random in an attempt to offer the reader a cross section of an average bush pilot's life style, often cutting across months and years, also no apology is offered for the some times coarse language or colorful descriptions that go along with creating a vibrant scenario.

Bush flying in and of itself a cruel mistress that demands total and unswerving allegiance, and as about as easy to give up as breathing, comparable only to the unrelenting thirst of an alcoholic or the insatiable cravings of a drug addict.

No question about it about my making the best of my long career as a bush pilot, filled with enthusiasm, anxious energy, optimism, romance and most of all dreams of the future.

My home town of Red Lake Ont, a small mining town where an endless
Appearing stream of a seemingly vagrant population restlessly seething to and fro on the muddy streets bent on one purpose or another lending the air of excitement and diversity that made a lasting impression on a precocious child such as I who took note of their activities with great interest.

But best of all the town being the gate way to the north boasted of numerous aircraft of every type and description, one and all they filled me with a strange longing, my spending every available moment observing their activities as they came and went along with my tending toward being curious about all that transpired around me.

In them golden days people pretty much lived their chosen life style in what ever manner or location they chose to being free to do so as at this time the enervate of the pen had as yet to rear it's ugly head.

How I envied them swaggering larger than life pilots as they blasted off the ice or water with a mighty ear shattering roar leaving me hungering to accompany them, my mind conjuring up the sights, sounds and smells of far away and mysterious places.

Having eventually worked my way in to the good graces of the local airways chief (and only) base engineer who literally took me under his wing in putting my burning desire to learn more about the intricacies of aircraft operation and maintenance to good use, my learning quickly and well until totally trusted to correctly perform what ever job placed before me.

It soon became apparent that the aviation environment suited my make up, totally mesmerizing me. There was no turning back, my spending every available moment learning as much as possible each day, my first ride in an aircraft leaving me in such a state of wonderment and ecstasy I existed solely for the next one. This state of affairs of course solidifying my resolve to obtain my pilot's license at the first opportunity, but as green and uninformed of the challenge that lay before me still knew with a certainty if that momentous occasion ever to occur, a drastic change of pace required on my part in seeking suitable employment that would in time allow my garnering sufficient funds to see myself through flying school.

This eventually took place with my spending two consecutive years working as a diamond driller during the winters and as a hunting and fishing guide during the summers until acquiring a sufficient amount of long green to hike myself off to Thunder Bay to begin my flying lessons.

Completing the training regimen in good time eventually returned to Red

Lake with a brand new shiny Pilot's License and justly proud to have acquired it.

Still retaining a good portion of my hard earned money and anxious to move ahead, common sense dictated if one were to obtain any degree of flying experience then it best to acquire my own aircraft. This I did by taking the bus to Winnipeg to make a visit to the War Assets Corp. Where a brand new De-Havilland Tiger Moth still sitting in its crates awaited me.

Placing aside protracted details of how it went from there, only learning the hard way of the horrendous cost to have it assembled by a certified engineer that in my estimation took unfair advantage of my burning desire to have it assembled as quickly as possible in order to begin flying it and when finally completed the hair raising flight back to Red Lake Via Kenora to in an aircraft I could barely control at best.

There being no such thing as an airport in Red Lake at the time I had wisely for one with so little experience previously scouted out and marked what I felt to be an appropriate landing strip in an area known as the "slimes", a relatively flat area of crushed rock that had been dumped at one time by the long defunct Howey Gold Mine prior to making my way to Winnipeg to hopefully purchase a suitable aircraft.

The evening I arrived over head of the town after a long tiring harrowing trip in a state of near exhaustion from the unfamiliar stress of making an exceedingly long cross country trip in an unfamiliar aircraft to unwisely circle the town a few times unthinkingly bringing on unwanted attention to myself by doing so and being so totally hammered forgot to remain uptight to somehow manage a landing that didn't turn out to be an unmitigated disaster, oh god how good it felt to be back after enduring such a long stress filled day.

Upon shutting down the engine, at first only able to sit there enjoying the feeling of being back on solid ground in one piece before suddenly becoming aware of a crowd of people gathering around me. Climbing stiffly from the cockpit, stood on the wing in view of all to make a slightly theatric bow to the onlookers who gawked curiously at the aircraft as if uncertain what to make of it doing there filling me with pride of accomplishment, (Weston has arrived, mother's, lock up your daughters). Yes this was my moment to shine, posing on the wing of the aircraft like some kind of a Greek god imagining myself to cutting quite the imposing figure decked out in my WW11 sheepskin flight jacket complete with leather helmet and goggles slid up onto my forehead with a resplendent white scarf hanging jauntily from around my neck (shades of snoopy). Oh Christ what an arrogant ass I must have appeared to the crowd that of a certainty included well experienced bush pilots. No doubt some them wondering who the god dam fool was who possessed the unmitigated gall to fly a single engine aircraft into Red Lake on wheels yet, well for what it was worth they were free to accept my presence into their ranks any way they saw fit.

From then on it was a learning experience, honing my skills as a pilot every day possible, oh yes I certainly did at one point became cocky and overconfident but a few bad scares and a lot of good advice from the old timers eventually settled me down to survive my initial trials without inadvertently visiting disaster upon the machine or myself with good luck more often than consummate skill saving my bacon.

Well as it went the summer season flew on by all too quickly with the chill winds of late September swirling the dead leaves restlessly about while seemingly endless dark skeins of migrating geese wove their way through the azure sky bound for warmer climes.

If I wished to utilize my yellow peril during the long winter months that lay ahead, then it was a certainty it would have to be ski equipped. Putting off doing so as long as possible, finally made my way to a phone with the measured tread of a convicted felon on his way to the electric chair.

Upon Wally (my original engineer that initially assembled the Tiger Moth for me) who being quite astute could not help but to detect the quaver in my voice when asking for assistance in locating and installing a set of skis on the moth, the long dreaded "well my boy" boomed out of the receiver, it just so happens I know where a set of appropriate skis to fit your moth can be found, but they don't come cheap, and of course a set of axle bushing will have to be machined to fit the skis along with making up a set of bungee cord harness that requires manufacturing, not to mention the many special fittings to be welded to the air frame to attach them to, etc etc, by the time he ended what appeared to be an endless litany of requirements my eyes had crossed with my knees going weak, threatening to buckle at any given moment.

Fortunately having managed to a marked degree replenish my bank account selling sight seeing rides to an unsuspecting public, but realizing no where enough to satisfy Wally' sure to be usurious demands, it became abundantly clear my having to take a crash course in the fine art of ass kissing in order to see myself through.

The return trip to Winnipeg my initial trip in reverse, but this time carrying extra fuel and oil with me not wishing to be burned again by the high price of fuel at the Kenora airport. Arrogant I might have been, but still not stupid enough to attempt cross country flight over many miles of thick bush and half frozen lakes, even though in doing so it would have cut the approximate length of the trip in half.

By the time the skis had been installed and ready to go the bottom of the financial well had been near scraped dry, when it came to the soul shriveling time to settle up the charges Wally had levied against me I almost dropped to my knees there and then upon becoming fully aware of the horrendous burden entailed while owning and maintaining an aircraft, but be as it may, one wisely did not quibble over mere money with the great master if they intended to rely on his expertise in the future,

With my nerves all atremble and lips strangely stiff producing a high pitched quaver in my voice chirped out a stammering apology for not being able at the time to meet the full amount of the bill as presented squeaking out my intention to remit the balance within a reasonably short space of time upon returning to work.

This unexpected turn of events earned me a black look that well and truly informed me of his being less than overjoyed at my unexpectedly coming up short, but astute enough to realize their was little to be done about it short of seizing the aircraft, and that he realized to be counter productive reluctantly agreeing to accept my terms, his being well aware I would have sooner sand papered a polar bear's ass in a phone booth than stiff him.

The return trip mostly uneventful with the moth gaining about an indicated eight miles in air speed producing a blistering eighty three miles per hour. On arrival soon making it known to all and sundry of my being available and it being an opportune time for me as the world of aviation in Red Lake had taken an abrupt upturn with the advent of gold mining interests moving en masse into the area taking up the services of every available aircraft leaving the tardy or less fortunate scrambling to find what ever became available in air transport, this is were I came in to a limited degree having maintained an easy relationship with the owner of Chukuni Airways, an affable personage by the name of Joe Mackle who didn't resent my intrusion in the least, instead generously welcoming my services offering all the (as he referred to it) shit work I could handle plus being welcome to make use of the company's facilities greatly easing my logistical problems.

The internal capacity of the moth's front cockpit improved on by removing the instrument panel, seat and dual controls, installing a heavy plywood floor to cover over the gaping hole left behind.

Most of the work consisted of transporting trappers and fishermen, it definitely turning out to be a learning experience first jamming in the sleigh dogs who got the worst of it within the confined space and then piling the supplies on and around them, it always remained a wonder to me why they didn't perish from suffocation, but none ever did to my knowledge, them buggers must have been some tough!

Actually the hapless passenger on the average fared equally as badly forced to sit on whatever available with the remainder piled around and in some cases on top of them, never once did I know of anyone to complain, seeming to accept it all with good grace and infectious good humor. On arrival at the trap cabin or fish camp they would be dug out displaying no signs of experiencing acute discomfort except for the poor dogs who's unobvious lot evoked my sympathy, their being last out could barely wobble about on cramped stiffened legs, but that got them little if any sympathy from the trapper who once having his sled or toboggan untied from the wing struts cruelly yanked them into their harness and with a few telling blows from his birch club convinced them to move stiff and sore or not.

This more or less describes how it went with me that winter with my flying my buns off every day possible, often ending up totally exhausted from enduring the debilitating cold and long hours spent in the cockpit, more than happy to see the end of the day often ending up more dead than alive, but man did I rake in the bucks big time managing to clear off Wally's debt within six grueling ass busting weeks of almost non stop driving it, but knew if I intended to have a set of floats installed come spring, and if the cost of having the skis installed considered usurious, well then one could expect the worst.

As it must the winter flying season eventually came to an end, it being far thinking on my part to have driven it as relentlessly as I had to garner every dollar possible, often pushing atrocious weather conditions so cold and demanding as to cause one to hesitate and often question their mental state. Gradually the vicious man and machine killing winter months abated much to my relief with much more bearable conditions relieving the cold weather demands turning the corner for me to fly longer hours without placing undue stress on my near exhausted body and mind.

Once unable to no longer straddle the fence and put off the inevitable with my cringing inwardly at the very thought of voluntarily placing myself under another financial yoke that appalled my very senses to the point of near deciding to say the hell with it and beach the moth for the summer months knowing full well to do so would leave me ahead of the game, but seeing as common sense and aviation do not speak a common language leaving me in a quandary wavering mightily when the siren call to fly the moth on floats transcended any doubts

I may have conjured up with my overwhelming desires often creating black periods of self doubt berating myself for being weak willed to even consider

Relinquishing the hard earned money I had labored so slavishly to obtain only to have that fat assed moon faced wheeler dealer son of a bitch so effortlessly relieve me of it, but resist as strongly as I did for some time, in the end temptation proving far too overwhelming eventually gave in throwing caution and common sense to the dogs when finally deciding to go for it.

After many aborted attempts to force myself to contact Wally, finally knuckled under, during the interim between contacting him and waiting for him to come to the phone pondered the cruel fates that stripped one of the will power to resist baring one's very soul to the tender mercies of such a predator, who with consummate ease manipulate those of my ilk who by chance or design forced to depend on his skills, my past dealings with him left me with little doubt of his being the master strategist who understood the desires of green horns and shamelessly prepared to profit handsomely from it at every given opportunity.

What made it so much worse was my knowing with dread certainty of his having long anticipated my eventually requesting his assistance in locating and installing a set of floats on the moth, and had without further ado already gathered up all the required components and materials beforehand.

When he finally deigned to answer my call one could clearly envision the self satisfied smirk of inner satisfaction creasing his swarthy jowls with my swearing to detecting a contented purr in his oh so cultured smoothly modulated voice that gave me the chilling insight of how a cornered mouse being cruelly played with by a cat must have felt before being deep sixed.

Wally I managed to croak out of a suddenly parched throat, is it possible for you to locate a set of floats to fit the moth?, the no doubt smoothly orchestrated silence that seemed to hang endlessly between us before his answering seemed to last for an eternity with just the hum of the open connection to be heard with his suddenly coming back on line with a "well my boy", as I cringed at what I knew must come next he jovially boomed out in his best I've just hooked a big fish (sucker) tone of voice, you're in luck, it so happens I know of some one who has a set their willing to sell, but be warned they don't come cheap (what did with him?), and by the way they don't come with the required rigging spreader bars etc, on hearing that my knees all but buckled, it was in the back of my mind to tell him to forget it, being far to rich for my blood, but as if another part of me took over my thoughts, for some perverse reason lost to me at the time that could never be rationally explained, against my will managed to squeak out that's okay with me, upon hearing my verification and before I could change my mind rumbled on to say he would have all ready within a week and to get myself back out there, at that he hung up.

Stunned beyond coherent thought and not yet having the foggiest notion of what financial hell I had so foolishly let myself in for doomed to find out the hard way.

To end this story of a green horns auspicious beginning in to the demanding and often colorful realm of "Bush Pilots", the installation of floats onto the moth went without too much of a hassle, but mother of Jesus upon being presented with the cost of doing so it came within a hair of reducing me to ashes, it taking me the better part of two ass busting years of making hefty payments before being able to settle the debt in full.

But can one truly place a price on the satisfaction that by and large transcended the horrendous financial cost, yes they proved to be anything but water tight, leaking so badly one was forced to beach the aircraft every to prevent from sinking out of sight, but a quick job of fiber glassing them took care of that problem, not to mention the benefit of gaining much slipperier planning bottoms that greatly enhanced take off performance.

It will suffice to say the moth taught me a lot while opening up a diverse life style that can never again be parallel in the good many years I flew it before moving on.

A Demon Called Fear

AT FIRST UPON FINDING MYSELF lying on my back in a state of confused disbelief and not yet fully aware of what had recently transpired until an agonizing pain began to slowly move up my right arm like a river of fire followed by a state of rising nausea that threatened to incapacitate me further as the sickness that had suddenly invaded my mind set off waves of uncontrollable retching leaving me weak and uncertain what had gone wrong and what to do next.

Eventually the brisk cold air revived my senses allowing my eyes to once more focus correctly though the excruciating waves of pain made it difficult to make sense what had previously transpired.

In time the nausea and the pulsing agony of my injured arm finally began to even out enabling me to struggle to my feet while shakily attempting to make sense of the confusing situation while still in a partially dazed state of mind and as yet not fully aware of the sequence of events that had recently taken place.

Once able to fully realize what had occurred I lost It, dazed, frightened and unsure of what to do next began to laugh, starting out as a mirthless chuckle slowly building up to a full throated roar, not at all a pleasant laugh, In fact If there had been any one close enough to hear they would have given me a wide berth as nothing of It indicated the presence of a person with a tight grip on their sanity.

How long I remained In this mental half world of a demented person I have no recollection, only coming to my senses when the tears in my eyes turned to ice, the discomfort of frozen tears clinging to my eye lashes exacerbated by the agonizing streaks of pain relentlessly shooting through my arm rudely brought me back to the present, It taking a concentrated effort on my part to bring an end to the hysterical laughter and brush away the frozen tears. At this juncture something perhaps a will power I didn't know I possessed at the time laced with mind numbing fear quickly brought me back to my senses with my suddenly becoming fully aware of the dilemma facing me, the shocking gravity of it all transcending all other emotions save for fear, the chilling realization if I where to survive while having no one or nowhere to turn to for assistance had to somehow get past the near insurmountable problems that bedeviled me on my own, forcing myself to remain calm and not allowing the burgeoning panic to take hold.

At first my fear burdened mind refused to function in any sense of order leaving me terribly confused as what to do next, but the rapidly dropping temperature quickly reminded me the short winter day fast coming to a close leaving me to face a long cold night I wasn't at all certain could be survived in my weakened condition without a shelter of some sort, but the over riding fact if I intended to leave there that day it was imperative the engine on the tiger moth had to be started and soon before it became too cold soaked to do so with out pre heating it, a daunting task I felt certain to be beyond my ability given the precarious circumstances I labored under, but what made further hesitation unwise was the fact the oil reservoir that sat externally apart from the engine had to be drained into a five gallon pail every night while the oil still hot or as it cooled it would eventually turn into the consistency of road tar. If that were to occur it would doom me to remain there without the faintest hope of forthcoming aid, not at all a pleasant prospect.

Having no other alternative but the engine be started as quickly as possible or face an uncertain future for be it ignorance or foolish pride on my part as usual neglected to inform any one of my destinations or when expected to return, thus no one knew what part of that vast area of the north I could be found in if experiencing difficulties along the way, a glaring omission on my part that could all too easily end up creating grave consequences leaving it solely up to me to extricate myself as best I could being all too aware no assistance to be forth coming.

It had all began when having delivered a trapper to his trap line over a hundred and forty miles north of Red Lake and then unwisely as it turned out agreeing to make a slight detour on the return trip to pick up some frozen moose meat at another lake were he had previously cached it to deliver to his family back in town.

The loading of them awkward frozen chunks of meat proved to be more difficult and time consuming then first thought when attempting to fit them into the narrow confines of the front cockpit taking far longer to accomplish than I could have wished.

I never could remember for certain what caused my being so careless or unthinking actions, but for what ever reason when spinning the propeller of the now gone cold engine that was when my troubles began.

Later on while making my way back to Red Lake the intervening pain filled interim gave me plenty of time to review the past sequence of events, eventually arriving at the conclusion it had been solely my impatience and stupidity that had placed me in the life threatening position I now found myself in, sitting helplessly with an injured arm half frozen in the narrow confines of an unheated cockpit shaking violently from the debilitating effects of pain, freezing cold and near overwhelming fear helplessly locked in a battle to survive.

Our slow progress over the rapidly darkening landscape gave me more than ample time to ponder the series of gross errors that had placed me in such an uncompromising position, the sickening realization it had been mostly impatience on my part that had brought on my problems.

Once having completed the onerous job of loading the moose meat, my state of mind not one of kind wishes toward my fellow man went far toward my becoming impatient and careless when performing the ticklish task of starting the cold engine. It wasn't that I remained ignorant of the engine's nasty propensity to backfire when cold, on the contrary my usually being extremely cautious when doing so as it could on the occasion be a real bitch to fire up at such times, and depending on one's state of mind while doing so could prove to be at times quite vexing.

Swinging the prop through many cycles failed to elicit a response allowing frustration to override common sense thus setting the stage for near disaster by not waiting the usual space of time normally required in allowing the engine to cycle through a backfire as it was often prone to do, instead impatiently moving forward while reaching up to give the prop another shot just as the engine suddenly reversed it's normal rotation causing the propeller to strike the top of my upraised arm just above the elbow, the severe blow to my arm sending me spinning backwards to end up lying on my back in the snow dazed with disbelief and shock, the pain would come later. Some how through the haze of confusion staggered to my feet and in a much weakened mental and physical state to with great difficulty infused with mind numbing fear it would fail to start eventually managed to accomplish doing so much to my relief, a procedure made doubly dangerous by being forced to use my left arm, an awkward procedure that called for extreme caution on my part, but for better or worse my choice remained limited being a case of doing so successfully or remain where I was, at times the physical demands required to spin the propeller came perilously near bringing on hopeless despair when my body in it's weakened state threatened to fail me before that faithful engine finally roared into vibrant life, it being well it did, my rapidly weakening from the effort required and the increasing agony from my injured arm.

Shakily observing the engine as it contentedly rattled away thinking that nothing ever sounded so beautiful leaving me grateful beyond words while freely giving reverent thanks to the old timer aircraft mechanic who had patiently taught me the intricacies of maintaining an aero engine, keep that engine in top running order at all times boy, his words now echoing in my mind as you never know by having done so it may one day save your life, Christ how prophetic.

Gathering up my remaining will power and strength against the full-blown pain that threatened to incapacitate me at any time struggled with great difficulty into the welcome confines of the narrow cockpit. Giving the sight glass below the gas tank a worried glance noticing the position of the cork bobber that informed me of just having sufficient fuel to make it to my gas cache which lay approximately sixty five long cold miles away from where I sat.

God dam how uncertain I felt sitting in that frigid cockpit near paralyzed with creeping fear that bordered on the edge of panic while impatiently waiting for the engine to reach operating temperature, frightened almost beyond human endurance as the what ifs scenario took over my thoughts leaving me deathly afraid of not having sufficient fuel to make it to safety, something that simply didn't bear thinking about not having any other choice but to risk it, and with that all too real fear riding heavily on my shoulders made the take off to face whatever fate had in store for me.

Navigating over the rapidly darkening landscape in a less than fully conscious state of mind proved to be far more difficult than expected exacerbating the fear of wandering off course and possibly missing the lake the gas cache located on, becoming increasingly restless and agitated as time dragged on by while the fuel level bobber indicated a lesser quantity each time I fearfully checked it with the aid of a flashlight, gone now was the feeling of cold and pain replaced by a numbing fear that threatened to overwhelm me, for if by chance or faulty navigation missing the fuel cache, if that were to occur there remained little hope of survival.

Rattling helplessly along desperately attempting to keep accurate track of my progress on the map, frozen to the very marrow of my bones while grimacing against the pain that emanated from my arm each time I inadvertently bumped it against the side of the cockpit, frightened half to death in my loneliness desperately willed the aircraft to fly faster.

Ensconced in a cold narrow cockpit that night one learned the true nature of raw fear, a fear that insidiously developed into an all encompassing mind numbing paralysis that gradually eroded ones mental and physical performance to the point of disaster, little did I realize at the time that in the future them same mind numbing fears would be confronted time after time throughout the years, gradually exacting their toll reducing one's confidence a little bit at a time until one either quit the game or met up with an unknown reckoning, but that eventuality lay far in the future.

Time seemed to drag by on leaden wings with the bobber in the sight glass sinking inexorably downwards towards the empty mark, the fear and anxiety continuing to grind remorsefully away at what little hope I still retained of arriving safely at the gas cache, gradually mounting to the point of being almost unbearable causing my squirming restlessly in the narrow confines of the cockpit in a near state of becoming a mental and physical wreck.

As if I didn't already have enough on my plate a quick perusal of the oil pressure gauge came near to bringing on a coronary on viewing with nerve jangling alarm the indicating needle on the oil pressure gauge beginning to fluctuate giving one the bad news the oil reservoir to be near running dry, the shock momentarily freezing me into a state of mind numbing terror before remembering with palpable relief a recent position check on the map had indicated our only being a few miles away from the gas cache and relative safety, that we had made it thus far without running out of oil only managed by an oversight on my part when inadvertently failing to shut the oil tank cooling vent door thus the cold air keeping the oil temperature much cooler than normal reducing the oil consumption, not good for the engine but proving to be a saving grace for me.

Upon initially sighting the lake clearly outlined in the frosty moonlight gave reverent thanks to the powers that be to within a relatively short space of time able to pin point the location of the cache to with an immense sense of relief then gliding in for a landing while reflecting on what a near thing it had been, but had to ask myself could it have gone any other way?, It wasn't that I didn't know the oil tank required replenishment before further flight but the debilitating effects of shock, pain and the fear controlling my thoughts and actions at the time had transcended all else, my only wanting to be gone from that place of misfortune as quickly as possible, at any other time it would have been no more than a necessary chore to have to land and replenish the oil, a normally lengthy task as the oil required heating up before it would pour readily, some thing I didn't think possible of accomplishing at the time given the severe injury to my arm.

Finding it difficult to fly the aircraft and manipulating the throttle at the same time with one hand the initial touch down on to the unseen rock hard drifts jarred my teeth as we bounced to a near stop, but it sure felt good to have made it down safely rough landing or not thankfully taxiing over to the prominent point of land where the gas cache had been located some times before in anticipation of needing it in times such as this.

I wasn't too certain for how long, but once shutting down the engine must have passed out for a time from pain and fatigue suddenly waking up so stiff from the cold it took a great effort on my part to rouse myself causing a galaxy of stars to cloud my vision during the process.

When finally able to regain my senses a horrible feeling of panic swept over me in fearing the engine had cooled off beyond the point of being able to re-start it without first pre-heating it as I slept, my relief at finding it still warm almost brought me to my knees to quickly as my physical condition allowed using one hand and a length of rope managed to drag the engine cover in to place, the effort leaving me gasping from the spasms of pain in my arm that had flamed up anew from the forced activity, the one benefit derived from remaining in a near frozen state was it dulled the excruciating pain to a near bearable degree.

Sick with unrelenting pain, half frozen and almost incapacitated with fear still fought desperately to carry on knowing to stop for a rest even for a few minutes could well doom me to sleep the sleep that never ends, my inevitably freezing to death in the now well below temperatures that continued to drop even lower as the night progressed making breathing painful.

At first only managing to stumble around in mindless confusion unable to focus on what needed to be done next, but that unproductive state of mind soon transcended by the bitter cold that viciously reminded one of the all encompassing need for warmth and the sooner the better, I knew my injured arm wouldn't kill me outright but if I allowed the cold and panic to take hold it would spell the end very quickly.

Eventually through a debilitating miasma of confusion and misery coherent thought gradually asserted itself with my forcing the weakness and despair to one side managing to retrieve the plumbers pot from the baggage compartment leaving myself weak and dizzy with relief at having successfully done so, but even at that I knew the hard part yet to come as preparing the pot for service required a lot of physical effort on my part to pump up the pressure, this normally simple procedure turning out to be an exercise of pure undiluted hell in using one hand, the strain producing waves of agony that coursed down the length of my arm often forcing me to halt my feverish efforts for a spell in order to allow the pain to subside to a dull throb, renewing my efforts when able till finally building up sufficient pressure for the pot to operate efficiently. Once having been successfully lit off a short rest taken until it had warmed up to operating temperature and upon cracking the fuel control valve instantly rewarded with a miniature volcano spouting a blue white incandescent warmth that gave me much needed comfort, never had anything seemed so welcome as that white hot flame did as it bellowed out of the burner coils leaving me to experiencing a growing confidence in making it through the life and death trial so long endured.

While crouching on my knees staring mindlessly at the blue white flames emanating from the blow pot enjoying the first all consuming warmth I had known for many hours eventually became mesmerized soon forgetting all my troubles. At one point I must have dozed off only to being rudely awakened when toppling over to one side fortunately on to my good arm. That period of rest as short as it was had given me a much needed respite of forgetfulness, also seeming to have gained in strength of mind and body leaving me feeling much rejuvenated enabling me to once more tackle the onerous tasks that still lay before me. The mind easing knowledge of now being in possession of a source of comforting warmth that could be used at my convenience allayed the gnawing fear of succumbing to exposure that had so long sorely beset me had now vanished, If all else went wrong at least I knew a ready source of life giving warmth awaited me ensuring survival.

With renewed energy once more began the clumsy one-handed task of locating and laboriously digging out the ten-gallon fuel drums out of the deep snowdrift where they had been previously cached. If I may digress for the moment in order to explain to the uninformed reader, storing or otherwise placing fuel and oil for future or emergency consumption in a secret location that is normally only known to the person or persons placing it there being referred to in aviation lingo as a "fuel cache", and in my case consisted of five gallon cans and ten gallon drums as they fit easily into the confined spaces of the moth plus they where much easier to handle by one's self than the larger forty five gallon drums used by commercial operators.

Additional fuel occasionally added as time and chance permitted, usually taking place if one happened to be flying by empty on a trip to pick up a trapper or a load of moose meat, fish or what ever. This practice insured one of having emergency fuel when most requiring it as I did at the time, often utilizing it as found necessary as the tiger moth had not been designed with sufficient tank age to enable it's being capable of extended flight being primarily a trainer, neither did they come equipped with any creature comforts such as a cabin air heater only coming equipped with what we jokingly referred to as a "North Winds" heater, one simply endured by bundling up against the ferocious cold that seemed to seep into the cockpit from every where possible.

Well as the story goes, by the time two ten gallon drums of fuel had been painfully dug out of the snow bank with the demanding effort costing me dearly leaving me once more in a state of near exhaustion necessitating my once again taking the time to rest and warm myself up from the life giving heat exuding from the blow pot while listening to the contented bubbling sounds emanating from the five gallon can of oil previously placed on top of it to warm up. What I wouldn't have given at that moment to be able to drink a hot sweet cup of coffee or hot chocolate, even though both being available from my survival kit it would have taken more time and effort on my part than I could spare, but still terribly tempted to do so almost hallucinating at the thought. Once again my fevered mind wandered into semi consciousness while staring uncomprehendingly at the blue white flames licking up around the bottom of the pail with my once again pitching slowly side ways to be cruelly jarred back into groggy wakefulness, but this time around failing to rally any further source of get up and go having already used up whatever reserves I may have retained.

Being exhausted as I was desired only to lie down and sleep, but realizing with a pang of alarm that to cease my efforts even for a short while would conspire against my efforts in completing what must be done before being able to leave.

The demanding job of digging out the fuel drums proved to be a picnic compared to what lay ahead of me, the fuel tank on the moth mounted between the upper wings at it's highest point making it difficult to get at, a simple solution to eliminating a fuel pump the fuel being gravity fed to the carburetor. Fortunately footholds had been incorporated into the sides of the forward fuselage to assist one in climbing up in order to re-fuel the nineteen-gallon tank. This innovation may have worked quite well with narrow toed boots but did not readily accommodate my fleece lined flying boots, the toes being far too wide making it increasingly precarious for me.

A quick perusal of the seemingly insurmountable problems that that lay before me left one uncertain of being able to surmount them, once again the latent pangs of debilitating fear assailed me, how in the hell was I going to manage to climb up on to the leading edge of the lower wing never mind climbing up to the top of the fuselage while lugging a pail of gas with only the use of one good arm not to mention the clumsy funnel had to be first inserted into the filler opening?. Refueling the aircraft away from base had always proven to be difficult and time consuming, not at all straightforward as when using a pressurized fuel hose.

The hopelessness of it all caused tears of frustration and anger to well up into my eyes, it simply couldn't be done, not in my weakened state that made the lingering fear of inadvertently slipping causing further damage to my arm or worse yet immobilizing further action on my part Cursing the day I had ever heard of god dam airplanes which next to the female species, could be the most frustrating and daunting of creatures designed to torment man.

Momentarily giving up in helpless frustration to walk away from the source of my frustration far enough where the roar of the blow pot subsided to a faint hiss to in my misery stare at the myriad of twinkling stars so clearly outlined in the back ground of a velvet sky seeming to appear so close as to be plucked effortlessly from their heavenly perch.

Standing there all alone in that most beautiful of moon lit night with no other sounds to be heard apart from the occasional pop of a frost swollen tree, only then did I fully begin to realize and truly appreciate the endless hard work and good fortune that had brought me this far even when taking my current dilemma into consideration, as undesirable as it seemed I realized that with determination and fortitude one could eventually overcome their seemingly insurmountable problems if one persevered. The old timers who had long preceded me must have often as a matter of course faced mind numbing challenges on a regular basis, if I failed to over come such minor obstacles as presently lay before me then I wasn't worthy of being called a bush pilot!

That short interlude of peace and soul searching did much to ease my gnawing fears, comforting my troubled thoughts to a degree of enabling me to once more face the onerous tasks that still lay before me with increased confidence.

I can't speak for any one else, but when I am faced with seemingly insurmountable odds, the first order is to vent my spleen railing impotently against all and sundry, then upon exhausting a host of vituperative ratings getting down to doing what must be done. With this in mind somehow knew I would eventually succeed if continuing to use deliberate caution and common sense, my not being a quitter no matter how daunting the situation.

Doing my best to ignore the dull throb of pain and threatening exhaustion tackled the problems with re-newed vigor finding them to be far less confounding with my now being able to solve them with relative ease, but still it turned out to be a real mind bender to move the drums over to the aircraft, as difficult as that had been it turned out to be the easy part as the struggle to place one slippery metal drum on top of the other would have tried the patience of "Job", if one has never attempted to place a slippery metal drum full of gas on top of the limited space of another equally slippery ones using just one arm then there is no easy way to describe the frustrating trials experienced when initially attempting to do so, it requiring many aborted attempts that tried one's patience to the limit before finally succeeding, but unable to accomplish that difficult feat until coming up with the idea of placing the upside down shovel blade next to a standing drum to give me the extra height required to successfully tip the drum into place.

Once having succeeded in that next removed the top bung then carefully rotating the drum sideways to allow it's contents to pour into a three gallon bucket only filling it about two thirds full knowing my not having the strength to lift too heavy a weight straight up, a normally easy job, but this time it's proving to be a real bitch when forced to use only one hand to initially maneuver the pail into place on the lower wing, my ending up spilling copious amounts of precious fuel before getting the hang of it. Once that had been accomplished a long rope tied to the bail of the bucket and draping the slack end over my shoulders before attempting the precarious climb up to the tank pushing the funnel ahead of me my legs shaking so violently from the strain it left me in some doubt as to my being able to continue on, but having no other choice but to struggle on even as the pain in my arm intensified from the terrible exertions forced upon it to the point of almost paralyzing further moment, only by gritting my teeth and doing my best to ignore the burning agony managed by dint of great efforts to finally succeed in climbing up to the top wing and to brace myself as best I could while one handedly twisting open the tank filler cap to successfully insert the funnel into the filler neck despite the burning agony produced when using my injured arm to hang on creating a fresh burst of tears that froze almost instantly clouding my vision.

The increased height of the funnel on top of the tank only added to my manifold problems but it was unthinkable to not use it as fuel taken from a drum without question is invariably contaminated with a host of carburetor plugging undesirables that without fail must be filtered out of the fuel through a felt cloth or a chamois placed within the funnel, to fail to do so invited potential disaster in the form of engine failure usually occurring at the worst possible time.

Once having successfully inserted the funnel into the tank began the tricky one handed job of pulling up the pail of gas as far as possible while performing a balancing act cinching the rope around my neck then carefully reaching down to grab the rope with my good arm then re cinching the rope around my neck repeatedly until able to grab the bail to then hoist the pail of gas up to the funnel to empty its' contents into the tank.

This slow and painful process repeated time after time over a protracted period of time with my being frequently forced to stop and rest, each trip taking it's toll until becoming increasingly difficult to continue on but with grim determination managed by using up a reserve of strength and will power I never knew I possessed up till then finally succeeding in filling up the tank with sufficient fuel to see me safely home, making absolutely certain to carefully replace the filler cap with palsied fingers, it wouldn't have done to have neglected to have done so after what I had just gone through.

Only once had I made that mistake my fortunately noticing the presence of vaporized fuel swirling behind and beside the canopy shortly after take off alerting me to my error before any further problem presented itself, a lesson learned and not soon forgotten.

As soon as my state of mind and body allowed the empty drum stowed away in the front cockpit. If one should wonder why I bothered at all considering my state of affairs in the first place the drums being painted a bright fire engine red would have clearly advertised the location of my gas cache to any passing aircraft, it not being unknown then as it is to-day to have an unscrupulous pilot who had spotted the cache to make use of some free fuel leaving one who depended on it being there caught short and the fact they where expensive and hard to come by.

Christ I was tired, so giddied tired my head spun wanting only to lie down and sleep but as mentioned beforehand that option remained out of the question with my still facing the formidable task of replenishing the engine oil. Normally that is a straight forward job being a simple matter of hoisting a five gallon can of warm oil up to the filler neck pouring in whatever required, but that with good reason remained out of the realm of possibility, another method would have to be used.

Well one does what one must, ripping the filter cloth out of the funnel placed it into the oil reservoir filler neck and without thinking grabbed the bail on the five gallon can of hot oil to lift it off the roaring blow pot forgetting how hot the bottom had become placed it on an upturned drum so as to be able to pour the hot oil into the bucket pulled out the metal pouring spout then unthinkingly grabbing the bottom of the pail in order to tip it over and rotate it into the pouring position filling the bucket half full, and then to clumsily pour it with one hand in to the funnel, the oil being so hot it poured like water but still making a hell of a mess each time another measure added until full. Hurting like all the devils in hell I may have been but still couldn't help feeling a smug sense of satisfaction at having overcome what at first had seemed insurmountable odds when taking into consideration my questionable physical state.

But as smug as I may have felt at the moment, a very high price had been extracted for the super human efforts demanded to accomplish what I had leaving me weak and dizzy to the point of wondering if it was possible to force myself to go on any further. At that juncture my suddenly becoming aware of a sharp tingling sensation emanating from the palm and fingers of my left hand that gradually turned into a searing agony that quickly roused me out of my slump, upon removing the heavy leather glove observed a perfect crescent shaped line of fast rising blisters that stung something fierce when exposed to the cold air and when inspecting my glove no surprise to find the same crescent shape branded into my heavy leather mitten and clean through the wool liner, that painful error shows how easy it is for one to make a serious mistake while laboring under great pressure and stress.

Well be as it may there was precious little to be done but live with it, my continuing to clean up as best I could in order to leave little or no evidence of my ever being there, and when satisfied at having done so busied myself with starting up the now cold engine, once having completed priming the intake manifold system carefully set the throttle then while practicing great caution swinging the propeller as hard as my remaining strength allowed, eventually to my everlasting relief rewarded with a full throated bellow from the exhaust pipe as it burst into life.

One simply could never begin to adequately describe the sense of accomplishment that washed over me upon successfully starting the engine, the euphoria of having overcome such diabolical obstacles leaving me in a light headed and giddy state of mind, that along with near terminal exhaustion of mind and body all but doing me in, sick and shaky I might have been but the will power and determination to keep on and to over come all barriers not quite done with yet, with a last careful look around to ensure that nothing had been forgotten for unwelcome eyes to possibly see wearily dragged my complaining body into the narrow confines of the oh so welcome cockpit, then waiting impatiently for the engine to reach operating temperature, upon it doing so rapidly advancing the throttle to full open making a short take off run before beginning a slow climb into the beautifully moon lit sky to begin the most hellish flight of my short career retaining very little recollection how I managed it, navigating through the still of the night by the light of the full moon over what seemed to be endless miles of trackless wilderness while in a semi conscious state of mind, existing in a surreal world filled with hallucinations interspersed with periods of absolute clarity, the remaining miles to safety seemingly endless until the first faint incandescent glow of the lights of Red Lake became faintly visible on the far horizon, only then did I fully realize and appreciate my questionable navigation had led me in the right direction more by good luck then skill or good judgment.

As the faint glow of incandescent light that hung over the town grew in intensity reflecting the crystals of ice fog hanging over the town like a star studded mantle, it's welcoming beacon assuring me all would now turn out well leaving me grateful beyond words at having succeeded against all odds to eventually carry out a safe landing that if the truth be known more of a controlled crash than a normal arrival.

Once having taxied cautiously into my usual parking spot and wearily shutting down the faithful engine that had once more delivered me safely home sat back to allow my confused and jumbled thoughts to settle down before attempting to drag my reluctant and near frozen body out of the confines of the cockpit. I must have passed out almost immediately lulled by the soothing knowledge that all to be well only to be awakened a while later by the freezing cold that seemed to have inundated my entire body clear to the bone reminding me of the persistent throbbing of my injured arm, how much time had passed I could never say but the near frozen state I now found myself in told me it must have been a good while only being able to extricate my well stiffened body out of the narrow confines of the cockpit with the greatest of effort at first finding my legs at first refusing to support my weight until experiencing renewed circulation that brought tears of agony to my eyes as my feet began to sting so fiercely at first I couldn't bear to walk on them, standing there somewhat confused by the series of past events still able to savor my good fortune at having survived a hell of my own making somehow feeling different as the bone chilling realization of just how easily it could have gone the other way but for good fortune and determined resourcefulness, the very thought leaving me beyond words, but also recognizing the fact my recent life threatening experience had tempered my very make up leaving me with the profound knowledge I would never be the same callow youth I had once been, then it dawned on me, I had been tried and found not wanting, my having faced down a demon called fear. The pain shooting down my arm like a river of molten lava brought me back to the present to suddenly recall the words uttered by an old bush pilot that had seen his share of hell during the course of his long career. When visiting him in the hospital where he lay recuperating all bandaged up with a leg and one arm in a cast along with a host of purplish appearing bruises from injuries sustained when being forced to crash into the bush when his engine failed during take off, upon my matter of factly inquiring as to how he felt he immediately snarled at me with a venomous hiss, goddamit heartless be grateful you can still hurt after an accident, then you at least know you aren't paralyzed and will eventually recover to continue on with your life to what ever degree your able! Yes he spoke the truth as admittedly I hurt like all the devils in hell but still able to get around on my own, if I wasn't man enough to be able to bear a little pain along with a dose of misfortune then I didn't have what it took to be called a "Bush Pilot".

Now being assured safety lay before me, suddenly became befuddled and confused, not at all certain what to do next having fought so hard for so long against uneven odds had become punch drunk. As if on signal the river of agony shooting down my arm intensified painfully reminding me of the fact I required medical attention pronto, so with the weary shuffling gait of an old man began what seemed to be an endless journey of what in reality no more than a block in order to reach the local taxi stand, strangely enough there seemed to be very few people to be seen on the street that night, perhaps it was far too cold to be wandering about instead choosing to spending their time in the local pub or in the warmth of the restaurant where I desired with all my heart to go to and drink an oh so welcome cup of hot coffee, but the agony running down the full length of my arm precluded that luxury my getting to the hospital taking precedence over all else.

I must have stood there staring uncertainly at nothing for some time swaying unsteadily back and forth like a drunk attempting to make a decision as the taxi driver peered out of his nearly frosted over window with curiosity written all over his face as he studied me as I stood there probably wondering what I had in mind to be. Sick and fatigued to my very soul finally dredged up the will power to make a shaky entrance into the taxi stand staggered at the sensation of the real all encompassing warmth felt for many long hours that suddenly brought on an almost overpowering desire to lie down on the hard wooden bench and sleep, but knew with a certainty the taxi driver an overweight mean minded individual would without fail construe that as the act of a drunkard seeking refuge from the cold immediately throwing me out. Remaining uncertain as to what I had in mind intently studied me with his close set piggy eyes before curtly inquiring in a tone of voice that lacked the least degree of respect as to what he could do to help?, having witnessed his on many occasions brazenly slapping half drunk native people around had seized me up as a potential drunk to be fleeced but still remaining circumspect as I was hardly a stranger to him.

In a slurred croak asked him to take me up to the hospital, at that his eyes flashed with greed and anticipation and now sure of his ground demanded I produce my money first. Fumbling for my wallet painfully extracted a twenty dollar bill which he rudely tore out of my unresisting fingers not offering the change due as the fare only coming to two dollars, but lacked the necessary strength and willpower at the time to fight back, he would be dealt with on a one on one basis later. Then with a self-satisfied smirk on his moon face preceded me out of the door not offering the slightest assistance. As we made our way the short distance to the hospital reflected on people such as him, the "jackalls" of society that ranked lower than the bar tenders to be found in the "snake pit"(local beer parlor) that shamelessly bullied and ripped off any of the native population that dared to enter and woe unto them that proffered any more than the exact price of a bottle of beer.

Upon arriving at the entrance door to the hospital shakily rang the night bell to be soon greeted by a nurse who involuntarily stepped back in shock upon initially confronting my sickly green pallor my over long hair wildly askew framing a set of red rimmed eyes, by this time it was all I could do to move my lips in a feeble attempt to mumble almost unintelligible words instead gesturing weakly at my injured arm, If that angel of a nurse had been any less astute I don't know what I would have done but she wasted no time in quickly sitting me down as my trembling legs threatened to give way at any time. Now overwhelmed by the life giving warmth and the sure knowledge of being in good hands I lost it, no longer having to be the man of steel fighting desperately for survival could now give into grateful relief allowing copious tears to course down my cheeks, the demeaning shame of crying like a baby flooded through me, grown men don't cry, especially bush pilots, (do they?)

I must have drifted off into an exhausted sleep as the next thing I knew a male doctor attempting to shake me awake, once he had me somewhat aware of my surroundings and able to relate my woes informed me they had to first remove my heavy winter parka, removing the sleeve off my left arm proved to be excruciating as in the course of doing so placing added pressure on my damaged arm but nothing that couldn't be tolerated, the removal of the right hand sleeve proved to be impossible my arm by now having become swollen far past it's normal size as to make removal impossible without creating unbearable agony no matter how gently they tried with my breaking into a copious sweat while almost passing out from the excruciating pain at each attempt leaving them with no recourse but to cut it off. This proved to be easier said then done, being extremely difficult to accomplish as the material consisted of very tough canvas interspersed with layers of insulation in between.

At one point once the parka had been removed vaguely remembering the nurse giving me an injection in my left arm, the next thing I knew was my groggily coming back to consciousness lying on a gurney with my arm in a cast slowly shaking off the effects of the drugs eventually coming fully awake to suddenly realize the unrelenting pain that had dominated my very being for so long now no more than a dull ache allowing my thoughts to dwell on other aspects of the situation began to feel extremely foolish lying there in my working clothes that where coated with blood, fish slime, fuel and oil stained, urine, dog shit and Christ knows what else?, little wonder they had wheeled me to the furthest corner of the hallway to recover! The odor that emanated from my filthy work clothes was referred to in the flying circles as"Eu De Aviation".

Well stink I might, but that was actually my last concern, god dam how awful I felt this being my first taste of the effects of anesthetics and not ever partaking of alcoholic beverages remained a stranger to the agony of a hangover now had a good idea of what it entailed plus my feeling as if I had gone one to one with a freight train my wildly spinning head threatening to fall off my shoulders every time I attempted to move it not to mention every muscle and joint I owned ached in unison with pain in my head.

Well like the old timer said if you're a hurting then you ain't a dead. Yes I thought to myself as the thoughts of the last dread filled hours came rushing back with the past events chasing through my head one after another, I'm not dead but the way I feel at the time it might not be a bad thing. But be as it may it could have just as easily gone the other way but for chance and good fortune not to mention a healthy dash of home grown ingenuity.

Once being released from the hospital took it very easy for the first while till my strength returned the mending of my arm taking about six weeks before the cast could be removed, the doctor had taken the time and effort to show me the x-rays which indicated a greenstick fracture with razor sharp shards of bone cutting into the muscle at every movement, one of the most agonizing fractures one could ever experience causing the terrible agony I had endured for so long and the inescapable fact that being forced by extenuating circumstances to use the arm only served to damage it further.

For the first week reluctantly remaining fairly quiet despite entreaties from my customers to do otherwise almost going bonkers with the effects of forced idleness, the encroaching boredom driving me to make many a visit to check out my yellow peril that I yearned with all my heart to fly once more, each long night spent restlessly re- living the course of events that had led up to the near disaster circling endlessly through my tortured mind like a stuck record till I wanted to scream enough. The sobering thought of my having once been such an arrogant ass that thought he knew all the answers to now fully realize just how mistaken I had been, the knowledge of past mistakes survived irrevocably branded into my consciousness, from that day on becoming a much wiser pilot not ever for a minute forgetting the lesson had been a costly one but had in the long run had gotten off cheap, the grave overtones of how it otherwise could have gone not lost on me.

Then as now I have always claimed it was only the intervention of the twin gods of fate and chance that saved my bacon that long lonely night and I stick with my convictions re-gardless of what others may think, that they in battling perpetual boredom much as us mortals do must have spotted a "live one" in me intervening as required that night as they continued to do throughout my long and sometimes hazardous career keeping one of their prize players alive and well to live another day for even they in their infinite wisdom could never be absolutely certain when I would step on my "dick" again.

Perhaps this could be construed by some as being outright arrogant and assuming on my part, but this is my unshakeable belief and the fact that I survived to tell my story while many others failed to do so and no longer casting a shadow speaks for itself Yes I will be first to admit to have become jaded after a long and illustrious career as a bush pilot, but doing anything less challenging bored me to tears.

Well as it went my arm eventually healed, when the cast was finally removed my whole upper arm found to be one massive bruise (color me purple) that slowly faded away. During the interim settling the score with the errant taxi driver, his wisely offering no argument with my now returning to deal with him in good health and carrying a big stick that convinced him it would be in his best interest to make immediate restitution. After the first week of recuperating though remaining a little shaky spent a few hours a day cleaning and checking over my faithful steed. Reluctant at first to reveal the extent of my stupidity failed miserably in hiding the fact of what had transpired from the astute base engineer who knew without a doubt what had taken place blandly stating my being extremely fortunate the aircraft having sported a wooden propeller at the time and not a metal one leaving me standing in embarrassed silence with my face and ears beet red humiliated beyond words, chuckling at my obvious embarrassment assuaged my well stung pride by informing me of his having located a "fairy reed" metal propeller designed to fit the engine of the tiger moth for a paltry fifty dollars from a friend of his in Hudson Ontario. This bit of good news made my day having contemplated contacting the great dzogan to locate one for me but reluctant to do so knowing the price would be at least ten times what the engineer had quoted. Once installed I simply couldn't believe the degree of improvement in performance the aircraft literally coming to life with a noticeable enhancement of take off and climb performance while also gaining slightly in air speed.

As my arm slowly healed began to once more make short flights finding it difficult at first to hold the control stick due to the fact the blisters on my left hand not completely healed over yet and tender as all get out but still remaining bull headed and determined carried on many's the time gritting my teeth in agony when inadvertently banging my still very tender arm against something or another soon learning to be more cautious there being no such animal as recovery therapy in them days.

One could say there is something good to be found in any situation, perhaps so having learned well from that soul searching experience never again leaving without informing some one or leaving a detailed flight plan where I could be found if turning up missing. My remaining time with the tiger moth taught me a lot before moving on to other jobs and more sophisticated aircraft, but the moth has always remained as my first love in the world of aviation.

Green machine

THE MONICKER "GREEN MACHINE "HAD absolutely no relationship what so ever with environmental issues in any sense of the word, actually being as far apart from that contentious issue as possible, in reality being an old (by todays standards) double winged fabric covered bi-plane known as a De-Havilland fox moth, a derivation of the ubiquitous De-Havilland tiger moth that had been used extensively by the armed forces to give potential armed forces pilots initial training during world war two. The fox moth emerged as a post war commercial version of the tiger moth but having a much larger fuselage that boasted a closed in passenger cabin directly behind the engine, while the pilot sat in splendid isolation in a snug cockpit well back on the fuselage enclosed in a sliding bubble type canopy. In direct comparison with the tiger moth a virtual Cadillac of the air (that was for the pilot), both cabins being comfortably heated by an efficient hot air system that kept one comfortable even in the coldest weather. This being a quantum jump from the rigors of flying the tiger moth where one literally froze their balls off flying in well below temperatures.

Unfortunately the fox moth didn't belong to me though would have gladly traded the tiger moth for it on the instant with my endlessly hungering to fly it once being checked out and discovering just how much more comfortable and easy to fly in direct comparison to my yellow peril.

The commercial fisherman that owned it didn't fly himself but had purchased the machine with the intention of guaranteeing his catch flown out to town while still fresh from his lakes which in itself brought higher prices. Up till then his being some what disillusioned and angered beyond tolerance, refusing to do any further business with the local airways that at best only offering him poor service, instead choosing to cash in on the far more lucrative mining work so widely available at the time only picking up fish when and if time allowed thus leaving the field wide open to me during the winter months when fishing at its heaviest.

In due course a deal that benefitted both of us had been worked out whereupon I would fly his catch out to town three days out of every week, the times in between the aircraft mine to use as I saw fit, a hell of fine arrangement that worked out well for both of us with my keeping busy making as many charter flights as possible each day flying all over hell's half acre from dawn to dark

Of course at the time remaining totally ignorant of the terrible discomforts my passengers suffered while confined in that tightly closed cramped and extremely noisy cabin directly behind the engine not to mention seats of any sort a luxury that simply did not exist, instead sitting on their luggage or supplies of which they unfailingly barfed all over during the course of the flight. My passengers as a rule normally consisted of trappers along with a host of snotty nosed children and their fat assed wives and of course the usual retinue of scruffy half starved sled dogs with their ribs sticking out like animated wash boards along with moose or caribou meat, fish, furs supplies and Christ knows what?, it all got jammed in one way or the other, weight and balance computations some thing I hadn't learned to spell yet never mind understand enough about to make use of it and caring less, stuffing in all one possibly could until all that could be seen of the passengers where eye balls and teeth with creature comforts being the last thing to be considered, what couldn't or didn't fit in to the cabin such as toboggans, sleds or an extra long pair of snowshoes or what ever tied onto the wing struts or flying wires in direct contradiction to the rules of aerodynamics.

The ongoing fact that the passengers invariably appeared to suffer severe air sickness to an unusual degree that left them almost comatose at the completion of the flight totally lost to me though admittedly didn't much care to have to clean up the indescribably repulsive mess of half digested stomach contents that would have given a hyena the dry heaves, usually they where considerate enough to barf all over each other and on to their luggage. But what really blew me away was the plight the poor dogs suffered usually the first to be unceremoniously heaved into the close confines of the cabin to be stuffed tight against the fire wall that separated the engine from the cabin actually only a thin sheet of aluminum covered with a light layer of insulation that must have done little to muffle the roar of the engine and also must have been the hottest part to have endured being literally covered over with baggage or what ever, the combination of heat vibration and fear must have all went to-ward their eventually losing control of their bowels invariably spewing a repulsive mess of unbelievably foul smelling greenish black slime over themselves and every thing within reach. My being comfortably ensconced well back from ensuing mayhem like some big assed bird totally unaware of what took place happily enjoying the flight.

Upon arrival at our destination the puke stained passengers would literally throw them selves gratefully out of the confines of the horrendously stinking cabin gasping for breath while even with my standing well back the revolting stench still assailed my nostrils often causing my stomach to lurch violently in protest. Never before had I witnessed so many green tinged native people with red eyes with my at the time failing to understand why though must admit to at times finding the situation highly amusing but wisely never letting on to doing so being quite certain my sense of humor wouldn't be appreciated, the usually good natured native people possibly taking it to heart and tomahawking me.

Though they never once complained about the sub human conditions they so stoically endured I'm quite certain they failed to find it to their liking in doing so what so ever but always remaining too polite to complain. Usually within a short space of time the cold fresh air dispelled their sickness with the green cast of their skin slowly fading to once more return to normal, as did their irrepressible sense of humor. On the average they where great people to get on with my respecting their life styles and enjoying their company no end which cannot be said for the majority of white people one dealt with.

Well as it went the situation being unknown to me remained uncorrected while the ongoing accumulation of fish slime and blood mixed in with a corresponding amount of puke and dog shit along with Christ only knows what else gradually made it's presence known to the point of eventually becoming over powering and that was during the cold weather, but my only having to brave that footed stench on the occasion gave it little thought, not for a minute realizing the warm air entering the tight confines of the cabin inevitably stirred up and enhanced that foul stench beyond human endurance, lord it must have been one son of a bitch of a trial for any one or anything to endure throughout the course of the flight, but other insidious factors unknown to me at the time diabolically contributed to the on going discomfort of my passengers, it was little wonder then they turned grayish green!

This situation could have well gone on for the remainder of the winter but for the appearance of an old grizzled prospector who it turned out to be of sour disposition totally lacking the slightest sense of humor approached me one fine day to fly him out to his mining claim on a remote lake. Upon loading up his equipment and supplies tucked him in and we where off. The location of his claim a fair distance away it took just over an hour before arriving at our destination my barely having touched down and sliding to a stop some startled to see the cabin door suddenly pop open with the prospector frantically climbing out of the close confines of the cabin to roll off the wing into the deep snow all the while retching uncontrollably. When able to speak immediately fired off a broadside of heartfelt curses at me in a hoarse choked voice interspersed by periods of gulping in huge gasps of air followed by bouts of violent retching that almost brought him to his knees. When able to renewing his tirade of abuse against me in a manner that set the hair rising on the back of my neck as he viciously confined me and my god dam stinking piece of shit airplane to various and colorful hell's. As abusive and demeaning I found his lusty tirade against me, one couldn't help but to mentally applaud his award winning out burst, but for the life of me couldn't begin to understand what had set him off to re-act so violently to-ward me, he must have had one hell of a good reason!

Suddenly it all made sense, the native people who had suffered to various degrees the very same hell the prospector had recently endured far too polite to complain, but the old prospector retained no such compunction as he informed me in no uncertain terms the oil fumes leaking back from the hot engine had all but gassed him. Well be as it may my never suspecting for a minute such an awful state of affairs could exist never mind happen, the possibility of such an unimagined   incident taking place had never once occurred to me, but when one thought about it the all too real possibility of that occurring seemed most likely given the propensity of the English built engine to piss oil onto everything within the confines of the cowlings including the hot exhaust which without question could definitely produce a great amount of noxious eye and lung burning throat choking oil smoke and fumes that had obviously been filtering through minute openings of the firewall into the passenger cabin. This would have made little difference while flying a load of fish as I have never known a dead fish to complain, though it not being unknown for them on the occasion to raise a stink, It would be difficult to envision the absolute living hell my poor uncomplaining native passengers had been forced to endure especially when taking into consideration the presence of the already existing exotic stench produced by the well marinated floor boards when interacting with the heady odor of burnt oil fumes, oh man It didn't bear thinking about, my only being able to term it as the tortures of the "dammed".

On parting the prospector made it abundantly plain he would never fly with me again, but admittedly that failed to make an impression on me with my being totally fed up with his non-stop complaining about everything he could possibly construe as being my fault. The take off at first leaving me uneasy and feeling some what exposed for a time as it was not unknown for a slighted or "bushed" prospector to take a pot shot at an aircraft and not being desirable of finding out the hard way immediately ducked behind the first island I came to only then breathing a ragged sigh of relief when considering myself to be safely out of gun shot range.

The remainder of the winter went on by pretty much on the same note excepting my finally taking the time and effort toward securely sealing off the bulkhead between the cabin and the engine not wanting any one else to have to suffer the same fate, but their was little to be done about the terrible lingering stench that emanated from the cabin that refused to react to repeated attempts of emoting harsh cleaners and disinfectants, my efforts failing miserably in removing the cloying stink, if any thing only adding to the already exotic odor causing my retching violently each time I stuck my nose into that footed cabin, in the end it was concluded their remained only one thing to be done and that was to rip out the existing floor and replace it. Once this had been accomplished with a great amount of cursing, violent bouts of retching and generally carrying on rewarded with the atmosphere inside the cabin definitely taking a turn for the better making my passengers much happier.

Well to my ever lasting sorrow the winter and my love affair with the fox moth eventually came to an end about the same time the fisherman who owned it, much to my dismay had decided his being unable to carry on much longer due to advancing age and failing health had seriously considered during the long harsh winter months to giving up or selling the licenses on his lakes and retire, but first offering both the fishing licenses and aircraft to me on an equitable terms, but sadly my lacking the necessary backing forced to relinquish both leaving a huge gap in my life for some time to come.

Now the reader understands why the fox moth was dubbed with the unlikely moniker of "Green Machine".

My how times have changed, the uncomfortable drafty, noisy vibrating contraptions that brave people who once as a matter of course dared to risk life and limb to the uncertainties of early aviation, and when they did during the winter months in most cases finding themselves in an unheated bare bones aircraft that lacked the simplest amenities often finding themselves sharing limited space with quarters of frozen moose or caribou meat along side of bags of flour and cases of lard and not what have you while not at all considered unusual as a passenger to have to sit on one's own luggage or bags of frozen fish. Never did I ever know anyone to complain about enduring the hardships involved, the atmosphere usually being one of gaiety and good cheer as they nipped from a quasi concealed bottle of spirits, and also never up to then noting a single incidence of an inebriated passenger becoming violent or obnoxious as they waited patiently to be delivered to their homes or jobs at some remote mining camp invariably arriving cramped and stiff from the cold but still retaining their good spirits never for a second considering their lot to be harsh and uncomfortable, that's the way it was and accepted as such.

Now days it seems that people in general cannot find enough to bitch or complain about, often without good reason suing all and sundry on the premise of real or imagined slights (blame the lawyers). One of my upbringing and background cannot help but to wax nostalgic for the past when flying was dangerous and sex was safe.

Yes there was once a time when people took pleasure in the simple things, times back then may have appeared harsh by to-days standards, but then the people I knew stood tall, not at all the petty small minded whiners that a good part of the population tends to be to-day.

Perhaps there is hope for them who find themselves unhappy with their present state of affairs as they may one day realize the best things in life are free.

A Learning Experience

IT CAME ABOUT ONE DAY while having a gab fest with an older, very experienced bush pilot who I idolized who off handedly mentioned the fact a rat shit outfit located at the old abandoned air force base in "Netley Manitoba", located about fifty miles or so north of Winnipeg was in the market for none too bright hard working low time would be bush pilots willing to depart from the common sense world to act as crew members with the possibility of upgrading to captain on an ancient world war two relic such as the Anson mk. 5 or a small Cessna twin engine trainer known as a T-50 crane, the work totally consisted of hauling freight and fish to and from diversified and remote areas all over north eastern Manitoba.

Well the line had been cast and the bait taken my hungering to try my hand at flying something that would pose more of a challenge then the trusty old tiger moth soon found myself on the phone to the operations manager at netley who upon hearing of the great amount of flying experience snapped me up like a hungry bass would a worm.

At first a near terminal case of cold feet assailed me with the thought of the uncertainties that lay before me, and if at the time my having entertained the least idea of what lay before me would have immediately dropped the idea cold, but the beguiling siren call of perhaps being given the chance to fly larger more powerful aircraft wiped out any shreds of common sense or doubts that that may have remained soon finding myself on a bus headed for Winnipeg and eventually netley airport to view what at first appeared to be a grave yard of derelict air craft lying around in ordered confusion.

Shortly after arrival being introduced to the operations manager by the name of "percy hoarsely", or as I would soon learn everyone referred to him as" prissy horsefly" an outgoing energetic sort that seemed to forever buzz around from one task to another like a bee in a flower garden seeming to be every where at once, but not lingering in any one spot for too long, who in turn introduced me to the chief engineer "johny myrons"a short stout dour person that gave off an air of intolerance toward green horns initially being abrupt and rude toward me, it didn't take too long to learn of his being a dyed in the wool piss tank supreme never becoming more than a quart low on booze at any time though in all the time I spent there never once catching him taking a snort of booze, the next one to meet was the janitor with an unpronounceable polish name one would require a ten piece band to get it right, everyone loosely referred to him as the night watch man who introduced me to the bunk house where I involuntarily recoiled in disgust at the meanness of it being certain the rats had abandoned it in disgust, but for better or worse it would serve as home for the next six months, a thought that initially caused me to quail inwardly but consoled myself with the thought if others can do it, well so could I.

Well the honey moon soon came to an abrupt end with my plunging into a life style one could only have imagined, starting out as a "crew man assisting the pilots to ready the aircraft for flight, The aircraft I was initially introduced to somewhat shocked me as they must have been the motlyest collection of poorly maintained piles of winged scrap I had ever gotten close to, but some how in spite of their pathetic mechanical condition they appeared to perform marvelously well considering the abuse they suffered on a regular basis.

If at first starry eyed soon became baggy eyed, the wake up call seeming to coming hard and fast being rousted out of bed before five: am every morning to stagger out to the flight line while the stars still danced heel and toe, the cold some times being so intense as to make it difficult to catch one's breath, for those who have never suffered the misfortune of having to venture outdoors unwillingly or otherwise to face skin searing well below temperatures during the bleak hours of a harsh winter's morning will never be able to understand just how low a man's life forces can sink at such times, it taking all the willpower one can muster to grit their teeth and carry on. Fortunately for us "crew dogs" the engines where kept warm by electrical strap heaters, a boon to us half frozen slaves, if on the occasion a heater failed it was up to the crew man to bust their ass to laboriously fire up and place blow pots under the engine to warm it up, an unwelcome job no one appreciated having to perform.

Then came the mind numbing job of re-fuelling, once having accomplished that unenviable task one then retrieved the five gallon pails of hot oil that was drained from the oil tanks every night and placed on a massive sheet iron stove to keep warm, a job that always guaranteed excessive and colorful cursing, then lastly came the job of installing the battery which of necessity removed every night to be re-charged and also to keep them from freezing, then the engines started. One simply didn't get to crank up them expensive delicate engines without a complete and thorough check out in the correct starting procedures by Johny Myrons, once he felt satisfied with your competency one was left on their own.

Once the engines had been run up to operating temperatures they where then shut down and the insulated covers re-installed to keep in the warmth, that being done prissy horsefly would appear almost as if out of the blue with a cube van loaded with freight bound for various Hudson Bay stores, that was the simple beauty of the operation the aircraft hauling in freight and paying the way to back haul a load of fish on the return trip profiting the operator both ways.

My being a crew dog cum pilot would ostensibly accompany the pilot under the shallow guise of training as a future captain (at best a long shot), if the real truth of the situation be known we acted more as low paid over worked indentured slaves spending long hours in unheated aircraft as the owner operator deeming it too great an expense to have gas heaters installed for our comfort, and why would they with a seemingly endless supply of not too bright pilots willing to freeze their nuts off for miserly compensation (color me blue). Never did I fully comprehend the make up of a bush pilot, not withstanding the fact of my eventually against better judgment ending up making a career of it, was it that we took misguided pride in enduring great privations?, though many where eventually to pay dearly from the vicissitudes of enduring long miserably cold hours exposed to the worst the elements could offer for too many years compounded by age. Well setting aside the fact of facing miserable conditions on a daily basis admit to being thrilled to sit in the right hand seat of the MkV twin engine Anson fondly referred to by those who flew them as the "bamboo bomber" being constructed almost entirely of ply wood and metal tubing, but god dam flying in one of them drafty hulks proved to be almost unendurably cold even bundled up to the eye brows and that in itself took some of the new found thrill out of flying in them even after having spent many an hour of freezing cold discomfort while flying the tiger moth.

As the pilots gradually became accustomed to my presence they're soon becoming aware that I was not a completely clueless green horn my quickly absorbing the intricacies of handling the Anson quite competently with their in time allowing me to carry out take off and landing practice when empty. By the time we reached our destination we both looked forward to dragging our benumbed bodies out of the frigid cockpit to stumble on wooden feet to the welcome warmth of the store or fish camp, at least the captain initially did my having to remain behind to place the covers over the engines and to assist in unloading the freight, some thing one learned to do with alacrity in order to make a mad dash to a place of warmth which often to my dismay proved to be woefully short if the captain who had gotten there well ahead of you decided to be warmed sufficiently and raring to be on our way to the fish camp where upon arrival the scene would be repeated with me stuck dragging stinky canvas bags full of fish inside the cabin until fully loaded before being able to make my sorry way to the camp to if time permitted quickly gulp down a hot cup of coffee as all too soon we would be on our way back to netley with a gross overload of fish that caused the aircraft to fly sluggishly through the cold air. Admittedly at that point I didn't know much about flying a twin engine aircraft, but regardless of my inexperience astute enough to realize it could be hurt city or worse if we where to experience engine failure at the wrong place or time, fortunately for all concerned no one up till then having experienced that happening though why it failed to occur on the occasion well beyond my comprehension they're being flogged unmercifully day in and day out while enduring what appeared to be a general lack of any form of maintenance what so ever, only seeing the inside of the hanger if some thing broke or failed to function any further.

Depending on the duration of the trips we could sometimes get in three in a long day if all went well, but the completion of the last trip didn't spell the end of my labors it remaining my responsibility to prepare the aircraft for the night by first draining the still hot oil from the engines and oil tank lugging it over to and placing the metal five gallon pails on the stove to keep warm, next removing the battery and completing the chore of placing the strap heaters into the engine cowlings assuring the fact they functioned correctly, finally wrapping up the engines with insulated covers, only then could I gratefully drag my benumbed weary body to the cook shack for a well deserved hot meal that once finished to then spend a little time gabbing with the crew before hitting the sack as morning seemed to come awfully early.

For the first month on the job it seemed all one had time for was to work like a galley slave flying from early morning leaving on the first trip of the day while still dark and landing from the last trip at or near dark day in and day out with never a break or day off to collect one's self, just wanting to at the end of a fourteen hour day to eat a hot meal and hit the sack shortly after so god dam beat out it was all one could do to remember their name or reason for being their in the first place, seeming to have just tucked my poor abused body into my cozy sleeping bag to instantly drop into a deep sleep before feeling the rough shaking of the night watch man who appeared to derive a masochistic pleasure out of waking us poor exhausted buggers up. Each consecutive morning becoming increasingly difficult to face, totally worn out in mind and body from the brutal cold and constant toil prayed reverently for a spell of bad weather that would ground us for a few days, Christ I grumbled to my self on many the occasion just what in the hell have I gone and done this time around?, but regardless how grim a situation it could well become never had been a quitter when the going got rough, only determinably soldiering on till the end. But not all of the would be young aspiring pilots who had started more or less when I had could hack the seemingly endless cruel and demanding regimen heaped upon them, the constant vicissitudes of unceasingly long hours and grueling hard work while existing in an isolated area that offered nothing in the way of entertainment excepting booze and nightly card games, eventually this Spartan life style took it's toll with many of them leaving in disgust to pursue a less arduous career. In hindsight have often wondered if I would have fared as well in tolerating the cruel regimen if not already having to a marked degree experienced much the same travails we now faced on a daily basis, of the eight that had begun with such exuberance and hope with stars in our eyes, only three of us stuck it out to the end, the process of elimination cruel and deliberate as there is no place in aviation for the weak willed as the unforgiving demands of bush flying soon weeds out the unfit leaving only those who where determined to succeed at all costs to eventually attain their lofty goals. Those of us who had grimly hung in there re-gardless of how difficult where richly rewarded, not monetarily (heaven forbid) but in garnering priceless flying experience. It certainly wasn't the money that lured us on if one would care to call a hundred and fifty dollars a month with board and room (such as it was) an incentive to work our buns off twelve to fourteen hours a day seven days a week well so be it.

Well as it went we finally got a spell of much prayed for inclement weather that effectively cancelled all flying for the duration much to the relief of all, (save for the owner operator) finally allowing me the long overdue chance to meet all of the pilots at one time in one place, one would have been hard pressed to meet a more colorful diverse collection of independent case hardened bush pilots all at one time, almost to a man they where supremely dyed in the wool piss tanks (hard drinkers) but on the average astute highly experienced individuals who chose of their own free will to be where they where and doing what they did best, living the life style they had chosen without being forced against their will to observe the strict beaucratic hoopla that stifled their natural independence. It had taken some time on my part to feel totally accepted as an equal with these taciturn hard bitten individuals, my readily understanding their all consuming desire to remain free of societies restrictions and demands being of like mind.

Naturally living in such close quarters among the great unwashed brought out the best and worst of all concerned, at times making it an absolute trial to co-exist in harmony, but as it must it certainly had it's days with all of us at one time or another finding it at times increasingly difficult to tolerate each others idiosyncrasies within such a confined space though rarely did violent disagreements flare up and if they did cooler heads ultimately prevailed in preventing potential mayhem. Some days it became a trial to endure the same boring conversation that never seemed to vary in content, sex, flying stories, good and bad brands of booze, more sex etc etc till one got to the point of wanting to drive a screw driver through someone's ear just to give them something new to talk about. On the rare days when inclement weather curtailed flying operations the general past time consisted largely of playing cards and of course the inevitable and tiresome discussion of sex interspersed with a good old fashioned B. S. session where the unbelievable at some point during it's course would occur, happily fortified with many a sip of old grandad`s"panther piss"(rot gut booze) or some other equally evil brand six or more rambling conversations would simultaneously start up at one time, layered and meshed with the others, cross firing, misfiring and spit firing with never a thread of the conversation that some one didn't pick up and hang themselves, it is not only possible, it's unstoppable. Often It has been surmised that the "great being" created those lovable rascals in a successful bid to avoid crushing boredom that even the God's who in their perpetual wisdom suffer as much as us mortals do. To them same gods I give the credit for often bailing my sorry ass out of successive and deep layers of the stinky brown stuff in all likelihood to keep me in the world of the living just to see what brain dead stunt I would pull off next.

The pilots may have pretty much ran the show as far as flying the aircraft went, but the camp cook held sway over all who would dare to enter his jealously guarded domain unless invited to do so, woe unto any of the unwashed misfits who by accident or design pissed him off (it took very little). As far as cooks went they didn't come much more skilled in the art of culinary skills then he did, all of us wondered at one time or another what such a talented cook was doing in such a hellhole as netley?

But for whatever reason he chose to be there remained his personal business, our only being appreciative of his culinary skills as nothing can be more demoralizing than having to look forward to an unappetizing meal prepared by a slovenly dirty cook. His being of French extract tended toward the feminine side, but Jesus was he volatile and emotional often going into a tantrum over the least slight be it real or imagined keeping the iron hard crews tip toeing around him when appearing to be in a flighty or irritable mood, when one took the time to give it much thought the existing situation left one with very little lee way. On the rare occasion all hell breaking loose if some one inadvertently created a real or perceived slight to his person, it immediately bringing on a passionate spell of flying hands accompanied by his breaking into heated vituperation directed against the perpetrator in his native language, then exiting the kitchen in a self righteous huff, no matter how unintended or slight the cause the offender forced to run the gauntlet of an angry crew in facing the indignity of having his ass well chewed out, needless to say no one ever made that mistake more then once if at all.

As the days dragged by in a monotonous routine my ever expanding knowledge of the intricacies of flying a heavily loaded twin engine aircraft in less than ideal conditions while landing and taking off from ice strips that varied considerably from one location to another, but generally they where well maintained by the tracked bombardiers that dragged huge logs behind them at every new snow fall thus maintaining the integrity of the hard packed surface. But the one situation that all the pilots feared and hated to have to endure was every so often a new fish camp location would be established calling for one of the ansons being jury rigged with ski gear enabling their operating on an unprepared deep snow landing strip on the ice, if the truth be known the installation of skis on an Anson never visualized by the manufacturer even in their wildest dreams and to be totally illegal to do so. (As if that mattered to anyone). As mentioned beforehand the pilots despised having to fly them with good cause as the added weight and drag of the extended gear that could not be retracted once the ski gear had been installed noticeably degrading the aircrafts performance. As it went each and every pilot had little choice but to fly it when their turn came up, it seeming I got stuck with it on every occasion whither I liked it or not, in reality no one asked or much less cared what I thought my just doing as told not realizing at the time the hard won experience would serve me well in later years.

The fact that the aircraft's performance degraded to a marked degree didn't alleviate the fact we where still expected to carry substantial loads both ways, it some times creating all sorts of problems when attempting to take off in deep snow that placed a horrible strain on the engines and our nerves, but the worst was our struggling mightily to remain air borne at speeds barely above the stall until sufficient fuel had been burned off thus gradually lightning us up until finally able to maintain a more acceptable air speed.

The consumption of prodigal amounts of fuel proved to be a two edged sword, yes it did increase our performance as it burnt off, but on the other hand it could create a dicey fuel reserve situation that to say the least could make it interesting. For whatever reason no one seemed to, or if they did dwell on the fact of incipient engine failure it was never mentioned outright, the feeling being if it should happen then one dealt with it accordingly with our not having the luxury of full feathering hydromantic propellers in the end it was all academic. The one bugaboo even the most experienced dreaded was the inevitable crossing of lake Winnipeg in bad or questionable weather conditions as none of the aircraft came equipped with blind flight instruments one could rely on often forcing us to turn back to a place of safety though on many the occasion crossing that formidable stretch of near invisible expanse of white ice forced to barely remain at a height judged to keep us safely above the jagged peaks of rock hard drifts with our fingers clenched painfully tight on the control wheel and ones heart in their mouth, some of the pilots actually swore on the occasion to having glanced the ski equipped Anson off a higher than normal drift scaring them half to death, the very thought of having that occur made my blood run cold though I did hear the following winter one of the ansons snagged a larger than normal drift smearing its self over about a mile of unbroken drifts but strangely enough neither of the two people aboard received severe injury though they where forced to spend a very cold and uncomfortable night burning parts of the wreckage to keep from freezing.

Without a doubt some of the hairy experiences one survived went far toward creating a well-rounded bush pilot out of me. At first while riding along as a crew man the pilots would only allow me to herd the aircraft along while in cruise mode but gradually as they viewed my increasing competency at handling the machine slowly began to introduce me to the rudiments of landing and taking off a twin engine aircraft on a hard packed runway, but at first as mentioned previously only when being empty on flights to the fish camp gradually extending their tutelage to include taking off and landing when fully loaded, under their expert guidance one quickly absorbed the extensive and complex requirements of doing so competently in a short space of time with my becoming proficient in all phases.

My getting on well with all the senior pilots by dint of taking the time and effort toward learning their individual idiosyncrasy's and using the knowledge gained to my advantage, but my all around favorite turned out to be a tall gangly taciturn pilot by the name of Norm Kerns, a totally unflappable personality who never became upset no matter how dire our present circumstances at the time, his craggy face which it appeared to me to have been custom carved out of the volcanic rock found on "Easter Island" never to my knowledge ever betraying any form of emotion, no matter how daunting the circumstances, my eventually learning that while his laboring under a period of stress displayed a tendency to puff on the cigarette that perpetually hung out of the side of his mouth with increased regularity, the only time I ever failed to notice the absence of one hanging out of his mouth was when eating or drinking, and not for too long at that, my often wondering if he smoked while sleeping or having a shower, otherwise a cigarette dangled from his square cut jaw at all times like some omnipresent appendage. As it went his turning out to be one of the best of the lot to fly with and learn from and the first to completely trust me to perform fully loaded take off's and landings. As my pilot skills improved the other pilots I flew along side of under his encouragement also began to slowly demonstrate trust in teaching me their individual techniques with my alternating between the right and left seats as we flew alternate legs.

This fortunate turn of events was to bear fruit much sooner then one could have ever hoped for as one of the regular line pilots who had over a period of time developed a deep consumptive cough that eventually developed into a severe case of pneumonia, not surprising in the least considering the trying conditions they worked under leaving us a pilot short without the means of locating a willing replacement within a short period of time.

I never was able to discover how it came about but absolutely thunder struck to learn I had been chosen to replace the sick pilot, oh yes I ached to one day be a captain of a twin engine Anson knowing without a doubt to having acquired the expertise to do so but still had to admit to my continuing to rely on the captain to make the decisions, now it would be up to me to make my own. One could truthfully admit to it being a heady wine upon taking my place as captain in the left hand seat with a less fortunate co-pilot who had started the job the same time as me sulking enviously in the right hand seat, but the initial euphoria of being El Captain evaporated quickly as the awesome responsibility suddenly and unexpectedly thrust upon me asserted it's self, but it turned out the old timers had taught me well my performing my flying duties with the same cautious measured pace of the more senior pilots, it would not have bid well to betray their trust, the very thought of doing so unthinkable in my books.

Being so taken up with my new responsibilities hardly noticed the passing of the winter flying season finding after my initial tenseness of finding myself in command of my own aircraft to be quite comfortable in the role of captain with a lesser mortal to perform all the menial labors I had once been subject to, appreciating no end the fact that rank has it's privileges, but never once letting that knowledge go to my head playing fair with my less fortunate co-pilot in passing on the opportunity to learn the intricacies of handling the aircraft in much the same manner I had been taught, but as it turned out much to his ever lasting regret disappointment and disgust the season ended far too soon for him to gain sufficient experience to hope to be able to captain his own ship.

As the crews settled their individual affairs with the company upon my being called into the flight office just about dropped my jock strap on being requested to ferry one of the ansons to the Winnipeg International airport.

At first finding this request a bit odd as their was far more qualified pilots than I to do that, but upon inquiring further blithely informed non of them wished to have any thing to do with it what so ever for whatever reason, but my still retaining a some what inflated opinion of my abilities agreed to do it though admitting the thought of doing so threw me for a bit of a loop as my total experience in flying in or out of controlled airports limited to my flying training days, also the fact that the aircraft boasted no such luxury as a serviceable radio justifying a call to the Winnipeg tower operator who assured me I could respond to the colored lamps still in use at the time. The short flight to Winnipeg a pleasure to be sure as very rarely having the opportunity to fly an empty Anson but never the less some what apprehensive at the thought of flying into a controlled airport, but in the end it all turned out well with my following the lantern signals to a letter perfect landing on the long runway and taxiing into the revetment in front of the Winnipeg flying club feeling very much like a grizzled old pro. Once having shut down the engines and completing the after landing checks climbed out of the cabin that reeked something awful of dead fish due to the effects of warmer weather to bustle importantly around the aircraft upon noticing the student pilots clustered by the picture window staring (as I would have liked to think) enviously at me and the aircraft, so taken up with my cock sure self importance failed to take notice of a stocky figure emerging from the back door of the flying club and walking toward me.

Busily involved in retrieving the control locks from the rear cabin just about jumped out of my skin upon hearing a deep gravelly authorative voice greeting my successful arrival causing me to quickly spin around to greet the interloper who had dared to intrude on my moment of glory coming nose to nose with "Doug Crayton", the head honcho of the department of transport air regulations division, a man one wisely did not trifle with if they desired to legally remain in the field of aviation, his staring insolently at me with an obvious glint of amusement in his steely blue eyes while the cigar that was his perpetual trade mark as always stuck prominently out of the side of his mouth like some displaced member. Christ now what I thought to myself?, as my heart took a nose dive toward my toes, then it all suddenly became crystal clear why none of the older pilots had chose to ferry the aircraft to the airport being all too aware of the possible pit falls that awaited one at the hands of the Dept. Of Transport, god dam that bunch of sorry assed piss tanks, they had knowingly thrown my innocent ass to the wolves, my shock and dismay must have been mirrored in my eyes upon becoming aware of his struggling to retain a straight face, but he simply couldn't manage to after my greeting him in a very unmanly shrill falsetto. Once he had by dint of supreme effort managed to place his normally stern visage business face back in place conversationally asked me for the aircraft log books and pleasantly inquiring if I had spent a good winter on the job, my not daring to speak thus making a further fool out of myself only nodded dumbly in affirmation, with the log books tucked under his arm he flashed me another huge grin while blowing a cloud of vile smelling smoke in my face then turning away while saying alright then see you at ten to-morrow morning for your twin engine check ride be there!, again I only dared to nod dumbly but this time he failed to notice, his basking in the sure knowledge of holding all the winning cards and thoroughly enjoying the fact.

Once again I cursed them rotten sons of bitches I had once called friend back at netley who by now where probably prostrated from laughter at my expense, oh Christ how I stung in absolute shame at being arrogant to the point of letting it blind me to their wiles, now I could only pay the piper one way or another.

The night spent in a flea bag motel seemingly endless, gray dawn finding me at the Salisbury house for breakfast but all I could handle was a few cups of coffee with my poor stomach rolled up into a cold ball by my twangy nerves that had become stretched almost beyond human endurance while waiting out the long sweat filled hours for the much dreaded appointment to come about, and since arriving back at the airport must have pre-flighted the aircraft and warmed up the engines at least three times flitting nervously about like a cat on a hot tin roof as the appointed hour came and went leaving me in a ragged state of mind as my nerves almost reached the breaking point while wondering impotently if he sat smugly in the flying club enjoying a last cup of coffee while chewing contentedly on his cigar finding my nervous pacing highly amusing as I waited in ever growing anticipation for his eventual arrival, no doubt about it he knew exactly what he did and by doing so gave me the opportunity to back out gracefully, a new game to me at the time but one that would be confronted many times in future years as I became cognizant of the wiles that that low grade civil servants exhibited in their unending lust for power. Eventually being able to settle my ragged nerves to a degree upon recognizing the rules of the childish game he played at my expense finally got my back up with my deciding to wait him out no matter how long it took as cold anger at being played for a fool transcended nervousness, if and when he deigned to show himself he would find me ready and waiting for what ever trials he wished to inflict during the course of the check ride. At exactly an hour later then the first agreed upon time he reluctantly sauntered across the intervening distance that separated us, the obvious look of impatience on his face informing me that I had best be in fine fettle if I hoped to pass the "ride". Once he had settled in to the right seat spoke for the first time snarling that something must have died and rotted away in here, wisely I kept quiet only agreeing with his observation where upon he ran me through an intense half hour of oral questioning on all pertinent facts as applied to the flight characters of the Mk. V Anson, something that had been beaten into my memory to the point of quoting it verbatim, once satisfied with my response directed me to fire up the engines, my being careful to not omitting any and all required pre-start up and taxi checks, and upon his say so off we went my meticulously carrying out all the pre-flight checks so loved by dept of transport personnel with out a hitch.

At no time during the check ride did I experience any difficulty in performing the exacting maneuvers he put me through as the aircraft an absolute pleasure to fly with no heavy load to degrade it's performance to the point of almost enjoying myself, the entire flight coming off without any obvious problems to be contended with leaving me with an unexplained feeling as if had somehow been cheated it in it's entirety ending so anticlimactic. On landing and taxiing in to the revetment and shutting down the engines in the prescribed manner Doug asked for my pilot's license to sign me off blowing a final cloud of smoke in my face before climbing out and departing.

The next few days spent in settling up with the company collecting my meager pay a princely sum of nine hundred hard earned dollars then taking the bus back to Red Lake to take up the life style I had left in a vain hope of bettering myself. Yes one had to admit the rigorous winter had taught me a lot so not entirely wasted in and of itself if not profitable at least I now possessed a good many hours on a twin engine aircraft plus a twin engine rating endorsed on my license, but somehow I knew that life style not for me, it's passing only leaving a great gulf of despair and emptiness deep down inside, the hard won knowledge that flying such poorly maintained derelict aircraft not the way to go For a long spell my emotions took a tumble in attempting to decide what else one could do with their lives that be construed as being satisfying, but eventually forced idleness brought about common sense thinking as my summer of discontent flew swiftly by with the brisk fall air rejuvenating my normal what the hell outlook on life as it always had.

When the geese began their annual migration I better understood the forces that drove and shaped me, their plaintive honking causing me to become irritable and restless as the riddle of my discontent slowly unfolded revealing the answers I had vainly sought for so long, I too was of the wild goose and not to be restrained or forced to remain in one place for too long as the restlessness within me drove me on to seek new places and new adventure, to seek out whatever I would, only the erratic and uncertain world of aviation offered what fulfilled me, thus a life time spent in aviation and it can be honestly said one could have never made a better choice even if at times regretting having done so, one can truthfully say it certainly had it's days that made one think twice about the wisdom of it all.

Trying Times

THE ONE CONSTANT A GREENHORN would be bush pilot could rely on was the absolute certainty of receiving all the short length labor intensive and dirty trips that usually consisted of fish or back breaking mind bending diamond drill hauls that generated a lot of hard work but very little in the way of remuneration as we did not receive hourly pay for our physical labors but only straight line mileage pay.

As it went one fine day in early march a scheduled fish pick up trip came up with my being low man on the totem pole got the unenviable job of carrying it out. What made it so challenging was the fact we had just received a much greater than average dump of snow making an already bad situation that much worse, the slush conditions to be found on just about every lake that didn't boast a hard packed runway without fail guaranteed back breaking grief when unfailingly becoming bogged down in knee deep slush, the existing conditions to be the worst anyone could recall experiencing for many years calling for extreme caution on the pilot's part when landing on unbroken snow.

The lake I was to visit one that retained a bad reputation for difficult conditions being part of a large fast moving river system, that in itself guaranteed trouble for the unwary as I was soon to find out upon arriving over head in a Norseman aircraft, dismayed to view the length of the packed runway which without a doubt far too short to accommodate a heavily loaded aircraft, it being a certainty if one where foolish enough to attempt to land, they where with a certainty guaranteed to go sliding off the end, and if only one sensing there was no way in hell of preventing doing so immediately fire walling the throttle while hoping to gain sufficient speed to drag themselves clear.

My being the god dam arrogant fool I was brashly thought even if one did overshoot the short runway remained confident beyond all common sense it being possible to power the aircraft back into the air or by completing a large circle until once more able to climb back upon the solid surface of the packed runway, so unthinkingly attempted the impossible with predictable results sliding a good distance past the far end of the short hard packed runway to eventually come to a shuddering halt despite the fact of having rammed the throttle balls to the wall with the aircraft refusing to move forward another inch in the deep clinging mixture of deep snow and water.

After a completely useless attempt to free myself forced to give up and shut down the engine in futile despair cursing them god dam fishermen for failing

46

to pack down a runway of sufficient length to accommodate the Norseman, but more so cursing my stupidity for being arrogant to the point of believing I could beat the odds, now I would pay in spades. At first only sitting there in helpless anger and frustration impassively listening to the tinkle of cooling metal as the now silent engine gave off it's heat while feeling very sorry for myself devoid of the will to rail impotently against the deity being far beyond mere words, only experiencing a deep down inside sickness for having pulled off such a boner, all my arrogance and bravado had vanished like the early morning mists, my no longer feeling the arrogant smart ass that was going to show all and sundry how a professional carried it off successfully. Glumly viewing the tendrils of steam rising from around the well buried main skis not at all looking forward to the gut wrenching knowledge of the inevitable humiliation that faced me if I ever got out of there, the very thought almost causing me to curl up in a ball and give up in disgust.

As if I didn't have enough on my plate the two fishermen came up to the aircraft on snow shoes demanding to know why I just sat there instead of turning around and taxiing in to the loading area? It took my all to restrain myself from screaming at them in pent up frustration, but common sense prevailed as being more or less at their mercy it would do me little good to lose my cool and getting off to a bad start with them, instead grimly explained through painfully clenched teeth my problem as it existed to them, they in turn sympathizing with my plight but never so much as offering a minutes assistance only advising me they where on their way to lift their nets!

Upon their leaving with my still refusing to accept the gravity of my unenviable situation could only sit a while longer reflecting on the dubious glamour of a bush pilots life before the insidious cold began to creep in cruelly reminding me of what yet lay before me. The sobering thought of my being abandoned to my own resources in extricating myself as best I could reluctantly dragged out and donned my snow shoes to begin the daunting task of freeing the aircraft from it's slush filled prison. Grabbing up my saw and axe with my heart all but sunk to my toes laboriously commenced to pack a trail to the nearest shore line, a demanding task of slogging through deep snow and a goodly layer of slush that soon had me panting heavily, often requiring a lengthy stop in order to regain one' breath and to make a feeble attempt to shake off the accumulated extremely heavy slush that inevitably built up to the point one could no longer lift them. Once having arrived at the shore line having to steel oneself to begin the onerous task of cutting and limbing a number of poles, once having accomplished that sweaty mind numbing job began the back breaking task of lugging them out to the aircraft two at a time stumbling awkwardly on the snow shoes often ending up sprawled my full length in the slush. By the third trip my leg muscles had began to protest vehemently forcing me to call it quits for a while so with trembling legs that threatened to give out at any time staggered to the fishermen's shack in hopes of finding a refreshing cup of coffee, upon entering that darkened foul smelling cramped hovel my senses instantly revolting at the over powering stench of rotten food and unwashed bodies, it remaining a cold certainty that having nowhere else to turn one had best get used to it, for it was an absolute certainty it would require a minimum of two days of excruciating effort on my part before hopefully being able to leave.

Upon close investigation and to my ever lasting relief a near full pot of hot coffee sat simmering on the back of the wood stove, after a few cups well laced with sugar along with a good rest in a warm cabin my once gloomy outlook improved considerably, but god dam it how my aching muscles screamed in agonized protest when stumbling back outside on wooden legs and then attempting to strap on my snowshoes, the agonizing pain of attempting to manipulate well abused muscles bringing tears to my eyes, the very effort reminding me this was merely a prelude of what one could expect if one were to judge by just how stiff and sore my thigh and leg muscles had become in that short stretch of time, it becoming all too obvious my being unaccustomed to such demanding use of them as they spasmed terribly at first making it absolute hell to force my unwilling body back to work. At first my best intentions went by the wayside, thwarted by the intense agony that shot through me like red hot needles until a gradual loosening up my much abused muscles responded as the continuing work progressively exercised them, there remained no question about it hurt city was to be my fate for the next few days.

That first day of almost unceasing slave labor seemed endless in producing the mandatory amount of poles required to build a platform to place the skis on once freeing them from the slush, at best a terrible job of using a hydraulic jack placed into the freezing cold slush to laboriously lift each of the main skis one at a time until high enough to place poles under, once clear no time could be lost in scraping the bottoms clean of clinging slush before it had a chance to freeze to the consistency of flint, to not have done so before giving up for the day courted disaster big time as they would have ultimately frozen in to the slush in one big unmanageable lump, impossible to break free of without a lot of hard work and support equipment. By dint of almost superhuman effort which called for kneeling and sometimes lying in the soggy frigid slush for extended periods of time finally completed that most demanding of jobs to my satisfaction, and a good thing I had with my by now beginning to run low on energy, my physically exhausted state allowing the cold to slowly infiltrate my weary body, as much as I yearned to call it a day there still remained two very necessary jobs to be done yet, the engine had to be started and the required oil dilution procedure carried out, to fail to do so would certainly doom me to remain there until support equipment could be brought in as the oil left undiluted in the tank, oil cooler and engine would become as solid as road tar, a very unappetizing and sobering thought.

Upon dazedly completing that remaining but absolutely necessary task wearily dragged my half frozen complaining carcass out of the cockpit to laboriously locate and drag the engine cover into place fastening it securely, next removing the battery and tying a rope to it to aid in dragging it back to the cabin and gathering up my sleeping bag to eventually complete a trek on shaky legs that threatened to buckle beneath me at any time to an uncertain welcome at the foul smelling cabin on what felt like two frozen stumps for feet, on arriving hesitated momentarily before entering to find it's inhabitants preparing their evening meal, one couldn't help but notice neither had bothered to wash the blood and slime and Christ knows what else off their hands from gutting and packing their catch, their unbuttoned sleeves festooned with silvery scales that flapped freely occasionally dropping a liberal dose of them into the food, well who was I to be fussy not to mention my choice being severely limited one would have to live with it.

Placing aside any misgivings I may have initially entertained concerning the lack of hygiene etc. gladly accepted what they offered being near famished from not eating all day and working like a dog, the food tasting delicious as did the hot sweet tea we drank out of filth encrusted tin mugs, Christ on a crutch one didn't want to dwell too deeply on just what form of wild life existed on the rims of them cups, one sure had best place aside any thoughts of being squeamish if they intended to make bush flying a career. There being only two bunks available left me with only the option of a dirty cold floor to lay my sleeping bag on, but quickly consoled myself it beat sleeping in the frozen interior of the aircraft all to hell. Once the meal had been eaten the two fishermen quietly discussed their day in Swedish while they smoked their foul smelling pipes and drank tea. By this time I was so god dam beat it was all I could do to remain in a state of half stupid wakefulness, they never knew how grateful I felt to have them finally turn in for the night with my sleepily laying out the sleeping bag crawling in fully clothed except for my parka that got used in lieu of a pillow. Boots and sock which where hung over the stove on a drying rack to dry as were my boots, but totally dragged out as I was sleep evaded me, kept awake by the agonizing muscle cramps that caused me to double up in knots as my poor tortured body struggled vainly to accommodate itself to the hard cold floor that offered little in the way of creature comfort, the tossing and turning accompanied by muffled moans and groans of pure agony finally ending when sheer exhaustion won over my litany of discomfort, eventually falling into a deep troubled sleep fraught with nightmares of the aircraft sinking into the slush up to it's wings while I impotently rushed ineffectually to and fro in an aborted attempt to save it by jamming huge over long poles under the wings.

The stars still twinkled merrily in their lofty perch outlined by a velvet sky that promised another clear cold day when being reluctantly awakened by the movements of the fishermen who obviously where early risers. Being near comatose from lack of sufficient rest along with my well stiffened muscles protesting violently creating wave of excruciating agony bringing copious amounts of tears to my eyes, my first attempt at rolling over to rise off the floor almost doing me in, but gritting my teeth against the pain shooting through my well abused body by dint of sheer will power managed to finally stagger shakily to my feet on legs that felt as if they where made of wood, it taking a great amount of concentration to make them obey the command to move, at that juncture my life spirits all but vanished leaving me wondering in a near state of panic how I could possibly face the awesome challenge that yet awaited me. To make a bad situation worse my unwelcome presence in that smelly cramped hovel not at all to the inhabitants liking, their on the most part ignoring me as they puffed blue clouds of nauseating smoke that had no where to go in the close confines of the cabin only lingering within the confines of the low ceiling to make it's way into every conceivable corner causing my eyes to burn and water, in a burst of gallows humor visualized my expiring from the smoke, when my death finally becoming common knowledge the news papers trumpeting head lines of "well known great Canadian bush pilot overcome by noxious pipe tobacco smoke found dead in lonely cabin on a small remote lake, the world of aviation mourns his passing". Well it wasn't quite that bad, but there remained little doubt things were about to get a hell of a lot worse before my finally being able to extricate myself from the grip of the slush, how ever it turned out it was guaranteed to be a humbling experience.

Well for what it was worth, there wasn't much to be done but face the music and to carry on as best one could. Not daring to say it in so many words but still remaining some pissed off the two fishermen who never once offered a minutes assistance leaving me to flounder on by myself, only grumbling about not getting their fish to market while still fresh. Personally if the truth be known I could have cared less if it never got out, all I knew was once out of there, very little chance of my ever returning.

Once they had departed in to the still cold gray dawn to begin their day of lifting nets, my life force sank lower than snake shit leaving me feeling sulky and unloved for the next hour until my naturally buoyant spirits once more manifested themselves with the coming of dawn, the early morning sun beginning to show itself over the eastern horizon promising another fine if not bitterly cold day, Christ it was cold, all one could do to catch their breath but that bode well for me in serving to freeze the slush to the consistency of concrete.

Well cold it may have been but that precluded the use of snow shoes my easily walking out to the aircraft on the previously hard won trails now frozen rock hard. One at first cringed inwardly while making the first few halting steps in an agony of tender feet chafed raw by the snowshoe harness.

Upon viewing what yet required to be done a terrible sinking feeling of helplessness assailed me almost causing me to lose my resolve, but the stark fact that if I wished to leave I had best get on with it and do what must be done. Mentally cringing at the mere thought of once more donning the by now dreaded snow shoes did so with great reluctance as to not do so guaranteed a long stay neither I or the fishermen would appreciate, without question a runway of sufficient length would have to be laboriously packed down to freeze solid over night.

Laboring mightily hour after hour each foot gained wearing me down just that much more leaving me afraid my strength would run out before completing the runway, taking a break at what I estimated to be the half way mark and if at all possible to make things worse upon ceasing my efforts it didn't take too long for my overworked muscles to begin to protest violently knotting up and burning painfully denying a protracted rest period, it didn't take too much convincing before arriving at the conclusion it being best to continue on before becoming totally incapacitated, it taking tremendous will power on my part to forcing myself to go on knowing I couldn't quit until a sufficient length of runway satisfactorily packed down, to fail to do otherwise would most likely result in my failing to gain sufficient flying speed before running out of hard packed runway, the very specter of that scenario gave me cold chills and a hardened resolve to keep on and not short change myself no matter how difficult it became to carry on.

At about the approximate half way mark one of the pilots flew over in a small aircraft to check me out on a return trip, making an extended cycle before flying by low and slow as if to tantalize me, one could clearly see his grinning from ear to ear with a row of white teeth clearly visible below his dark sun glasses, my being in a sadistic state of mind sincerely hoped he would be foolish enough to land as misery loves company, but wisely on his part declined to do so much to my disappointment instead giving a cheery wave and rocking his wings in goodbye soon disappearing over the trees leaving me feeling more alone than ever to continue with the mind bending task of completing packing down the runway.

Well having little choice but to do so kept on with the sure knowledge of the gales of laughter that where sure to follow the pilots arrival back at base, the very thought of what he would be telling the rest of the crew causing me cringe in shame, almost being able to hear the hoots of amusement at learning my plight, well well, that smart ass son-of-bitch Weston slugging his guts out attempting to extricate himself out of that slush hole, hardy har har, hope he's enjoying his humble pie!

Gritting my teeth in frustration doubled my efforts as my manly pride had just received a royal shit kicking leavening a host of bitter thoughts that plagued my mind making me forget how difficult it was to plow on over the sodden snow surface that constantly reminded one of attempting to walk over muskeg with only a pair of running shoes on, the torturous going regardless of the risk of enduring muscle spasms forced many a short break, but not daring to take too long a period of rest as each time I did so it became that much more difficult to renew my efforts keeping doggedly on till what seemed an eternity finally completing the run way to my satisfaction.

The trees had begun to cast long shadows by the time the runway completed with the short (long) day having progressed to the point of not leaving me much time to do any thing else so gladly called it a day reluctantly making my way to that sorry hovel of a cabin my heart sinking to my toes at the thought of being forced to spend another excruciatingly long uncomfortable night in that cramped stinking space with two taciturn fishermen that made no bones about resenting my unwelcome intrusion into their ordered lives, well be as it may we where stuck with each other for at least another night.

The two fishermen had long returned with their day's catch and once more my being treated to the revolting sight of blood and slime on their unwashed hands as they prepared the evening meal, actually if the truth be known my being so famished would have gladly eaten the north end of a skunk heading south. As we ate a quiet meal by the feeble yellow glow of a smoky oil lamp, a tasty dish of Swedish style fish pudding along with fresh baked bread they had just baked up, that meal that was found to be absolutely delicious, never had I enjoyed anything so much and in turn complimenting them on their gastronomical expertise that earned me a grudging smile. As before no one stayed up too late once the early darkness took over the land. A short venture out of the cabin to relieve myself revealed the velvet sky beginning to sparkle with bright stars, god, how truly beautiful nature in her natural glory is, in staring intently at the clear star studded sky, pondered why man becomes so taken up with things that hold very little if any meaning but to reflect the apparent success of the owner, some how I knew how ever it went with me I would never trade my freedom for financial or material gain. On re-entering the smoky cabin found the inhabitants involved in playing cards, one couldn't help but to reflect on their simple life style they're seeming to be quite content with their lot in life, for some odd reason a pang of regret ran through me in remembering having given up such a life style to enter into the uncertain world of aviation with its poor monetary rewards, demanding of one's time along with posing a constant risk to life and limb, pushing these somber thoughts to one side volunteered to do up the dishes of which am most certain to be the first time that winter. By the time that simple but demanding chore had been accomplished my eye lids had begun to droop with my fighting desperately to remain awake, I don't think I had ever felt so completely thrashed out in my entire life, fortunately for me the two fishermen had decided to call it a day before too much longer retiring to the comfort of their bunks much to my everlasting relief, by the time they had done so I had reached a stage of near stupidity dazedly laying out the sleeping bag to gratefully crawl in again fully clothed stinking of sweat and god knows what else but could have cared less, all I desired was drop off into a restful sleep which I did with my head no sooner having hit the parka cum pillow before falling into a deep dreamless slumber, and in doing so all my aches and pains forgotten. Morning came all to soon, I would have sworn to having only slept for only a short spell of time but twelve hours had flown by before my reluctantly being awakened to find myself in the same position I had assumed upon first crawling into the sleeping bag, but man did I feel well rested and willing to go.

One of the fishermen busied himself starting a fire in the wood stove while the other had begun to slice bacon for breakfast while I groggily rolled up my sleeping bag mentally bracing myself for what lay ahead. After consuming a delicious hearty breakfast of pancakes bacon and coffee well fortified with sugar, shrugged on my heavy parka and boots to once more resume my labors, at first it was pure hell to force my protesting muscles to co-operate but my spirits soared at the thought to-day would be the day I would be able to leave, but strangely enough a part of me rebelled at the thought of returning to a world I was so ill suited to, somehow the inner man longed to return to the solace of a remote location far away from the never ending demands placed on one in what is referred to as modern society. Upon my advising them that all would be ready on their return the fishermen agreed to return to camp no later then two in the afternoon to prepare their fish for loading onto the aircraft. Once they had departed walked out to inspect the well frozen runway finding it to my liking though somewhat surprised to have the weather remain so cold for such an extended period in late march but who was I to complain! My how beautiful the vista of frost covered trees appeared in the glow of the early morning sun as it rose majestically over the eastern horizon, only them who live and work in the north can truly appreciate it's beauty at such a time. Shuddering against the early mornings icy grip that almost seared one's lungs dragged out the blow pot in preparation of warming up the now well-frozen engine. Once successfully fired up placed it beneath the engine to begin the long thawing out process that could in some cases take up to three excruciating hours.

Keeping a wary eye on the some times recalcitrant blow pot being all too familiar with it's alarming propensity to suddenly flare up spraying raw fuel over every thing and in some cases setting the engine on fire wisely kept my snow shovel within easy reach to quickly dampen down a potential conflagration if it should occur while cautiously diverting my attention for short periods of time to inspect the wings and tail for frost and or any damage that may have occurred sliding through the slush pleased to find all well.

After a period of a little over two hours the engine appeared to be ready. Next returning to the cabin retrieved the battery and installing it in preparation for starting. Now it is never an easy proposition starting an engine after it has been pre-heated, for some obscure reason lost to me, often retaining a miserable propensity to back fire with it not being unusual to shooting great gouts of flame clear back to the tail, a sight guaranteed to reduce the boldest to quivering jelly, much to my relief upon initial start up the engine behaved itself only creating a minimum of fuss with my keeping a wary eye on the oil pressure gauge till the indicating needle stabilized. Once satisfied all to be well left the engine to warm up on it's own took the time to roll the three drums of fuel out of the cabin into the snow, then placing the fish tubs beside them in preparation for filling with fish.

Once the engine had reached operating temperatures shut it down and replacing the engine cover to keep it warm till ready to leave. With nothing else to do during the interim made my way back to the cabin to thaw out and enjoy another cup or two of the fishermen's crank case coffee and make further inroads on the left over pancakes and bacon while awaiting their return. As promised they showed up almost to the minute with our working together soon having the fish packed and loaded. Once being satisfied all to be well made a last inspection of the bottom of the skis to make certain no residual slush remained that could ultimately spell the difference between success or failure on take off, in truth only delayed my departure as long as seemed prudent as part of me willed me to leave immediately while another part urged me to stay not to mention the fear of all not going as it should lay heavily on my mind. Knowing I couldn't delay the inevitable any longer with the short winter day rapidly coming to a close reluctantly removed the engine cover and giving the skis a last good belt with my axe to break them loose crawled into the pilots seat to crank up the engine allowing it to once more reach operating temperature while checking the propeller function and perusing the engine gauges for at least the hundredth time knowing full well the time to hesitate had passed, with a feeling akin to desperation rapidly advanced the throttle to full power while kicking the rudder pedals madly back and forth to assist in breaking loose the skis the aircraft suddenly lunging off the pad of logs roaring and clattering noisily down the length of my makeshift runway slowly picking up forward speed, to my anxious state of mind far too slowly, our thundering right to the very end of the packed runway with my heart in my mouth with the aircraft only barely beginning to fly as we used up the very last inch of available runway barely staggering into the air at the last second to leave us wobbling uncertainly until the airspeed built up sufficiently before daring to begin a slow climb. At that point realizing having forgotten to breathe finding myself suddenly gasping for air.

Well for what it was worth I had by the dint of using my own resources and ingenuity managed to extricate myself from a difficult situation contemplated the demanding events of the last two days calculating that for two long days of absolute slave labor had earned the princely sum of one dollar and sixty cents, pharoses slaves surely fared much better than that.

Well in any case all had turned out well and if I would have had the least inkling of what lay in the future it is most certain I would have considered pursuing a far more lucrative if no less exciting career. In no sense of the word am I religious or hold religious beliefs except for that of Buddhism which makes me a fatalist believing that much of life is preordained and the path you travel is your destiny, one can only meet what ever fate is in store for you with dignity if not pure spirit.

One can only ponder the fates that leads one into the uncertain life style of a" bush pilot" in truth there has never been much written on the subject in a sense leaving us who dared made out to be some sort of an oddity that everyone at one time vaguely hears about but very few know or cares to know more about, our very existence in their minds just one of them strange occurrences that take place.

I have never at any time been too certain of what drives a normally sane person who having the chance to earn a decent living for some reason known only to them instead choose to flog some worn out barely serviceable collection of aerial junk for lousy pay and long hours, either facing searing heat from the engine on a hot day or freezing near to death in a drafty unheated aircraft during the long cold winter months and of course one must justly take into consideration the soul crushing problem I had just faced. Yes it could well turn out to be a demanding career that defines the measure of a man to reveal if he has what it takes, bush flying is not for the weak or faint of heart but for those who excelled at it and accepted it's idiosyncrasies and risks were rewarded with unlimited opportunity to experience far out adventure and travel to out of the way places that few have ever visited and as always remaining the realm of the bush pilot. We where who we where, doing what we wanted to do simply because we chose to, and given that there always more good times than bad could never imagine my being anything other than what I was, how many people can say that?

Shadows on the Wind

LIKE ANY ADVENTURE OF NOTEABLE significance this one too started out innocently enough when with my long time friend Jim Lindokken, the only child of Oscar & Jeanette Lindokken who ran a successful trading post in a remote area known as "deer lake, a good one hundred and ten miles north of red lake Ontario they're having administered to the needs of the native population for over thirty years. Jim growing up as an only white child in the remote settlement with no other children but those of the native people, and as could be expected speaking the native ojibway language fluently along with Cree and various other dialects while learning the intricacies of the fur trade from his father reaching a degree of skill in the fur trade few white people ever have.

In time as he became of age acquired his pilots license with his father purchasing a small aircraft on floats, soon demonstrating himself to be a natural pilot quickly learning the complex issues that flying entails while transporting supplies into the post and fish on the back haul thus making it pay both way's.

Within a period of two years they upgraded to a fine aircraft known as a " Cessna 180"one of the finest best performing aircraft either one of us had flown up till then. Having made a lasting acquaintance with Jim's family soon adopted by them as a second son accompanying them on many a fur buying expedition hopping from trap cabin to trap cabin purchasing all the fur available in the area. I was never certain of the details of how it first came about with Jim successfully negotiating a deal with a well heeled fur auction company located in Winnipeg Manitoba to have them (Illegally of course) purchase all the raw fur we could possibly obtain through the winter trapping season.

Well however he managed it, some how convinced them to bank roll the operation, no mean feat in it's self when considering the company owned and operated by a family of exceedingly cautious and astute people of Jewish descent, but it is my firm conviction the deal only went through on the strength of his fathers fair dealings with them for over a period of thirty years as very few would invest in such a risky venture unless absolutely certain of who they dealt with.

Now one would wonder just why anyone would be willing to stick their necks out so far? For us a certain monetary windfall along with the challenge of experiencing endless adventure more than made it worthwhile. By purchasing the raw fur at source we bypassed the mandated obligation to pay out the ruinous "royalty" imposed by the province of origin on every pelt. For those who have no knowledge of the system that can only be viewed as archaic and self serving dates back to the inception of the notorious Hudson Bay Co. which over a period of time spread their tentacles the width and breadth of Canada annually reaping huge amounts of fur by cheating the unsuspecting natives. At the time all the furs obtained through a series of the companies trading posts where eventually gathered and packed at a central location and eventually shipped to the Hudson Bay's auction house in England to be sorted, graded and auctioned off. This is where the catch comes in with each pelt becoming subject to a tax known as "royalty" to be paid to the king or queen of England once a year.

Understandably once the trappers through out the provinces became aware of this royalty being imposed on their hard won fur, many of them reacting in justifiable anger viewing it as a "royal rip off" to whenever possible selling their furs to illegal buyers or in the United States thus avoiding the royalty thus receiving a higher return for their labors. Of a certainty this state of affairs viewed as threat to the bottom line of the Hudson Bay Co, they're being such a powerful entity immediately went about lobbying the Canadian government to enact protectionist laws proclaiming it illegal to sell or export raw fur across the line without first paying the royalty. To ensure the law rigidly adhered to, no time was lost by the provincial governments to introduce a self locking numbered metal tag that was distributed among fur dealers who dealt in the fur trade who by law bound to attach and record a numbered tag to every single pelt except for squirrels and weasels. How it came about as far as the royalty payment to the provinces went I never knew.

It is also a definite no to transport or cause to have transported fur between provincial borders without obtaining the appropriate export permits. But of a certainty not every one be it trapper, fur dealer or otherwise cared what the laws dictated, it was their fur and they would do as they chose by passing the system by dealing with what the law makers refer to as "shady dealers" who in their own right often took great financial risks in carrying out their dealings, but as noted before hand if one could remain judiciously out of harm's way the practice proving to be enormously profitable, justifying their illegal dealings.

As it went once all had been agreed on and our being trusted to perform well, the fur company initially financing an up to date state of the art radio in the Cessna 180 that came equipped with all the necessary radio frequency crystals as found in every and all federal and provincial enforcement agency's aircraft and ground stations allowing us to passively tune into at our discretion thus giving us an edge we could have never survived as long as we did. In order to pay our expenses and have the necessary large amount of ready cash on hand to make our purchases soon setting out to make our first forays just out of the boundaries of the deer lake area where Jim and his father where well known and trusted by the native population, but not so close to the post as to adversely affect the dealings that where normally transacted there. This initial foray gave us a sense of the possibilities that lay open before us with our soon garnering a far greater amount of fur in a shorter period of time than at first thought possible making it necessary to have the fur expeditiously retrieved by the auction people who upon request immediately arranged to have a trusted associate pick up our cache with great discretion much to our relief while at the same time re-supplying us with as much fuel and what ever else we desired at the time or as could be carried along with a vastly increased sum of cash, a staggering amount that far outweighed what we had initially begun with now that trust in our venture justified.

Once stripping an area clean of as much fur as could be garnered, it called for a nerve shattering transfer of our ill-gotten gains, something we never did get used to. Eventually out of sheer necessity we ventured ever further afield as each of the areas we worked in became exhausted of all available fur we moved on to the next with our increased foray's in time taking us clean to the west coast of Hudson's Bay, a very remote demanding and dangerous area to operate in being costly in time and fuel not to mention if one were to make a grievous error it could well be ones last, that unforgiving part of the country brooked no errors no matter how mundane, but talk about rewarding in fur purchases with our soon running out of cash to transact deals with necessitating another infusions along with the surreptitious retrieval of the secretly stashed furs that in any case could not be left in safety for too long in case of accidental discovery and also leaving it for an extended period of time could easily result in it's being mouse damaged.

Jim being the fur quality expert bartered all the purchases, my lacking his extensive knowledge in both the language and the fur buying trade kept an accurate record of the fur purchased and the cash distributed, his being able on the most part able to sway the most reluctant to part with their furs upon the presentation of ready cash, most if not all of them long fed up with the Hudson's Bay's normally miserably compensation that held them in a thrall of perpetual debt but able to do little about it forced to accept the status quo. As the weeks flew by the ever increasing amount of fur we garnered soon became a great concern to us necessitating frequent supply and pick up trips over an ever increasing distance, though the pick up's went without a hitch much to our relief we still found the naked feeling of being exposed during the period of transferring the furs to the larger aircraft to be harder on our nerves than anything else we had done up till then leaving us as jumpy as cats on a hot tin roof, our overriding concerns of possible detection as unlikely as it was taking into consideration the vast area we worked within, regardless of our isolation that alone guaranteed the near impossibility of accidental or otherwise detection our imaginations ran riot with our hearing a virtual armada of aircraft bearing down on us during the entire time it took to complete the transfer, no question we were always deliriously overjoyed to observe the pick up aircraft's departure and to watch it gradually disappear over the far horizon. Our being more than aware of having kicked over a hornets nest knew that the longer we remained in a certain area the more it required increased vigilance.

There remained little doubt we where stepping heavily on the toes of a long established company that had operated almost solely in the area for over a hundred years considering the area to be their exclusive domain, not only that they had powerful allies to call upon at will if found necessary to do so, from here on every move would have to be meticulously planned and carried out with utmost discretion by employing our skills, high mobility and whatever resources available, also we knew without a doubt there was them who idolized the company in every settlement gladly reporting our presence to the post manager each time we had occasion to land at a settlement to renew our supplies or just to mingle with other people of our ilk and above to luxuriate in a hot shower or soak in a tub of hot water for as long as one chose to. For them who have never resided in a smoky trappers cabin for weeks on end without a change of clothes, eating bland unappetizing food on a regular basis and surviving each day as it came as best one could one can easily understand our dilemma. Of a certainty the dyed in the wool usually scotch post managers more or less attempted to keep track of our movements by use of their stoolies who demonstrated a great show of friendship to- ward when ever we made an appearance at a settlement, button holing us in a hopeful attempt to pry out information regarding our operation, of course we fed them a line of b. s that appeared to satisfy them, we never knew if they followed up on the false trails we made. Once we departed a settlement, the post managers if awake at the time employed their powerful radios to advise others of our departure but other than that not too much else. But our strict policy of not arriving at a settlement until just before night fall and sometimes after depending on how dicey or threatening the situation before us appeared to be at the time, such as an unidentified aircraft sitting there, or how our well honed instincts for survival re-acted at the time, while never at any time having any fur on board for we well knew the risk at landing at a settlement could present an unpleasant surprise to the unwary it being a simple matter to leave a government agent within the population, and always weather permitting leaving the next morning while the stars still danced heel and toe in a velvet sky, not ever returning twice in a row knowing the manager at the Bay had alerted all and sundry to our unwelcome presence within the area.

We continued to brazenly deny the Bay their staple resource, our buying a good ninety percent of the available fur to be obtained within the area, but they remained totally ignorant who their enemy was or how we operated relying totally on innuendo leaving them impotent and unsure as to how to deal with our grab and run tactics until in frustration they passed the problem to the higher up's who in turn used their powerful political position to call in the big guns, namely the minions of the empire building MNR-(Ministry of national resources), we laughingly referred to them as the ministry of national recreation, they're eventual appearance on the scene bothered us not at all having a low regard for the abilities of them pampered beyond belief government wimps, we knew beyond a certainty the forbidding conditions they faced in attempting to way lay or track us down would soon wear thin and they would soon give up and return to their warm comfortable offices with their tails between their legs.

Little did they know when they eventually arrived on the scene their presence had been long anticipated, but still we felt a tinge of alarm knowing they would be tracking our every move and from here on the rules of the game would change with our being far more cautious than ever before.

Well they didn't hold all the winning cards, the fur auction people where no fools nor did they suffer fools, their placing a huge amount of trust and resources on our expertise in being more than able to operate and survive the many vicissitudes entailed by such a high risk venture, they had spared no expense in equipping our Cessna 180 with a state of the art radio and survival gear that allowed us to monitor any radio frequency we chose making it possible to know who was where at any time, if It hadn't been for the advent of the radio we wouldn't have been instantly aware of the presence of the M N R single otter who apparently summoned by the post managers to bring in a game warden to put a stop to our depredations had quietly moved into the area without our knowledge until breaking radio silence when discussing our probable location at the time with one of the post managers sending waves of alarm through us, things where getting just a little too hot with one aircraft already on the prowl and the all too certain probability of an RCMP aircraft on the way.

Having shifted to new ground for a little over a week a radio transmission between the two aircraft intercepted one fine cold morning as they discussed our latest activities over what they mistakenly assumed to be a discrete frequency, it going some thing like this, well boys I hate like hell to rain on your parade but we've chased them two buggers all over hells half acre for a week now and haven't seen hide nor hair of them as they never seem to be where last reported, I understand you have an obligation to apprehend them as soon as possible, but if you by the remotest of chance manage just that and doubt very much you ever will, take my word for it they will drag you all over the country only making fools of you at every turn, them boys are top of the line extremely resourceful bush pilots that know the country and the game their playing far better than you could possibly know, take a bit of good advice and don't be foolish enough to think for a minute you can match them at their game, give up before you get in too deep or mark my word you will most likely have cause for regret, have fun guy's it's all yours now as I'm heading back for Sioux lookout, with that they signed off. The M N R pilot was well known to us as he often had cause to visit the trading post at Deer Lake and in our opinion an amiable decent person. We of course were hardly encouraged by the MNR pilot's high regard for our abilities, for we knew deep down inside that like all other government employee they lacked drive and motivation. As for the RCMP, well that was another matter, if one were wise they did not ever take their abilities lightly, they're being highly motivated stubbornly adhering to the dictum, they always got their man.

Much to the regret of the R C M P officers we ultimately caused them no end of grief and horrendous expense in fuel and manpower during their fruitless pursuit. One of the side benefits of knowing the right people that worked in our favor was the illegally obtained MNR map issued to all of their pilots with the location of every well stocked fuel cache location which naturally we used up to our advantage saving ourselves a lot of time and expense while allowing us to range further afield in our quest for available fur which turned out to be of the highest quality either one of us had ever seen before.

The constant vigil and the seeming never ending pressure required of us while carrying on our daily affairs eventually wore us down, our now appearing haggard and frost burned while slowly losing weight on the meager diet we where often forced to subsist on, and when becoming too exhausted to continue on safely would hole up at a remote trapper's cabin to rest and recuperate for how ever long it took to regain our energy and will to continue on as we knew all too well one never fought the north country but went along with it's moods if one hoped to survive, plus it turned out to be an added benefit in bewildering our pursuers with our sudden disappearance with no sign or trace of our being in the vicinity leaving them most likely angry and frustrated in failing to quickly round us up. We would have been willing to bet the farm the advice received from the MNR pilot rang hollow in their ears.

No doubt about it we played a high stakes risky game that took an increasing toll on our health and nerves by forcing us to remain on high alert at all times, and regardless of how exhausted we became getting a good nights sleep almost an impossibility due to the pent up anxiety that came with the awareness that our good fortune we had enjoyed up to date in successfully evading the law could suddenly turn against us at any time on top of never knowing when and where the rules of the game could suddenly change, we weren't foolish enough to believe it could happen at any time

But stubbornly we kept on as best we could while the creeping symptoms of fatigue and the ravages of being constantly exposed to numbing cold for hours on end with our finally realizing we had all but reached the limits of mind and body and our resources to be infinite. Reluctantly acknowledge the all too certain fact we faced imminent disaster if remaining in the area it being a certainty the RCMP would eventually tumble on to our area of operation. Having pretty well stripped the area of all available fur to decided to pull up stakes and move our activities closer to the Fort Severn area on the west coast of Hudson Bay where a substantial amount of cached fuel awaited our arrival.

Once having arrived at our chosen area we immediately established a secure base out of a remote trapper's cabin to began our depredations in Ernest, harvesting all the fur we could handle while making the odd discreet visit to Fort Severn in order to stock up on supplies that could only be obtained through the good graces of a few teachers that resided there and being old friends of ours always delighted to have us drop in even if unexpectedly welcoming us into their dwelling to enjoy a much needed shower and change and wash of filthy clothes as our life style led one to eventually become rather "gamey"

Not for a minute did we entertain the foolish notion the RCMP would not be duly noted of our arrival and continuing presence by the Bay manager who would have had us shot on sight if our daring enough to enter his store.

For the first while we played it cautiously, never coming near or landing at the post unless being absolutely certain of not inadvertently meeting up with an unwelcome visitor. But basing our faulty logic of the great amount of fuel required in flying the single otter such a vast distance from big trout lake over the most remotest of terrain foolishly relaxed our guard when breaking our cardinal rule of arriving late and leaving early, perhaps it was because of our becoming weary of the constant isolation or fearing the inevitable onset of the "shack Wackies" requiring the company of our own people and a welcome respite from our unceasing toils

Well against our foolish predictions the RCMP once being informed of our unwelcome presence by the post manager chose to visit that out of the way remote corner of the earth, seemingly appearing out of the blue when they did while unexpectedly doing so coming as close to nailing our pelts to the wall as they ever had, it being by the merest of chance one of the old trappers who had lived in that forbidding part of the country all his life and intimately familiar with the vagaries of the local weather systems that often with little warning came screaming off the bay with a vengeance to inflict a living hell on all and sundry, taking it upon himself to come to the teacher's residence were we lounged in absolute comfort while enjoying a gab fest with our hosts to warn us of an extremely violent and turbulent weather system to be fast moving in off the bay cautioning us it best to leave as soon as possible and to take refuge from the storm in a relatively protected trapper's cabin located far inland he pointed out to us on the map.

No doubt about it, that was discouraging news at best, but our being far too familiar with the intensity and ferocity of the storms that blew madly off the bay having on many the occasion battled our way through them at one time or another wisely chose to heed his warning even though sick at heart at having to leave the cozy comfort and warmth of the teacherage reluctantly packing up our sparse gear to glumly make our way to the icy discomfort of a frozen cockpit and then in a foul dark mood make our way to the remote trapper's cabin were we would hunker down through the duration of the approaching storm. As was to be expected we where warmly welcomed by the inhabitants to stay as long as we wished as the native people as always warm hearted toward strangers reveling in their company as it goes far toward relieving what can often be a monotonous existence.

Of course we had no knowledge of their arrival at Fort Severn at the time, but still one cannot help but to wonder at the frustration experienced by the RCMP upon landing at Fort Severn only to learn of our departing a bare half hour or so before their unexpected arrival. Securing our aircraft against the ravages of the approaching storm as best we could, gathered up our survival kit and gear to move into the comforts of the cozy cabin to wait out the storm in comfort.

In time we realized our now having the opportunity to completely relax for the first time from accidental discovery, the fast approaching storm would see to that giving us a much needed rest and ample time to run the past events and recent happenings through our minds with both of us arriving simultaneously at the conclusion that the pilot of the RCMP aircraft to be on the rather astute side and not to be dismissed lightly while our remaining certain barring evidence otherwise he had recently without a doubt tumbled onto the fact that we could at will hack into their radio frequencies giving us a leg up on their daily movements, thus explaining the sudden cessation of radio transmissions between them and the post managers, their most likely hoping our mistakenly assuming they're having given up on us. The very thought of the chances we had recently taken while uncertain of their positioning left us cold, we should have known better, but ceaseless toil and strain along with the creeping symptoms of fatigue had taken it's toll numbing one's ability to think clearly, only chance and good fortune had seen us through, but it was much later on before becoming aware of just how fortunate we had been that day.

The storm when it moved through our area proved to be a real mind bender with our remaining eternally grateful to have escaped the mind boggling fury mindlessly unleashed at Fort Severn while we reclined in total comfort, one could only begin to imagine the terrible conditions one would experience in the unprotected wide open spaces of Fort Severn were the unimpeded fury of the storm howled madly off the vast reaches of Hudson's Bay with all the unbridled might and abandon of a runaway freight train, shrieking insensately like a demented soul around the crude dwellings, threatening all that would dare venture out with white death, in truth we did wonder how the local population could deal with it, but they did so with admirable aplomb. In truth the violent storm benefitted us in allowing a much-needed respite from our incessant and demanding labors, tired pilots make mistakes and in that totally unforgiving part of the country one's first mistake could all too easily prove to be their last. To be certain we made the most out of enjoying the safety and comfort of a cozy cabin that allowed our tired minds and bodies to rest and relax secure in the knowledge that their existed no way in hell of being detected even by the most ardent of pursuers, the violence and the intensity of the storm saw to that.

With little else to do but to plot our next series of moves once the storm cleared or to carry on long rambling conversations with our hosts about the land, the people who inhabited it and their fascinating legends and of course to sleep to our hearts content and to partake of the native fare as one saw fit. One day while helping myself to a bowl of savory smelling mouth watering stew that constantly simmered on the back of the stove without thinking stirred up the contents of the pot, then casually transferring a ladle full of stew into my tin bowl to be somewhat taken aback when noticing a tiny animal skull with it's empty eye sockets and a set of prominent orange yellow incisors staring accusingly at me causing me to momentarily hesitate having become unsure what to do next before catching myself and continuing to tip the ladle full of stew into my bowl with the sure knowledge my hosts covertly observed my every action, to not accept their proffered largess in what ever way shape or form it came in would construe the worst form of insult. Knowing there to be no way around it bravely popped the skull into my mouth and to suck noisily on it before losing my resolve, the act of showing my appreciation for the fine food offered me extremely difficult to say the least, Jim who had been smugly sitting back watching my antics with unabashed amusement dancing in his eyes, no doubt got a huge kick out of my squeamishness as such an occurrence hardly new to him having lived among the native people all of his life and quite accustomed to their life styles, actually if the truth be known it was only a matter of one's state of mind..

Certainly we were concerned about the safety and security of our aircraft, but knew better than to even consider venturing out to check on it as one would soon become disoriented in that maelstrom of screaming wind and swirling snow that effectively blotted out any thing more than a few feet away, if one were foolishly inclined to have done so they ultimately faced certain death from exposure when almost instantly losing their bearings to the safety of the cabin, we could only hope for the best as we had made certain it to be well secured and fairly well protected from the worst of the storm. Eventually the storm exhausted it's fury after five full days of doing it's worst, but the welcome respite left us in a far more positive state of mind, well rested and raring to go. The night of the cessation of the storm with the manic winds dying down to a vagrant breeze the stars at given intervals began to peek out from behind the high racing cloud formations that eventually moved off allowing the stars to once more fully dominate the velvet sky, how beautiful the skeins of aurora borealis that suddenly appeared as it writhed across the clear moon lit sky hissing and crackling as it wound it's way over the visible horizon.

Early the next morning while the stars continued to dance heel and toe we made our way out to the aircraft, the first pink flush of dawn on the horizon had only just began to make it's awesome presence known appearing as a demarcation between the first light of day in contrast to the still darkened sky giving off the promise to all who thrived in that remote land of a fine bright day.

Not until coming up to the aircraft did we notice upon opening the door the cabin to have a heavy dusting of fine snow through out it's interior necessitating a little work in removing it. One could only ponder the fate of anyone being caught out in the exposed spaces of Fort Severn.

We had yet to learn that was exactly the fate that befell the RCMP crew who unbeknownst to us had landed shortly after our timely departure, the native population there had on the average little respect or regard for policemen or government officials in general, deliberately failing to inform them as they had done for us of the violent storm bearing down on them, thus leaving them to face heart breaking misery. The pilot upon realizing they were in for a violent storm and knowing there was no hope of escape, him and his crew barely managed to by dint of frantic measures to lash a number of drums of fuel oil to each wing and tail section while placing as many as possible on top of the skis, then just only managing to make their way to the safety of the post at the last minute before the storm roared in completely blotting out the landscape, only to learn from the post manager much to their dismay of our having departed shortly before their unannounced arrival, I for one would have dearly wished to have known their thoughts upon being apprised of our recently having been there and to have once more slipped away into the vastness of the north shortly before their arrival, one can safely assume them to have been quite black.

Our having eventually having cleaned out the aircraft's cabin to our satisfaction and filled our wing tanks from the drums we had brought with us, but still we hesitated to climb into what closely resembled an ice cave. Strangely enough neither one of us retained any desire to leave our cozy haven that day, we may have been well rested of body but still remained near exhausted in mind, the constant requirement of living on the edge at all times had exacted it's toll, instead agreeing to stay put one more day with my deciding to strap on my snow shoes and explore some of the surrounding vicinity, delighted to discovering numerous forms and varieties of fascinatingly diverse snow sculptures shaped by the whims of the fierce winds that had swirled with wild abandon across the lake, one only had to permit their mind to run free in order to truly appreciate mother nature's finest, to remain as man was meant to be, to be able to view the awe inspiring sight of a copse of straggly wind blasted pines etched darkly against the background of an azure sky with the hummocks of drifted snow to give them depth, what more could any man ask but to remain free to wander were they would or to do what they chose, to make the most of nature's bounty unfettered by the cloistering demands of modern society.

Yes I thought to myself, my present state of affairs is fraught with chance and potential danger, but I for one would have never forsaken a minute of the time spent in that fascinatingly remote part of the country that appeared to offer so little but offered so much to those who respected it's moods and appreciate it's savage beauty, some how, some way the stark emptiness of that vast unspoiled land appealed deeply to my awareness as very few of the numerous places that had been visited at one time or another had ever done .

The following time spent in that part of the country consisted of early morning starts while the stars danced and twinkled merrily overhead with our on the occasion venturing up and down the formidable boulder strewn coast line that on the occasion caused one to cringe inwardly upon viewing up close the awe inspiring sight of the house sized chunks of drift ice that appeared haphazardly along the entire coast line, one could not help but to remain in awe of the sublime forces of nature that had placed them there, not exactly a good spot to experience mechanical failure, our always breathing a collective sigh of relief upon gratefully turning back inland.

Our ongoing level of success in purchasing fine furs would have had to be seen to believe necessitating frequent pick ups to relieve us of our burgeoning collection that as always kept us on edge.

Our being well aware of the fact the trapping season fast coming to a close forcing us to increase our efforts as the trappers within the vicinity would be soon moving back to the settlements.

Not being aware of what had become of our nemesis, not having picked up more than a few garbled messages that told us nothing for some time kept us on edge. The weather slowly becoming increasingly mild and less daunting, the long hours spent in the cockpit increasingly endurable as the long winter wore on easing the constant strain imposed on our tired bodies.

Often while Jim took his turn as pilot in command and my not too taken up with the demands of keeping track of our progress and ground position on the map while traversing what would appear to the untrained eye as endless miles of wind swept barrens as we made our way to the next potential fur buying site pondered the circumstances that had allowed my participating in an extremely daring risk filled venture that took me to places were very few had ever dared go aside from the occasional native trapper or hunter and of course damn fools such as us not to mention the exceedingly remote chance of meeting up with another aircraft lost to infinity, not at all a good place to lose one's way and run out of fuel or to experience mechanical failure, the possibility of that occurring never straying too far away from one's mind at any time adding to the stress.

Eventually as it must, our great adventure with our in the end having attained an unprecedented level of success. But before it all came to an end our becoming increasingly nervous at not knowing the where abouts of the RCMP aircraft, discreet inquiries at some of the smaller outlying settlements we dared to visit on the occasion revealed nothing of their being in the vicinity for some time creating an increased level of nervousness, there was no way in hell we could have possibly known they're having left the area and would not be returning, something I would only find out by chance many years later.

But our remaining ignorant of the fact at the time maintained our usual vigilance, not having become arrogant to the point of believing for a minute our having seen the last of them and all too well aware of their reputation of always getting there man, and by a rare combination of luck, chance and design having up till then evaded their grip, outfoxing them at every turn and that accomplishment in it's self guaranteed their pulling out the stops in an all out effort to nail our pelts to their office door.

It always has and remains so to this very day a pet peeve of mine that powerful moneyed corporations always have the minions of the law at their immediate disposal to make certain lesser mortal are discouraged from competing with them Personally I have never been shy about making my lack of respect for the law known.

Well as it went the long looked forward day finally rolled around much to our relief having become tired beyond human endurance by the unceasing demands constantly visited on us Another worrisome problem that came about from time to time was the difficulty experienced in establishing a line of communication to our backers to arrange a pick up date and location, fortunately to the collective relief of all our last effort went off without a hitch. Once that most nerve wracking of experience had been accomplished it left us free to make a final stop at a smaller cache on our way through to deer lake and from there on to Winnipeg.

For some strange reason that could not be rationally explained a pang of regret at leaving the now familiar barren chunk of real estate that had offered us manifold adventures and thoroughly exciting times that would never again be repeated or would we ever return to assailed me, but all things must come to an end be they good or bad. Eventually disposing of the last of the incriminating furs to the care of the auction house though we where not that naive to presume it to be a done deal between us and the law, they had been thwarted but would still be demanding their pound of flesh one way or the other, thus we were required to remain on the discrete side of life until it blew over, little did either of us realize at the time a heavy price for our misdemeanors had yet to be exacted.

Once a full accounting had been laboriously enacted by the companies bean counters, it taking an entire week to accomplish to the satisfaction of all decided during the interim to take some time to rest and clean up and if at all possible to wind down to a mild scream in our hotel room and to take advantage of what passed for normal to ordinary every day people Both having access to more ready cash than either of us had held in our possession at any time in our lives. On my part knowing the potential danger of flashing a large sum of money that was certain to attract unwelcome attention for some time to come left the bulk of my share in care of the auction house not being that green or uninformed of the far reaching powers of revenue Canada and the RCMP to pry at will in to one's bank account, and remaining absolutely certain mine would be closely monitored for some time to come as not believing for a minute the law was not at any time unaware of our identities regarding our past activities but lacked the hard evidence required to lay charges against us and they are bad losers.

After a time becoming weary of it all and having been absent from my home for an extended period of time yearned to return to a semblance of peace and quiet, exhausted to very core of my soul and having more than my fill of existing as a fugitive from the law. My entreaties to leave fell on deaf ears, Jim being on roll with a motley assortment of hanger owner's that appear as if out of nowhere who with their genius in spotting a prize sucker to be fleeced. Instantly tacked themselves on to Jim. I was never certain it to be a genetic or an opportunistic fault in his makeup, but it being abundantly clear his being unable to handle any level of success without his seemingly childish desire in making it clear to all and sundry that he had, foolishly blowing his hard won gains on upscale hotel rooms replete with wine women and song and god knows what else to a degree of totally disgusting me.

Knowing any further attempts to convince him to leave his juvenile desires to be a sugar daddy to be futile dispiritedly took the bus back to Red Lake to await his eventual return not being aware at our final parting in the hotel room that it would be the last time I would ever see him alive as he never did arrive.

As the circumstances of his last hours unfolded the most likely scenario being after completing an intense period of out and out non stop debauchery had finally run down or exhausted all his resources and while in a sick and sorry state of mind taken off in the same faithful aircraft that had served us so well for so long to return home only to mysteriously disappear while enroute, it taking eleven days of intensive search before the wreckage of the aircraft discovered, it being obvious his having for an unknown reason to have crashed into the trees while in an almost vertical descent killing him instantly, and so ended the short life span of a close friend and a fine young man in the bloom of youth. Upon learning of his premature death, the knowledge of his passing shattering me, our having shared a common danger for so many months while depending on each others skills for survival, no two brothers had ever shared the endless dangers and privation in such close quarters for so long a period of time we had, to me it was ironic that he should die so ignominiously leaving a large hole in my life that remains to this very day.

This is only an opinion on my part and never substantiated by the autopsy performed on his remains, but I retain a deep suspicion that prior to his departing Winnipeg, his being by whatever means having been dosed with a slow acting drug without his knowledge that eventually incapacitated him during flight causing loss of control with the aircraft diving almost vertically into the ground killing him immediately. To my way of thinking and there is no one more qualified in expressing their opinion, he was at all times no matter his state of mind or unsureness of body just too astute and skillful a pilot to have as it has oft been erroneously stated to have simply passed out over the controls, my firmly maintaining to this very day he was never aware of ceasing to exist. It is only conjecture on my part, but would I have suffered the same fate if having partied with him instead of returning home? Yes, I firmly believe so. It is left up to the individual reader to arrive at their own conclusions, and that the truly astute of them will quickly and accurately arrive at the correct one.

Well regardless of what, life goes on with my after a long and circuitous career in aviation eventually found myself as a flight engineer on DC-3 aircraft based out of Churchill Mb. One morning while sitting and drinking endless cups of coffee in the airport cafe along with many other crews impatiently waiting for the weather to improve as promised by the local "Met" boys whiled away the time by striking up conversations with other aviation personnel as there is no such thing as a stranger in the aviation profession the world over.

As the long boring hours slipped away by chance struck up a conversation with an elderly quiet pipe smoking pilot who as it turned out flew the RCMP's twin otter, for some odd reason it was felt that he had been covertly studying me for some time and that it was not random chance he struck up a conversation with me. Having behaved myself for a number of years had little to fear from the law but my curiosity to see how far protracted conversation would go led me on and I was not to be disappointed upon his revealing for reasons best known to him during the course of our conversation to be the very same pilot that had once pursued us all over hell's half acre in a futile attempt to apprehend us with the "corpus delecti". Why he chose to reveal that odd bit of information to me at that time failed to come clear to me until much later on when relating the story in it's entirety.

My knowing what he represented remained guarded even when informing me of his pending retirement that lay less than a year away, an event his obviously not looking forward to. A Dreamy sort of a look seemed to appear in his eyes as he continued to reminisce on some of his fondest memories that occurred during his long career, openly admitting to having a high regard for the bush pilots of his era, admiring their manifold skills in being able to with relative ease navigate over the most barren and trackless wastes of the north during the dead of winter while using mostly maps and acquired knowledge of the featureless terrain they traversed, going on to say their ability to thrive under the most trying of conditions never ceased to amaze him, openly admitting to his never having had it in him to be a bush pilot.

At one point his dialogue appeared to lag leaving me uncertain if his having said all he was going to on the subject or mulling over where to go next as his eyes once again took on that dreamy long ago far away look that seemed to reflect past glories never to be re visited, one I had now begun to recognize. After an extended period of contemplative thought suddenly turned to face me with an intent look on his face surprising me no end upon inquiring if I had ever made the acquaintance of Jim Lindokken?, somewhat taken aback by the suddenness of his unexpected inquiry must have momentarily hesitated before admitting, yes he was once my brother in law and the closest of friends. Upon hearing that admission his lips and eyes immediately crinkled up at the corners in amusement that at first left me wallowing in total confusion before it struck me he well knew who he was talking to and enjoying leading me on.

Well if that was the way he wished to play the game it would prove interesting to find where I stood in the scheme of things before inadvertently stepping on my dick, his having long struck me as being rather astute and noteworthy opponent.

Not for a heartbeat did I lose sight of the fact that at one time we had stood on opposite sides of the fence, and also the possibility of his still smarting inwardly after having experienced total failure in apprehending us even after all the years that had passed and the RCMP never forgives or forgets.

Call it what one may, while having little cause to retain my enmity toward police officers, the very notice of their presence causes me to bridle finding something sinister and threatening about their ill concealed arrogance, that feeling especially applies to female police officers who it appears carry a lot of baggage with a burning desire to prove their worth.

He must have sensed my passing enmity as his features momentarily took on a resigned look of sorrow. Somehow that made me feel slightly guilty as at no time during our extended conversation did I get the feeling of his attempting to trap me or to involuntarily hang myself, but instead it becoming readily apparent his desiring to relate something of import to me.

With a soft shuddering sigh he took another long pull on his pipe as his face once more took on the satisfied look of one who has pleasant memories they wish to share, and this he commenced to do relating in great detail of a noteworthy time during his career spent in attempting to track down and arrest two renegade bush pilots engaged in the illegal practice of purchasing raw furs without a fur buyers license directly from the native trappers. It appears the Hudson's Bay Co.'s top brass had filed a formal complaint against us upon being informed by near hysterical post managers of our ongoing depredations in their stock in trade, reporting a severe drop in the amount of fur normally procured. It was the native workers who remained curiously loyal to the HBC that first gave them the bad news of our unwelcome presence.

This unruly state of affairs could not be allowed to continue to exist but in injecting a little humor into an other wise humorless situation on our being apprised of the expected but totally unwelcome presence of the RCMP in the area I couldn't help but to concoct a scenario of a team of police officers decked out in their traditional garb of scarlet red jackets with smoky bear hats perched over their lantern jawed granite visage features, steely eyes intently focused on their mission as they bravely set forth to uphold the honor of the Hudson's Bay Co. from the ravages of two insignificant and obviously arrogant renegade bush pilots that dared to infringe on their profits, riding antlered moose with snow shoes attached to their hooves.

Puffing sedately on his pipe creating a wreath of aromatic smoke suddenly peered at me as if just having arrived at a momentous decision, hesitating momentarily as he took the time to knock the dottle from his pipe before fixing me with an intent stare saying I don't rightly know as I should be telling you this, but what the hell can it matter in the short run as I have less than a year left till I'm forced to retire, aside from that it is my understanding you are not one to randomly shoot your mouth off, this statement surprised the hell out of me our previously having parried and thrust for some time with the conversation often drifting off to totally unrelated subjects, but invariably returning to the subject matter he appeared to want to reveal, once certain of his ground launching into a fascinating story that left me in a totally bemused state of mind.

Once having completed the excruciatingly long and boring flight from Winnipeg Mb. To the Hudson Bay's most lucrative post located on Big Trout Lake were they set up a base of operation of sorts. Then began an immediate inquiry as to how many perpetrators were known to be operating in the area, the answer they initially received left them in a state of confusion as if the hysterical reports being sent out from the outlying posts were to be believed there was no less than a dozen of us floating around engaged in illegally buying fur. One could not help but to have a good chuckle to think we had managed in such a short space of time to having created such confusion amongst the post managers that had mistakenly placed us at more and varied locations at one time than humanly possible.

Yep he went on to say, it turned out to be a fool's errand from inception, our being tasked with tracking down two well-experienced highly mobile bush pilots that intimately knew the lay of the land and the people who populated it. Each time they followed up on a report of our present where abouts, by the time they got their act together we had moved on, but in the process they sure shook up a lot of transient pilots that had the misfortune to be sitting there at the time of they're arrival, and so it went time after frustrating time till they began to question the validity of our existence or only the figment of a bunch of badly bushed or hysterical post managers. As the pilot of the RCMP aircraft put it so succinctly at the time them two if they exist at all where as "Shadows On The Wind.

In time their frustrations at failing to apprehend us up till then began to fray their nerves while weighing heavily on their pride. He surprised me all to hell and back when openly admitting to having developed a grudging admiration for our seeming ability to continue to operate with seeming ease in such a demanding and hostile environment where one bad mistake or mechanical failure could well spell out certain disaster, and surprising enough in time admitting to fear for our safety if by chance they did manage to apprehend us, not at all certain of being able to control the frustrations of a young police officer who at first had arrogantly predicted they would be able to round us up in no time flat, as it stood their ongoing failure to have done so up till then had obviously unbalanced him to the degree he had been overheard muttering threats to blow our fucken heads off once accosting us.

On hearing that, waves of ice-cold fear coursed down my spine not doubting for a second the sincerity of his statement. In giving it some thought it was a simple matter of getting in to the head of the young officers frustrations, not being that long out of training and finding himself totally out of his element while remaining in the brain washed state of mind his instructors had drummed into him leading him to keep believing himself to be of superior intellect in comparison with the average man, taking our lack of co-operation to heart nurturing an unreasonable all consuming hatred that fed on itself each time we outmaneuvered them thus prolonging their stay. His being a city boy would not fare well in traversing such a remote and barren area of frozen muskeg mostly bereft of any signs of mankind save for the occasional trapper's cabin, that must have gone far toward loss of confidence that terrified him, his only desiring to having their task successfully concluded as quickly as possible and be able to return to the comforts and familiarity of city life.

It so came about one day while futilely involved running down a possible sighting of our where abouts that as usual had led nowhere the pilot misjudged his fuel reserves leaving them far too short on fuel to make it back to the post necessitating an emergency fuel stop at supposedly secret MNR fuel cache marked on the map. One can only imagine their severe frustration and dismay on arrival to be met with nothing but recent ski tracks and empty fuel drums to mock them. This awkward and unexpected turn of events clearly placed them in a quandary not having sufficient fuel to attempt to reach safety had little choice but to accept their present lot and make the best of it until forthcoming assistance could be rendered.

The pilot being unable to make radio contact with the post manager waited until night fall when radio reception at it's best, but as fate would decree it the northern lights made their appearance crackling and hissing through the star filled heavens completely wiping out any hope of radio reception leaving them to set up camp to endure a long cold night while dining on unpalatable emergency rations. The next morning the pilot lucked in when being able to contact an airliner flying by far overhead who passed on their plight to Winnipeg who in a round about convoluted manner managed to contact the post manager who in turn arranged to have fuel flown in at what we where certain had to be an atrocious cost.

Our being well aware of their dilemma having overheard their calls for assistance would have presented same if found necessary to have done so, but once having fuel delivered to them eventually made it back to their base on their own, but we sure wouldn't have cared to come afoul of them for the next while if the tone of the intercepted radio transmissions were anything to judge by, it would have proved interesting to have known the young police officer's reactions.

To add insult to injury we took full advantage of their plight by making a surreptitious visit to the settlement during their absence to enjoy a hot shower, a change of clothes and above all a chance to imbibe in food stuff far superior to the usual bland and monotonous native diet, of course one of the faithful immediately took it upon themselves to inform the local post manager of our presence who to his consternation could do naught but to grind his teeth in helpless anger and frustration with our rubbing it in by not departing until it being no longer judicious to remain. No doubt that audacious act placed us well up on the endangered species list. In a sense even though our pursuers having almost unlimited resources to aid them we held the advantage of being intimately familiar with the area we chose to operate in like our back yard often utilizing the cover of the vicious storms that swept unimpeded across the vast stretches of barren land picking our way from cabin to cabin at will occasionally being forced to hole up when the weather becoming far too severe even for us to handle. Of a certainty we made the most of them breaks from our almost constant demands as we too subject to creeping fatigue. Of course the RCMP pilot not being any one's fool knew better than to take on such uncalled for risks by attempting to match us, chose to sit the storms out in comfort and as he put right happy to do so.

The days marched by in monotonous regularity with each one bringing us closer to exhaustion of mind and body, the high level of stress brought on from the unrelenting strain of playing cat and mouse against a determined pursuer who wanted nothing more than to bring an abrupt end to our activities and return to the comforts of their homes.

Only the fact our state of the art radio allowed our freely monitoring their radio frequencies as they contacted the various post managers giving us the advantage of being aware of their intentions and positioning preventing our unintentionally blundering into harm's way, but regardless we remained extremely cautious regarding radio transmissions as they could all too easily be misleading with our never at any time being absolutely certain that a member of the crew had not been planted at any one of the various settlements to arrest us in the event of our inadvertently risking a landing there. If that were to occur it would doom our venture to failure as they could without justification detain us for a lengthy period of time when our ongoing success depended on reaping all the available fur we could during the few productive months open to us. The fact that we in theory operated solely on our own and unable to if apprehended expect help from any source in extricating ourselves be it financially or otherwise

Fortunately for our peace of mind we were never aware if they had, and if so our luck held up with our being elsewhere at the time.

Another advantage we held over them was our ability to become mobile long before the last star winked out by utilizing the incomparable services of a small catalyst heater that was placed into the engine compartment at the end of each day and then tightly wrapping an old sleeping bag around the cowlings that effectively keeping the engine toasty warm through out the long cold nights, it only taking us a matter of minutes to prepare our selves for flight and shortly after be on our way while preparing the single otter for flight a daunting task that would tax the patience of the most staunch to the limit forcing them to begin their daily struggle well before sun rise when a man's life forces have reached their lowest ebb if they intended to capitalize on the short winter day, we certainly didn't envy their lot.

Eventually it came clear to the astute pilot that we must have access to their radio frequencies, how else could it be explained our slipping through their fingers at every turn making it highly unlikely in any event they're apprehending us any time soon if at all by futilely pursuing us from pillar to post came up with the idea of laying an ambush. At that juncture taking another hefty swig of his long gone cold coffee and a few more deliberate puffs on his pipe in order to bring it back to life, once seeming satisfied with it's performance once again sat back uttering a short bark or two of laughter before continuing his fascinating narrative, yep he intoned we where absolutely certain our ruse would see our nailing the pelts of them two maddeningly elusive buggers to the door our having set it up with the post manager to play along with us in leaving a member of the crew to apprehend us in the most likely event of our showing up while acknowledging over the radio to the post manager it was not their intention to return that day, instead planning on remaining overnight at another settlement.

That simple statement caused a shiver of cold fear to run up and down my spine, once more re-living that well remembered close call, for at the time of our intercepting the false radio transmission we sat not too many miles away desperately requiring access to a phone in order to pass on our coded message for much needed pick up along with a request for fuel and supplies, not to mention the almost overwhelming desire for a most welcome shower and a change of clothes and above all good food in the presence of friends. Nothing but mile after mile of sere non descript muskeg and dimly lit trapper's cabins paled on one after an extended period of time rendering the siren call of our favorite settlement almost irresistible. Upon hearing their plans to be away for the night we were almost beside ourselves with glee at being able to spend the night without fear of being apprehended. But in thinking it over further we soon came to the conclusion it was too pat and rehearsed leaving a lingering residue of uncertainty, a falseness that literally screamed of treachery with our reluctantly but wisely choosing the option of bowing out, instead disappointedly returning to the isolated safety of a trapper's cabin, oh yes we certainly did question our motive for staying away from the settlement, but concluded we hadn't managed so far to remain out of the iron grip of the law by ignoring our instincts and retaining an ongoing proclivity for caution at all times.

As I was to learn much later on we had by the merest of chance by disregarding the almost overwhelming human desire for the better things in life unknowingly avoided a well thought out ambush.

At the conclusion of his narrative, once again stared me directly in the eye stating emphatically that during the course of his career having met up with some exceptionally astute and clever people, but goddamit them two beat them all hands down.

Our previously having come to the obvious conclusion the area to be pretty much cleaned out of available fur moved our operations much farther east to range along the forbidding and daunting coast line of Hudson's Bay were we felt comparatively secure from the attentions of the RCMP though knowing full well it to be only a matter of time before their being apprised of our presence in the area by the local post manager.

We hadn't really established ourselves with the local trappers as yet, but the very remoteness of that vast and unforgiving land wore badly on our nerves within a brief period of time before out of sheer desperation seeking solace with our own kind at the remote settlement of Fort Severn only managing to remain for a few days before chance once more stepped in with the advent of a long time friend of mine who had become too old and feeble to trap anymore warning us of a pending storm front moving in rapidly from off the bay and indicating a likely spot on the map were we would remain secure and comfortable at a trapper's cabin for the duration of the storm avoiding the worst of it.

It was to be many years later before my learning of what had taken place during our unplanned absence from the settlement our remaining ignorant at the time of the unexpected arrival of the RCMP. It appeared we had reluctantly taken our departure only a half an hour or less before their landing at the settlement just ahead of the fast approaching storm to face a mind-numbing ordeal they had not expected and would bring on much grief along with unexpected consequences before it was over.

We of course remained totally ignorant of their presence and their pending ordeal back at the settlement our being comfortably ensconced within the confines of a snug and cozy cabin while the steadily increasing fury of the storm raged wildly around the cabin shrieking madly as it tore at the ragged curtains of drifting snow causing them to swirl wildly in ever changing patterns across the open expanse of the lake while we sat in secure comfort idly discussing with our hosts what it took to endure the ravages of the violent storms that rolled off the bay into the unprotected settlement, our mutually arriving at the consensus it not a good place to be at such times.

The pervasive silence as he puffed away on his pipe obviously engrossed in how to tell me what he had in mind next became almost ominous before finally giving off a slight shrug as if he had reached further into his memories to suddenly taking up where he had left off relating the terrible times the onset of the unexpected storm had forced him to endure, goddamit a man would have to had the death wish to even consider venturing out into a storm of such unbelievable intensity, as it was we barely had time to tie down the wings and tail of the aircraft with barrels of fuel oil that were conveniently placed there before that doozer of a storm roared in with our making a hasty exit to the safety of the post managers dwelling, man that experience was one not soon forgotten. Yep he intoned almost as an after thought we were forced to sit it out for five god dam long days with little to do but drink cheap Hudson Bay Co. coffee, eat canned goods until we almost barfed at the thought, and play cards with my almost worrying myself sick about the safety of the aircraft, and to be honest about it I did wonder where them two had holed up but having more or less arrived at the conclusion they where quite capable of looking after their interests as they have proven many of the time, at that he once again lapsed into the now familiar thoughtful silence that characterized his demeanor for a time before once again startling me with an explosive "Christ on a crutch" did I receive an unpleasant surprise once the storm had blown over upon making our way to the aircraft which much to the surprise of all had survived the storm without apparent damage except for the engine tent being torn to rags by the violent winds, but god dam it man did I get a shocking surprise upon opening the rear cabin door, at first unable to believe my eyes upon discovering the entire cabin space to be solidly jam packed with rock hard drift snow the ferocious wind had caused to be driven in through every available crack and cranny, as if this wasn't enough to make any staunch man quail inwardly he knew with a sinking feeling of what he was sure to find once removing the inspection panels on the wings and tail section, and sure enough upon doing so finding them to also be packed solid with drift snow.

Stunned at that unexpected turn of events that dismayed him almost beyond human endurance, secretly wished the wind had totally destroyed the aircraft as he now faced a quandary that left little hope but to do what ever they could to render the aircraft flyable it requiring two days of intensive mind boggling labor to clean as much of the snow out of the interior of the cabin as possible, but there was little to be done about the wings and tail, if he wished to chance flying the aircraft back to Winnipeg he had to accept the risks that offered a chancy proposition at best.

To add to his grief the chief engineer back in Winnipeg who had been duly apprised of the existing situation cautioned the pilot to not attempt to use the cabin heater that normally maintained a reasonable cabin temperature in the coldest weather as the melting snow posed the hazard of trickling into the belly of the aircraft where the flight control cables were located and to possibly freeze in their pulleys causing the cables to jam solid, it couldn't be risked, he had no choice but to bite the bullet and get by without it. He then went on to say they refueled to capacity with horrendously expensive fuel obtained from the post manager before taking off with heart in mouth to fly the one hundred and seventy miles to Big Trout Lake, the long cold flight as he so succinctly put it a real white knuckler being forced by necessity to keep the throttle advanced far above normal engine power settings in order to maintain a semblance of flight while battling a fierce head wind of which in the course of using up a prodigious amount of precious fuel to barely scrape their way half frozen with cold and fear into the safety of the settlement by the skin of their teeth much to the everlasting relief of all aboard.

Having had all the excitement and heart stopping adventure he could handle for one day wisely elected to remain overnight.

The next morning it was all he could do to summon up sufficient courage to continue on in what he somberly described as a winged deep freeze that retained all the flight characteristics of a manhole cover. Having completed the telling of that part of their travails, once more looked me straight in the eye as was his wont while saying, goddamit but them two hardy buggers must have been some tough to have endured such terrible privation as long as they did, I on the other hand enjoyed the comfort of a gas heater not to mention unlimited resources backing me up, I plain and simply will never understand to my dying day how they did it.

As the rest of his fascinating story went they eventually managed to white knuckle their way to Winnipeg, a memorable trip that left him haggard and worn down to a nub from experiencing a fair share of grief while involved in doing so to be almost immediately upon arrival brought up on the carpet to explain to their superiors as to why they had failed to apprehend us with the resources available to them. Upon the telling he emitted a loud snort of utter disdain saying in a voice tinged with disrespect, them desk bound political ass kissing weenies seem to have the answers to everything except reality, they simply don't have a clue what it takes to survive way out there or the near impossibility of matching wits with two highly resourceful bush pilots that outclassed us at every turn in that god forsaken patch of real estate, attempting to nail them two elusive buggers enough to make a hyena weep, and by god if the truth be known I simply must admit to admiring their resourcefulness in having done so no end. Then on a sudden his mood appeared to alter in a manner that left me wondering as to what was to come next as his eyes once more took on the now familiar far away long ago look that left a pregnant silence hanging over us leaving me unsure if perhaps he had related all he cared to and had dismissed my presence. But within a short space of time letting out a resigned sigh to slowly and haltingly as if unsure how to continue before finally being able to collect his thoughts before taking up the threads of the conversation in stating that during the course of my life always the "safe man" who made it his goal in life to acquire a well paying position that offered job security along with eventually receiving a substantial pension, that with wise investments that guaranteed a high return on my money assured my financial security during my retirement years, always kept that requirement foremost in my mind, with out question doing what ever it took to accomplish these goals, no matter the cost to my well being or state of mind, but in hindsight what for?, only while hotly involved in pursuit of them maddening buggers had I really lived, felt so alive and as one with nature as during the time spent attempting to match wits with them two endlessly resourceful renegades who incessantly led us on a merry chase from pillar to post only to be outfoxed at every turn with their leading us from one end of that god forsaken barren chunk of real estate to the other to no avail, only then did I really come alive for the first time I can remember throughout my dismal career, god dam how I enjoyed the challenge even though having long realized with unshakeable certainty to have gotten in over our heads and the only way we would ever nail them would have to be a matter of luck, chance or by accident.

Yes without a doubt my retirement future is monetarily secured, but at what price to myself has yet to be assessed once my flying career is over leaving me with nothing tangible to look forward to, and that is not that far into the future, my reason for living will become a little less certain as my past employment leaves little to base poignant and treasured memories on, you at least have that, and believe me they are worth far more than one can possibly imagine, at that we stood up to shake hands in parting with his going on to say that meeting up with me as unexpected as it was had finally put a face on a ghost of the past, who's identity had for so long haunted his thoughts, with that he gave me a parting grin that reflected an inner satisfaction, we were never to cross paths again.

Bad Penny

ON ONE OCCASSION THAT STRICTLY bordered on one's requirement to earn a living took a position as a pilot flying for the local airways, there being no such foolishness as dress codes in them days, one simply attired themselves as one saw fit, my usual get up could be best described as casual, reporting for work during the summer months in a pair of short shorts, a baggy usually un-ironed shirt with buttons missing or mismatched, high top leather boots with an Australian outback floppy Tilley hat that completed my bush pilot's wardrobe.

To the uninitiated, me and others like me in all respects appearing like a misbegotten collection of orphans, unloved, unwanted and most of all unappreciated.

It had never been openly stated by anyone at any time but it was a sure bet our outlandish appearance did little in the way of instilling any degree of confidence to our startled passengers who upon viewing us climbing into the pilot's seat wearing a semi stunned expression on our usually well whiskered faces partly concealed by a pair of reflective sun glasses to when firmly settled into our seats to immediately commence to stare stupidly at the instrument panel as if it was something foreign to us while mumbling incoherently under our breath totally confused by it all and not certain what to do next, this no doubt must have given more than a few innocent and unsuspecting passengers pause for thought.

One of the more hilarious incidents taking place one early Sunday morning shortly after a load of carping irritable demanding fishermen who hailed from the lone star state of Texas waited impatiently for a flight to one of the numerous tourist traps that dotted the area, once the dock hands having completed boarding the passengers on the aircraft and as usual with such people who are anxious to be gone immediately they soon set up the usual round of bitching and whining about the poor customer service complaining bitterly if for one reason or another there was a slight delay, all the usual crap we were forced to endure every day many times a day till one rode the bare edge of completely losing one's patience and screaming at them, enough already. In this instance upon they're being informed of having to wait a little longer for the relief camp cook's arrival which he eventually did in good time, the cab driver upon arrival skidding to a sudden halt in a cloud of dust wearing a look of pure disgust on his face literally bouncing out of his seat to violently yank open the back door of the cab and to forcefully drag the protesting obviously well inebriated cook who promptly lost his balance to take a nose dive into the gravel drive way.

Upon being assisted back on to his shaky legs begin to wobble unsteadily onto the dock intending to board the waiting aircraft leaving a nose crinkling stench of long unwashed body in his wake that came perilously close to nauseating all within sniffing range, Christ that dude sure did stink exuding an exotic cloying odor of old sweat, puke, well matured shit and worst of all the mind numbing odor of partially digested booze, man but that dude sure was some fragrant, it was definitely a certainty his fellow passengers not likely to be overjoyed with his odious presence within the cramped confines of a hot aircraft cabin.

While making his uncertain way to the aircraft either tripped or lost his precarious balance taking an unplanned dive into the lake, at first we were sorely tempted to leave him to marinate for a spell, but his frantic splashing and piteous cries for help convinced us otherwise, our dragging him out with the aid of two dock poles as no one ventured to touch him, on being dragged to safety he began to flop around like a beached fish to suddenly shit himself as the most horrendous stench that defied description began to waft from his person immediately forcing all and sundry observers to take a step or two away from him to catch their breath.

Disgusted with his antics we seriously contemplated heaving him back into the lake to flush him off, but again no one wanted to get too close.

At that point the ensuing commotion must have piqued the curiosity of one of the passengers, curiously sticking his nose out of the cabin door to inquire in an almost unintelligible west Texas twang, ah sez boy, who all in tarnation thyar be thyat fellow a flopping about on the dock creating such a ruckus, haint the cook ah sure nuff daint reckons?, we all sure enough wants no truck with that thyr boy!, at hearing that my as usual not giving any thought to the possible consequences once more shoved my foot in my mouth retorting, hell no, that's your pilot, he sure don't appear too impressive at the moment, but he will be o'kay in a few minutes and you can be on your way.

The look of pure consternation that washed over his emaciated features quickly turned to one of wide eyed disbelief giving him the look of a skinny gargoyle as he took in the disconcerting sight of the cook who had somehow struggled to his knees feebly rocking back and forth while drooling copiously in confusion, with his eyes almost bugging out of his head the startled passenger doing the inquiring quickly ducked back into the cabin where a short but heated discussion took place with the remainder of the passengers who had been unable to witness the revolting

Sight of the cook's antics.

I had no idea of what transpired between them but much to the surprise of all they suddenly began to exit the aircraft, unreasoning haste, anger and confusion reflecting from their grim visages as they thundered on by almost trampling anyone who got in their way, as they tore on by in mass confusion one of them was clearly heard to utter a less than complimentary "god dam canucks, they're all fucken nuts", to with righteous anger converge in to the startled dispatcher's office yelling incoherently at him, of course his having absolutely no idea of what had transpired back on the dock it taking much persuasion on his part to shout down the highly pissed off fishermen in order to eventually make some sort of sense of it all, when finally able to get to the bottom of it, could do little but in helpless frustration apologize for the sick joke perpetrated on them by a pilot with a weird sense of humor.

Once the dust had settled and the sulky less than impressed passengers who by now totally disgusted with the way it had gone so far, if one were to judge by the looks of pure malice cast my way it was a sure bet they to a man had taken a very dim view of my off the wall sense of humor, that on top of having little if any degree of confidence in my less than inspiring appearance it taking some tall coaxing to get them to re-board the aircraft. When finally on our way an extremely tense atmosphere continued to pervade the confines of the cabin, fortunately for all concerned minus the cook, to have placed him on board in his present condition would have most certainly created a mutiny, as it was the uncomfortable sensation of their staring saliently at the back of my head kept me uneasy during the entire time it took to arrive at our destination.

As expected upon arrival the camp hosts who met the grim visaged passenger and upon hearing their tale of woe, the forced plastic smiles they normally plastered on their porcine features when greeting a new set of paying guests quickly turned into what could be best described as a rectus to privately inform me in no uncertain terms hissing through clenched teeth that from that moment on my services no longer required (as If I cared). Needless to say once being apprised of that decision the chief pilot who I had always considered to be a brown nosing wet blanket type immediately lobbied to fire me on the spot for unbecoming behavior, but the airways facing an acute shortage of qualified pilots at the time, cooler heads in management elected to keep me on, banishing me to what was considered to be less desirable freight and fish hauls which of course suited me perfectly, my not in the least retaining any desire to further tolerate foul mouthed overbearing fat assed Yankees.

The reader is warned beforehand the following may be found offensive, perhaps creating shock and outrage that such a terrible happening could and did occur and very much part and parcel of what bush pilots view on an ongoing basis Take it from one who personally witnessed this shocking act on more than one occasions, Regardless of what anyone including the public in general thinks it does and always has taken place, only the fact of it's usually being practiced in total isolation far away from prying eyes shields it from becoming public knowledge.

One sobering occasion that has been vividly retained in my memory through the ensuing years occurred while making a side trip from the settlement of Poplar Hill to an outlying lake with the odd name of Old Shoes Lake that for some unexplained reason reminded me of the many disturbing scenes of the cruelty the native people often imposed on their sled dogs.

Having to wait while the native fisherman who had chartered the aircraft to gather up a load of fishing equipment he wished to take back to Poplar Hill unwittingly became a witness to a past act of unparallel cruelty toward animals upon stumbling across the remains of numerous sled dogs that as it turned out perished from hunger and thirst upon being abandoned to their fate when the winter camp had been evacuated for the summer. Upon making inquiries concerning their terrible fate, looked on by the fisherman as if having taken leave of my senses in asking such foolish questions, retorting in a matter of fact tone of voice, they are only dogs, aren't they?, my god what a terrible fate for any animal no matter how lowly or despised to be forced to suffer, better they had been quickly dispatched on the spot sparing them the agonies of hell they no doubt had endured for some time.

But it didn't end there, at a later date my once again unwillingly or otherwise witnessing a wanton act of unbridled cruelty that made my blood run cold when accidently viewing boat loads of unwanted animals that had been rounded up on the reserves and transporting them to an isolated island located a goodly distance from the main land to be unceremoniously tossed overboard a short distance from the island to either make their way to a certain fate or attempt the long swim to the safety of the main land as many did, only to eventually become exhausted and ultimately drown, their bodies could be seen randomly floating on the surface for some time. These I later discovered to be as cruel as it sounds the fortunate ones. To me the most heart breaking scene consisted of confused half grown pups that had been cruelly torn from the only home they had ever known to be transported to the island and unceremoniously tossed overboard to in their fright and confusion frantically attempt to climb back aboard the boat only to be clubbed into submission leaving them with no other alternative but to swim to the island or drown, those who did drown as it turned out as tragic their cause of death to be the fortunate ones.

It was never revealed to me just how many of them unfortunates met their end on that lonely island, but that very day witnessed over thirty helpless animals abandoned to a horrible fate.

One doe's not require too fertile an imagination to visualize the horrors that ultimately transpired on that remote island as the laws of nature dictated only the strongest and the fittest survive, the half grown pups along with the smaller and weaker first to succumb, torn to bloody rags within minutes of gaining the perceived safety of the island by the larger stronger animals that fought viciously among themselves to gain a share of their victims still living flesh with the correspondingly weaker next to be hunted down and ultimately devoured until only the fittest remained. These brutes of a certainty constantly visited horrible degrees of mutilation on each other in establishing pack hierarchy until the end. It so came about by accident one day my striking up a conversation with a long time prospector who related a harrowing story of narrowly escaping a terrible death by a pack of fear and hunger maddened dogs marooned on an isolated island near a native reserve, as the story unfolded he described how he and his partner had been tracing a promising vein of mineral bearing ore that appeared to extend out towards a small remote island were his partner dropped him off from their canoe in order for him to cut and place claim posts and then returning to the mainland to finish off doing the same.

The prospector "John Caswell" immediately set about completing his tasks, and while busily engrossed in doing so began to develop an unexplained sense of unease that he was being bodily threatened, by what he at first could not say but being a veteran of frequent bear attacks during his long career far too experienced in his profession to ignore his self preservation instincts. Now fully alarmed carefully surveyed the surrounding heavy brush covered area suddenly horrified to find himself being surrounded and stalked by a pack of hunger maddened feral dogs who having long lost their fear of man were intent in making a meal of him, instantly realizing the danger and having only an axe to defend himself with immediately sprinted towards the closest and largest tree within sight, only the fact of his being in top physical shape from a summer spent prospecting was he able to reach and shinny up a large pine tree with the alacrity born of mind numbing fear, only just managing to do so ahead of the largest and meanest brute which had lunged madly at it's escaping prey to almost succeed in dragging John off the tree when gaining a hold of the heel of his boot, his only managing to avoid being dragged off by desperately hanging on with all the strength he could muster as the brute yanked and worried the boot heel until eventually losing it's grip allowing him to climb higher till reaching safety. Near paralyzed beyond words from debilitating fear gave fevering thanks to have been able to make his narrow escape, frightened to death he may have well been, but never the less extremely grateful beyond words to have escaped possible debilitating injury and to be safely beyond the reach of the pack of wildly milling dogs that had set up a fearsome dirge of uncontained anger while viciously from time to time turning on each other from the frustration at losing their intended prey.

The uncomfortable period of time spent awaiting the arrival of his partner the longest of his life, but as his heart rate settled to a mild roar it gave him the opportunity to gain a perspective of the feral dogs that snapped and snarled ferociously at each other with such murderous intent it chilled his blood, noting that on the most part their being terribly emaciated along with many fearsome appearing battle scars inflicted from constantly attacking each other, time never had seemed to drag by so slowly until much relieved to eventually spot his partner returning to pick him up and who upon coming closer some startled to see John perched high up on a tree like some kind of big assed bird yelling his head off. At first being confused by the ludicrous scene of john perched on top of a large pine tree unable to at first understand why being unable to see the pack of dogs milling below the tree in the heavy brush cover, they're being well screened from his immediate view by the shrubbery, once cautiously coming close enough to hear john's frantic warning instantly alerted to the danger quickly grabbed up the high powered rifle they always carried with them to if found necessary deal with bear problems managed to dispatch two of the boldest that dared or desperate enough in their ravenous hunger to leave the concealment of the thick brush to challenge him before the remainder got the message melting out of sight into the surrounding scrub allowing John to gratefully clamber down from his perch. Terrified stiff and sore as he was, still quite capable of hot footing it as he so succinctly phrased it in ten foot jumps to the safety of the canoe. Man he was to tell me I could sense them brutes snapping at my precious ass every inch of the way.

Upon questioning him about the possibility of escaping the attentions of the feral dogs if having by chance arrived on his own, a far away and long ago look came into his eyes, finally saying in a grave tone of voice, not too good I would think, them buggers had time on their side, in fact I wouldn't be here talking to you now as over a period of time I faced exhaustion from fear hunger and thirst becoming weaker by the hour until eventually becoming unable able to hang on, finally tumbling to the ground with predictable results. Once again that far away and long ago look came into his eyes as he lapsed into a protracted period of silence as he mentally re-lived that horror.

Involuntarily a shudder of cold unreasoning fear coursed through me just thinking about it, my god what an awful soul searing experience to have endured.

Life as it always has went on as usual with my having many and varied experiences but basically the same shit, at times giving up on the flying game to do other things, but always returning to flying, Aviation gets in your blood.

All In A Day's Work

A MEMORABLE FLIGHT WORTHY OF note took place one day under extremely trying conditions that proved so daunting it remains seared in my memory. It's taking place one cold wintry day in late December while flying side trips out of a remote native settlement known as "Poplar Hill" while flying an odd ball of an aircraft known as a "Fairchild Husky", in and of itself a truly marvelous performing comfortable aircraft to fly on skis.

Having delivered a load of freight to the post of the local free trader turned my attention to carrying out a number of pre arranged side trips for the local trappers and their families that wished to return to their trap lines the easy way. Once completing a number of them waited anxiously for the last family to arrive in order to finish off the last trip of the day as the short winter day fast coming to a close with random flakes of snow already beginning to swirl restlessly around the waiting aircraft that told me a full blown blizzard to be in the offing. Not in any sense of the word desiring to remain there until the coming storm blew itself out immediately upon their anxiously awaited arrival hastily began to load the usual mélange of the families house hold goods, numerous snotty nosed children and finally six of the rattiest appearing hump backed mean tempered sled dogs I had ever seen up till then, it remaining a certainty they're not being overly enthused about their forthcoming ride in the very rear of the aircraft viciously snarling and snapping at each other until unceremoniously receiving a sharp rap from an axe handle across their sensitive snouts from the no nonsense trapper, a move that quickly took the fight out of them, finally topping off the load with the trapper and his humungously wide assed wife leaving us clear to be on our way.

At about the time we had reached the approximate half way mark drawn on the map we ran into a curtain of light snow that gradually got heavier the farther on we flew placing me on edge as it promised our eventually encountering a full blown blizzard. Eventually the forward visibility worsened to the degree of forcing our flying closer over the tree tops than I normally cared to in order to maintain visual flight, our present state of affairs at first causing little concern on my part being part and parcel of the bush flying game.

As we continued to drone along I began to feel a slight prickle of unease as the ever decreasing visibility gradually forced our flying much lower than normally considered healthy calling for me to rivet my undivided attention on avoiding flying into the trees, (something like that could all too easily ruin one's day.) while also attempting to make the decision to fight it through or turning back while still able to do so leaving little time to take note of anything else. Finally having decided to have pushed it far enough and not at all certain of our ground position turned in my seat to advise the trapper sitting next to me of my intentions, his being quite astute had taken notice of my growing confusion pointed out on the map exactly were we were which fortunately for all proved our chosen destination to be not much further on, always I have marveled at the intimate knowledge they had of the terrain they trapped or had traveled through even when flying over it.

Now the final decision to turn back into more acceptable weather conditions or to chance it by keeping on lay heavily on my mind knowing all too well the sometimes fatal consequences of "get there it's", but for what ever reason be it foolishness or just plain stupid bravado on my part threw caution along with common sense to the wind bull headedly forging on. It was the trappers sudden and unexpectedly sitting bolt upright while turning in his seat to stare fixedly into the rear cabin that first alerted me to the alarming fact all not to be well behind us, but having little time for anything else being wholly taken up with maintaining our scant few feet above the tree tops for if anything the visibility had worsened taking up my entire attention just to maintain level flight leaving me with the certain knowledge we were now wallowing in deep fried shit with absolutely no idea what was taking place behind me, but upon observing his suddenly vacating his seat while grabbing up his axe gave me an awful start.

Peering anxiously into the gloom desperately hoping to locate a large enough lake to safely land on being uncertain as what to do next when as if by some unexplained miracle we suddenly broke through into a relatively clear patch were the visibility in the blinding swirl of the snow storm improved considerably no longer near liberating the surrounding landscape to the degree it previously had. Taking advantage of the opportunity to gain precious height immediately climbed the aircraft a few hundred feet higher giving a little more welcome clearance between us and the threatening trees allowing a little more room for error.

Feeling a little more secure ventured a timid glance into the interior of the cabin to see what the rising commotion that had slowly seeped into my consciousness was all about soon wishing I hadn't upon witnessing a sight that came near turning my blood to ice water upon taking fearful notice that some of the sled dogs had some how broken loose and obviously not at all pleased with being trapped within the confines of a noisy vibrating aircraft had panicked taking out their fear and frustrations on each other and the ones still tethered helplessly in the rear of the cabin creating an unthinkable fur ball of yelping, snarling fear maddened dogs mindlessly bent on each others total destruction.

As if these going ons didn't constitute enough of an uproar, the by now thoroughly frightened women and children had set up a hair raising blood curdling howling and wailing that could be audibly heard over the roar of the engine setting my already over stretched nerves a little further on edge, goddamit I thought to myself, what else can possibly go wrong?, It wasn't much longer before finding the answer to that much sooner than expected and not at all in a manner one could have wished. The free for all between the dogs and the trapper who had wasted little time wading into the thick of the fracas to begin swinging the flat side of his axe wildly in an attempt to subdue the tussling mutts with it's on the occasion inadvertently glancing off the bulkhead with an audible clang behind my seat placing the well cowed women and children in imminent danger from both sides as they frantically attempted to dodge both the ravages of the maddened mutts and the danger of being struck by the wildly flailing axe head, it had most definitely turned into a situation that would jangle the nerves of the staunchest.

Gritting my teeth while hoping for the best we hadn't proceeded much further when being startled by a sudden and unexpected shift of the aircrafts center of gravity that caused the nose of the aircraft to suddenly pitch up scaring the hell out of me, upon immediately gaining control a quick glance behind me revealing the alarming fact the entire contingent of women and children had somehow managed to switch places with the dogs and now huddled in the very rear of the cabin adding greatly to my already considerable difficulty in controlling the aircraft causing my immediately rolling in all the nose down trim available barely managing to attain a modicum of balanced flight in doing so, but it seemed my troubles had just begun upon noticing with alarm the fur ball of tussling mutts were on the verge of invading my space, a definite no something had to be done to prevent the unwelcome intrusion and god dam quick.

Jesus Christ Hail Mary and all that shit I certainly didn't need any further hassles at such a critical time. At first uncertain what to do next just sat there in frozen indecision occasionally flashing nervous glances at the hassling hounds as they edged ever closer to my hallowed space, transfixed by the impending disaster that promised to make life in that cramped cockpit a little more interesting than usual, the blood chilling thought of a pack of out of their minds kill crazed mutts acting as co-pilot did little to ensure one's peace of mind.

The hair on the back of my neck suddenly bristled when one of the trappers wild swings glanced off the bulkhead directly behind my seat narrowly missing my right shoulder causing me to instantly cringe away in absolute terror from the threat as far as possible which if the truth be known not very far at all having no place to go. Sitting there half paralyzed with fright at the disturbing thought of unintentionally being done in by the trapper's wildly flailing axe or being rended into bloody hamburger by a myriad of very long very sharp mad dogs teeth, not finding the existing situation to be in my best interest my survival instincts roared into full afterburner to without thought of the possible consequences suddenly slamming the control column full forward violently placing the aircraft in a full nose down position that within seconds left me eyeballing the tops of the trees rushing up at me in a nose to nose blur, a firm pull back on the controls quickly arrested our near vertical descent bringing us back to level flight and not a moment too soon, my swearing to hearing my anus shut tight with an audible clang as the bottoms of the skis sheared through the very tree tops with a malovent hiss.

Surviving that most necessary but near disastrous maneuver more a matter of good luck than skill on my part, but that violent roller coaster ride proved to work in my favor though the trapper and his family no doubt had experienced a bad time of it, the trapper not expecting what so suddenly took place, much to his surprise found himself plastered against the cabin roof as did the tussling mutts then as suddenly being smashed back onto the floor violently enough to knock the wind out of him and effectively taking the fight out of the well stunned dogs of which during the process had lost any interest in creating further mayhem long enough for the trapper who fortunately recovered before they did allowing his taking advantage of their confusion by administering well aimed sharp blows to their snouts that left them senseless. Next came a broadside of harsh commands directed at his family to immediately cease and desist their high pitched caterwauling or they too would receive a sample of what the dogs had just received. One couldn't help but to experience a slight pang of pity for them poor frightened buggers considering what they had just gone through and still half out of their wits with fear, and who was to blame them?, but that cut little slack with the trapper, his for real no nonsense threats producing the desired results with the wailing and sniveling ceasing without further ado.

Once the situation had returned to a degree of normality given the existing circumstances, suddenly began to take notice of a footed stench that pervaded the cabin soon causing my eyes to blur with tears with my involuntarily beginning to gag and retch in a futile effort to catch my breath, soon realizing the source of the extremely pungent odor to be produced by an exotic mixture of dog shit, puke, blood, urine and god knows what else laced with the all pervading odor of plain old fear. Christ it was all one could do to be able to take tiny breaths of air without one's stomach threatening to erupt at any second, never mind being kept busy wiping the copious tears from my eyes so I could fly the aircraft and see were we where going eventually being forced by sheer desperation to crack open the side window to use my nose as a snorkel to draw in great draughts of fresh mind clearing air.

Eventually and grateful to have done so after a spell of convoluted wanderings in order to avoid the worst of the blizzard we finally arrived at our destination to the relief of all, my giving heart felt thanks to have done so safely. The near lifeless dogs that still remained somewhat groggy from their ill treatment were unceremoniously flung out of the door into the snow like so much baggage, all the fight taken out of them and wanting nothing more than to get back to the security of their log kennels, the lot of an Indian sled dog leaves much to be desired, but they if nothing else incredibly tough and resilient and would continue to survive.

Next to gratefully emerge was the badly shaken puke spattered wife followed by a pack of also puke spattered children with tear stained eyes and dribbles of snot hanging off their chins, once clear of the aircraft they immediately received a few terse commands from the trapper that soon had them collecting up their baggage and huge bundles of bedding to lug up to the trap cabin with big momma breaking trail, one couldn't help but to notice the man of the family remained absolutely in charge at all times!

Once the initial confusion of unloading the aircraft and the trappers organizing the family affairs that followed our arrival had some what abated the entire family as if on some unheard command sort of lined up in what appeared to be a very sorry lot suddenly to as if on signal bursting into gales of heart felt raucous laughter with genuine tears of mirth filling their eyes, at first being some what taken aback by that unexpected outburst of genuine laughter soon recovered my aplomb to join in on a good belly laugh, one couldn't help but to compare their reaction to our out of the ordinary adventure to how it most likely would have strung out if it had been white folks, to be absolutely truthful I really don't think one would care to know.

Yes without the least doubt felt I had learned an indelible lesson concerning the vagaries of life, one that humbled me to the point it would never be forgotten, the seeming resilience of them fine native people who could experience an otherwise upsetting state of affairs to without conscious effort make light of it all by bringing out the humorous side of an otherwise upsetting experience, that they could so spontaneously do so simply blew me away. When one compares the self serving attitude of the white man who by and large view the native population as ignorant savages, if we were able to put aside our arrogance there remains little doubt much could be learned from them fine people, for without question their outlook on life in general puts our society to absolute shame, but no doubt as outside interests continue to infringe on their life styles that too will change in time and I for one will be saddened to see it happen.

Now that the excitement of having arrived safely behind us, wearily began to mentally brace myself to face the long cold lonely return trip while at the same time congratulating myself for being able to live and experience a life style that offered such a gamut of unalloyed fright and unabashed hilarity all within a short space of time, the thought bringing on a smirk of self satisfaction that just couldn't be suppressed.

The trapper with a wide grin plastered across his face shook my hand while thanking me for the fine service in transporting his wife and family to their trap grounds while his wife shyly gave me a good bye slobbery kiss with snooze (Copenhagen Tobacco) stained lips while the ring of silent children looked on in wide eyed wonder.

The watery appearing late winter sun had already begun it's inexorable descent into the western horizon promising a soul searing totally unwelcome flight of a hundred miles or better over unmarked forbidding terrain in marginal weather conditions.

The long cold return trip by all rights turned out to be one of physical and mental endurance being accompanied by a near state of nausea the whole time from that god awful stench that emanated from the rear cabin with my coming near on many the occasion to adding to it.

During the interim my thoughts wandered back in time to our near brush with disaster, pondering the intercession of the fates that brought us into a patch of relatively clear weather allowing the gaining of sufficient height that had spelled out a narrow margin between success or failure, but for that providentially taking place one could only speculate as to how it would have gone otherwise.

By the time the faint blur of light over the town of Red Lake finally came into view appearing in all respects to be giving off an incandescent ethereal glow as it reflected off the ice fog crystals that hung like an iridescent curtain over the town. Was I some pleased to have finally arrived as my tortured stomach muscles had reached a wretched state during the long cold trip that had seemed to take forever as we plodded our way over the darkened terrain with only my random thoughts and the merrily twinkling stars for company, at such times one really gets to understand the true meaning of being totally alone, but being no stranger to that raw emotion having endured it many times throughout the years accepting it as a matter of course.

The advent of finally spotting the light over town just beginning to loom over the darkened horizon gave me a twinge of renewed hope not thinking for a minute of my having a hope in hell of surviving, it remaining an even toss up of either freezing to death in the confines of that icy cockpit or expiring from the effects of that pervasive stench that against all odds and freezing cold continued to plague me leaving little choice but to reluctantly crack open the side window that allowed what felt like thunderous gale of frigid air into the already deep freeze cockpit, the only benefit being that super cooled air some what keeping the stench almost bearable.

God dam how good the welcome rumble of the skis contacting the rock hard runway felt with my gratefully taxiing in to the revetment and shutting down the engine while enjoying the luxury of a long drawn out sigh of relief as it clattered to a stop to then complete the cockpit shut down check.

The dock hand who had come out to meet me and prepare the aircraft for the night as usual flung open the rear cabin door to check if any freight required removal, once having done so involuntarily staggered back with eyes as large as golf balls struggling to regain his breath as the waves of putrid stink washed over him causing his recoiling in disbelief while continuing to gag and choke until finally being able to regain his breath gasped out in a hoarse strained voice, Jesus Christ hart, what in the hell died in there? I must have become somewhat inured to that god awful stench being totally taken aback by his re-action upon opening the cargo door, it wasn't the wisest thing to do considering the circumstances involved but simply could not restrain myself from breaking into howls of laughter at his plight, man if it still stunk that bad in them well below temperatures, it would have been beyond human endurance if the cabin had been heated?, I decided it best not to know. Slowly and stiffly forcing my near frozen limbs to respond struggled painfully and carefully out of the cockpit with unfeeling feet that began to sting unbearably as increasing blood circulation slowly restored, then to grab up my map case and sleeping bag to gingerly shuffle my way to the welcome warmth of the office not in the least aware of pending mayhem my soon to be unwelcome presence about to create.

As usual upon entering the office received a sneering glance from the over done bleached blonde twit who happened to be the managers current "Gal Pal" who in a condescending tone of voice that literally dripped with ill concealed contempt requested my handing over the day's receipts and paper work. Ignoring that saccharine request much to her consternation instead unzipped my smelly parka to drape my near frozen body over the large oil heater placed directly in the middle of the room to ensure spreading it's warmth evenly, as the oh so welcome warmth began to work it's way in and around my person my thoughts turned to the sulky young lady that ostensibly acted as our current dispatcher, but if the truth be known she lacked the mental capacity to dispatch a ham sandwich, well be as it may one could only console themselves with the knowledge her type came in every shape and form and in our collective thinking only qualified in one thing best not mentioned.

As the welcome warmth slowly penetrated the folds of my parka and insulated flying suit which of a matter of course had become thoroughly marinated by the foul stench I had been forced to endure for so long began to exude from them but in the process being ripened and enhanced by the warmth surrounding me to noticeably waft throughout the room and as it did so my noticing with grim satisfaction the over done twit's pug nose beginning to twitch like a nervous rabbit while her normally pale pallor taking on a light green hue before suddenly bolting to-wards the bathroom while screeching in a high falsetto to get my stinking self back outside where my kind belonged and stay there, well well I thought to myself with great satisfaction, revenge certainly is sweet.

Just at the very moment she had shut the bathroom door with deliberate force one of the other line pilots came crashing through the door (bush pilots don't as a rule walk through a door like normal people) only to stop dead in his tracks with a puzzled look of pure disbelief mirrored in his eyes that quickly changed to one of undisguised revulsion as he vainly gasped for breath, finally being able to croak out a "Jesus Christ Weston did you just shit yourself ?, well goddamit man at least have the common decency to change your shorts and wipe your ass!, with that said immediately made a hasty exit back out into the fresh air.

Meanwhile one could distinctly detect the sounds of violent retching emanating from the confines of the bathroom where the bleached blonde twit had vainly taken refuge, between copious bouts of honking her guts out screaming at me in a choked voice between bouts to immediately remove my rotten stinking person out of her office when knocking on the door in order to inform her of my intentions to leave the day's receipts and paper work on her desk, well being the consummate gentle man I am complied with her heart felt request leaving for home sporting such a self satisfied grin it hurt my cheeks.

One can assume with a certainty my reception at home not exactly one of wholesome welcome, my wife not being in the least impressed with the overpowering stench of "eau de aviation" firmly insisted on my disrobing out side of the house and leaving my smelly parka outside to air out (it never did) which in due course attracted every dog in the neighborhood to make an appearance in order to thoroughly investigate the source of such a mélange of tantalizing odors that continued to exude from it.

As it went even after giving the aircraft's cabin a through going over with powerful detergents and solvents, it turned out when all had been said and done that time consuming effort that tried the perseverance of the dock hand to the limit proving in the end to have accomplished nothing in the way of eliminating that god awful stench as the god awful stench remained despite many futile efforts to remove it persisting in lingering on throughout the remainder of the winter.

Every pilot that reluctantly flew it from there on referred to it as the "dog shit express. As it happened my moving on before the advent of warmer spring weather that no doubt greatly enhanced that mind bending stench most likely beyond human endurance. Often I wondered how long it persisted and how it was finally dealt with?, oh well one certainly cant deny the fact that bush flying has it's just rewards.

Short End Of The Stick

ONE OF THE MANY SHORT comings communally endured among many other bush pilots learned to live with was the lack of toilet facilities in their aircraft mainly because it at large not required except in the case of passenger only types, of course the lack of space and even if it being somehow managed to squeak one in ninety percent of the time it would prove to be impossible for anyone to access as our flying loaded to the nuts most every trip thus one became quite adept at voiding their bowels before committing themselves to a long flight or at the worst holding on till relief became available but one can be absolutely certain it sure could and often did play holy hell with a hapless passenger.

The twin beech of which I flew at the time normally carried out the extended trips because of its long range and load carrying ability. Fortunately for the pilot the aircraft came equipped with a simple device known as a relief tube consisting of a plastic horn one urinated into, being attached to a long rubber tube that had been routed through the floor and belly skin allowed the urine to vent freely into the atmosphere during flight, now this worked just great during the summer months but not advisable to attempt to make use of when the temperatures began to drop as the drain tube had a maddening tendency to gradually freeze solid with frozen urine until warmer weather once more came around in effect putting an end to any further use unless one cared to risk their urine flooding back onto their lower extremities thus creating a very uncomfortable and sometimes dangerous condition for the unwary that constituted a definite threat to the family "jewels".

But being who we where soon found a way around that minor inconvenience by utilizing what is referred to in aviation parlance as

"Sik Saks", a plastic lined moisture proof paper bag the passengers with weak or unsettled stomachs could retch into at will during flight in rough weather, thus the moniker "Barf Bags" soon became coined and referred to as such by all and sundry in the aviation circles. As mentioned before hand our being creative we soon found they served marvelously well as a " Piss Pak", once having urinated into it the bag carefully sealed and toss it out the window. Of a certainty we where questioned at intervals about the unusually high incidence of air sickness that seemed to be occurring especially through the winter months when one took into consideration we carried very few passengers that weren't hardened to flying in bush planes, but we always managed to wiggle our way out of it by shamelessly stretching the truth or telling outright blatant lies.

If by rare chance female passengers where aboard on a long flight they where warned well ahead of time to desist from drinking excess fluids prior to flight being as there was no toilet facilities available for their use, and if they at their peril chose to ignore the warnings and to experience the agonies of an over full bladder well"Ce La Vie.

On one memorable flight the buxom well rounded wife of the local Indian affairs agent, who had often heard told of the many far away and seemingly exotic places we flew into decided she would like to accompany me on an exceedingly long flight to a remote settlement located on the coast of Hudson Bay a little over three hundred and fifty miles one way to deliver another load of saw mill components. Her ample girth posed minor problems when attempting to squeeze through the narrow roof hatch leaving her some what red faced and embarrassed before successfully accomplishing it as the crowd of onlookers who had taken an interest in her travails cheered her on, one could say she definitely filled the seat to overflowing taking up considerable space in an already cramped cockpit.

All went well as it normally did until we had droned our way over the seemingly endless terrain until reaching the approximate half way point where we would be crossing "Big Trout Lake", It's wide expanse of fifty miles from shore to shore made it more of an inland sea than a large body of fresh water that I never dared to cross in bad weather unless flying in reference to instrument as the water and sky melted into one eradicating any reference to the horizon, truly a crown jewel of the north with it's crystal clear waters and endless sandy shore lines and offering the most fantastic fishing for monster lake trout one could care to imagine, but from that point on the coniferous forests gradually thinned out with the vast empty area that extended from there on became a low lying muskeg area, to the untrained eye appearing to be a featureless sere expanse of wasteland interspersed with numerous small shallow lakes that stretched clear to the barren wind blasted shores of Hudson Bay. As we continued on our way the landscape gradually began to change with what few trees that managed to take root in that inhospitalable environment appearing as straggly wind twisted sticks protruding randomly from the muskeg.

At this point the overwhelming urge to urinate made it's self known and fortunately for me not being of shy or retiring nature matter of factly informed my passenger of my intentions and without further ado yanked down my short shorts to relieve my self with the aid of the relief tube the well practiced bladder emptying procedure going smoothly allowing returning to my duties in a much more relaxed state of mind but also well aware she had viewed the whole proceeding with undisguised curiosity opining it to be a neat trick though she did have the common decency to blush a deep red at her seeming boldness though putting on a pretence of doing her best not to appear too interested by occasionally glancing out of the side window for brief periods of time before giving into the urge to direct her attentions to what must have seemed to her more interesting scenery. We hadn't flown on much further before the power of suggestion manifested it's self as it was surely bound to do with her beginning to show signs of visible distress casting tight glances around the narrow confines of the cramped cockpit as her eyes began to widen with her ever expanding need to urinate but not quite certain how to manage it.

My being all too aware of the signs of portending distress having witnessed it a score of times before knew it only to be a matter of time before nature's overriding demand to relieve one's bladder be complied with immediately one way or another, either way it was definitely going to prove interesting before it was over. As predicted we hadn't proceeded much farther along before her informing me in a tight voice she had nearly reached the end of her endurance and must soon relieve her bladder and could I please land immediately, this heartfelt plea uttered in a hoarse strained manner prompted my immediately pointing out the endless expanse of sere muskeg dotted with a confusion of randomly shaped tiny shallow lakes asked her in a droll tone of voice, where?, her being rather astute quickly got the drift in realizing no one in their right mind short of an emergency would ever consider landing in one of them, but even if by chance we had been flying over large bodies of water I would have been forced to refuse to comply with her wishes for two very good reasons as it is of necessity a complicated procedure to land or take off a heavily loaded beech craft, the lengthy procedure taking up a lot of time effort and fuel, secondly one never if at all possible allowed a passenger to step out on to the wing reason being it all too easy lose their footing on the slippery surface with predictable results, the lady in question having no other choice would have to face up to what ever came next.

This of a certainty placed her maidenly reluctance to expose her self to perceived, humiliation but having no options available out side of letting go and severely wetting herself, her remaining options had dropped down to zero, finally after a short struggle with modesty and a painfully extended bladder gave in to the inevitable asking if I by any chance had a suitable container she could use to urinate into with my wordlessly handing her a barf bag that she initially viewed with initial confusion and dismay, but realizing she had no other options requested I keep my eyes averted as she dubiously viewed the bag deciding how best to utilize it. Having complied with the lady's wishes by staring out of my side window to be soon treated to an amusing medley of squeals curses and grunts occasionally accompanied by some very unlady like expletives as she struggled mightily to slide her fortrel slacks and panties over her ample hips, no doubt a truly a daunting challenge in such a cramped space. After the struggle had gone on for some time the lady near shocked me off my perch when stating in an obviously agitated tone of voice I can't get these god dam slacks over my fat ass and I'm pissing all over myself, your going to have to help before it's too late!

It taking all the self control one could muster in attempting to maintain a straight face while dryly informing her that was simply not possible considering your request I keep my eyes averted, at that she snarled at me in a very unlady like tone of voice so who gives a shit if you have to look, your not about to see anything you haven't seen before, maybe just a hell of a lot more than usual!

Well what was one to do but to assist a maiden in distress with my being the consummate gentleman at all times in the presence of the fairer sex assisted her as requested. As if the poor women didn't have enough on her plate we at that very moment in time ran into an area of severe turbulence that is commonly encountered on a hot day over an area of muskeg causing one to bounce all over the sky, normally this phenomena bothered me very little but in this case it kept me busy on the controls in a futile attempt to ease the severe gyrations but to no avail as after a few good wallows and dips she screeched at me with a venomous for Christ's sake cant you keep this fucking winged contraption still for at least a few minutes, I'm pissing all over my god dam self, quickly taking note of her dilemma reached behind my seat to retrieve a towel from my kit bag and to place it as she gratefully requested under her ample buttocks as she arched her buttocks upwards in order to make room to do so "WOW". Having finished up she handed me the over full bag to dispose of, a job that proved to be easier said then done my facing the difficult proposition of attempting to control the wildly bucking aircraft that had just entered another area of severe turbulence in a timely manner, if one ever needed three hands it was then with my performing the most adroit of juggling acts managed to keep the aircraft in a semblance of level flight, slide open the side window, seal the bag and then pitch it out all without spilling urine all over myself. Once having accomplished that near miracle turned my attentions back to the lady to inquire if she needed any further assistance to be somewhat taken aback in receiving a smoldering look from her half closed eyes and in taking notice that she still contentedly sat there with her knickers remaining at half mast, for what ever reason obviously having lost all trace of maidenly modesty as if for the first time in her life enjoying a daring new found expression of freedom.

Now this sudden and unexpected change of heart left me somewhat confused and not at all sure how to handle the existing state of affairs took a little time to think over this rather unusual turn of events. If the truth be known she was a rather attractive women in a solid sort of way and I only being human could only assume her most likely to be frustrated to near tears with her uncompromising holier than thou church going husband, a stolid staid rigidly formal Scotsman who viewed the world in either black or white along with possessing the sense of humor of a hyena. It must have been a mind-bending trial for her to have to daily endure his sour demeanor and stark outlook on life. In the short time we spent in close confinement I had soon learned she basically posed an outgoing demeanor of being a kind loving women with an outgoing personality who longed for a change in her predictable rigidly unswerving life style, so if by chance she experienced sexual fantasies brought out by her present state of affairs, who was to blame her. Even if I had wished to take advantage of the situation it remained an impossibility in any case unless one cared to flirt with suicide or capable of strenuous sexual gymnastics that remained totally out of my realm not much of anything out of the ordinary about to take place while remaining air borne, besides that who was I to complain about my good fortune as it wasn't every day an attractive female bared her charms to my appreciative gaze in the confines of my normally sterile cockpit, admittedly it did much in the way of dispelling the usual mind bending boredom one normally endured on a long trip.

It appeared to me once having gotten over the initial shock of her unaccustomedly behaving in such a bold and daring manner took it all in a stride as if challenging herself to keep up the play acting that must have gone a long ways in helping her toward accepting the fact she was an individual with the individual right to do as she saw fit or be what ever or who ever she chose to be, after all it was her body and her life! One could almost visualize the conflicting play of emotions that must have been running rampant through her mind in savoring every moment of her daring show of new found freedom, but one wondered at what point the very audacity of what she dared would catch up with her dyed in the wool sense of modesty and female decency to bring it all crashing to a sudden halt to slink ashamedly back to the boring security of a trite marriage, however it went it remained her call.

When we where still about a half hour or so from landing regretfully advised her it time for her to pull-up her slacks, this she began to do immediately with unseeming alacrity, perhaps she had begun to experience a sudden sense of shame or modesty struggling impotently in a futile attempt to draw her slacks up past her knees where they immediately snagged on the edge of the seat leaving her panting in frustration, and once more I played the part of the devil's advocate in assisting her in completing that difficult task while she growled at how god dam difficult it was to wiggle into a pair of still damp panties over her ample ass on a god dam narrow confining seat yet, once that had been accomplished to her satisfaction, the equally difficult struggle to pull on the fortrel slacks took a goodly while with my taking alternate turns flying the aircraft and leaning over to help her as the remaining the miles rapidly slipped by until the dark smudge of the low forbidding coast line of Hudson's bay slowly slid into view. When pointing this out to her much to my surprise she stared me directly in the eye not saying a word, only receiving another high voltage smoldering look through half shuttered eye lids that only a highly aroused woman can portray to a man leaving me all aquiver, once getting her message across she asked me in all sincerity to keep what took place between us to myself, for if it by chance got back to her inflexible unyielding husband as she explained it was something he would not and could not begin to understand or be tolerant of, this I of course readily agreed to assuring her us bush pilots kept our own counsel and it would go no further being a code of honor among us that was rarely if ever broken.

Upon completing an extremely hairy approach in the face of the fickle winds that normally gusted off the bay, managed to accomplish a reasonably safe landing in the treacherous stretch of river that fronted the shores of the settlement to gratefully taxi cautiously into the dock

Keeping in mind the sudden switching of the swirling currents that could with very little warning cause one to instantly lose steering control and drive one into the pilings of the fixed dock. It seemed the entire citizenry of Fort Severn had flocked out to meet our arrival standing and gawking curiously at us like so many wooden statues. Once having successfully docked without problems heaved a sigh of relief as Fort Severn topped the list of places I hated to visit due to the treacherous wind and tide conditions that prevailed with one always sure to find one or the other or communally both to bedevil one in the fast flowing river mouth excepting by good fortune one arrived at slack tide. Upon completion of unloading the sawmill components that included a brand new diesel engine still in its crate and a huge circular saw blade among many other crates and packages and related components that went toward constructing a workable saw mill.

Just before casting off on our return trip she suddenly asked me where the nearest toilet facilities could be found, only to become crest fallen on learning the nearest to be at the school a half a mile away from the dock, her look of absolute despair made me feel sorry for her plight and still having a little over an hour before the tide went out cautioning her of the possibly of being stranded if we delayed our departure too long decided to accompany her to the school which earned me another smoldering glance of appreciation. From the disgusted look on her face upon emerging from the antiquated facility one could assume she was in no way impressed with it, but I would have been willing to bet she had found a new appreciation for her modern up to date plumbing she enjoyed as a matter of course, in a perverse way I enjoyed her discomfort, like it or not she probably for the first time of her life got a glimpse of the real world and now she could better understand and appreciate what us pilots where forced to endure on an every day basis.

The return trip as usual long and boring with my reading a book as it had become readily apparent there was not to be any further out of the norm excitement forthcoming to while away the time and quite content to do so having to make use of the relief tube once more to her apparent consternation for without a doubt she would have exploded before being forced to endure her previous travails, once obviously being enough, only sitting and appearing to stare disinterestedly out of the side window pretty much the during the whole time. One could not help but to wonder about her innermost and secret thoughts, perhaps now that she had experienced a slight but heady dash of the spice of life, just enough to create a sense of intrigue and to upset her predictable static life style or maybe she had frightened herself at her unseeming boldness in exposing her maidenly charms to another than her husband voluntarily or otherwise, now no longer understanding or certain of being the woman she once was most likely wrestled with her conscience and conflicting desires that would continue to haunt her for some time to come, either way I never saw her again but it remains a certainty it was one experience she would never forget, to my knowledge never again did she ever venture out on a long trip.

In concluding this story I wish to point the conclusive fact that there is 109

No available source of timber of saw mill quality to be found any where close to Fort Severn as the trees that do manage to exist are poor quality stubby twisted wind blasted sticks totally unsuitable for producing lumber or much of anything else of value except firewood.

If one should ask why then would a complete saw mill be flown in at a staggering cost when it is apparent there is no viable use for it, the answer if one should exist at all lies with the federal beauacrats in Ottawa where common sense to any degree fails to exist, we of course didn't care one way or the other only being hired to do a job not question the why's or where fore's or sensibilities of projects that didn't add up in our or anybody outside of Ottawa's minds as we if the truth be known witnessed many questionable decisions on their part, the average tax payer living in a world apart from basic reality has very little knowledge of the profligate and senseless waste of tax dollars, and why should they care, the dominion of Canada appears to be bursting with workers willing to pass over a usurious chunk of their hard earned pay cheques without a whimper.

Often have I wondered what the public reaction would be if availed of all the costly brain dead projects thought up by the hacks in government under the guise of Department Of Indian Affairs And Northern Development, If I have read the general demeanor of the Canadian public correctly most likely nothing!

As it stands to day only the people who are closely involved within the hierarchy of the dept of Indian affairs and of course the bush pilots who are by the very nature of their jobs aware of the many dead end make work projects that start with nothing and end with less and the endless but usually costly schemes that usually fall on their faces once the funding runs out and believe me this is predicated on an ongoing basis are acutely aware of the mind boggling amount of tax payers money squandered on meaningless non productive projects throughout the north.

Subsequent trips to Fort Severn eventually revealed the loss or disappearance of much of the costly saw mill components, some of the heavy cross beams no doubt ending up as high priced fire wood while the brand new extremely costly diesel engine and circular saw blade that had been unceremoniously dumped off the pier in order to create additional space and to date can still be seen at low tide lying ingloriously in the mud next to the piers resplendent in a blaze of orange rust, a fitting tribute to the powers that be.

Bitter Medicine

OF THE MORE NOTEWORTHY FLIGHTS that involved a rare combination of what could only be adequately described as an unbelievable combination of skill along with a large dose of good luck, and as always the timely intervention of chance and fate, an adventure so far out and brazen that it remains forever locked into my memory.

This memorable incident taking place solely by chance when just having completed a series of time consuming side trips out of a remote settlement with the remainder of the day becoming short leaving me weary in mind and body and only wanting to return to base and to relax over a cool bottle of beer with the rest of the pilots.

Having just taken off from the site of the last completed side trip had barely begun to climb to a comfortable cruising altitude when the radio suddenly crackled into life with my unthinkingly picking up the microphone and answering it, an act that I would have just cause to regret in the near future. The transmitted message instructed my making a slight detour to pick up a load of fish at a near by fish camp, my being empty at the time had no choice but to reluctantly comply all the while cursing my unthinking stupidity in answering the god dam radio and the inescapable fact of their ever having been invented as it gave the dispatcher the opportunity to extract additional profit at the pilot's expense.

Tired to the very core of my being and totally pissed off when taking into consideration it would prove to be a tight race to pick up the load of fish and still be able to make a landing back at Pickle lake before dark as the setting sun now barely hovering over the rim of the western horizon.

The native fishermen at the fish camp who I got on well with having previously picked up many a load of fish from their camp understood my dilemma setting up a rapid pace in filling and loading the tubs while I anxiously stood idly by admiring their easy going life style with my once again pondering and questioning the little understood forces that drove me on, and as usual the answer evaded me. By the time the loading had been completed the sun had set noticeably but after taking off and beginning my climb out all appeared to be well with the bright ball of sun appearing to be hanging well above the horizon giving one the impression of still having many hours of remaining daylight, but from long experience knew all too well it to be an illusion for as one climbed to a greater height the sun remained correspondingly at the same level as the horizon due to the curve of the earth, but the long shadows that had begun to invade the lower reaches of the landscape preceded my progress informing me otherwise leaving me with the unsettling knowledge of facing an unwelcome night landing, something even for a highly experienced pilot, best avoided with a heavily loaded aircraft if at all possible.

To the uninitiated when one is flying high over the landscape at sunset the terrain appears to be an endless black carpet, but the lakes remain clearly outlined in a silvery relief. But one must eventually descend to lower altitudes where upon the lakes lose their reflective surface melting in to the darkened landscape.

Having little else to do during the interim but to stew over what had now become certain to be another unwelcome night landing before my working day came to a close, could still gaze appreciatively at the sylvan panorama of the surrounding area sliding slowly by below my wings, taking in and appreciating what so few people get to see the especially the radiant blush of the setting sun that hovered just over the now darkened horizon grandly setting up an awesome spectrum of light rays radiating outward from behind the occasional cloud banks, having become totally immersed in my mental wanderings almost jumping out of my skin when the radio once again crackled into life. This time being sorely tempted to ignore it, and as future events would dictate would have ample time to wish I had of, but curiosity and perhaps a misplaced sense of duty got the better of me assuming the bozo of a dispatcher back at base requesting an estimated time of arrival. But the terse message received over the radio from one of the dock hands advised me one of our native workers involved in building a new dock at one of our satellite bases located on a river had inadvertently stepped on a broken bottle while wading bare foot in the shallow water severely gashing his instep and severing a main artery while doing so leaving him in the unenviable position of eventually bleeding to death unless receiving prompt medical aid, but as it stood that remained an impossibility due to the fact the nearest help lay over a hundred land miles away placing immediate medical assistance out of the question.

At first my remaining somewhat confounded by the message relayed to me as there was precious little one could do to offer assistance as the satellite base located on a narrow river one I hated to have to land in even during daylight hours and now lay in total darkness.

While wrestling in confusion as to what could be possibly expected of me in alleviating the situation the head nurse from Osnaburgh house nursing station who had obviously been contacted by some one at the main base or directly by the injured man's co-worker for first aid instructions unexpectedly broke into our radio conversation to inquire if it was at all possible to land and pick up the patient, the enormity of her request almost jarring me senseless, it taking a few long seconds to once more gather my now totally confused and jumbled thoughts into a cohesive pattern, my god I thought to myself she has absolutely no idea of the gravity of what lay before me or the high degree of risk it would entail in attempting to land a heavily loaded aircraft on a narrow darkened river, to even consider doing so bordered on madness, and even if by an unbelievable stroke of luck or exceptional skill managed to do so without wiping themselves out in the process, still faced the daunting prospect of stabilizing the injured man, an undertaking best left to trained medical personnel, then if successful in staunching the flow of blood attempting a takeoff in total darkness within the confines of a narrow river, the very thought made my blood run cold.

Switching frequencies on the radio enabled me to converse with the injured man's partner at the river base who at first being in a rattled state of mind his initial attempts over the air waves transmitting as an incoherent babble, after a few attempts on my part to calm him down he finally managed to collect his wits sufficiently to allow his more or less being understood.

During our radio conversation it turned out his having initially contacted the main base at Pickle Lake who in turn had contacted the head nurse at Osanburgh house who in her turn got on the nursing station radio to pass on first aid advice of how to bind the wound to staunch the copious loss of blood. The well rattled co worker being rather restricted in medical supplies ended up using a dirty towel to bind the wound but that course of action failing miserably when within a short time also becoming soaked with blood. Upon his informing me of his difficulties in preventing further loss of blood gave him the best possible advice advising his immediately removing the towel and packing the wound with ashes from their wood stove, then to apply a tourniquet using a belt or a rope, whatever was available to do so and to loosen it off every fifteen minutes to allow the blood to momentarily flow to the injured foot before tightening it up again, at first his remaining hesitant and uncertain as how to proceed, some what confused by my barrage of information, but finally agreeing to do his do his best.

On pondering what to do next that could possibly assist in alleviating the situation, mentally ranted to myself that all concerned without saying so waiting to see were I would go with it, goddamit how I hated having an impossible situation laid on my door step as theoretically the saving of a man's life lay in my hands, yes one could attempt a landing but common sense coupled with years of experience dictated it could only end up in disaster gaining nothing along with the certainty of losing a lot more.

By the time of my arriving within the vicinity of the river only a winding ribbon clearly outlined by a silvery sheen hemmed in by a threatening verge of trees that lined the riverbank, what could be seen from my vantage point at the moment I knew would entirely disappear once descending to tree top level leaving nothing but a black hole upon descending to tree top height leaving one without any form of height or directional reference what so ever, common sense dictated it simply could not be done.

At that very moment of decision to attempt the near impossible I seemed to enter an area of cold and uncaring indifference to my fate if failing to succeed that seemed to leave me in drifting as in a vacuum were I was no longer myself, now totally devoid of my normal codes of fear and danger whose meaning could no longer be comprehended, characterized by an abnormally heightened state of mind that led my thoughts and actions from that moment on. Strangely enough my mind remained crystal clear, unnaturally so as the pending actions of the impossible situation that lay before were weighed up and the disastrous consequences that could all too easily follow, my overloaded mind racing ahead in a feverish attempt to formulate a plan that could offer the least chance of success. After a protracted period of time eventually came up with a plan that in itself quite simple but suicidal so with the possibility of failure so high it seemed inevitable, but no other choice remained to me if one were to complete the act leaving me no less determined to succeed. To this very day still fail to understand what unexplained force gave me the inspiration to direct the worker to as quickly as possible grab up two gas lanterns and to place one on the middle seat of the crash boat and the other as far forward as possible and then to take up position in the approximate middle of the approach end of the river to give me a semblance of the height and directional references required to make a night landing. This he reluctantly agreed to do so and who was to blame him for being hesitant, never the less his alacrity in carrying out my request astounded me for within a few minutes two tiny pin pricks of light moved away from the dock to soon remain stationery in what one could only hope to be the middle of the river. Still despite my new found bravado and determination driving me on a burgeoning fear coupled with growing indecision at the folly of my decision raged within me, my descending from a long line of long lived cowards, like it or not my unwillingly having become the star player in "don't let this happen to you". How I ever managed to place my new found fears to one side when making the final decision to chance it against my better judgment I could never say, it just happened, almost as if another part of my subconscious mind took command shoving aside the uncertainty and indecision that continued to plague me giving allowing one the courage and impetus to flawlessly complete the most blood curdling night landing of my entire career. The bravery of the worker in risking his life in a bid to help save the life of another also had to be commended, his later admitting that upon my thundering over head of the boat at what he shakily described as scant feet frightening the be Jesus out of him.

Having touched down fairly heavily without bending or breaking anything managed to slow the aircraft down enough to allow it's finally falling off the step without my inadvertently driving us up onto the darkened shore line my cringing in absolute terror at the thought of doing so as one could not be absolutely certain during the approach phase of the landing to be lined up with the middle of the river once dropping below the tree line having no other reference to judge the landing by except the pin prick glow of the two gas lamps that instantly disappeared once overflying the boat leaving me to blindly feel my way down to the water, once falling off the step relieved beyond measure to having avoided doing so more by the intervention of good luck than skill on my part, the palpable relief experienced at that moment allowing most of the terrible tenseness labored under for far too long to finally dissipate leaving me weak and totally disoriented, at that stage my remaining uncertain of my position on the river that could well be any where when taking into consideration the effects of the fairly swift current that could all too easily sweep me on to the rocky banks of the river dictating that it would be a wise move to as quickly as possible switch on and to make use of the landing lights to slowly and carefully turn the aircraft while hoping not to be to close to either bank and possibly snagging a wing tip, and once having successfully done so to taxi slowly into the dock were the worker held up a lantern to guide me in and upon shutting down the engines finding myself to be soaked with sweat while my knees knocked so violently that when it came time to crawl out of my seat it took a tremendous effort on my part to accomplish that normally simple task before climbing out of the hatch and slide of the wing to initially wobble along on rubbery legs that came perilously near failing to support my weight as I cautiously made my way onto the dock having to go very slowly until gaining sufficient confidence in their holding up before attempting to make my shaky way up to the bunkhouse. Upon beginning a dialogue with the well shook up worker my not having quite recovered from the tenseness of my hairy landing it now became my turn to become unintelligible of speech, my teeth continuing to chatter so violently my words initially came out in a series of meaningless gobbles and quacks, if the situation had not been so serious our badly rattled efforts at intelligible conversation would have appeared hilarious to an onlooker the overall scenario being better suited to a Monty python episode than a life or death discussion between two concerned and well shaken individuals, but eventually calm prevailed with our eventually settling down to the degree of finding ourselves capable of communicating with each other. My first sight of the injured man as he lay near lifeless on his bunk indicated his having become almost comatose from loss of blood, his sickly gray green pallor showing up clearly in the diffused glow of the gas lanterns leaving me wondering if perhaps it was too late to attempt to save him, but the fact he still continued to breathe albeit it raggedly one in good conscience had to if at all possible try.

Having made a cursory check of the tourniquet and loosing it to allow the blood to flow for a few tense minutes before re tensioning it we wrestled that two hundred pound man from the bunkhouse to the aircraft with great difficulty albeit at times none too gently when one of us stumbled and to load him into the rear cabin as there being no way in hell it possible to place him in the front passenger seat. Once having accomplished that extremely difficult task his co-worker entreated me to allow his accompanying us being near spooked out of his tree by the series of past events and not wishing to be left alone, but as much as my regretting to have to refuse him explained my requiring his ongoing co-operation in taking the boat about a mile further on from the dock, a very necessary request as there being no other way to judge my take off within the confines of the stygian river cautioning him to take the time to judge his position in the middle of the river as accurately as possible my not having any other references to go by.

While watching his progress as he reluctantly moved away in the darkness with the glow of the two gas lanterns gradually diminishing in intensity until once again resembling two pin pricks of light, the butterflies that had taken residence in my stomach had now grown to the size of bats causing my guts to flutter wildly at the soul shriveling thought of what yet lay ahead of me. Yes I had a lot of experience flying a beech craft in all conditions, but never under such trying demanding circumstances leaving me uncertain of my ability to handle such a daunting prospect as taking off in the narrow confines of a darkened river?, as much as I dreaded to attempt what in all respects to be nothing more than a fool's errand, nevertheless with considerable effort swept aside the mind paralyzing fear and reluctance that threatened to inundate my senses hesitantly climbed into my seat and strapping myself in tightly all the while wrestling with a near debilitating fear that threatened to overwhelm me at any time. Dread fear being the only emotion left to me causing my badly shaking hands to fumble with the controls while starting the engines. When taxiing out into the black hole of a river something of significant and meaningful importance I had overlooked nagged at me, but my near paralyzed mind refused to function clearly with my failing to put my finger on what it was at the time and in doing so unwittingly setting the stage for potential disaster.

Having placed the nagging doubts and fears to one side as best one could considering the awesome challenge awaiting me, knew without a shade of doubt if hesitating for even a second or two longer my flagging resolve to keep on would disintegrate entirely, steeling myself against what ever came next fire walled the throttles to begin the most nerve wracking flight of my entire career. Thundering down the black hole of a river with the pin prick glow of the lanterns rapidly growing brighter as the intervening distance between us and the helpless worker in the boat shortened rapidly, but even as we did so time appeared to become suspended, almost if our being contained in a vacuum with our finally becoming airborne far closer to the helpless worker in the boat than would have proffered, as taken up with mind numbing fear and with the muscle knotting intensity of controlling the aircraft as I was at the time still retained the presence of mind to admire the fortitude of the worker who grimly held his position fully aware if I was to have misjudged my take off he didn't stand a chance in hell of survival, only able to watch in a state of helpless acceptance as the speeding aircraft relentlessly bore down on him, he was to inform me much later of his clearly being able to hear my progress and to watch with mounting dread as the flashing navigation lights moved ever nearer as we raced toward him leaving him feverently hoping not to be run over with only at the last second hearing the deafening roar of the engines and vaguely observing the blue white glare from the exhaust pipes as we roared on by scant feet overhead soaking him to the skin with the residual spray off the floats with the effects of the violent prop wash coming near to causing the boat to flip over as it spun in a half circle from the near hurricane effects inundating him as we passed overhead.

Once having cleared the boat no longer had lights or any other visual reference to assist my progress forcing my reverting to looking up at the tops of the trees lining the river that were outlined in black relief against the glow of the sky contrasting with the darker shadows of the river bank, not a very accurate method of avoiding the all too real possibility of snagging a wing tip on one side of the river or the other, but it had to suffice having no other recourse.

Forced by necessity to momentarily remain below the tree tops until my airspeed built up sufficiently to initiate a slow climb out to relative safety when unexpectedly the area immediately in front of me becoming pitch black instantly informing me of the wide but not too severe a bend in the river that in my overriding haste to be gone had completely forgotten about it's turning to the right, a frantic glance at the airspeed indicator quickly shot down the option of clearing the offending trees that lay directly in my path by climbing over them as to attempt to have done so unless having attained a much higher airspeed guaranteed a fatal stall. Having no choice but to take my chances wracked the aircraft to the right hoping to avoid contacting the trees with either wing tip to somehow by unbelievable chance succeeding in doing so.

To this very day I remain uncertain as to how close one or the other of the wing tips came to contacting the trees, for all I knew perhaps one of them did, but one could bet the farm my having come far closer than one would care to dwell on.

Upon successfully completing that hairiest of turns my senses instantly reoriented themselves to the glow of the night sky allowing my continuing on until gaining full control of the existing situation when finally able to climb out of the narrow confines of the river to establish a slow but steady rate of climb to with vast relief reaching a safer altitude before my resolve failed me as my knees knocked so violently my feet had commenced to dance a jig all over the rudder pedals.

Feeling the worst to be over futilely attempted to unwind from the terrible stress labored under for far too long, the collar of my shirt had begun to noticeably chaff my neck where the sweat had pooled and dried only to appear again as a new wave of near debilitating fear washed over me, a tide mark of my successive fears that escalated the rank cloying odor of dried sweat pervading the close confines of the cockpit.

Having made it safely thus far by some miracle, fearfully contemplated the remainder of the endlessly dark fear ridden miles that yet lay before me, the soul crushing thought of what it entailed causing my involuntarily quailing inwards, but having no viable options, committed to what ever fate had in store. As time dragged by on seemingly leaden wings my state of mind more or less reaching the point where my confused and fragmented thoughts once more began to coalesce into some form of order, decided it high time to perform a cockpit systems check, in doing so whatever slight wisps of confidence that had been painfully scraped up cruelly torn asunder when checking the fuel gauges, their indicating to read far below the requirements that would see us safely at our destination, but why?, then it hit me like a bolt of lightning, the extra miles flown to the fish camp, two extra fuel gobbling take offs and climb outs, and worst of all allowing my overriding concern for the injured man in neglecting to unload the god dam tubs of fish at the river base plus the inescapable fact one could have so easily added on extra fuel from the base, but due to my overloaded state of mind had failed to do so, the blood curdling fact of my having screwed up big time now hung around my neck like an albatross. In hindsight the chilling realization of just how great the amount of stress and pressure I had been subjected to in the last while, and just how badly it had clouded my judgment became all too apparent. Oh Christ did that mind numbing oversight hit home upon fully realizing the consequences in having done so, it's extracting from whatever slim hope of survival we might have had.

The blood chilling realization my time on earth now measured by the dwindling amount of fuel remaining in the tanks swept through my near panicked mind to all but paralyze further thought process, only with the greatest of effort succeeding in throwing off the god awful feeling of icy despair and to admit to the gut wrenching knowledge I still faced an extremely thorny problem of navigating a heavily loaded aircraft short on fuel at night over many miles of trackless wilderness without benefit of electronic navigation aids having to rely on the magnetic and gyro compass to maintain as direct a course as possible in conjunction with my extensive familiarity of the terrain we would be traversing with my realizing my margin for error to be absolutely non existent.

God dam my poor head ached fiercely, brought on by the effects of my adrenalin charged system that also caused my limbs to involuntarily jerk spasmodically, almost like a marionette. The dread certainty that emergency measures needed to be instituted immediately gave up on the idea of gaining additional height, instead throttling back the engines until barely remaining airborne before reducing the propeller rpm's in effect leaving the manifold pressure higher than normal, finally leaning out the mixture controls until the engines began to protest, these desperate measures of a certainty played havoc with them but my choice of doing otherwise remained starkly limited being forced by overwhelming circumstances to trade off one advantage to gain another, having done all that was possible to stretch our fuel reserves it now lay out of my hands, one could only wait and see what would transpire next.

Wearily sitting back in my seat desperately attempting to choke back the burgeoning fear that threatened to inundate my senses at any time causing my overwrought mind to attempt spinning in all directions at once as I vainly searched for alternate ways out of our dilemma, but finding none resignedly accepted the cold hard fact that what would be would be to absent mindedly watch the minute hand of the clock mounted on the instrument panel make it's inexorable sweep around it's face, in doing so could not help but wonder just how many more times it would continue to do so?

Idly glancing out of the cockpit window became instantly transfixed by the monotonous blink of the red navigation light on the wing tip while occasionally observing the exhaust flaring brightly in a blue white stream from under the wing's trailing edge.

My reverie rudely interrupted when a disembodied voice suddenly crackled through the ear phones near causing my jumping out of my skin being in such a tense state of mind, it turned out to be the head nurse from Osnaburgh house nursing station her asking how it was going with me at the time and to the condition of the injured man, the silence that followed my informing her of having absolutely no idea how he fared at the present time as he lay in the very rear of the aircraft and I of course in the cockpit and unable to observe his progress hung heavily over the air waves. This terse inquiry immediately followed by an inquiry if it was at all possible to land at the small shallow lake that fronted the nursing station? Now this was a new twist as no one I knew had for what ever reason landed there during daylight hours, never mind being requested to do so at night, however the upside of doing so if at all possible offered the opportunity of it's being twenty five miles closer than Pickle lake our chances of survival went up a notch if it could be accomplished.

Fearfully daring another glance at the fuel gauges immediately set my overstretched nerves to jangling like a harpsichord on speed when discovering to my horror all five tanks to be registering near empty or not too far off the mark, Christ on a crutch, if they read accurately we were dead meat, but as every pilot is intimately aware of the idiosyncrasies of fuel gauges and not to be implicitly trusted invariably reading more or less than the fuel tanks actual contents, oh god dam how I feverently hoped they're reading on the low side hopefully offering a little more time in carrying out a safe arrival and landing, but for what it was worth it had now become a moot point.

Running the nurse's request through my mind realized my not being the least familiar with the lake in question, but even at that knowing it to be all but impossible to accomplish a safe landing at night without some form of assistance.

Keying the mike horridly outlined a plan that had suddenly formulated in my mind having previously arrived at the conclusion the head nurse to be astute and organized, well able to handle most any crisis with relative aplomb requested that she as quickly as humanly possible rally every available boat on the lake and to have them prominently display whatever manner of lights they could come up with and to form a double line the length of the lake keeping the two lines of boats approximately two hundred feet apart.

My still being some miles away from the lake so rigidly tensed up from expecting the engines to cease running upon reaching fuel exhaustion at any given moment my breath came in labored gasps bringing on a state of mind so jam packed with tense emotion it cannot be adequately described, only another pilot who has had at one time or another faced much the same dilemma can truly understand almost collapsing with relief upon coming closer to the lake allowing my being able to observe a faint ragged line of pin prick lights beginning to appear.

117

But the overriding fact that I still had to get there weighed heavily on my mind with my hoping against hope my fast dwindling fuel supply would prove to be sufficient to see us through to a safe landing.

Safety now seemed so close but yet so far, goddamit I swore vehemently to my self, another totally unwelcome night landing and this one promising to be far more demanding and hairier than most, forced by dire necessity to do so under less than favorable circumstances, I couldn't help but wonder if my nerves were up to it considering my mental demeanor remained rather on the ragged side.

One could not help but to admire the unstinting bravery of them native people voluntarily placing themselves in harm's way as there was no absolute guarantee of my being able to maintain adequate directional control of the aircraft on touch down.

Tense with mounting dread the engines would quit at any time due to fuel exhaustion time seemed to stand still before eventually to my everlasting relief able to maneuver into position to carefully line up the nose of the aircraft between the ragged line of lights with my hands literally flying over the controls in setting them up in preparation of making a landing while cautiously retarding the engine power settings to maintain a safe approach speed just managing to complete the last of the pre landing checks as the right hand low fuel pressure warning light flashed on startling me half out of my wits even though expecting it to happen at any time, if at all possible my becoming further tensed up as it began transmitting it's grim message blinking ominously with the chilling reminder of a having at most another minute or less before the engine quit from fuel exhaustion, far too short a time to set up a heavily loaded aircraft for a night landing, to make matters that much worse not having proceeded much further before the left hand low fuel pressure warning light also flashed on to blink in mesmerizing concert with the right hand one with my involuntarily gripping the control wheel tighter than ever while coldly dismissing the possibility of not making it before running out of fuel grimly concentrated on making the final descent towards the ragged rows of lights that could yet prove to be my salvation with my coming near to misjudging our higher than normal vertical speed barely having the time to check our rapid descent toward the surface of the lake by ramming on full throttle a split second before heavily impacting onto the water with such force it resulted in a fair sized bounce with our barely settling onto the lake surface the second time just as both engines began to mill to a stop, the second impact with the water almost as heavy as the first jarring my teeth but oh man it sure felt good, but the results of the bounce coming near to causing momentary loss of directional control which in turn created a flutter of panicked mayhem among the boats with their highly nervous operators wasting no time in scattering in all directions in a wild attempt to avoid my charging through their ranks. As the now silent aircraft settled off the step to gradually lose all forward speed eventually drifting to a near stop before two boats cautiously came up along each side to latch onto the floats in order to tow us into the dock. Only then did I remember the plight of my passenger, my wondering if he still survived up till now being far too taken up with the almost insurmountable problems of ensuring our survival to have given thought too much else.

As we moved slowly toward the dock suddenly becoming aware of the total silence that now engulfed me, the absence of the sustained yammer of the engines seeming strange to my ears while continuing to experience difficulty in comprehending the fact we had against all odds somehow survived to live another day when by all rights we shouldn't have, a few precious minutes in our favor had spelled the difference between life or death. Perhaps it was my distorted view of the time span brought on while laboring under such terrible stress but it remained unexplained to me why the engines continued to produce power long after they should have quit from fuel exhaustion, I couldn't help pondering that perhaps a divine providence that decides in it's wisdom to spare well meaning fools such as I, holding one in thrall for some other momentous occasion further on down the road of life.

Once the excitement and euphoria of our near miraculous survival had some what abated to a mild scream, began to experience the debilitating effects of an adrenalin hang over, my suddenly feeling dizzy and nauseous, the following adrenalin induced confusion leaving me uncertain and undecided if one should first piss their pants in relief, shout hosanna or simply break out singing the ride of the valkyries, wisely I managed with concentrated effort to avoid all the above being absolutely certain of the fact the bevy of nurses and curious onlookers that had gathered on the dock to welcome our safe if not unorthodox arrival would have had their suspicions of my being a crazy white man confirmed beyond a shadow of doubt, only deserving of being quietly led to the loony bin strapped tightly in a canvas tuxedo before causing further mayhem or worse yet being set loose to fly another day.

The head nurse who had immediately taken it upon herself to begin administering first aid to the now comatose passenger who against all odds continued to survive, making an oblique reference to the hastily applied makeshift tourniquet and the slimy mess of blood soaked ashes, for what ever obscure reason lost to me at the time pointedly made an issue of the consequences involved in not relieving the pressure at given intervals, but in truth when one took into

119

consideration the circumstances involving that unavoidable oversight, it wasn't difficult to understand why. Little did I know at the time the consequences of my actions or lack of them would come full circle to haunt me in a manner one could have never begun to foresee or it's taking place in the unforeseen manner it did.

Later on when all the hollow compliments, meaningless hoopla, blame placing and condemnation of the innocent had more or less been accomplished the excitement of the moment eventually dying down to mild roar, the head nurse and I sat alone in the kitchen discussing the past events over a cup of coffee, it still taking a supreme effort on my part to steady the cup while attempting to drink out of it without chipping the enamel off my front teeth. After my having somewhat settled down to a semblance of forced calm and swallowing a number of pills she offered me to alleviate my pounding headache and calm my overstretched nerves she went on to inform me the patient to now be heavily sedated and presently stable but remaining in a state of deep shock from loss of blood with her succinctly adding his if not for my daring rescue had very little chance of surviving for another fifteen to twenty minutes on the outside without receiving medical aid so great was his loss of blood, then while studying me through her horn rimmed glasses in an intense manner that left me feeling noticeably uncomfortable complemented me on my pilot skills and my humanity toward another, secretly my take on it all is why had I attempted such an extremely risky undertaking that by all odds should have ended in disaster, an act that unselfishly involved taking such grave risks in offering succor to a gravely injured man who otherwise had no hope of survival at all, but again in retrospect, who was he to me that I would so foolishly risk my own life to possibly save his? Her well intentioned words of praise rang hollow in my ears for be as it may the deed for what it was worth had been done and the need to ponder the wisdom of it all and perhaps arrive at a satisfying conclusion would come in good time.

Eventually two dockhands who had been reluctantly roused out of their rooms arrived to pick up the load of fish that had almost been our undoing and to offer me a lift home. Upon arriving there found myself incapable of settling down to any degree due to the cumulative effects of enough adrenalin charging through my veins to jump start a locomotive on top of enduring mind searing stress for far too long, the combined debilitating effects coming down on me like a truck load of bricks leaving me feeling far to rocky and ragged of mind to even consider attempting to rest, instead sitting there by myself in a darkened room running the scenario of the past events through my tortured mind over and over again not unlike a non stop closed loop until ready to scream, enough already. After enduring an endlessly long and sleepless night that included much pacing restlessly back and forth as if attempting to find mental equilibrium to finally with palpable relief welcome the first life giving rays of the early morning sun upon it's appearing over the eastern horizon, the new day finding me in such a ragged state of mind I wisely chose to have another pilot ferry my aircraft back to base. When finally able to reach a somewhat coherent state of mind discreetly inquired into the series of events leading up to my near disaster, to be taken aback upon learning it had been a dock hand who had first received the distress message from the worker at the satellite base, and being unable to contact the dispatcher who had ostensibly gone home for the day and removing his phone off the hook the dock hand upon failing to reach him for advice and being of astute nature took it upon himself to switch radio channels and relay the message to me.

As it went with my learning much later once the dispatcher having been brought up to speed on the past sequence of events, immediately took upon himself to draft up a written report denying any and all responsibility on his part while irrevocably stating as to my having acted solely of my own volition without requesting prior authorization to proceed as I did to recklessly and without prejudice unnecessarily subject a company aircraft and innocent passenger to grave risk, thus in one fell swoop personally absolving himself from all possible blame while distancing the company from any future liability, and in doing so securely placing the noose around my neck.

Well as small minded and of little consequence as I initially found the whole affair to be and not expecting it to go any further than it already had, some what chagrined to discover the authorities in co-operation with Indian affairs who after a lengthy and no doubt costly investigation into the facts surrounding the affair had seen fit to make much ado of it all by bringing in the RCMP to investigate the possibility of my knowingly and without due regard breaking many airworthiness rules and once completing their findings to ultimately charge me with reckless abandon (whatever that is?), flying at night in an improperly equipped aircraft (imagine that), landing at night at other than a lighted airstrip (they lie, I did so have lights) flying an aircraft while having less than the minimum amount of fuel aboard to fly safely to my destination plus sufficient fuel to fly to an alternate airport and to top it plus forty five minutes reserve (I wonder what they were smoking?), thoughtlessly and without exercising due regardwhile   endangering life and property, blah blah blah, and so it went, not a word of commendation for saving a man's life at great risk to my own.

In summation during the court case but for the head nurse's unselfish testimony on my behalf, it could have all too easily gone very badly for me as it unfortunately turned out the patient required having the foot amputated due to complications brought on by my failure to relieve the pressure on the tourniquet at given intervals.

This effectively placed me between a rock and a hard place, some of the ridiculous charges made against my person were eventually dropped due to lack of concrete evidence, but it would appear that those worthies who infest the civil court system hungered to add another notch to their gun stocks in order to enhance and advance their careers no matter what the cost to an innocent person ultimately through much argument and perseverance eventually worked up a raft of nonsensical charges that stuck, the judge finding me guilty as charged levied a hefty monetary fine while admonishing me it was only the fact of the nurse's testimony on my behalf and the terrible risk I had taken to save another man's life that kept me from serving a lengthy jail term, it took two years to pay off forcing my having to declare personal bankruptcy plus to add insult to financial injury suffered the loss of my commercial pilot's privilege for a period of six months severely restricting my ability to earn a decent living during that time.

This miscarriage of what can only be construed as "Justice" left me in a totally disillusioned and confused state of mind for some time to come, the system having unjustly branded me as a "Felon", that could well be as my in the first place having very little or no respect for the environs of the law, the carnival of so called justice that took place in the court room did little to reinforce my positive beliefs, the end results could only be termed as "Bitter Medicine".

Overload

ON ONE OCCASSION DURING MY flying career found myself flying a twin beech for a company known as Neptune Fisheries out of a small mining town known as Lynn Lake Manitoba, a real loser of a burg that offered nothing in the way of a decent life style or social life unless one happened to be an out and out boozer, which I wasn't, but man did it offer up unbelievable hordes of mosquito's and black flies that guaranteed making one's life a living hell during the short hot summer months and of course one either endured the frigid Siberian style winters that seemed to stretch out forever or one departed for warmer climes.

One of our main customers being the South Indian Co-op Fisheries located on a huge lake of the same name that offered a frightening smorgasbord of huge snow drifts and pockets of deep slush that plagued the lake's surface most any where one went making it wise to land only on well packed runways, but the worst being the unpredictable and frequent weather systems that swept rapidly through the area.

Never before had I encountered such adverse flying conditions, fiercely cold for days on end putting a halt to flying until moderating, and when it did most often bringing on severe icing conditions that effectively brought flying activities to a sudden halt as to challenge it guaranteed disaster, thus placing every one involved in the business of air transport between a rock and a hard place.

One day when no longer able to tolerate the crashing boredom brought on by endless days and longer nights of inactivity and fed up with the constant bitching of the fishermen demanding our services in picking up their fish consented to attempt a flight, unwisely as it turned out in doing so even though aware of possibly encountering severe icing conditions along the way, the entire situation throughout most of the winter had become ludicrous, first it being far too cold to risk flight when metal became brittle, then when it did moderate to an acceptable degree one faced life threatening icing conditions, try explaining that to a gang of frustrated fishermen.

Loading up five drums of fuel and a pesky young bank clerk that constantly lobbied for rides to view the outlying camps, contrary to better judgment started out with a growing feeling of unease nagging at me as the conditions we encountered along the way not at all to my liking, becoming increasingly agitated and not at all sure to be doing the right thing each time another aircraft reported turning back due to encountering heavy icing conditions, but for some unexplained reason my not running into severe enough conditions to warrant turning back, reluctantly pushing on while dodging the occasional curtains of ice saturated fog until finally arriving at the fish camp.

At the time it was common practice to dispense with smelly fish bags and heavy metal tubs in order to save weight, instead employing a canvas bin to load the fish into, the only drawback of employing this method it made it all too easy to place a gross overload of fish within it's confines without the pilot's knowledge.

Having gained trust in the fishermen who had loaded the aircraft many times before to place the correct weight of twenty five hundred pounds aboard, failed badly that day in not exercising due caution when taking into consideration their growing desperation of getting their fish to market while still fresh, instead taking a short break to thaw out and enjoy a cup of hot coffee at the bunk house, as it turned that cup of coffee coming near to being my last,

Upon returning to the dock it was immediately noticed with some surprise a large compliment of them still hovered within the vicinity of the aircraft as if in anticipation of some as yet unknown event about to occur, now that struck me as being rather odd and out of context as they usually dispersed rapidly once completing loading the aircraft, for some reason that could not be readily explained their strange and as yet unexplained behavior unsettled me but passed it off as just one of them unexplained happenings that on the occasion took place among the native people.

Upon starting the engines the aircraft suddenly settled further down on the oleo struts, something it had never done before, that unusual occurrence in itself should have given me ample warning something to be amiss, but being more concerned about the deteriorating state of the weather along with a terminal case of get home its bone headedly chose to ignore that subtle warning thus setting the stage for a life threatening experience one would never forget, instead when ready applying full power for take off with my instantly sensing the aircraft to be initially reacting abnormally heavy and sluggish, failing to accelerate as rapidly as it normally did, but for what ever reason once again ignoring the warnings putting it down to sticky snow conditions, only upon finding it far too late to abort the take off it was noticed with some alarm that full forward pressure on the control yoke failed to lift the tail up into flying position as it normally did upon reaching the required take off speed, with growing alarm at my rapidly worsening situation instantly realized my having no other choice but to if at all possible become airborne before running off the end of the packed strip where it was a certainty the huge rock hard drifts that concealed deep snow and slush without fail guaranteed to rip the gear off if we plowed into them leaving no choice but to continue on with my desperately doing the unthinkable by ramming the throttles into the over boost position while selecting flap full down to barely stagger into the air in an extremely dangerous nose high tail low attitude upon reaching the very last foot of packed runway with my frantically dancing on the rudder pedals in an attempt to keep the wings level as they slewed from side to side as we thundered along barely clearing the tops of the huge drifts that seemed to menacingly reach up as if attempting to impede our precarious progress.

With my not daring to make the slightest of turns in order to avoid the area of thin ice that lay directly in our path and at the same time being all too aware of the abnormal strain being imposed on the laboring engines, the pressure on them had to be reduced and god dam soon if one wished to avoid possible damage to them or worse.

Eventually safe flying speed reached as the flaps were slowly raised a few degrees at a time allowing a corresponding reduction in the power output of the engines and none too soon the cylinder head temperatures having crept into the never exceed red zone.

Soon finding that even with full nose down trim rolled in, it still called for my maintaining a constant pressure on the control yoke to prevent the nose from climbing.

It must have taken all of ten miles or better to gain sufficient flying speed before daring to attempt a slow and careful turn in order to if at all possible returning to the fish camp to offload the excess weight, that is until the sickening realization rolled over me like a tidal wave if my being foolish enough to attempt a landing on that relatively short strip at the high speed approach required to remain airborne, we wouldn't stand a chance in hell of being able to stop before sliding off the end with predictable results, for better or worse we were committed to keep on going while hoping for the best and expecting the worst.

After having white knuckled ourselves through a hair raising turn that frightened the hell out of me each time the tail section hammered out a warning of a potential stall we managed to take up a rough heading for Lynn Lake, a most trying maneuver that left my nerve ends raw as the aircraft continued to wallow through the air like a gut shot goose, but gradually building up speed as fuel burnt off. The situation having eased off some what took the time to check out my passenger who for the most part had sat in frozen immobility through it all in bug eyed fear, stared beseechingly with his mouth moving soundlessly before once again finding his voice and able to scream in a high pitched voice, hart do something, anything but get us down alive, I don't want to die, well as far as that went neither did I, but his uncontrolled panic attack served to ratchet my already overstretched nerves up another notch, yes he had ample reason to experience paralyzing fear as the area directly in our path almost completely socked in with heavy snow and ice crystals we didn't stand a chance of avoiding, Christ, wrestling that highly unstable aircraft through the snow storms endless gloom fighting off successive waves of black incapacitating fear that rode heavily on my shoulders as we continued to white knuckle our way to perceived safety, once through it the near overriding fear of losing what little control I had over our badly out of trim and terribly unstable aircraft that had so sorely beset me eased off somewhat for a time, but the absolute certainty of our encountering patches of severe icing that couldn't be avoided would place us into further jeopardy for if we were to acquire even a slight coating the aircraft would eventually take on all the aerodynamics of a manhole cover sealing our fate, but having little choice but to do otherwise we desperately continued to hang in there.

After a time the constant and unrelenting pressure demanded of me on the controls to keep the nose in level flying position had by now caused my arms to go numb to the point of requiring immediate relief before my muscles began to spasm and lock up, the absolute necessity for immediate assistance in relieving the pressure required much screaming and pleading on my part for assistance, only just managing to coax my terrified passenger to take up the required pressure on the control column before my overtaxed arm muscles gave out. Once he had assumed control cautiously allowed the quivering painfully knotted up muscles on each arm to slowly relax while keeping a wary eye on his questionable ability.

It seemed to take forever to limp our way across that featureless terrain in next to zero visibility seeming to be suspended in space and time, but with a combination of good luck and navigation skills we had made it thus far, at one point when just emerging from claustrophobia inducing snow squall we ran directly into a heavy gray curtain of icing that could not be avoided, goddamit I managed to shriek in a whisper, what in the hell else can go possibly go wrong next?, fortunately for our existing state of health and peace of mind it turned out to be a very narrow band, but still the thin sheen of clear ice it inflicted upon us it caused a slight loss of precious air speed while glazing over the windshield further reducing my already limited forward visibility.

Many an anxious glance at the engines cylinder temperature gauges assured me the engines were holding up well considering the constant and unrelenting strain being imposed on them, they're not overheating though the head temperature indicating needles tending toward remaining slightly on the high side.

But still one remained in a constant state of anxiety as if either engine as much as coughed for being in the precarious flight condition we were there remained little doubt if that were to occur our immediately losing control and rolling over with no chance of survival, not the sort of thoughts one cared to have riding on their shoulders.

Another grave concern surfaced upon checking our remaining fuel contents which indicated an alarming propensity on the part of the engines to be consuming far more fuel than normal due to the required high power settings making it questionable if we still retained a sufficient amount in the tanks to make it the remaining distance to Lynn Lake, the only good thing that could be said about it as the fuel burnt off the aircraft became correspondingly lighter allowing a slight but welcome increase in performance, Christ, talk about being impaled on the horns of a dilemma.

Eventually to my ever lasting relief flying over and recognizing an abandoned fish camp on the west shore of a large lake that informed me of having slightly less than twenty miles to go, upon fortuitously sighting that welcome landmark hope sprang anew, but goddamit how my poor tortured arms ached from the unremitting pressure required of them, while my eyes burned from the constant demands imposed on them while peering through a partially iced over windshield in an attempt to keep track of our plodding progress. My head also pounded unmercifully threatening to fall off my shoulders at any time due to the effects of all the adrenalin being pumped into my bloodstream.

The constant tension on my back muscles eventual caused painful knotting bringing tears to my already burning eyes, severely limiting my control inputs adding to my growing concerns.

Finally after what had seemed to take a life time gratefully sighting our destination through the winter day's watery gloom, not daring to take the chance of circling in order to assess the wind direction due to the highly unstable status of the aircraft and our shortage of fuel, instead electing to make a straight in approach to the runway, one that had to be without question done right the first time as there wasn't a hope in hell of going around if blowing it, we had one chance to get down safely and one chance only, goddamit how my poor head ached on top of being soaked with sweat and all torn to hell with blood curdling fear and indecision, my thought processes almost refusing to function being too long on the bare edge of overload, but as I had done many times before while laboring under duress dipping into a reservoir of strength and determination while retaining my cool and not allowing myself to become over anxious to get it over with my ever so gently and cautiously maneuvering the aircraft around as required using only rudder control not daring to bank a wing in the least lest it stall out until lining up with the runway to my satisfaction, my planning on using up every available inch, the high landing speed required to touch down safely left me unsure of how much available length would be required before coming to a stop.

Only upon being absolutely certain to safely making the threshold of the runway were the flaps cautiously lowered by degrees into the full down position, once having done so irrevocably committing ourselves to a landing, finding all to be going well cautiously eased off on the throttles a hair or two, upon doing so instantly experiencing the most horrendous shudder from the tail section as it hung on the bare edge of a stall, at a critical time like that one does not have the luxury of protracted analysis, one either instinctively acts to correct the situation if at all possible or one meets with potential disaster, in my case immediately without thought fire walling both throttles narrowly avoiding slamming tail low onto the rock hard runway, if that had occurred it is most likely the aircraft would have broken it's back, as it was the touchdown proving to be feather light, no thanks to skill on my part but in doing so having increased our forward speed somewhat by the sudden application of engine power, our arriving like a runaway locomotive with my swearing to leaving a trail of sparks from the skis once they firmly touched down on the frozen hard runway surface as we rocketed down the runway, it taking the better part of the three mile long stretch to finally slow to a shuddering halt, at no time during that headlong charge down the runway did I retain any semblance of controlling our forward speed, just hanging on and hoping for the best while keeping the aircraft centered on the runway as best one could by judicious application of rudders hoping for the best while expecting the worst.

Upon shutting down the engines and giving shaky thanks for our safe deliverance the now noticeable crash of silence all but deafening me, at first so stunned by the rapidly unfolding turn of events only able to sit there in stunned silence for the first while in dumb acceptance of our miraculous delivery, but it appeared my erstwhile passenger retained no such compunctions, immediately upon our shuddering to a stop, his quickly unlatching the overhead escape hatch to scramble out of the cockpit with remarkable alacrity giving me a parting smack me on the side of the head with his boot heel, so much for appreciation.

At first finding it difficult to accept our having overcome such terrible odds, but soon reminded of the cost to my back and shoulder muscles as they continued to spasm and burn so painfully it brought tears to my eyes making my exit from the cockpit awkward and difficult, upon sliding on to the wing it was found my rubbery legs refused to support me until the blood circulation resumed.

Being as there was no way in hell that aircraft could be taxied into it's normal parking spot as long as that terrible overload remained on board the fish packers truck had to come out to me to retrieve the load. During the interim it was decided to inspect the aircraft as best I could for damage and or visible signs of being overstressed, gratefully finding none but some shocked at the amount of clear ice found to be layered on the leading edges of the wings and tail section, little wonder then the tail section had come within a hair of stalling when unthinkingly retarding the throttles, god alone knows how we managed as well as we had, something's can not be rationally explained, physically or otherwise.

It took the fish packer two good sized loads to empty out the aircraft instead of the usual one, the gross tally coming out to an amazing thirty eight hundred and forty two pounds of fish, plus one stocky passenger who topped a hundred and ninety pounds for a grand total of four thousand and thirty two pounds disposable load, an overload of fifteen hundred pounds, just hearing that shocking bit of bad news came near to causing my knees to give way as at no time did I ever exceed a maximum of twenty five hundred pounds. One simply cannot begin to comprehend how that marvelous aircraft ever got off the runway never mind remaining airborne despite the creeping erosion of precious air speed brought on by the effects of ice building up on the leading edges, if we by chance we had encountered severe turbulence their remains little doubt the wings would have parted company from the aircraft.

That most sobering of experiences left me shaken to the very core of my being, if trust is a two way street then I had invertently taken a one way, never again taking anyone's word or trusting them to load my aircraft unless personally supervising the procedure.

As for the errant fishermen who took advantage of my trust, thus placing me in dire straits. One could never be absolutely certain of the fact at any time, but my one way or the other arriving at the unmistakable conclusion more than a few of them were some surprised on my returning safely to the fish camp, they're having assumed we had crashed through the thin ice that lay before us shortly after completing our hairy take off and immediately disappearing into a heavy snow squall that instantly muted the roar of the engines as we began our mind bending trip from hell.

Needless to say, that unthinking act of the fishermen deliberately overloading my aircraft to the degree of placing one in peril quickly spread to all the other operators who immediately took steps to prevent a further occurrence. And to my knowledge never took place again.

Inferno

THE LONG SUMMER MONTHS THAT year having remained unusually hot and dry with little if any rainfall to dampen the tinder dry forests, created an unprecedented fire hazard aided by the frequent bouts of dry lightning that for the most part proving to be little else but sound and fury, only on the rare occasion producing an isolated rain shower.

Fortunately the bulk of the fires remained in isolated low threat areas were they eventually burnt themselves out doing more good than harm in reducing the heavy scrubby undergrowth allowing a new crop of seedling to gain a foothold and accelerated growth.

The down side of it being the heavy layer of smoke that blanketed the area creating hazardous flying conditions for all as on the occasion the forward visibility dropped to less than half a mile or less creating the nerve wracking risk of a possible mid air collision that weighed heavily on our minds at all times during flight.

The local aircraft kept close tabs on each other by radio during flight our having jointly set up outgoing and arrival corridors that every pilot adhered to as accurately as possible, the main threat to us arriving in the form of transient pilots barging into the heavy traffic zone unannounced, the very worst of them being the American pilots who on the average unthinkingly sailed unconcernedly through the area to on more than one occasion frighten one of us half to death as they blithely cruised on by, suddenly appearing as if out of nowhere.

Fortunately, if it can be construed that way the heavy blanket of smoke on the most part extending thirty miles or so to the north, it always being a profound relief to finally break out into clear air, but just the same one had ample time during the interim to ponder and fret over the sometimes gut wrenching trials involved during the return trip that called for hanging over the trees at near zero feet either on your way out or returning, each time we went out and came back without incidence it became increasingly difficult to bring one's self to repeat it.

No pilot, no matter how bold or daring could tolerate such nerve wracking stress day after day with our finally giving it up upon finding ourselves turning in to hollow eyed caricatures of our former selves, requiring two hands to hold a cup of coffee to our lips without spilling most of it on one's self or chancing chipping the enamel off one's front teeth. Without fail the brass viewed our voluntary stand down as next to mutiny, nothing ever changed with them, all that mattered was the bottom line, no matter how dire the circumstances surrounding our decision, it remaining first last and always the god dam bottom line, our welfare came in last.

Of course the dispatcher who being a dyed in the wool company man predictably jumped into the fray going near ballistic upon being apprised of our decision threatening all sorts of mayhem if we carried out our Stan down, that is until being braced by one of the more outspoken pilots who's nerves had been severely tested that very same day when experiencing a near miss with an unidentified aircraft, suggesting in a saccharine manner that if he (the dispatcher) was so god dam gung ho about getting the trips done, then he (the pilot) would be the first to volunteer to go, but only if the dispatcher accompanied him, no more needed to be said.

As if nature deliberately conspired against us, the light wind that sporadically came and went dispersing the smoke some what up and died completely leaving an eerie dead calm that allowed the dirty gray layer of smoke to thicken considerably.

The MNR, as we facetiously referred to them as "the ministry of national recreation" it appeared having their share of troubles upon one of their much required aircraft badly damaged a float in one of the black water lakes placing it out of service for the duration.

That sort of incident being common place we paid little attention until monitoring a radio exchange between the main base and a crew of fire fighters who found themselves being threatened by a sudden and severe wind shift that placed them directly in the path of a fast moving fire, they're taking refuge in the waters of a fairly long narrow body of water that by the damndest coincidence to be one of my favorite fishing holes were they awaited evacuation.

As it turned out there being a crucial demand for every available aircraft except for the beech craft, they're not being suited to carry out the requirements of getting in and out of small lakes, a shortcoming that suited us beech craft drivers just fine, not wanting to be part of the unfortunates forced to fly in the smoke. The search for suitable aircraft rapidly becoming critical as none to be had within the vicinity being taken up by fire suppression duties elsewhere.

As the situation facing the trapped crew of fire fighters wore on it became increasingly critical, for what ever reason lost to me, be it bravado, ultimate stupidity or an honest concern for the unenviable plight of fellow men or what ever one cared to call it, I truthfully could never say when consenting to make a cursory venture to check out just how critical or life threatening their situation had become, not really planning or desiring to do much else, for as it was flying a beech craft at tree top level in such visibility restricted conditions bordered on near madness when asking the aircraft to perform in an environment totally unsuited to it, not to mention the all too real possibility of unintentionally venturing too close to a smoke shrouded wall of flame that potentially concealed violent wind shears and unthinkable down drafts created by the insatiable demands of the fire for oxygen that could all too easily suck an unwary pilot into the maw of the inferno with predictable results.

Why I volunteered to place my and the young pilot,s life on the line can not as mentioned previously be rationally explained when taking into consideration the past shabby treatment suffered at the hands of righteous self serving government minions who's reasoning powers or lack of it continuously fail to take reality into account at any level, to me there has always existed an unbridgeable gap between their brain dead mode of reasoning and common sense, would this time be any different? I hardly thought so but in good conscience could one use that as a valid excuse to at least try.

While taxiing out into the murk cursed the very devil that drove me to once more face unknown adversity, such blatant boldness or otherwise lacking a suitable description, plain and simple stupidity that only had a place in fiction.

Being well aware the attempt for what it was worth could well turn out to be a fool's errand nevertheless elected to carry on even when taking into consideration the beech craft, s forward and side view short comings that only got that much worse when flying in restricted visibility.

Shortly before advancing the throttles for take off the visibility had dropped to near zero almost convincing me to abort the attempt, but within a short period of time clearing off sufficiently to allow a take off that pretty much made by reference to the flight instruments, once clearing the water one could only see straight down to view an eerie landscape entirely wreathed in smoke that caused our eyes to burn and tear copiously, we certainly had our work cut out for us for we were informed upon our return of our disappearing into the smoke even before leaving the water, the listeners only able to keep track of our progress by the roar of the engines until they're eventually becoming muted by the sound deadening smoke.

Initially electing to climb over top of the smoke layer, once accomplishing that simple maneuver took up a heading in the direction the lake lay in an uncertain state of mind having absolutely no idea what we were committing ourselves to afraid to keep on, afraid not to knowing it would only be by the longest of shots to even think of locating the lake in question, and if by the rarest of chance we did, then what? Only time and circumstances would eventually answer that equation.

Having spent some time circling above the smoke layer in the area where the lake was more or less estimated to be and while completing our last turn before giving up any hope of locating it even though certain of being close to or within the area we thought it to lie in before giving up and returning to base fate stepped in with our suddenly receiving a scratchy transmission from the fire crew's radio coming faintly through our ear phones informing us of our just having over flown their position. That information as sketchy as it was more or less informed me of our position in relation to them and being aware the area surrounding the lake to be fairly flat cautiously eased our way down through the heavy layer of smoke till arriving at what we estimated to be a few hundred feet above tree top level, remaining there until flying through a thinning layer of smoke that allowed our being able to make out what appeared to be an alien landscape, we must have at one point come far closer to the frontal area of the fire than intended as the aircraft suddenly began to shied and buck so violently it would have pitched us out of our seats if not for our previously having the foresight to ensure our being tightly strapped to them in anticipation of sooner or later encountering the effect of the violent thermals created by vicious currents of air being sucked in to feed the voracious demands of the inferno greatly intensifying my control inputs that sorely tried one's stamina until able to break clear leaving both us soaking wet with sweat from fear and demanding exertions, again as if by some weird twist of fate as we once more circled the area but this time not venturing as close as before. By some whim of nature the pall of smoke for what ever reason suddenly cleared off to a reasonable degree allowing a smoke distorted view of the lake with the co- pilot sighting men standing in the shallow water along the shore line. By the remotest of chance we found ourselves perfectly lined up with the lake, once realizing we had been offered a golden opportunity without conscious thought of the possible consequences yanked back the throttles while lowering the flaps in readiness for a landing to be met by a terrified yelp of dismay from my co-pilot about my being fucken nuts.

One can only ponder the make up of our mental and physical world and how it controls our thoughts and actions, especially while laboring under great stress, my not having made any prior decision to land it almost seemed as if another part of me took control, the pilot animal within taking over command of mind and body, the same element of cold calculation that had on many the occasion saved me from certain disaster, turning me into a flesh and blood machine that lacked feeling and emotion, save for the basic concept of survival that existed deep within, the other personality, the human element stayed back to observe as it had on many occasions with no other emotion except that of raw fear. Little can be clearly recalled about the landing except it's being among the shortest I had ever accomplished in a beech craft up till then, once falling off the step the engines shut down to allow the aircraft to drift toward the men in the water. Only upon finding ourselves on the water and almost entirely surrounded by a ring of fire that advanced inexorably toward us a sudden thrill of alarm began to course through me upon viewing with growing concern the number of men standing up to their waists in the shallow water, expecting no more than six counted eight of them wading to- ward us, good Christ there was no way in hell we could ever make it off within the restricted space of the lake with six water logged men and all the gear they still toted with them, never mind eight. This being a one shot deal that had as yet to be accomplished and one could bet our chance of successfully doing so did not come with an iron clad guarantee, well desperate situations call for desperate measures with my hoarsely shouting at the first man to wade up along side the float to strip off his water logged boots and clothes and dump them into the lake as quickly as possible, only to be met with a questioning stare as if I had lost my mind, my throat being raw from breathing acrid smoke for too long my voice carried little authority. God dam you stupid bastards I screeched in a whisper as they milled confusedly about as if on some kind of Hollywood "Let's make a deal" group effort, get your Asses in gear or were all dead meat. The sudden jolting and rocking motion that suddenly seized the aircraft informed me the fire to be rapidly advancing on us and if we were to leave at all it had to be soon.

My entreaties for the men to do as asked only met with stubborn resistance on their part, the increasing amount of burnt pine needles and ash that had begun to randomly swirl about and rain down on us along with a noticeable shortage of oxygen beginning to making it's self apparent decided me on our having exposed ourselves to life threatening danger long enough, I had up till then at great risk offered them some hope of rescue that they for some obscure reason stubbornly failed to embrace, well to hell with them my life came first as far as I was concerned, in desperate haste instructed the near panicked co-pilot to shut the rear door while quickly sliding into my seat in preparation of starting the engines, the foreman who had just made his way to the aircraft took instant note of our desperate actions shouted desperately for me to wait, as difficult as a request it was to do so hesitated momentarily in hopes of his being able to talk common sense into the recalcitrant crew reluctantly held off starting the engines while repeating my prior request to have the men strip and to dump their gear. To his credit they without further hesitation complied immediately, fortunately for all his being respected as being astute and quick witted, once having stripped to their skivvies reluctantly climbing into the cabin to huddle fearfully, by the time the last man had climbed aboard my nerves were completely strung out from the near mind paralyzing fear that we had tarried for too long, desperation fortifying an all consuming desire to be on our way before the situation deteriorated to the point of becoming impossible to do so, the co-pilot who had been monitoring our erratic progress as we drifted and swung every which way at the whims of the erratically shifting winds that on a sudden began to blow strongly off the nose of the aircraft briskly shoving it backwards to-ward a shoal of exposed boulders that had made their threatening presence quite plain by the sheets of white water suddenly smashing off them desperately hollered at me to start the engines, fortunately for us they're previously being readied for a quick start managed to without hesitation bring one of them to life just as the rear of one float contacted a boulder with a resounding clang that sent a shudder all through the aircraft leaving me all atremble while starting up the other engine and to without further preamble fire wall both of them to the stops.

Initially the aircraft appeared to respond sluggishly as it initially began to plow ahead, fortunately the shallow water worked in our favor, for as we gained forward momentum began to compress under the floats placing us on the step far quicker than normal with our rapidly gaining forward speed as the smoke once again began to blanket the area effectively blotting out forward visibility, as we gained flying speed the aircraft bucked and shied viciously from the effects of the rapidly shifting gusts of wind hammering on it from all sides requiring my continuously dancing on the rudder pedals slamming them from one stop to the other in an almost vain effort to counteract the effects.

Having previously instructed the co-pilot to monitor the air speed and to inform me within good time if at all possible our approaching the far shore line, we must have accelerated down the length of the lake much quicker than initially thought my suddenly being alerted by a frantic screech of pure terror from the co-pilot, having just lifted my eyes off the airspeed indicator upon noting our fast approaching a safe lift off speed met with the heart stopping spectacle of a seemingly solid wall of burning trees directly in front of us galvanizing me into desperately heaving back on the control column to almost within seconds of clearing the water crashing in to the thick of them as if launched from a giant slingshot driving headlong through the flaming barrier accompanied by the nerve wracking tattoo of broken off branches bouncing off the wings and fuselage as the wildly spinning propellers slashed through the tree tops like twin buzz saws creating a blinding swirl of pine needles and other debris that in flying back onto the windshield like a black cloud further reducing our already severely restricted forward visibility while causing both of us to involuntarily throw up an arm to protect our faces, our precarious passage through the copse of burning trees seeming to last an eternity before finally breaking clear, but in all probability only a hellishly long duration of only a few seconds.

As the aircraft jolted and shuddered it's way through my control inputs displayed all the effects of attempting to manipulate a wet noodle so ineffectively did they respond, fortunately the engines never missed a beat though undoubtedly ingesting a large amount of pine needles into the air intakes.

Once breaking clear with my more or less gaining control for some reason not apparent to me at first the aircraft refused to gain additional forward speed seeming to wallow sluggishly through the air, a frantic check of engine and flight instruments failed to indicate the cause, not until doing a systems check were the flaps found to still be in the full down position, retracting them a few degrees at a time rewarded us with a gradual increase in air speed as the aircraft responded to the decreased drag, and not a second too soon as the engines out of necessity held far past the maximum time allowable in over boost, they were amazingly rugged engines, capable of absorbing severe abuse for extended periods of time, but even at that they had their limits and guaranteed to self destruct if pushed too far, and after what we had just gone through it would go badly for us if experiencing engine failure.

Throttling back the engines we continued to wallow all over the sky while

Flying through an area of violent thermals with my seething inwardly over the

Co-pilot's neglecting his duties, soon got something more to be concerned about upon glancing at the cylinder head temperature gauges, shocked to finding the indicating needles almost pegged out at the never exceed red lines, on top of that both engines emitting streaks of blue black smoke from their cowlings almost giving me heart failure, a near panicked perusal of the engine fire warning lights thankfully failed to indicate engine fires. Then it came clear to me in a flash of inspiration, of course the cylinder heads cooling fins had to be packed almost solid with pine needles received from our inadvertent passage through the tree tops markedly restricting the air flow over them, that explained the smoke pouring out of the engines, well we couldn't continue on like that for too much longer, shit and goddamit what else can possibly bedevil us?

My mind locked into a state of near paralysis when for the first while finding myself unable to decide what to do next, unless somehow managing to bring down the head temperatures pronto, we had little choice but to make an emergency landing on the first suitable lake that could be located. One can never be certain how an answer to a dilemma can suddenly come about while laboring under great mental stress, but almost if out of the blue a trick I had picked up somewhere along the way suddenly came to mind, my quickly placing the ram air selectors into the hot air position, thus feeding heated air into the carburetors, this in effect richens the fuel mixture to the engines, the excess fuel acting as a coolant, gradually to my ever lasting relief the indicating needles slowly began to edge out of the red line zone to finally stabilize at a far higher temperature than one could have wished, but there is a penalty to be paid as in doing so it noticeably reduces available engine power while ratcheting up fuel consumption.

No sooner having averted that threatening crisis, fell headfirst into another upon completing a check on our remaining fuel, jolting me to the degree my feet began to involuntarily dance all over the rudder pedals, Christ what next, I already had enough adrenalin charging through my blood stream to jump start a diesel locomotive, violently shaking the co-pilot to rouse him out of his seeming paralysis yelling at him in a voice hoarse from breathing smoke to monitor the fuel tanks and engine fuel pressure warning lights and to be god dam quick about switching over to emergency fuel if either began to blink it's warning of low fuel pressure, my being too taken up with navigation and preventing the aircraft from inadvertently scraping the tree tops while at the same time desperately attempting to keep a sharp lookout for the power line right of way we must soon cross at a ninety degree angle according to our rigidly held compass course, if by chance we were to miss spotting that life line to home we would find ourselves in deep trouble having absolutely no idea of our present ground position.

With my eyes burning and smarting found it extremely difficult to focus on the smoke shrouded terrain passing below us as we bumped and swayed all over hell's half acre, the co-pilot never did see the power line as it flashed by with my by the merest of chance doing so while wiping away tears and sweat out of my burning eyes while momentarily glancing out of the side window just in time to recognize the right of way to immediately turn back to-ward it and once more acquiring it and verifying our compass heading to be correct began to follow it to Pickle Lake.

As the endlessly long minutes slowly dragged by our situation became increasingly tense not being at all certain as to how much longer our fuel supply would hold out, just about the time of my despairing of our finding the lake before it became too late to do so the familiar swampy area at the north end of the lake hove into view, that welcome sight gave one the feeling of having a piano lifted off their shoulders, but we were not entirely out of the woods just yet as a large island lay directly in our path, not daring to attempt circumventing it due to the poor visibility it left me with no other choice but to overfly it before attempting a landing.

Even though being expected, it's suddenly looming out of the gloom directly in front of us, it's menacing presence nevertheless coming near to causing both of us to jump out of our respective skins as we scraped our way over top of it.

Once certain of being clear throttled back to begin our landing approach utilizing full down flap to assist in stabilizing our descent, we couldn't afford to be overly cautious having only two miles or less to touch down safely before inadvertently running into the far shore line, something like that could well ruin one's day.

The smoke and lake surface having merged as one making it appear as if one were suspended in a glass of milk, when the initial touch down did occur it totally caught me by surprise startling me into yanking back on the control column while ramming on full throttle, a bad reaction on my part leaving us suspended in a near stall, not daring to attempt a controlled fly down with power on descent due to the distance required to do so more or less allowed the aircraft to mush onto the lake until once more contacting the water heavily enough to jar one's teeth, but glad enough to have arrived safely instantly yanking off the power as soon as the full weight of the aircraft had settled onto the lake surface fearful of running up on the far shore line or break water at any time.

From here on in what ever took place next could only prove to be anticlimactic when taking into consideration what we had just endured.

The muted rattle of the idling engines music to my ears as they told me we had survived in spite of it all, coming down from my adrenalin high found myself vibrating all over the cockpit with terribly dry throat and lips, not daring to attempt to speak knowing it would only come out as an unintelligible croak.

Shutting down one engine to taxi slower instructed the co-pilot to stand on the back of the seats and stick his head and shoulders out of the hatch in order to gain a better perspective of what could suddenly appear before us, with his before too long shouting something inaudible with my immediate reaction being to shut down the still idling engine thinking we were about to collide with as a yet unseen obstacle.

Peering myopically out of the windshield finally able to spot what appeared to be a sickly diffused yellow glow of flashing lights with my overstressed mind at first refusing to recognize it for what it was until the co-pilot joyfully slid back into his seat with an alacrity not observed on his part for some time informing me they were the lights from a vehicle a quick witted dock hand had driven to the end of the dock and to continuously flash the head lights to assist in our locating the dock before running g in to it, I could have gladly kissed that astute young man for showing such initiative, the flashing lights making it a simple matter to make our cautious way to that most welcome place of safety we had departed from it seemed a life time ago. Once successfully docking the aircraft without bending or breaking anything only able to sit there for a time, happy to have made it back in one piece, Christ I thought to myself if that's what it takes to be some kind of a tin hero, I would be content to spend my life as a craven coward, god dam how my poor head pounded, that and the rank odor of my sweat soaked body almost revolted me, coming down from an adrenalin high as usual took it's toll on me leaving every muscle in my body as one huge mass of over tensed protoplasm that continued to spasm uncontrollably, as yet not daring to attempt an exit from the cockpit being well aware my palsied limbs would refuse to obey, so wisely chose to remain in my seat while desperately willing my teeth to cease chattering and my knees to quit jerking spasmodically, once able to concentrate on my surroundings distractedly observed the crowd of onlookers that had gathered as if out of thin air who stared in unconcealed awe at the still smoking engines and the assorted collection of well scorched chunks and pieces of pine tree sticking out of the cowlings and randomly jammed into the float struts and fittings. Well from there on the following course of events pretty much taking place as expected as the fire fighters exited from the aircraft to huddle sheepishly in a group acutely aware of wearing only a pair of shorts until being rescued by a fast thinking worker from the rangers station who quickly collected a set of coveralls for each man with their gratefully donning them. It seems upon their doing so collectively appeared to within a short period of time to re-gain their aplomb and self confidence, reacting in their respective manner toward me that ran the gamut of thanking me profusely for risking my life in order to save theirs, others subjecting me to prolonged and severe verbal abuse that sickened me to the core of my very soul for exposing them to such a life threatening ordeal.

Down deep inside though badly stung and shaken to the very core of my being realized I shouldn't let it get to or bother me to the degree it did knowing their reactions to be brought on by what must have seemed to be a never ending duration of fearful hell while crouched helplessly in the confines of the cabin unable to see or understand what was taking place, only existing in an environment of fire, smoke and pounding engines, unable to do anything but to wait in mind numbing terror to meet whatever fate had in store for them.

But be as it may, in spite of it all we had survived near impossible odds that left me wondering what was to come next, having acquired a bitter legacy from past dealing with government personnel made it a certainty in no way had I heard the last of it, them low life home steadying sons of bitches that without fail staffed all levels of government who with cowardly mien being their forte lacked the guts to stand up and be counted except when absolutely certain in doing so worked in their favor, making up for their shortcomings by roundly castigating them who dared, my not for a minute expecting things to be any different this time around if the usual cover your ass scenario so diligently played out to the extreme at such times by them worthies as they usually did with it being a dead certainty my once again facing condemnation.

Well what would be would be, once certain of being able to control my rubbery knees to a acceptable degree shakily exited the aircraft to make my way to the hotel for much needed refreshments, the gaggle of pilots accompanying me all attempting at once to query me about the details of the flight, hardly able to grunt much less talk my throat being terribly dry and raw from breathing smoke for so long at first unable to go into lengthy detail until the first bottle of cold beer some what alleviated my near dehydrated condition.

God dam it sure felt mighty fine to have survived such unforgiving odds and to once more be enjoying life amongst friends, only those who have experienced a similar life threatening ordeal can readily appreciate just how precious life is and most of all what is important in a man's life is not what we do, it's who we are. Once the pilots had heard me out, some turning pensive as they thought over the possible ramifications of my story, others mirroring absolute awe, with some remaining in a state of total disbelief, some reacting toward me in a sly manner as if the story as related to be a figment of a fertile imagination and could not have possibly taken place in the prescribed manner until the co-pilot who had for the most part restrained himself from jumping in to assist in the telling of the story took it upon himself to in no uncertain terms corroborate the course of events as they took place and to having occurred as stated, if the truth be known what any one chose to believe or disbelieve mattered not to me one way or the other, what was done was done and now considered a closed issue and it would be left at that.

After a while the conversation moved on eddying and flowing around me in a random manner as my scattered thoughts whirled around endlessly in my mind like a closed loop, futilely attempting to come to grips with my seeming penchant to place myself in harm's way, why had I with a free will chosen to place my precious body so far out onto a limb to save if at all possible the lives of others doing so at grave risk, in truth it failed to add up in my mind, from here on I would choose the way of the craven coward, but then again being who I am would I?

Unable to come down from my adrenalin induced high and suffering from a pounding headache that threatened to split my skull asunder along with mentally quivering like a tuning fork, quietly took my leave to seek solace from it all in the quiet and security of my own home.

That as it turned out proving to be an exercise in futility, unable to dismiss the feverish mental trauma that continued to torment me as the past series of hellish events refused to cease thrashing about in my overloaded brain until driven in desperation to seek out some form of succor finally drove back to the base to resignedly flop out onto the ratty couch to doze fitfully, often coming wide awake in a near panicked state of absolute confusion and terror as life threatening scenarios endlessly chased each other through my tortured mind leaving me afraid to doze off again but unable to prevent doing so thus suffering re-occurring night mares over and over again until the first gray streaks of dawn once again stained the early morning skies.

For all the world, feeling and most likely looking like shit stared vacantly out of the window as my world welcomed a new day, pondering what was to come next and what the repercussions of the loss of several thousands of dollars of equipment we had by the direst of necessity forced to leave behind, strangely enough when all had been said and done and my submitting a comprehensive written report nothing more came of it.

As was bound to happen in such a small town my eventually meeting up with the MNR pilot who had originally dropped the men off at the lake in question, and who related his version of the near disaster as he knew it, only upon his suddenly slamming his bottle of beer onto the table top with such vehemence it caused me to come near jumping out of my skin with his precipitate actions inevitably garnering the attention of every other set of eyeballs in the room, man he loudly intoned for all within range to hear, this bit of news is going to frost your balls big time, going on to say as it went the chief ranger who was originally responsible for unnecessarily ordering his placing them fire fighters in harm's way when there was very little reason to have done so in the first place as the location of the fire so remote it threatened no one, has believe it or not has recently been promoted to district ranger for displaying superior judgment while laboring under severe stress that ultimately led to the safe rescue of the beleaguered men by the judicious deployment of local resources, well needless to say it certainly did frost my balls, but that's the way the government circles operate, one is promoted to the level of their incompetency.

In completing this story I can not resist taking a dig at the depths of the inefficiency and ongoing incompetency that runs rife through the hallowed halls of the empire building MNR

On one memorable occasion me and many others including a long time MNR employee who flew an otter out of the base at Pickle Lake along with many other interested parties who one fine late evening personally witnessed a case of gross incompetency by one of the senior MNR pilots who as we were to later discover at the time of the incident ferrying a brand new fresh off the assembly line gold plated plushy appointed twin otter from the Dehavilland Aircraft factory in Downsview Ontario to Sioux Lookout Ontario, and had only dropped in to Pickle lake in order to refuel, thus offering the local low life an unprecedented insight of one's tax dollar at play. Once completing re-fuelling at the local MNR base and during the ensuing take off the pilot for what ever reason badly misjudged the requirements of his take off run from the glassy waters of Pickle Lake in the process barely managing to clear the west wall of the rock filled breakwater enclosure he had for what ever reason chose to take off toward instead of utilizing the wide open expanse of lake that lay before him. The front two thirds of the huge floats at lift off barely clearing the wall of rock while the aircraft passed over it in an unusual nose high attitude with the last third contacting the top of the wall of stone with a resounding and no doubt prohibitively expensive crunch of precious metals being violently rearranged scattering chunks of stone like miniature projectiles everywhere, the aircraft despite all the sound and fury being produced appeared to hesitate momentarily before assuming a sudden nose low attitude to disappear into a spectacular welter of spray and foam that all but oliberated the entire forward portion of the aircraft for a few seconds before it's once more popping up and staggering into the air trailing impressive plumes of silvery water behind the floats for some time, one can be certain the sudden and unplanned baptism undoubtedly led to the red hot turbine blades to be found within the horrendously expensive turbine engines to having received a fair dash of icy cold water with the effects of the thermal shock so suddenly induced upon them must have without question created grave problems some where down the line, also one must wonder how the delicate gear case and propellers fared when all had been said and done?.

Well as it went we were to learn much later the aircraft managed to make it to Sioux Lookout, but we did wonder if the pilot's first act upon arrival was to change his shorts?, of course none of us commoners were to ever learn what transpired upon the brass being informed of the incident or the immensely prohibitive cost of repairing the extensive damage to them mind bogglingly expensive floats and in all probability the two turbine engines, plus what ever collateral damage that may have occurred, that revered information has no place among the tax paying commoners who are by and large generally viewed by the political hacks found within our accredited government bodies as the revenue producing sheep of industry who it appears labor mightily in the interest of maintaining inefficient incompetent government beauracracies. To my knowledge and at no time have I heard otherwise no matter how many MNR personnel had been discreetly questioned concerning this incident, it has somehow regardless of the nature of those most often in the know to shoot their mouths off, it to this very day remains as an in house hush hush report, though we did often wonder how the top brass viewed the pilot's big time screw up in bending up their brand new multi million dollar gold plated wonder machine, but one can be certain that if they stuck to their usual protocol, the pilot advanced another notch in seniority along with a substantial raise in pay.

As for the long time lowly MNR otter driver who had filmed the complete sequence of events on his camcorder for some reason lost to me (ahem) not retired from the MNR at the end of the season as scheduled, managing by what could be construed as persuasive argument to remain in their service for a further six years until retiring voluntarily, How does that grab you?.

Skating On The Edge

OF THE MORE INTERESTING TIMES of my lengthy career took place when the insurance company that underwrote of all the company's insurance requirements convened a gathering of all company pilots including me to select one that met their criteria in flight testing re-built aircraft and the taking off of float equipped aircraft while placed on a dolly, and to land float equipped aircraft on the grass.

To be sure we underwent a grueling session of oral and written tests along with unquestionable proof of experience, log book certifications etc. It certainly left me some shocked upon learning of my beating out all the competition including the chief pilot for the position, it seems the powers that be where impressed with my extensive and varied experience on so many different types of aircraft, their reasoning that any one who could survive the number of years I had under such trying conditions to be eminently qualified to carry out their requirements.

Well it goes with out saying that decision left a few hopefuls more than just a little burnt up and envious about failing to be selected.

Initially a feeling of trepidation came over me, not quite sure what to expect while awaiting the first test of my abilities to come about. The first job assigned to me was the salvaging of a Cessna 180 floatplane that had flipped over on it's back while touching down on glassy water. Once having turned it right side up and carrying out field repairs as necessary in order to ferry it back to Gimlet Mb. for re-build. The catch being the aircraft to be landed on the grass adjacent to the hanger. Never having experienced that before increased the pucker factor about ten fold while cautiously circling the field gauging the wind and the intended touch down area. Of course the word had gotten out about my intended landing attracting quite a large audience with there being no doubt that some among them feverently hoping to my screwing up grievously, wrecking the aircraft and possibly myself, now that sort of happening one wished to avoid if at all possible. Relying on past experience made a careful approach to touch down gently onto the grass, but even expecting and ready for it the sudden and severe deceleration still startled me although the aircraft indicated no tendency what so ever to nose over at any time, one simply jolted to a halt.

At finding our still sitting upright and in one piece just sat there attempting to appear nonchalant but if the truth be known the affected delay in climbing out of the aircraft was to give myself time to bring my violently knocking knees under control before exiting the aircraft. This was the first of many hairy landings that were to eventually became routine.

145

Another forthcoming aspect of my new found job involved taking off float equipped aircraft mounted on what was referred to a "Dolly", a sturdy four wheeled cart that sported large low pressure tires mounted on the rear of the cart and a set of full catering dual wheels on each side of the front. My very first experience on the dolly began with a float equipped Cessna 180 the hanger crew had placed on it. This being a totally new experience for me the butterflies that had formed in my stomach was having a field day with my having absolutely no idea of what to expect could only depend on my past skills. The 180 not having near enough power to propel the dolly to the required lift off speed of sixty five miles per hour it was towed down the runway using a pickup truck, once lined up and ready to go full power rammed on assisting the pick up to accelerate rapidly with my holding the control wheel full forward to pin the aircraft to the dolly, as the speed rapidly built up the aircraft began to buffet madly from the disturbed air flowing over the truck cab threatening to tear me off the dolly well before being ready to lift off, if that where to occur then one did not stand a chance in hell of survival. To put it mildly there was definitely a short space of time one could say the situation became rather dicey before the air speed indicated the desired numbers with my instantly releasing the pressure on the control wheel while yanking on full down flap simultaneously, at that the aircraft literally shot upwards and forward to instantly shoot past the speeding pickup, but as the aircraft transited the short space between the dolly and the truck a momentary violent buffeting startled the hell out of me, one had to admit that first dolly take off while being towed not something soon forgotten. If the truth be known as many times as I performed that hairy task, never did became accustomed to doing it, one simply had too much working against them for peace of mind.

The first time I had the opportunity to take off a Beech-18 floatplane on the dolly it proved to be a snap, once being towed out to the runway and having completed all the pre take off checks, the tow bar disconnected and the all clear signaled it remained a simple matter of applying full power, the Beech Craft being so powerful and nimble accelerated rapidly and before you knew it one was airborne, simply breath taking and of course I loved It.

Now the astute reader may wonder what become of the dolly as it continued to career down the runway at a high rate of speed totally uncontrolled once the aircraft had lifted clear?, well that was supposedly taken care of by a unique braking system that was actuated by a light but strong length of cord attached to a convenient spot on the tail or float of the aircraft with the other end attached to a spring loaded brake master cylinder lever on the dolly. Once the aircraft lifted off it instantly yanked the lever upwards activating the braking system which quickly brought the dolly to a wheel smoking halt, but if for some unexplained reason or another the system failed to function as it sometimes did, the dolly continued to hurtle madly on down the runway until it either ran out of inertia coming to a stop of it's own accord or as in most cases veering violently off to the side of the runway demolishing a few runway lights on it's way through, and in some instances began to weave wildly back and forth until flipping itself end over end before coming crashing to a halt, it must have been well constructed as never at any time knew of any lasting damage to occur, but it sure gave one a blood chilling sensation to observe what losing control at high speed promised, it simply didn't bear thinking about.

As mentioned previously, taking a Beech Craft off on the dolly a pleasure as one retained complete directional control at all times by using asymmetric thrust from the engines as required to assure the dolly's remaining on the center line, this ability absolutely critical while taking off with a cross wind to contend with, but taking off a single engine aircraft on the dolly called for a totally different technique.

On one occasion a De-Havilland beaver came up for delivery to Red Lake Ont, as was usual towed out to the runway and once lining me up and removing the tow bar (a very necessary procedure, as to not have done so could have easily ruined one's whole day, if not a hell of a lot more). Left to my fate, again this being a first for me hardly knew what to expect. Rapidly but smoothly applying full take off power the aircraft accelerating with the snap of a mile long freight train barely seeming to sidle down the runway in the most casual manner before lifting off so gently and easily as to be almost boring, but again that was what one could expect from a high performance aircraft.

With each new experience easing my initial trepidation the exhilarating dolly take off's and ferry flights to various destinations enjoyed immensely often taking advantage of my new found freedom to wander at will within reason of course all over hell's half acre, it sometimes to my everlasting pleasure take a few days before a return trip to Gimlet Mb. Became available.

In between times when there was no work ferrying aircraft, acted as a field man traveling to where ever an aircraft was down with maintenance problems the company supplying a small twin engine aircraft known as a Beech-B50 available for my use, up till then not ever having the opportunity to fly such a modern well equipped aircraft requiring my seeking the assistance of one of the more skilled pilots to familiarize me with the intricacies of the at first bewildering and complex array of modern state of the art radio, navigation equipment and a fully automated blind flight instrument panel. Many a happy hour spent playing with my newfound toy while enrooted from one place to another, inclement weather conditions rarely holding me back.

On the occasion a Cessna-206 utilized in lieu of my favorite steed having an over large cargo door made it possible to load a complete DC-3 wheel and brake assembly on board or whatever over large equipment required at the time, the 206 easy to fly but excruciatingly slow compared to the Beech, but regardless happy to be flying whatever available at the time.

On the occasion my flights would take me to Churchill Mb. And beyond and often as far and throughout the province of Quebec, one certainly got around on that job.

On one memorable occasion returned a Beech-18 on floats from Pickle Lake to Gimlet for an engine change and major float repair, the catch being it was to be landed on the grass adjacent to the hanger. Having landed a Beech on ice many a time before didn't feel it would be much different accepting a probable high rate of deceleration. The actual touch down surprised me no end, the aircraft assuming much the same nose low attitude as it did landing on ice easily sliding over the grass with no noticeable deceleration force, intrigued to hell and back decided to experiment with it's ability to make a turn one way or the other soon learning it could actually be done effortlessly without excessive use of power, in fact feeling totally confident in it's ability to take off on dry grass taxied effortlessly back to the far end of the grass strip to turn back into the wind and apply full power, surprisingly the aircraft accelerated far more rapidly then first thought possible being empty and light on gas quickly assuming the familiar nose low attitude it took on during a take off on ice, past experience had taught me it mattered not how hard one pulled back on the control column the nose could not be raised an inch, the trick was once reaching a speed of no less than seventy miles per hour one simply dropped flap to the full down position, the aircraft almost immediately lifting off almost straight up but still maintaining a nose low attitude, but as the forward speed increased and flaps retracted it soon leveled out climbing rapidly. In retrospect did not find the take off on a dry grass field noticeably different than taking off on ice except it taking a few seconds longer to accelerate to lift off speed. Once more circling the field in preparation for landing suddenly noticed a small red jeep sitting beside the runway, oh shit I thought to myself; It's Barney Lamb (the president and owner of the company). Mentally cursing my bravado that without question had irrevocably placed my ass in a sling, what the hell was he doing there any how?, according to my understanding he was to be out of town that day! Making a cautious text book approach and landing drove the aircraft right up to the grass verge with the left wing directly over the jeep, what the hell

I thought, in for a penny in for a pound. Climbing out of my seat consoled myself with the thought if he fires me on the spot at least I would go out with panache.

As it went my fears turned out to be groundless with his initially staring fixedly at me through his Ray Bans, a huge grin suddenly began to crease his features, turning to the parked aircraft shaking his head in wonder while drawling in his Yankee twang that seemed more pronounced than ever, ah's ever wondered if one of them thar machines could manage to do that, well dang it now ah can be most certain it can, hop in I'll give you all a lift to the hanger. As expected met at the front door by the entire hanger staff who no doubt had not missed a thing, staring coldly at me as if I were the village idiot while waiting in delicious anticipation for Barney's verdict regarding my latest prank.

Once having climbed out of the jeep, methodically surveyed the hushed and expectant crowd while rolling his omnipresent cigar from one side of his mouth to the other, always the politician remained a past master at capturing and holding the attention of an audience. As the pregnant silence wore on they began to squirm under his unnerving gaze giving me a great sense of satisfaction, then after what must have passed as an uncomfortable age he turned to me with another huge grin creasing his face to clap me on the back loudly proclaiming at least we have one man here that knows how to keep life interesting, with that said sauntered grandly off to his office trailing a cloud of foul cigar smoke

One can only imagine their collective dismay at my unexpectedly escaping instant dismissal.

A De-Havilland DH-3 single otter had just emerged from a major re-build which as a matter of course entailed a complex series of taxi and eventually flight-testing trials. Once assured all to be as it should a full take off and extended flight to ascertain stability and control response adjusting flight controls as required. Upon completion of the flight trials the next step consisted of installing and rigging a newly rebuilt set of floats in readiness to be placed into service. But of course it first had to be flown off using the dolly. The otter is not and never would be an aircraft I cared to fly in any configuration as it retained strange flight characteristics that did not appeal to me, so avoided them as much as possible.

No one I ever knew or heard of had ever taken an otter off on a dolly, thus suffering a dearth of available information on how it best done leaving it solely up to me. Failing at first to take into consideration the otter retained a very strange take off attitude that could prove to be critical contingent to lifting off the dolly during take off. As it went my coming within a hair of rolling up a newly rebuilt aircraft and myself up into a ball of bent and twisted aluminum and mangled flesh because of my lack of knowledge concerning it's flight characteristics.

The hanger crew that had placed the otter on to the dolly in preparation for take not being any wiser than me concerning it's flight characteristics erroneously posisitioning it on the dolly in much the same attitude as a Norseman, slightly nose high and not as it should have been in a nose low tail high attitude as required. Not having a lot of experience flying an otter the glaring error going unnoticed by me and many others.

During the interim it took to tow the aircraft out to the runway an unsettled feeling that all not to be as it should nagged worrisomely at me in spite of my careful attention to detail in making absolutely certain all that needed to be done prior to take off had been done, still something didn't seem just right keeping me on edge, I was to find out soon enough almost to my everlasting sorrow.

Once having received the all clear signal with not yet understood misgivings advanced the throttle lever to full take off power setting, the initial acceleration could only be termed glacial at best our slowly rumbling down the runway with my expecting the otter to lift off easily between sixty five to seventy miles per hour instantly realizing something amiss as the airspeed indicator needle shot rapidly past eighty miles per hour and climbing without any indication of the aircraft taking flight, one didn't require being a rocket scientist to realize that something to be going very wrong, but had no idea what the trouble could be, when the tail began to lift off of it's own volition tilting the nose down further while threatening to fish tail the aircraft off the dolly, my efforts in hauling full back on the control column came to naught, the otter continuing to cling stubbornly to the dolly as if afraid to let go and launch itself into the air, even when the airspeed needle crawled past the ninety mile per hour mark. Not having the option of chopping the power and aborting the take off due to the fact we where only seconds away from crashing into the barrier of used automotive tires that blocked the runway, to have done so could only end with the aircraft being suddenly catapulted off the dolly to predictably cartwheel into a pile of flaming junk wiping precious me out in the process. These terrifying thoughts ran feverishly through my near panicked mind as we irrevocably raced ever closer to sure destruction.

One can never be certain why one does what they do while laboring under stress, to this very day I will never know just what prompted me to suddenly grab the flap pump handle to desperately pump the hydraulic flaps to the full down position just managing to do so with the otter popping off the dolly a second or two before the dolly impacted with the barrier barely maintaining flight while remaining in an unimaginable nose low position with the floats barely clearing the top of the barrier continuing to stagger along in that frightening half controlled state of flight until suddenly remembering to relax the back pressure on the control column whereupon the otter responded instantly climbing out steeply in a nose low position as it was designed to do gaining precious height to continue on our shaky way to Kenora Ont.

It took a fair amount of time for my knees to quit knocking and the sweat to dry while my heart rate and labored breathing gradually dropped to normal, to be truthful I hesitated to check my shorts afraid of what I might find.

Once reaching a safe cruising altitude and flying sedately along began a mental post mortem on just what the hell had gone so wrong on that near disastrous take off, mentally ticking off each step of the way leaving out nothing it suddenly hit me like a bolt of lightning, Christ how stupid and bone headed can one be and still survive?, mentally berating my failing to take note of the improper mounting of the otter onto the dolly, strangely it wasn't only me that overlooked that gross error that came so near to creating a spectacular disaster, the chief engineer and more then a few of the crew leaders had also done so. One could only put it down to a fixation of placing all the other aircraft on the dolly in the normal position, but the otter can hardly be termed a normal aircraft as it did everything according to my lights ass backwards. Still it boiled down to the inescapable fact that in the end it remained the ultimate responsibility of the pilot in command in making certain of it's correct placement on the dolly, I had screwed up big time at almost the cost of my life.

It appeared my troubles not quite over yet, as after cruising along normally for some time it suddenly became apparent the aircraft to be slowing noticeably while gradually losing height, now what?, a rapid perusal of the engine gauges almost sent me in to shock, the manifold pressure having rose far above it's normal cruise setting while the propeller RPM had for some unknown reason dropped back from it's normal nineteen hundred revolutions per minute to slightly less than fourteen hundred, a drop of more than five hundred RPM , little wonder the aircraft had begun to stagger along through the air, fortunately being empty loss of height could be kept to a minimum even if barely so.

The otter being so unbearably noisy with the augmenter tubes situated directly behind one forced the warring of a set of noise cancelling head phones, that was probably the reason for my failing to detect the increasingly labored engine beat, setting the propeller pitch control into the full fine position evoked no response what so ever, for some reason lost to me the propeller blades had experienced internal mechanical failure resulting in being frozen in the high pitch position. With the aircraft barely making decent headway the cylinder head and oil temperatures edged ever closer to the never exceed red lines leaving me with the all too real possibility of blowing a cylinder on the newly overhauled engine, the very thought did little to relieve my already highly stressed state of mind though at no time did I find myself in danger if things went to hell there being many suitable lakes along the way to conduct an emergency landing on if found necessary to do so.

Slugging slowly along the overwhelming desire to rid myself of that recalcitrant bitch of an otter as quickly as possible over rode common sense with my pushing on, again it was the cautious deployment of the flaps that saved the day with my playing with various settings eventually discovering the aircraft would maintain height if barely so while holding less than desired air speed staggered grimly on until eventually making a safe landing at Kenora. While taxiing to the dock the interim between landing and taxiing in giving rise to the disturbing thought of what would have most likely occurred if the propeller had acted up during the critical phase of the dolly take off, there remains little doubt this story would have ever been written.

Having reported the propeller malfunction to the base engineer it was learned some time later the propeller had been subsequently removed and returned to the overhaul facility for repair, the ensuing inspection and repair report sent shivers down my spine upon reading of the internal pitch actuating mechanism located within the hub having been improperly assembled to somehow pass what is normally a very rigorous function testing procedure thus placing me in a possible world of hurt or worse, it being nothing less than a miracle my not experiencing catastrophic propeller failure during the near botched take off.

As it went continuing to do my job as required, but the god's weren't finished playing cat and mouse with me yet as further as further involvements with close calls still loomed on the horizon.

My next interesting adventure posed no real problems, just a small but still alarming matter of incompetence and finger trouble. Normally taking a beech craft off on the dolly considered a pleasure, but the one I took off the dolly that day certainly gave me pause for thought. Once receiving the all clear signal advanced the throttles to maximum take off power, or at least that was the intention as for some reason unknown to me at the time the manifold pressure gauges failed to indicate their normal readings even with the throttles fire walled, being far too late to consider aborting the take off and considering the fact engines both ran smoothly continued on though the aircraft appeared to lack it's usual nimble characteristics though still getting off in good time.

Climbing up to altitude it was noticed the manifold pressure dropped far quicker than normal as we gained height running out of steam at four thousand feet, hmmm that's odd, actuating the carburetor heat levers produced no visible changes in the manifold readings, the entire situation fast becoming stranger by the minute though the engines continued to run smoothly prompting me to continue on to Red Lake Ont. The trip in its entirety proved to be uneventful experiencing no further surprises.

Upon arrival at Red Lake immediately recruited the base engineer David Fiorito, a no nonsense highly skilled mechanic who brooked no guff from god or man while maintaining an ongoing sneering disdain for the brass and the incompetence that seemed to emanate from the Gimlet hanger crew on a regular basis.

Once removing the cowlings from one of the engines he snorted in disgust at what he found, to my surprise he pointed out the ram air scoop to be missing, not only that, he soon found the carburetor hold down bolts to be installed only finger tight, all that kept the engines running was the immense suction of intake air, also it was soon found the throttle actuating rods where not safetied and could have easily vibrated off at any time, only the advent of my holding the throttle levers hard against the stops had kept them in place, these ongoing close calls due to carelessness and ongoing

Incompetence that appeared to be gaining momentum directly concerning my state of health had reached a point of being a bit too much to take, how many times could one avoid potential disaster while facing such adversity, it seemed that knowingly or otherwise there was too many troublesome variables working against me, this alarming and potentially deadly situation definitely called for greater caution on my part in future dealings.

Well it certainly got the maintenance supervisor's attention when Dave laid a horrendous blast of shit on his door step making no bones about the incompetency of his and the hanger crews he supervised, of a certainty Dave's outburst definitely put a few noses out of joint, but the risking of injured pride came second to mine and many others continuing safety.

Needless to say my eventual return to Gimlet met with open hostility and if the truth where known could have cared less, my being there to do a job not to build up a mutual admiration society or to involve myself in kiss ass hanger politics.

Then came the ultimate challenge, the company had recently completed the rebuild of an Mk. V Norseman, nothing unusual about that except it had been totally metalized except for the tail empennage which for some unexplained reason lost to me remained fabric covered. The aircraft had recently been placed on a set of shiny newly overhauled floats sitting there in pristine splendor awaiting its first flight. The required test flying would all be carried out on floats but first it required launching off the dolly.

153

The day finally rolled around when all stood ready to go with the aircraft placed on the dolly in preparation for take off. Yes I must truthfully admit to a growing concern at the thought of performing the initial flight test of an aircraft fresh out of rebuild and to make it considerably more interesting off a dolly yet.

Waiting for an early calm morning to make the initial take off before towing the aircraft out to the runway made certain it to be placed well to the right side of the runway, a very necessary precaution when taking a Norseman off on a dolly as the tremendous torque produced by the propeller initially overcame rudder control that only became effective above fifty miles per hour initially torquing the aircraft to the left. The all metal wings did not accommodate the usual wing tanks, instead having three separate fuselage belly tanks that incorporated an engine driven fuel pump with an emergency electric fuel pump for back up to supply fuel to the carburetor.

The take off regardless of my tense state of mind went smoothly as could be expected but for some reason unknown to me at the time the aircraft's initial acceleration felt unusually sluggish though the engine delivered full power according to the gauges, outside of the propeller rpm that indicated fifty rpm or better on the low side, that and my overly tense state of mind that perhaps made it appear that way as the other Norseman previously taken off on the dolly had appeared to feel much livelier.

Other than the low propeller reading the take off and further hour-long flight went well. Once on the water the propeller governor adjusted, still the aircraft continued to act "doggy" until well into the fifth hour of test flying over Lake Winnipeg the propeller suddenly freezing into the same high pitch setting as had previously occurred on the otter, mmmmm "déjà Vue "all over again, this time it hardly fazed me at all but keeping in mind the wording of the report concerning the last propeller malfunction wasted little time in getting back down to safety. Only after having landed did it hit me, all of a sudden a burgeoning fear of the unknown inundated my senses, coursing through my thoughts like river of fire, that was twice I had narrowly averted disaster brought on by faulty equipment. It had always been my firm belief everything came in three's be it good or bad luck, but be as it may what happens for a reason, for without question the inevitable equation of the odds conspired against one, the more hours one flew the more risks one took, in the long run it all bunched together makes it almost a certainty that one will eventually meet with disaster. Yes the close calls jolted me some what, but that would pass in time, where else could one have such endless adventure and blood chilling excitement on a regular ongoing basis and get paid for it yet.

In due course a replacement propeller installed on the aircraft, oh man what a world of difference it made with the aircraft thundering off the water in less than half the distance it had taken previously becoming an absolute joy to fly. Then came the real fun part, the necessary wing adjustments could only be done in the hanger requiring the aircraft to be landed on the grass strip adjacent to it.

This was to be a new one for me never before having landed such a large heavy single engine aircraft on the grass as usual did not rightly know what to expect with huge black butter flies forming in my belly to have a field day at the thought soon feeling as if they had taken on the size of bats. Perversely intimidated or not welcomed the challenge, choosing to do so during the early morning hours when the grass still lay wet with dew. My initial attempt at landing a Norseman on the grass went exceedingly well regardless of all the horror stories presently circulating of Norsemen flipping over onto their backs when attempting to land on dry grass riding heavily on my shoulders leaving me wondering if the aim was to shake up my confidence.

Having no idea how best to carry it out reverted to my years of hard gained experience Initially overflying the field to get a better sense of it noticed a large crowd of early morning "gawkers" who having got the word had gathered to watch "Weston's Flying Circus" in action, goddammit I swore to myself just what I didn't need, my nerves where twangy enough without the added pressure of performing in front of a crowd.

Well what the hell, in for a penny in for a pound, setting up a precise power assisted approach initially dragged the float skegs on to the grass surface as gently as possible, but as the aircraft settled it's float keels fully onto the grass the sudden and severe rate of deceleration almost catching me by surprise with my coming within an ace of ramming on full power to go around again for another try before only just catching myself adding on sufficient increments of power to prevent a too sudden deceleration that was sure to pitch the aircraft over on it's back before it's gradually sliding to a shuddering halt with the engine roaring at almost full power. One could not help but to make a comparison between Norseman and the beech craft in regard to ease of landing on the grass, the Norseman if nothing else certainly kept one on their toes.

When first attempting to pry myself out of the seat soon found myself forced to sit down again as my shaky legs refused to support my weight forcing me to hesitate until re-gaining control of them, after all it wouldn't do to have any one notice "Super Pilot himself tottering about on shaky legs, bad for the image eh what. Instead pretended to sit there for a brief period of time while ostensibly viewing a flight test form until certain of my legs, my shorts would be inspected a little later in privacy.

That being the first of many successful landings onto the grass field with various Norsemen, each succeeding one becoming a little easier, but never at any time allowing my becoming over confident while doing so.

Of the many Norsemen flown, CF-OBE without question one of the finest best performing ever flown, to this day it still has a place in my heart.

Time as it always has moved on with my enjoying a constant change of life style people and places I had never had the opportunity to visit before, in between times carrying on my usual routine of keeping myself perpetually frightened out of my wits, one of the more memorable incidents being taking a Beech craft off on the dolly, nothing new about that for if anything it had become rather routine but a shorts staining experience soon changed arrogance to fear.

The take off as usual started out auspiciously enough with the aircraft smoothly and rapidly accelerating down the runway with the airspeed indicator nearing the established lift off speed when suddenly and unexpectedly finding myself violently catapulted off the dolly, from there on the following sequence of events occurred far too rapidly for the human mind to assimilate, the next thing I knew the runway was staring me straight in the eye, at a time like that one doesn't have the luxury of protracted analysis concerning the why's and where for's of an immediate problem, one simply reacts with my instantly yanking frantically back on the control column while ramming the throttles to the stops with the aircraft barely leveling out a split second or so before the float keels impacted the runway with a horrific bang causing the aircraft to immediately ricochet back into the air vibrating violently like a tuning fork while barely maintaining level flight as the tail assembly hammered violently in the throes of an incipient stall. How losing control was avoided and predictably contacting the ground and rolling up in a ball of tangled wreckage goes beyond human comprehension as the aircraft staggered along barely maintaining flight for what seemed an eternity with my white knuckling it until finally reaching a safe flying speed before cautiously beginning a slow climb out.

Soaked with sweat and still uncertain what had gone so terribly wrong took the time to settle my ragged nerves and allow my pulse rate to settle down to a mild scream. Once feeling to have a handle on my emotions fumbled the microphone close to my lips to squeak out an inquiry to the ground crew as to what in the hell had happened. It took a few minutes before the maintenance supervisor answered to hesitantly inform me of the shocking fact they had just found the brake actuating handle that for what ever reason had come loose from the master cylinder assembly prematurely activating the braking system to instantly eject the aircraft clear of the dolly. Christ I shakily thought to myself how fortunate can one

156

be?, if that had occurred at a slightly lower speed than I had fortunately attained at the time, there left little doubt as to the eventual outcome.

Much later I was to learn the ground crew who enjoyed witnessing a dolly take off at first thought my having screwed up royally by attempting to lift off before reaching sufficient air speed, only after a closer inspection of the dolly braking assembly was it noticed the actuating handle to be missing, only after driving a fair ways further down the runway was it found where it had twisted loose from the aircraft, only then was it fully realized what had occurred.

Remaining unaware of how much damage the aircraft had sustained upon impacting the runway I found myself uncertain as to what to do next. Circling the field requested the ground crew to stand by while making as low and slow as I dared fly by in order to give them a chance to evaluate the damage as best they could, the news when it came not good as it appeared both step compartments to be crushed and mangled, oh man them floats where just fresh out of a complete re-build, not only that, both rear float struts visibly bent out of shape, and there existed a good chance of other collateral damage not readily visible.

That bit of disturbing information made it an absolute certainty of my not daring to attempt a landing on the water to chance the risk of digging in and flipping over, the very thought of that occurrence left me in a cold sweat definitely cancelling out any thoughts of a water landing leaving me with little choice but to risk a landing on the grass and hope for the best and expect the worst.

With my stomach tied in knots radioed the crew of my intentions and to have the mobile fire extinguisher unit standing by just in case, cautiously white knuckled the aircraft down to a landing as slowly as possible literally dragging it on, the initial touch down and subsequent deceleration as we ground to a shuddering halt had gone far more smoothly than first anticipated even though the damaged floats tore up great strips of turf during their brief passage and somehow the rear struts held up throughout it all, at no time did I feel the aircraft indicated any tendency what so ever to nose over, the violent nerve rattling deceleration only made it feel that way.

Once the dust had settled and my being certain my shaky legs would support me climbed out of the hatch to survey the ragged gouges created by the passage of the damaged floats marveling at their depth and length. Yes once more fate had allowed my escaping unscathed, but if any one had taken the time and trouble to inquire if I had at any time felt fear concerning that dicey situation, they would have been succinctly informed of my not at any time being scared, just plain and simply terrified.

The follow up investigation concerning the failure of the brake-actuating handle proved to be inconclusive. Poor workmanship and lack of proper maintenance one thing that could be tolerated to a degree, but the other could not in any sense be atoned with my from that time on making it a point to thoroughly inspect the dolly from one end to the other thoroughly satisfying myself it to be serviceable before each take off.

As if the God's of fate hadn't finished toying with me yet, about a month later a Beech Craft on wheels required ferrying to another base, well nothing could be easier than that, or so my thinking at the time. All going well after take off until setting the gear retraction lever in the wheels up position with the gear having transited about half way through it's retraction cycle when all of a sudden all hell broke loose with a terrific din emanating from the right hand side startling me half out of my wits with my still remaining some jumpy about the last close call, only by placing the gear selector in the neutral position after reselecting gear down did the nerve wracking grinding cease with the unsafe light for the right hand gear blinking ominously while the left hand light glowed green indicating down and locked.

Concerned about creating more problems left well enough alone radioing in to inform dispatch of my current problem. A low fly by indicated the right hand landing gear flopping uselessly back and forth in the propeller slipstream. With no way out of it elected to land on the grass strip, but first feathering the right hand propeller to avoid damaging it on touch down if at all possible.

The single wheel landing went smoothly enough and as the airspeed bled off it gradually allowed the right hand wing to gently contact the grassy surface the ensuing friction causing the aircraft to turn slightly to the right before gently sliding to a halt, the only visible damage being a bit of paint wore off the bottom side of the wing tip.

Future investigation revealed the right hand torque tube had failed due to lack of lubrication, the damage being slight the aircraft soon placed back into service non the worse for wear, there it was again, careless or none existent workmanship had caused the problem in the first place as was eventually revealed to be the cause of another torque tube failure on another wheel equipped Beech Craft prior to my incident, again pause for thought. And so it went.

In the real world of bush flying we often as a matter of course faced a variety of hazards, some known and dealt with accordingly, others that were often totally unexpected occurring by random chance.

One especially trying incident that would be a long time remembered took place one early morning as six dejected looking hard bitten diamond drillers who where reluctantly returning to the job after a week off from their month to month seven day a week incessant labors obviously to a man suffering the debilitating pangs of a monstrous hang over that had a good many of them nursing an almost unbearable physical agony.

They're on the most part appeared to be bleary eyed and subdued giving off an air of resignation as if all the fight had been taken out of them posing little risk, that is excepting the corpulent mean looking bastard of a foreman who for some odd reason lugged a small tool box with him that must have went fifty pounds or better wearing a grease stained well ripped up pair of coveralls that had known better days, his outward demeanor unmistakably projecting the air of being an arrogant hard drinking bully and a brawler to boot.

Before taking his place in the aircraft he sneered evilly at me while uttering the less than complimentary slur of "fucking panty waist pilots", a chilling remark that caused the hair on the back of my head to rise in alarm for if trouble personified looking for a place to happen ever existed it was him. One could tell by his confrontational attitude toward any or all who dared to oppose or challenge him or them of his like who gladly welcomed a brawl as what was left of his broken teeth attested to, that along with filthy sausage shaped fingers that sported split nicotine stained nails that protruded like jagged claws, his malovent demeanor causing a wave of uncertainty to wash over me as he sized me up with his piggy watery blue eyes I knew there and then he was not the type of dude one would care to confront on a dark moonless night intentionally or otherwise. For some reason totally lost to me and only known to him obviously had taken an instant if unreasoning dislike to me even though we had never met until that morning.

Foolishly consoling myself they would as usual pass out as they communally did upon reaching higher altitudes as the rarefied air tends to affect those with residual alcohol remaining in their systems placing them in a state of torpor or sleeping heavily, but be as it may not a rock solid guarantee that would always be the case with one remaining cautious and on guard at all times when transporting any one who was just coming off a knock em down drag em out snot dripping bender or having shown signs of recently coming off a week long drunk with our absolutely refusing to even consider allowing any who appeared to be remaining in the throes of intoxication to board the aircraft.

As the first five well-subdued appearing drillers took their seats I took the precaution of placing an innocuous bedraggled appearing one in the front right seat who instantly passed out once settled in.

The foreman being the last to get in left me some troubled on my noting his sneering attitude plainly indicating one of being loaded for bear and just spoiling to create problems. If I had had the least inkling of the life threatening hell that lay before me the flight would have never taken place with him on board as it is not my bag to knowingly place myself at risk if at all possible, our getting enough of that without deliberately seeking it out!.

As much as that piggy eyed oversized chunk of mean minded protoplasm disturbed me it still gave me insufficient grounds to refuse the flight as up to then he had made no overt threats or created any outward disturbance outside of uttering an uncalled for nasty remark to-ward my person, hardly sufficient grounds on which to base a bad vibe on and in light of that fact made a bad call by ignoring my instincts, and in doing so placing my precious body in harm's way. Hindsight as always would prove me right, but that was cold comfort when struggling mightily to survive and only managing to do so by the skin of my teeth in a virtual life and death aerial ballet scenario.

Once taking off pushed the engines hard in order to climb to a higher altitude as quickly as possible in hopes the rarefied atmosphere would do it's job of causing potential troublemakers to pass out and remain in a deep sleep until arriving at our destination. As we passed through eight thousand feet with no problem throttled the straining engines back to cruise mode with my just beginning to settle down for the long flight ahead of us almost jumping out of my skin when something that sounded heavy bounced off the bulkhead behind my seat with a loud metallic clang that was clearly audible to me even over the roar of the engines and wearing ear phones, startled out of my wits by the unexpected suddenness of it all took a quick glance into the cabin area to if at all possible to discover the source, my curiosity almost resulting in my near being brained by a second unidentified object that only just missed, whatever it was caroming off the edge of the bulkhead frame behind the co-pilot's seat. In my initial confusion at first failed to comprehend what was taking place until spotting two very large pipe wrenches lying on the floor where they had fallen after bouncing off the bulkhead, as it was barely managing to get my head back around the corner before a third and better aimed projectile smashed into the lower half of the control pedestal, the gut wrenching realization the projectiles had been deliberately aimed with the murderous intent of inflicting severe injury or totally incapacitating me, that mind numbing revelation temporarily immobilizing any further action on my part until the advent of another heavy object clanging off the bulkhead finally spurring me into re-acting though being so badly frightened my breath came in painful gasps as the mind bending realization that sick minded son of a bitch had every intention of doing me in. As the situation stood mine and many others lives hung in balance, our ultimate fate lay in the hands of a demented drunkard totally out of control and no longer retaining any sense of reality of the inescapable fact his fate sealed as surely as ours if he succeeded in braining or incapacitating me.

The confined space I sat in offered very few options but fortunately for all of us the passenger in the right hand seat remained comatose through it all drooping in his seat like a rag doll in deep slumber and for our sake and his it was feverently hoped he would remain that way as it could have gone badly if he was to suddenly awaken and panic at learning of the desperate straits we unwillingly found ourselves in.

A cautious glance around the bulkhead near caused me to experience a coronary upon viewing the nut case to be unsteadily weaving his way up the short aisle brandishing another large wrench in his grimy paw while portraying a determined leer on his porcine features obviously bent on putting the coup de grace on me once and for all, he must have completely slipped over the edge in not seeming to realize or care he would also forfeit his life if successful in dispatching me!.

Having no recourse it left me with no other alternative but to resort to desperate measures. (Déjà vue all over again) having been this way before knew with cold certainty what had to be done even though the threat factor that existed in doing so extremely high, but had to be chanced if we where to have any hope of survival. With a fiercely pounding heart and my breathing becoming increasingly ragged with all consuming fear dared a quick look back in order to better judge his present position to just about shit in seeing his having advanced much closer then first thought with my alarm factor jumping up a couple more notches upon noticing his having risen off his knees brandishing a huge wrench with what could only be described as a look of pure malice etched on his twisted features as lunged wildly at me, this immediate threat to my person gave me the much needed impetus to make a desperate move abruptly slamming the control yoke full forward pitching the aircraft into a sudden dive that all but lifted me off my seat against the safety harness, his being free of any restraints instantly flew off his feet to crash heavily into the cabin roof with a force that would have snapped the neck of an ordinary individual or at least have fractured their skull, my immediately reversing control with the same intensity hauling back viciously on the controls to reverse our sudden descent causing him to smash back onto the floor with a resounding crash that must have sent vibrations throughout the entire airframe.

This violent maneuver is not recommended at any time especially when heavily loaded except as in my case one is facing the direst of emergencies as it places severe and sudden negative and positive "G" force loading on the wings and tail emphanage that could possibly result in structural failure, some thing best avoided in the continuing interest of one's health if at all possible, but what choice was left to me?, as either way it was do what one could to prevent sure disaster or face the certainty of his imminently doing me in My not being in the least desirous to have that happen decided on taking my chances yanking back on the throttles to initiate a rapid descent that would hopefully take us to the dubious safety of the ground while he still lay stunned holding a near wing bending steep turn that I feverently hoped would help in keeping him pinned to the floor while spiraling downward as rapidly as I dared while futilely screaming at some of the other drillers who had been rudely jolted out of a sound sleep to jump on him and restrain him from coming at me again, but for what ever reason be it fear of him or if their still foggy brains left them unaware of what had recently transpired between us, they just stupidly sat their staring in stunned disbelief at the refugee from the stone age who lay in an untidy heap covered with blood from a severe cut to his head with not a one of them making the slightest attempt to assist me, he sure must have had them well cowed and absolutely no help to me, for better or worse I was on my own and I feared the worst greatly.

Taking advantage of the temporary lull frantically called the base over the radio outlining my dilemma as quickly and best I could in a panting hesitating voice considering it would have been a bad move to take my eyes off him for more than a few seconds at a time and that I was presently attempting to return to base if at all possible and to summon the local police officers to meet us if by chance I managed to get down safely, all this uttered in a sequence of jerky breathless sentences that should have alerted any one with half a brain to my obviously laboring under great stress. The current idiot of a dispatcher being rather new at the game when finally replying with the brain dead inquiry, are you certain of your emergency?

God dam him to hell and back for displaying such blatant stupidity literally screeched at him to do as asked.

I simply couldn't believe it when his hesitating for a short time before inquiring in a neutral tone of disbelief "what ever for".

Being far too fearful of taking my eyes off that maddened gorilla for more than a few seconds at a time continued to maintain a close watch on him and it turned out well I had as he to my great disbelief and horror somehow despite his obviously suffering a horrendous concussion had against all odds had managed to struggle back on to his knees shaking his bullet shaped head spattering blood every where including onto the terrified men who impotently attempted to shrink away from him while cringing in naked fear he might turn on one of them, my blood instantly turning to ice water as he shakily staggered to his feet with blood running freely from his broken nose and the deep gash in his scalp casting me a look of pure salience that shook me to the very core of my soul at it's naked intensity. With grim determination he once more began an uncertain shuffle toward my sacred place bracing himself as best he could against what he even in his demented state of mind was certain to come, oh shit I thought to myself here we go again but knew with a cold certainty my next move would have to be very finely judged in order to derive the maximum effect from it, at this juncture I didn't know which I feared more, structural failure or his murderous intentions, (Actually I feared both equally as it was academic, either way we where all dead.)

I didn't know or much less care what the other passengers thoughts where concerning the severe and unusual manipulations of the aircraft they had recently experienced, but for what it was worth they where about to be treated to a whole lot more before it ended one way or the other.

Christ I could hardly believe the terrible concussion the gorilla had sustained along with obvious facial injuries hadn't totally incapacitated him; he must be one hell of a tough cookie to have survived such terrible abuse without something being permanently damaged, as the severe abuse he had recently received would have easily killed a lesser mortal.

My arms and legs had begun to ache terribly from the unrelenting strain imposed upon them plus my lap and shoulders burned from the excessive pressure of the restraining harness while my breath continued to whistle hollowly through clenched teeth as my tortured lungs strained for air, it having now become a certainty of my being unable to continue to bear the physical and mental strain required to exercise the violent exertions for too much longer, some thing had to give and god dam soon one way or the other.

Having gradually descended to approximately two thousand feet above ground very little error if any in judgment could be tolerated, as it could all too easily prove disastrous if misjudging a critically violent maneuver. Sure enough another frightened glance revealed his having some what gotten his head straightened out and now sure of victory this time around making a desperate lunge for the cockpit in a final effort to finish me off, regardless of the fact of my being almost paralyzed with fear still prepared for him to make his final move once again catching him totally off balance upon once again performing the violent air frame straining maneuvers that so far had saved our bacon, I never was absolutely certain as to just how close we came to plowing into the trees before managing to level out in just the nick of time as nothing but green tree tops filled the forward view of the windshield for what seemed an eternity, but in all probability only a few very long seconds before disappearing beneath us, we had now blown our last wad and if the hairless ape had somehow survived that second vicious pounding well then we where in deep fried shit as there was no where else to turn to. A quick fear filled glance revealed his lying in a motionless heap on the floor that now closely resembled a slaughterhouse, secretly I hoped he had broken his neck.

How in the hell the wings and tail managed to survive the terrible stress imposed on them and still remained glued to the aircraft well beyond my powers of imagination but grateful beyond mere words to be able to give feverent thanks to Walter Beech and his workers that had built such a marvelously resilient aircraft!. But we weren't out of the woods yet as the hairless ape had unbelievably once more begun to twitch as he slowly came around giving me the bad news we had only a very limited window to get down as he appeared to be rapidly recovering much to my dismay. It came down to my either making a controlled landing within the next few minutes or so or not at all, my doubting very much the aircraft or I where capable of taking much more of the metal twisting mind shattering stresses imposed on us for far too long. With this raw truth searing my very mind threw caution to the winds performing the most blood curdling approach and landing of my entire career driving the aircraft recklessly down onto the water in a manner that would have made a fighter pilot green with envy, something I would have never dared to think about, never mind to attempt under normal circumstances, but these where far from normal circumstances and one does what one must do without the benefit of protracted thought in order to save one's self.

Without giving it any consideration what so ever to proper docking procedures literally drove the aircraft up on to the sand beach that fronted the base, the aircraft barely slowing to the point of falling off the step before ramming the floats up high and dry decelerating from the sudden drag of the sand on the float bottoms so violently it pitched everyone forward, the painful cutting in of the restraining harness totally ignored while yanking back the mixture controls and opening the escape hatch all in one smooth motion with my exiting the cockpit almost before the aircraft rocked back on it's heels with an alacrity that would have had to be seen to be believed, fuelled by the overriding fear that he might have recovered sufficiently to grab my legs as I frantically attempted to scramble clear not hesitating for a second in jumping off the wing into the shallow water to make my way to the safety of the shore only then feeling I had managed by the skin on my teeth to have escaped certain death at the hands of the booze crazed hairless ape.

Wading to the dock to meet a collection of totally confused dock hands who having absolutely no idea of the life and death struggle that had recently transpired stared uncomprehendingly at me as if not certain I hadn't lost my mind and best avoided from watching my unexplained aerial antics to desperately running the aircraft up on to the beach wasting little time evacuating the cockpit and jumping frantically off the wing into the water as if all the devil's from hell where hot on my heels, (that wasn't too far off the truth)Upon reaching the dock inquired in a hoarse quavering voice if the cops had arrived yet only to be met with a negative response from the bug eyed dock hands. Some of the pilots who happened to be there at the time and having witnessed my last near suicidal maneuver at first certain to my having gone in when momentarily disappearing behind a hill before soaring once more into view in an unusually nose high attitude before wheeling madly into a landing approach and touch down that had left them collectively holding their breath not sure of what I had in mind until sailing on to the beach at a fairly high rate of speed that all but flipped the aircraft onto it's back with my suddenly popping out of the hatch like some one had goosed me with a cattle prod to come flying off the wing not hesitating to put as much space between me and the aircraft in the shortest time possible.

Fortunately as it turned out one of the more astute pilots recognizing the desperation in my voice took it upon himself to over ride the dispatcher's objections to call the police. Why they where so slow in responding they never said but the screams and frightened wails of men being savaged by the maddened gorilla who having lost his primary victim turned his frustrations on them, the ensuing results of his carnage to be clearly heard over the intervening distance.

The dock hands at my insistence having armed themselves with what ever they could lay their hands on guarded the main cabin door to ensure he didn't escape and come after me once more until the cops deigned to show their presence.

But for the timely arrival of the two police men god only knows what degree of carnage would have prevailed as the hairless ape had gone clean over the edge cruelly whaling away at the confused still half dazed men strapped into their seats, their remaining in a totally confused state of mind being for the most part unaware of what had transpired between the hairless ape and I while helplessly enduring the most terrifying ride in their lives leaving them totally stunned and uncertain as to expect next. Those who still retained the sense to do so quickly unstrapped their safety belts to rapidly bail out the door not bothering with the steps but jumping directly into the shallow water in their panicked haste to escape the attention's of the maddened foreman, others who had been beaten insensible slumped in their seats covered in blood.

The two officers upon their eventual arrival to their credit wasted no time in wading out to the rear door of the grounded aircraft to confront that maddened beast, it must have been some titanic battle in such a confined space but determined to incapacitate him before he managed to kill some of the helpless men employing all the force deemed necessary to subdue his maddened depredations freely applying their police batons onto his thick skull with complete abandon until rendering him unconscious, once subdued hand cuffing him rendering him helpless to fight on. Imagine our surprise to suddenly and unexpectedly observe that hulk of a driller come flying out of the rear door to land head first into the shallow water creating a monstrous splash and then being left to either struggle to his feet on his own or drown, but to my everlasting dismay he somehow managed to roll over to end up sitting in the water, If I would have had my way he would have found my foot on his neck and held under until he ceased to struggle, but as much as I greatly desired to put a final end to him that was not to be allowed. Much later having inquired of the police officer in charge, a good friend of all the pilots about the Neanderthal's abrupt departure from the aircraft he only grinned saying he would have hazarded a guess he must have tripped over some thing on his way out. (Yeah his foot). Once having frog hopped the hairless ape up the slight hill, a procedure that had called for a fair amount of less than gentle prodding with their night sticks on their part convinced him it was in his best interest to do so, when it came down to forcing him to get into the cruiser get into the cruiser he once more balked, I can still hear the hollow sounds of the batons glancing off his rock hard skull and the sight of blood streaming down his face as they convinced him otherwise prevailing until his finally relenting in the end with their carting him off to a jail cell to cool off for a spell before being removed to another jurisdiction to face numerous charges of assault and battery, the worst injured of the drill crew where taken to the osanburgh nursing station for first aid, some requiring being flown out to Sioux Lookout for a lengthy hospital stay before eventually being able to return to work.

Well as for me, that most nerve wracking of close calls left me in a heightened state of mind and as yet to deal with the effects of the large doses of adrenalin still singing through my veins that ultimately created an adverse reaction to my nervous system to eventually cause my becoming nauseous to the degree of barfing my guts out, from then on my state of health and mind improved rapidly. Once the dust had settled to the degree of once more being able to concentrate on the mundane and the ordinary sensations of life suddenly noticed an acrid odor and an uncomfortably wet sensation emanating from my crotch telling me that somewhere along the way due to the high degree of stress labored under for too long having in all probability pissed my pants in fright more than once, but actually some surprised and grateful it hadn't gone any further than that, but feeling little or no embarrassment over that involuntary happening when taking into consideration the absolute undiluted patch of hell recently endured, it taking sometime for my mind to come to grips with the fact that only by a combination of luck, skill and a fine aircraft we managed to survive at all. Two hours later one of the police officers returned to the base to take down my statement and to find out if I wished to press charges of which I declined as much as I wished to, having found out the hard way many years before it best to remain clear of the machinations of the law if at all possible, besides that he no doubt faced multiple charges that would see him incarcerated for some time to come arising from those he had so viciously savaged for no good reason other than a sick desire to inflict injury on others. Those of the drill crew who were fortunate enough to have escaped serious injury at the hands of the crazed foreman on the other hand retained no such compunctions almost to a man desiring to press charges against his person being fed up for some time with his constant bullying and ongoing threats of personal injury while on the job, some of them where in such bad shape physically and mentally from the effects of the roller coaster ride they had been forced to endure while helplessly strapped into their seats not knowing at any time if they where about to die, on the average just sat quietly while drawing absent mindedly on a soggy cigarette or every so often as if compelled to do so by nervous reaction to shuffle aimlessly around the room most likely in a vain attempt to make sense of their near demise and miraculous survival, so shaken up by the soul searing experience it left them incapable of deciding what to do next.

Once having completed and signed the written report inquired of the police officer in a shaky tone of voice that still retained a noticeable quaver if it would be legally overlooked by the local constabulary if one were to methodically break the dispatcher's arms and legs one by one utilizing the slowest and painfully method one could possibly devise?, at hearing this he gave off a huge grin stating he didn't doubt for a minute it he had it coming but advised against such violent recourse as it constituted assault and battery (exactly what I had in mind) a serious charge best avoided, but "ahem" there is no laws that I'm aware of at this time that prohibits one from discreetly laying on a well deserved verbal assault especially if there is a dearth of witnesses, take my advice it would be in your best interest to assure it happens that way, have fun, with that he departed leaving me to pick up the pieces of my near shattered state of mind the best I could while nursing a smoldering rage that threatened to fan itself into a full blown anger at any given time. With my desiring to settle the issue once and for all finally stormed into the office to tear into the hapless dispatcher with all the pent up fury one could justifiably dredge up gradually working myself up into such a towering rage at his stupidity and seeming incompetence more than a few of the pilots who stood by during my tantrum at one point fearing I was about to lose control of my emotions and inflict severe and lasting bodily harm upon his person, eventually taking it upon themselves to step in between us just in time to prevent my doing just that when it appeared my seriously considering grabbing him by the throat and shaking him senseless, their timely intervention eventually allowed my gradually winding down to a mild scream, but not before assuring his having been reduced to cowering wreck from the incandescent fury of my verbal attack, fortunately for him he had not at any time during the course of my verbal attack dared to squeak out a single word in his defense being all too well aware of his having erred grievously in not recognizing the significance of my emergency and failing to do as requested at the height of the dilemma, a wise move on his part in sensing my highly disturbed state of mind appeared to be dangerously near to slipping over the edge.

It would appear my caustic outburst having gained an appreciative audience as at it's conclusion the office space found to be close to bursting with pilots and ground crew crowding in to hear the much despised dispatcher receiving his long overdue come uppance, the ill concealed grins plastered all over their homely mugs gave rise to the fact of their obviously enjoying his silent discomfiture and embarrassment at being roundly dressed down in front of them by a mere line pilot yet. Directing one last malovent stare at him that literally reeked of violent promise causing his cringing further back into his chair, concluded the affair leaving him to lick his wounds while we trooped out of the office to a man wearing shit eating grins with they're swearing on an oath to not having heard a harsh or threatening word exchanged between us at any time during the course of the civil conversation we had recently concluded. Feeling as if I had been run over by a Mack truck followed by a freight train took some good advice when walking over to the hotel for a desperately required cool beer to allay my burning thirst while we conducted a post mortem on the how's and why's of the series of events leading up to my near disaster and the grievous company policies that allowed it to come about in the first place, with our eventually concluding that changes of policy regarding our ongoing safety as well as that of other innocents when knowingly allowing inebriated or marginally inebriated passengers who potentially could create problems prior to or during flight to enter our aircraft, any decisions regarding the passengers suitability would remain the sole responsibility of the pilot in command who would decide on a one to one basis even if it meant refusing the flight on grounds of potential threat to one's personal safety.

In the end that most terrifying of experiences written off as just one other things, but I for one had learned a valuable lesson about heeding my instincts.

Strangely enough a very thorough inspection of the aircraft that had sustained such terrible stress factors during the course of my wild maneuvers to the surprise of all not found to have as much as popped a rivet, now that's one hell of a sturdy aircraft!

Wild Life

SOME OF MY FONDEST REMEMBERANCES were irrevocably branded into the memory banks of my mind while living and working as a bush pilot in the extremely remote out of the way tiny hamlet that once boasted two actively producing gold mines referred to by the locals as Central Patricia, aka Pickle Lake Ontario. It took no time at all for me and my family once having settled in to embrace it's anything goes free wheeling life style, my originally being born and raised in the free swinging mining town of Red Lake Ontario soon found myself fitting in immediately appreciating the fierce pride and independence of the diverse and outgoing population that on the whole presented as about a colorful lot one could wish to encounter. The town such as it was more or less boasted a permanent population of approximately two hundred souls, also seeming to as a matter of course having an equal amount of stray ratty looking mongrels that could be seen skulking everywhere one cared to look, but it was the huge retired "Clydesdale" known to all as "Moose", an ex logging horse that was owned by the Koval Bros. The towns local business people that left it to wander throughout the town as it pleased, at first viewing it's size and demeanor totally fascinated me as it made it's daily rounds summer or winter scrounging up offerings from the local hotel and to take advantage of every opportunity as it presented itself.

"Moose" as he was known by all and sundry retained little if any respect for the sancticity of garbage cans or their enclosures quickly stomping them into almost unrecognizable chunks of galvanized metal and shattered wood to pick out the choice delectable while scattering the remaining contents everywhere for the hordes of ravens that perched on his back hitching a free ride everywhere he went to pick over what ever little he didn't devour, and believe me that wasn't too much, Pickle Lake could definitely lay claim to having a local celebrity and a living breathing garbage re-cycling machine.

During the five enjoyable years spent there, a time that flew by all too quickly the towns transient population either swelled in size in direct proportion to the latest influx of mining interests or shrunk accordingly when interest faded until the town once more dozed in obscurity until the next wave of transients made their appearance.

The town being relatively small in size and population at best only able to offer a limited amount of after hours entertainment, the transient workers who sought any form of entertainment normally wore nothing fancier than scruffy jeans and faded shirts that without fail exuded the rank sweaty stink of long unwashed bodies that went far when crowded into a closed near airless space such as the local hotel beverage room toward creating an extremely exotic atmosphere, but that minor inconvenience really bothered no one to a great degree, they're delighting when ever the opportunity presented itself to create how ever they could their own bizarre mode of entertainment, nightly jamming the local bar to near bursting and for the most part competing passionately for the favors of a bevy of dusky maidens who in their own right consummate experts at extracting the most from the panting swains while giving out the least.

Fighting within the confines of the bar at any time for any reason not tolerated to any degree, to do so guaranteed instant and lasting barring from entering the hotel, a policy strictly upheld by the management, but on the occasion despite the best of intentions it did occur. The battles when they for what ever reason suddenly flared up normally taken outside of the hotel where an expectant crowd of onlookers would quickly gather to watch the promised entertainment and to goad the adversaries on with delighted shouts of "kill the bastard" or less complimentary jibes of encouragement. The local constabulary to their ever lasting credit chose to ignore such crass going on's as unworthy of their attention or as long as the combatants refrained from using any other weapons but their fists or feet, scratching, biting, gouging and tearing out each others hair allowed along with what ever variety of street fighting came to mind, what really made it interesting was when some of the local mongrels would get caught up in the excitement to join into the fray, always a highly amusing spectacle to observe as one or both of the combatants desperately attempted to shake or kick loose one or more of them from their ankles, and often while engaged in doing so futilely attempting to ward off their opponents who taking the opportunity to rain blows on them, of course this had the effect of setting off the onlookers to howling with delicious delight.

Eventually the combatants due to exhaustion or just plain running down would cease their impotent tussling with it's accompanying sound and fury that if the truth be known usually resulting in very little harm if any to either of the participants.

As entertaining as the nightly free for all's by the amorous swains could prove to be, they paled miserably in comparison when one of the local belle's perceived a competitor trespassing on what they jealously regarded as their turf, all hell guaranteed to break loose with one or the other casting disparaging remarks concerning their competitors womanhood or lack of it, the men having witnessed it all many times before knew with delicious certainty what was bound to come next slyly urging them on until one or the other lost it to fling herself in blind fury at her opponent who on the average not likely to back down resulting in the fur flying while tearing and clawing at each other, not unlike two feisty game cocks, my god how they fought with a no holds barred determination to maim and mangle each other that caused us lowly males to cringe in delightful horror as they clawed, bit, spit and scratched wildly attempting to inflict the greatest amount of damage to each other in the shortest possible time, occasionally managing to get a good hold of each others long tresses to yank out great hanks of hair while screeching like two banshees with their butts dipped in turpentine laboring mightily to tear the clothes off each other, often succeeding much to the collective delight of the male onlookers as flashing thighs and ample breasts became exposed to the glance of appreciative males bringing out an audible sigh of inhibited lust accompanied by an increasing rumble of heavy breathing in the event one or the other not having a pair of under pants on, that commonly being the case as in their profession the wearing of them tended to slow down natural proceedings as in their profession time equaled money.

Eventually the cat fight would lose momentum as they became exhausted or being pulled apart by the self appointed bouncers who had initially stood back to appreciate the show and who having correctly gauged the mood of the crowd knew it not in their best interest to interfere until appearing to have lost it's momentum.

Once separated they immediately rounded on each other screaming vehement curses in such colorful descriptive terms it often had the effect of causing the hardiest among us to blush unashamedly.

They're being some what ruffled in appearance after completing such strenuous activities, contritely wiped away the blood sweat and tears to separately retire to the lady's room to repair the damages to their make up and clothes, once satisfied with the results of their efforts once more go about their business as if nothing out of the ordinary had taken place. Often I wondered while watching them combing out their long glossy hair, or whatever was left of it, why we didn't have nearly bald local belle's going about their affairs.

Once the excitement of the moment had died down to a full throated roar the girls would soon make contact with a hot blooded paramour who previously having his desire stirred to a fever pitch by the sights and sounds of the battling belle's anatomy, money would discreetly change hands where upon they would casually saunter off into the night to complete their tryst, mosquito's be dammed, nothing got in the way of true love.

At one point during a pitched battle between two women, one of the French men I had befriended breathed hoarsely in my ear in an almost incomprehensible mixture of rural Quebec patois and fractured English, sacre bleu artley, dat's god dam women's fights like god dam alley cats, make like hell for my blood run hots like bastard, no. If anything finding the simple rustic charm and child like simplicity of the French workers I dealt with on an every day basis who on the average came from the remotest areas of Quebec much to my liking, they're innocent uneducated out look on life always remaining cheerful and upbeat, being well aware of the extremely harsh existence they had for generations eked out within the rural villages that were tightly controlled by the catholic church that kept them existing in a state of abject poverty all of their lives in northern Quebec until being hired on by a local diamond drilling company that treated their workers with respect, and they in turn being pathetically grateful to having a decent paying job displayed an unbending willingness to work harder than any one else I had ever seen, never has there been a more willing harder working crew of men. Having taken an interest in learning Quebec French, they're appreciating my efforts immediately adopted me as their intermediary as few spoke more than a few halting words of pidgin English, naturally my initial attempts to construct a formal sentence in their patois often met with bouts of undisguised hilarity when getting it all wrong, but all the same endlessly encouraging and assisting me over the rough spots until my eventually becoming fairly fluent. The ability to converse with them in their native tongue went far towards an improved working relationship with the foremen of the drill crews, for whenever requiring supplies or setting up a move one of the foremen would get on the radio to yell art, translates out as "Hartley" over and over again until I answered on either the base or the aircraft radio. On one occasion while this was taking place one of the pilots commented, Jesus Christ hart, it sounds like a dog with a sore throat barking.

If it so came about my happening to be standing by and being immediately available to answer the radio, the dispatcher with apparent relief yelling at me for Christ sake Weston answer that god dam frog before he drives me around the bend with his insistent art, as it usually went our two way conversation to the uninitiated must have sounded like a free for all dog fight as we exchanged a virtual babble of fractured French and shattered English, incomprehensible to all within listening range but the foreman and I with some of the more curious eavesdroppers who not having the faintest clue of what transpired during the course of the conversation rolling their eyes upwards in total disbelief at the seeming gibberish, leaving it up to me to translate the message to the mystified dispatcher. As was bound to occur sooner or later my being absent from the office or most likely on a trip, to the dispatcher's ongoing dismay the by now much dreaded nerve rattling art would come booming in over the radio to be endlessly repeated while the dispatcher frantically attempted to contact me on my aircraft radio and depending on my availability or state of mind at the time would either answer immediately or if in the mood for a little blood letting deliberately ignoring his calls allowing him stew in his own juices for a while until many failed attempts to elicit a response from me had him on the verge of foaming at the mouth in wild eyed frustration with his voice gradually rising an octave or two in intensity at each attempt until almost becoming a desperate screech. Upon his reaching that stage I normally took pity on his plight consenting to answer the radio to be met with a teeth-grinding request to switch frequencies and get that god dam frog off his back.

On my return to base it remained a sure bet he would have immediately jumped on me with both feet for as he so succinctly put it taking my sweet god dam time in answering him on the god dam radio, of course my in a well practiced wide eyed innocent manner denying complicity in deliberately ignoring his frantic calls as honestly I was monitoring the radio all the time, don't give me your usual line of shit he would invariably hiss venomously at me, I know god dam well you heard me but chose to continue playing your childish games, and in the future if you know what's good for you answer the god dam radio post haste when called or else.

Affecting an air of injured pride would make a frosty exit from his office while doing my utmost to conceal a shit eating grin that took a fair while to wipe off my mug on my way to the hotel for a cup of coffee and to enjoy a good laugh over the poor bugger of a dispatcher's never ending frustration and despair that renewed itself daily from trying to deal with a crew of hard core nutty pilots.

Eventually the day came about with his unable to tolerate the insistently nerve wracking demands of the job that included non English speaking French foremen and the endless frustrations of attempting to deal with a pack of stubborn willful pilots on an every day basis eventually gave in to the pressure throwing up his hands in despair and pulling up stakes to seek employment that took him far away from and didn't involve working with a crew of unrepentant physcos.

One of the highlights at the end of our working day was to straggle individually over to there hotel for a coffee and a gab fest or if a hot summer day for a cold beer, it being late in the day one invariably found one of our more colorful local maidens "Sophie Bell" waylaying prospective customers, it never really came clear to me and having the good sense to not inquire why the proprietor of the hotel, a very socially upstanding tiny English lady of rigid demeanor that brooked no guff from god or man appeared to so matter of factly accept Sophie's daily efforts to solicit customers in the lobby of her hotel without a quiver, but for what ever reason known only to her, she plainly did and as stated previously one could remain certain no one including me was to the best of my knowledge ever to have what it took to inquire why, something's are best left unrevealed.

Sophie in her own supercilious manner that I always found refreshing in it's simplicity proclaimed herself as being a high class seductive native call girl looking down with a haughty air of unconcealed disdain on her co-workers who she acidly referred to as being nothing more or less than "common sluts".

Always appearing clean and well dressed for the occasion, a notably attractive women who artfully waylaid every male who happened to pass by on their way into the bar with a throaty "eh mizter', you want a good piece of dale?, two dollars and pifty zence, but you got to make it fast I'm a busy girl, normally at the height of the season she did a brisk trade and to whenever not involved otherwise took the greatest pleasure whenever the opportunity presented itself in pissing off my wife who by the way retained the sense of humor of a hyena when it came to women of Sophie's ilk. Sophie who it seems for what ever reason mutually despised her made it a point of openly accosting me every time we came by possessively taking me by the arm and whispering in a sibilant hushed tone of voice "eh ardley", I got a becial biece of dale I'm saving for you and as you know can take as long as you want, I make it good for you, adding for good measure, any way's Ardley, why don't you get rid of that scrawny white bitch you call a wife and get a decent women like me? Any way's I luff you Ardley.

Grinning foolishly from ear to ear from her repartee would discreetly give her a fond pat on her well rounded bum much to my wife's disgust while passing over a couple of dollars with the admonition to be sure to save some for me, this salient request gaining me a rich heartfelt laugh and a no broblem Ardley, I keep it warm for you. She was to privately inform me one day which of the local pilot's, married or otherwise who availed themselves of her services on a regular basis, that being quite the revelation at the time wisely kept it to myself.

One late summers evening as every one made a bee line for the hotel my wife having remained behind for a few minutes longer to clear up some last minute details, with our bringing up the rear we happened to pass close by the small alcove that fronted the hotel steps faintly detected muffled grunts and groans that sounded suspiciously like what us pilot's referred to as mortal combat of the beast with two backs, curiosity as always getting the better of discretion pushed aside my wife's snarled admonition to mind my own god dam business for a change decided to investigate the source much to her disgust poking my crooked beak into the dimly lit interior to find Sophie lying flat on her back with a bored expression on her face while a half pissed Frenchman straddled her, upon spotting me looking in a wide grin immediately creased her pleasant features that didn't betray the slightest tinge of modesty at being discovered in such an uncompromising position saying "eh Ardley, don't go away now, be right with you now that I got it all warmed up and ready for you, at hearing that a hearty chuckle at her sense of humor escaped my lips when digging out and tossing her a few dollars while informing her of my being tempted but far too tired in mind and body from putting in a long hard day's flying to be able to take on such a sexy women, thas ogay Ardley, I unerstan being a hard working girl myself.

Grinning foolishly from ear to ear made my way into the bar to be confronted by a stiff frosty faced wife who had in a pique of self righteousness had flounced off to the bar on her own to face good natured teasing from the crew of co-workers who had preceded us and to a man well aware of what had most likely transpired took great pleasure teasing her about Sophie's ongoing competition.

As has often been stated the north country inevitably attracted or produced some of the most unforgettable or far out individuals one could wish to meet, one of them being a commercial fisherman from Duck Bay on Lake Winnipegosis Manitoba who's very name defied verbal description, one would have to have played it on a piano with a violin compliment to get the desired pronunciation, we in desperation quickly dubbed him "rotten nose Pete" because of the over sized nose that appeared to have been carelessly slapped on to his moon face between a set of buggy eyes with a trowel, to add to it's fascination the pasty gray surface of his nose randomly dotted with a series of huge craters that sprouted long black curly hairs complimenting a perpetually vacuous grin that he wore at all times, putting his weird appearance aside once we got to know him, his turning out to be one hell of a fine man who made friends with all he met and in doing so making no bones about the fact life to him was to be enjoyed to it's fullest and he by what ever means available fully intended to do just that.

In time our becoming acutely aware of Pete's bizarre and often controversial sex life, his seeming to have an insatiable penchant for the company of the filthiest lice ridden, snooze chewing, snot dripping unspeakably foul hags to be found anywhere, and if they came simpering vacuously up to him trailing a cloud of flies and a pack of mangy half starved mongrels sniffing excitedly behind them, all the better. Upon eventually dredging up sufficient nerve to do so discreetly inquired about his seemingly exotic tastes in such unattractive women, at hearing that his moon face lit up in a huge lop sided grin with his simply stating he much proffered his women to be on the ripe side, for the life of Christ no one could begin to understand how any one could possibly entertain such vicarious tastes, he must have really hated his mother. Aside from the revolting desires that made up his bizarre sex life, a fact generally considered by all to be his personal business, we were to remain close friends for many years.

Some of the pilots sought solace from our some times ongoing and often monotonous labors that lacked any form of diversion save for the local bar once their flying day done in drink, others like me who largely abhorred the degrading effects of alcohol, as an outlet from unrelenting boredom often deliberately went out of my way in tempting fate by deliberately pushing my luck past the envelope of common sense. On one memorable occasion relegated to flying an aircraft with a history of having a troublesome engine that retained an unexplained but alarming propensity to without prior warning threaten to shake itself off it's mounts, an insidious problem no amount of engineering expertise could uncover the cause continuing to baffle the most experienced as it would just as suddenly begin to run smoothly, but never ceasing it's alarming propensity to suddenly belch huge gouts of oil out of the exhaust creating a disturbing trail of heavy blue gray smoke that trailed behind the engine for some time scaring the life out of the pilot and passengers until reaching the point all the pilots but me refused to fly it. Naturally it's alarming idiosyncrasies concerned me but not to the degree of being afraid to fly it, but as it went my finding it had in the long run a lot more to offer than first expected.

Having made a trip in it to a remote settlement with a young would be pilot for company with the engine behaving admirably all the way there and half way back lulling me into a false sense of security, actually if the truth be known I should have known better as it is a well known axiom in the world of aviation that whatever can go wrong will at the least inopportune time, in this case belying the fact for once the engine would behave itself, that assumption soon to be proved to be in error as the engine without any warning what so ever suddenly hiccupped giving off an alarming belch of smoke and flames completely enveloping the engine while dragging us severely to the right as the propeller began to go into over speed due to lack of oil pressure causing my without hesitation instantly regaining control of the aircraft from my startled passenger to rapidly begin the emergency engine shut down procedures then feathering the propeller before any other unexpected problems such as an uncontrollable propeller over speed situation, the interim required between shutting down the engine and being able to activate the fire extinguisher system seemed endless, if there was anything I feared it had to be the loss of control or in-flight fire, every pilot's worst nightmare as either one could quickly spell one's doom.

The tense period between activating the fire suppression system and awaiting the results left me in a heightened state of mind not being able to do much more at the moment than stare impotently at the trail of grayish black smoke continuing to stream from the engine that after what seemed to be an interminable period of time gradually began to taper off leaving me weak with relief, if it had been the case of the fire extinguishing system initially failing to suppress the fire it would have forced my doing the unthinkable by diving the aircraft at high speed in hope the increased velocity of the air passing through the engine would blow out the flames, not wishing to prove that theory, grateful beyond words to have gotten off so lightly though requiring a concentrated effort on my part to will my feet to cease dancing all over the rudder pedals.

As nerve wracking experience it had been for me, it had been absolutely traumatic for my passenger who sat there as if made of stone staring fixedly at the now silent smoke blackened engine in glassy eyed silence, I didn't realize it myself at the time but before our flight ended he would have a hell of a lot more to think about.

Eventually my nerves settled down to a primal scream now that the crisis had passed with the aircraft handling marvelously well on one engine with my remaining confident all would turn out well, as if the devil finds work for idle hands for some obscure reason lost to me began to speculate on the unknown at the time flight and glide characteristics of a beech craft with both engines shut down and both propellers feathered as up till then had never heard of anyone attempting it, the more I thought about it the more intriguing the idea became to the point of mildly alarming my sense of survival, Christ what sort of a madman had I become to even consider tempting fate twice in a row.

It has always been my firm belief that if I had been alone in the cockpit the idea would have been dismissed outright as being downright fool hardy until glancing at my passenger who I had cautiously turned over control of the aircraft to allow his getting in some single engine practice, the smug self contented look on his face betrayed the fact of his looking forward to boasting of his recent mind shattering experiences and how well he took them in his stride to his class buddies as he nonchantly pretended to be totally unfazed by our close call by playing the part of captain cool.

What took place next in my mind could only be described as a terminal case of uncontrollable madness on my part that ran rough shod over common sense with my perversely deciding to give him something concrete to think about for the rest of his life. Once set on what could well be a suicidal course of events once more assumed control of the aircraft to slowly begin retarding the throttle on the active engine until reaching the idle position as he helplessly observed my unexplained actions with the fixed intentness of a rat powerless to save itself as a snake advanced on it, while I completed shutting down the engine and feathering the propeller.

Upon completing their last shuddering revolutions as the propeller blades rotated into the full feathered position some surprised to sense the aircraft momentarily surge ahead but other than that almost undetectable reaction continuing to respond crisply to my control inputs with my lowering the nose slightly to maintain a constant airspeed of one hundred and ten miles per hour giving us a controlled descent of five hundred feet per minute indicated, at our present altitude gave us an approximate unpowered flight duration of fifteen minutes, more than ample opportunity to restart the engine many times over if deemed at any time necessary to do.

How strangely quiet it had become with the engine noises absent, only able to detect the rush of air as it flowed smoothly past, a quick glance at my passenger found him to be perched rigidly in his seat staring helplessly out of the windshield, so quiet and unmoving he could have been carved from stone.

Eventually arriving at a position only a few miles from Pickle Lake with the altimeter still indicating three thousand feet above ground and all seeming to be in order with my feeling confident all to be as well as could be expected when taking into consideration our unique circumstances decided to go for it and complete an engineless landing, one that would no doubt require absolute skill and total concentration on my part as once we dropped below a thousand feet one did not have sufficient time remaining to fire up the engine, a scornful glance at the would be bush pilot in the right hand seat found him staring intently at the fast approaching lake waters while futilely engaged in attempting to slide his rigid frame up the back of his seat while still strapped in and facing forward.

From that point on my being wholly taken up with concentrating on setting up my approach parameters placing his presence out of mind, only focusing on the forthcoming touch down, it just wouldn't do to screw up so late in the game.

Concentrating on my landing failed to take notice of four men on the dock, only after completing a successful landing and firing up the engine to taxi back to the dock were they noticed, only later it being revealed these same men had gotten the surprise of their lives upon being alerted to our presence by the eerie whistling of the wind through our float struts as we ghosted almost silently over the trees lining the shore with both engines silent and propellers feathered to a perfect landing, well well I thought to myself that's how it's done, all very good but wouldn't care to attempt it again short of an emergency.

Once docked the passenger cum pilot shot out of the top hatch like a turpentine dog on speed, imparting a stinging kick to my right ear on his way through to completely disappear never to be seen again, one could only surmise his having re-considered a flying career to be out of the question if forced to train under the tutelage of far out psycho pilots who obviously entertained the death wish.

As it turned out much to my initial dismay, the four men who had witnessed my unusual landing, three of them being Department Of Transport inspectors on an unannounced base inspections, the fourth being none other than the president and owner of the company himself, oh Christ I couldn't have timed my questionable escapade to occur at a worse time, for certain I'm dead meat.

For some odd reason when all that required being said and done had been accomplished without too much ado, not much made out of the unusual incident. Upon they're initially inspecting the smoke blackened engine and feathered propeller did little but to stare curiously for a protracted period of time, all the while making hushed comments as if not certain what to make of it while I fidgeted nervously near by doing my best to appear nonchalant about the whole affair.

Once more or less satisfied with their cursory inspection, they talked among themselves for a few minutes, gesticulating wildly and shaking their heads as if in disbelief at what some thrill crazy bush pilots did for a rush before retreating off the dock while at intervals casting uncertain glances over their shoulders, I would have bet a years pay my engineless landing was a widely discussed subject among them for some time to come.

As for the owner, his only curiously inquiring about the beech craft's flight characteristics during engineless flight, nodding his head sagely while I related my first hand version of the affair from start to finish only to have him surprise the hell out of me when admitting to it having been one of his long time desires to have done the very same but never doing so for what ever reason, a rather strange admission from a man who's aviation background made mine appear modest in comparison.

For some time there after the dreaded registered letter from the powers that be awaited with growing trepidation, the much feared recriminations outlining the charges laid against my person that would once more hang my well tattered pelt out to dry, but for reasons best known to them none of the beauracratic hoopla they are so inordinately fond of dishing out at every opportunity failed to materialize much to my relief, one could only assume there is no specific laws or rulings prohibiting engineless landings, though one can bet their sweet ass they turned their voluminous rule books inside out in a futile attempt to locate one.

As strange a happening as could possibly occur took place shortly there after with my for the first time ever failing a Dept Of Transport proficiency check ride for shutting down an engine and feathering the propeller during flight, my unthinkingly frightening the accredited inspector clean out of his wits in doing so immediately terminating the check ride as a failure, my of course being somewhat confused on this unusual turn of events on inquiry it was determined the Canadian air force training syllabus does not include full feathering procedures to be carried out during flight except in the case of the most dire emergency, only carrying out a simulation procedure.

Well that most unexpected turn of events left me unqualified to fly twin-engine aircraft until successfully passing a re -ride. As if this in itself didn't create enough grief for me, the pilot who had flown the "stone boat" (single otter) for some time with the promise of eventually being promoted to flying twin engine aircraft the very same day I failed my check ride reached the point of despairing that eventuality would ever take place after completing a very difficult period of time that left him haggard and worn from wrestling diamond drill equipment into boggy shored lakes almost non stop for over a month suddenly up and quit making it clear to all and sundry if he was to be a god dam stevedore he would seek employment at some sea port and at least receive decent pay for his labors.

This unexpected turn of events sent cold chills chasing up and down my spine knowing all too well it was inevitable of my being relegated to taking over that winged manure wagon, but I had other ideas about that ever happening knowing to consent to completing even one trip would doom me to remaining on it full time, and despite many entreaties and not so veiled threats to do so or else from the dispatcher stubbornly stuck to my guns despite also weathering a barrage of thinly veiled threats from head office gurus that left my future with the company less than certain unless my immediately complying with their demands, but in spite of it all steadfastly refused to do so.

Locating a qualified full time otter driver at any time remained a tall order as only very few pilots except them on the way up and more than willing to fly them in order to gain precious experience that would give them a boost further on down the road. That untenable situation went far toward jeopardizing my already tenuous position, eventually the situation became desperate as the customers who had long lost their patience demanded action immediately or they would take their business elsewhere, this no nonsense dictum forced the owner of the company to leave his plush office to unwillingly, but having little choice otherwise assume the demanding task of flying the otter in order to complete a long overdue diamond drill haul contract that could only be accomplished with an otter.

His no doubt having been long aware of my present status pounced on me as an albeit unwilling otter driver by making no secret of the fact that replacing a Beech craft pilot of very little consequence as every aspiring pilot out there hungered to be assigned to one, otter pilots on the other hand a very rare breed indeed.

My reaction and equally dark thoughts at being sadistically informed by a smug dispatcher who tartly informed of my being assigned to being checked out by no less personage than the owner himself would not be printable, it will suffice to say that bit of expected but bad news left me royally pissed off only serving to all the more determinedly dig in my heels, no one, no matter who they were or what their position about to black mail me or dictate what I would or wouldn't do, or assume that my being insecure enough regarding my employment I could be manipulated.

Upon confronting the big man with fire in my belly discreetly informed him in no uncertain terms that regardless of the consequences there being no way in hell of my ever consenting to fly the otter, end of story.

Upon his receiving that written in stone edict just nodded sagely like some animated budda, and then in an oily dulcet tone of voice as if attempting to reason with a recalcitrant child he managed much against my will and better judgment to persuade me in accompany him on just a few trips to give him a break, not wanting to be viewed as being totally unreasonable reluctantly agreeing to do so.

Having very little experience flying an otter and wishing to keep it that way, the first take off with my finding myself in the left seat and some what confused how he had managed to persuade me to do so in the first place did not go well, the sluggish performance of the heavily loaded otter reminding me of a lead sled, little wonder it had assumed the well deserved title of "stone boat", my less than laudable performance at wrestling that ungainly beast off the water left us barely hanging on the thin edge of disaster with his white face twisted in sheer disgust at my less than laudable performance, but with his aiding in the control inputs when the situation appeared to be spinning out of control we managed to get air borne.

Once having arrived at our destination after crawling across many miles of barren muskeg while my confidence further evaporated by the minute, just about dropped my drawers, tightening up in horror upon first viewing the minute lake we were to land in, Christ on a crutch, there was no way in god's green earth I could ever hope to land that ungainly contraption in such a limited space, his more or less expecting my reaction upon spotting that tiny lake had taken immediate note of my all but freezing up at the controls sneering at my cowardice while attempting to placate my fears by coaching me step by step in the correct procedures required to conduct a safe landing.

With everything a tremble and a rapidly failing will power more or less did as instructed with the jerky movements of a robot in setting up for a landing. With all more or less proceeding as normally as the tense situation would allow until passing over the scrubby trees that bordered the shores of the lake in an alarmingly nose low attitude that seemed suicidal rattling me further. It wasn't one of my better moves when totally losing my nerve at almost the last second to without thought of the possible consequences in doing so ramming on full throttle while yanking up the nose of the rapidly descending aircraft to what appeared to be a more sensible attitude catching him totally unaware of my intentions and being far too late to salvage the landing forced to sit there in frozen horror as we barely managed to remain airborne while staggering across the narrow width of the lake barely clearing the stunted trees on the far side with the aircraft hung precariously on the ragged edge of a stall, I remain certain to this very day if it had not been for his timely intervention in bleeding up the flaps and whatever else he did to save us, it is a certainty we would have without the faintest doubt eventually mashed into the surrounding muskeg as I had no idea what to do next.

Upon recovering a semblance of normal flight and a safe altitude he ashen facedly screamed at me to get the hell out of the pilot's seat before killing both of us, a request gladly complied with, once in control he expertly swung that heavily loaded aircraft around in a vicious turn that all but turned me into a gibbering idiot to line up and perform the shortest most cold blooded approach and landing I had ever witnessed, literally dumping that ungainly beast into that piss pot sized lake with absolute aplomb leaving me breathless and well shaken by it all, as we taxied in to the make shift dock not saying a word to each other with a grim look of disgust etched all over his features, the tightness of his eyes reflecting our near miss with disaster, upon shutting down the engine turning to me and openly scoffing at my lack of skill and guts, if there had been any other way of getting out of there including walking out I would have gladly embraced it, but as it stood my choice of leaving there remained limited, either fly out with him or stay. Once unloaded and taking on a cargo of empty drums and propane bottles reluctantly forced my trembling body aboard to strap myself tightly into my seat having a fair idea of what was to come next, Jesus Christ, hail marry and just plain goddamit, the exceedingly cold blooded hairy take off he performed while getting us out of there with it's seeming to me our coming within a hair of unavoidable disaster that came near to causing me to piss my pants in fright as he yanked it off the water to immediately drive it in a frighteningly nose low attitude directly to-ward the low lying shore line before beginning to climb over them with it appearing our coming uncomfortably close to clipping them as we staggered on by.

The return trip made in a heavy hostile silence with his eyes continuing to mirror absolute disgust at my past and less than laudable performance that had come uncomfortably close to doing us in, but what ever the price to be exacted I felt totally vindicated at getting off so cheaply for it was a given my pending future as a potential "stone boat" driver dying a borning. After completing many tiresome trips over a period of days one could readily see the demanding pace had become more than he could sustain for much longer

In sheer desperation latching on to a cocky young beaver pilot who had showed a budding interest in the otter, his waxing ecstatic upon being chosen out of the blue to fly an otter so early in his budding career, as it fortunately turned out for all concerned from the first proving to be a natural to within a few days of intensive operation finding himself promoted to captain at the end of his last day of training, the newly minted "stone boat" driver upon being so informed immediately taking to strutting importantly around amusing all no end with our reasoning if he was brain dead enough to embrace the dubious career of a flying stevedore, who were we to judge, he would learn it's failings soon enough.

As for me when it came about easily passing a second check ride given by a far more seasoned inspector who found it difficult to believe my having failed the first time around.

The long hot busy summer moved on heralding another winter season's flying with me happily employed flying my beloved beech craft knowing far more adventure lay ahead. Proceedings, and to them time was money.

Medicine Man

IT IS FELT TO NOT relate in detail this strangest of stories as difficult as it may prove to be to make sense to the reader as even to me it has never come clear how it came about that some way my having without being fully aware of it at the time participated both mentally and physically in the strange series of events that go toward the creating and telling of this story.

To begin with my earliest memories of Bob Sheppard where to say the least unfavorable at the time of his being posted on McKenzie Island, a one time thriving gold mine community as a police officer. My initial hatred and distrust of him began upon his targeting me as potential law breaker all because of his envy of my owning and flying an old by to-day's standards De-Havilland tiger moth, it was only much later on I was to learn he hated his job as an police officer and yearned with all his heart to be a pilot and do what I did, why he chose to come down as hard as he did on my commercial flying activities that if the truth be known had absolutely nothing to do with his duties one could never say, thus it became in my best interest to avoid his attentions as much as possible. I wasn't alone in receiving his unwanted attentions as his arrogant brutal manner toward the populace included all and sundry, abusing his authority as member of the O. P. P, (Ontario Provincial Police to a degree of becoming alarming. It is my firm belief he was only a short time away from being dismissed from the force as unsuitable to carry out the duties of a responsible police officer when he made the grave mistake of grev1ously assaulting the local native medicine man. A more bitter caustic man I had never met, his unjustly and indiscriminately meting out his twisted authority against all who dared to cross his path on the least excuse paying special attention to the native population of whom it appeared he held an unreasoning if not fully understood grudge against dealing out unsurpassed brutality against them on the slightest pretext, of a certainty they avoided his attentions as much as possible but in such a tiny communities that could often prove difficult to do.

Well one day he went just a little too far when apprehending and without just cause other than the fact he was found to be slightly inebriated from imbibing a potent concoction brewed up by the native people and known as "moose milk" laid a severe beating on the local medicine man "Robert Perrault", the vicious beating with a night stick (baton) resulted in coming within an inch of taking his life for no reason other then he must have feared the respect and authority the "medicine man" received as keeper of the spirit world from the local native population, the end results of the severe beating inflicted with a night stick left the "medicine man hovering at death's door for some time, it requiring much intensive hospital care and a long period of convalescence there after before fully recovering from his numerous injuries but remained blind in one eye.

My having from the first of my school days had befriended and associated with the native population of the surrounding area of Red Lake and for an extended period of time choosing to live among them which of a matter of course allowing my becoming steeped in their language traditions and customs and once getting past my fear and awe of him gaining a great respect for the "Medicine Man" who's strange unexplained mysterious powers of which when demonstrated always left me in a bemused state of mind, for as much as I hungered to delve further into his mysterious art, only at certain times were the innermost traditions of tribal spirit ceremonies revealed to me, and only then because of my close association with them. On rare occasion the elders allowed my taking part in certain cultural1 ceremonies that gave me the opportunity to witness strange and disturbing séances that could never be logically explained leaving me to ponder at leisure the mystifying difference between their spiritual world and ours as taught by the church, but respecting the activity of the native peoples beliefs chose to not question the how or why of it, just accepting it for what it was thus not in the least surprised upon one of the elders I held a great abiding respect and trust for one day unexpectedly informing me the "Medicine Man" who had recovered sufficiently to resume his duties had just completed a sacred ceremony in private that resulted in his placing a curse on Bob Sheppard that time would prove it's placing would lead to a series of related events resulting in his living a near hell on earth existence and ultimately leading to his death in a violent manner as previously foretold.

Not being all that aware of the ramifications of having a curse placed on one remained somewhat confused for some time about the consequences involved. In time the elder's eventual portent of the curse revealed to me, but only upon his gaining full permission to do so from the Medicine Man, my not realizing at the time by involving myself would at one point figure in during the course of the curse to inadvertently prevent Bob Sheppard's premature death in a manner one could have never have began to predict. It couldn't be honestly said I feared the strange powers of the Medicine Man out right, but one could say I sure as hell respected him!. Upon being apprised of the curse not in the least surprised about it's eventually coming about having a very good idea how it had originated, for at different times during the ceremonies I was allowed to participate in often included a spirit dance with my on the occasion witnessing a series of hair raising events brought on by the Medicine Man's strange powers as he sat cross legged by a smoky fire looking for all the world like a stone idol besides the open fire staring intently into it's flickering flames with strangely luminescent eyes while muttering incomprehensible incantations, at no time could I ever be absolutely certain of how it came about as we collectively sat in a circle silently waiting for whatever came next, mesmerized by the smoky tendrils of flame licking out from the fire I could have sworn on many an occasion to having observed strange wraith like figures that took shape while appearing to dance and twist in the slowly rising smoke, this strange state of affairs always accompanied by the muted pounding of the skin drums, their monotonous cadence seemed to take over one's mind separating it from reality leaving one strangely disembodied while one's life spirit hovered just above the smoky flames dispassionately observing the proceeding as if viewing it from another dimension with time seeming to become meaningless. Once this out of body experience passed and our having returned to our watchful selves crouched around the smoky fire intently observing the proceedings with great interest as the medicine man who with a great show of theatrics sprinkled some sort of powder into the flames that instantly resulted in clouds of heavy tangy scented smoke oliberating him from view, once the smoke cleared in a short space of time a dirty brown cone shaped tent which had not been there before sat directly over the spot where the Medicine Man had sat.

At first the silence hung heavy with no one as much as daring to breathe too loudly with nothing of note taking place for a protracted period of time that had us all squirming uncomfortably until with out warning the tent suddenly begin to shake and vibrate as if taking on a life of it's own, then to just as suddenly settle down followed by a heavy eerie silence that seemed to dominate one's very senses as the drums suddenly as 1f on an unheard s1gnal ceased their monotonous pounding.

Almost if planned the excruciating silence would seem to stretch on interminably to the point of beginning to grate on one's nerves where upon almost jumping out of my skin at the onset of an unexpected terrible scream that ripped the silence to shreds followed by a repertoire of grunts, squeals, and heavy coughing sounds finally terminating in the harsh and discordant croak of a raven, again to be followed by an eerie silence. The sight of so many native people sitting in a ring rigidly mesmerized like so many huddled up brown skinned statues made of stone amused me no end, but wisely never letting it be known.

The scenario as described could and often did vary from time to time but in effect always proving to be of mystifying interest to me. The one séance that I had been forbidden to attend because of my being non native it turned out had gone much further after the usual ceremony had been completed, as something is always lost in translation I can only repeat what was revealed to me in my words, it going something like this, following the usual ceremony, on a sudden a very ghostly hollow sounding voice that rang with throbbing authority had issued from within the confines of the tent intoning, Bob Sheppard now hear this, I alone will know of your death as a white man, now you will become as us, you will know privation and suffering as we do, as one of us you will forsake the way's of the white man taking one of our women as wife to live as we live, you will never again know peace of mind as you seek your way, and lastly you will die as a bird, now hear this Bob Sheppard I have spoken and it shall come to pass.

Upon being informed of the curse laid on him immediately made it my business to keep a close eye as possible on his activities without giving myself away, not only out of morbid curiosity to observe just how long it would take for the curse to take effect, but also to avoid his unwanted attentions as he had been ragging me unmercifully of late, much more than normal the last while about questionable concerns involving my flying activities.

At first nothing worthy of notice seemed to occur with my almost for a time forgetting about the curse placed on his head until about three months later the disquieting information of his having becoming increasingly violent in nature, more so than ever before to the degree of turning his frustrations on his family, on one occasion beating his wife within an inch of her life while threatening native and whites alike with his hand gun. I never knew at one point he was fired from the force and how it went from there for he had mysteriously disappeared for some time and when just as suddenly appearing again it was all I could do to recognize him for who he was his physical make up having changed so drastically appearing to be more native than white man it eventually becoming common knowledge he had forsaken his one time life style to take up and live in the native style with a comely native girl by the name Martha Keeper who had mysteriously appeared from her reserve in Little Grand Rapids Manitoba.

The local natives shunned her as a trouble maker referring to her as the "devil's grand daughter", my getting to know her well throughout the years found their estimation of her amazingly accurate as it turned out if she could create any form of deviltry either by direct actions or innuendo she would immediately do so given the chance but strangely enough I never knew her to have anything to do with liquor. Well for what it was worth the first part of the prophecy had come about with bob going "native", now it remained only a matter of time before the next part of the curse came due!.

For a period of time he seemed to disappear but my through discreet inquiry eventually finding out he had taken up the life style of a trapper in the Ear Falls area south of Red Lake, he couldn't have picked a more formidable area as it is widely known as a "snow belt" where copious amounts of snow built up during the winter months making travel on snow shoes difficult if not impossible. To my knowledge very few native or white men had chose to trap there for some time and it was my honest guess he would not fare out too well and as it ultimately turned out he didn't almost losing his life while attempting to do so but faced little choice otherwise there being a birth of available areas and definitely not daring to take up a trap line anywhere within the Red Lake area his remaining more than aware of the residual hatreds of the native people he had once wronged still continued to smolder, it would have taken very little to fan that smoldering hatred into a full blown conflagration and they would have soon seen to it in short order that he would mysteriously disappear without a trace with my remaining absolutely certain Martha would have met the same fate even though she had done them no wrong, but it didn't seem too likely they would have been foolish enough to have left a living witness to their depredations, that in itself would be certain to create unwanted and far reaching problems for them knowing her penchant in creating trouble, wrong a native and you have gained an enemy for life .

As fate would decree it my making a trip to return a trapper to his line on Uchi Lake which lay some distance away from where Martha and bob where supposedly trapping, but for some reason lost to me to this very day decided for no good reason once departing uchi lake elected to follow a chain of lakes that more or less paralleled the areas bob supposedly trapped in that would eventually lead me to Ear Falls, the late spring day being absolutely gorgeous with the pristine landscape standing out in vivid relief in the bright sun that beamed warmly down from a clear blue sky, it just didn't get better than that making it a fine day to be alive and to be doing long what one enjoyed best flying the aircraft you loved above all!.

Having reached a point about thirty air miles or so from Ear Falls while curiously following a set of tracks that meandered almost the complete length of a long narrow lake known as "white mud" on the map suddenly spotted some dark objects that stood out from the blinding white backdrop of the lake's snow surface with my at first taking them to be caribou or wolves, curiosity as always getting the better of me swung over for a closer look in order to identify the unknown objects, but upon coming closer it became clear they where not what I first thought to be as whatever it was it did not attempt to flee as any wild animal would immediately have, but instead remained huddled up in one spot at the end of what appeared to be a wavering snow shoe trail.

Coming around again but this time much lower could have sworn it appeared to be two people crouched in the snow staring back at me, not being all that certain of what I first saw took my eyes off the lake surface momentarily to in the process of my brief inattention almost digging in a wing tip scaring myself half to death in the process as the wing quickly jerked back to level flight, another more cautious fly by finally revealed them to be what I had first thought as they feebly flapped their arms as if signaling for assistance. Now the last place I cared to land had to be was in the middle of that notoriously slush and deep snow filled lake, but obviously something had to be done to offer assistance regardless of the all too great possibility of becoming inextricably bogged down in deep slush, the very thought of that occurring almost caused my curling up in a ball of abject fright, as much as my instincts screamed at me to forgo a landing the pathetic sight of they're appearing to be in desperate straits hardened my resolve to at least try, making another low pass for some distance along their snowshoe trail failed to reveal the tell tale black stains that invariably indicated the much feared presence of slush but that was not always the case as had been oft learned the hard way, but still that left me between a rock and a hard place and more uncertain than ever what to do, with my heart in my mouth and my sphincter as it usually was at such times almost wrapped around my neck made a delicate touch down on to the lake surface, cautiously placing the weight of the aircraft onto the snow covered surface by degrees for a fair ways without being able to detect any noticeable drag on the skis before applying power for a go around to check my tracks for the dreaded tell tale black stains that indicated a deep pocket of slush that was certain to mire the aircraft if foolish enough to place myself in it's grip to be relieved beyond mere words to have seen none, then coming around again to much against my better judgment completing a cautious touch down that all but left my heart in my mouth and tense with the anticipation of suddenly sensing the aircraft bucking to a rapid halt as we broke through the surface snow into the clinging slush before much to my ever lasting relief sliding to a stop almost beside them without that dreaded scenario occurring, relieved beyond mere words to have somehow been fortunate beyond measure to have landed on a dry area of the lake, why this should be one couldn't say, only being thankful it had. They where to tell me later the very spot they had reached before becoming unable to go on any further due to complete exhaustion had up till then found to be the only dry area within the entire length they had so painfully traversed that was found to be free of deep clinging slush that made snowshoeing an absolute hell on earth sapping their remaining strength, unfortunately for them the slush and the snow conditions that winter remained exceptionally heavy and deep for late march.

The ragged emaciated figures that staggered over to greet me at first left me some what stunned upon viewing their haggard appearance, one would have been hard pressed at first to tell if they where natives or whites they're being so sun and filth blackened, but it quickly became obvious the smaller of the two was a female, but the taller of them being over six feet gave him away as being bob Sheppard. My god were they terribly emaciated, nothing but skin and bones, how they ever managed to struggle as far as they had while laboring under the most trying conditions defied description, when they staggered up to the aircraft it became readily apparent they're having reached the point of being too weak to walk, right there and then it was decided they required immediate assistance, my reaching into the rear compartment to drag out the ration kit and blow pot in order to cook up and eventually be able to feed them hot tea, sugar and oatmeal mixed up with raisins and dried milk to bolster them until able to fly them into Ear falls. Quickly firing up the blow pot soon had snow melting in a pot for tea to fortify their sagging spirits, up to this time they had hardly croaked a word, mostly remaining huddled up or in a crouched position staring at me as if they couldn't quite believe I was real or a figment of their imagination or maybe an angel of mercy that had dropped out of the sky to save them, in a way one could say there was some truth to the angel part as without question if I had not by the greatest of unexplained chance happened to come by when I did it remained extremely doubtful of their surviving another frosty night without benefit of food or shelter as their terribly run down condition indicated their being in the last stages of starvation and exhaustion, chances were otherwise they would have given up to gradually sink into the sleep that never ends. Now there is chance and there is chance, but to this day I still ponder the fates that convinced me to fly over to that certain area, as I really had no valid reason to do so. (Some how some way I figured in the scheme of things) I have my theories for what they're worth but that's all they ever will be, it plain and simply stood in my way of thinking to not be Bob's time to die as it still remained for him to fulfill the curse to it's conclusion, the spirit of it fully intended toward keeping him alive until the time came about for him to die as a bird, however that would come about yet remained to be seen. I cannot ever be certain he was at any time aware of the curse the medicine man had laid on him, and if so did he believe in it and live in fear of what it portended?.

Once the water had boiled and the tea steeped sufficiently I poured each of them a tin cup full laced with enough sugar to stand a spoon up in it of which they accepted gratefully with handshaking so violently with need and anticipation it was all they could manage to prevent themselves from attempting to gulp down or spill the scalding hot liquid and injuring themselves. Once having greedily gulped down the first cup of scalding hot tea as quickly as possible he was finally able to croak out an almost unintelligible heart felt thanks for my unexpectedly coming to their rescue and of course inquired as to how it had come about that my seemingly out of the blue happening to come along and rescuing them just at the most opportune of times for as he put it they didn't stand a chance in hell of survival in their present condition, all I could honestly tell him it was just pure chance on my part in doing so not having any valid reason at the time for coming so far out of my way outside of the fact it seemed the right thing to do at the time though normally I never deviated from my flight plan, as vague an answer as it was it seemed to satisfy him as he never pursued it any further once making his initial inquiry. Upon my having fed them well sweetened oat meal boiled up over the blow pot and they're having made an impressive inroads into the plain fare my ration kit had to offer they sat back in contented repletion to relate his woes.

It seems it had all started out badly the last early September when they had begun their trip out to their trap line location by canoe, all going fairly well until his foolishly insisting on attempting to run a rapids instead of choosing the safer but tedious back breaking labor of portaging their winter supplies and canoe despite the fact he lacked the skills required to safely do so unwisely ignored his native wife's warning it was too dangerous his ultimately as she had predicted striking a submerged boulder unseen in the frothing white water swamping the canoe spilling him and their winter supplies into the icy raging waters, they're only able to salvage a portion of them after much hard labor. The grave loss of precious supplies placed them at a grave disadvantage in surviving the coming winter.

He never really said as much but one could only assume his initially being stung by his obvious imputed so early in the game or simply failing to realize the import off the loss of critical supplies at the time or worst of all stubbornly refusing to admit to it perhaps due in part to misplaced male pride. Whatever the reason it eventually proving the loss was as a matter of course to have far reaching consequences for them. In hind sight the wise course of action would have been to swallow his pride and reluctance and have returned and renewed their supplies, but as it went his having little knowledge of what lay ahead of him and foolishly refusing to listen to his native wife who wise in the ways of her people and the land knew all too well the potential risks they faced when placing themselves so far away into the wilderness for the winter with inadequate supplies to see them safely through and what it eventually portended begged him to reconsider, but bull headedly he chose to tough it out and in doing so coming within a hair of dooming both of them. As it went his insisting they carry on to eventually reach their designated trapping area after experiencing a rigorously difficult time of it took up residence in a long abandoned trapper's cabin, his native wife Martha wise in the ways of her people and long having realized it has been left up to her to ensure their well being as best she could soon had their fish net set out into the near by river netting numerous white fish she preserved by smoking a large quantity for their own consumption and drying a large part of the catch for bait or if necessary emergency supplies, from what Martha was to inform me in private much later on it had been well she had the foresight to do so even though bob managed to bag a moose within the first few days of their arrival but now certain of his "bush" prowess ignoring Martha's entreaties to harvest more of them before the snow began to get too deep for easy hunting. Winter that year when it did come, doing so unusually hard and fast and much earlier than normal bringing on an abnormal fall of heavy snow. Bob being new to the game as a trapper forced to rely on Martha's skills to show him the ropes, but as it ultimately turned out most likely due to his bull headedness when forced to take advice from others his proving to be a poor trapper obtaining little in the way of saleable fur. In due course coming down to a struggle for survival as the snow continued to deepen to the degree of making it extremely difficult to snowshoe any appreciable distance from the trap cabin. Also as a hunter he failed miserably not being able to get his sights on another moose due to his ineptness in managing to do so, a remarkable feat in itself as they abounded in great numbers within the area, only his wife's native bush smarts in snaring rabbits and squirrels kept them meagerly supplied with meat, but if the truth be known there isn't much needed fat to be found on either of them leaving them fat starved and in poor health.

Judging from what he related to me they had endured one hell of an excruciatingly long agonizing winter that had tried their physical well being and mental capacity to it's utmost, on the most part barely subsisting on a near starvation diet that eventually sapped their will to survive to the breaking point before the early spring weather eventually came reviving their flagging spirits.

It doesn't take too vivid an imagination to imagine the high degree of desperate boredom endured during the unceasingly long days and longer nights of forced idleness enhanced by the seemingly endless long months of total isolation, but having little choice to do otherwise could do not but stoically endure their travails. With the excessively deep snow restricting the checking of his trap line on a regular basis, for the most part remaining cabin bound with little to keep mind and body occupied outside of ensuring their having an ample supply of firewood. This was by their own admission the way it went until the long awaited spring thaws settled the deep powdery snow that had up till then made snow shoeing any great distance all but impossible had shrunk in depth to the degree that they could safely chance snow shoeing their way out or at least he assumed as much, but as always due to bob's poor planning or lack of it nothing worked out that way, the arduous winter of existing on a poor diet that barely offered bare survival had sapped their strength to a greater degree than first thought generally leaving them in a state of being in too poor a physical and mental condition to attempt such a demandingly trying journey on snow shoes. The early spring weather and lengthening days finally convinced them to leave while they still could being on the edge of running out of patience and most any form of sustenance save for a bit of near moldy flour a few dried fish and some dried meat from the rabbits Martha was able to snare, taking what little remained hoping to be able to shoot some game on the way set out one early morning to begin the long trek down the chain of lakes that on the most part presented terrible snow shoeing conditions that that went far toward slowing down their progress and sapping their remaining strength, only after slogging determinedly on hour after endless hour did they manage to make it part way down the length of white mud lake on the morning of the third day of their forced march to where by the merest of chance I had located them. It had now come clearly apparent to me the second part of the prophecy had run it's course, from here on it could only become more interesting. As it turned out Bob's First year of attempting to live as a native trapper turned out to be his last,

Once feeling their confidence to be restored to a greater degree than when first finding them and they're being strong enough climb up onto the wing to with almost indecent haste to ensconce them selves into the front cockpit of the tiger moth all the while grinning like two school kids. Almost immediately upon their settling in the overpowering stench of long unwashed bodies and unthinkingly filthy clothes marinated with what I really didn't want to know began to permeate the confined atmosphere of the cockpit all but causing me to gag uncontrollably until finally able to dredge up the presence of mind to slide my canopy open again to quickly revive myself with a breath of fresh air, it may have been an exceedingly crude method of travel to the average air traveler but to them it must have felt it to be as luxurious as a first class air Canada flight when considering what they had recently endured. Flying them the rest of the way to Ear Falls and landing almost at the door of a friend of mine who lived on the edge of the lake who some surprised at seeing me appear as if out of nowhere. Once explaining the situation to him he suggested I contact the local police officer who much to my relief instantly upon his eventual arrival took charge of their welfare. Once having bid them good bye took the time to imbibe in a hot cup off coffee and a delectable snack of roast moose meat sandwiches offered by his wife before thanking him for his valued assistance in taking care of my wayward passengers, then taking my leave to fire up my trusty steed in order to fly the remaining forty miles to Red Lake with a lot more unanswered questions to occupy my mind for the next while then I had started the day with. Upon first realizing that pondering the imponderable only confused the issue that much further gave it up for the time being placing it in to the back of my mind to be thought over later.

Eventually It was learned through various sources that once he had recovered from his ordeal had found a job guiding fishermen for a local tourist trap while Martha found employment with the same camp cleaning cabins and not what have you during the summer months with bob working in the bush as a logger during the off season. Some where along the way he managed to squirrel away sufficient funds to put himself through flying school, something he had long hungered to do. Upon completing his initial pilot's training   managed   by dint of unstinting perseverance to gradually upgrade his flying skills through the intervening years by taking on less desirable flying jobs that allowed his obtaining sufficient flying hours to train for his commercial pilot's license, there being a dearth of available pilots at the time he was soon able to land a full time job flying a small aircraft for a tourist camp. As one is bound to sooner or later in the world of aviation we bumped into each other on the occasion, the last time I was to ever see him alive took place in Big Trout Lake while passing through while flying an American filming crew throughout the north country in Green Airway's Stinson Gull Wing, the very same one he had always admired and lusted after so openly. I never knew how much longer he remained there flying a Cessna 180 for some small outfit after our chance meeting, but some where along the way completing his tenure at Big Trout Lake with his eventually moving on, and in doing so my completely losing track of him for many years until one day being informed of his death in the mountainous area of northern B C. It would appear he had brought on his own demise (or did he) by losing his way in bad weather and inadvertently flying into a box canyon, upon realizing his mistake far too late to save himself attempted a panicked emergency turn in order to get out of the rapidly narrowing confines of the box canyon snagging a wing on a projecting over hang during the process tearing it loose from the air frame to helplessly end up cart wheeling end over end to his death on the jagged valley floor far below, often I have wondered if at the time of his demise and if during the seconds left to him of his being aware of the curse placed on him by the medicine man, and if he was what his last thoughts? Thus the final part of the curse came about as prophesied by the medicine man, his dying as a bird!.

Again it is once again left up to the individual reader to view this strange story as they see fit. But one must remember at all times there are strange things done beneath the sun in this beautiful world of ours that often defies logic or scientific explanation.

If there is a moral to this story, I for one would subscribe to the logic of it not being a wise move to piss off a native Medicine Man.

An Experience Out Of Reality

THE AUTHOR WISHES TO MAKE it clear to potential readers that during my long tenure as a Bush Pilot, random chance would dictate that on the rare occasion my experiencing strange phenomena that can not be readily explained, and in some cases exceed the boundaries of credibility as this story does, but it is left up to the individual reader to accept or reject it as they see fit.

The writing of this particular story only coming about due to the rarest of chance meeting up with another individual many years later who also by the rarest of chance experienced much the same unexplained and baffling phenomena at the very same location I had, but only a few years later. Our by the remotest of chance meeting up in the tiny hamlet of Pickle Lake, the odds of our ever doing so lost to infinity as the settlement we met in being so remote and far off the beaten track few being aware of it's existence save for a mere handful of itinerant Bush Pilots and adventurous foot loose wanderers seeking asylum from the maddening crush of humanity, out handful them very few dared the excruciatingly long lonely drive to reach it.

My being employed by Severn Enterprises as a pilot flying a twin beech our main source of work at the time being INCO.{International Nickel Co.} who had fielded a large mineral exploration program in hopes of locating viable mineral deposits of base and precious metals and being informed at a later date to also be actively seeking diamond bearing locations.

As a matter of course the necessity to fully prove out the potential of promising ground as located by their geologists called for a massive diamond drilling program requiring a legion of drilling companies to locate into the area creating on the average far more work than we could possibly hope to handle as they where individually located far and wide through out a vast area straining our resources to the absolute limit.

Having in due course struck up friendships with all of the site drill foremen being in my best interest to do so.

As it happened one of them moved in next to me making our social intercourse an ongoing thing with our gradually becoming more at ease with each other to the point of openly discussing our past experiences regarding the varied areas we had one time or another lived and worked in with his surprising me all to hell and back upon admitting to have recently worked out of Churchill Mb., this revelation struck me as being some what unusual as to my knowledge there is very little in the way of mineral exploration carried out in that remote part of the country.

My curiosity being piqued inquired as to the location where their drilling program had taken place, surprisingly enough his remaining somewhat reluctant at first to pursue the subject to it's conclusion, it taking some doing on my part to appraise him of my being quite familiar with the area and it held no surprises for me, this matter of fact statement eventually convinced him to haltingly relate his strange story eventually becoming increasingly confident upon the telling I would not view him as some one with a vivid and fertile imagination.

At it's conclusion I could only at first stare dumbfounded at him feeling as if some one had unexpectedly fetched me a mighty blow to my chest so difficult had it become to catch my breath, it turned out the only noticeable difference between his experience and mine was the time frame and the number of witnesses.

My now presuming the readers curiosity to be sufficiently piqued the remainder of this strange and fascinating story will be further revealed.

It had it's beginning while on a return trip to Churchill from a remote lake set well back within the boundaries of the North West Territories where the fish producing company I flew for had just begun to set up a commercial fishing operation to harvest the much prized land locked arctic char.

The weather picture that day at best remaining less than desirable with low cloud and many areas of heavy rain scattered throughout the duration of the flight often creating difficult forward visibility problems that made accurate navigation over bleak and forbidding terrain that boasted few lakes of any note creating an unexpected series of flight difficulties that resulted in using up more fuel and time then flight planned for and upon finally arriving at our destination my being immediately beset by a myriad of problems concerning the setting up of the new camp thus further delaying my departure well past the time I should have left on the return flight if wishing to arrive back at Churchill before dark.

As it turned out the following events would prove it would have in the long run been circumspect on my part to have taken my chances with a sudden wind coming up and no secure dock yet to safely tie up on or a suitable beach to heel the air craft up on for the night and unable to anchor out in deeper water not as yet having a boat to ferry me back and forth and not in the least motivated to swim in them icy waters, so lacking an alternative unwisely as it turned out took off to return to Churchill triggering a series of events that set in motion one of the strangest experiences to ever take place in my entire career as a Bush Pilot.

The weather which had not at all been to my liking on my trip in had now lowered considerably presenting a brooding ominously gray black overcast setting my nerves further on edge. Deciding it best to not chance flying low over that forbidding terrain decided to climb on top of it into clear conditions and if at all possible tune in to the Churchill radio directional beacon, it being in my best interest to find out what the local weather conditions over that way before doing so called Churchill radio for a weather report only to receive the blood chilling news of they're being totally socked by a weather front that had moved off the bay ruling out any hope I had entertained of making it back that day, the unexpectedly bad news gave me quite a mental jolt leaving me shaken and uncertain what to do next. Having flown in the general direction of Churchill for some time estimated my being approximately half way there placing me over some of the worst stretches of forbiddingly barren terrain one would never wish to be caught over in marginal weather as the few shallow lakes to be found in the area totally unsuitable to make an emergency landing in, that nerve shattering knowledge did little toward alleviating the pressure of having to locate a suitable landing area and god dam soon as the weather continued to worsen dropping the visibility even lower the further on I flew, but having no other choice than to attempt to return to the fish camp, but it was a fool's paradise to even think one could possibly locate it considering the state of the weather and my ever shrinking fuel supply.

Having inadvertently boxed myself in to a dilemma that didn't bear thinking too heavily on with the remaining daylight rapidly fading due to the ominous presence of the heavy black clouds that now filled the sky forcing my flying ever lower. Once again the familiar icy cold fingers of raw fear crawled down my spine, fear, gut wrenching bowel loosening debilitating fear that turned one's very blood to ice water and one's brain to mush, with one's knees involuntarily beginning to knock so violently one's feet began to dance all over the rudder pedals.

Once more cursing my unthinking stupidity in allowing the situation to deteriorate to such an alarming and threatening degree as mind numbing anxiety washed over me in ever increasing waves it became crystal clear of my being in deep trouble with no obvious way out, but still retaining enough presence of mind to realize one had best get immediate control over their emotions before committing a grave error in judgment, gradually being able to allow my survival instincts to assess the situation in a clearer state of mind.

The flat featureless terrain offered no hope of salvation save for my fortuitously running across one of the fast moving rivers that randomly flowed through the area, until doing so, having run out of options one could do little but to carry on. Having all but reached the point of despairing of ever locating one of them before running out of daylight, suddenly to my ever lasting relief flashed over top of a river that more or less flowed toward the coast, the palpable relief felt upon finding the river left me weak with relief, bringing on new found hope of locating a suitable stretch of water to make a safe landing on.

Desperately attempting to keep track of the wildly meandering river kept me busy weaving from one side to the other seeking a suitable landing area before running out of what little remained of the murky day light.

Time as it always does when laboring under high stress seemed to stand still while continuing on in hope of soon locating a suitable stretch of clear water with overstretched nerves hovering on the bare edge of the breaking point as the encroaching gloom threatened to blot out what little of the terrain that could still be seen when as if out of nowhere the river being followed suddenly joined forces with another that at first appeared to be a far larger and powerful if one were to judge by the foaming cataracts that appeared to blanket the rivers course from bank to bank seemingly endless before suddenly smoothing out in a stretch of calm waters.

Having run out of options no indecisions as what course of action to take next plagued my overstressed mind elected to without further hesitation to land on the proffered stretch of calm waters regardless of the consequences, as the badly degraded forward visibility had worsened noticeably upon the advent of our encountering a light drizzle that coated the windshield further cutting back on forward visibility by creating distracting streaks that forced my having to revert to looking out of the side window a desperate option that at best offered very limited visibility and judgment, but regardless the time for procrastination had long since passed, if one hoped to survive a chancy landing on an unknown stretch of water, it's having to be carried out post' haste'.

Lining up the aircraft for a landing as best one could considering the less than ideal circumstances the blurred outlines of what appeared to be in my peripheral vision those of buildings set far back from the river bank, but put it down it down to an illusion caused by the refraction of the rain on the windshield or perhaps wishful thinking on my part, instead dismissing as being highly unlikely to concentrating on hopefully getting down safely without damaging the aircraft or my precious self to somehow eventually managing to do so with a combination of skill and good fortune to heavily contact the river's surface with a jolt that was severe enough to jar my teeth creating a spectacular bounce with my allowing the aircraft to settle back down on it's own being afraid to apply power uncertain of what lay ahead of me, grateful to not have snagged a wing tip on either of the by now almost invisible river banks, as the speed bled off with the aircraft wallowing off the step found myself bracing for the inevitable collision of the floats with an unseen underwater obstacles that could possibly lay in my path, grateful beyond measure to eventually find myself sedately taxiing against the current. It took a concentrated effort on my part to come down from my adrenalin induced high and to allow a gradual unwinding of over tightened nerves, it taking some time to cease clenching my teeth, the terrible pressure endured for so long had taken it's toll leaving me soaked with rank smelling sweat and trembling in relief at our deliverance, it all too easily could have gone the other way.

Switching on the landing lights cautiously eased my way into the river bank pleased to finally feel the front of the floats gently slide up onto the muddy shore line.

Upon shutting down the engines, at first somewhat startled at the cessation of engine noises emitted a shuddering heart felt sigh of relief that the mind-shattering ordeal had ended without my having met up with disaster. At first remaining totally confused and uncertain as what to do next sat there in contemplative silence as the light rain that had moved in shortly after landing pattered softly across the cabin roof to eventually create a series of twisted rivulets that coursed down the slope of the windshield, their wavering meanderings coming near to mesmerizing my thoughts as the all pervading silence that totally encompassed the confines of the cockpit only being broken by the muted whirr of the gyro instruments as they slowly wound down.

Too numb in mind and body to at first give it much thought, the fact that having faced near insurmountable odds and survived in spite of it all suddenly washed over me, once more the twin god's of chance and fate had intervened to save Weston's sorry ass.

Finding myself in a mentally exhausted and bone weary state of mind while getting over a severe case of close call jitters remained in the security of the now darkened cockpit for some time before reluctantly prying myself out of the seat to grope between the seats for the tie down ropes that were always kept within easy reach then popping open the hatch to toss them onto the now well darkened river bank with my cautiously climbing down off the slippery wing to securely tie up the aircraft to some huge boulders that were conveniently located far up on the bank for the night.

My curiosity about what had briefly appeared in my peripheral vision as buildings against the back drop of the rapidly darkening sky during the landing some what overrode my weariness and reluctance to leave the security of the cabin to seek what ever it was if anything at all, grabbing up my flashlight to check further up onto the river bank in hopes of verifying the sighting, a short stroll brought me almost up against what was to my surprise a buildings of sorts that suddenly appeared within the beam of the flashlight, I couldn't for a minute understand why they had been placed there but my god talk about blind luck in unsuspected beaching the aircraft directly adjacent to them, a few hundred feet on either side it remained most likely my not stumbling upon them as I invertently had, otherwise their presence would have remained unknown till the next morning, to say the least their unexpectedly being there at all startled the hell out of me, solid proof I had not been hallucinating after all.

Staring open mouthed at what could be seen of them made me wonder just what they were doing there, and what could be their purpose be in such a remote area?, not to mention contrary to normal practice their location and purpose not printed on any of the maps in my possession though in no way could the cartographers be ignorant of their existence, but for what ever reason failing to print their location on the map, well everything is done for a reason no matter how obscure, in time their unexpected presence would be clarified to my satisfaction, as it turned out I would have cause for regret for ever having stumbled onto them.

Further but cautious investigation proving that one of the smaller buildings to once having been a bunk house for the inhabitants that once populated the place having six spacious partitioned rooms placed on either side of a wide center corridor, further investigation showed them to be furnished with old fashioned steel bed frames complete with well mouse chewed mattresses, but what could not be readily explained and what gave me an unexplained sense of growing unease was the degree of destruction visited on the furniture that lay in shattered disarray throughout the rooms appearing in all respects to have been viciously vandalized, but why and by whom, and what purpose in doing so could it had possibly served? All my questions only blown away in the wind as no answers were yet forthcoming.

At that very minute I would have given most anything to have had the reassuring company of another individual to share the awful feeling of complete and utter loneliness that washed over me at that very minute, rarely had I ever felt so vulnerable and alone.

Hesitantly playing the flash lights beam throughout the middle space to center the beam on the far wall that appeared to have numerous large rusty appearing splotches of what could have been blood splatters and randomly interspersed streaks that stained the wall clear to the floor, the flashlight beam when shone on the space directly below also indicated wide areas of rusty appearing stains that appeared at one time to have puddled on the floor, these puddles of what could only be assumed as once having been pools of blood appeared to occur through out the room at random giving of the miasma of terrible violence at one time having been enacted within the confines of these walls, that unexpected and totally confusing reminder of past and terrible violence at first paralyzed further moment on my part for a brief space of time before being rudely jolted back to the present with my coming within a whisker of bolting out of there in panicked flight to the perceived security of the aircraft before catching myself and reassuring my well shaken state of mind that nothing within them walls offered any sort of threat regardless of the less than inviting atmosphere that pervaded the room, and upon taking into account just how cold and clammy it could be lying on the cabin floor of the aircraft during the long cold night in the metal cabin of the aircraft, finally able to convince myself of being slightly overwrought and a victim of fatigue and over stretched nerves managed to shake off any lingering doubts before making my way back to the aircraft to retrieve my sleeping bag and travel kit to reluctantly return to the well darkened bunk house choosing a bunk as close to the main door as one could get, why I chose to do at the time I didn't know for sure.

Once more or less settled in to my new digs lit up four candles that immediately dispelled a large part of the overwhelming gloom that seemed to settle over one like a suffocating blanket. Still partially remaining in the throes of an adrenalin produced high found it all but impossible to cast of an intense state of anxiety that prevented my unwinding sufficiently to drop off to sleep, instead finding myself staring restlessly at the flickering candles, each of which cast individually weird and distorted shadows that appeared to take on a life of their own as the flames guttered and flared against the back drop of the bedroom wall with my in a distracted manner imagining the rising smoke to be creating diaphanous images that were subject to the workings of one's mind.

On edge as I remained for some time exhaustion finally won over with my eventually drifting off into a fitful sleep, lulled by the warm comfort of my sleeping bag. During a period of restless sleep sensed more than heard the resonating mutter of the rising wind as it swept around the cornices of the building, it's chattering dirge vaguely disturbing my rest.

Some where along the way when the long night hours are at their darkest rudely being brought to full wakefulness by what I was absolutely certain to be a long drawn out quivering scream of pure agony that eventually ended in a phlegm gurgle and a disturbing series of explosive coughing as if some one was drowning in their own blood and about to expire leaving me in a paralyzed state of terrible fright with my hair standing on end, now I wont make an issue of my being as terrified of the unknown as the next person but one can be absolutely certain them strange sounds went far toward further upsetting my already uncertain state of mind.

Eventually all seemed to somewhat settle down with my eventually dredging up the nerve to re- light another set of candles with hands shaking so violently it was all one could do to light a match and hold it to the candle wick, the others having burned down during the course of the night, the flickering flames quickly assuring my overwrought state of mind all to be well with no unpleasant surprises confronting me. After a protracted period of time finally able to convince myself that what had so rudely awakened me to be a night mare brought on by an overwrought state of mind and being half dead from exhaustion decided what would be would be blew out the candles to once more drop off into a fitful sleep.

A good many hours must have passed as the first grey fingers of a watery gray dawn had begun to filter through the grimy windows but still leaving the interior of the bunkhouse fairly dark requiring a source of light if one wished to identify certain objects within the room when once more being rudely jarred awake by a resounding crash of splintering wood work accompanied by what sounded like hoarse panting and the heavy agonized grunts of bodies locked in mortal combat to be suddenly accompanied by the most blood curdling stentorian screams of pure agony that turned my very blood to ice water, eventually ending in a spate of heavy labored breathing and panting moans interspersed with a short spell of unintelligible gibberish finally ending with some awful sounding gurgling noises.

My remaining wrapped up in my sleeping bag through it all totally immobilized with unspeakable fright paralyzing my mind and body couldn't have left that bed if the devil horns and all had jumped in along side of me, it was nothing short of a miracle of my not experiencing cardiac arrest as my poor overworked heart threatened to pound it's way out of my chest. So there I remained, totally bereft of all emotions save for pure raw undiluted heart stopping fear, petrified to remain there, but more petrified of confronting some nameless horror as I attempted to flee.

Eventually as before all appeared to once more settle down as did my heart rate, once more or less settling down doing my best but failing miserably to convince myself the past happenings being nothing more than an all too real nightmare, but try as I might my overwrought mind refused to accept any simple explanation, and as time slowly ground on by fully justified in not doing so as no sooner having collected my wits and gotten my blood pressure and heart rate something within the realm of normal, what ever the hell it was that did such a fine job of upsetting my peace of mind suddenly re-commenced with the ghastly sounds of mortal combat once more echoing off the walls.

To be absolutely honest about it I really have no conception of the time frame taken up by each set to of mind numbing terror, only of near being reduced to a blubbering idiot, though in stark reality each set to most likely of brief duration, my overtaxed imagination did the rest.

During one of the quiet periods timidly ventured to re-light the candles that for some unexplained reason had been suddenly extinguished by the advent of a sudden but violent gust of air that defied explanation, with hands that still shook so violently it was all I could manage to accomplish that simple task, once the feeble but vastly welcomed light cast off by them, to a great degree dispelled the fears of the threatening darkness along with the manifold terrors of the night allowing my by now well subdued state of mind to almost return to normal. Picking up my till then forgotten flashlight timidly dared to crawl out of the sanctuary of my sleeping bag and venture to the doorway of the cubicle to warily probe the farthest and darkest recesses of the main room of the bunk house half expecting some unimaginable horror to suddenly leap out of the shadows brandishing a club and spear intent on seeking another warm body to dispatch, relieved beyond words to find all to be as I had originally found it.

Any further thoughts of sleep now banished leaving me fearfully wide eyed awake while feverently wishing for the coming of dawn to hopefully put an end to my ordeal, but eventually the endlessly remaining hour or so left between false dawn and what passed for a new dawn crept slowly by allowing the watery gray light of a new day to filter through the grimy windows replacing the smothering darkness with it's feeble light before daring to blow out the candles that had burned down to about half of their original length.

The coming of dawn, as heavy and gray as it was still found by me to be most welcome in banishing the awful dread that had pervaded my very being. Bone weary from lack of sleep and suffering from an overdose of old fashioned sheer terror that lingered in my overwrought mind groggily gathered up my meager kit to make a hasty retreat to the security of the aircraft while casting fearful glances over my shoulder as if half expecting some nameless horror to be pursuing me. Once ensconced in the cabin of the aircraft laid out my sleeping bag to hopefully grab a little more shut eye, but my adrenalin charged system would have non of it finally forcing my giving up in despair to rouse myself to the point of being able to break out my ration kit and portable stove to cook up a pot of oatmeal liberally laced with sugar, powdered milk and raisins, the welcome repast going far towards bolstering my sagging spirits.

While involved in eating my breakfast my wandering gaze kept returning to the strange building that in the strengthen day light it was noticed their somber brown coloration came near to blending in with the surrounding landscape, little wonder my having failed to notice their presence until flying by almost on top of them, but what really caused me to catch my breath in startled fright was the unexpected sight of a tall steel tower that could barely be made out against the back drop of surrounding hills projecting from behind one of the buildings, Christ on a crutch, one could have all too easily snagged a wing tip on one of the myriad of guy wires that supported it or worse yet not being aware of it's presence have flown directly into it, my remaining appetite vanished like smoke in a gale leaving me with a hollow feeling of despair and an overwhelming desire to quit that place of dread and mystery.

As much as I desired to leave, the inclement weather dictated otherwise leaving me with little choice but to wait it out until it improved. Not desiring to sit around and become increasingly uptight and antsy, decided to check out the mysterious buildings to if at all possible discover their purpose, the first of the smaller buildings proving to be a generator shed housing two long dormant Lister diesels, the fact that the two huge fuel oil storage tanks had been artfully concealed beneath the ground to conceal their presence from prying eyes did not go unnoticed. The next building investigated turned out to be a storage shed that held numerous wooden crates with USAF stencils embossed on them plus many other types of mouse chewed cardboard cartons that dated throughout nineteen forty five on, the last building explored being the largest gave me quite the surprise upon finding the gloomy interior crammed almost to the ceiling with huge gun metal gray radio transmitters and receivers along side of what appeared to be weather recording paraphernalia that must have dated as far back to world war two vintage, that and the steel tower informed me beyond a doubt of my the merest of chance had stumbled on to clandestine weather reporting station obviously built by the American Air Force to gather information for their long range nuclear deterrent bombers that had once flown out of Churchill.

All fine and good, but that still left me non the wiser of how and why the extensive damage to the furniture in the bunkhouse had come about, not to mention the huge splotches of what were obviously blood stains splattered on the floor and walls to be seen every where one cared to look, the unexplained mystery of it all left me in a terribly upset state of mind as what ever had taken place must have in all respects been of extreme and brief violence.

Having satisfied my curiosity to a degree now only wished to leave that place of mysterious happenings and let the past be the past.

But mother nature still held the winning hand it being obvious by the low lying clouds it would be a while yet before chancing it, having had enough of bad weather flying and pushing my luck to the limit the day before.

Eventually working my way up to becoming increasingly uptight and restless and not knowing what else to do decided to explore the surrounding area, and having only walked no more than a few hundred yards toward a slight rise glimpsed what I took to be a boulder lying half buried in the tundra, but something about it's unusual shape prompted my picking it up to examine it, soon discovering it to be a human skull, as I studied it the empty eye sockets appeared to stare accusingly back at me bringing on a fresh wave of unease and an unexplained uncertainty prompting my carefully replacing it back in exactly the same position I had first found it.

Continuing on toward the rise in an increasingly sober state of mind suddenly taken aback when first spotting the profusion of bones that lay scattered randomly across the tundra, one could never say for certain lacking hard evidence to the contrary there remained little doubt the area had once served as a killing ground, and again by whom and why?, upon witnessing the remains of what had once been living breathing humans my first reaction was to get the hell away from there as quickly as possible, but morbid curiosity got the better of common sense drawing me in closer to examine the numerous skulls and scattered bones, a detailed examination of some of them indicated without a doubt that death had come upon them swiftly and in the most violent manner, the horribly shattered condition of some of the bones suggested they're being subjected to an unknown but intense form of brutalization, what ever or who ever had done the unspeakable damage to them, it spoke volumes of being commensurate with a force that had shattered some of them almost beyond recognition, closer examination of the skeletal remains that lay scattered randomly across a wide area of tundra indicated they had obviously been subjected to the same trauma, the only difference being where they fell.

Viewing the pitiful remains of what had at one time been living breathing people, could not help but to wonder what terrible calamity had overtaken them to create such wide spread carnage, what ever the cause it spoke loudly of short duration and extreme brutality, having seen all I wished to and somewhat upset by it all decided it best to leave that place of violent death and allow the remains to lie in peace.

Back at the aircraft in a thoughtful somber mood some pleased to note an improvement in the weather as the heavy gray clouds slowly moved off improving to the degree of my willing to chance it, a call on the radio to Churchill affirmed the weather picture improving by the hour. Once having cast myself loose from the river bank cautiously allowed the current to take me downstream with the nose pointed upstream ready to hit the power on a split second's notice if unexpectedly coming into contact with an unseen submerged obstacle, in doing so it allowed an extended take off area and the time to mull over the fates that had so fortuitously provided a clear landing area when most required, that it existed at all an absolute and almost unheard of anomaly for that part of the country where the rivers on the most part consisted of non stop cataracts, that I mused the precise reason the weather station had been originally located there.

Once having made a departure from the river without further incident climbed to a suitable altitude to re-gain my navigational bearings to Churchill eventually arriving in a pleased but somewhat confused state of mind over the past happenings and a greater respect than ever for the normally unstable moods of the weather patterns that could unexpectedly roll in from the coast, it would take some time to get over such an unorthodox experience.

From then on when having occasion to fly past or near the site of the clandestine weather station soon discovered one had to approach it at exactly the correct angle making use of the clear stretch of water to line up to be able to briefly observe the buildings, who had ever located them must have been a master of disguise to have so effectively concealed their presence from all but the closest of scrutiny, their mysterious presence save for an unseen emergency landing would have also remained unknown to me, though for what ever reason I wasn't sure of kept it's existence to myself.

Never again did I choose to re- visit that place of unexplained mystery and intrigue, once being enough as the experience of once having done so leaving me in an unsettled state of mind as the unanswered questions left me uncertain if I had been hallucinating or the victim of a fertile and overactive imagination brought on by exhaustion until one day quite by accident making the acquaintance of a well worn grizzled barren lands trapper who retained an abiding respect for bush pilots, and who was in the long run able to shed a lot of light on the mystery by eventually revealing his being quite aware of the mysterious presence of the clandestine radio station as it had once lay within the boundaries of his trapping grounds. From there on as his trust in me grew he began to reveal an extensive knowledge of what had once transpired their upon my admitting to have spent a night there, relating a story that left me absolutely spell bound.

As the story went the weather station deliberately or unknowingly placed directly within the boundaries of an ancient caribou migration route where they had crossed the river for countless generations, consequently the disruption brought on by the building of the radio station was to eventually prove instrumental in bringing about the cessation of the massive herds of barren land caribou that had twice annually crossed there, changing their migratory route elsewhere with the fall and spring hunts the Inuit people had depended on for generations falling off to the point of the Inuit hunters only being able to procure a few stragglers that still passed through leaving the people in dire straits that eventually resulted in starvation claiming the lives of many of the very old and very young during the course of the long winter months.

As the trapper's story went, it seems that the shaman {Medicine man} who had long nurtured a burning hatred and distrust of the kabloona {white man} further inflamed by the unthinking and deliberate encroachment of their sacred hunting grounds had convinced some of the desperately fear ridden people of his tribe the spirits of the caribou had been angered by the infringement of the white man on their hunting grounds and only the complete destruction of the inhabitants of the station who in his mind not having the right to be there and must be removed would appease the caribou spirits, only then would they once again re-appear in their original numbers. The elders of the tribe wisely did their best to discourage this destructive course of action for they greatly feared the might of the white man knowing to harm even one of them for any reason guaranteed severe retaliation, but it seems they protested in vain, the shamans flaming oratory succeeded in convincing a small group of younger hunters who also thirsted for revenge against the interlopers to take up their spears.

One can never be absolutely certain of the course of events that eventually transpired as nothing had ever been recorded publicly but it must have been the group of renegade hunters that had under the cover of darkness sneaked up on the unsuspecting station inhabitants pulling off a surprise attack on the occupants of the bunk house, and if one were to judge by the wide spread damage and what could have only been blood splotches on the floor and walls. One can only begin to imagine the surprise shock and horror of the viciousness of the confrontation, still it seems they had in spite of being surprised at the suddenness of the attack while being weaponless and helpless to defend themselves on top of being out numbered put up a desperate battle for their lives only to shortly becoming overwhelmed by the sheer number of kill crazed Inuit's with blood lust driving them on. One should not be too hard pressed to imagine what took place next upon the station personnel failing to report in on schedule to the military base at Churchill, therefore the reader is left free to conjure up any scenario they see fit as to what most likely occurred next concerning the state of the shattered bones.

Fate often works in strange and mysterious ways with the advent of the drill crew arriving at that very same spot to be surprised as I was when observing the unexpected presence of the weather station, and to be further perplexed by what they found while checking out the buildings and surrounding area.

It is not deemed necessary to go into a lot of detail concerning what they experienced when choosing to sleep in the very same bunkhouse I had, only that they remained in there just one night, the very next morning hastily moving across the river to set up their camp site, if six case hardened tough as nails men who had been near frightened out of their wits by the course of events that must have taken place that night, then it doesn't take too vivid an imagination to conjure up the state of living hell I had experienced being alone.

By some unbelievable stroke of fate the foreman of the drill crew and I destined to meet and compare our strange adventures that in so many ways parralled each other, though his off handedly mentioning the unexpected sight of three half burnt down candle stubs left as mute testimony besides the bed had left him wondering who had been there ahead of them.

In summation of this strangest of stories, the reader is advised the old barren lands trapper who I deeply suspected to be well aware of the violent course of events that had taken place, but never at any time admitting to it for reasons best known only to him, perhaps his doing so with good reason, if I had been in his shoes there remains no doubt of my doing exactly the same in the interest of one's continuing good health.

To quote Robert Service, There are strange things done beneath the midnight sun.

Bacon Rind Repair

STUDENTS OF BUSH FLYING AS a rule are on the most part knowledgeable of the trials and tribulations Bush Pilots faced as a matter of course and their uncanny ability to often extricate themselves from difficult and sometimes dire circumstances, relying solely on their resourcefulness when doing so for as is often the case the closest assistance at best many miles or days away, often effecting simple repairs that allowed their returning home. During the course of my career there where times I found myself unable to continue on due to float damage or minor mechanical failure, unless it turned out to be far past my abilities to effect a temporary repair due to the sometimes extensive nature of the damage usually able to correct a minor problem that in time saw me on my way.

The one certainty every pilot faced at one time or another when flying on floats was to unexpectedly strike an unseen underwater obstacle, usually shallow boulders or jagged edged reefs that lurked dangerously near the surface and extremely difficult to detect in dark brackish waters. No other nerve wracking sensation quite equals the shock of suddenly and without warning to jolt over a boulder strewn reef or coming to a grinding halt upon becoming impaled on a jagged rock, or experiencing the sickening lurch and dull thump as your float bottom rides over a flat top reef or large boulder, either way one often finds themselves in serious trouble, the degree of which largely depends on the extent of the damage. incurred to the float bottom at the time. If one is fortunately close to a sand beach or shallow shore line and the damage to the float bottom not too extensive, one may be able to run the aircraft up on either one of them before the float fills with water which in an extreme case can cause the aircraft to turn turtle, a dreaded scenario that fortunately during my entire career never forced to endure that soul searing experience, but the ones who had assured me it was not something one forgot for a long time to come if ever especially if one happens to have passengers on board who's fate is some time sealed upon finding themselves in a confused and panicked state of mind that often renders them incapable of saving themselves upon finding it extremely difficult or down right impossible to differentiate up from down negating a successful escape from the confines of an submerged aircraft.

One of the few times I had by accident severely damaged a float on a lake located about as far away a remote area as one could choose to be, in this case not too distant from the arctic circle on a beautiful lake known as "Dubawnt", a body of water so large as to be an inland sea. Having left Lynn lake that morning to make the excruciatingly long flight with an elderly obviously well heeled prospector who wished to spend the short summer months on Dubawnt lake doing his thing, though for the life of me at the time failing to understand why anyone would choose such an out of the way remote area, and all by his lonesome yet. Eventually after a long and boring flight arriving at and circling over the spot on the north side of the lake he had previously selected on the map I couldn't help but to take in the pristine landscape in it's natural state as it had remained for many a millennium and as yet not touched by the destructive hand of man, also taking note and marveling at the absolutely crystal clear water of the sylvan lake and the wild untamed beauty of the raging river as it thundered in a series of awesome eye catching white water that boiled unchecked through numerous stretches of rapids as it made it's way to the coast, my being totally mesmerized by the awesome beauty of the remote area surrounding us to such a degree I failed to take notice of a line of boulders that lay a short ways out from the sand beach under a cloak of shallow sun glittered water, the very spot chosen by my passenger as a good place to set up his camp. Once landing and taxiing in toward the sand beach the unexpectedly sudden and sickening lurch as the left float impacted and rode over an unseen obstacle startling both of us badly as it momentarily swung the aircraft slightly to the left before the forward momentum dragged the float clear, stunned and dismayed beyond comprehensive thought it took a few long seconds before comprehending just what had occurred and getting over the initial shock long enough to drive the aircraft the remaining distance while feverently hoping no further shocking surprises lay in wait ending up on the beach before taking on too much water into the float, it turned out well my having reacted as rapidly as I had as the left wing now due to the increase of weight in the float now sat much lower than normal. Shakily shutting down the engines reflected on the deep despair that pervaded my entire being, mere words proving inadequate in describing the terrible feeling of helplessness that washed through me, leaving me sick with fear to my very soul, it took some time but finally managing to work through it by degrees until able to with legs so shaky as to almost refuse to support my weight making it difficult to exit the cockpit and with reluctance begin the arduous task of unloading the prospector's supplies.

The demanding job of unloading made all the more difficult by the fact the aircraft faced inward and with the cargo door located well back on the fuselage forced our having to wade to the rear of the floats in order to access it, as we initially entered the icy water it's shocking cold embrace at first causing one to momentarily hesitate while gasping in agony from the painful cramping sensation experienced in one's lower groin, by the time that onerous job had been completed no one had to explain the meaning of "numb nuts" to us. By the time the heavy load had been by dint of perseverance and will power finally removed the float had risen much further allowing my being able to power the aircraft further up on to poles placed under the floats on the sloping beach enduring several more unwelcome baptisms that ultimately left me blue with cold even though the day was fairly warm leaving me wondering if I would ever thaw out, but little did I know at the time that was only a minor work out with much much worse yet to come. After completing that mind and body numbing task had absolutely no idea where to turn to next as outside help totally out of the question leaving me inescapably and irrevocably screwed and on my own without the remotest chance or hope of receiving any form of assistance in the near future Removing the access panel off the top of the float in order to assess the damage entailed the frustrating job of removing a multitude of balky screws that came perilously near to giving me a severe case of the fits, but eventually won out in the end to be rewarded with the blood chilling sight of a foot long gash on the bottom skin of the float, my very first thought was shit and god dam, now I'm totally screwed every which way come Sunday.

The very worst part of it was the cold unassailable fact I sat many hundreds of miles away from any source of assistance, however one feverishly tossed a myriad of possible solutions around in their mind, the all too real knowledge that all but left me in black despair of having no where or no one to turn to, forced by the unforgiving circumstances surrounding my present dilemma to solely rely on my ingenuity to some how affect a temporary repair employing what ever resources available to assist in extricating myself. Normally the damaged float would have to be jacked up to effect ready access for a permanent repair, but that remained out of the question, the tools and support equipment required to accomplish the job would have to be flown in at a ruinous expense, not an option at the time. These mind boggling problems eventually caused my mind to tune out and become totally blank with ongoing confusion being the order of the day, my wisely deciding to leave things as they where until once more being able to think clearly as my poor overloaded mind only capable of spinning in circles. I had often found if one leaves alone what at first seems to be an insurmountable problem, if one leaves it be for a spell a viable solution that just may be the solution to one's problems often in good time present itself.

Meanwhile as I fretted and stewed over my dilemma the prospector true to his calling had taken it upon himself to explore the awesomely beautiful point of land busily engaged in snooping behind a huge sand beam pushed up by the ice suddenly giving off an excited shout for me to join him, quickly dismissing my present problems clambered up and over the beam to see what had set him off to view a sylvan park like clearing with much to my surprise not ever suspecting for a minute that some one had once lived here in splendid isolation as the remains of an old log cabin attested to, now nothing turns me on as much as exploring old camp sites or ghost towns, the sight of the log cabin gave my heart an excited leap at the thought of exploring the remains, but my god it simply boggled the mind when attempting to reason out how had they found their way to such a remote area in the first place, It could only have been one of them hardy barren land trappers, a one time exceedingly rare breed that so little has ever been known or written about. In any case who ever it had been had seen to it that the cabin well situated, being adequately protected from the vicious winds that must have raged off the huge expanse of lake during the long cold winter months and a goodly supply of standing timber that in it's self a rarity in that part of the country that offered easily accessed fire wood. The construction of the cabin had been done by an expert, the logs being of the finest quality lying straight and true while the corners beautifully notched in the dove tail fashion, rarely had I ever seen a trappers cabin built with such care, it no doubt having proved to be warm and cozy during the harshest of winters. As we dug our way into the furthest corners and every nook and cranny I discovered an old fashioned brass compass that continued to function perfectly belying the numerous years of being exposed to the elements lying by the remains of what had once been a window sill, spurred on by my discovery and using my extensive knowledge of trapper's ways and habits eventually rewarded by locating an old style Winchester rifle that appeared to be in surprisingly good condition when taking into consideration how long it too had been exposed to the ravages of the elements, but for the fact it having lay concealed under the overhang of a log thus for the most part well protected went a long way toward preventing it's deterioration, this certain rifle remains in my possession to this day as have since found it to be of a rare Winchester 25/20 caliber. Meanwhile my partner some what miffed at my good luck grumbled to himself in a far corner of what had once been a tiny kitchen replete with shelves containing various rusty tins he spent a lot of time worrying the rusted lids off, finally letting out a whoop of joy upon finding an old time stained diary in a lard can. We spent a few interesting hours perusing the written entries of the personal life and times of a solitary person who for what ever reason best known to them had not written down his name or where he had first come from or how he happened to end up trapping in such a remote area, actually this was nothing new to me having at one time or another associated through the years with many of them taciturn and elusive men who generally shunned civilization and they're having in no uncertain terms made it abundantly clear it not being wise or circumspect on one's part to ask personal questions or to inquire from whence they came. But what fazed us was to how he had first arrived at that certain spot, obviously he must have traveled from some settlement with it's remaining most likely to having traveled up the coast from Churchill Manitoba or some other remote settlement located further along the coast by means of a coastal steamer that once plied the waters of Hudson's Bay during the late fall and by dog team further inland to trap. But that would have been an extremely difficult time consuming endeavor considering the distance to be covered and forbidding terrain he would have been forced to traverse, it only being possible to have done so in the dead of winter, it remains and always will continue to be a mystery as to how these rugged individuals accomplished what they did in traveling over unmapped terrain while providing themselves with the necessities of life. We where further mystified upon reading the date of his last entry which preceded our arrival by thirty eight years to accidently find and read his diary that stated he would be away from his cabin for an estimated total of ten days while making his final round to pick up his traps as spring had put an end to the season, for what ever unknown cause failing to return to his cabin, but then again maybe he had and for what ever reason neglected to indicate his having done so in his diary, just another one of them unexplained mysteries of the north. As we completed reading the last entry we were suddenly startled by what we didn't rightly know, whatever it was it instantly caused our freezing in position not saying a word or having any clear idea as what to do next while staring uncomprehendingly at each other with our eyes reflecting the alarm brought on by the sense of a strange presence, one that could not be construed in any sense of the word as being threatening, just that we where trespassing, feeling as if we had just been caught dead to rights with our hands in the cookie jar we decided without further ado to leave well enough alone with our making a hasty exit back to the beach my feeling uneasy about removing the rifle and a few of the rusty traps that hung on some of the trees.

Still not wanting to face up to the onerous task that haunted my thoughts and hung heavily on my shoulders instead decided to check out the area adjacent to the cabin to find various pieces of equipment scattered throughout with an axe head still sunk in a block of wood, the well weather-beaten handle still attached to it with a rusty buck saw lying on the remains of what was once a saw horse, a pile of fur stretching boards lay concealed against the ravages of the weather in a small log shed that had some how with stood the seasons along with a roll of unused stove pipes lying within a galvanized wash tub, but what really got me was the fair sized pedal powered grinding wheel still sitting in it's cradle and a huge cast iron frying pan lying in the middle of a fire pit ringed with small boulders, one couldn't help but wonder why any one would go to the trouble of lugging in such heavy ungainly pieces of equipment from so far away under such trying conditions?, but who's to say why any man does what they do! An old meat cache that still stood on shaky poles caught my interest but wasn't foolish enough to attempt to climb the time rotted ladder to check it out. Having satisfied my curiosity thus far wandered down to a small cove where the remains of what had once served as a dock constructed of logs lay pushed way up onto the beach by the ice, but no signs of a canoe or home built boat to be seen but the stubs of two roughly carved oars still gave mute testimony to the fact a boat of some sort had once existed. A cluster of strange looking stones lying near the dock caught my attention, closer scrutiny proved them to be drilled anchor stones commonly used at one time to act as weights for the old fashioned linen nets of the era, again I pondered the folly of putting out such a great effort to transport such heavy gear from so far away, but in retrospect realized a fish net is an absolutely necessary item to a trapper in order to obtain fish for himself and his dogs, drying and smoking much of it for future use as food or bait.

Having more or less satisfied my curiosity in that area decided on a whim to range a little further afield to were the trapper had originally cut the logs to build his cabin and to gather fire wood, my instantly noticing the various heights of the stumps, this in effect indicated the depth of the snow at the time of the tree being cut down, but being acutely aware that very little snow falls in them latitudes could only surmise the snow that did build up around the trees to have drifted or swept in off the surface of the huge lake by what must have been fierce wind storms that slammed into the protective beam dissociating it's energy and allowing the now gently moving snow to settle into the treed area.

All the trappers I ever knew and they were many invariably chose to build their cabins on the small side in order to conserve their wood supply not to mention a smaller area required less effort to keep it warm and cozy during the long cold winter months, another reason they're on the average being solitary by nature choosing to have only their sled dogs for company, thus a small living space suited their requirements admirably. It was obvious by the remains of the log kennels he had once kept a team of six dogs.

Well as soothing to the mind my interlude had been, the nagging problems waiting to be solved still lay before me, the very thought of it went far toward sullying an otherwise beautiful day, the grinding seriousness of my dilemma almost causing my dancing a jig in frustration as no matter what scheme I hatched up it seemed to on perusing it (pardon the pun) have holes in it. As it became increasingly obvious the answers would continue to evade me that day, gave up beating up on myself by deciding to take time to enjoy what promised to be great fishing. Fetching my collapsible fishing rod and a few extra artificial baits as did the prospector with lights of anticipation reflecting from his eyes.

Taking our time in threading our way past and around the immense boulders that lay in scattered profusion along the river banks, some of them equal in size to a small house, standing there openly admiring their immensity, couldn't help but to ponder the implacable force that had originally forced them so far up onto the river banks, that would have been an awesome sight to have witnessed when the warm west winds in the spring loosened and driven incalculable tons of ice before it, pushing and piling it layer upon layer until the combined weight sinking some of the floes clear to the bottom of the lake to scoop up the huge boulders from the bottom of the lake and to eventually deposit them high up on the shore line.

Having made our way to a likely looking pool that boasted a back eddy lying below and slightly off to the side of a thundering cataract of foaming white water, made my first cast in high anticipation of catching a good sized lake trout watching the lure flash invitingly as it wobbled downwards in the crystal clear waters with it's barely having sunk out of sight when suddenly being struck by a large fish, it doing so with such shocking fury it came near to yanking the pole out of my hands.

Once getting past the initial strike induced shock set about playing whatever it was that had seized the lure with such viciousness watched the incredible rate of line melting off the spool at an alarming rate with near disbelief as what ever it was continued to tear in a headlong rush almost across the entire width of the pool before settling down to a stubborn sulk my eventually coaxing it up to the shore line to be rewarded by the sight of a beautiful lake trout that could have easily topped the scales between thirty five or forty pounds which was carefully released to return to the depths from were it had first come. It was obvious by the amount of whooping and hollering my fishing partner enjoying equal success. After an almost non stop period of catching and releasing mostly large fish, forced by necessity to call it quits our arms and wrists becoming worn out from the constant exertion imposed on them, our only retaining a few of the smaller ones for our evening meal. It didn't take too much of an imagination to conclude that outsized monsters lurked within the icy depths of that huge lake that up till then mostly remained untouched by human hands. Upon returning to our makeshift camp, immediately filleted and cooked up with thick slices of bacon fresh cut from a huge slab.

Having surfeited ourselves to our content, sat back to enjoy a cup of fresh brewed coffee boiled up in a well blackened tin pail over an open fire, not saying much, our remaining satisfied to sit there in compatible silence, each deep in their own thoughts, that was on the occasion broken by snatches of desultory conversation as my eyes for reasons I could not at the time begin to comprehend kept wandering over to the slab of bacon lying there, not being able to fathom my sudden interest in a slab of bacon dismissed it from my mind, or so I thought.

As what passed for nightfall in them latitudes descended on us we eventually gave up our campfire vigil grateful to roll into our sleeping bags. Sleep did not come easily to me, my remaining unsettled and restless wrestling with the devils that continued to plague my overwrought mind keeping me on edge until finally succumbing to exhaustion falling into an uneasy slumber only to experience recurrent convoluted dreams of futilely attempting to plug the gash in the float with a slab of bacon that obstinately refused to co-operate frustrating me almost beyond human endurance by it's stubbornly refusing to remain in place.

Upon awakening in the first light of early dawn feeling for all the world of having labored mightily through out the night on what one could not rightfully say, but the pertinence of my convoluted dreams suddenly assailed my mind with full force, maybe just maybe that could be the answer and it might well do the job.

The cup of cold coffee I had been absently sipping on now forgotten with my retrieving the slab of bacon from the prospector's grub box to hurry over in anxious suspense to wedge myself inside of the damaged float to in a fever of anticipation place the slab of bacon over the gash, weak with relief upon discovering it to fit perfectly. But my uneasy dreams came crashing back to haunt me, how in the name of Christ would it be possible to keep it in place against the immense water pressure generated during take off and landing?

Baffled and frustrated to near tears decided it best to leave well enough alone for the time being, instead for no good reason other than not knowing what else to do made my way back to the ruins of the trapper's cabin.

Once arriving at first just glumly sitting there while great waves of despair washed over me absent mindedly staring at the remains of a robust hand hewed table, suddenly like bolt out of the blue the answer to my dilemma struck me, tearing off two of the fairly wide planks that had once served as a table top and all four of pole like table legs, gathered up my spoils to hustle quickly back to the aircraft to dig out my emergency buck saw and hatchet, carefully measured and cut the still sound planks to the desired length to lie both forward and sideways, then with great care gauging and cutting the correct length of table legs that were to act as uprights to hold the boards when placed on top of the slab of bacon that when placed against the gash on the very bottom of the float hopefully seal it off. Being forced by necessity to once again venture in the icy water didn't sit well with me as at first nothing worked as planned causing many the heated vituperation to escape from my lips, only managing after numerous frustrating attempts in preventing the wet slippery slab of bacon from sliding all over hell and back each time one attempted to place pressure upon it, the demanding effort required in doing so bringing me to the bare edge of near madness with my almost giving up on many the occasion from the burgeoning pain of my by now raw and well scraped knees.

Finally when almost reaching the point of not finding myself unable to take much finally completed that demanding and onerous task, one last check on the quality of my work satisfied me all to be well gratefully dragged my near frozen well stiffened complaining body out of the near suffocating confines of the float compartment to complete the job from the outside by installing and nailing the two uprights through the top of the float deck and cross pieces into place using the old fashioned rusty nails removed from the table top boards.

Once being satisfied that all that could possibly be done had been done retrieved the float pump and commencing to pump the remaining water out of the compartment, after what seemed to be an endless chore of pumping finally to my ever lasting relief rewarded by the most welcome sucking sounds that indicated a dry space. And just as well it happened when it did as my back and arms muscles had begun to spasm creating painful knotted muscles that screamed for cessation of my labors.

Worn down to almost a standstill from being forced to crouch on my now painfully raw knees while humped up like a dog attempting to screw a football for an extended period in ice cold water that all but numbed my extremities beyond feeling, all the while working in a suffocating tight space desperately attempting to convince a recalcitrant slab of bacon that seemed to have developed a mind of it's own to stay put in one place long enough to allow my hammering the retaining uprights into place, and upon successfully doing so barely having the strength and willpower remaining to wiggle out of that hell hole and shuffle wearily back to the camp fire springing back into vibrant life upon inhaling the delicious odors of fresh brewed coffee and frying bacon that instantly revived my flagging spirits and whetting my appetite.

The prospector that had continued to snore peacefully through my filching his precious slab of bacon and the time spent on the ensuing mind boggling labors upon awakening had sleepily fumbled through his grub box in a futile effort to locate the original slab of bacon, a look of absolute consternation and perplexity still remained on his craggy features upon having failed to do so. At my informing him of it's being used for another purpose at first refusing to take me seriously certain of my pulling his leg until finally convincing him to come over to the aircraft to view my handy work. One can be sure of his hardly being amused at the demise of his slab of bacon, his darkly growling about it being a waste of good bacon and in all probability ending up as an out and out failure as he couldn't see it holding for any appreciable length of time, but still able to retain the good grace of marveling at the ingenuity of the repair.

Well for what it was worth I had done the best job possible when one considered the extremely limited resources available for me to work with, now all that could be done was to wait and see. Our at the time remaining totally ignorant of the mind bending toils that still lay before us, happily returned to the camp fire for a hearty breakfast feeling a little more buoyant and a little less uncertain of the future. Fortunately the prospector still had a good supply of bacon, most of what remained for his future consumption consisted of the canned variety, little wonder his being put out with my running off with one of his slabs of fresh bacon making it a point of warning me he would guard the remainder of the fresh stuff with his life, one couldn't help but to have a good laugh at his levity. After our enjoying an excellent breakfast topped with a cup of delicious tasting fresh brewed coffee while openly admiring what we both considered to be the most beautiful of setting that lay before us, that any man could ask for more to be totally unthinkable, this was the way a man ought to live, if nothing else it sure gave one pause for thought. As we once more sat in companiable silence gazing in awe and wonder at the overwhelming expanse of beautiful lake that seemed to stretch endlessly before us, it being so vast it made it impossible to view the far shore with the shimmering sun light glancing off the placid waters, how crystal clear it remained, as yet free of man's penchant to destroy or pollute all they came in contact with, the profit motive justifying the destruction of all that's good and decent. My god how good the coffee tasted, brewed in naturally clear water totally free of the chemicals that unfortunately has become man's lot to bear, for the younger generation born of the big city warrens they will never know of any but the chemical laden variety throughout their lives.

Not feeling up to tackling the mind boggling job of attempting to return the aircraft into deeper water just yet, instead electing to sit for a while longer in the rays of the soothing sunlight engrossed for a time in our own private worlds, for reasons best known to him he seemed to have an inner need to talk to someone he respected and trusted about why he had been driven to seeking closure in such a remote area, perhaps in the hope of finding elusive peace and comfort from the devils that pursued him in the silence of the north, and if seeking justification for having done so.

In time the onerous truth of what still remained to be accomplished ahead of me began to nag at me, to be honest about it I had absolutely no idea as to how to begin the difficult if not near impossible task of moving the aircraft back into deeper water but knew I couldn't procrastinate for much longer even though the ramifications of what it entailed left me weak in the knees as no matter how one viewed it, the job bound to be a bugger as floats moved ahead much easier then backwards on sand as the weight tends to move rearward when attempting to force them to move backwards as the float skegs on the very bottom of the step compartments tends to dig in when attempting to do so. Goddamit how we sweated and slaved for almost the entire day on that heart breaking task to in the end having accomplished very little except to near freeze our nuts off while being forced to wade in the icy cold water, our lower extremities may have been blue with cold, but the air surrounding us superheated from our sweat and heated cursing. It shouldn't be too difficult to imagine the immensity of the herculean task we faced in attempting to lever a dead weight of almost seven thousand pounds of recalcitrant metal sitting in soft sand backwards into deeper water where it would float free. As I knew they would the skegs created all sorts of difficulties when predictably digging in forcing me to bite the bullet and out of dire necessity to reluctantly submerge my protesting body into the frigid water to frantically attempt to dig out the sand from around them using only a tin can to clear away a sufficient space to allow the placing of a short pole under the skeg. There is simply no easy way to describe how increasingly difficult each following dive became, even when taking the time between session to partially thaw out in the warm sun with my ability to endure the feelingly cold water for any length of time becoming shorter between each successive attempt until being forced to cease before expiring from the debilitating effects of hypothermia, but not before barely managing to jam two short poles under the skeg of one float.

If I had found the digging clear the skeg of the first float almost beyond human endurance, that most onerous of tasks proving to be a mere prelude of what still lay ahead of me with my once completing my last immersion found it almost impossible to thaw out even after drinking a pot of scalding hot coffee and basking in the rays of the hot sun wrapped up in my sleeping bag shaking like a dog pissing razor blades, found the thought of once more being forced to endure the rigors of submerging my severely quaking much abused body in icy water almost more than one could bear, but having little choice but to do so and some how with supreme effort fuelled by sheer desperation mustered up the will power to finally do the first of many dives, succeeding in accomplishing what I had set out to do if barely so before running out of endurance and will power, upon the completion of the final dive emerging feeling sick and dizzy, unable to control the violent trembling that wracked my very being for some time to come, the violent reaction signaling my having reached the end of the rope for that day spending the remainder of it in thawing out and regaining my strength.

The following morning we once more tackled that most difficult but necessary task of freeing the floats from the sand by digging along side of them until the water flowed under them and then placing poles under each of the floats for the keels to ride on until able by dint of excruciatingly hard labor managed to with the aid of a series of long poles to act as levers and an ample supply of home grown ingenuity coupled with a fierce determination to succeed eventually inch by hard won inch re floating the aircraft much to our profound relief. With trembling limbs we gratefully swung it around to heel the floats into the beach securing the aircraft to some large boulders that had been driven far up onto the beach by the ice pack's irresistible force, again I had to marvel at how effortlessly the unthinkable power of the ice made it all seem, the indescribable powers of nature relentlessly driving untold millions of tons of thick unyielding ice that effortlessly moved, crushed and scoured all before it as it implacably advanced onto the shore line. One could only marvel at nature's unlimited powers and at how puny the powers of man outside of his mindless penchant for destruction.

The huge sand beam that lay back a good distance from the beach the results of the ice being driven by the wind with it's effortlessly bulldozing untold tons of sand before it where the wave action and wind would eventually see to the final sculpturing and smoothing of the ravaged beach and sand beam, if one cares to take the time to observe, much of natures beauty and design is self explanatory if one cares to study the how and why's it occurred in the first place, it's there for all to plainly see and appreciate if they would only spare the time to do so.

A few hours later a hesitant check made inside the float to find it still remained relatively dry much to my everlasting relief, and with good conscience replaced the access panel, by the time that minor job had been accomplished a great weariness came over me, worn out from the incessant hard labor and stress endured for so long as to have to fight off an overwhelming desire to drop in my tracks.

After napping for a couple of hours and eating a decent meal once more felt reasonably fresh and renewed to the point of making the suggestion we go fishing again feeling we deserved some time to relax after our daunting labors. This time we ventured further afield until coming to the bottom of a large stretch of rapids to find a pool of relatively quiet water, as before the lure had barely struck the water when a mighty explosive swirl of agitated water off to one side of were my bait had hit the water startled me and a few seconds later receiving a terrific jolt on the fishing rod, but this time not caught unawares with the line again singing rapidly off my reel as a large fish ran with the lure to finally stop shortly before my reel running out of available line going deep to sulk, these actions convinced me it wasn't a trout but not at all sure what it was until after spending some time playing it managed to coax it up into the shallow water by the rocky shore line to just about drop the rod in amazement when viewing the outline of the largest northern pike I had ever seen or heard of, the prospector who had come over to see what all the fuss was about his eyes coming near to bugging out of his head upon first sighting the impressive size of the massive pike to breath in awe, Jesus Christ man I never knew they existed this far north or they could possibly get that big, god dam it must go at least fifty sixty pounds or better, my god what a hell of a fish! As we admired the monster pike out lined in the clear water the white bars against a dark green background looking for all the world like a huge speckled green log lying dogo in exhaustion fanning it's over large gill plates while occasionally shaking a head that appeared in all respects to be the size of a five gallon pail. To my way of thinking that magnificently superior creature was meant to be released to continue procreating a superior line of northern pike, it's somehow surviving untold odds in it's eat or be eaten world to have attained the size it had deserved a far better fate then ending up in some sportsman's trophy room, my not being one who seeks recognition in the slaughter of fish or game simply for the sake of boast decided there and then it be released cut the line to watch in unconcealed awe it's return to the murky depths from where it had first come gliding silently down to disappear from sight, I could sense that the prospector had approved of that decision by the pleased look in his eyes. As could be expected we once again began to hook smaller fish once the large pike had disappeared into the depths, my getting quite the surprise to reel in a hefty white fish, normally they don't readily bite on artificial lures but we continued to catch a good number of them before calling it quits for the day.

Having little else to do again sat up for half of what passed for night fall in them latitudes discussing every thing in general and nothing in particular, my finding him astute and widely read on top of being well informed on any subject one cared to discuss before calling it a day and rolling up gratefully into our sleeping bags to enjoy a well earned rest. Morning as it always does when one is at peace with the world seemed to come far to early with breakfast turning out to be a sober affair, both of us reluctant to part company and as much as I desired to remain there with him the obligations that awaited my return demanded I leave immediately.

After having shaken hands with him reluctantly departed to return to the crush of the every day world. The long boring return flight gave me ample time to reflect on the happenings of the last few days, the strange unexplained guidance that led me to make use of a slab of bacon and other available materials required to make an effective repair job to the float, again it is left to the individual reader to arrive at their own conclusions. During the latter part of august once more made the dauntingly long trip to Dubawnt lake but in a more trying and demanding manner being forced into Churchill by foul weather for three long days before the conditions improved marginally enough to allow my traveling part of the way up the forbidding dodging spates of bad weather and patches of fog coast line before turning inland to nervously pick my way from lake to lake the rest of the way in to Dubawnt lake to retrieve the by now badly frightened and near hysterical prospector who had tears of relief running down his cheeks upon my arrival having convinced himself to be stranded for he didn't know how long before being rescued if at all, in my way of thinking he should have by all rights left two weeks earlier to have remained on the safe side for as it was we experienced a hair raising time of it in making our way back to Churchill returning much the same way I had come, relieved beyond words to barely be able to sneak into landing lake at Churchill before the weather closed in again with our gladly holing up for another four days before eventually arriving at Lynn lake in less than ideal weather conditions, I would like to think he learned it is not wise to remain in that part of the country after the first part of august. Well so ended another strange adventure, as mentioned at the beginning there are strange things done, beneath the midnight sun!

Nu-Elthin-TUA

The Lake Of The Island that sleeps like a man.

AT ONE POINT IN MY career as a bush pilot eventually found myself bored to death with flying the same old tired out junk de jour on a regular basis chose to seek employment outside the immediate area for available flying jobs lucking out when a commercial fisherman friend of mine informed me the fish company he dealt with had been seeking a high time pilot to fly their float equipped beech craft based out of Lynn Lake Manitoba. At first this seemed rather odd to me as their certainly was no dearth of experienced beech craft drivers but decided to follow up on it any how.

Making a hasty trip to Winnipeg after making an appointment over the phone to meet with the owner Roy Page of Neptune's Fisheries. His immediately accepting my qualifications and shortly being approved by the insurance company plus the fact he was impressed with my holding a valid Air Craft Engineers License, the job beginning on the first of May of that year with his extensively outlining the extent of the area we would cover at one time or another a demanding program that would definitely keep one busy from break up till freeze up as it covered just about all of Manitoba, Northern Saskatchewan and Alberta, the North West Territories and finally North Western Ontario, quite the ambitious program for one aircraft.

Having spent two weeks checking over the aircraft at Riverton Manitoba where it had been stored for the winter prior to beginning the season, looked forward to flying a spirited beech my having drooled over and longed to fly one of them for some time feeling a thrill shoot through me each time I watched one of them marvelous aircraft thunder off the water in such a rapid and effortless manner it made my senses swim.

Well the day finally came around when it was time to strut my stuff, never having up till then flown a beech on floats or any other configuration as far as that went totally unprepared for what came next. The boss Roy Page had unexpectedly come out that day to accompany me on my maiden flight not being the least aware of my having blatantly lied about having previous beech craft experience.

Once the aircraft sat in the water ready to go the engines cranked up in what I assumed to be a well practiced professional manner taxied out in to the middle of the river were a brisk wind blew straight down the pike, once completing the required pre-flight checks (all very professionally of course) yanked up the water rudders as if I had been doing it in a beech craft for years then to rapidly advance the throttles to full take off power while still remaining mentally locked into the "Norseman" take off mode, what happened next left me totally stunned as the aircraft being empty and light on fuel literally leapt up on to the step to within a very short space of time to virtually rocket into air and begin a rapid climb out with my initially hanging on while going along for the ride for the first few seconds before being able to utter a mental "Jesus Christ, Hail Mary and god dam what a beast and all that sort of shit, my being awed beyond belief at it's magnificent performance, actually if the truth be known it had not been planned on my part to perform such a cavalier take off in the best of cow boy style, but that marvelous aircraft from the first simply left me in it's dust.

The owner Roy Page who I was most certain would have been hardly impressed with such a hairy first take off surprised the hell out of me by emitting a loud exuberant whoop and slapping me on the shoulder in appreciation of what I considered to be less then professional performance, enthusiastically exclaiming I sure as hell could get that aircraft to perform, man you sure are one hell of a beech pilot. I have often wondered what he would have thought if he had ever become aware of it being my very first time as pilot in command (well almost) of a beech craft?.

From then on it proved to be a non-stop torrid love affair between the beech craft and I!.

My first trip for the company consisted of flying the full length of lake Winnipeg to eventually end up at a beautiful spot at it's top end where the play green river mouth began known as 'Warren's Landing".

located at the narrowest part where the fast flowing currents could only be described as absolutely vicious with crystal clear waters that seemed to magnify the nearness of the Volks Wagon sized boulders strewn all across the bottom appearing to be only inches below the surface initially scaring me half to death upon landing. It took a few days to completely swallow my anus back down to it's normal position. Roy Page got quite a charge at my fright assuring me the water to be quite deep and safe to move through but I just never did get used to that place though flying in and out of it many times without mishap. As it went our spending many the hour flying all over hell's half acre visiting a score or more of potential customers finally arriving many days later at Lynn Lake. Once settled in began the first part of the summer operation flying into the vast and extremely beautiful Reindeer Lake to a location know as "Jack Pine Island" where I was to meet a huge bluff man about three hundred and fifty pounds with a shiny pate and bulging eyes known as "Ingevar Stolberg, an entrepreneur of the local fishing industry, our hitting it off immediately my finding him to be one of the most kind hearted considerate people I had ever met up till then, his proving to be a pleasure to work with. One could say with absolute certainty of his being lionized by his considerable sized crew of native and a sprinkling of hard-core white fishermen.

In time as we got to know each other through long and close association eventually became the best of friends.

The fishing operation he oversaw one of the largest and most efficient in scale I had ever laid eyes on, his must having at the least fifty full time fishermen producing copious amounts of fish on his behalf every day of the week, Among his retinue where six white men who had gone "native" having married Indian women ultimately producing the most handsome and intelligent half breed children I ever had the pleasure of meeting (the young ladies could only be described as absolutely stunning) they're being as a matter of course pampered outrageously by their white fathers, though admittedly very outgoing, polite and well mannered with most of them being well educated. Once they got past their initial shyness with me we became very close.

As it went Ingevar`s total production alone proved to be far greater than could be efficiently handled by one aircraft even flying up to ten trips a day. It had become apparent there was no way in god's green earth I would even begin to handle the pending production from Kasba (white partridge) and Neultin (Nu Elthin tua) lakes on top of Ingevar`s daily production. To the company's credit after my outlining the fact of my rapidly becoming overwhelmed by the sheer volume of fish produced recognized this eventual short coming and purchasing a fine performing Norseman CF-BEM to handle the short hauls with my helping out whenever possible with the beech craft.

One of my extraneous duties consisted of taking a cheque presented to me by Ingevar made out to "cash" for the sum of anywhere between fifty to seventy five thousand dollars to be converted into cold hard cash depending on that weeks scale of production, the money was made up in various denominations by the bank clerks as the fishermen where always paid in cash every Friday.

This as can be expected an awesome amount of long green to be responsible for as lugging it around town while carrying out other demanding errands naturally kept me on edge until being able to place into the security of my cockpit and to eventually see it safely delivered to it's rightful owner. The very first time I innocently took one of them large cheques to the bank it produced quite an unforeseen kerfuffle among the bank staff who up till then had never laid eyes on me, it going to the extreme of my being covertly accused of forging the cheque with the manager out right refusing to honor it threatening to call the police on me if not evacuating the premises immediately, of course this totally unexpected situation leaving me humiliated to a stand still at the raw treatment received from their pig headed stupidity, embarrassed and angry from the needless rejection received from the bank manager and his smug staff returned to jack pine Island still seething inwardly to inform Ingevar of what had transpired. What made it so much worse it happened to be pay day with the dock lined to sinking with expectant fishermen waiting to be paid as they usually where once a week. Upon receiving the bad news I feared he was about to experience a case of apoplexy with his moon like features instantly turning a hideous mottled purple with burgeoning rage, appearing to swell up like an oversized bullfrog to bellow out a thundering "Py Tundering Cheezus" in such a loud voice all the confused onlookers involuntarily cringed while stepping back a foot or two. Eventually regaining control of his emotions he began to speak in a quivering voice so choked up with ill concealed fury and emotion I feared he was experiencing a heart attack. Turning to the fishermen gathered on the dock he assured them he would look after the situation as he had always had and would be accompanying me to town to straighten out a certain bank manager. Placing him in the right hand front seat prior to loading no mean feat for a man of his girth where he quietly sat while quivering in great indignation until the loading completed and on our way.

God dam I thought to myself, I would not care to be in that insufferably arrogant bank managers shoes when Ingevar latched on to him. By the time we arrived he had worked himself up into a towering rage rumbling incoherently under his breath. Once reaching the bank experienced great difficulty in suppressing a smirk of grim satisfaction at what I knew must come, Ingevar didn't enter the bank as much as explode into it bellowing at the top of his stentorian voice demanding to know vere iss dat shit head of a manager as he strode malovently forward like a runaway bull dozer to stick his sweaty face next to the trembling female clerk's who involuntarily cringed away, once certain to have her undivided attention he let out another thunderous bellow that shook the very rafters when demanding to see dat shit head of a manager god dam quick like that of course caused every one in the building to turn to-ward him in alarm, if nothing else he sure knew how to get the onlookers undivided attention. As soon as the thoroughly frightened female teller could re-arrange her ruffled feathers she scuttled back to the managers office to summon him post haste, without question he had been duly alerted by Ingevar`s initial thunderous bellow and now cringing fearfully in the dubious safety of his office had little choice but to make a shaky appearance with a sickly look on his pasty features where upon Ingevar instantly pounced on him demanding to know in no uncertain terms who in the "tundering cheezus" he thought he was refusing to honor his cheque as he waved it in the flustered manager's face reducing the poor helpless bugger to ashes while threatening to change banks. Each time the manager impotently attempted to placate Ingevar by squeaking out soothing words they only served to inflame his ire to a greater degree. By this time Ingevar had once more worked himself up into a towering rage with my fearing for his health decided against better judgment to step in and attempt to calm him down if at all possible my gently but firmly taking him by the arm calmly advised him to back off and settle down before he suffered a heart attack, strangely enough to my ever lasting surprise he first looked questioningly at me then becoming instantly docile subsiding to muttering dark threats under his breath.

The bank manager finding himself in a terrible state of helpless embarrassment stripped naked by sheer fury of ingevar's attack in front of the customers and bank staff with a sick look having taken over his usual bland features stuttered his final apologies taking the opportunity afforded him upon my stepping in to attempt to calm ingevar down wasted no time in scuttling back into the sanctuary of his office to lick his wounds and salvage what remained of his shattered prides, from that moment on all other bank transactions temporarily halted while we waited impatiently for the required sum of money to be counted out and placed into a canvas bag with ingevar continuing to rumble and growl like a long dormant volcano slowly awakening, but once having settled the situation to his satisfaction had agreed to accept an apology from the well shaken manager.

The huge amount of cash much to my surprise being put together in record time by the clerks who no doubt only wished to see ingevar gone and their usual dull routine restored worked at counting out the required amount with great efficiency until completed, upon receiving the canvas bags of cash we made our way back to the base but not before making a slight detour to pick up a special order of "Glen Fiditch" finest of scotch whiskey's from the local liquor store. Once loaded with drums of fuel and fish tubs returned to jack pine island to pay off the now ecstatic fishermen Needless to say from then on no further problems of any sort arose with the bank with nothing further coming about to embarrass me upon my personally presenting the cheque, the money always ready within the hour no questions asked. The first long trip to Neultin Lake came about in late spring, a distance of slightly over two hundred and fifty miles one-way. No one could be certain if the ice on that huge expanse of lake had gone out but the company willing to chance the considerable expense involved for the sooner they could set up a viable operation the sooner the high quality fish products could be flown to market. As it stood the all too real possibility of the lake surrounding the camp still being frozen over with my loading an eager crew of Lake Winnipeg commercial fishermen we where off to what lay ahead of us we where yet to know. Arriving over the south end of the huge lake we noted the ice had just recently broken away from the shore in places, that made it almost certain we weren't about to find open water further north where the main fish camp was located. Upon arrival it was as I first suspected it would be, only an endless glittering expanse of blue white ice to be seen clear to the horizon. Of course the eager fishermen who had feverently hoped it to be otherwise where understandably bitterly disappointed at the apparent delay they now faced in setting up in preparation of the coming season. Not willing to give up in defeat just yet flew as close as I dared in order to check out it's surface, pleased to note it on for the most part appearing to be as flat and smooth as a billiard table with consecutive low fly by's convincing me it worth the risk. Consulting the crew on my upcoming plans to make a landing on the ice though being a new and unique experience for them met with instant approval when assuring them it not to be much different then landing on water or so I feverently hoped as it was virtually impossible to make a slow approach and touch down in a heavily loaded beech craft, our minimum touch down speed being slightly in excess of one hundred and five miles per hour.

Having perused the chosen landing area more or less to my satisfaction even though my belly suddenly came alive with butterflies the size of bats decided to go for it hoping against hope a ridge of ice hadn't gone unnoticed as it would only take a very minor one to severely damage the float keels. On completing what could be termed as a scorching touch down and as the aircraft gradually slowed down it's full weight gradually settling onto the floats with a noticeable tightening of my scrotum taking place in fear full anticipation of sliding over an unseen ridge of ice bracing myself for the possibility of an impact, to my everlasting relief we slowly slid to a smooth stop without incident, when all had settled down to a muted roar my initially experiencing slight difficulty unclenching my fingers off the throttle levers and control wheel and settling down in my seat with a heart felt sigh of relief thinking to myself "Look for a fool and you will find him here. Yes fortunately for me all had gone well and could expect an accolade from the company for showing great initiative, yet I knew deep down inside if it had gone wrong what one could expect for attempting to pull off what would be viewed as foolish daring.

I didn't doubt for a minute the crew of fishermen had collectively held their breath as we began the approach and touch down as they unexpectedly gave off a mighty cheer as we slid to a stop unscathed. I am not in the least ashamed of admitting to at first being unable to totter out of the aircraft on shaky legs so great had been the tension experienced on landing, I had taken a calculated risk and won and as stated previously sure to be applauded for my expertise and daring, but not fool enough to not understand the consequences one would have faced if it had gone otherwise.

When able to walk without fear of collapse climbed out of the cockpit to supervise the unloading, the crew who had eagerly piled out of the door upon our coming to a full stop and anxious to get moving, some dispatched themselves to the nearest shore line to cut small pine trees to be used to mark out the safe stretch of runway we had so fortuitously had managed to land on using the straight line marks cut into the surface of the ice by the float keels while others busied themselves cutting small holes in the ice with needle bars to receive them. From then on it was a ridged practice by the most trusted among them to carefully examine the entire length of the runway every day before my daring to land knowing all too well the ice surface could shift at any time, one simply didn't take chances if at all possible to avoid doing so, fortunately the ice held all during our initial tenure though admittedly each landing and take off an adventure unto itself.

Once having done all I could to help the crew unload, now came the time for my very first take off on ice with a beech craft on floats, having personally scouted the take off area quite a ways ahead of my potential take off path as their was just no way it being possible to turn an aircraft of any size on an ice surface as the keels cut in deeply preventing anything but a straight line take off run. Not sure what to expect it proved to be a very tense but exhilarating experience as once having applied full power the aircraft jumped ahead like a turpentined dog accelerating rapidly, but the faster we went the lower the nose seemed to dip no matter how hard one pulled back on the control column the aircraft stubbornly refused to leave the ice surface, by now we where thundering along at a very high rate of forward speed momentarily leaving me with the awful fear it would never unstick, In unthinking desperation the electrically controlled flaps where lowered to the full down position, as they came into the full down position against the rapid air flow the aircraft literally exploded into the air climbing like a home sick angel in the most horrid nose low attitude ever experienced keeping me busy dancing on the rudder pedals, retracting flap and re-setting the trim, all in all a very busy few moments. So that's the secret of flying a beech off the ice I mused to my self, a lesson well learned.

Well that most unique experiences gave me something to think about fortunately for my peace of mind the reaming supply trips proved to be straight forward though each landing on the ice a unique experience, one much like the other and yet no two alike with no surprises upsetting our routine except on the very last trip .

Shortly after landing and still in the process of unloading the aircraft one of the crew suddenly spotted a diminutive dark wizened figure standing beside a team of three wolfish appearing sled dogs, who ever he was to us seeming to have appeared out of thin air but remaining well back from us as if uncertain of his welcome, needless to say his sudden and unexpected appearance startled everyone no end none of us being aware of another living soul within three hundred miles or better, but there he stood big as life staring curiously at us as we jointly stared back open mouthed not sure just what to make of his totally unexpected presence. Studying him closely it being noted he couldn't have been more than a little over five feet tall, weather beaten and whip cord lean, his elfish face clean shaven with deeply inset twinkling blue eyes that squinted at us against the glare of the shiny ice surface. Without a doubt to an onlooker we would have appeared as a frozen "tableau", all visible movement having instantly ceased with each man freezing into what ever position he may have assumed at the time upon first spotting the stranger, almost if time stood still.

After what seemed to have been a protracted period of time he made the first move when retrieving his snow anchor from a small sled to bury it firmly into the soft ice then uttering a guttural command we found out later to be Swedish to his three beautiful appearing wolf dogs who then reluctantly but warily lay down on the ice never taking their yellow eyes off us .

Having some what recovered from the initial shock of unexpectedly meeting up with some one in such a remote area finally found our tongues offering him a friendly greeting while apologizing for our outwardly rude behavior upon initially becoming aware of his presence as we really hadn't expected company where upon we shook hands and introduced ourselves. It was only then the realization I had finally gotten to meet the elusive barren grounds trapper I had oft heard about but had never met up till now. He was to my knowledge the only resident trapper in the whole area of Neultin lake and I was to find out much later having resided and trapped there on a year around basis for the last sixty one years living alone all that time with just his dogs for company, somehow I found it difficult to imagine how he had managed to do it.

Adhering to the inflexible code of the North we offered him refreshments back at the camp, one couldn't help but note how his eyes lit up at the prospect of imbibing in much different fare than he was used to, his accepting with alacrity yanking up the ice anchor and shouting a command at the dogs made off for the camp helter skelter. Of course it took much longer for us to walk to the camp where we found him busily erecting an exceedingly filthy appearing one man tent back behind the main cabin, nervously we looked around for his wolf dogs as they where not to be seen, while talking to ragnar the hair on the back of my neck began to resemble a hair brush, turning slowly to be able to look behind me almost jumped out of my skin with fright to find one of them less then five feet away staring unblinkingly at me with cold yellow eyes, a totally fascinating and unnerving experience that left me unsure of my self as we sized each other up for a short spell of time before it gracefully turned then appearing to vanish like a puff of smoke, now that really gave me a bad case of the willies.

The fishermen where to inform me later they had at one point become almost afraid to leave the safety of their cabin individually in fear of the dogs, my eventually having to tell ragnar if he wished to remain within the vicinity of the camp he would have to either remove them elsewhere or chain them up, he did not welcome this edict at all but within the period of a few days reluctantly deposited them on a nearby small island once the ice had gone out where he took food out to them by boat every day so they did not suffer unnecessarily.

As it went once ragnar had completed setting up his "mobile Home" he appeared expectantly at the cook shack, upon entering removed his filthy beyond belief heavy caribou skin parka as it was quite warm, he didn't appear to stink of accumulated body odors but more of the pungent odor of a carnivorous wild animal, best described as a blood and fur sort of smell. For some strange reason that cannot be readily explained the strange odors emanating from him caused all of us to feel uneasy, almost as if being in the presence of a wild animal,

threatened but not threatened, during their entire stay the fishermen never became truly at ease in his presence .

Within a short period of time since he sat down at the table he had greedily gulped down several cups of over sweetened tea while choking down a good quantity of large camp cookies with the single minded voraciousness of a half starved animal leaving us awed with his seemingly endless capacity. Covertly observing him shamelessly stuffing himself with sweet tea and cookies it suddenly dawned on me he had been sugar starved for over a year, existing on a monotonous diet of caribou and fish and a little flour having run clean out of staples long before we arrived there.

Eventually he was to grudgingly relate a tale of woe that shocked me to the quick upon informing me we where the first people he had seen in the last two years, having become too old and fragile to further endure the travails that would have to been his lot during the long overland journey to Churchill or Brochette on Reindeer Lake could only wait and hope for the arrival of the supply aircraft that would never come, and up to the time of our unexpected arrival a very faint hope any one having just reason to venture into that barren area.

As it went it had by his own admission become a close run thing his having near given up hope had in helpless despair gradually sunk into a morass of apathy resigning himself to his fate. It wasn't until my unknowingly flying almost overhead of his cabin on my second trip on my way to the fish camp did he realize that something had to be taking place at the long abandoned fish camp. With hope springing anew he managed to dredge up the will to rouse himself from the deep lethargy that leads to death that had come so near to claiming him to slowly make his way there with his half starved wolf dogs, an exceedingly difficult trip his being weak from the ravages of old age and poor diet taking him the better part of two days of travel with the added burden of uncertainty of not knowing if anyone to be found at the fish camp upon his arrival, well aware if called for he would have never had the strength to return to his cabin. As it was he only had about another ten miles or so to go when he observed me making my landing approach with floats instead of skis leaving him uncertain what I had in mind for as he well knew there was no open stretches of water to land in within the area that time of the year until coming close enough to see much to his surprise the aircraft sitting on the ice, at first being confused thought he was seeing things as he had never heard or seen any pilot do such a thing before, but in any case overwhelmingly happy to see us no matter how unique our manner of arrival.

If he had been surprised to see us then we where that much more so, It seems he had in the past heard a few aircraft flying by but always at a great height, it was a good feeling to know one had putting aside the fact of inadvertently doing so saved another's life, I was to eventually become a close friend as he in time learned to know and trust me, his seemingly taciturn nature gradually thawing out as he once more became accustomed to being near people again.

One early summer evening when having chose to remain overnight we sat companionably with his being well fed and having tobacco for his pipe, his world all well again with a much improved outlook on life puffed contentedly on his ancient stinky old pipe for all the world resembling a miniature wizened steam engine obviously enjoying the tobacco he had craved for so long being without for over a year now in all respects appearing to be doing his best to make up for it. He was wearing his usual now familiar to me far away and long ago look in his shuttered eyes having become so withdrawn as to almost blend in with the shadows produced by the glow of the gas lamps that didn't quite reach the far corners of the room, after a protracted period of time he would rouse him self almost reluctantly to mutter inaudibly to himself while knocking the dottle from his pipe in a half dreamy fashion as if returning from a long journey in the recesses of his mind gazing absent mindedly around him as if not having quite made up his mind to go or to stay. If the mood happened to be right it would require very little prompting to have him relate in great detail the many years spent as a barren land's trapper on Neultin Lake, the more he revealed the more fascinated I became with his daring exploits.

On my last trip that late spring season the ice surface having become far too treacherous to push it any further called it quits. Estimating it to be at least a week to ten days before being able to return at open water, our not having reliable radio communication left me to more or less guesstimate when the ice would move out. That was when ragnar`s vast knowledge of the ice conditions on Neultin Lake came in to play, his confidently predicting to the day when the ice that averaged ten feet or more in thickness would be broken up and moved out by the wind. Also we made good use of his long time knowledge of the lake in pointing out to the fishermen the prime locations in which to set their nets marking each spot clearly on the map enjoying himself hugely in being able to be of some assistance to us. The fishermen if not totally at ease in his presence had by now become quite fond of him referring to ragnar as their "hungry Mascot" referring to his willingness to eat huge amounts of food at any time of the day or night rightfully earning him that moniker. We where all amazed and pleased to see the change that good and substantial food had brought over him our being well rewarded in witnessing his returning energy and zest for life becoming openly energetic and "Chirpy" as he lost his reticence toward the fishermen taking great pleasure in offering to help them prepare and set their nets in highly productive areas.

The men were to inform me on the day of the second last trip Ragnar had mysteriously disappeared, when thinking on it the only logical place he could or would have reason to go to would be his cabin for reasons only known to him returning to the camp on the afternoon of my last trip in until open water with his sled piled high with jute sacks stuffed with a variety of fur, mostly species of timber and arctic wolf pelts, his total harvest of the last two years requesting my taking them back to Lynn Lake with me, this request not one to be taken lightly as it indelibly demonstrated his total trust in me, judging from what could be viewed of it the total market value would easily exceed fifty thousand dollars, when readily agreeing to do so presented me with a smaller bundle saying this is a small gift of appreciation for what you have done for me. Later investigation proved it to be two extremely rare prime whitish yellow long furred arctic wolf pelts of considerable rarity and value.

On the prescribed day the ice had been forecast by Ragnar to have gone out my heart fell to my toes upon sighting huge floes of ice jamming the south end of the lake with miles of solid ice as far as the eye could see, god dam talk about anxious minutes while flying over it's seemingly endless expanse until nearing the site of the fish camp to be relieved beyond measure to discover a large ice free area surrounding it.

Ragnar of course met me at the dock wearing a grin you could see a mile giving off a self satisfied hearty chuckle went on to say hah, I'll just bet what your thoughts were upon flying over the south end of the lake, snicker snicker, obviously he enjoyed being dead on about the ice going out when he predicted it would, well one could say my being grateful he had been, later on one of the fishermen privately informed me the ice had only moved out four hours prior to my arrival, now that's calling it mighty close.

It proved to be quite the occasion upon presenting Ragnar with two years of accumulated mail that had been forwarded from Churchill to Lynn Lake on request along with a receipt for his fur, his eyes really lit up on spotting the cartons of outdated magazines, books news papers etc.

The fishing being so productive I flew on the average two round trips per day weather permitting till the end of the season, sometimes remaining overnight to give myself a brief respite from my never ending flight duties and to rapturously listen to Ragnar's endlessly captivating tales of his life as a barren lands trapper. When ever he chose to fire it up when making one of his visits to the island to feed his dogs we all got the dammdest charge out of his ancient outboard engine known as a "water Witch", one of the strangest weird appearing contraptions any of us had ever laid eyes on, one could hear it coming or going for at least twenty miles on a quiet windless day giving off a prodigious stuttering cough that assailed one's ears at close quarters when running that appeared to be far out of proportion to it's size while emitting copious amounts of foul smelling bluish white smoke, for all the ear shattering sound and fury emitting from it, to the onlooker appearing to produce little in the way of noticeable thrust as the canoe barely created a ripple at the bow with our laughing ourselves weak every time we watched that diminutive shapeless bundle crouched over in the stern of his totally unseaworthy canoe with his old fashioned soft billed salt and pepper hat placed on backwards and firmly pulled down to his eyes as if he were running flat out at the "Daytona Five Hundred" while his three dogs stretched out of sight on the bottom of the canoe as if embarrassed to be part of the scene.

Then as if out of the blue Ragnar inquired if it would be at all possible to wangle a few days off as he had something of interest he wished to show me. Having by then become some what ragged from the unceasing demands of flying long hours every day badly needed a break from my demanding routine, in due course having arranged it made it a point to arrive back at Neultin Lake at late evening to secure the aircraft safely to the mooring buoy for the night to return to the cook shack for a delicious meal of fresh caught lake trout and fresh brewed coffee and of course an enjoyable gab fest with Ragnar.

Try as I might, no amount of persuasion or cajoling could induce him to reveal what he had in mind. The next morning saw us on our way making use of a hefty fifty horse power out board engine with one of the fishermen who chose to accompany us out of curiosity that quickly sped us to the far north west corner of the lake expertly guided by Ragnar who stood in the bow seemingly impervious to the icy blast of wind created by our rapid passage across the wind swept lake until reaching a group of small rocky islands, as we neared them Ragnar cautioned the fisherman to go dead slow until coming much closer to a high jumbled rocky head land that initially gave no indication of allowing a way past it, only when coming up along side of it did the narrow entrance suddenly reveal itself immediately finding ourselves entering an almost perfectly concealed inlet flanked by sheer rock walls that towered well above us on both sides of the narrow channel, very rarely had I ever had the pleasure of witnessing such awesome beauty, mother nature the ultimate artist had certainly out did herself in creating that unforgettable and alluring bit of landscape. But we were soon to learn that remote place had a poignant down side to it. The crystal clear water we carefully made our way over offered a slight current setting towards the entrance while revealing the alarming presence of huge boulders that lay on the bottom in scattered profusion appearing to loom within mere inches of the surface as if to snag the unwary at first startling the hell out of a few of us, that is except for ragnar who assured the helmsman the water to be of sufficient depth for the out board motor. After what seemed to be an interminably long period of twisting and turning in order to avoid shallow water and rocky outcrops made a final sharp turn around a breath taking pinnacle that jutted straight up out of the water like an inert sentinel we immediately spotted what appeared to be a an ancient camp site that boasted numerous circles of small boulders that had obviously been used at one time to hold down the skin tents of the inhabitant who had once camped there against the wind.

Upon disembarking we began a closer inspection of the what obviously had once been a heavily populated campsite. While busily engaged in exploring the camp site, out of curiosity picking up one of the what I thought at first to be strangely shaped small grayish green boulders, one of many that appeared to lie randomly through out the camp, at first upon picking it up to examine it quite shocked to discover it to be a human skull, the two gaping empty eye sockets immediately spooking me leaving one uncertain as to how to take this unexpected and grisly discovery could only stare at it in speechless confusion until ragnar who had noticed the confusion mirrored on my face came over to matter of factly inform me that we were standing on the site of a cold blooded massacre perpetrated by a roving band of Chipewyan caribou hunters, ancient and deadly enemies of the Inuit people who had often in times past when intruding into the domain of the Inuit people usually during the fall caribou hunt when availed of the opportunity to do so crept up on the unsuspecting Eskimo families as they slept, murdering them before they could collect their senses, it would appear that a great majority that had initially managed to escape the initial onslaught were to be mercilessly hunted down to be cold bloodedly dispatched.

Not being at all certain as to what methods the Chipewyan's employed in dispatching their victims, inquired of Ragnar if he perhaps knew, that being quickly answered upon his picking up one of the skulls to point out the evidence of blunt trauma {a heavy or severe blow to the head by a blunt object} as the skull indicating to have been severely crushed as if by a club or the flat side of an axe, most of the skulls we examined displaying the same trauma, some of them to the extent they closely resembled crushed egg shells, especially those who judging by the size of the skull to have been those of infants and young children. Ragnar admitted to not being certain to how many had been massacred but obviously if one were to judge by the remains it had once been a good sized tribe, ragnar conjectured the skeletal remains to consist mainly of women, children and the elderly as it to be certain the younger and more capable of the men who were the hunters had been most likely out on the land in pursuit of the caribou herds, otherwise the Chipewyan's would not have dared to attack the camp, it being most likely they're patiently waiting until the hunters had unsuspectingly left the camp in pursuit of the caribou herds leaving the helpless women, young and very old on their own before sneaking in while the camp slept. As much as I desired to clarify to a greater degree his seemingly extensive knowledge of the time and place the massacre had occurred then he had voluntarily revealed up till then and also how he had come across the location of the secret camp site and the perpetrators method of attack, but something warned me not to pursue it any further with my deciding it best not to inquire too deeply, but one could not help but to dwell on it's ramification.

Poking through the remains of the camp site only produced a few flint spear tips and a broken oil lamp, it being plain either the attackers had looted all of value or the survivors upon their return had claimed what little remained of their sparse possessions it proving very little of interest to be found.

Distractedly picking up another of the larger skulls to examine it closely in hope of determining the cause of death suddenly felt the hair on the back of my neck began to rise as a deathly cold chill swept over me near causing my fumbling and dropping the skull, at first some what uncertain of what had transpired momentarily taken aback by the unexpectedly strange sensation hesitating only briefly before hastily replacing the skull in the original depression in the moss to have the overwhelming feeling of dread leave as quickly as it had first come, this not being the first time to have experienced such a strange phenomena, having felt it a few times before, one is free to interpret the described sensation however they see fit, but to me it was an indelible message the spirits of the long dead continued to hover within the confines of the killing grounds.

For many years afterwards the chilling thought of them innocents being so cruelly attacked while they slept with the survivors methodically hunted down to be dispatched for no other reason but ancient tribal hatreds, one at best can only begin to speculate on the all consuming terror and panic of them who initially succeeded in escaping their would be murderer's initial attack.

Our eventual return to camp found me introspective and in a some what depressed state of mind, wishing feverently to have never been witness to man's inhumanity toward man though wisely keeping my thoughts to myself.

As it always has the course of events returning to it's normal but monotonous perspective with my flying two trips a day weather permitting The longer my association with Ragnar endured, the more my respect and liking him for the man he was grew, his presence at the fish camp the one constant I looked forward to never before having met up with such an independent and capable individual, my never seeming to be able to get enough of the tales of his survival in a cruel and demanding environment for the many years he had, something that only a few iron men of his ilk could have managed.

Often as we sat enjoying each other's company while we studied the placid waters of the lake his long subdued sense of humor would manifest itself when out of the blue taking a notion to yank my chain he would suddenly begin to study me with a mischievous grin plastered all over his weather beaten mug suddenly blurting out "I feel sorry for you, working your heart out for some else and living in that anthill of humanity in between times, initially rising to the bait would heatedly challenge his statement with a rejoinder soon coming to realize my having reacted exactly as planned it being quite plain his enjoying my outraged re-actions, now having tumbled to his ploy now only laughing at his futile efforts to turn my crank. But never was he reminded it was people like me with our marvelous technology that had barely saved him from starvation and supplied him with his worldly needs, some things are best not said.

When one takes into consideration his successfully having spent over sixty years in that most hostile of environments as a trapper without companionship of any kind save his sled dogs to share his life or thoughts with remaining against all odds marvelously astute and well informed of world events, his grudgingly admitting to having a dry cell battery powered radio which was used sparingly to conserve the battery. One day as we sat there discussing any worthwhile subject that came to mind suddenly got the notion to inquire of him as to just how he had gotten his fur to market in the past, my at first thinking it would have been most likely his having traveled by canoe to brochette located on Reindeer lake by making the arduous journey down the Cochrane river system that ran south out of neultin lake, his succinct reply near floored me when blandly stating his having often made his way by canoe down the seal river to Churchill, his stating that super human accomplishment so matter of factly my jaw must have near dropped clean to my knees, not certain of having heard him right the first time again inquired in a small voice, did you say Churchill via the seal river route?. At that he slowly removed the pipe from his mouth staring at me as if I had become totally de-railed and shaking his head as if trying to get a point across to a clueless child prompting me to make a quick trip to the aircraft to procure the appropriate maps for the area in question. When once placed before him he patiently pointed out his route from neultin lake to another large body of water known as "Seal Hole Lake" quite a ways north of our present location, to then make his precarious way down the full length of the seal river that offered a daunting series of torturous rapids, shooting the ones he safely could and portaging around the one's deemed unsafe or suicidal to attempt, my god I thought to myself what a hell of a man to be able to successfully descend such a terrible fast moving river my having had occasion to follow the length of it's entire course when coming in from Eskimo point on the coast of Hudson's Bay could only marvel at his aplomb, Christ it was almost unbelievable that any one could accomplish much less survive such a formidable undertaking, but did learn much later it to be done as a matter of course on a seasonal basis by many of the inland dwellers who traversed it's entire length when heading for Churchill to sell their furs or for what ever reason, if one cares to pursue the truth of the matter a well known author who wrote extensively of the barren land people also claimed to have made this treacherous journey, if so he then would be of the very select few white men to have done so and lived to tell about it.

Well as it went he gave me another thorough shaking up when going on to say once having reached the treacherous estuary of the seal river

he still faced a daunting journey of if my memory serves me well another ninety or so miles of shallow rock studded coast lines to at any given time remain subject to the vagaries of ferocious on shore winds while battling the uncertainties of formidable tides, all this in a fragile cockle shell of a canoe before reaching Churchill. Again one had to marvel at any one's accomplishing such an amazing feat of endurance, the very thought of doing so gave me pause for thought, though appreciative of the coast line's awesome beauty, not ever becoming comfortable with the omnipresent threat it presented when flying down it, even when traversing it's course in a reliable modern twin engine aircraft.

Not only did he knowingly face the aforementioned tides and the all too likely possibility of encountering high winds, treacherous currents and fogs that often without warning blanked out the area, all having to be overcome by a single individual without the benefit of modern navigation aides, only relying on his magnetic compass and weather sense to see him through, all accomplished in a fragile cockle shell of a canoe, no question about it that man had "chutzpah" I sure as hell didn't possess, Christ on a crutch just sitting there thinking about it made my knees go weak. One couldn't help but to admire such a man as he sat there unconcernedly puffing away on his pipe seemingly so contented with his lot in life, now a time worn shadow of the man he had once been, now an aging diminutive old man, so worn and fragile now, what a power house he must have been in his prime!.

Not remaining satisfied for long in hearing only part of his daring adventure, insisted on questioning him further, at first the best that could be gotten out of him was a derisive snort, and every so often a terse , why do you need to know for?, having by now figured out his moods played the waiting game having learned of his propensity to draw things out as long as possible patiently waited for the tell tale puffs of smoke that he rapidly gave off upon having decided to continue on, once he began to study his odiferous pipe as if it had bitten him on the ass when his attention had been directed elsewhere and then to knock out the dottle while muttering uncomprehendingly in Swedish to himself with dreamy eyes that had once more taken on the now familiar long ago and far away look as they wandered aimlessly around the room, a look I had long ago learned to recognize.

During the course of my career as a bush pilot which naturally put me at various times and places in close contact with many of them elusive individuals who for reasons best known to them chose to live apart from their fellow men in the remotest areas one could wish to visit, they where for the most part an extremely resourceful hardy breed of men, they had to be in order to survive the vicissitudes and demands of their chosen profession. But very rarely have I ever met them of ragnar`s ilk who where as capable in the art of survival in sub arctic conditions as he, having successfully thrived in a totally unforgiving environment with nothing more than his enduring ability to survive and thrive as a matter of course the most hostile and harsh of living conditions the land had to offer, but remarkably he did for over sixty years not only surviving but prospering as he appeared to have done. Perhaps unfortunately or otherwise their very nature itself failing to produce following generations of their stature, time as a matter of course eliminated them till this day non that I have any knowledge of remain on the land.

Never again will we know of such "Iron men", they where a breed apart, my respect for them and their abilities to this very day knows no bounds.

After what seemed to be an eternity he gave off a non committal shrug removing the odious pipe from his mouth, once again to knock out the dottle with a studied indifference, a definite sign he was willing to keep on relating his fascinating story. Upon re-charging his pipe and re-lighting it, satisfactorily puffed a few clouds of aromatic smoke while casting a glance around him as if not too certain where to begin. After some hesitation a shrug of the shoulders and emitting a great sigh of indifference, resignedly took up the threads of his story to continue relating a tale of such unbelievable endurance and daring that the very telling of it left me spell bound. Upon his eventual arrival at the estuary of the seal river at an opportune time as the tide was out, patiently waited for night fall when the on shore winds ceased to blow and the evening tide to rise sufficiently to safely float his canoe out through the treacherously narrow channel that led out of the mouth of the estuary, only then leaving the relative safety of the river mouth cautiously poling the canoe into sufficiently deep water to eventually crank up his water witch outboard engine, an ancient but obviously reliable one to motor approximately twenty miles out from the low lying shore line in order to avoid the treacherous shallow boulder strewn inshore waters for the dubious safety of deep water, this also gave him clear access to watch for the guiding beams of light from the powerful rotating beacon from the Churchill airport that could easily be seen for an unbelievable distance at night and even to a great degree during an overcast day, using this and setting a ridged compass course he would make his painfully slow way to Churchill taking any where from ten to twelve hours depending on the wind and tide conditions, if all went well he could easily home in on the flashing beacon, but still it must have taken some skill on his part to once having reached button bay were the out flow of the mighty Churchill river clashes with the tides creating a maelstrom of treacherous viciously swirling currents and to have safely navigated it's course until reaching calmer waters.

The mind numbing thought of finding myself out in the far reaches of the bay subject to the capricious whims of nature in a fragile cockle shell of a canoe floating on that god awful treacherous stretch of threatening waters for endless hours with the full knowledge if a sudden wind storm where to hit him he had very little chance of survival if swept into the shallow jagged shore line, the very thought of it gave me a supreme case of the goose bumps, but again one must give credit were credit is due, if nothing else he knew exactly what he did and knowing exactly what he faced tide and weather wise no decision concerning his ongoing safety and ultimate survival throughout that precarious journey ever made randomly.

Well for what it was worth, few men I ever knew would have attempted such a daring venture in a canoe outside of a few select Chipewyan's who accomplished that feat on a regular and ongoing basis, but it would seem he knew his stuff as he always arrived safely to peddle his furs to the H. B. C. purchasing his next years supplies to be flown in to Neultin lake either by Lamb Air or Arctic Wings.

On eventually becoming jaded with as he put it the overcrowded and boisterous town of Churchill and once again longing for the wide open spaces of his beloved Neultin Lake would begin to make his long and difficult journey back the way he had first arrived. Upon questioning why he chose to do it the hard way as he could have saved himself a lot of back breaking man killing effort by the simple expedient of flying back, this earned me a pronounced snort of derision, testily retorting he enjoyed the challenge that offered a break from his normal routine.

In a sense he had already bowed to the advent of air transport as previously having met up with a band of roving Chipewyan's who introduced him to the Seal River route, themselves on the occasion making a one way trip to Churchill as a change from their usual one to the Hudson's Bay post at Brochette on Reindeer Lake, but the difference being they're waiting until well after freeze up to make their way cross country to return to their normal trapping grounds unwilling to endure the man killing hardship of having to make multiple back breaking portages with their winters supplies upstream against the powerful and treacherous currents of the Seal River, ragnar on the other hand had his supplies flown in.

Gruffly informing me that prior to the availability of air transport he had often single handedly made the long and grueling journey to Brochette via the Cochrane River as soon as the ice retreated from the lake to peddle his furs at the Hudson's Bay Co. when for the most part disappointed in the on again off again presence of the free traders that when the price of white fox fur high enough to warrant their presence at the outpost located at Windy Lake on the south east corner of Neultin Lake deigned to appear, a hit and miss proposition at best, not to mention often being woefully short of supplies to trade with.

Besides that he looked forward to a break from his monotonous routine, the few short months of summer demanded his leaving as soon as possible and to not linger for too great a period of time as the arduous return journey against the river's current and many portages to cross packing his winters supplies on his back over each one, but admitting at the time totally reveling in the challenge.

At the time air transport being in it's infancy making it all but impossible to procure at Brochette eventually decided him on going the more difficult Seal River route to Churchill were air service though largely unreliable still available to a greater degree.

Reluctant to admitting to his advancing years and gracefully accepting that obvious fact, refused to bow to the knowledge of his not being as capable as he had once been, instead attempted one last trip that came near to being his undoing with the advent of less than ideal weather conditions delaying his return trip to the mouth of the seal river arriving well out from it's mouth just as the tide had ebbed. As it had become impossible to continue on due to the inescapable fact the water level had dropped to the degree he soon found himself on the verge of becoming hard aground surrounded by stinking rock strewn mud flats having little recourse but to wait out the long tension filled hours until the tide once more rose, totally at the mercy of the elements, for the first time in his long adventurous life as the long monotonous tension filled hours slowly dragged on by became truly aware for the first time in his long life of the debilitating effects of mind paralyzing fear.

Upon reaching that juncture of his fascinating narrative, he visibly gave off a slight shudder as if re-visiting the terrible memories of that ordeal, hesitating longer than usual as he performed the now familiar routine of re-packing his pipe that gave him the time to collect his thoughts, when once more lit and drawing on it furiously until satisfied with it's performance before once more taking up the threads of his story.

During the interim one couldn't help but to ponder his unenviable life threatening dilemma he unwillingly found himself in, forced by circumstances beyond his control to endure the terribly long fear filled hours trapped many miles away from the safety of the river perched precariously on a huge boulder surrounded by miles of stinking rock studded mud flat resignedly waiting for the tide to turn and what ever terrors and tribulations it brought with it, what his thoughts had been all through them endlessly long tension filled hours as he waited for the tide to turn he never said, but one can bet the farm they must have been some bleak, wisely I never inquired though burning up with morbid curiosity.

As it went the tide eventually turned as it always has with the rising waters viciously sweeping in aided by a cold wind that numbed him to the very marrow of his bones, as if that wasn't enough a vicious deluge of icy cold wind swept water rolled completely over the huge flat rock he was marooned on soaking his lower extremities to the skin compounding his already considerable misery on top of half filling the canoe with water he was forced to bail out as quickly and best he could. As the water level slowly began to rise the fragile bottom of the heavily laden canoe now at the mercy of the waves that unceasingly swept under it causing it to buck and pound as if taking on a life of it's own, time and time again bumping heavily against the rocky surface it had previously rested on leaving him with no choice but to leap overboard into the cold stinking mud in a desperate attempt to lighten the load and to if at all possible prevent it's being damaged from pounding against the unyielding boulder surface or at the worst being swept off the relative safely of the boulder into the jagged rocks surrounding him, fearfully accepting the fact if he failed to prevent that potentially disastrous occurrence or preventing it's gradually being pounded to pieces by the increasing wave motion, one way or the other he didn't stand a chance in hell of survival. To add to his considerable woes the rising waters also began to produce increasingly huge waves that frequently inundated him becoming ever larger dissipating their energy onto his precarious perch threatening his ability to retain a hold on the canoe against their implacable force much longer as the water continued to deepen, to have the canoe holed or to lose his desperate grip on it would have quickly spelled the end.

Fortunately for him as the water continued to deepen the canoe began to float free greatly lessening the threat of being damaged on the boulder's surface and when the depth of the water reached his waist he managed to clamber back aboard with great difficulty, a feat that in itself almost miraculous considering the difficulties he labored under, but some how managing to do so even being numbed by the protracted immersion in the icy waters that all but left him beyond feeling but in spite of it all grateful to have survived thus far, but fully cognizant of the fact the battle had not been won yet as he must at all costs if he hoped to survive prevent the wind and tide from hurling him on to the jagged boulders that guarded both sides of the river's mouth and also knowing the chilling possibility of when attempting to navigate it inadvertently encountering the rock strewn shallows lining the sides of the narrow channel that torturously threaded an uncertain path through the mud flats into the safety of the river estuary, to do so guaranteed tearing out the bottom of the canoe.

Despite herculean effort on his part to avoid such a happening soon to his increasing dismay finding it to be a losing battle in preventing his being swept onto the rocks like a chip in a mill race, the wind and waves easily overcoming his puny efforts with the end seeming inevitable until a huge wave unexpectedly came in from behind him to curl under his canoe and as it swept by the crest gradually losing it's energy dissociating as it did so miraculously depositing the canoe more or less gently onto a large flat shelving rock that lay only inches below the troubled waters jarring him soundly and cracking a few ribs in the canoe, but fortunately for him only considered to be minor damage to the canoe's structure much to his everlasting relief.

While being numbed almost beyond feeling from his previous immersion in the ice cold water that knotted his muscles so painfully they almost refused to respond, nevertheless still retaining the presence of mind while ignoring the burning pain of his knotted muscles to once again leap overboard in an effort to prevent the canoe from smacking against the flat rock as each succeeding swell curled under it seeming to give it a life of it's own at times gyrating wildly with the successive passing of each huge wave threatening to tear it loose from his benumbed unfeeling hands, only by sheer will power and an iron bound determination to survive did he manage to retain his desperate hold until the water reached up to his arm pits, only then by the greatest effort of will power barely managing to climb back onboard near the end of his endurance but more than willing to fight it out to the bitter end if it came down to that. Exhausted and frozen almost beyond human endurance continued to grimly fight on in a superhuman attempt to avoid being swept to destruction, only receiving a minor reprieve from certain fate when the violent wind that had pummeled him for so long suddenly abated slowing down his inevitable collision with the rock bound coast line that upon contact would have immediately wiped him out of existence.

The near miraculous dropping of the wind gave him the slight chance he needed, taking advantage of the situation calling on a reservoir of determination and strength he didn't know he possessed up till then to assist him in doubling his desperate actions paddling fiercely with aching arms that felt as if they were made of lead managing to more by good luck then good judgment to scrape his way past and through the pounding surf and treacherously shallow convoluted twisting channel that led into the safety of the river's mouth to finally find himself in sheltered waters within it's welcome confines.

Beaching his canoe, shakily set about hanging out his well soaked tent and whatever else required immediate drying, then building an ample fire to begin thawing out as best he could and to cook up some hot food while boiling up water for a pot of tea fully aware of his requirements to as quickly as possible imbibe of hot food and liquids in order to build up his badly depleted strength and to above all avoid the pit falls of hypothermia, once having accomplished these life giving necessities painfully erected his now dry tent to gratefully turn in for a much needed rest.

The following day the rigorous demands previously made upon him left him physically incapable of carrying on forcing his resting and building up his strength for the next three days giving him ample time to reflect on the magnitude of the formidable journey that still lay ahead, the thought of the terrible hardships he as yet faced almost convinced his giving it up and returning to Churchill to fly back to Neultin Lake, but the resounding crash of the huge breakers smashing against the boulder strewn shore line went far toward convincing him he could never again take on such formidable odds in his present condition and expect to survive, the grim reminder of having already endured such a harrowing ordeal and his surviving at all only a matter of good fortune, no matter how daunting the journey that still lay ahead of him would be he knew he had little choice but to attempt it or perish realizing it to be pure folly to even consider making his way to Churchill on foot as the impassable terrain he would encounter could only be traversed in the dead of winter, that and his fear of being caught out by the first of the violent winter storms that would soon be blowing off the reaches of the bay irrevocably trapping him were he was totally unprepared to face a long harrowing winter without adequate supplies and shelter, if that were to occur it without fail guaranteed his demise.

That amazing story of survival against all odds gave me pause to reflect on the fact that only one man in many thousands could have managed to overcome the soul shattering ordeals he had endured and survived, it must have come as a severe jolt to his pride to realize his not being the iron man he once was, no longer able to do as he had once done with consummate ease, as much as the reality of the situation must have galled him, reluctantly accepted the fact he had reached the cross roads of his life as all mortals must.

Well aware the season to be well advanced leaving him with no time to waste reluctantly forced himself to begin the formidable journey that still lay many demanding days travel ahead, the journey taking a total of two excruciating weeks to accomplish, fighting the river current and crossing the man killing portages every inch of the way, often despairing of having the strength and will power to continue on, but the grinding fear of being caught out by an early blizzard followed by freezing temperatures would in all likelihood create conditions beyond his ability to overcome forcing his driving himself unmercifully until finally reaching the security and safety of his cabin drawn and exhausted from battling the river and early storms that had bedeviled him most of the way.

Pausing to stare vacantly at nothing after that lengthy recital for a protracted period of time, suddenly muttering an unexpected confession that came within a hair of flooring me, It doesn't feel right anymore, it's not the same, now I'm afraid of being alone!

Now that coming from one who above all had once treasured his solitary existence left one wondering as his having recently established a close friendship with us it had been noted he very rarely ventured too far away from the camp, obviously having his fill of being a solitary soul now craved constant companionship.

After another lengthy silence and once again completing the now familiar ritual of cleaning and tamping his pipe with fresh tobacco to once having lit it with much ado to puff away determinedly until satisfied with it's performance, heaved a deep heart felt sigh continuing on as if determined to bring the story to it's conclusion now that he was in full cry.

It would appear the aircraft that finally did make it in from Churchill only 258

days before the lake froze over bringing in only part of his winter supplies, an unforeseen and totally unexpected state of affairs that left him in an alarmed state of mind, but the pilot for what ever reason falsely assured him the remainder would be coming in the following day some what alleviating ragnar's anxious state of mind.

Watching the aircraft take off and to eventually disappear from sight and as it faded from view a sudden and totally unexpected change of resolve overtook him, for the first time in all the years he had resided there accepting with equality the crushing burden of loneliness and complete isolation in a vast land were no others existed, a sudden desire to quit the land and return to Churchill coming over him, never before in all the long years spent in total isolation had he felt so utterly bereft, the allure of that vast empty land having now deserted him. At that point he decided to leave that brooding isolation behind, taking the next supply plane back to Churchill, but unbeknownst to him at the time it was not to be, not for another year while seeing no other living soul during that time as the market for white fox fur had crashed disastrously with most if not all barren land trappers leaving the land and deserting their trap lines.

Also unbeknownst to ragnar the pilot who had promised to return the next day had suddenly left the employ of the airways and failing to pass on the message to his superiors it was imperative that the remainder of ragnar's supplies without fail be delivered before freeze up, a happening that late into the year could take place anytime within the next few days., .

This in itself not an unusual occurrence as it takes place more frequently than the public is aware of, in some cases leaving a solitary trapper or prospector to be abandoned to a terrible fate while hopefully awaiting the aircraft that may never come except for the hardy few that were able to walk out on their own, but on the average they were few and far between.

As the short fall season rapidly came to a close freezing over the smaller lakes and shallow water bays on the larger ones, ragnar finally despairing of the supply plane returning and being picked up before the lake froze over and the land once more reverted to a long cold harsh winter hastily set his nets out to catch as many of the spawning trout and whitefish that crowded the still flowing rivers in order to sustain himself and his dogs during the course of the winter.

Once having caught all he could before the rivers froze immediately set out to hunt for the few remaining caribou that he knew still straggled through that part of the country on their southerly migration. He admitted to at one time killing an average of three hundred caribou each year leaving the greater percentage of them where they fell to act as bait to lure in wolves and arctic fox employing both traps and poison as deemed necessary. It being so late in the season the major herds had already passed through only managing to kill about a dozen stragglers that he wisely kept for himself.

By the time he had more or less prepared himself to facing the vicissitudes of what he knew all too well would prove to be a long harsh winter as the cold weather had recently set in with a vengeance with the day's becoming progressively shorter and colder, there comes a time in them far northern latitudes when the weak winter sun fails to make much of an appearance, barely showing itself above the horizon during the long cold months of mid winter, the somber landscape for the most part becoming bathed in a twenty four hour gloomy darkness that if allowed to will steal away a man's vitality and life forces leaving one's very soul to wither away on the vine.

One can hardly begin to imagine his feelings of soul crushing alones, the barren landscape totally bereft of all life save that of the animal inhabitants along with Ragnar who only had his dogs for company who with fading hope waited for the plane that would never come, it finally becoming more than he could bear with each short winter day and interminably long winter nights increasing the strain of waiting reluctantly returned to his normal trapping activities setting out traps, poisoned baits and building many dead falls to catch arctic wolves, in doing so more to alleviate the mind numbing endless hours of boredom than a desire to trap.

Often during the interminably long nights when sheer boredom and desperation beset to the degree of almost losing his ability to retain coherent often giving him reason to contemplate attempting the long arduous journey to Brochette, but his being well experienced in the vicissitudes of what it would take to make such a demanding journey on snow shoes through a harsh and demanding landscape difficult at any time to travel over especially in the dead of winter, deeper consideration of what it would entail made him realize he now lacked the strength and fortitude to overcome the demands of bitingly cold weather and the deep snows that can quickly sap a man's strength and the will power to keep on.

The challenge of taking on the barren lands that he once thrived in doing had now lost it's allure, locking him in as securely as any prison made of iron bars. Experience having taught him that isolation along with cabin fever{going shack wacky}could eventually derange one's mind to the degree of attempting to do the impossible with predictable results, strived to keep himself occupied as much as possible, be it cutting wood to fuel his stove, checking his traps and deadfalls, skinning and curing the furs as they became available, thus whiling away the excruciatingly long dreary winter to eventually welcome the appearance of the sun as it once more peeped over the horizon, gaining in time and strength each passing day giving Ragnar's morale a much needed boost, but also knowing with a certainty he must above all else when the opportunity to do so presented itself leave the land and to make his way south if necessary to do so at first open water.

Fate often intervenes in strange ways, our setting up a summer fishing camp inadvertently allowing Ragnar a whole new lease on life with his remaining close by during the short intense fishing season electing to leave with us once we had completed closing down the fishery reluctantly releasing his wolf dogs to run wild shortly before leaving on our last trip out knowing they could never adapt to life in close proximity of a busy crowded town, that final act of kindness toward the dogs he had lovingly raised since they were tiny balls of feet and fur affected all of us.

And so it went for the next three years with his gladly returning each spring to the land he loved, never ceasing to marvel at my ability to land smoothly on the spring ice surface with floats.

Eventually taking up a new career as a fishing guide for Hank Parson's recently established Tree Line Lodge enjoying spending time keeping the guests spell bound while relating tales of the many years spent on the lake as a barren lands trapper, not to mention his unfailing ability to take them to where the Lunker lake trout could be found, quite the change for a once elusive and solitary barren lands trapper.

Unfortunately for all our tenure on Neultin Lake after completing our third year coming to a grinding halt when the newly elected NDP government in it's social leaning wisdom and lack of foresight created a monstrous beaucracy controlled fish marketing board with far reaching unlimited powers that eventually revoked all the commercial fishing licenses of non native corporations or companies that had successfully flourished in the province of Manitoba for generations, instead turning all rights over to various first nation fishermen while supplying considerable financial backing to assist them to get a viable fishing operation up and running, as time would prove to no avail, each and every native controlled fishing operation after a time failing miserably as predicted, only succeeding in incurring great monetary cost to the tax payer. This unthinking act of creating a bloated with home steaders and political hacks fish producing corporation by incompetent bone headed self serving politicians who understood nothing of what it took to succeed in such a far reaching enterprise by and large eventually failed miserably in the end but not before permanent and lasting damage had been inflicted on the industry on the whole.

The fish producing company I had flown for eventually forced by economics to shut down their extensive operation selling their aircraft and abandoning the expensive equipment and supplies at many of their far flung fishing operations to rot or be vandalized.

Ragnar upon being informed of the sequence of events leading up to our eventual demise understandably took it very badly, what his thoughts were concerning our leaving he never ventured to say, only shaking my hand with his weather beaten craggy features mirroring absolute dismay at my leaving as we had become close friends.

Years later I was to learn of his passing at the ripe old age of ninety four, remaining to the very end the anachronism that he had always been, one of the rare breed of "Iron men".

I have always felt my life to have been considerably enriched by associating with him and proud to have called him "friend".

Never again will we know such a rare breed of men as time and fate has contrived to decimate their numbers that at no time numbered many, it is my sincere belief that none survive to this day.

Muskeg Express

STRANGE, COLORFULL OR OUTSTANDING APPEARING CHARACTERS are rarely if ever viewed with suspicion or distrust throughout the remote reaches of the north were they are most likely to be found, they're choosing by their very nature to habitate out of the way places and considered by all who work and reside their to be part and parcel of the landscape as much as they, so very little attention if any paid to their chosen life style whether coming or going or carrying on with their normal activities.

Arriving back at Pickle Lake after completing an early morning trip upon entering the flight office immediately took notice of a hard bitten appearing older man who by his very demeanor gave notice of being quite astute in knowing his way around the north country sitting quietly in the furthest reaches of the office saying nothing, but obvious to all who took note of his quiet presence to be extremely aware of what transpired around him. His type being nothing new to us and accepted for what and who they were with our respecting their penchant for privacy. Every morning for the next while he appeared at an early hour to sit throughout most of the day quietly observing the hustle and bustle of a busy flight office and every so often copying copious notes into a pocket diary until our eventually becoming quite accustomed to his quiet unassuming presence accepting him as part of the decor. Every so often he would get up and quietly leave only to re-appear within a short period of time reeking of scotch whiskey, but never once did he appear in any sense of the word to be inebriated or did he ever slur his speech when greeting us.

After a period of time we tumbled to the fact there was a hell of a lot more to him then first met the eye, but little did we realize at first his spending time covertly gauging each pilot's personality and expertise, closely observing our individual performances in great detail be it flight planning or taking off and landing. After about a week of being part of the decor he appeared to feel comfortable enough in our presence to bring his ever present bottle of scotch into the office to be nipped on at intervals, of course that bothered no one our practicing a live and let live principle as long as the person in question did not step too far out of line, but in his case he unfailingly conducted himself in a polite charming old world manner we thought of as quaint.

By now we had tumbled to the fact that his for what ever reason best known to him expertly evaluating the every day efficiency of our flight operation and would only show his cards when he felt the time to be right. When he finally consented to do so it surprised the hell out of all of us upon his revealing his credentials of being the chief geologist for "Ethyl Corp", a subsidiary of Esso Oil Ltd, a well heeled corporation if there ever was one and as we where to eventually discover spared no expense in meeting their desired goals.

One can only imagine my surprise upon my being apprised of their having leased the beech craft I normally flew for a period of no less than four months exclusively for their use with my being chosen as pilot in command. Pleased beyond measure at this unexpected turn of events but remaining uncertain as to what would transpire next sat back and waited for further events to unfold as they would, soon learning my new boss to be extremely astute in dealing with people, going to great lengths to assure his recruiting only the best of workers to assist him, also as it went my soon learning his being well versed in bush flying lore.

Having worked out a system that allowed only the dispatcher and I to be privy to his daily plans concerning visiting and working pre planned exploration areas, our first jaunt turned out to be a long one with our taking on full fuel and two extra forty five gallon drums along with a hand pump and not much else but a good sized lunch . With an flight endurance of eight hours it promised to be a long day.

Once on our way to the prescribed co-ordinates as laid out on the map it quickly becoming apparent to me his maintaining a close watch on our progress even though discreetly attempting to conceal the fact. Upon reaching our initial destination we lined up on one of the first of many grids lines he had previously drawn on the map with our spending the next four demanding hours adhering to rigidly held gyro compass course the entire length of each grid as he scribbled incomprehensible notations on the a map relating to the geological formations that presented themselves until much to my relief being almost prostrated with boredom and compass fixation we finally completed the last one to his satisfaction.

By this time our last grid flown brought us within sighting distance of an a long abandoned dew line site that bordered on the settlement of Winisk located on the west shore of Hudson's Bay, the long abandoned site still boasting a serviceable paved runway, many out buildings and a control tower and it being time to re-fuel before making our way back to base decided it would be as good a place as any to do so landing on the snow covered runway and parking adjacent to the long abandoned control tower. It didn't take too long before curious onlookers arrived on their ski-doo's from the small settlement that lay just across the river from the air strip to see who had broken up the mind bending boredom they endured on a regular basis and also bringing a bundle of letters etc. for us to mail upon returning to Pickle Lake, a common courtesy that's normally practiced by all bush pilots.

As I busied myself transferring the fuel from the drums to the wing tanks and replenishing the oil in the engines Alex took a great interest in investigating the interior of the control tower and adjacent buildings. Once having satisfied his curiosity we took off on our long return trip home to arrive shortly before dark. While preparing the aircraft for the night I thought to myself if every day goes as well and easily as to day did I for one have no cause to complain.

For reasons best known to him during our second week Alex disappeared to some where for a full six days leaving me to enjoy idling the time away much to the envy of the other flight crews who were on the average driving it day in and day out on a near continuous basis while I sat around in leisure being paid a minimum of one thousand miles a day whether I flew a mile or not, this of a certainty suited me just fine.

On Alex's return it signaled the beginning of a very busy winter, but how he chose his destinations always remained a mystery to me but we were eventually to end up flying the width and breadth of the barren wastes that made up the Hudson Bay low lands, a vast area of sere muskeg that extended for many square miles with our main base of operation being located less than a hundred miles off the coast. The area we worked in consisted of endless tracts of featureless muskeg only broken by a myriad of small shallow randomly shaped lakes that varied greatly in size and geological formation with no two being alike. This being my first foray into that certain part of the country finding it's diversity to be endlessly fascinating even to the awe inspiring snow drifts piled up by the fierce winds that on the occasion blew off the bay with unparalleled vengeance. What really titillated my senses was the complex variations of huge sculpted snow drifts that could be frequently observed, they're appearing in truly awesome shapes and sizes being randomly formed by the fierce winds that blasted unchecked across the width and breadth of the wide open area, but for some quirk of nature only to be found on some of the lakes while on others within the same area the ice surface remained relatively smooth!. The lake closest to where Alex wished to begin his explorations sported a long narrow neck of land created by a granite up thrust randomly lined with rows of wind blasted scraggly pine trees with their roots clinging precariously to the shallow soil, it was well the neck of land lay as it did as it completely sheltered a large half moon shaped bay from the incessant winds offering excellent landing and take off condition prompting Alex to set up a permanent camp, the only draw back being we only had a maximum distance of eighteen hundred to two thousand feet maximum to touch down and stop in before shooting by the neck of land to end up endangering the aircraft and most likely ourselves if one where to collide with the monstrous drifts that marched grandly in serrated rows beyond the tip of the up thrust, if one where to misjudge their landing and not be able to go around, hurt city for all aboard definitely guaranteed.

Fortunately I had previously made it a point prior to being accepted to when ever the opportunity presented itself to do so practice short landings in all conditions mainly because of enjoying the challenge, this we where to soon find out worked to our advantage, the landing area available actually quite sufficient to land in safely if carried out in the well practiced manner, but one could be absolutely certain it would do little in the way of easing the unsuspecting passengers state of mind having it's drawbacks, cautioning Alex to not become duly alarmed at the unorthodox method I would be employing in the first forthcoming landing, he just flashed me a wide smile while giving a thumbs up signal of approval.

Selecting a prominent granite up thrust as a base for beginning the initial approach from what I roughly calculated to be about three miles distant from the lake and while attaining a height of approximately a thousand feet above ground slowed down to a hundred miles per hour indicated selecting full flaps while setting up a relatively nose high power on approach discreetly varying trim and engine power as required to maintain a vertical descent of fifteen hundred feet per minute as indicated on the vertical speed indicator, fine tuning the descent as required to maintain a constant glide slope until the nose passed over the margin of the lake with our hanging on the ragged edge of a stall, then at the very last second ramming on full power momentarily to check our vertical descent then as quickly pulling the throttles back to idle to settle on to the surface of the lake so gently as to be hardly noticeable coming to a full stop in less than a third of the available distance to turn around and taxi into the bay and shut down the engines. Alex who hadn't said a word until the silence unbroken by the now silent engines suddenly spoke up saying Jesus Christ hart, I've flown with some pretty god dam good beech craft pilots but never before have I known any one to literally parachute one of the god dam things onto a lake like you just did, I'm impressed all to hell and back but I don't think for a minute any of my crew are going to be overjoyed about it he commented with a sadistic chuckle.

After having made a number of trips into the lake to bring in fuel and supplies including two ski-doos to move their equipment over the expanse of muskeg, my pretty well having the ridged procedures to safely perform the hairy landing down to an inexact science, the only variations confronting me being the load and wind conditions which could and often did make for an extremely dicey situation at times.

Alex having decided after our spending a busy time in preparation as ready as could be to begin his winters exploration work loaded the four men he had recruited from god knows where on board the next day to start them off in preparing the camp and what ever else he had in mind. Upon our eventual arrival at the lake the four innocents not being forewarned of what to expect could only stare out of the windows in disbelief at our proposed landing area, having throttled back the engines our clearly hearing one of them loudly proclaim in a voice that came out on the shrill side with helpless uncertainty, Jesus Christ on a crutch we aren't going to land there are we?, then it came clear to me that mean minded sadistic old bugger purposely neglected to warn his crew of what to expect upon arrival, that explained the shit eating grin plastered all over his homely mug. He was most accurate in forecasting they would in all probability be less then thrilled as we began to plummet downward like a runaway elevator our clearly over hearing a collective moan of ooooooooohhhhh shitttttt that carried on until touch down where upon it turned into a collective gasping sigh of relief at their safe deliverance. God dam that old goat, to me that was not fair play my failing to derive any pleasure out of frightening some one half to death, this was my first glimpse into a twisted and convoluted side of Alex I found disturbing, but not my last. For them poor unsuspecting buggers it must have seemed we where about to crash and once having landed safely just barely able to exit the cabin on shaky legs to stagger as far away from the aircraft as practible ashen faced and uncertain as to what they had let themselves in for as they shakily attempted to light up a cigarette with fumbling fingers that refused to co-operate as their fear numbed minds hadn't quite caught up with the fact they were alive and well. Once they had some what accepted that fact and more or less settled in Alex immediately put some of them to work sorting out the large collection of supplies we had previously dumped their and others to begin erecting the tents to be used to protect the perishables and above all a slightly larger one to be used only as an emergency shelter complete with a large oil stove, survival gear and ample food supplies to see us through if found necessary to hole up if caught by   by bad weather and forced to hole up.

Once having set things in motion to his satisfaction, Alex decided on making a short jaunt over to another nameless pot hole lake he referred to as" pan lake".

Selecting one of the more astute workers to accompany us who obviously having second thoughts about accompanying us with his acting as if making his last steps to-ward the gallows, dragging his feet before reluctantly placing his unwilling body into the aircraft. Not having been to pan lake for some time not at all sure what to expect in the matter of snow drifts, it being high noon with the sun directly over head made it a good time to check the shadow heights of any drifts that may have built up since our last visit but to our immense relief the existing conditions found to be acceptable for landing on though they did jar the hell out of us as we slammed over them. This part of the country never ceased to fascinate and amaze me with its never ceasing anomalies that seemed to occur randomly from lake to lake, pan lake an almost perfectly round lake about two miles in diameter that boasted unusually high marshy banks surrounding it to some how prevent the buildup of monstrous drifts that appeared to form as a matter of course on most of the lakes.

It seemed that each and all of the many lakes we visited throughout the winter found to be in one way or the other unique unto themselves, all in one way or another retaining individual characteristics that reflected nature's finest schemes with my never becoming jaded from viewing the stark beauty of the wind blasted black spruce trees perched precariously at the edges of the lakes outlined majestically against a back drop of an azure sky, often enhanced by the wispy white clouds slowly drifting by, no artist no matter how skilled could begin to compete with natures brush!. So awed by what few have ever had the good fortune or opportunity to witness, I could have stood there for hours humbled by the awesome panorama that lay before me deeply appreciating the raw scenic beauty that mere words failed miserably in adequately expressing, this was a wilderness cathedral where silence held lease, broken only occasionally by the harsh croak of the ubiquitous raven that called that most barren of wonderful landscapes home, but I well knew this was only one of the many faces nature wore, as beautiful and as captivating as it appeared to-day it could as suddenly turn vicious and uninhabitable except by those that came uniquely prepared to meet it's many moods head on being marvelously adapted by nature to survive it's violent moods.

My reverie was suddenly and rudely imposed on by Alex's strident summons for us to leave having accomplished their task of setting up base line with wooden stakes and fluorescent ribbons and selecting a suitable site to erect an emergency tent, actually a very good idea in case of our by chance fluorescence to remain by the advent of bad weather suddenly closing in, an all too real possibility of that occurring at any time in that part of the country with the weather conditions never getting too far away from my thoughts. Upon approaching the aircraft in preparation for imminent departure noticed the young man who had so reluctantly accompanied us staring intently at it as if it would suddenly jump at him and bite him on the ass, one didn't need to be a physiologist to know his thoughts transparent as they were, but regardless of his state of mind had little choice but to climb physiologist here was no other way out short of remaining there by himself and that remained totally out of the question.

We must have given the awe struck men who had remained behind a preview of what to expect in the future upon performing my parachute type landing complete with all the sound and fury that accompanied it in front of them, actually I pitied them as it couldn't have been a great feeling sitting in the rear cabin belted in their seats impotently awaiting what ever fate had in store for them.

On the return trip the crew treated for the first of many times to what I referred to as our "Nantucket" sleigh ride as we sizzled flat out over the pool table flat areas of muskeg at less than twenty feet or less from the surface of the muskeg giving the illusion of traveling twice as fast as we really where. I didn't know what their thoughts where upon our eventual arrival back at Pickle Lake for when they bid me a good night not one of them made any reference to it only giving me a quizzical look as if remaining uncertain if their immediate future lay in the hands of a capable pilot or a mad man with the death wish riding on his shoulders. As Alex bid me a good night he did mention with a gleeful chuckle, oh they'll be alright, though it wouldn't surprise me a bit if more than a few of them might have to change their underwear, but they'll get used to it, with that he took his leave with a poorly disguised look of pure glee written all over his craggy features.

Well the job went on more or less as expected with my noticing our hauling in barrels of JP-4 (turbine engine fuel) as consumed by a helicopter. At first I assumed that some where down the line Alex planned on bringing one in to assist them with they're work, quite surprised when inquiring about it he answered hell no, there to god dam expensive and they use up so much costly fuel, besides that there isn't much they could do for us we are already doing with the beech craft!. Well that left me some what puzzled as to it's ultimate purpose for a time, but eventually he saw fit to enlighten me by pointing out it being a long time practice of his to mix approximately twenty five percent of that volatile fuel with seventy five percent common fuel oil explaining that it kept the feed lines to the oil stoves from congealing in the frigid temperatures and it also gave off a much higher ratio of BTUs (British thermal units)per gallon burned, this of course raised proper hell with the stoves but they where expendable.

As the tent accommodations now being equipped with a heat source and emergency food supplies with a thick foam mattress for each man plus we always as a matter of course kept our woods five star sleeping bags in the aircraft at all times in case of a forced landing away from the main camp, mainly using the tent to warm ourselves up and thaw out our usually well frozen sandwiches and to make tea or coffee over a small propane stove. The all too real possibility of being caught out by a freak blizzard weighed heavily on Alex and I having four green horns to watch out for and it was always safety in mind first last and always.

On this day it had been noticed during the trip in the sky on the average remaining as a high watery overcast with the sun dimly peeking through on the occasion creating a multi hued halo that gave it an eerie appearance that for what ever reason deeply disconcerted me, but the visibility remaining excellent throughout the duration of the trip, but still it continued to be of concern even though the latest forecast for the region did not predict any disturbances off the bay for the next twenty four hours, all well and good but my well honed weather instincts warned me it to be otherwise, my sensing our being in for one hell of a blow within the next twelve hours or less keeping me on the edgy side being all too well aware the weather systems that randomly raged off Hudson Bay very rarely played by the rules, the possibility of that occurring increasing my nagging sense of unease that increased as we flew south eastward to pot lake maintaining a good height not daring to descend to fly just over the muskeg as we usually did in order to enjoy our sleigh ride, it being far too chancy to risk low level flight at high speed due to the fact the snow surface and the pewter gray sky tended toward blending together as one making accurate height reference next to impossible.

We hadn't spent more then five uneasy hours at pot lake with my keeping tabs on the weather by listening in hourly to the available weather broadcasts and had just decided to tell Alex to call it quits and get the hell out of there before being caught by the storm I strongly suspected to now be bearing down rapidly on us, but much to my lasting regret knew then with a sinking feeling of having left it until too late upon detecting a low moaning sound that had just began to vibrate through the air as a curtain of random snow flakes suddenly began to dance around us, a precursor of much worse to come, Alex being an old hand in the north instantly recognizing the low moaning and what it portended immediately yelled at the men to drop what ever they where doing and get into the aircraft as we where leaving post haste before the brunt of the storm hit. I on the other hand entertained no such foolish idea knowing even if we did manage to take off ahead of the storm knowing it had already curled in behind us in an anti-clockwise direction as it always did in affect trapping us. Informing Alex of my hard and fast decision to stay put where we at least had a modicum of shelter and it best if we quick like grabbed our gear and place it into the dubious safety of the tent while we could still safely so, thankfully he didn't argue with my decision though initially appearing to be somewhat hesitant but remaining undecided for a short time before taking my advice and instructing the men to do as told and well he did as quickly as he did our barely having the time to accomplish that and at my insistence to place numerous drums of fuel all around the tent to act as a wind break and to help pin it down against the fierce winds that were sure to inundate us.

Having barely accomplished this very necessary task shortly before the full force of the storm raged over us like a de-railed locomotive instantly blotting out all visibility as the blizzard accompanying the shrieking wind slammed in full fury across the granite up thrust that partially sheltered us from the ravages of the storm. Christ I was sick with worry about the aircraft but there was nothing to be done, given time we would have lashed drums of fuel to the wings and tail but time was a luxury we couldn't afford, the safety and security of the tent came first for without it's fragile shelter we where all dead meat.

Unbeknownst to us that morning we had unwittingly run smack into the middle of what is referred by metreoligists as a "bomb", a rapidly developing and intense "low" that created fierce winds that with unimpeded fury literally exploded across the wide open areas of the muskeg while capable of shifting direction without warning at any second, any way one cared to look at it we where in for a bad time of it.

Nervously settling in to our make shift surroundings, it became quite plain by the diffused light cast from the gas lantern Alex had the foresight to light the four workers had the first stage of full blown panic mirrored in their eyes a happening that could not be allowed to occur and had to be immediately nipped in the bud, it being a dire necessity our collectively continuing to work together in order to survive our pending ordeal depended on keeping a firm hold on reality calling for Alex and I to ease their fears of the unknown consequences of the storm by informing them that the dilemma we presently found ourselves in nothing new to me or as I strongly suspected to Alex, only the place, time and circumstances being different.

Only able to impotently lie there attempting to make desultory conversation with one ear cocked to the ever building fury of the storm as it raged around us. Having experienced and survived similar situations many times before able to relax with the hard won knowledge that what would be would be and fretting about the what if's of it all not about to change a thing giving me the time to reflect on the varied levels of survival skills one garnered through the years as a bush pilot, the acquired ability to overcome the many and varied often troublesome circumstances that one frequently found themselves immersed in, most experienced and time hardened pilots have developed the capacity to withstand the multiple stress factors produced by the exigencies of the profession. Invariably this confident attitude can and often does lead one to some times mistakenly believe they are capable of overcoming or mastering any situation no matter how dire as presented at one time or another, but this sometimes misplaced confidence has it's limits, familiarity as it is oft said breeds contempt, but on the other hand hard won experience also teaches one that at any given time imminent catastrophe remains a constant unforeseeable and sometimes unpreventable occurrence.

Well for what is was worth all we could do was hope for the best while waiting it out cognizant of the fact that when one immersed themselves in the flying game as deeply as I had, one never knew when their ticket to hell would be punched. Actually short of the catastrophic event of losing the tent we where basically in sound shape with an ample supply of food, warmth and gas lamps for light even though they often danced and swayed alarmingly when ever a solid gust of wind hammered against the tent roof, how ever long it would take the storm to blow it's self out no one could even begin to hazard a guess, but during the interim no one allowed to venture out side of the dubious shelter of the tent no matter how compelling the reason for wanting to do so!

Well it wasn't a case of whether or not we looked forward to our remaining trapped for the duration, that decision had been made by the powers that be, our retaining absolutely no control of what would conspire next. With precious little to be done but to patiently as possible considering the charged and tense atmosphere that inundated the interior of the tents wait it out and hope for the best, however long the storm raged it would weigh most heavily on the four workers nerves as this was an entirely new found and frightening experience for them being as unexpected as it was. The constant nerve singeing whine of the wind guaranteed to play hell with their imaginations to a much greater degree then it would on mine and Alex's, our being far more familiar with the weather phenomena one often encountered while working and living in the north or the far reaches of the muskeg areas.

I n a convoluted sort of way it appeared so ironic, us superior human beings, lords of the earth (or so we like to think), not feeling quite so high and mighty now, we six tiny sparks of life trapped in a fragile tent surrounded by a huge empty wilderness of barren muskeg beset by horrendously wild storm conditions that threatened to if given the chance to do so snuff us out of existence at any given moment. We didn't tell the four workers our chances of survival uncertain at best, they where frightened enough as it was, it would serve no useful purpose to upset them further.

As my mind wandered about it came to me about often having read about brave men struggling to survive against hopeless odds, the outcome reserved for the god's to decide, my not being so arrogant as to think the gods if they existed at all would have been bothered to take note of our passive endurance with their lofty and detached curiosity, I'm certain they had more important and demanding matters to occupy them abandoning us to fare however we would.

As the first long day of our enforced confinement wore on the gloomy atmosphere in the tent gradually deepened as the banshee howl of the wind rose to a maniacal crescendo causing all to shrink further into themselves to cringe in helpless fear. At first the constant nerve wracking slap of the wind hammering remorsefully on the tent canvas for the most part going unnoticed our initially being far too taken up with other more pressing concerns, but once becoming fully aware of it's monotonous repetition it's soon becoming a major concern as the incessant slapping of a loose fold of canvas somewhere on the tent began to torture our overwrought imaginations as the gale force winds seemed to be doing it's best to rip it to shreds, god dam I for one grateful beyond mere words it being brand new and only exposed to the elements for a short duration, one couldn't help but to cringe at the thought of it being a half rotted well used one, if that had been the case our fate would have been sealed long ago, as it was no one knew or wished to hazard a guess just how much abuse thin canvas could tolerate even though manufactured with the highest quality materials?

But even under the most trying of conditions one must eventually seek rest if only in brief snatches of restless sleep. To further add to our ongoing discomfort the wind appeared to suck away any vestige of heat produced by the oil stove forcing all to wear their heavy parkas with the hood pulled over our heads in an attempt to retain body heat.

Well be as it may, regardless of the dire circumstances surrounding us one still had to eventually heed nature's summons, fortunately our having the foresight to retain a five gallon oil bucket for such an eventuality to use as a commode, but the use of it left little room for modesty.

As bad as the situation had become it was bound to become much worse as Alex had feverishly nipped on his perpetual bottle of scotch with an ever increasing frequency it only lasting well into the following day when the last drops disappeared down his throat, it didn't take too long before his predictably becoming increasingly agitated and irritable along with his incessant bad tempered growling and grumping endlessly pacing the restricted confines of the tent setting every one's already stretched nerves a little further on edge.

The endlessly long dreary hours dragged by on leaden feet, the only way one knew the excruciatingly long day had passed into an equally long tension filled night and after what seemed to be an eternity what passed for morning had arrived was by referring to their wrist watch.

Though the endlessly long night had dragged on by the storm had not abated the least in intensity, if any thing it seemed to have gained in violence shrieking malovently around the tent like a lost and demented soul seeking sanctuary. Alex who had in desperation born of a burning thirst and withdrawal pains fought his raging desire for the coveted bottle of scotch he had mistakenly left behind in the cabin of the aircraft his making it obvious his being on several occasions been sorely tempted to retrieve it, but fortunately the fear of the for certain consequences involved in attempting such a foolhardy quest kept him from doing so, if he had chosen of his own free will to have done so there was little we could have done to restrain him, if he made up his mind to go it was his call.

But for that matter he managed to exert a terrific will power in restraining himself from doing something that would have without question resulted in tragedy, god dam how I wished with all my heart the storm would end, but that eventuality would not be realized until three agonizing days and nights had dragged by But at the time perhaps fortunately no one knew that, our only being able to crouch in boring misery enduring our fear in silence as any meaningful conversation had died a lingering death after the first long night leaving us individually wrapped up in our thoughts while miserably wondering if the storm would ever end? To add another dimension to our enduring Alex's wholly unpleasant withdrawal symptoms the nauseous stench of our make do commode and rank odor of six sweaty long unwashed bodies mixing and mingling with cooking odors and the ever present acrid lung burning odor of burnt lamp gas soon created a heady atmosphere that would have given a hyena the dry heaves, at the end of the third day becoming almost beyond human endurance the near unbearable stench almost taking on a life of it's own and sprouting fur, but still we didn't dare to crack open the tent flap even an inch to allow for the circulation of much needed fresh air in fear of the furious wind getting a hold and tearing it clean off adding to our already considerable difficulties.

And so it went, one interminably long day after another of mind boggling boredom along with the increasing discomfort of our sleeping bags as they became damp and lumpy making sleeping in them almost unbearable, but still having no other choice one could only endure until the storm to our relief eventually began to blow itself out after four terribly long days and almost unendurably long nights and just as well it had our being on the ragged edge of our endurance, filthy of body, bewhiskered caricatures of our former selves on the verge of eating each other from the mind eroding effects of fear and frustration endured for far to long churned to a froth by crushing boredom.

On the early morning of the fifth day Alex if one were to judge by his ragged shaky appearance to have weathered the storm very badly took a cautious peek out of the tent flap to inform us stars could occasionally be seen between the racing patches of scud that still blew raggedly across the early morning sky promising a fine day in the making much to our collective relief, our thankfully being able to crawl out of that foul smelling tent we had been confined in for far too long on shaky legs that almost refused to do our bidding being terribly cramped from being forced to remain inactive for so long to be greeted by the welcome sight of a star studded sky with the promise of a clear sunny day if one where to judge the soft yellow glow on the eastern horizon. As the wind continued to abate, we dared to venture further away from our tent prison to view a world completely alien to us, one we hardly recognized as we stood there gawking in profound disbelief at the changes brought on by the storm blinking like so many unkempt owls at the unaccustomed weak rays of ever increasing sun light.

The welfare of the aircraft being my greatest concern at the moment relieved beyond measure to seeing it by some miracle to be still remaining upright, but still something seemed out of place as I stared at it, then it came to me the aircraft had been blown backwards at least two hundred feet till the tail ski had wedged against the frozen verge of the marshy bank of the lake obviously doing little or no damage.

Christ that must have been some god awful wind force that most likely having reached a velocity of at least eighty miles per hour probably gusting up to well over a hundred at times at the height of the storm, only upon seeing how easily the wind had moved the aircraft did we truly realize just how fortunate we had been in not having the tent plucked up and torn away sealing our doom.

It didn't bear thinking about! God dam how I marveled at the raw power of nature, that must have been some awesome wind force to have further increased the size of the already magnificent drifts into absolute breath taking monsters behind the point where the full fury of the wind could play merry hell with any thing in it's path, one could only be grateful the aircraft sat mostly sheltered from it's full fury but even at that it had been much to my everlasting surprise moved back a goodly ways, my surmising that only the fact it was a low winged aircraft prevented the wind from generating sufficient force to flip it over on it's back though remaining certain it must have come precariously close to doing so at the height of the storm. When finally able to make my way to it with Alex feverishly leading the way we found only the very front of the nose section and one wing tip sticking out of a huge drift that otherwise completely inundated the entire aircraft. Initial poking around revealed the drift to be as hard as concrete, oh man we sure had our work cut out for us for the next few days. Mean while Alex was frantically clawing at the drift attempting to gain access to the rear door in a desperate attempt to retrieve his bottle of scotch with negative results, the wind blasted snow was just too hard and would have to be patiently cut into chunks and removed piece meal, but the look of pure frustration mirrored on Alex's drawn features told me his being near the end of his endurance his vibrating and shaking almost as if having a severe case of the palsy. requiring a "fix" as soon as possible.

Returning to the tent to dig up some metal kitchen utensils to begin our initial attempts to dig our way in to the rear cabin door decided out of morbid curiosity to inspect the tent and upon circling it some what taken aback to discover a rock hard drift slanting almost to the top of the tent completely inundating the drums we had initially placed there, we then knew without a doubt the barricade of steel drums we had so fortuitously placed there at the very last minute before the storm broke over us with all it's insensate fury had without question saved our bacon acting as an immovable wind break against the gale force winds thus preventing the loss of the tent and in all likelihood our lives to exposure, a very sobering observation at best that gave one pause for thought.

Well be as it may we had survived that terrible storm if just barely against all odds and grateful beyond words to have done so.

But now the hard work that promised uncertain results beginning with the back breaking job of extricating the aircraft from the rock hard drift snow, but hardly knowing where to begin that is except Alex who quickly solved that equation upon our discovering him industriously employed playing the part of a human mole as he desperately hacked away at the unyielding snow drift with a piece of wood. God he looked awful in the full light of day, being denied his life giving scotch made him look like a man from the grave as he exhorted

267

the four men to work harder and faster toward digging out as he phrased it, that god dam door. They certainly faced a challenge as until access to the rear door had been successfully accomplished they where denied the use of the axe and shovel to be found in the rear cabin. As it went their initially forced to use chunks of dead trees and what ever else could be employed to dig with the work proving to be a real bitch in making any degree of headway. Alex's feverish antics amused us no end as we detachedly watched him digging madly away like an oversized gopher, but then he had the incentive we lacked. Our being on the bare edge of exhaustion from enduring many long days and longer nights of strength draining fear, lack of sleep, cold unappetizing canned foods that one soon reached the point of being unable to choke down and just plain lethargy soon ran down as did Alex who reluctantly gave up his frantic efforts reluctantly agreeing it was in our best interest to take the time to cook up a decent hot meal and a much needed cup of hot coffee, but regardless of our weakened state it was discovered much to our dismay (that is except Alex) much of our required cook ware, bread bacon and coffee where still in the rear cabin of the aircraft and if we wished to enjoy them in the near future we had little choice but to force ourselves to carry on with the excavating, doing so with new found incentive until after much stubborn persistence on every one's part finally accessing the rear cabin door taking turns until finally being able to wedge open the cabin door stunned beyond words to find the entire cabin packed tight with drift snow, that discovery as dramatic and unexpected as it was only slowed Alex down momentarily before resuming his frantic search for the grub box only to find it after much frantic digging to eventually produce his precious bottle of scotch whereupon he wasted little time belting down a snort that would have staggered a water buffalo instantly producing a remarkable transformation with the color returning to his face and his eyes taking on a glitter we hadn't seen for some time

Mean while out of curiosity my digging out the escape hatch above the cockpit to find not at all to my surprise also tightly packed with drift snow, oh Christ I breathed to myself we got ourselves a mighty big hairy problem, how in the name of all that's righteous could we manage to ever get the aircraft dug out of that concrete like drift never mind somehow having to make certain it remained in flyable condition with our meager resources!

Well there wasn't any sense in worrying as what would be would be, after taking time to cook up a decent meal we all felt much better with the future not appearing to be as bleak as it first had with our getting right to it again with a much improved attitude, but this time around having the added concern of one of the now exuberant men becoming a mite careless or a little too hasty while wielding the axe or shovel close to the fragile aluminum skin of the aircraft as they chewed their way through the rock hard drift in an ongoing effort to free the aircraft from it's icy tomb with Alex haranguing them on now well fortified with false courage and bravado.

If the truth be known I was frightened almost to a stand still upon encountering the seemingly insurmountable problems that confronted me, but not daring to voice my fears to the others as they too where already clearly confused and visibly uncertain by the unexpected turn of events. After the short but intense day of mind boggling labor had ended we where all so worn out from our labors coming on top of the mind altering stress we had endured previously we could hardly place one foot in front of the other as we made our way gratefully back to the sanctuary of the tent.

No one bothered to eat much being too dog tired to even make the effort of lighting up the stove and warm up a meal, just nibbling on some canned meat and bread washed down with coffee only wanting to lay down and sleep to give our tired bodies time to rest up for what ever came next. I must have fallen asleep as soon as my head hit the pillow it being so cozy and for once quiet in the tent now that the wind had abated, god dam how good it felt to once feel secure in the knowledge the tent wouldn't be ripped out from under us at any moment and to for the first time in many days to be able to remove one's parka and boots though it must be admitted the rank odor of many pairs of smelly socks further pervaded and enhanced the already heady atmosphere that lingered to a greater degree, but being too tired to care much less notice though my socks as they dried out began to feel a bit brittle.

Was I some surprised upon awakening early the next morning to look at my watch and see I had slept soundly for a good twelve hours and finding myself in the same position initially assumed upon lying down, but oh man did that long sleep revive my body and spirits leaving me feeling much refreshed, the uncertainties of the past nights spent in mind numbing fear a thing of the past! Though it was early morning the stars twinkled merrily in the still darkened sky but there remained much to be done yet before we could even think of leaving. Upon waking Alex he snorted angrily a couple of times before fumbling for the bottle of scotch he kept under his pillow fortifying himself with a hefty snort that caused me to shudder clean down to my toes, Christ it was always more then I could begin to understand how any one could tolerate that fiery brew at any time never mind first thing upon awakening?, he must be one hell of a tough customer to withstand it's corrosive effects.

Now that we all felt more alive then we had for some time after a good night's rest our appetites returned full force making gluttons out of ourselves with a substantial breakfast of hot cakes and canned bacon washed down with fresh brewed coffee, filled to repletion we faced the coming day and whatever travails it had to offer with much renewed hope and vigor.

Once again it was circumspect of me to caution the men to exercise great care as they exuberantly hacked away with the axe and shovel, even though their new found enthusiasm was more then appreciated neither I nor Alex cared to explain an aircraft chewed all to hell by well meaning workers. As the men fought diligently to cut the iron hard snow from under and around the aircraft I busied myself in digging out the cabin using kitchen utensils to claw away the resisting snow, it all went well until reaching the cockpit where it really got interesting being forced to almost stand on my head to dig out from around the cramped space between the rudder pedals, if nothing else full and free control of them had to be assured as one could not risk the off chance of them jamming up on me at a critical moment. Once having completed that demanding job to my satisfaction took on the most terrible of tasks cleaning out the packed snow from around the control console the cabin and cockpit in general, when done as best it could be still appearing to be nothing short of an ice cavern and just as cold and gloomy. The short day again flew by all too quickly leaving us bone tired but ever so much more light hearted and more certain than ever all would turn out well in the end.

After a sumptuous meal of canned stew and bread with stewed dried apples for desert lay back with a cup of hot well sweetened tea on my foam mattress for the first time in many days more or less content with our state of affairs with my thoughts once more turning to the seriousness of our dilemma couldn't help but to emit a wry chuckle, all this fun to be had and get paid for it yet, my oh my how good does it get?. With that lighthearted thought easing my mind rolled in for a good night's rest.

As was usual for me up and at it in the early morning hours long before full dawn once more bathed the landscape in it's pearly glow well rested and raring to go went out side into the frosty dawn to relieve myself, one couldn't help but to marvel at how of crystal like clarity the sky appeared to be in that remote area, the memory of another time during the early day's of my flying career coming back of my having stood in awe of the clear velvet sky that gave one the impression one could reach up on tip toes and pluck the twinkling stars from their heavenly perch, so entranced had I become with my mental wanderings had momentarily forgotten a certain parts of my anatomy still hung exposed to

the harsh elements with a sharp reminder it best be immediately tucked safely away into a more agreeable environment if one wished to retain it.

Having done so with alacrity just about to go back into the tent when the sudden appearance of a colorful skein of northern lights (Aurora Borealis) began to dance and writhe across the heavens in breath taking splendor once more causing my forgetting the well below temperatures while watching in awe and delight as they filled and folded in endless succession from horizon to horizon until the sharp chill of the early morning air brought me back to my senses reminding me it was time to return to a more mundane world.

After breakfast it was time for us slaves of high technology to return to the demanding task of preparing the aircraft for flight as best we could for departure that day if at all possible. As the men reluctantly returned to their uncompleted task of digging us out my attention turned to the snow packed well frozen up engines, upon removing the remains of what had once been a set of pricey insulated engine covers now reduced to mere tatters by the fierce winds. Digging out the wing covers which fortunately had not been installed draped them over the engines to serve as a make shift tent, then firing up the trusty blow pot (plumber's pot) began the heart breaking maddening job of thawing out the frozen engines. That normally simple job all but drove me to distraction as the snow packed cowlings warmed up they began their inevitable shower of melted snow that trickled down giving the blow pot fits as it sputtered and flared giving me conniptions every time a sudden deluge would pour down effectively drowning it and leaving it hissing angrily at such shabby treatment until being dried out and re-started, what normally took an hour stretched into two. Not wanting to have to face that daunting task all over again with the second engine wisely removed the cowlings to bust out as much snow as possible from around it's circumference minimizing my grief to a marked degree.

As the problem of heating up the engines resolved itself a thornier one still lay ahead as to how to heat up the oil in the tanks that had all but congealed into the consistency of road tar, until that most necessary of tasks completed we weren't about to be going anywhere, something had to be done but what and how?, the use of the blow pot could not be considered except in the direst of emergencies as the oil tanks where situated in the very top of the wheel well nacelles where many delicate accessories and bundles of wiring that could all be too easily damaged by the fierce heat given off by the blow pot if one where foolhardy or desperate enough to attempt it!.

Bedeviled by mounting indecision had begun to cast desperately about in futile search for a way out allowed my attention to wander over to our tent camp, standing there in complete bewilderment of where to turn next idly watched the thin wavering waves of smoke and heat emitting from the chimney and like a bolt out of the blue it came clear to me just how it could be done safely and easily. Rounding up two of the men we began the onerous job of yanking the hot oil stove out of the tent and over to the aircraft, while the men busied themselves dragging over and setting up the drum of fuel oil to feed it while I opened the wheel well doors and swung them out of the way in order to access and allow the removal of as much hard packed snow as possible then placing the oil stove directly underneath to allow the exhaust smoke and heat produced to rise up and begin the long process of warming up the oil tank having hung my sleeping bag over top of the nacelle to help retain the heat thus speeding up the process.

The only fly in the ointment was Alex who continuing to suffer terribly from the effects of soul crushing withdrawal symptoms came near driving us around the bend with his continually finding fault with all we did bitching endlessly about our efforts being a fucken waste of time and effort, my already being terribly overwrought with the overriding concerns of being certain the aircraft could be made flyable finally had my fill of his surly attitude angrily braced him as to how he would have gone about it if it was his responsibility, the set to ending up with our being nose to nose in angry confrontation informing him in no uncertain terms of my being some what pissed off with the way he had been unfairly haranguing the men at every turn who through it all had continued to labor diligently to free the aircraft from the huge drift that entombed it. Surprisingly he was first to back, off but the fact of my having made a bitter enemy of him by challenging his authority in front of the men did not sit well, his being accustomed to being the man in charge at all times and my having the temerity to contest his authority well meaning or not had earned me an implacable enemy that I knew with indelible certainty would seek redress one way or the other for embarrassing him at the first opportunity. Alex having sulked off somewhere to sulk in private we resumed our duties as if nothing of consequence had transpired.

Well it was "déjà vue" all over again the residual snow melting and raining down on the hot oil stove created volumous clouds of steam that all but gave me conniption fits, but in the end it did the job very efficiently warming the oil to the desired consistency, then it was on to the other engine to began the mind bending regime all over again. As the oil slowly warmed up on the second engine the first one started by the time honored method of hand cranking, some thing I happened to be an old hand at as both batteries having frozen solid and split wide open rendering them useless. The wasp junior engines usually started easily as did this one with me hot footing it back into the cockpit to add more prime as required to make certain the engine continued to run and to keep a close eye on the oil pressure gauge while the engine warmed up till reaching operating temperatures where upon it was shut down and tightly wrapped to retain it's internal heat. Once having both engines warmed up to my satisfaction we took a break from our incessant labors to replace the oil stove in it's proper place and to enjoy a hot meal having been hard at it well before the sun made it's first welcome appearance on the eastern horizon.

Sitting there in glum silence it was noticed the strain on the men's faces had become quite apparent as the morning light strengthened, I knew all too well where their innermost fears lay, in the same place as mine did, all of us wondering but reluctant to say as much, would the aircraft be flyable? That question which lay so heavily on the minds of all could not be answered until our attempting flight, something the very thought of having no choice but to do left me in a terrible state of indecision, but if we were to ever leave that place of hardship and misery and return to the creature comforts we longed for, flight with all it's promised hazards had to be attempted.

Regardless of their fears the men on the average standing up well to the strain, almost hyperactive with the thought of the risky take off yet to be made along side of the comforting knowledge we would soon be leaving, but Alex continued to sulk like an overgrown child with our largely ignoring his frequent outbursts at every opportunity degrading our efforts as futile as he struggled to regain the unquestioned authority he had recently lost.

All appeared to be going well as could be expected considering the trying circumstances we labored under, but still something intangible continued to nag at me, something that could well affect future decisions and as captain of the aircraft remained solely responsible for the lives of all who would be boarding and should be at all times aware of all the possible hazards facing me before attempting a take off in the limited space available.

Running the most recent sequence of events through my mind the blood chilling realization came to mind that if the cabin and other areas of the aircraft found to be packed tight with drifted snow, then it logically followed it would be an absolute certainty all the other structural spaces were drifting snow could enter through the narrowest of openings, it stood these spaces would have suffered the same fate, so why not the wings and tail assembly?, not as yet wanting to voice my suspicions went over to the aircraft absolutely certain as to what I would find and upon opening the first of the inspection panels located on the wings and tail empennage the evidence of what had first suspected leaving me weak and unsure what to do or think next, breathing heavily cursed the god dam day I had ever wanted to be a bush pilot, as if the crushing fear that had already taken over my thoughts not enough, my latest discovery riding heavier than ever on my already overburdened shoulders. After a time clear thought transcended all else including mind eroding fear, for what it was worth there was nothing to be done but to accept what was and live with it. I couldn't be certain, but the disturbing fact the weight of the densely packed snow within the wings and tail could add immeasurably to our take off weight, Christ I thought to myself and having little reason to think otherwise that alone would almost place us at the maximum or better allowable take off weight even before loading on six big men and then having little choice but to do so if we ever wished to leave somehow perform what was guaranteed to be a hairy take off in a restricted space where one tiny error in judgment guaranteed disaster.

Deciding it to serve no useful purpose at the time in informing the men of our present crisis as it would only serve to frighten the poor buggers further, Alex on the other hand being quite astute and sensitive to my moods had already sensed something to be amiss forgot his sulk coming over to question me in private. Upon my informing him of where we stood at the present time his pallor immediately took on a sickly gray tinge and for once forgetting to resume his sulk only staring helplessly at the aircraft as if it had suddenly sprouted a set of horns, but after some deep thought agreeing with the decision it best not to spring that disturbing bit of news on the crew our remaining uncertain of their reaction upon being apprised. At he stood there with absolute bewilderment clouding his craggy features for some time before inquiring of me in a hoarse whiskey falsetto if there was anything that could possibly be done to alleviate our situation, his query earning him a negative shake of the head, that immediately sent him in to a frantic flurry of attempting to locate his non existent bottle of scotch he usually kept concealed within the voluminous fold of his parka, but to no avail having drained the last of it some time ago.

As put out with the juvenile demeanor he had so recently demonstrated toward us my sympathy toward his plight somewhat tempered my anger as he stared questionably at me with red rimmed eyes, the depressing thought came unbidden to mind that the poor bugger who had once lived such an interesting and rewarding life style now reduced to a mere shadow of the impressive man he must have been in his youth, time and excessive dependency on fiery spirits to fortify his fears and flagging confidence in his continued abilities had gone far toward reducing him to the pathetic wreck as I now viewed him, one couldn't say so with absolute certainty but it being most likely for the first time in his undoubtedly long and colorful career no longer in complete control of the ongoing series of events that unfolded as they would before him, leaving him with little choice but to go along with whatever hand fate dealt. My having arrived at the conclusion some time ago of his having reached his nadir, it being quite possible that this field trip once having reached it's conclusion in all likeliness to be his last, his usefulness to the multi national corporation he had selflessly put his all into forwarding their interests for so many years would eventually see him as no longer useful cold bloodedly terminating his position with the company leaving him with little choice but to reluctantly accept retirement, if that were to occur it was anybodies guess how it would go with him. Actually nothing new in the fast paced world of large multi national corporations who without regard to one's years of loyal and faithful service, their board members who dealt only in the results of the bottom line would without regard or due conscience matter of factly consider it' feasible and good business practice in replacing the old hands with the new crop of "whiz Kids" that were emerging in the world of high technology who would eventually take over his duties but never begin to equal him in doing so.

As it stood if we were to attempt leaving that day, a decision had to be made and soon as the truncated arc of the short winter day's sun had now passed it's zenith placing the remaining daylight on the short side.

Gathering the four men around me to without elaboration or fan fare laid our dilemma as it stood directly on the line leaving out nothing, giving them the option of taking their chances with me or remaining behind to wait for a future pick up that could well be a long time coming, as frightened as they were of chancing it in an aircraft that could well prove to possess questionable flying qualities they still trusted my skills as a pilot implicitly, to a man agreeing to accompany me come what may being more afraid to remain behind then to chance it, their childlike trust left me floundering uncertainly, but if there remained any way possible to get away from there we would certainly try.

Having satisfied my self that all that could be done had been done loaded up my fear ridden passengers ensuring their being tightly strapped into their seats. As tense as the situation was it was all one could do to prevent myself from grinning from ear to ear at the sight of four sets of bulging eyeballs staring hopefully at me, they're reminding me of a quartet of frogs perched on a lily pad, as for Alex he as always benignly sat there hunched over and so still as to be made of wax. Once the engines started and quickly brought up to operating temperatures shifted uneasily in my seat checking the engine gauges and controls for the umpteenth time before steeling my self to face what ever lay ahead reluctantly advanced the throttles to shake the aircraft loose noting immediately once it began to move sluggishly ahead demonstrating all the characteristics of an unsprung and severely overloaded Mack truck with the air frame groaning and protesting from every joint, god dam now I really began to question the possibility of becoming airborne within that impossibly short stretch allotted us the aircraft generally feeling so terribly heavy and unresponsive, and if by some miracle we did become air borne and to hopefully clear the huge drifts that awaited would the wings stay attached?. Making a series of turns within the confines of the bay to warm up the Teflon bottoms of the skis an absolute necessity in order to decrease resistance almost having to apply full power on one engine to complete a full turn, the god dam thing steering like a stone boat.

Once satisfied as I ever would be considering the less than laudable circumstances facing us, knew with a dread certainty if hesitating much longer sure to lose my nerve. Having previously completed the necessary pre take off check lowered the flaps to their full down setting knowing by doing so it would initially decrease our acceleration to a slight degree, but would immeasurably aid in raising the tail up to flying position that much sooner, a very desirable configuration to be attained as quickly as possible when taking off in a short space.

The consequences of failing to reach flying speed before encountering the huge rock hard drifts that lay in waiting before us not something one cared to ponder too deeply. Taxiing into the furthest corner of the bay in a desperate gambit to utilize every available foot of space to once lined up to my satisfaction fire walled the throttles exceeding the normal settings as much as I dared, at first our glacial acceleration appalled me but within a short period of time our forward speed began to increase rapidly as the power caught up with the weight.

Time seemed to be suspended as we raced toward the end of the short strip slowly gaining speed with my utilizing every short take off procedure ever learned through the long years of flying a beech craft, our to my over anxious mind seeming to have reached the runway's outer limits all too soon with the airspeed barely indicating a safe lift off speed but the clumsy heaviness of the aircraft indicating it still not quite ready to fly forcing my using up more of the limited runway space then originally intended before our flashing past the point of land that marked the extreme boundary, it was now or not at all with my gently coaxing the reluctant aircraft to take to the air, and not a second too soon as barely having lifted off the rear section of the skis glanced off the crest of a rock hard drift as we staggered on by creating an ominous jarring sensation that vibrated throughout the entire air frame almost causing my curling up into a ball of thoroughly frightened protoplasm and no doubt scaring the living Jesus out of our unsuspecting passengers who unable to see or to have possibly known what had transpired, but regardless of the near consequences of that most frightening occurrence we managed to remain airborne if barely so staggering along for the first of what seemed to be many very long seconds barely hanging above a stall before much to my relief finally clearing the lake and entering an area of much flatter terrain, man that was about as close as I had ever come to buying it, but too deeply involved in maintaining flight to dwell on the what if's with our continuing to wallow along slowly gaining precious airspeed with my cautiously raising the flaps a few degrees at a time, but due to our being so overweight any variation in control input created a slight but unsettling tendency to cause the wings to wobble slightly from side to side like the cheeks on a fat lady's ass while climbing a set of stairs until sufficient air speed had built up.

The gross instability of the aircraft detracted badly from it's normal nimble performance creating tense seconds of mind bending anxiety for me, especially upon discovering that each time the rudder pedal applied past a certain degree of travel it immediately causing the tail to lose lift resulting in it's hammering violently as it entered an incipient stall, the first time it occurred the frightening and totally unexpected reaction sending my blood pressure and heart rate clean off the scale with a cold sweat running down into my eyes and shirt collar while gripping the control wheel with such intensity as to almost squeeze the juice out of it. As it went the impossible situation we faced could only get that much worse if not soon turning on a compass heading for Pickle Lake as like it or not we were unwillingly headed for Hudson's Bay, something had to give and god dam soon. At this point the heavily straining engines had begun to overheat from the continuous higher than normal power settings imposed on them for far too long not to mention the fuel consumption running off the clock.

Having no other recourse breathed a shaky sigh while muttering goddamit, hail marry full of grace, and just plain shit began to with absolute caution accompanied by an over dose of over riding fear to execute an extremely dicey turn delicately employing tiny increments of rudder pedal to induce a slight skidding motion towards the desired direction not at any time daring to allow the wings to leave their level position being deathly afraid to apply aileron pressure fearing greatly it would fail to return to level flight. Each time I gathered up the courage to apply a touch of rudder the tail invariably gave off a horrible shudder that left my poor stomach wrapped around my backbone. By the time the much desired and exceedingly crucial turn that had seemed to take forever to accomplish my brain had all but turned to mush and as it went having done so none to soon as the engines cylinder head temperatures had crept into the never exceed red line zone.

It required a concentrated effort of will power on my part to steady my violently shaking hands that at first refused to do my biddings to finally be able to reduce the power settings to near normal cruise mode, the head temps quickly stabilizing in the cold air.

Upon gratefully reaching the flat muskeg area we commenced our Nantucket sleigh ride, not for the thrill of it but upon doing so immediately gaining in ground speed which in turn reduced fuel consumption but diligently avoiding the many obstacles that often popped up in our path well in advance keeping in mind the aircrafts normal nimble performance to be almost non existent. The relatively bright rays of the late afternoon sun aided immeasurably in aiding one to better judge the critical height above the muskeg's surface, if it had been overcast we would have had to forgo our sleigh ride as it is virtually impossible to accurately judge height as the overcast sky and the snow surface tend to blend together as one.

Actually safety in our critical condition lay in height, the one luxury we could ill afford at the time. As the fuel burnt off the aircraft became progressively lighter beginning to by slight degrees improve it's response to control inputs eventually allowing a further reduction of required engine power greatly extending our fuel endurance.

After what seemed to be an eternity of wrestling an unresponsive aircraft in a tense atmosphere of thundering engines, sweat, fear and frozen hell over what seemed to be endless miles of wind swept barren terrain we finally and gratefully arrived overhead of Pickle Lake with the gas gauges all but indicating empty tanks, it was high time to set down, may pronto. Foregoing the usual direction of approach elected to sizzle straight in to the two mile long well packed ice runway not daring to reduce the power a hair during the approach, only lowering full flap when assured of making the runway to scorch the bottom of the skis onto the icy surface and allowing the over weight aircraft to slowly and gently settle onto the hard packed runway before daring to fully retard the throttles, a few of the dock hands who observed my high speed landing swear to this very day to have witnessed sparks emanating from the ski bottoms as they initially made contact with the hard packed surface, once having fully retarded the throttles continued to slide along a goodly distance before slowing down sufficiently to allow blasting the aircraft around to taxi back into my normal parking space, that no sooner being accomplished before both low fuel pressure lights began to blink their warnings.

Upon shutting down the engines, a strange heavy silence immediately inundated our space with Alex gathering himself like a cougar about to spring on it's unsuspecting prey to with an alacrity I would have never previously dreamed of his being capable of, feverishly unlatching the top escape hatch to adroitly spring out onto the wing and to literally bound onto the ice surface to hot foot it up the hill with determined intensity to his room, obviously to retrieve a much required bottle of scotch, the four vastly relieved workers exited in a more leisurely manner being stiff from the long cold flight to offer a heartfelt thanks at delivering them safely and to bid me goodbye as they wearily but gratefully made their way to their rooms with the intent of resuming a more acceptable life style.

Having due to circumstances beyond my control remained out of the loop for some time and having my own tales to relate elected to hang around the flight office in order to catch up with the latest gossip (bush pilot's are inveterate gossips), not expecting to see any more of Alex that day some taken aback to see him suddenly appear in the office door, it being obvious his having fortified himself with a hefty belt or two of scotch as he literally reeked of it while the ruddy blush had returned to his craggy features, one could safely bet in his desperate haste to guzzle a much required swig of the fiery panther piss with wildly shaking hands having managed to pour as much on the outside as he had the inside, it must have been a sorry sight to witness. All the banter fell silent with our remaining uncertain as to what he had in mind as he stared morosely across the room his eyes casting back and forth as if uncertain of what to do or say next, his unkempt demeanor reminding me of a wet dog seeking somewhere dry to lie down before shuffling over to take a seat and as if in defiance taking up his ever present bottle of scotch and downing a hefty belt that left us gasping in awe and admiration, that old boy sure was some tough.

As he appeared to be in a mellow state of mind, just for the hell of it foolishly as it turned out inquired of his thoughts concerning our latest hairy adventure (big mistake)at that he directed a dark glance of what could be best described as pure malice at me as if all the past misfortune we had endured strictly my fault, then thundering out in a stentorian tone of voice, what the fuck am I supposed to think , were here alive and well aren't we for Christ sake?.

That unexpected attack upon my person at first leaving me speechless (an unusual state of affairs), this was not the man I thought I had gotten to know and understand, he now appeared in all respects to be a frightened shadow of his former self desperately attempting to reclaim his self worth and to hang on to a semblance of the only life style he had ever known and now totally consumed in fighting down the devils that pursued him, at that he suddenly rose to his full height to cast an accusing beetle browed glance that reeked of pure malovence at us as if having just discovered our in some obscure way perpetrating some manner of back handed dealings against his person, then with another equally black look that tookin the entire room took his leave with that peculiar stance common to an inebriated person striding out the door not unlike a storm cloud moving across the sun.

His recent and unexplained hostile attitude toward us left me in a confused state of uncertainty, our finding it quite shocking to have observed that usually taciturn normally unflappable Scotsman for what ever reason only known to him so visibly shaken, we could only assume the heavy load of responsibility he shouldered along side of the cumulative effects of a series of unavoidable but trying circumstances such as we had recently endured had begun to rattle him.

Well what would be would be, shrugging off his tirade as just one of them things we trooped off to the hotel for a long overdue hot meal and a bottle of beer, camp fare such as it was got old very quickly.

Once seated in the overheated hotel bar removed my parka which within a short time brought on the advent of all sitting near me to wrinkle up their noses in unalloyed disgust as the over ripe odor of a long unwashed body encased in rank sweat soaked undergarments marinated and enhanced by the heat rolled over them in cloying waves bringing on many the uncomplimentary remark, the less staunch moving to another table, their precipitate actions informed me the exotic stench of a week long accumulation of unspeakable filth and sweat that coated my skin and permeated my clothes combined with a near terminal case of foul breath that in all respects capable of bowling over a water buffalo at forty paces, fuck em if they can't take the smell of a real man I thought to myself, having just returned from facing the rigors of an excruciatingly long week that included facing life threatening circumstances that even though we had survived the near impossible circumstances that had spun way beyond our control the very thought of the terrible risks we had been forced to take still caused cold chills of fear to run down my back while them panty waists who had sat out the storm in relative safety and comfort felt justified in passing judgment on my present state of hygiene, who the hell did they think they were?, with that thought clearing my mind commenced to let it all hang out getting snot dripping drunk for the third time in my life with my fellow pilots eventually scraping my smelly remains off the bar room floor and bundling me home to sleep it off.

The next morning upon awakening and feverently wishing I hadn't when a pounding hang over that all but reduced me to ashes made itself abundantly apparent calling for a quick trip to the bathroom to honk my guts out, man, talk about the bitter taste of defeat. After somewhat getting past my hangover and once more or less capable of marshalling my jumbled thoughts had absolutely no recollection of what had transpired the night before much less of how I had gotten home or what time of the day it was, soon giving it up as unworthy of further thought promptly dropped off to sleep again. It took a few long seconds for it to sink in that the insistent clamor of the god dam phone had roused me out of a deep sleep, my waking up to once again be greeted by waves of pure agony coursing through my skull threatening at any second to split it wide open with my blindly groping for that curse of mankind, my fumbling efforts that came within a hair of causing me to lose my precarious balance and pitching onto my head, the effort required in attempting to gain a coherent state of mind only exacerbating the waves of agony to the degree of almost bringing me to my knees with a very upset stomach threatening to erupt at any given time, eventually able to with eyes that refused to focus snatched up the offending instrument with near nerveless fingers to snarl into the receiver, who the fuck is this and what do you want?, it turned out to be the dick head of a dispatcher who first made it quite plain his not being impressed with my odious greeting, then without pause blandly informing me of the aircraft sitting there gassed up and ready to ferry to Thunder Bay for a much needed thawing out and a long overdue inspection. What I had to say to him at best unprintable, but one can be absolutely certain of my not failing to take the opportunity to direct unkind and disrespectful references toward his ancestry. Upon angrily slamming down the phone once completing our heated exchange with such vehemence it was a wonder it didn't shatter to resignedly sit back in consternation at the unmitigated gall of that turkey, Christ on a god dam crutch, having just endured a week long stint of horrendously pure undiluted hell that saw our very existence hanging in doubt for a good part of it now expected to jump through his hoops at his imperious command, not much caring what management or for that matter what anybody thought of my militant attitude, as far as I was concerned they could line up and kiss my (stinky)ass.

Still in a nauseous half dazed sleepy state of mind stumbled into the kitchen to with fumbling hands that still shook copiously managed to by the dint of great effort brew up a pot of coffee, and while impatiently waiting for it to

281

complete brewing my senses slowly came back on line gradually becoming aware of an exceedingly foul odor emanating from my person that would have brought tears to a sea gulls eyes convincing me beyond a shadow of doubt my requiring a long hot shower and to burn my clothes, but first an oh so refreshing cup of life restoring fresh brewed hot coffee that went far toward encouraging my will to live, gratefully sipping on my coffee pondered the combined effects of exhaustion, adrenalin and alcohol, mixed together sure as hell could pack one mighty wallop as my present state of health attested to leaving me feeling totally derailed, too much so to even remotely consider climbing into that iced over death trap of an aircraft, just thinking about it brought on an economy sized case of the "willies", oh Christ in my present condition and unstable state of mind it could be construed as nothing less than voluntary suicide, no way in god's green earth did I intend to offer myself up to such foolishness. Well it was off to the shower to hose off the odiferous accumulation of grime from my poor abused body and to shave off a week longs growth of begrimed whiskers, the mirror almost appearing to writhe in horror upon my presenting my unspeakably wild countenance that included red eyes, on top of that it almost requiring a whip and a chair to drive my filthy underclothes into the laundry basket, if remembering correctly picking my unspeakably filthy shorts up with a stick and depositing them into the garbage considering them to be long past salvation, god dam how good it felt to be clean and presentable and wearing a fresh change of clothes. Now convinced there existed a fifty chance of survival elected to wander down to the base to discover who else's feathers could be ruffled rather disconcerted upon finding it was mine that got the full Monty upon being apprised of the dispatcher and Alex having conspired behind my back to convince another of the pilots to ferry the aircraft to Thunder Bay with no takers much to their chagrin.

Now that sort of underhanded dealing thoroughly pissed me off, what ever respect I may have once retained for Alex vanished like the morning mist vowing that from here on to only do the job expected of me but no more than that.

Stubbornly sticking with my decision to wait for two days despite endless entreaties to do otherwise before reluctantly considering ferrying the ice cavern of an aircraft to Thunder Bay enjoying pissing Alex off while slowly recovering from the culmination of a nerve wracking ordeal and a debilitating hangover before finally working up the nerve to ferry the aircraft, though in no sense of the word looking forward to doing so. Once airborne without the added weight of five passengers the aircraft still to a large degree possessed all the aerodynamics of a man hole cover, one could only marvel at the desperate risk we had taken in attempting to fly an over grossed aircraft out of such a short and confined take off area much less flying the vast distance we had in an aircraft that retained less than desirable aerodynamic. Even though having far less weight to contend with it still continued to fly horribly, one could only attribute our daring and bravado at accomplishing the near impossible at the time to the debilitating and to a large degree the mind numbing effects of exhaustion and sheer desperation, one can only say that desperate situations call for desperate measures. But again there is far more to it than meets the eye, to the average person a machine is just an inanimate object designed to perform a specific task, and to them it lacks innate personality, they could not have been more mistaken in that assumption as any sailor who spends a great amount of time on their ships can attest to as their vessel becomes as one with them in personality and demeanor, and so it is with most pilots and their aircraft who become totally attuned to their machines, no longer separated mentally as flesh and metal but as a living entity melded as one, such being the case with my aircraft, we understood and respected each others individual personalities and abilities reacting accordingly as we did that frightful day, skill and luck can only account for so much, from there on it is left up to the aircrafts response to the pilots needs.

There is no appropriate way of describing my elation at finally arriving safely at the Thunder Bay airport where a blistering landing high speed landing performed adjacent to the runway to be greeted by an expectant ground crew who awaited my arrival who without hesitation immediately got about placing the aircrafts skis on four wheeled dollies, while jacking it up in order to do so one of the crew commented on how unusually heavy it appeared to be. On informing them of the hard packed drift snow to be found throughout the wings and tail and of course under the floor boards they failed at first to take me seriously scoffing openly at such an absurd claim until one of them having the presence of mind to open an inspection panel and to see for himself, needless to say that sure got their undivided attention with one of the younger of the crew inquiring as to how it handled in the air?, they had a good laugh when quipping, it having demonstrated all the aerodynamics of a manhole cover.

Once laboriously placed on the dollies it then taken into a heated hanger to begin a lengthy thawing out. Having no sooner walked in the door immediately collared by the chief engineer who without further ado demanded my producing the log books, my with out conscious thought putting on my best liars face and assuming a righteous air of injured innocence apologized for forgetting to place them on board before ferrying the aircraft as during the heat of the moment it had slipped my mind, but he could be assured that upon my return to Pickle

Lake they would be shipped down post haste as sure as the sun rose in the west and settled in the east, but this time around his having become totally frustrated with my past shenanigans climbed up one side of me and down the other, but in the end it did little to allay his immediate concerns impotently making an overt threat to keep the aircraft grounded until the log books produced. That threat I knew with a certainty lacked teeth and to only be a paper tiger, our already being so woefully short of serviceable aircraft and also secure in the fact the almighty dollar came first last and always.

There remained a justification on my part in refusing to relinquish the log books as the aircraft I flew had long since reached engine expiry and due to be replaced, but my being reluctant to exchange the time proven engines I trusted implicitly for a set of newly overhauled ones that required breaking in and not to be relied on for a time, my type of flying required the absolute dependability the old but reliable engines offered. Having successfully run the gauntlet with the chief engineer our calling it a draw immediately made myself scarce for a few days until a surreptitious inquiry informed me the aircraft ready to go back into service.

Needless to say upon presenting myself back at the hanger met with black scowls from the management, but as to be expected they of a matter of course got me in the end they're always having an eye for opportunity the aircraft sat there loaded with freight to be delivered to a remote settlement that would take me a long ways from a straight line return to Pickle Lake. Actually this turn of events phased me not at all being more than pleased to cover new ground.

Upon my eventual return to Pickle Lake Alex met me at the parking area chomping fiercely at the bit and anxious to once more resume our duties. The day we returned to Pot Lake sure gave me something to be grateful for when taking the time to view the awesome changes visited upon the surrounding area by the storm, the huge drifts formed and carved by the ferocious winds that appeared to march in staggered rows toward the eastern horizon made it abundantly clear our only escaping annihilation by the skin of our teeth, it isn't very often one gets the chance to survive that violent an experience.

The days from that point wore on in much the same manner without anything worthy of note occurring to mar the monotony of our routine, but it seemed fate still held another life threatening occasion in store for us yet.

Since our set to during the aftermath of the storm Alex and I had little to say to each other short of terse instructions applying to my duties taking the fun out of the job, his surly attitude also began to have an effect on the crew, their not seeming to be enjoying their duties to the degree they once had, perhaps the lingering fear of a repeat performance of the past storm occurring continued to hang over them as they often appeared to be keeping a close eye on the weather, well they could be assured so was I, from here on no risks taken with our abandoning the job at the first sign of bad weather moving in on us no matter how minor it appeared to be at the time or how badly it inconvenienced Alex's programs.

Actually having become somewhat bored with the ongoing sameness of my flying routine began to look forward to the end of the season, for as much as I enjoyed the work it had by now become old hat, but we were soon to have a little unexpected excitement injected into our usually monotonous routine during the course of a return trip, our just having completed our usual sleigh ride as usual climbed to a higher altitude to cross the sparsely treed area that stretched all the way to Pickle Lake eventually being forced to drop down to a much lower altitude upon encountering a band of low lying cloud directly in our path with my choosing to remain just slightly below the cloud base. Cruising blithely along with my mind in neutral a strange threatening uneasiness suddenly began to pervade my consciousness, a quick perusal of the engine instruments indicated nothing to alarm me nor could I sense any form of suspicious vibrations, but yet something tangible nagged at me, not really understanding why suddenly chose to make a rapid descent to get away from the cloud base and be that much closer to the ground if as a yet to be determined emergency dictated it be so, Alex must have felt the same premonition I had his suddenly sitting bolt upright in his seat to cast inquisitive glances out of the windshield as if expecting to see something out of the ordinary.

We hadn't descended more than five hundred feet or so when Alex suddenly gave off a startled yelp of shock and surprise just as a massive object hurtled by scant feet overhead, my busily concentrating on the height remaining to the ground below us never did catch sight of what it was, the next thing I knew the aircraft suddenly becoming totally uncontrollable yawing and twisting all over the sky with our rapidly descending in a half controlled state almost to ground level before reaching an area of stable air to only then begin to recover from an near inverted position that went far toward creating some tense moments before finally regaining full control, when all was said and done there remained very little space between us and the stunted trees.

For the first while no one seemed to be capable of speech as we struggled to come to grips with whatever the hell it was that had come so near to wiping us out of existence. After a time Alex who had finally managed to regain his composure after imbibing a couple of hefty snorts of scotch with near nerveless fingers leaned over to inquire in a whiskey falsetto, just what in the name of Christ happened back there?. My not as yet having fully recovered from the shock of that close call could only respond by shaking my head, at that he treated himself to another healthy snort before managing to gasp out, Christ hart, I have no idea just what in the hell it could have been, but all I can recall is catching a momentary glimpse of what could only be described as an aluminum overcast suddenly passing overhead of us, and when it did that was when all hell broke loose, I don't know how close it came but goddamit man it appeared to be god awful huge only missing us by a friggin hair, with that said he began a vicious assault on his bottle of scotch while mumbling to himself, I'm too god dam old for this shit, then continuing to stare nervously out of the windshield while fidgeting restlessly in his seat the rest of the way in.

My remaining in a state of total confusion and still badly shook by the unexplained incident that had come so near to wiping us out mulled over the inescapable fact that by the merest of chance we had avoided a mid air collision with an as yet unidentified aircraft that in passing had created a violent vortex of tortured air that all but spelled our demise upon sending the aircraft almost out of control with our coming near to spinning to certain doom, my barely regaining control and saving ourselves at the last possible second.

One could not help but to ponder the possibility of two aircraft converging into the same air space at exactly the same moment in time, the odds of that ever occurring beyond infinity, but obviously it could and in our case almost had but for my unexplained but fortuitous descent to a lower altitude, and in doing so narrowly averting disaster, it would appear the gods of chance were on the job that day.

Still the exceedingly rare possibility of such an occurrence taking place in such a remote area encompassing thousands of square miles continued to nag at me, as was to be expected we were never to know who it was or why they had chosen to descend through the cloud layer in the first place, and by doing so had unknowingly come perilously near to colliding with us, but we after much soul searching surmised it to be a four engine Canadian Forces aircraft returning from a long and boring arctic patrol, the flight crew most likely seeking a diversion from endless hours of crushing monotony the flight crew having out of sheer boredom descended over what they most likely considered an extremely remote and safe area to carry out their version of our Nantucket sleigh ride. But always I wondered why they had failed to detect our presence on their ultra sophisticated radar systems, obviously the operator(s) had most likely been sleeping at the switch. The well-rattled crew in the rear cabin had to wait in understandable confusion until we landed before our being able to divulge just what had occurred. It was a gray visage shaky crew that soberly disembarked from the aircraft that had come within a whisker of becoming our coffin to totter gratefully up to the office.(something like that could ruin one's whole day).

The young know it all dispatcher being of the smart ass type upon taking note of our shaky demeanor and ashen pallor's offhandedly inquiring in a smarmy tone of voice if we by chance had seen a ghost, then flashing all who had overheard him a self satisfied smirk at his sense of humor.

At first ignoring his presence as being unworthy of our notice went on to relate our near miss to a crowd of rapt listeners, upon hearing it the dispatcher rolled his eyes upwards as if in disbelief to inquire in a tone of voice that literally dripped of sarcasm as to what had we been smoking, the worst possible attitude he could have assumed at that time considering our confused and terribly upset state of mind, he should have known better, Alex who's overstretched nerves finally snapped suddenly rounded on him with a black faced fury one would have had to witness to be believed, pouncing on the now hapless dispatcher who had realized his gaffe far too late now received a taste of Alex's pent up and unbridled emotions that shocked us as he railed, you insignificant little prick what do you know about anything except sitting comfortably in your ivory tower playing tin god?, once having reached full cry there was no stopping him, and if the truth be known no one cared to intercede on the dispatcher's behalf as Alex continued to tear great bloody strips off the offender, it became increasingly obvious to all the strain of the long winter's travails stoically endured up till then had boiled to the surface fuelling his frustrations with the unmatched fervor of the righteous. We could only stand there in rapt awe at the incandescent intensity of the scathing spiel that spewed forth from the very same man it near taking a jackhammer to pry two consecutive words out of at one time. As he towered over the by now well cowed offender he appeared to swell up to twice his normal size, his passionate tirade reminding me of an enraged grizzly.

As his voice became hoarse from such unaccustomed use, paused momentarily to belt down a hefty snort of ye olde glenfiditch scotch whiskey that would have done in an ordinary man without once taking his burning eyes off his victim, upon returning the much depleted bottle back into the volumous folds of his parka and then casting a black look around the room as if daring anyone to contest him, the silent but appreciative audience to a man involuntarily taking a step backwards as if in obeisance, seeming to be satisfied with the results again took up his attack on the hapless offender with renewed passion and vigor spraying spittle and scotch whiskey into the cringing well subdued dispatcher's face continuing to mentally tear him into bloody quivering rags.

Upon being satisfied to having made himself abundantly clear, momentarily hesitated for a heart beat or two before violently slamming a huge hairy fist onto the desk as if enforcing his long winded discourse with a resounding crash that almost caused us to jump out of our skins with the well cowed dispatcher coming close to flying out of his chair backwards in fright.

As if satisfied with having gotten his point across, once again fished out his bottle of scotch to take a huge snort of scotch as if rewarding himself for portraying such an outstanding and commanding performance, suddenly wheeling around to cast a malignant beetle browed glance at what he most likely considered as lesser mortals, then grandly taking his leave with the overt threat to take his business elsewhere hanging in the air, at his departure someone began to clap their hands with the rest of us soon joining in, that is save for the well humiliated dispatcher who relieved to have watched Alex disappear out of the door had begun to fuss about in a brave attempt to smooth his ruffled feathers while vainly attempting to avert a beet red face while doing his best to ignore our knowing grins.

To celebrate that momentous occasion we all trooped over to the hotel to enjoy a cold beer with shit eating grins plastered all over our faces to discuss at great length the finer points of Alex's colorful theatrics that in our (uneducated in the arts) opinion, felt to have rivaled or even to have surpassed to a marked degree that of Byron or Plato for real life presentation (as if we knew the first thing about it)laughing ourselves weak from our antics in attempting to recreate Alex's metaphor failing miserably by invariably flubbing our lines at every attempt, in short are enjoying ourselves at the dispatchers expense, but one hell of a fine method of dissociating built up tensions. The following day it was business as usual, and to me a good thing as if one were allowed to dwell to long and heavily on the "what might have been" it could all too easily turn one into a mental cripple. Alex as if sensing our boredom suddenly as if out of the blue added a new dimension to our normal routine. Our having on many the occasion flown through an area dominated by a series of huge dome shaped granite up thrusts that marched sedately along a huge expanse of a pool table flat expanse of muskeg we normally traversed, they had long become familiar to us as a noticeable landmark, but one of them far larger in diameter than most stood out so imposingly it could be clearly seen for many the mile on a clear day and often used as a navigation way point being so prominent.

Alex surprised the hell out of me one fine cold morning when expressing a desire to land adjacent to the large up thrust but not offering any valid reason why he desired to do so. At first hesitant to comply with that odd request fearing the snow crust not sufficiently hard enough to bear the weight of the aircraft allowing it to bog down if not worse in what promised to be very deep snow upon slowing down, the very thought of that occurring causing me to cringe inwardly, he soon eased my mind upon assuring me it's wind swept surface being capable of supporting the weight of a far larger and heavier aircraft than the beech craft, having learned to trust his judgment implicitly as he had never in the past misrepresented any situation for his benefit, taking him at his word made a cautious touch down to find much to my relief his being absolutely correct, the surface found to be as hard as concrete and as flat and smooth as a pool table. The smug look that momentarily flashed across his homely mug after we had taxied in close to the side of the up thrust and shut down the engines told me he enjoyed being right, well be as it may it being a small relief to have someone make a critical decision once in a while though being the captain of the aircraft making such momentous decisions regarding the safety of the passengers and the aircraft usually my call.

How Alex went about choosing his areas of interest he kept to himself, but having gotten to know him quite well, aware that he never did anything randomly being too much the experienced professional, he hadn't risen to the lofty position of being the chief geologist for a multi national corporation without good reason. But for the life of me could I begin to imagine just what he could be possibly seeking in the midst of a remote and barren area of muskeg, well what ever it was he must have valid reason for having me land here, only in later years it was found out his seemingly random search for the elusive where with all also extended to diamond bearing lodes. But for what ever reason we had landed there it left me pleased beyond measure as the rare opportunity to have done so, it not being likely the chance to ever do so again would come my way again.

Time has since proved his hypothesis concerning the likely areas he had once (as I saw it at the time) fruitlessly prospected to eventually prove to be diamond bearing as rich lodes have since been found to exist not that far away from his endeavors.

Always the cores produced from the relatively shallow holes the crew drilled on a regular basis, the ones I managed to get a sneak peek of with the assistance of the drill crew intrigued the hell out of me seeming to largely consist of a yellowish type of lime stone interspersed with narrow bands of a coarse bluish appearing sand stone and often coming with numerous bits of ancient sea shells and marine invertebrate that informed us the shores of Hudson's Bay had once extended a lot further inland than first thought. This theory verified beyond a doubt the day we had occasion to land along side of an ancient boulder strewn beach that extended for as many miles either way as one could see, our spending many days there drilling for sand cores and bagging the coarse surface sands that were carefully labeled. As usual my insatiable curiosity ran rampant as Alex continued to keep his secrets to himself leaving me none the wiser.

One day out of simple curiosity drew and measured a line on the map from the ancient beach to the existing coast line on Hudson's Bay revealing the waters had receded a total of one hundred and twenty five miles more or less from were we now stood on the shores of what had once been an ancient shoreline.

Having retained a healthy curiosity of the nature of the huge granite up thrusts that continued to intrigue me no end, and now presented with the opportunity to investigate one of them set about doing so. The snow being packed rock hard by the incessant winds that must have regularly howled across the open stretches with unbelievable intensity making it easy going with my scaling one side of the up thrust to once having attained it's very crest able to behold a grand view of the surrounding area, god dam I breathed to myself, what impressively raw beauty to behold, nature at her finest and as yet unspoiled by man kinds voracious greed and relentless quest to destroy and sully all that's good and decent in pursuit of the golden wherewithal.

While admiring the awesomely unrestricted tapestry of the surrounding area it gave one the indelible impression of standing on the very crest of a sparsely treed island in the middle of a huge white lake dotted with smaller islands, seeming to stretch into the distant horizons, only then realizing the good fortune of my having been given the rare opportunity that very few would ever gain the opportunity to do so and to be able to observe the natural and wild beauty that surrounded me, humbled to have witnessed what very few ever have or ever will.

So entranced had I become while taking in the awesome vista that ringed me almost missed seeing what first appeared to be a well weathered table constructed entirely from the sparse stunted spruce trees that grew raggedly in the more sheltered areas of the up thrust, at first couldn't believe what my eyes told me much less conceive how it happened to be there, closer investigation revealing what I had first thought it, a crudely constructed table obviously created by human hands with an old fashioned well rusted buck saw hanging off one end. Now that really gave me pause for thought, how who ever had arrived in such an unlikely and remote area in the first place and why?, no trapper in their right mind would even remotely consider setting up camp on such an inaccessible wind blasted treeless place. Further investigation led me to conclude more than one man had once been here judging by the number of rusty bed springs and frames along with all the accoutrements that had at one time went toward a crude kitchen with a collection of old fashioned pewter and cast iron utensils lying randomly about.

At first assuming their having arrived in much the same manner we had, the bush pilots of long ago if nothing else did not lack courage or fortitude in landing their ancient contraptions in such a remote area. That assumption pretty much went by the wayside upon stumbling onto an ancient well-rusted steam powered diamond drill with many lengths of large bore steel drill rods lying beside it. Also there appeared to be a number of well rotted jute bags that once had contained coal lying in a fair sized pile besides a well rusted steel boiler mounted on what had been at one time two huge timber skids with bands of heavy steel attached to their bottoms, scraping away the drifted snow from behind the boiler revealed an old fashioned geared winch that still had a length of rusted cable wound around the drum, good Christ how had they ever managed to winch that monstrosity up the side of the steeply slanted dome, but in order not to allow it to sink out of sight in the muskeg come spring when it once more reverted to floating bog it required doing, obviously who ever they had been no doubt planned on returning and perhaps they had, but for reasons lost to me it had been abandoned.

Having pretty much satisfied my curiosity summoned Alex and the crew to have a look, at first they could only gawk at the ancient machinery in stunned disbelief finding it incomprehensible that some one some how had arrived there long before we had, they must have been one hell of a tough and determined crew of hombres to have made their way to such an isolated area dragging in such unwieldy and cumbersome drilling equipment and how had they known their ultimate destination while traveling through such impassable terrain and for what purpose?, one could only cringe at the thought of the adversity they must have as a matter of course been forced to endure while involved in doing so.

Alex conjectured they had arrived there well before the Second World War having made their way in from the frozen shores of Hudson, s Bay traveling during the dead of winter over the frozen muskeg utilizing teams of horses. Alex proclaiming they're most likely to have extensively drilled parts of the immediate area though we found no evidence of their having done so outside of the ruins of what had one time been a semi permanent camp site, It being next to impossible to ascertain how long they had initially remained there, be it just one season or many?, but for whatever reason failing to return to claim their machinery, it could have well been written off as being economically unworthy or could have been due to the burgeoning shortage of man power and materials at the time, or found to be uneconomical for what ever reason only known to them to further pursue the drilling program, but still how had they had ever managed to accomplish such a super human feat in it's entirety at all evaded logic.

My being totally fascinated by ancient machinery took it upon myself to examine the workings of the antiquated steam drill with great interest knowing there was usually a manufacture's plaque made of cast brass riveted to the structure eventually located one almost completely hidden by a layer of black lichen that once scraped clear revealed the name of "Boyles Brothers" diamond drilling from Port Arthur Ontario, one hell of a long way as the crow flies from were it sat, The plaque proved to be next to impossible to remove except by the use of heavy duty tools prevented my removing it as a keep sake, perhaps some day some one else will unexpectedly stumble on it as we did, but that eventuality remains some what doubtful during my time being located in such a remote, inaccessible and out of the way area it will remain unknown except to a few, probably forever unless by chance man in his unending quest for the golden wherewithal should by the remotest of chance wander into that truly fascinating wonder land in the middle of no where, for as any one who has spent time in the vastness of the north knows there are strange things done beneath the northern sun. Alex having satisfied his reasons for landing there we continued on our way but for reason unclear to me it found me strangely reluctantly to leave that place of strange occurrences and many unanswered questions never to return.

As it went we continued to traverse the width and breadth of that vast muskeg, it's complexity and endlessly changing wonders became as familiar to me as my back yard with my thoroughly enjoying the opportunity to do so, perhaps to the uninitiated it appearing to be nothing more than a vast tract of sere sterile muskeg, actually it abounded with a diversity of wild life, with wolves, caribou and moose being abundant and to be seen just about everywhere we went along with signs of seldom seen smaller animals such as mink, marten, fox and weasels, no doubt they could be found in every partially sheltered copse of scrawny wind blasted trees that usually bordered the meandering rivers and creeks that wound their way throughout the entire area, also harboring a large variety of northern species bird life that appeared to thrive in the muskeg they called home, and of course one can not fail to mention the ubiquitous raven that magically appeared out of a seemingly empty sky no matter were we went. What made it all the more interesting and kept me on my toes when moving along at high speed during the course of a Nantucket sleigh ride were the small herds of woodland caribou and on the occasion a moose that without warning seemingly bolt out of no where to stampede recklessly in front of us as we thundered along forcing an immediate and abrupt pull up in order to avoid a collision, such a happening could well ruin one's whole day thus keeping one alert to the possibility of spooking an unseen animal out of a copse of wind blasted trees at any time.

As the days relentlessly marched on, the constant effort required to get the job done placed a great strain on men and machinery, in our heightened efforts to complete the program as laid out by Alex before the approaching spring thaw curtailed our efforts. It had been noticed for some time the left hand throttle travel had become increasingly sticky making it extremely difficult to coordinate smoothly with the right. This unknowingly created a deadly combination of familiar contempt along with exhaustion of mind and body that insidiously crept in lulling me into ignoring the potential danger by assuring myself the season to be soon ending, this foolish oversight came as near to spelling the end for all of us as one would ever care to come.

One fair early spring day with my feeling totally dragged out and not in the least up to flying that day and feeling more dead than alive after completing the long trip from Pickle Lake with my slouched in the seat most of the way half dozing in the warmth of the early spring sun that came through the windshield, the mesmerizing roar of the engines combined with the comforting warmth of the sun conspired to create a torpid state of mind that left me far less alert than I should have been. On arrival over our destination reluctantly roused myself sufficiently to begin the normally demanding parachute landing and as usual upon the nose of the aircraft just beginning to pass over the shore line to ram on full power at the appropriate time to check our rapid descent with the engines faithfully responding as always to immediately upon touch down pull the throttles full back to idle, that is the right hand throttle responded normally but the left hand throttle lever did so without any noticeable resistance what so ever leaving the engine roaring madly at full power immediately causing the aircraft to slew wildly to the right with my recognizing within the space of a split second the throttle cable had snapped leaving me with no throttle control over the engine to with lightning speed born of desperation making a grab for the mixture control levers to snap them back into the full idle cut off position effectively shutting down both engines, as quickly reacting to the emergency as

I had we only just averted piling into an unyielding wall of granite with only a few feet to spare.

Once all had more or less settled down to a primal scream with all counting their blessings in having gotten off so lightly, Alex who at first continued to sit staring at the menacing granite wall in front of us with stunned disbelief etched all over his craggy features that had turned a pasty gray blinking like an owl in the bright sunlight his first words being, goddamit Hart, I'm too old to put up with this shit, what in the fuck happened?, at that he began to fumble about in a futile attempt to locate his omnipresent bottle of scotch, so badly rattled making tiny squeaks of relief upon successfully locating it to belt down a hefty snort that would have laid a lesser man low, at that point in time I was sorely tempted to join him.

Having more or less recovered from my initial fright managed to chirp out in a high pitched falsetto it being a sure bet the throttle cable had snapped, the mind numbing thought of what was sure to have transpired if the cable had let go before the engine reached full power in unison with the right one didn't require being a rocket scientist to foresee the calamity that would have ultimately taken place if that were to have occurred at such a critical juncture with our barely hanging on the edge of a ragged stall just short of touch down, without question we would have immediately without warning flipped over onto the right wing to cartwheel to destruction.

Alex upon finally realizing the full import of our dilemma went near ballistic with concern, snarled Jesus jumped up Christ, now what are we going to do now? in a surly tone of voice that implied it to be all my fault as if secretly doing so to bedevil him..

Waiting until his wrath and frustrations had abated to a spate of angry mumblings informed him it presented a very slight problem for me to jury rig the throttle to a degree it would safely see us back home, but he would have to bear with me during the interim and to go about his work as if the situation to be of no consequence.

Removing a panel that allowed access to the accessories section of the engine removed the broken stub of cable from the throttle actuating arm in order to allow wire locking it in any position chosen as the engine could still be controlled to a sufficient degree by actuating the mixture control lever. While doing so mentally castigated myself for ignoring the obvious warnings the increasing stiffness of the cable had given for some time, actually in retrospect it being highly inexcusable on my part to having done so when taking into consideration the continuous and severe usage imposed on it, especially during the rapid advancing of the throttles during final flare and touch down during the parachute landings, how many more times could one tempt fate before one's luck ran out?, it really didn't bear thinking too deeply on.

Later on in the day after Alex had completed all the work his well rattled nerves could tolerate, gathered him and the crew into our survival tent explaining to them in great detail as was my policy in keeping them in the loop thus gaining their trust of what had recently transpired and how I planned to see us safely out of there.

Having pre warmed the engines and when ready to go had then shut them down and wire locked the throttle arm on the left hand engine in the full power position for take off.

Be as it may, I admit to not looking forward to what promised to be another hair raising take off loaded all aboard then starting up the right engine advancing the throttle to the point the aircraft threatened to pivot then quickly starting up the left engine which caught immediately with a throaty roar our practically leaping ahead as we zig zagged all over hell and back calling for some fancy foot work on the rudder pedals before finally gaining a semblance of directional control with my finally being able to herding the aircraft in a relatively straight line, being lightly loaded we took to the air in no time flat to commence a rapid climb with both engines hammering away at full power until reaching a safe altitude while making a bee line to a flat part of the muskeg, once satisfied all to be well commenced to perform some tricky adjustments of the left hand fuel mixture lever to reduce the power output of the engine, coordinating its power output to more or less remain in synchronization with each other, which if the truth be known not to be all that accurate as the uneven beat of the left engine on the occasion emitted a loud backfire that all but caused me to jump out of my skin each time it did so soon wearing badly on everyone's nerves until gratefully able to shut down the left engine and carry out a single engine landing onto on a chosen flat section of muskeg were the throttle arm re adjusted to an approximate high power cruise setting.

The reduced power setting during take off called for a considerably longer run than normal, but that requirement proved to offer no hardship having many a mile of clear take off space ahead of us.

On landing back at Pickle Lake after completing an uneventful flight it again proved to be an easy matter of shutting down the left engine and performing a single engine landing, only firing it up as required to erratically weave my way in to my parking spot with the ground crew wondering just what in the hell I was up to this time around, but by good luck more than good judgment managed it without colliding with anything.

The replacement of the throttle cable being quite time consuming and requiring a lot of technical expertise called for another trip to Thunder Bay much to Alex's chagrin, but pissed off about it or not there was no way out of it my flying down the next morning with the hanger crew getting right at it upon my arrival, my by necessity requiring as quick a turn around as possible due to the season getting short with much yet to be accomplished.

The following morning the head office received notification one of our beech craft missing, failing to return on a return trip from Pot Lake. On being informed on that unexpected bit of news it all but knocked me over as no one but me authorized to land there due to the high degree of hazard involved, something had a bad smell about it.

The completion of the cable replacement would require at least another day and failing in an attempt to elicit further information from any source about what had transpired during my absence forced to bide my time until the unfolding series of events revealed themselves. The growing suspicion that Alex had gotten his priorities all tangled up as he was often prone to do when under stress becoming unbearably contentious had no doubt bullied the dispatcher who knew better into sending another pilot in my place directly against orders from top management unless checked out by me to take on the hazards of pot lake, the more I thought about it the more certain I became that was exactly what had occurred with the end results being predictable, oh man, if some thing got bent or broken the shit guaranteed to hit the fan big time.

The tiresome routine of fending off the chief engineer took on a new dimension with his furiously threatening to ground the aircraft unless producing the log books pronto as he had enough of my silver tongued excuses, but as usual ignored his passionate outburst being well aware his impotent railings lacked conviction unless having the log books to provide the evidence to do so, and of course their was the bottom line to be considered.

The next morning the aircraft wheeled out to the runway fully fuelled allowing me to fly a direct course to pot lake and for once having the rare chance to fly an empty aircraft that performed nimbly in the crisp cold air greatly enjoyed passing over terrain I had never flown over before, a steady diet of sere muskeg got a little heavy after a while. At about two thirds of the way the heavily treed area began to thin out with the rolling terrain gradually flattening out as we flew ever closer to the coast.(And here comes the Muskeg Express).

At about twenty miles or so back from pot lake what first appeared to be a darker smudge visible against the back drop of white snow that could not be discerned until coming much closer it then becoming obvious to be one of our aircraft flipped over on it's back and all bent to hell as predicted almost smack dab in the middle of the huge drifts.

Still puzzled as to why the pilot had attempted to land there in the first place considering his lack of knowledge concerning the local conditions, but not in the least surprised to see the extent of the damage the wrecked aircraft had sustained, as to pile into them huge drifts at high speed guaranteed it's destruction, whoever the pilot, he had screwed up big time.

Circling overhead indicated at least five men standing on the ice, it now being obvious our four man crew had been aboard, all I could do at that point was to hope they weren't injured, and if so not too badly. Goddamit, just what in the hell was that pilot doing there in the first place without first being thoroughly checked out on the local conditions?, well for whatever reason what was done was done, but the confusing situation no doubt bode grim consequences for some one leaving them with some tall explaining to do before it was all over.

Performing my usual tried and true approach and touch down able to turn around in half the usual required space to taxi in and shut down the engines to be immediately mobbed by our crew who were extremely grateful to see me, but that didn't apply to the pilot who I recognized as being one that had never appealed to me, his demeanor being one of brash arrogance on top of being highly opinionated about most anything under the sun. His sarcastic sneering comment upon limping up to me concerning my highly unorthodox method of landing immediately set me on edge, but ignoring his empty comment as if he didn't exist being more concerned about the crew's condition, one of them had what I suspected to be a fractured arm, another badly bruised or cracked ribs his experiencing great difficulty in drawing a deep breath, the grayish pallor on his face informed me of his suffering to a greater degree than willing to demonstrate, the other two had gotten off fairly lightly only sustaining a series of painful bruises along with a severe shaking up, otherwise pretty much intact.

As for the pilot in question who appeared to be limping badly, I didn't inquire into his state of health for if the truth be known could have cared less if he dropped dead at my feet from his injuries.

Loading up the injured crew who in spite of their pain all sported huge grins, pleased to be flying with me once again as we blasted off for Pickle Lake, a now well subdued pilot who I had refused to allow to sit in the co pilot's seat sat morosely in the back cabin with the rest of the crew most likely contemplating his uncertain future. To my surprise upon landing met by none other than the president and owner of the company who had flown up in his private Beech craft to await our arrival, but Alex for whatever reason remaining conspicuously absent. As it was it had been a hell of a surprise to not find him among the crew at Pot lake, his absence leaving me somewhat confused as he had never in the past sent his men out alone, his without fail accompanying us, now his unexplained absence at Pickle Lake to see to the welfare of his men really threw me.

The four men were immediately taken to the Osnaburgh nursing station to have their injuries attended to, as to what had transpired between the errant pilot and the owner, we were never to know his disappearing the following morning as did the dispatcher who had in knowledgeable error dispatched the fateful flight to Pot lake against standing policy.

The next morning Alex suddenly re-appeared as if out of no where in an extremely foul mood looking for all the world like a man from the grave, coming on to all and sundry in a rude and brusque manner, and if the whole odorous affair had been solely my fault directed his built up frustrations straight at me, I got the message real quick like, but if the truth be known I could have cared less what he thought.

No one was ever the wiser just what eventually transpired between the owner of the company and Alex during their marathon meeting behind closed doors, but it was a safe bet that Ethyl Corp. not finding it in their best interest to quibble about the accident quietly paid out the loss of the aircraft, one can also be certain in doing so it failed to place Alex in a favorable position with the top brass.

Upon resuming our duties short one man Alex having become increasingly morose and withdrawn and if at all possible had taken to hitting on his perpetual bottle of scotch harder than ever, his surly attitude placing a black cloud over everyone further taking the fun out of the job, our three remaining men though more than willing to do their best even though still stiff and sore of a matter of course unable to carry out their duties with the alacrity they had shown in the past much to Alex's mounting frustration, but in spite of it all our eventually being able to complete the last of the job requirements, and none too soon as the late spring weather made it a dicey situation to land in certain areas of the muskeg except during the early morning hours when the snow surface still retained a hard crust, but even then it could prove to be a precarious undertaking that kept me on edge at all times making me more than happy to complete the last of them without incident.

Being called into the owners presence one morning behind closed doors, some surprised to hear his requesting my taking two of our apprentice mechanics and fly to Pot lake in order to salvage the expensive still serviceable engines and propellers, plus what ever else of value that could be claimed within reason before the wreck sunk into the muddy bottom of the lake, that Wiley old bandit just couldn't resist such a good deal, but what the hell given the opportunity would have done the same.

Eventually the season wound down with new faces appearing on the scene on a daily basis, Alex as most had in the flying business walked out of my life never to be seen again without so much as a handshake or a farewell kiss my ass, but one can truthfully say if nothing else he certainly gave me a winter to remember.

The ghosts of the past often parade by in my memories, but Alex among many others stands tall, them of his ilk are a rapidly vanishing breed of men, the likes of who will never pass this way again, they simply don't make them like that anymore.

A State Of Mind

NEVER AT ANY TIME CAN maps pertaining to the areas once frequently flown over during the time of my lengthy career be perused with out a flash back of past incidents, be they good bad, indifferent or otherwise. Some remembered with deep nostalgia, others with a repressed shudder of raw fear, in effect running through the entire gamut of human emotions, however they turned out I am still casting a shadow though by all rights shouldn't be if one were to observe the rules of statistics.

One of them worthy of note comes to mind that wholly encompasses all known human emotions involved in what could be best described as an exceedingly trying venture that to this day remain firmly locked into my memory banks.

It all came about one early morning upon receiving a desperate plea for assistance on the phone from Brian Maxwell, chief engineer for Slate Falls Air based in Sioux Lookout Ont. As it turned out they had a twin beech-18 stranded at Fort Severn on the forbidding coast of Hudson's Bay with an unserviceable engine and felt his present crew of young know it all eight to five time clock punching mechanics only used to performing their duties in an air conditioned hanger complete with all the support equipment one could possibly need and in his opinion not in any respect mentally or technology wise up to such a formidable task of taking on a possible engine change in such a hostile environment. To be truthful the thought of venturing out there at so late in the season being late October left me less than thrilled at the thought of venturing into such a remote area being all too familiar with the predictably atrocious weather conditions one could expect at that time of the year. One in good conscience could not let them down in their time of need for they in retrospect had always treated me with due consideration and respect when ever performing work for them even though my guts where doing their dammdest to wrap themselves around my back bone as the mind and body numbing problems and unforeseen difficulties my familiarity with the area in question knew with a certainty guaranteed to be a bitch on wheels leaving me unsure of having the fortitude to take on such a daunting task. But if the task ever to be done within the time remaining one could ill afford to waste precious time battling indecision or futilely pondering the imponderable made the decision to do it come what may, gathering up my tools and cold weather gear along with a healthy dose of trepidation riding my shoulders headed for Sioux Lookout. Once there immediately began the crucial task of collecting all the necessary support equipment one would require in order to do what was certain to be a difficult and demanding job, to overlook or forget even a few of the necessary tools could all too easily doom one to failure or in the least create unneeded expense and problems as there was no where or no one to turn to for help, with the combined expertise of the chief engineer we managed to round up everything one could possibly require or at least that being the idea, but still in my over anxious haste overlooked an item crucial to the job, the oversight creating far reaching consequences, as it turned out I would have ample reason to regret that oversight.

For a skilled helper chose a young native apprentice I had known for some time and respected his work ethics by the name of Eli Waboose, in my estimation a very willing and astute worker.

Once having completed the loading of another beech craft with the replacement engine and support equipment, soberly informed the owners we at best only stood a fifty chance of success considering the odds, but they could well be assured we would do our very best.

The next morning we where on our way in a grossly overloaded aircraft that flew ponderously for the first while until a fair amount of fuel had burned off and for the most part keeping me on edge throughout the first hour and half of the long cold flight. Before departing the tide tables for Hudson's Bay had been carefully consulted to ensure our arrival more or less coincided with the high tide cycle in order to be certain of utilizing the one and only fixed pier to safely unload our gear and replacement engine.

After enduring that long cold mind numbing ride in a draughty aircraft loaded to the nuts, the butterflies in my stomach expanding to the size of bats while somberly viewing the barren expanse of sere featureless terrain stretching endlessly below, upon our eventual arrival at the remote settlement of Fort Severn we circled once to establish the wind and tide conditions before committing ourselves to a landing, as we circled the dreary appearing settlement I couldn't help but to mutter to myself, good Christ what had I let myself in for this time?

Upon landing and docking met by a raw bitingly cold wind that did little to fortify my sagging spirits. Thus our arrival into a less than sylvan environment more or less set the scenario for the next few days. Well be as it may, we still had a job to do so we set to with a vengeance to unload the aircraft as quickly as possible, once having accomplished that demanding task the pilot Matt Mitchell couldn't leave quickly enough bidding us a cheery "have fun guys", blasting off on his return flight leaving us feeling abandoned, unloved and very much alone to face what ever came next. Viewing with growing alarm the disturbing sight of shell ice beginning to crust along the shore line despite the vicious currents that swirled along the muddy river banks cruelly reminding us our time to be short and above all demanding, needless to say that gave us added impetus to begin the job and to accomplish it as quickly as possible.

Viewing the fixed pier, couldn't help but wonder how many times it had been replaced throughout the years as without fail the spring ice floes that came crashing down the Severn river like a runaway locomotive it's head long progress hardly experiencing a moments hesitation as the unstoppable floes completely ripped out or badly damaged the deeply sunken pilings, snapping them off as if they where made up of flimsy bamboo annually requiring extremely expensive replacement. A lot of us wondered why it wasn't simply replaced with a floating dock that could rise and fall with the tides and be easily removed from the water in late fall. But then again that's asking a bit much of the political hacks that that governed Northern Affairs, perhaps a little thing like replacing a prohibitively expensive pier on an annual basis not worthy of consideration. Actually the on going replacement cost of the pier unworthy of comment in direct comparison with numerous other extremely costly and totally useless brain dead schemes randomly taking place in all the settlements at one time or another, for example at one point our flying in piecemeal the complete components of a portable saw mill with all the bells and whistles, an undertaking that consisted of flying two round trips a day from Pickle Lake, a total distance flown of seven hundred and twelve miles for one whole week, of course us pilots loved it considering it easy money, but for the life of us, no one could begin to comprehend the logic behind such an prohibitively expensive scheme as there simply is no adequate stands of suitable timber to be found any where in the area to supply the mill with raw fiber any where in the area. Actually useless conjecture as all the components that were required to set up a viable saw mill within a given period of time either vandalized or being indiscriminately heaved off the dock to make room, a good many of the expensive components ending up on the muddy river bottom to be eventually inundated by mud or washed away by the high rising fall tides not to mention the annual ice floes that annually decimated the pier had spelled the end of an expensive diesel engine and huge circular saw blade still in their packing crates along with numerous heavy steel components that had sat all summer long gathering rust, all eventually ending up ignominiously sinking out of sight in the silt of the river bed.

As it stood our otherwise having little choice in the matter but to do what must be done if we were to ever leave there before becoming frozen in reluctantly forced to accept the cold hard fact the sooner we began our onerous task the better for us.

Our first job consisted of moving the aircraft over to the pier while the tide still remained high to begin removing the stricken engine post haste, while Eli busied himself draining the cold thick oil from the engine and oil tank I took a precious half hour to arrange suitable accommodations at the teacher age being pleasantly surprised to find the two female teachers to be old friends of mine who welcomed us with open arms. One must in all decency give them credit for not only offering us hot meals and much needed moral support when most needed, for without question it would have gone badly for us through our darkest hours.

With grim determination and numbed fingers we labored straight through what remained of the day and with the feeble glow of two gas lanterns assisting us throughout the miserably endless night. Having at one point been forced to move the aircraft away from the pier due to the tide ebbing had no choice but to slog through the clinging slippery mud from the aircraft to the pier when ever requiring one thing or another making our job hell on earth only taking short breaks when finding ourselves unable to continue and to fortify our sagging spirits by literally inhaling great draughts of hot coffee and soup provided by the good hearted teachers, a kind hearted and thoughtful consideration that went far toward bolstering our fast weakening resolve, on the occasion when unable to further withstand the bitingly cold wind blowing off the bay we would give it up for a time to visit the teacher age with the welcome warmth often finding both of us nodding off at the table only to suddenly jerk ourselves awake more tired and worn than ever knowing we would once more have to return to our labors and face the daunting trials that lay ahead. Each time we made the short walk back to the aircraft in the dark and the cold of the night, it coming perilously close to withering away our determination to continue on.

Having at a crucial time discovered much to our regret we had overlooked the requirements to bring three twenty five foot aluminum pipes to use as a tripod, the mind boggling disappointment of having done so all but spelled the end for us, but if we were to accomplish the job our having little choice but to do otherwise had hired two of the locals with the help of the teachers to locate and deliver three of the tallest trees they could find in the area as soon as possible, some what taken aback upon their being delivered our finding them woefully short, not exceeding much more then fifteen feet in length when requiring a minimum of twenty feet, preferably more not to mention they're being warped and twisted almost to the point of being unusable, really of very little use to us but again having no other alternative had to make do with what we could get. God dam how I cursed my stupidity in over looking the critical need for a tripod as we could have so easily tied three aluminum pipes of sufficient length on to the floats, but again useless conjecture.

Assembling our makeshift tripod as best we could, the very sight of their squat ungainly and inadequate appearance really set off the butterflies in my belly. Once more having moved the aircraft over to the pier as the tide approached it's high water mark. My heart sank to my toes upon viewing the pathetic set up of wind blasted stunted poles that passed for a tripod with my impotently berating myself for overlooking such a critical component. As it stood our chances of success had sunk to an alarming level, but still we bulled on moving the aircraft into position as the rising tide eventually allowed the positioning the engine beneath our woefully inadequate tripod. To our dismay soon learning the chain hoist we had planned on using to lift the engine totally useless lacking sufficient height to allow our making use of it. At that point a sinking feeling of defeat washed over us wanting to give it up there and then, staring disconsolately at our seemingly impossible situation with tears of anger and frustration filling my eyes the answer suddenly came to me, certainly it would prove to be extremely dicey but having no other alternative reluctantly shinnied up one of the poles to remove the useless chain hoist and to secure a short length of cable to the very top of the tripod and down through the engine lifting lugs shortening them to the limit the rising tide allowed.

Now it was a matter of waiting for the tide to recede and for the restraining cable to tension. When checking on how little leeway we had to play with as the tide receded before the wing contacted the dock gave me a bad case of the willies, it would be a close run thing as there was woefully little else that could be done.

During the tension filled interim we made absolutely certain nothing had been inadvertently overlooked when removing all the control lines etc. if that where to be the case it could most certainly cause grave problems at a very critical time.

Taking advantage of the time span for the tide to ebb we took a much needed break, but found it hard to relax the gnawing concern about the suitability of our jury rigged set up saw to that. Anxious to the point of distraction that we might miss a critical minute or two that could spell the difference between success or failure kept a vigilant watch on the tide's progress, a nerve wracking past time that in due course leaving us almost numb from enduring the ravages of exposure to the bitingly cold wind and the debilitating effects of sustained stress brought on by the uncertainty of what to expect next as the tide inexorably ebbed the weight of the engine gradually taken up causing the poles to settle as had been expected but not to the alarming degree they did before stabilizing into the yielding mud, and in doing so coming near to giving us fits of despair as we could ill afford to lose precious inches.

Numb with anxiety and near despair at our catch twenty two situation that neither allowed our releasing the engine from the tripod cable or to arrest the inevitable fall of the tide, only able to impotently wait in tense anticipation while watching the scene before us unfold with cold horror as the bottom side of the wing verged on making contact with the surface of the pier, at the very last second desperately managing to pry the engine clear of the three mounting lugs and when the engine had swung clear screeching frantically at Eli to shove the god dam wing clear of the pier's surface, this he managed to do with alacrity grabbing the wing tip while desperately lifting with all his might barely managing to shove it clear in the bare nick of time at the cost of a little paint. Man I panted to myself as the wing tip scraped clear of the pier, that's as close as it gets.

Once that soul numbing crisis had passed, for the first brief while our only able to stand there weak with relief at avoiding what had been the closest of calls, not really caring to dwell too deeply on the consequences of the what if's dismissed the incident as best one could from my mind. Shaky from the unsettling effects of our close call but still grateful to have succeeded gave in to the release of the terrible tension we had labored under for so long breaking into gales of wild laughter that bordered on the hysterical, as the pent up tensions drained away, it wasn't too long before our newly found euphoria vanished as the morning mists upon becoming aware of the cold hard fact the engine now hung at least five feet away from the edge of the pier with nothing but sticky clinging mud below it.

Faced with the daunting task of figuring how best to sling the heavy awkward engine over without inadvertently toppling our tripod momentarily stumped by the enormity of what still lay ahead of us, wondered just how I happened to possess the seeming propensity in invariably finding myself up to my ears in deep brown.

Any moves made from here on called for extreme caution as to make a wrong one could spell imminent disaster, but however we did it our choice remained limited as we somehow had to shift the unserviceable engine over to the pier in order to ready the replacement engine for installation as quickly as possible and above all to have it ready to sling into place during the course of the next high tide. Our recent mind bending ordeal that had all but wiped us out had also turned my thought processes to mush, finding myself unable to respond to our next crisis wisely decided we required a short rest along with an infusion of hot food and coffee if we planned on continuing on without creating a disaster.

Once having fortified our sagging will power and feeling some what revived, still felt terribly bone weary, but at least now able to reason out our situation soon coming up with a viable plan. Fortunately having had the foresight to bring two cable come along and in doing so saved the day. Outlining my plan to Eli, gathered up my courage to reluctantly shinny up one of the shaky poles, an Endeavour that plain and simply scared the life out of me while doing so, at one point while doing found myself almost unable to continue when near freezing up with fright upon the unstable contraption we loosely referred to as a tripod for reasons never understood began to vibrate and shake as if inflicted with a severe case of palsy (I think it was only me), Having no choice but to continue on gathered my fast dwindling courage to shakily continue on albeit very slowly and carefully until reaching the very top, and once establishing a hold began the exceedingly difficult mostly one handed task of first attaching one of the cable come along to the tripod and then on to the short cable attached to the engine lifting lugs, then completing the extremely difficult job of hooking the cable from the second come along to more or less the bottom of the engine to then toss it to Eli who hooked his end to the far side of the pier. The mind searing job of carefully loosening off the cable clamps on the cable that took up the weight of the engine allowing it to slip sufficiently until the full weight of the engine taken up by the come along attached to the tripod, the excruciatingly demanding gymnastics demanded to accomplish the job all but doing me in.

Greatly relieved all had gone as well as it had, braced myself to begin the teeth clenching ordeal of lowering the engine one click at a time while Eli in turn took up the slack one click at a time. This excruciatingly slow but sure method gradually resulted in the engine being pulled toward the pier at an alarming angle.

As tense as the situation had become, we had little choice but to continue with the stress factor running off the scale, my finally deciding it would be circumspect on my part to place my weight as far out on the outside pole of the tripod as possible and still be able to work the come along, this in effect served to act as a counter balance, but Christ was it difficult to hang on and exceedingly difficult to work the come along calling for a lot of exhausting shifting of my body back and forth as required to do the job. By the time that mind shattering ordeal had finally been completed without accident or incident or any other unforeseen difficulties my mouth had become bone dry while my overtaxed muscles screamed in burning agony threatening to lock up on me from hanging on to my precariously shaky perch for so long, when first attempting to lower myself off the pole almost lost my tentative hold and plunging into the sticky stinking mud that lay in wait. I am certain to this day I left deep gouge marks as my finger nails raked deep grooves in the bark of the pole during my shaky descent, one can never be absolutely certain but might have even used my teeth a time or two in a desperate attempt to slow down my descent, but still garnering a few healthy slivers in my hands and belly during the process but grateful all the same to have gotten off so easily.

With smug if not shaky satisfaction of having safely accomplished that most difficult and trying of tasks we viewed the two engines now sitting side by side with a sense of relief momentarily washing over me until the nerve shattering thought it would have to be done over again in reverse assailed me sending cold chills racing down my spine, but this time with a new engine. My blood ran cold at the thought of once more being forced by absolute necessity to climb up that shaky contraption of a tripod to sling the engine back under it.

At that moment my resolve all but failed leaving me in serious doubt of my being able to dredge up the strength and willpower to do so, but again what choice did one have, what must be done would be done.

Tired and cold as we were we ignored the symptoms of fatigue as best one could continuing to labor mindlessly with numbed hands and feet all that long cold miserable day and far into the endlessly long night working by the feeble glow of two gas lanterns stripping down the stricken engine and building up it's replacement. To make matters increasingly difficult the cold wind blew threateningly off the bay throughout the long night making the job all the more difficult reminding us winter storms lay not far off. In a vain attempt to inject a little humor into an otherwise humorless situation commented to Eli we where extremely fortunate to not have to contend with hordes of mosquito's, this only earned a non-committal grunt in return.

At times when pushed far beyond human endurance we often considered giving it up for the night, but the nagging fear of being frozen in along with an overwhelming desire to get the job done and get the hell out of there mercilessly drove us on. As the first light of gray dawn filtered in we took a few precious minutes to gaze at and appreciate the beautiful flush of red sky in the east as the sun began to burn through the early morning mists, it's feeble rays offered little in the way of warmth but nevertheless the comforting sight of it bolstered our sagging spirits tremendously, but as beautiful as it was it still brought on a feeling of trepidation my knowing all too well what the red sky portended, we where in for a hell of a storm within the next day or two, but regardless of the coming threat one could not help but to admire the azure blue sky outlined by thin wisps of ragged clouds painting the horizon, how beautiful nature can be at that time of the year. Then came the seemingly endless skeins of geese etched against the limitless sky for miles around, they're plaintive honking echoing in our ears as they flew south to warmer climes, they're passage also foretold of the fierce winter storms yet to come, the icy grip of winter lay not too far off in the future. As much of a beautiful sight it presented to gaze appreciatively upon we knew we could ill afford the time to do so as every minute counted against us. How I envied them geese as they flew on by unburdened by the wants and cares we humans brought upon ourselves.

As they soared majestically overhead in great and endless skeins with their calls echoing plaintively in the cold air the almost unbearable longing to accompany them all but overwhelming me. Always having been one that truly appreciated the grandeur of the north felt proud to have been part of it my having extensively traveled the width and breadth of it's unparrelled beauty for many years.

Eli who had stood silently observing the high flying geese suddenly uttered this never to be forgotten statement, my grandfather once told me this is the time of the year man's spirits walk across the sky.

As much as we would have liked to remain gazing at natures wonders and bask in the warmth of the early morning sun's feeble rays knew all to well that would only be a fools paradise.

The rising tide told us we had best get back to work if we intended to use it's power in our favor, now facing the onerous task of slinging the new engine into place in order to mount it. I don't feel it necessary to burden the reader with the grim details of slinging the engine across the intervening space between the pier and the aircraft, it will suffice to say in doing so it left us worn to a nub and rubber kneed before the engine had been successfully slung back under the tripod and eventually re-mounted with very little difficulty onto it's mounts, no one in their right state of mind would ever choose to if at all possible to avoid doing so face such a terrible ordeal again, twice being enough for one lifetime. Our shaky contraption of a tripod had sufficed if just barely so, there is no easy way to describe the heart stopping ordeal we had recently gone through, if by chance our shaky tripod had given way at a critical moment, as it threatened to at any time, if it had we would have found ourselves in deep trouble that would have proved to be next to impossible to extricate our selves from given the short time frame remaining to us. To this very day remain reluctant to ponder the far reaching consequences we would have faced if by accident or bad karma had failed to accomplish our ends by dumping the new engine into the muddy waters, it simply does not bear thinking about.

Once the new engine had been safely mounted and our blood pressure returning to normal, my with great satisfaction at how well it was going urging me on to complete the required control hookups which for the most part went without a hitch much to my relief, then the propeller re-installed while the tide still worked in our favor.

Actually once we got past the mind shattering part of precariously slinging the new engine over the threatening water and mounted securely in place that critical task being accomplished with relative ease in comparison to removing the old one as the rising tide positioned the aircraft perfectly making it an easy matter of lining up the mount and sliding the new engine into place. Once having assured all to be well, it was with profound relief the engine disconnected from the cables on our shaky tripod, once having done so finally allowed our overstretched nerves to wind down to a mild scream and our trembling limbs to almost cease trembling and convulsing, finding things went much easier when not forced to labor under the added burden of high stress. Upon completing the final hook ups that went toward the completion of the engine change Eli busied himself heating up a five gallon bucket of oil on an ever faithful blow pot in order to fill the tank with hot oil. Having reached the point we had by forcing ourselves to keep on no matter what had now reached a degree of exhaustion that left us weary to the very core of our being, but still we were denied a rest period while the tide remained high as it allowed our continuing use of the pier thus easing the strain on us.

Upon the completion of the final hook ups and double checking my work to assure all to be as it should be, filled the oil tank with fresh hot oil and pre oiling the engine insuring instant oil pressure on start up. To our relief the new engine fired up immediately without too much fuss, this pleased me greatly as newly installed engines are often prone to be balky. After running the new engine for a short time it turned out to be something of a pleasant surprise for us upon only discovering a minor oil leak that was quickly acted on and a minor adjustments of the engine controls setting things right.

The short fall day had slipped by largely unnoticed our being so busily occupied, but the rapidly dropping temperature that closely followed the setting of the watery sun bringing on an early darkness. We would have much proffered completing the loading of the engine and support equipment even being as tired as we were, but the rapidly ebbing tide dictated otherwise leaving us with little choice but to have to wait for the next high tide.

Once more moving and securing the aircraft to the muddy river bank little suspecting our activities being covertly observed. Winding down after such demanding activities proved to be extremely difficult even after enjoying the first hot meal in some time, as the lively conversation of a group of friends and acquaintances eddied around me, mentally ticked off all we had accomplished so far in a vain attempt to remember if any critical component or control hook up or setting inadvertently overlooked and could possibly create problems in the future, coming up with negative results, but still something intangible and of grave import nagged at me, but for the life of Christ totally failed to ascertain just what it could be, but we would find out soon enough almost to our lasting regret.

As I knew it being bound to happen, my overtaxed mind refusing to wind down resulting in a much required restful sleep evading me, only restlessly tossing and turning throughout what seemed to be an endless night in a fever of anticipation to be on our way, impatiently awaiting the coming of dawn while hoping above all to be greeted in the morning with flyable weather conditions. The moon had not quite set with the first rays of dawn just beginning to peek over the far eastern horizon finding me giving the aircraft a final inspection which much to my chagrin and dismay found to be coated with a heavy layer of frost that twinkled and gleamed in the early morning light as if taunting our past efforts to once again make it flyable.

Cursing the elements that worked against us did little to assuage my frustrations, the weak rays of the early morning sun would hardly suffice in melting off the frost by the time we wished to leave necessitating our laboriously dousing it with water. Fortunately the tide cycle on the rise making it a simple matter once moving the aircraft over to the pier to complete the loading of the engine and support equipment.

Having taken note of the red sky that once again portended the imminent arrival of a vicious storm front, quickly rounded up our gear while bidding our teacher friends goodbye.

Once clear of the muddy river bank taxied in circles prior to takeoff while the engines slowly reached operating temperatures, uneasily watching the low lying scud that suddenly appeared tearing by in ragged streaks, their unwelcome presence adding to my concerns. Perhaps it was just plain carelessness or the results of an overtaxed mind that caused my overlooking a critical check on the fuel tanks. Having been assured by the pilot of the aircraft of his having refueled to capacity at Big Trout one hundred and seventy miles west gave our fuel reserves little thought, an oversight that came within a hair of producing grave consequences.

Just about the time the engines had reached their operating temperatures while completing the last half of a circle the aircraft suddenly gave a mighty lurch to the left coming near to dipping the wing tip into the muddy waters before the right hand float crashed back onto it's surface creating a huge welter of spray that came near to jarring us out of our seats, only the advent of our wearing safety harness held us in place, Momentarily stunned by the suddenness of it all at first suspected we had inadvertently run over an unknown reef and severely damaged a float, the very thought of having done so coming near to creating a state of overriding panic in my already overloaded mind, but my extensive knowledge of the river informed me their was no such thing, having no more than settled down from that nerve wracking and as yet unexplained experience when it just as suddenly re-occurring for the second time coming near scaring us out of our wits as this time it all but completely spinning the aircraft around in it's own length, then it came clear what was transpiring, as the rising wind tore across the flat relatively treeless area of muskeg facing the wide open spaces of the bay it eventually collided with the two hundred foot river bank the settlement was built on creating violent vortices that clashed with the surface winds on the narrow river creating an unexpected but dangerously threatening situation for us, we just might not survive the next one with my yelling at Eli to retract the water rudders while I horsed the aircraft around to face the wind in preparation for take off, upon applying full power the aircraft instantly becoming terribly unstable shimmying and jittering all over the surface of the water, the weird sensation produced akin to riding a flat board across a floor covered with marbles. No sooner had we come up on the step before being thrown violently into the air far before having attained a safe take off speed only to stall back onto the water with a bone jarring impact, this most upsetting state of affairs occurring a further second and third time before finally being able to keep us airborne with my frantically dancing on the rudder pedals in an attempt to keep the wildly swaying aircraft in a semblance of level flight, Christ it was like steering a wet noodle until reaching safe flying speed. One can only compare our initial phase of flight as going along for a ride in a winged roller coaster as we flew into the very teeth of the fast approaching storm, once having cleared the stunted wind blasted trees that had initially blocked the outer reaches of the bay from view making what we had already endured a minor preview of what we could expect that left me quailing in abject terror upon witnessing a humungous jet black storm front charging grandly across the tortured waters of the bay blasting up snow white spumes of feathery spray in front of it, the sight of that monstrous storm all but paralyzed further actions, but a severe wing rattling gust that vibrated the entire aircraft with both of us momentarily hanging in the restraints of our safety harness soon brought me back to the present. Deathly afraid to begin a turn away from the life threatening storm but more afraid not to as we were heading the wrong way making it imperative we turn around and damn quick, gingerly applying tiny increments of rudder and aileron that eventually brought us shuddering around in what could be best described as a horrendously frightening square turn that upon completion of found myself soaked with sweat while quivering like a dog pissing razor blades, it taking a combined effort of strength and will power to unclench my fingers from off the control wheel.

Pleased beyond mere words to safely find ourselves blistering along down wind heading in the desired direction, the memories of that mind numbing turn would guarantee high definition night mares for some time to come for it can be truthfully said that at no time during the execution of that hairy turn did I retain little more than a semblance of control over a madly bucking aircraft, only more or less grimly going along for the ride.

As we bounced and swayed on our way towards Big Trout Lake gradually managed to relax my overwrought mind down to a primal scream, gradually winding down until feeling all to be well, that is until taking stock of our fuel reserves, there is no simple way to describe the shock and dismay at the low readings that greeted me, initially my mind refused to accept the graphic evidence my eyes told me, how could that have possibly come about?, we should easily have had more than ample reserves to see us safely to Big Trout Lake now a dauntingly long one hundred and seventy miles away across the most forbidding landscape known to man, consisting of nothing but endless miles of sere low lying muskeg dotted with a myriad of tiny pot holes, very few offering an emergency landing area, like it or not we now found ourselves involved against our wills in a dubious race against time having no way out as a return to Fort Severn totally out of the equation, we could only continue on regardless of the consequences.

After a protracted period of indecisiveness that plagued my mind finally able to puzzle out what had become of our fuel when it dawned on me with cold clarity what had transpired, the unexplained at the time presence of muddy foot prints on top of the floats told all, someone within the settlement had a passing knowledge of the fuel drain petcocks located on the lower part of the wings and belly and had taken advantage of it to garner themselves some free fuel not knowing or not caring about the possible consequences to us. Only the advent of the aircraft being heeled up on the river bank at low tide and assuming a steep nose down angle that placed a goodly portion of the remaining fuel out of immediate reach as the drain petcock is placed in the lowest position at the rear of the tank, this is what remained to us, my calculating our only having sufficient fuel to remain airborne for a maximum of one hour give or take a few minutes either way as fuel gauges as a rule to be notoriously inaccurate.

This totally unexpected realization of the terrible dilemma we now faced left me with a strange hollow feeling in the pit of my stomach temporarily suspending my thought processes.

Our fuel without question had been stolen from us, but the real culprit was me in mistakenly assuming to have sufficient fuel aboard based on the other pilot's statement and in my haste to be gone neglecting to check the fuel contents within the tanks prior to take off.

Well for what it was worth wasting precious time laying blame not about to improve our existing state of affairs, gradually allowing the shock and disbelief to gradually fade away with my long experience exerting itself goading me into precipitate action in taking stock of our present dilemma and what could be done to assure our remaining airborne as long as possible. Being acutely aware of the stiff tail wind that gave us a blistering ground speed of slightly over two hundred miles per hour at normal cruise settings indicated it would be a close run race before arriving over the welcome shores of Big Trout Lake, the dicey fuel situation dictating it to be in our best interest to reduce our fuel burn to a minimum by placing the engine settings into maximum range mode, something not highly recommended for a new engine as it played holy hell with them, but if the truth be known our precious pelts came first.

Once having accomplished all that could be done vacantly stared out of the window at the sere muskeg sizzling by, unbidden thought of the blood chilling realization of how poorly equipped we were to survive if it came about our making a forced landing on the muskeg, a soul shriveling thought I soon banished having better things to ponder. Once again step on his dick Weston takes front stage in his famous one liner of Don't let this happen to you, one could all but to hear the twin god's of fate and chance chuckling to themselves over my latest screw up.

Time appeared to almost stand still as it always did at such times, almost as if we were suspended in a void, but that was only the workings of my over anxious mind manifesting itself, actually we were being pushed along by the violent storm surge that worked in our favor with our maintaining a high ground speed, but unable to ascertain just how fast lacking prominent landmarks to judge by.

Droning on over what appeared to be endless miles of featureless muskeg performed frequent checks on our remaining fuel as the needles on the gauges continued their inexorable descent toward the empty mark increasing the tension I labored under that worsened with each passing minute ultimately causing my grip on the control wheel to reflexively tighten to the point of my fingers becoming numb.

Eli who had sat there through it all wearing what I jokingly referred to as his wooden Indian face continued to stare impassively at the passing muskeg, one couldn't help but to experience a slight compassion for his unenviable state of affairs as being a passenger could do naught but to sit helplessly while events unfolded, at least I had more than enough to keep my mind well occupied in flying the aircraft and doing my utmost to maintain flight as long as possible.

As time ground on with nothing to be seen but endless miles of sere muskeg interspersed with shallow pot hole lakes it left me with absolutely no idea of were we where over that seemingly endless expanse, after what seemed to be an interminably nerve shattering length of time the fuel gauges now hovered barely above the empty mark telling me with a dread certainty we perhaps had gambled and lost, only a short space of time remained before matters would come to a conclusion one way or the other.

At that juncture a cold unreasoning anger swept through me, all our superhuman efforts would go for naught as any way one cared to view it we remained in deep trouble with most likely no way out. Repeated radio calls failed to elicit a response, only able to hear a sibilant hiss and crackling over the head phones bringing on the impression of being more isolated than ever. Just about the time my belly muscles began to contract in anticipation of a forced landing thinking all to be lost we suddenly flashed alongside of a long narrow body of water that suddenly appeared as if out of nowhere, it's totally unexpected presence shocking the hell out of me but our moving on by so rapidly it gave one little chance to even consider making an emergency landing, but as we sizzled past it my peripheral vision had vaguely spotted the remains of a long abandoned dock and what I knew with absolute certainty to having once been a diamond drill site on the far shore having immediately recognized it as one I had made many a trip into making my present ground position instantly known lifting a very heavy piano off my back, a quick glance at the fuel gauges confirmed our only having fuel for another few minutes at best, but the safety of Big Trout Lake lay only a few miles distant, it had only been the fortunate

315

advent of a stiff tail wind that had brought us safely over the muskeg now leaving us in a much better position to make an emergency landing if found necessary to do so. The interim between leaving the lake and the next one approximately five minutes or less flight time away, but them highly charged tension filled minutes seemed to last an eternity before the huge expanse of Big Trout Lake finally coming into plain view. The fuel gauges now indicating near dry tanks informing me our only remaining aloft by the dregs of remaining fuel, just as the nose of the aircraft crossed the shoreline of Big Trout the right hand low fuel pressure warning light flickered on with the engine quitting within a short space of time following the warning with my immediately descending to just above the water in order to utilize ground effect in a desperate attempt to stretch out every mile toward safety as possible, only managing to make it approximately half way across to the settlement before the left hand fuel pressure light began to blink it's ominous message for a short time before the engine quit from fuel exhaustion.

Landing a beech craft down wind at a high rate of speed is something that is not highly recommended at any time, but what choice did I have?, I can honestly say that high speed dead stick down wind landing on a following sea had the distinction of being one of the hairiest of my entire career white knuckling it as the aircraft did it's damndest to snap around and bite it's tail before finally losing all forward speed and slamming to a bone jarring halt with great gouts of water and foam being sprayed over the wings and windshield, man I thought to myself I don't think one would ever be lucky enough to survive another one of those.

As the aircraft settled in the wave pattern violently swung it into the wind with my no longer retaining any degree of control commenced as the now dead aircraft rolled and swayed from one side to the other from the effects of the huge white crested rollers that smashed into the floats at given

intervals making for a very uncomfortable pitching and rocking motion. Being bone dry of fuel we were left to drift helplessly at the mercy of the howling wind, frantically transmitting on the radio for immediate assistance

met with little success adding a new dimension to my growing fear and frustration, impotently cursing the frequent radio black outs that often occurred in the area without warning cutting out communications even being so close to the settlement.

Goddamit it was a real mind bender to have to helplessly witness our inevitable drift into a point of land that jutted out into the lake that offered a hostile environment of jagged boulders that lay clearly outlined against the wind torn sheets of foam and spray from the huge waves that smashed unimpeded against them.

One could do naught but to stare helplessly out the window with one's stomach tied in knots as we continued to inevitably drift onto what was certain destruction and total loss of the aircraft, an unlikely event one could not have possibly conceived of occurring even in their wildest dreams. As the hopelessness of our situation became increasingly apparent it left me to ponder the events of the last stress filled days, we had been through a lot in that time, perhaps far too much with our luck finally deserting us.

Just about the time helpless despair had seeped into every corner of my being from listening to the now clearly audible crashing roar of the huge swells lashing the jagged boulders of the rugged shore line, my near panicked thoughts suddenly interrupted by Eli yelling in my ear of having just spotted a boat slowly making it's torturous way through the huge swells to reach us, it's only managing to doing so not a minute to soon with our rescuer not wasting any time attaching a tow line to the front bollard of the float and ever so slowly towing us away from that threatening shore line to safety.

Once having reached the safety of the dock we found ourselves relieved beyond measure to finally find ourselves in a safe harbor, it being all I could manage to force my shaky legs to respond when climbing out of the cockpit. When finally able to martial my jumbled thoughts into a coherent state of mind inquired of our savior as to how it had come about his fortuitously rescuing us from certain destruction?, his replying that one of his grandchildren playing along the shore line had witnessed our hairy landing with both engines stilled, the native children being quite familiar with the normal comings and goings of various aircraft immediately realized our experiencing difficulties when failing to re-start the engines and taxi into the dock, wisely for one's so young taking it upon themselves to inform their grandfather of our plight, were he upon close examination of our drifting up onto the rocks immediately realized we required immediate assistance wasting little time in coming to our rescue. For his timely and unstinting assistance he was given a forty-five gallon drum of expensive aviation fuel and a five-gallon can of oil from the companies cache along with many profuse thanks, in truth a very cheap price to have paid.

Upon his realizing our being on safe ground, Eli's somber mood took an unexpected swing becoming light hearted and garrulous, quite the change from his normally stoic wooden Indian demeanor, but that was destined to be of short duration when as much as I hated to have to inform him that once we had completed re-fuelling and checking over the new engine for oil leaks we were once more on our way. Needless to say upon hearing that bit of bad news his new found euphoria came crashing back to earth, his face crumpling back into his now familiar wooden Indian sulk that reminded me of a dog caught out in the rain.

Actually if the truth be known my state of mind not being much better than his having fought off the numbing effects of debilitating exhaustion and bouts of high stress for extended periods of time, the combination of the two dragging me down by draining me mentally and physically and if at all possible would have gladly chosen to remain overnight, not in the least looking forward to battling the questionable weather conditions that lay ahead of us. Patiently explaining to Eli that the very same storm front that had fortuitously provided the stiff tail wind that had seen us to safety now fast approaching bringing in a horrendously huge and violent weather front that promised high winds, snow and freezing conditions as the speed of which the ominous appearing overcast that had appeared overhead within the last half hour attested to informing me in no uncertain terms we had best leave while we still could.

Satisfied all to be well we departed the waters of Big Trout Lake just as heavy snow laden clouds began to skitter across the huge expanse of the lake to all but blot out forward visibility, we had departed not a minute too soon being certain we faced the all too possible risk of being frozen in if we had remained.

Yes there was no doubt about it of the Big Trout settlement vastly superior to Fort Severn in all respects but alluring as it was still retained no desire to remain there, only looking forward to delivering the aircraft safely to it's owners and to eventually return to the comforts of my home. Crossing that huge expanse of water while dodging frequent snow flurries turned out to be a hell of a lot dicer than one would normally care to experience, the visibility at times becoming terribly restricted in the lowering gloom that now surrounded us. Casting a curious glance at Eli to see how he was holding up my heart immediately went out to him, his appearing to be completely listless and dejected, resigned to his fate what ever it would be with my almost expecting him to suddenly break out singing his death dirge. Actually one could easily sympathize with his plight, not being a pilot had for so brief a time enjoyed the security of solid ground when taking into consideration the harrowing flight he had so recently endured, only to be unwillingly cast back into the fray, in contrast my outlook being one of complete elation now that the worst lay far behind us, our now having an ample supply of fuel and the engines performing sweetly not to mention our now traversing what I had long considered to be part of my back yard, as familiar with the terrain we flew over as the back of my hand. Since departing

Big Trout the weather picture had continued to deteriorate with the forward visibility dropping to no more than two to three miles while at given intervals becoming much worse.

Making another attempt at making light of the existing situation by injecting a touch of humor, quipped, well Eli it seems your going to get a belly rub tonight, only to be met with his best wooden Indian stare reserved for brain dead white men, to then pointedly ignoring me by lapsing into his now familiar wet dog sulk as if the empty words of a forked tongue white man not worthy of notice. Having gotten the message in spades that this hardly being a good time for light banter clammed up and left him to enjoy his sulk.

The weather becoming increasingly atrocious as we charged along almost at tree top level with the heavy snow laden clouds often barring our way forcing our circumnavigating them, one could not help but to shudder inwardly when imagining what the state of the weather conditions at Fort Severn. As strange as this may sound to the novice the atrocious weather conditions we flew through left me feeling to be entirely within my element as what one does not fear one enjoys, the ultimate challenge of man versus nature gave me a vicarious thrill, but still one does not blindly challenge the elements by foolishly exposing one's self to imminent danger or flying into the face of adversity, as unthinkingly doing so often guarantees a quick end to those who fail to heed the warnings. In my way of thinking there is a time to stand and a time to retreat, only them who observed that simple creed survived.

Continuing to play hide and seek with the heavy layers of snow clouds that often forced our making a wide detour in order to circumvent them, had continued to make calls on the radio in hopes of raising someone, almost jumping out of my skin when a deep masculine voice boomed over my earphones curtly inquiring as to who in the hell is this and what my position?, up till then not being able to raise a response from anyone leaving me wondering if we were the only two people within that vast area foolish enough to be out that day. As it turned out upon questioning the voice emanated from another pilot holed up for weather at a small settlement known as Weagamow (round lake) using the powerful base radio at the local nursing station who obviously not at all pleased at hearing from me judging by his surly manner and agitated tone of voice that literally frosted up the airwaves, taking me to task about my having the unmitigated gall to be flogging around in what he proclaimed as adverse weather conditions no one in their right mind should be flying in. One could easily sense his disbelief upon informing him of our having departed from Fort Severn that morning and intending on going straight through to Sioux Lookout, this met with a protracted silence with one almost being able to hear them thinking it's that god dam bone head Weston pushing weather again, that prize idiot never did know when to quit.

At that point the realization of my inadvertently having kicked over a hornets nest awoke the mischievous streak within me it being a given that any radio station within receiving range would be tuning in to our terse exchange. It took only a short while before the expected querulous inquiries from varied operators who no doubt must have had aircraft operating within the area began to jam the radio waves overriding each others inquiries, all wanting to know the existing weather picture within the area I traversed, and to also acidly inquire in a no nonsense tone of voice why if Weston had flown in all the way from Fort Severn, then what was their problem?

In truth the weather picture remained nothing short of atrocious and anyone with a shred of common sense (that left me out) would have avoided flying in it. Well common sense not something I subscribed to on a regular basis, my enjoying playing the game by my own set of rules.

Working our way ever further maintaining a south west direction cautiously picked our way from one prominent land mark to another through an area as familiar to me as my back yard, all the while painting a rosy weather picture to all who inquired while barely hanging over the trees often holding an altitude of less than two hundred feet or less at any time. Normally I wouldn't have transmitted such misleading and false weather reports, but anyone who flew in that part of the country on a regular basis retained more than passing awareness of just how rapidly the weather situation could change within a short period of time so could not be held accountable. The pilots who received my misleading weather reports were no body's fools being well aware the false reports were bound to create great consternation at their home base, and this it did with spades, the operators making heated demands for their wayward pilots to get their collective butts in gear or else, one sincerely doubted that any of them would be sending me a get well soon card if by chance were to pile up.

It had been a long time coming but now it was my turn to place some of them holier than thou sons of bitches on the hot seat as they had at one time or another done without remorse or compunction to me, revenge certainly tasted sweet.

The terse demands from frustrated operators continued to jam the radio waves with demands to get moving creating an untenable situation for the stranded pilots, some of them obviously attempting to mollify their dispatcher through tightly clenched teeth as they made weak excuses that portrayed little sincerity on their part.

Eli who had forgotten to maintain his wet dog sulk while monitoring the exchange now appeared to be hugely enjoying himself with a shit-eating grin plastered all over his face.

Not being aware at the time, but only learning of it much later my having been the sole cause of disrupting a snot dripping, knock em down drag out the dead barn burning party, the planning of having been in the works for some time at the Round Lake nursing station and scheduled to take place that very night with the advent of the adverse weather conditions working in the transients pilot's favor, some of them it turned out having converged there secretly not being authorized to do so. There remains little doubt all would have most likely turned out well and the party a smashing success save for one of the pilots no doubt slightly inebriated at the time out of simple but as it turned out foolish curiosity answering my radio call as he was to learn much to his everlasting regret. Actually if my being aware at the time of what was transpiring at the nursing station would have kept quiet for as it turned out in the end it resulted in far reaching consequences for some of the errant pilots, some who to this very day despise my very name.

Having stirred up a hornets nest to my satisfaction continued to hedge hop our way until eventually reaching our destination worn down both mentally and physically almost beyond human endurance but right happy to have after experiencing many a hair raising venture while doing so arrive safely.

The two owners of the aircraft had been closely monitoring my radio exchanges came down to the dock to offer a heart felt greeting upon our arrival grinning from ear to ear. Once ensconced in the privacy of their office, on the telling they're being somewhat in awe of our travails and near miss with the storm front in Fort Severn. Having no sooner settled in the phone began to ring almost non stop with other operators wishing to speak with me, having foreseen that possibility had cautioned them to deny my presence for obvious reasons with the more outspoken off the two fielding the calls as he absent mindedly rolled the omnipresent cigar that perpetually jutted out of his mouth continually from one side to the other while listening politely to the callers request only to reply in his best no nonsense business tone of voice while winking at me saying sorry old man no can do, he just left to head for town to get a bite to eat and have no idea when he will be back and giving me a conspiratorial glance, thus putting a quick end to all the following inquiries in the same vein.

Meanwhile Eli upon exiting the aircraft had vanished like smoke in a gale, one could readily assume of his having had enough adventure and excitement for some time to come and not about to take the chance on being caught up in further travails.

The two owners had me repeat our experiences from start to finish, finding it difficult to believe how we had managed against such overwhelming odds to have accomplished what we did in such a brief period of time, but then again one would have to experienced the nagging fear of being frozen in at such an undesirable place as Fort Severn along with the grinding fear of the possible loss of the aircraft to the onslaught of the monstrous ice floes that regularly came crashing down the river sweeping everything away before them, that alone gave us the incentive to get done and to depart as quickly as humanly possible.

At the conclusion of my story, John C. the more outspoken of the two stated tongue in cheek from here on were going to send all our aircraft that require an engine change to Fort Severn along with Weston and Eli to do the job. No thank you I thought to myself, once in a lifetime will suffice.

No doubt that statement if by chance repeated would have gone over like a lead balloon with the hanger drones who were already hard at it checking over the quality of our recent installation no doubt hoping to discover a gross error or an overlooked hook up of a critical component giving them something to crow about, to their collective disappointment they failed to do so.

For whatever reason it generally took them the better part of a week to complete an engine change in a warm well equipped hanger, but then again one must take into consideration along with their eight to five routine interspersed with lengthy coffee breaks and not having to deal with a capricious mother nature while working under terribly demanding conditions that offered an overriding incentive to get the job over and done with as quickly as possible.

Once completing all that required to be done took my leave for the hotel to enjoy a much needed clean up and change of clothes, a sumptuous meal and a good nights sleep with the following morning finding me on my way home.

The long drive home gave me the time to reflect on the past events, pondering at great length what manner of inner devils pursued me to the degree of knowingly and deliberately risking not only my own precious neck, but also that of an innocent family man by pushing the envelope far beyond reason, the answer as it always had continued to taunt me, if one is not living on the edge, then one is only taking up space, not to mention during such times of unimaginable stress one felt so vibrantly alive.

Mississa

THE FIVE YEARS SPENT FLYING in the pickle lake area considered a time of wonder and adventure that since leaving the area has never again occurred.

To them who never having experienced the endless wonders of the land that changed greatly with the seasons, it is my opinion they have missed a once in a lifetime opportunity to witness nature at her pristine finest, but unfortunately except for the fortunate few it remains the garden of Eden to us bush pilots with it's seemingly endless verdant green forests, an unending plethora of jewel like lakes that glittered a deep blue in the summer sunlight or reflected an unbroken expanse of pure white during the winter season.

Very few of these pristine lakes or the endless tracts of virgin forests that abound there have known the intrusion or presence of a white man, pretty much remaining the private domain of the animals and birds that abound there along with a few native trappers that still pursue their chosen life style. But one can truly appreciate the wonders of the endlessly rolling expanse of muskeg areas that flamboyantly changed color with the passing of the seasons. As many times one ventured across it's seemingly endless expanse of verdant openness one could if they chose to be observant could always discover new and different sights and in some cases unexplained strange phenomena that could not be readily explained. In other words during the course of flight over it's boundless terrain one could if they took time to study the lay of the land one could always observe something of interest.

As much as I thought my becoming quite accustomed to the unusual to the point of being jaded, seemingly out of the blue being introduced to the strangest physical phenomena yet experienced up till then that began the day the owner of the company who had many and varied interests instructed me to fly three commercial fishermen into an extremely remote lake that up till then totally unaware of it's existence strangely enough located in the middle of a huge expanse of featureless muskeg, some how it's very presence defied the odds of it existing at all where it did. My not having been aware of it's existence up till then completely titillated at being given the chance to visit that intriguing strangely located body of water known by the natives of the area as "Mississa" lake, what that translated to in the English language I never was able to discover.

As it turned out the purpose of our initial visit was to revitalize an already existing sturgeon fishing facility (more surprises), one could have bowled me over with a feather at that revelation as yet but many more totally unexpected ones as yet awaited me.

Not being aware at the time who the fishermen where to be some taken aback and pleasantly surprised to see my old buddy "Rotten Nose Pete" and his cohorts appear at the office one fine morning with his remarkable proboscis literally glowing in shades of purple red speckled with the usual huge black craters as if to give it depth.

He hadn't changed a bit since I last saw him, his being as usual filled with repressive good humor and enthusiasm at the coming prospect of new adventure, it eventually came out he knew a lot more than I did at what to expect for it turned out the owner of the company still retained a valid sturgeon fishing license on the lake in question and had retained the rights for a good many years having set up a permanent camp complete with steel hulled boats and a caterpillar diesel to provide power, in other words the camp had existed for some time prior to my entering the picture and the license holding requirements dictated it be fished up to it's quota that year.

In truth I never was to be enlightened to as just how he had become aware of the existence of the large sturgeon that entered the lake by a totally unorthodox method, but could safely assume of his being informed of their presence by native trappers from the Winisk settlement located on the west shore of Hudson's Bay that once trapped within the area the lake lay in. Much later on having had the opportunity to discuss the uniqueness of the lake in great detail with a resident trapper from the Winisk settlement being some surprised to learn the lake had always been avoided by a good many native trappers who considered it to be haunted by evil spirits. This in part explained the absence of trappers cabins located within it's waters which of a matter of course always to be found on any large body of water.

My curiosity knowing no bounds perused the maps of the area to find the lake to measure approximately ten miles in circumference being almost perfectly round. It could only be rationally explained as an anomaly of nature sitting alone in vast splendor in the middle of a huge expanse of seemingly endless muskeg with only small shallow black water lakes and narrow twisted creeks surrounding it.

Being cautioned on the first trip to time my arrival to coincide with the high tide cycle on Hudson's Bay and if it so happened staying the night to be absolutely certain to anchor the aircraft well out from the fixed dock to an existing mooring float. Of a certain all this advice piqued my curiosity no end, but further inquiry met with a dead end only being further advised it would all be quite the revelation.

The day we were to leave dawned sunny and bright, the beauty of the late summer day making it a pleasure to be so alive and appreciative of natures bounty and to be doing what I did best. Man what a pristine day, as we made our way in a south easterly direction with only long skeins of wispy clouds to be seen anywhere on the horizon so ethereal they appeared as brush strokes by a master painter across an azure sky, it would have been difficult to not feeling pleased with life at such a time.

The late summer weather had allowed the early frosts to work their artistic magic throughout the expanse of the usually sere muskeg, transforming the local flora into a breath taking profusion of varied colors and shades that ranged from magenta to a flaming red blush that contrasted greatly with the startlingly bright yellow of random copes of tamarack, mother nature, the greatest of artists had skillfully applied every color available from her palette to create an astounding scenario few people aside from bush pilots ever got to admire and appreciate.

How I enjoyed traversing that part of the country in the first blush of late summer and early fall. Rotten nose Pete who sat in the right hand seat along side of me had begun to display a growing sense of unease as we droned over that seemingly endless muskeg, probably because he had never before had cause to venture over such an arid environment with the lakes becoming fewer the farther we flew, and what did exist at all consisting mostly of tiny shimmering pot holes, gradually his perpetual smile begin to run away from his homely face being replaced by a deeply concerned look that openly hinted at his wondering just what the hell he had gotten himself into this time around.

Eventually we arrived at and flew over the exceedingly remote strange appearing lake that was to be his home for the next six weeks or so with his confidence in the new venture visibly shaken leaving him uncertain if he had done the right thing in having agreed to come in the first place and the most likely scenario wishing he hadn't. His awed gaze at the strangeness of the lake that lay below us definitely something that neither of us had ever witnessed before, my being absolutely certain at that point that at any time my suggesting we give it up right there and then and turn back for pickle lake he wouldn't have hesitated for a moment in agreeing we do so.

Our having arrived almost precisely at the top of the high tide cycle and still remaining in the dark why it being so important to have done so made a normal uneventful landing to taxi in to the existing fixed dock.

Having out of pure and simple curiosity chose to remain overnight once having unloaded taxied out to the anchor buoy as previously cautioned to tether the aircraft for the night burning with the question as to why it's being so important to do so, but not foolish enough to disregard the warning.

Spending the remainder of the day in assisting the fishermen in readying their gear the hours flew swiftly by. One of the men who had decided to give fishing off the dock a try just as the tide began to turn astounded us by catching a nice string of golden yellow walleyes that not one of us had remotely suspected where to be found in such an unlikely environment. Once getting over our pleasant surprise we filleted and cooked them up for supper along side of fried potatoes accompanied by fresh boiled coffee, nothing could have tasted so good.

Consulting the tide tables almanac noted the time of the next low tide cycle still wondering what significance it held for me decided if at all possible to remain awake to see what could possibly take place. As it went my resolve going for naught, being well stuffed with an excellent meal of fresh walleye on top of feeling totally relaxed and pleased with my world soon dropped off into a deep sleep to be suddenly awakened some time later by the fairly loud gurgling and swishing of fast moving water accompanied at intervals by hollow sucking noises that instantly caught my attention to bring me instantly wide awake, grabbing up my flash light made a quick dash to the dock and lord did I get something of a shock upon directing the beam of the flashlight on what had once been many feet of water now only wet glistening sand. Focusing the powerful beam of light on the aircraft revealed it to be sitting high and dry on the sandy bottom, now I knew the answers to all my questions. There remained little doubt in my mind that the lake some how some way directly connected to the waters of Hudson's Bay most likely by huge tunnels that most likely ran through the lime stone bed rock but being too far inland to be contaminated by salt water as it was most obvious the level of the water in the lake somehow controlled by the cycling of the tides, now it came clear what that huge black depression we had noticed in the middle of the lake while circling overhead had been.

Well that most unexpected of sights totally blew me away, it having to be the dammdest phenomena ever witnessed in that part of the country up to now being long convinced to already having seen some of the strangest.

Having somewhat satisfied my curiosity returned to my well mouse chewed bunk to grab a few more hours' sleep. Early morning found us carefully studying the meticulously written instructions set out to initially aid the fishermen in their initial endeavors at fishing the lake efficiently and above all safely.

The instructions set out stated they where to set out the trot lines close to the huge opening in the middle of the lake as soon as the returning tide permitted, and the nets much further back and preferably fronting the many creeks and rivers that abounded in the area and to be certain to pull them short of the beginning of the ebb tide in order to give themselves sufficient time to clear the lines and nets of any sturgeon that may have been caught and above all to make it back to the camp before the water level fell too far to allow them to do so in safety.

Well that made absolute sense, to not heed the instructions guaranteed the possible loss of both fish and equipment or worse due to the awesome suction created by the retreating water into the huge opening as the tide ebbed. One day out of burning curiosity deliberately delayed leaving on the return trip not lifting clear of the tortured waters of the lake till the last possible minute in order to witness for the first time the phenomena of the water emptying from the lake while circling overhead, my gawd what an awesome wonder inspiring sight to behold as a powerful whirlpool suddenly began to form in the very middle of the hole eventually building into a monstrous ring of rapidly swirling water.

Another time I got to witness just how powerful the suction of the rapidly receding water could be as it swirled and sucked noisily at the sturdy piers that supported the dock, a hell of a lot of fore thought and hard work had gone into building that dock in order to insure it's survival for any length of time.

The ebb tide cycle never ceased to fascinate me, whenever possible observing the ongoing process as it began it's cycle, as it progressed the water began to move in an anticlockwise motion slowly picking up speed soon causing the water to surge violently past and against the dock pilings creating a slight vibration felt on the soles of one's feet, gradually the noise of the rapidly receding water would build up to an audibly muffled roar, within the hour the water had dropped about an average of fourteen feet to once more reveal the smooth sandy lake bed making it an easy matter to walk out to the grounded aircraft.

Often I wondered how the fish handled it, one can be absolutely certain they some how did as by absolute necessity they must have had to depart the lake to go wherever they did before the whirlpool formed, nature sure does leave us with many unexplained variables to ponder. One at best could only hazard an educated guess how the tide reacted during the winter months?, but that remains natures secret to this day, but if it where at all possible I for one would pay a lot just to be able to witness a winter season tide cycle, I'm certain it would prove most interesting.

The sturgeon fishing proved to be excellent, the size and quantity of those caught on the lines and in the nets never ceased to amaze me, very rarely did a set line not produce a good many sturgeon on a daily basis, the nets often undulating with large sturgeon attempting to break free, some of them weighing out dressed at over a hundred and twenty pounds. Them three fishermen labored like indentured slaves to pull in and tether the live sturgeon during the period between tide cycles.

The sturgeon which averaged between forty to sixty pounds where not dispatched on the spot, instead a stout line passed through the gill opening using a short round smooth stick then looped through a metal ring to be tied to the individual boats(I have witnessed a variation to this method when a snap ring placed on the tail) . It was quite a sight to observe three boats moving ever so slowly across the lake towing numerous black hued torpedo shaped sturgeon like a raft of so many submerged logs behind them.

It must be pointed out the sturgeon being of so high a value where never slaughtered until it being deemed a sufficient number caught to make up a load with the aircraft waiting at the dock with the pilot being absolutely certain of completing a return trip to pickle lake the same day.

As mentioned previously once the live sturgeon had been towed carefully back to the camp, they where immediately placed in a large rock ringed corral dug out of the lake bed with the bottom and sides lined with flat rocks. The corral retained approximately eight feet of water during the period of low tide, actually quite a nifty set up with sheets of plywood being placed over top of the corral during the period of low tide to protect the sturgeon from the direct rays of the sun on clear days.

When it was deemed to have a sufficient load waiting a radio message sent requesting an aircraft. Surprisingly enough the corralled sturgeon remained passive during the entire time penned up as they initially had during throughout the procedure of being retrieved from the lines and nets to be tethered, not creating much of a fuss at all during the entire procedure as long as the fisherman remained cautious in not allowing their heads breaking clear of the water, placing the tether through the mouth and gill opening without mortally wounding the sturgeon called for consummate skill and great caution on the fisherman's part. These oddball fish can sometimes become a real handful if by chance they for what ever reason becoming alarmed during the process of retrieving them from the trot lines or nets, then all hell breaks loose making it an absolute necessity in allowing them to return to the depths until settling down, at times this delicate procedure often had to be repeated many times before eventually succeeding. With the fishermen working under a severe time constraint between tides, it gave them a very small window in which to perform their laborious duties.

It was obvious to all the sturgeon and other scale fish that inhabited the lake could only return to feed during the high tide cycle, where they disappeared to at low tide only the fish knew and we could only surmise. Strangely enough once hooked or trapped in a net the sturgeon does not fight against the line, or net, mostly lying dogo until retrieved. The ones that are well hooked are left that way until being slaughtered where upon the large hook removed, the trotline having a nifty snap hook that can be instantly released and replaced from the main anchor line and transferred to the line on the boat.

On the average my completing two trips a week weather permitting and that in it's self sometimes proving to be a dicey affair as weather predicting in that part of the country hardly an exact science and being so close to Hudson's Bay the weather could and often did suddenly brew up terrible flying conditions almost as if out of nowhere sometimes causing my having to white knuckle it for mind numbing periods of time, on the occasion being forced to resort to scraping my way along fifty feet or less over the seemingly endless expanse of muskeg with a load of highly perishable and expensive sturgeon giving me the added incentive to complete the trip, one could rightfully say it certainly had it's day's.

The slaughtering of the sturgeon a sight I can honestly say not at to my liking once having made the some times risky decision the weather would remain flyable, only then were the sturgeon removed from the corral and towed to shore to be immediately dragged out of the water to have their throats cut allowing them to bleed out as they thrashed about in their death throes. Once having quivered their last immediately beheaded and gutted, the roe from the females placed in five gallon buckets for further processing into what is known as caviar. Little time was lost in preparing and loading the tubs of sturgeon as we all frantically labored under the constraints of the tide cycles and the ongoing threat of unpredictable weather that guaranteed to keep one's stress level high at all times.

When and if at all possible enjoyed staying over for a few days at a time and if not choosing to accompany them finding unique ways to entertain myself while the fishermen were away doing their thing by walking the endless tracts of exposed beach at low tide in search of oddball shaped stones, some of them having holes worn through them that probably took hundreds if not thousands of years to wear through. One of the anomalies being the discovery of large chunks of silky smooth pitch black "Basalt", a type of volcanic stone supposedly (as so informed by a geologist) only found in certain regions of South America, having in one instance taken samples back with me for analysis, presented them to a top Inco geologist only to receive a lot of unexpected and undeserved criticism that bordered on the bare edge of his accusing me of being an outright liar when informing him of it's source, put that in your pipe and smoke it.

They weren't as common being extremely difficult to find, but the occasional discovery of bright Red Indian bloodstone and another type of brilliant yellow stone that was never identified to my satisfaction added to my growing collection.

It remained a mystery to me how such a unique body of water found in such an unlikely location could have ever existed in the first place, actually the entire area presented endless anomalies of nature if one cared to take the time and effort to seek them out. From what I had gathered from the local native population of the nearby settlement of Winisk, many of the larger and deeper black water shallow appearing pot hole lakes and the narrow twisting rivers that connected them with my initially assuming them to devoid of aquatic life in fact teemed with many varieties of fish including monstrous northern pike and sturgeon.

Nature very rarely does anything by accident or chance, what ever the forces that created Mississa lake not to mention another lake much closer to Pickle Lake by the name of "Shabusquay" which in itself an anomaly also being located in the middle of a huge expanse of muskeg but boasting white sand beaches and Mediterranean blue water literally teemed with speckled trout. Regardless of how they where formed they are jewels in the midst of waste. The very fact that both these precious jewels of nature being located in the middle of a huge bog that so far visibly offer no known resources of value to be thoughtlessly plundered by uncaring greed driven corporations and hopefully to remain as a pristine anomaly of nature for ever.

If by chance one should wonder why some of the chunks of basalt had holes worn through them, well that took a while to discover the how and why of it, the answer came about, only by the merest of chance my stumbling onto the perfect combination for that rare phenomena to occur. This amazing discovery took place while searching for colorful or odd shaped rocks to add to my collection unexpectedly coming across a fairly flat piece of basalt lying just at the edge of the water at low tide, on top of it lay a fairly round chunk of what appeared to be flint or black chart, both composed of extremely hard and dense materials, the fact that the waters of the lake at no time ever lay still as some unknown dynamics that remained beyond my comprehension caused the water to constantly fluctuate creating an endless swirling motion along the shore lines which in turn during the periods of open water endlessly rocked the chunk of flint or chart sitting on top of the basalt to literally grind itself into it's surface to eventually create a hole that diminished in size as the rotating chunk wore away possibly taking untold eons of time to accomplish this phenomena. In one instance discovering a chunk of basalt that contained a perfectly round stone trapped inside of a chamber worn into a circular groove by the unceasing water action.

By the time the quota had been filled the incidents of bad weather had increased considerably, making many of the round trips at best a dicey situation with my often having to do white knuckle battle with the almost unceasing storms that roared off the bay like runaway freight trains moving far inland creating terrible flying conditions that kept me on edge on every trip. Having picked up the very last load prior to removing the fishermen forced to endure a hellish return trip when being overtaken by a violent weather front that all but blotted out forward visibility near giving me fits of anxiety while fighting my way through to barely arrive ahead of a three day blizzard that dumped a heavy layer of fresh snow on the surrounding country side and freezing over all the smaller shallow lakes.

But yet it still remained to remove the fishermen, but goddamit how I feared having to make that last trip into such trying conditions, but if at all possible would attempt it as three good men who called me friend depended on my doing so. As each day of forced waiting endlessly dragged on by with the passing of each one making the possibility of being able to get them out in time increasingly remote, but one could only wait and hope for the weather to improve to the point of allowing a rescue attempt, but that remained one exceedingly long shot.

The morning of the sixth day the men had been marooned found me warming up the engines on my aircraft long before day break as a rare window of opportunity awaited according to the prediction from the weather station, hopefully it would allow me enough time and clear enough conditions to pick them up and return safely, one could only wait and see.

Be as it may that that morsel of good news did little bolster my sagging resolve being all too aware of and having often experienced the vagaries of the rapidly evolving coastal weather systems that rarely turned out as forecast, and if any one had learned the hard way to respect it's ever changing moods it had to be me.

The first light of dawn found me well on my way into the somber grayness that perfectly matched my mood. My reluctance to carry on deepening with each passing mile my not looking forward to the struggle that was sure to come between man in his flimsy machine and the formidable powers of nature that still lay ahead of me. What made the successful completion of the trip so questionable was the chilling fact that little over a hundred miles of the total distance yet to be covered offered absolutely nothing in the way of a suitable emergency landing areas if all where to go to hell in a hand basket. These morbid thoughts constantly plagued my already fear filled mind while continuing to bore on through the encroaching gloom already being forced to fly at near tree top level with my almost at intervals losing the resolve to keep on with what already considered to be an extremely high risk and foolhardy venture into unknown conditions fraught with latent peril, but the thought of the three most likely badly frightened men who had waited in vain for so long for my hopefully returning for them drove me to fight on against the burgeoning odds of ever finding such a small lake in such a vast area constantly nagging at my fast eroding confidence.

It would be untrue to say that up till now that certain flight to be the most harrowing of my career as every difficult flight into bad weather or over unforgiving terrain creates it's own unique set of circumstances to be dealt with on a one to one basis, but it certainly came close to it, it having become increasingly difficult to navigate over the featureless snow blanketed muskeg that offered very little in the way of visible landmarks, only able to navigate by the use of the gyro compass and timing my progress as best I could constantly wrestling the controls as the aircraft bucked and shied like a frightened steed reluctant to keep on.

Since leaving the tree line some time ago remained uncertain of my ground position, only grimly maintaining a ridged a compass course as possible while attempting to on the occasion correct my compass heading to compensate for the effects of the violent cross winds that swept me sideways as much as flying straight ahead making an accurate time and distance computation a bad joke, all one could do was to guesstimate and hope to have more or less maintained an accurate heading as the all too real possibility of completely missing the lake made my blood run cold at the thought.

Time dragged by on leaden feet as it always had at such times with my nerves becoming increasingly twangy to the point of having almost convincing myself to have already missed the lake and on the verge of giving it up before placing myself in deeper trouble then had already done. But for some perverse reason one couldn't begin to fathom bored on frightened or not, and in no less then fifteen minutes on the outside it proved to be well I had, suddenly recognizing or maybe it was just wishful thinking on my part a cluster of small odd shaped pot hole lakes that lay not too far east of Mississa but the heavy mantle of snow greatly altering their physical features rending them difficult to recognize until coming much closer to be verified much to my relief at finding them what I first had hoped to be, but still the snow altered landscape continued to make it extremely difficult to locate Mississa with my stubbornly boring on heart in mouth hoping against hope to be heading the right way.

One can only begin to imagine the depth of my relief upon suddenly spotting the perimeter of the huge round lake looming directly ahead now only a few miles away. The palpable relief at miraculously locating the lake under such terrible conditions left me weak with relief, but the sobering thought of my only having barely reached the half way mark immediately brought me down to earth, the cold hard fact of what lay ahead of us during the long trip back caused my insides to shrivel while a safe landing and take off in unknown conditions yet to be safely accomplished.

My initial relief at successfully locating the lake short lived upon flying overhead, alarmed by the unwelcome sight of the huge pans of ice floating all over the main part of the lake, Christ on a crutch, that's all one needed, to hit one of them at high speed guaranteed severe damage to the floats and that all too real possibility could not be risked, some how a way had to be found to getting a clear shot at it. Goddamit I swore to myself as a feeling of gut wrenching helplessness swept over me having risked so much and fought so hard to have even gotten this far left me momentarily confused and in near tears with frustration leaving me unable to think clearly of what to do next, a terrible sense of despair dominating my senses when facing the unthinkable but all too real possibility of being forced by circumstances beyond my control to abandon the three men to their fate, the very thought of being forced to do so leaving me sick at heart.

During one of my indecisive overhead circles suddenly noticed three boats pulling away from the dock breaking up the huge pans of ice all the way out, at first failing to comprehend just what their plan of action could possibly be soon taking notice of them breaking up the huge pans of ice into manageable size with their steel hulled boats and to then to push them clear of my potential landing path.

Even though small random chunks of ice still lay in my path that caused some concern felt all to be as well as it could ever get went on to carry out the slowest landing possible, but still the nerve wracking clatter of random chunks of ice colliding with the floats set my teeth on edge before coming off the step to coast to a silent halt, how strange it seemed to be without the constant yammer of the engines assailing my ears, all one could hear was the whirr of the gyros accompanied by the distant clink of ice glancing off the floats mixed in with the sound of approaching out board motors.

It turned out my having arrived over the lake so unexpectedly it had caught them totally unaware of my being any where near them until suddenly bursting noisily overhead, repeated radio calls to them had elicited no response what so ever my eventually discovering the radio battery had failed leaving them without any means of outside communication what so ever.

They're not expecting or even entertaining the faint hope anyone foolish or brave enough to make an attempt to reach them in such atrocious weather conditions had all but given up hope of being rescued for some time, but my unexpected and most welcome arrival had instantly galvanized them into action, Pete being quite astute instantly realized the predicament facing me acted as quickly as possible to successfully alleviate the situation as best they could.

All three had tears of joy and relief in their eyes they made no attempt to hide boarding the aircraft without the least hesitation, Pete being the last to do so taking the time to return the three boats to the mooring buoy after picking up their gear leaving them to whatever fate awaited them with my taxiing over to collect him.

With everyone on board immediately began the take off grimly enduring the nerve shattering clang of the ice colliding with the floats at high speed with the ensuing racket causing all to cringe in their seats, pleased beyond mere words to finally rise safely off the threatening waters of the lake and to be on our way.

If at all possible the limited visibility endured on the way in appeared to have worsened forcing our flying scant feet above the muskeg to the consternation of all, it obviously posing a risky proposition being exceedingly difficult to accurately judge one's height above the surface as the leaden gray clouds merging with the grey snow covered muskeg made continued flight so close to it's undulating surface a genuine white knuckler. The entire distance flown under difficult and often adverse weather conditions made that long difficult trip home an all out no holds barred mind bender that came perilously close to driving me into a state of mental and physical exhaustion. Fortunately for me and every one else in general one didn't have to endure a gnawing concern about missing a critical land mark as I had on my way in making it far easier to navigate, especially when once more passing into the tree line soon over flying a fast flowing river that was immediately recognized with my quickly ascertaining our exact ground position.

Eventually after a long cold harrowing flight fraught with risk we gratefully arrived over pickle lake and not any too soon as our remaining fuel supply now having reached the critical stage with our having used up far more fuel than normal battling adverse conditions then originally planned on. Needless to say it was four very grateful men who wordlessly stepped back on to familiar solid ground. It having taken a little over six excruciatingly long hours from the time of departing from and returning to Pickle Lake fighting the elements every inch of the way, little wonder I felt so totally wrung out.

Once realizing they were now safe and feeling their feet once more on firm ground the gray visage faces of the three fishermen slowly regained their color with Pete's proboscis once more assuming it's normal purple red glow they're almost shaking my hand off at the wrist in appreciation for what I had done for them.

In retrospect one could question in all respects the justification or wisdom of taking on such a terrible risk to save them three good men from god only knows whatever hardships they would have had to endure until rescued, but again that's who I am.

Well nothing would do but to have me join them in the local pub for a . beer or two, though to be absolutely truthful my wanting nothing more then to return home and crawl out of sight under the bed for at least a week. Lordy did them three do it up brown, they're quickly becoming snot dripping pissed up with Pete at one point getting up and performing his impossible to follow Ukrainian folk dance while a few of his over ripe lady friends who had somehow gotten wind of his recent return to town simpered happily while looking on appreciatively at Pete's contortions bug eyed while drinking his freely proffered beer in great gulps, on the occasion drooling strings of brown colored saliva on to their already unspeakably filthy blouses, the situation rapidly building up to more than one could bear felt the time to be right to make an unobtrusive departure. Once having reached home had a good long shower to flush off the rank odor of fear induced sweat from my smelly body along with a fresh change of clothes, but still remained so wound up it was all I could do to prevent myself from attempting to walk on the ceiling, it taking the better part of the day and an almost entire sleepless night before being able to wind down to a mild scream.

The next morning found me in a wretched state of mind worn down to a nub, hollow eyed and feeling like shit and for all the world most likely appearing like it, in plain words just stretched out to the limit but still able to meet up with Pete and his cohorts at the hotel for breakfast. It never ceased to amaze me how them three could totally abandon themselves to partaking of unspeakable varieties of booze along with performing far out debauchery with their unspeakably filthy lady friends, the very thought causing me to cringe, and be able to do so non stop for twelve hours or better at a stretch and still be able to bounce back to life the next day as if nothing out of the ordinary had taken place all bright eyed and bushy tailed and ready to take on the world on equitable terms while poor miserable me only having one solitary beer felt as if had been on a week long non stop binge.

Once more thanking me profusely for taking such a great risk to rescue them many times over, informing me in great detail of their all but giving up hope of rescue any time in the near future when a huge lingering storm front had moved in off the coast bringing freezing temperatures and dumping a copious amount of snow, but they really began to feel terribly depressed when the lake froze over out to the middle, but Pete not being one to give in too easily cajoled his two cohorts to take the boats out on the occasion and bust up the ice just to have something to take their minds off their present dilemma and also to be prepared in the unlikely chance I would make it in, his quick thinking without question was all that spelled the difference between success and failure when my unexpectedly arriving suddenly over the lake startling the hell out of them but also galvanizing them into action. Prior to my suddenly and unexpectedly arriving overhead they had barely completed busting up the ice in front of the camp and returned to the warmth of their cabin in a gloomy state of mind to ponder what their eventual fate would be.

Then came the clincher, with Pete suddenly grasping my hand while saying at no time did I ever give up hope of your eventually showing up to rescue us being the man you are, knowing deep down inside you would take great risk in order to get us out if at all possible, but god dam it man I'm no pilot but when one takes into consideration the solitary vastness of the muskeg area the lake lies in how in the hell did you ever locate it in such terrible weather conditions?. Not wanting to go into great detail of the terrible time experienced in getting there at all decided it best to keep it on the light side to In a joking manner retort it had been easy, all one had to do was follow the smell of your long unwashed bodies, this light hearted statement completely broke them up their laughing so hard a copious amount of tears rolled from their eyes, wisely the subject left at that. These three where good men, in fact they where my type of people, the ones who made no pretence what so ever to who or what they were, living and enjoying each day to it's fullest being of simple and uncomplicated nature.

How I enjoyed their easy going wholesome camaradie, like me they wanted nothing of wealth, position, possession or grandeur, happy to live the simple life where and how they chose.

On the day of departure to return to their home at duck bay on the shores of Lake Winnipegosis Manitoba with my experiencing a heart felt pang of deep regret at their leaving. Once again having to bid adieu to some one I had come to know well and deeply respect who they where as close friends, but be as it may that is the very nature of the flying profession which rarely leaves room for lasting friendship.

Eventually it came about my making a visit to duck bay to be met by Pete at his home, never had I felt so welcome and as one with them good hearted outgoing people who lived there going overboard in showing me what real living was all about almost non stop for a period of well over two weeks, a plethora of good times with good and decent people never to be forgotten, my only reluctantly saying goodbye in order to return to the responsibilities of work and family life, something intangible while visiting Pete had noticeably paled, in retrospect if I had known then what I know to day there remains little question of my at the time would have without the slightest hesitation or regret cast off all my worldly responsibilities and what ever aspersions I may have retained up to then and to have remained there with them.

But again that's life, hindsight never changes anything only leaving us to deal with our present state of affairs be they good or bad or indifferent.

Fire And Ice

A Taste Of Frozen Hell

VERY FEW TIMES IN ANY of the publications on bush flying has any one described a comprehensive outline of the hardships and travails endured by the engineers as they worked hand in glove along side the Bush Pilot's while maintaining and keeping their aircraft serviceable while exposed to the most trying of conditions. Strangely enough it's almost if they hadn't existed at all, perhaps because their duties for the most part lacked the glamour and romance often portrayed by the editors of bush flying publications.

But the truth is they out of sheer necessity did exist, for without their unstinting efforts that often-included working under the harshest of conditions not much flying would have been accomplished. Yes the inescapable fact the pilot's at the time faced tremendous odds flying in unheated cockpits in well below temperatures often suffering frost bite and in some cases near hypothermia after enduring a long period of exposure that caused their body temperatures to drop dangerously low during a long cold flight.

But as difficult a time the pilots experienced in truth it was the unsung mechanics who labored mightily under the most adverse and trying conditions in order to maintain and prepare for flight recalcitrant often worn out engines to ensure that dated airframes remained flyable long past their useful service life solely relying on primitive or non existent support equipment that by all rights should have been consigned to the scrap heap long before.

Then it is little wonder on many occasions their tempers would flare, often having begun their day's labors while the stars still twinkled merrily overhead, a time when one's life forces have sunk to their lowest ebb with their wanting nothing more then to have had the luxury of remaining in their cozy bunks. The situation always guaranteed to be interesting when more then one aircraft stood there in frozen glory awaiting the engineer's attention. The challenges that awaited the sleepy foul tempered mechanics and in some cases novice pilots who rated the lowest on the totem pole who with valid reason dreaded having to face what they knew all too well lay in store for them .

It usually started innocuously enough, but some where along the way one of the already pushed to the limit frustrated engineers would when least desired experience greater then normal vicissitudes while laboring mightily under the most trying conditions imaginable to persuade a cranky cold soaked engine to start would sometimes find themselves tried far beyond human endurance, suddenly moving well clear of what ever piece of shit "Du Jour" they where attempting to coax into life to utter a heart rending scream of pure anguish often brandishing a hammer or large wrench clenched tightly in a white knuckled frozen fist as if coming within a hair of threatening to beat the object of their frustrations into submission.

As suited their individual personalities, some tended to-ward being far more vocal then others, a very few of the more controlled types suffered their frustrations in (pardon the pun) cold silence, but they for the most part a rarity. As vocal as I could be when in a thoroughly pushed to the limit pissed off state of mind freely venting pent up anger against the object of my frustrations most often appearing amateurish in comparison to some of my co-workers who when having reached their breaking point suddenly burst out with a heart felt," god dam this piece of shit" followed by a colorful tirade of fluent cursing and screaming unequalled in drive and force, vociferously damming with great imagination every aircraft ever built taking it's pedigree to task while consigning their designers, structural engineers and most of all the god dam brain dead workers who had built them pieces of shit to various and colorful hell's.

Then if not entirely fullfilled with getting that vocal atonement off their chest, rambled off into the by way`s of theology, mythology and if happefulfilled in top form that day often sinking into the depths of demonology in such a soul searching eloquent manner us less gifted mortals could only pause from our labors to bow in awed respect in deference to their superior oration, once having exhausted their repertoire would then as if embarrassed by their loss of control over their emotions taper off to an unintelligible series of mumbled curses. Of a certainty to a man our whole heartedly agreeing such rare vocal talent so capably demonstrated in such a colorful manner to be wasted working on mere aircraft, as any one capable of creating such heightened depths of flowery prose and verse highlighted with such color and feeling without question worthy of the stage.

But even then it was known that such incidents of high drama as impressive as it was often paled in direct comparison to the heightened antics of royally pissed off ground down to the edge of barely controlled madness of those who daily fought their frustrating battles against adversity not only fought balky engines but often forced to battle bitterly cold winds that went far to-ward grossly reducing an already near futile attempt to produce sufficient heat to thaw out a frozen engines with only the use of the ubiquitous blow pot (Plumber's Pot) to accomplish these ends.

Aviation at that point in time technologically only a step away from the

Stone Age, the use of electric heaters though in use in many other applications still in most cases lay far away from being adopted by the average bush operation. The "blow Pots" as they were most often referred to and widely used at the time actually an oversized Coleman stove but quite capable when properly employed of producing an immense amount of heat when in use. But as we all knew nothing comes easy in the world of bush flying, once the pot had been fired up and performing to one's satisfaction it was carefully placed inside the engine tent directly under the engine and if one were wise keeping a wary eye on it at all times they're possessing an alarming propensity to suddenly and without warning to flaring up spraying great gouts of volatile fuel and flame over everything, again if one where wise to the blow pot's idiosyncrasies a shovel full of loose snow always kept within easy reach to douse the inevitable fire that raged around the engine, no fire extinguisher I had ever used up till then had proved to be as effective. But for what it was worth one inevitably paid a price upon resuming the heating process as one not only had to re -light the blow pot while attempting to avoid the stinging hot drops of oil that incessantly dripped onto the red hot blow pot that even though not operating continued to hiss angrily until cooling off, but also the heavy drops of water produced by the melting frost and snow that often pooled within the engine cowlings could and often did when suddenly cascading on to the red hot blow pot causing it to have violent fits as it hissed and sizzled threatening at any time to flare up or just plain quit. As a matter of course one diligently suffered the agonies of hell from the noxious gases produced by the blow pot along with the occasional cloud of thick choking fumes from the burning oil creating an unbreatheable atmosphere that also stung one's eyes to the point of tearing copiously.

This situation soon reaching the stage of being untenable forcing one to seek temporary relief by poking your head out from inside the tent to gasp a breath of fresh air, but if one where to avoid experiencing a potentially dangerous state of affairs that inevitably occurred when one's attention otherwise diverted one did not dally for any too long a period of time as one could almost swear the god dam blow pot could actually sense your moment of inattention choosing just that moment to flare up. If that where to occur it sure got one's attention with one scrambling madly to grab the shovel of snow and to hopefully douse the conflagration as it not only set the engine on fire but also the oil soaked engine tent. As one of my fellow pilots who posed a droll sense of humor once stated, "Eh Hart" them god dam engine tent fires spreads quicker then a hot fart in a cold room, actually if one cares to ponder it, a very accurate and appropriate analogy.

As if that alone didn't present enough problems the advent of a windy day compounded one's grief as the wind gusts on analogyasion tended to billow the wind ward side of the tent directly over the hot flame of the blow pot to instantly catch fire, when this occurred a mad scramble made to rip the tent off the engine and roll it in the snow to douse the flames, then to laboriously replace the still smoldering tent back over the engine before it cooled off too much, this maddening occurrence greatly extending one's time spent in up the engine. If this where to occur more then once, and believe me it often did , not only blow pots flared, it being guaranteed the rising heat of one's temper rose in direct proportion.

If it so came about with one experiencing many failed attempts due to the wind the frustrations would become too much to bear it not being uncommon at one time or another to witness a blow pot being launched high and wide followed by a heart felt shriek of despair, "god dam piece of shit" usually accompanied by a virtual war dance as they frantically stomped on the burning tent to quell the flames all the while cursing the day they had ever heard of aircraft. Once all had settled down to a mild scream the party in question having vented their growing frustrations and having while muttering inaudible curses reinstalled the now worse for wear engine tent to begin the maddening search for their wayward blow

Once found it could well happen all over again with the engineer mindlessly attacking the object of their mounting frustrations with renewed fury kicking at it till it bounced in all directions, it was no small wonder they ever functioned at all considering the terrible abuse they received on a regular and ongoing basis.

This abject show of pure and undiluted frustration could and often did continue until their wrath subsided to a manageable level, once more grabbing up the much abused blow pot to return to their respective charge where it always remained a possibility the sequence of events could all too easily begin all over again, sometimes within a short period of time.

Many were the bitterly cold winter mornings with a light breeze stirring up the already frigid temperatures to give it a "bite", at such times one was guaranteed to within a short period of time to suddenly hear a heart rending wail of total despair followed by the heated expletive "god dam piece of useless fucking garbage" and with that resounding exclamation still hanging in the frigid air being treated to the amazing sight of a blow pot arching through the air followed by the afore mentioned war dance.

On the serious side blow potting a cold soaked engine at best a difficult and time consuming proposition.

One neat trick learned from the old timers early on in my career was while heating up the engine to closely observe the metal propeller blades that almost immediately on the application of heat would take on a fairly heavy coat of frost, as the engine gradually thawed out the frost on the propeller blade would slowly creep up it's length until finally disappearing into the hub, this told me the internal temperature of the engine and the propeller had stabilized. But again it did not pay to get antsy in hurrying up the starting procedure even if the engine felt to be sufficiently warmed up, my making it a practice to add an additional fifteen minutes or so to the total time being all too well aware even if the exterior of the engine felt warm to the touch, the interior remained damp and as any one with the most rudiment knowledge of engine operations in cold weather knows, wet or iced up spark plugs don't spark.

Then in some instances came the difficult task of filling the oil tank with hot oil, usually while attempting to maintain a precarious balancing act on a slippery surface, a sometimes difficult feat that would put a tight rope walker to shame. And then as was often being the case in making it all the more difficult when the wind curled around the lip of the pail inevitably caused the hot oil to spray back into your face creating all kinds of grief for one to endure.

The one spring ritual enjoyed by all consisted of piling our well worn oil soaked parkas and coveralls in a heap on the spring ice and to douse them with a good measure of aviation gas then setting them on fire to gleefully watch their initially creating great volumes of greasy smoke until burning down and in some cases smolder away for an additional three days leaving only a black smudge on the ice to remind us of their one time existence.

Aviation in them early days offered little in the way of creature comforts when performing necessary maintenance, often during the winter months, the only shelter available being flimsy canvas shelters whose longevity remained subject to the winds ever changing moods, on the occasion being blown completely away from around us. Eventually as aviation progressed we began to enjoy the luxury of unheard of up till then permanent shelters referred to as "nose hangers" normally constructed of insulated plywood walls, wooden floor, oil stove for heating and a heavy canvas cover draped over the front section to allow the placing of an aircraft's nose inside allowing the engine be worked on in comfort and considered by us to be the equivalent of an aviation garden of Eden. Being constructed of light weight materials and mounted on skids made it a simple matter to move from one aircraft to another as desired, man it sure was seventh heaven to be able to perform one's work in relative comfort with bare hands and our bulky parkas removed.

Yes one could say it must have been one hell of a tough way to earn a living, but be as it may no one forced us to go that route, individually choosing of our own accord to living the life style we chose as grueling as it could often be one felt a sense of freedom in doing what one chose to do and that in it's self rewarding. Due to the transient nature of aviation one was often required to leave the comforts of home for various periods of time, often forced to exist on poorly prepared food while taking up temporary residence in mind bending filthy accommodations that offered bug infested quarters even the rats had abandoned in disgust.

The pay scale at best miserly, risk to body and limb high, we all knew too well the gnawing hunger of lonely men for home and all that it means, the subdued feelings of frustration and anger that often threatened to overwhelm one, the isolation that could and often did broke the spirits of them less able to cope, the hopelessness of attempting to do a reasonable job while laboring under primitive working conditions. In the end it all went toward forging us into independent strong willed men proud to the point of arrogance of our accomplishments, this attitude of a certainty galled them of lesser mien, but to us who had endured if that be the price exacted for standing tall while overcoming great odds made it well worth it.

One may wonder where such rigorous experiences took us, well that's a fair question that can only be answered by the individual personality of those involved as each of us chose our own path to the top of our profession, some to go the way of the major airlines as line pilots or mechanics. I for one being too much the strong willed individual, far too independent of nature to labor under the iron grip of the unions or to tolerate the rigidity of working under a time clock or in general to have anything to do with the beaucracy of any large entity, instead choosing to remain where I belonged in the free spirit realm of the bush pilot's where simple contentment as an individual took precedence above all.

It is well I chose as I did as my very nature bridles against authority in any way shape or form, also regimentation has never appealed to me being too much my own man to tolerate it. If this can be construed as a failure to move up into the higher strata of aviation, then so be it, but strangely enough my satisfaction in attaining the level I did in having succeeded so marvelously well at my chosen profession as a career "Bush Pilot", a long and worthy career that led me down a path of an unimaginable life style that gave one the freedom to choose how and where they worked, as the old saying goes

"Freedom is the salt of life"!

Then if by chance there is them who would view my chosen life style as taking the easy way out, then I must commend their astuteness as that was exactly what I did as no other life style would have fitted half so well.

For if one is not skating on the edge, then one is only taking up space.

North Caribou Incident

AS IF THE GOD`S OF fate and chance had become bored with the human race in general requiring a break from their incessant boredom must have decided to place their favorite "captain step on his dick Weston" on the hot seat to liven things up a bit .

The summer months had worn on in their normal fashion with our doing whatever needed to be done including the much despised transporting to and from the fly in fishing camps hordes of whiny smelly foul breathed overbearing fishermen who to a man felt themselves to have been ordained by god and the president of the good old U. S. A so pronounced was their brain dead arrogance to-ward what they perceived as lesser mortals

Having just returned from a trip wandered up to the office to see what came next to my surprise to be greeted by six of the largest blackest Negros I had ever seen, they're towering over me by at least six inches, indeed making me feel rather short and runty. Their unexpected presence surprised the hell out of me, they're being the first I had ever known to come that far out of the way just to go fishing with my soon learning I was to fly them out to north Caribou Lake .

Well that suited me just fine my not harboring the least discriminatory leanings to-ward negro people, my generally finding them very polite and likeable which says a hell of a lot more in their favor than can be truthfully said of the so called as they perceive themselves superior Whiteman.

The dock hands who having loaded them and their gear aboard the aircraft in preparation for their flight commented to me later how pleasant and helpful they appeared to be, a far cry from the average demanding whining sniveling complement of white people we where normally forced to endure. Once airborne their infectious delight at viewing the myriad lakes and seemingly endless verdant forests prompted me to give them the extended scenic tour on the way out pointing out places of interest to them.

On arrival at the camp we where met by a group of six fishermen who had just completed a satisfactory week's fishing and now anxious to return to their homes and jobs,

most of them we where soon to learn hailed from "little rock Arkansas," a notoriously Negro discriminating state.

The large mean looking florid faced one who helped to dock the aircraft appeared to me in all respects to be the overbearing trouble maker type, It was soon found my initial appraisal being correct with what transpired next brought on by his reactions when at first viewing the Negros alighting from the cabin, his being the first to recover from the shock of seeing Negros in such close proximity immediately came out with a sarcastic cutting remark, Well bless mah soul boys it seems we all gotten ah selves a passel of coons hereabouts!, with a cruel snicker of self serving satisfaction following his depreciatory remarks.

It quickly became obvious to all he retained a very pronounced discriminatory hang up to-wards Negros in general who to their credit totally ignored the cruel undeserved jibes directed to-ward them, not seeming in the least fazed or intimidated by the discriminatory rantings of the red necked loud mouth, instead quietly going about their business of sorting through their gear in preparation of moving it up to the cabin. This deliberate act on their part of totally ignoring his uncalled for rudeness only served to further inflame his sense of righteousness as his attempts to goad the other five men into joining in with him in de- riding them meeting with little if any success, it being obvious they're choosing to refrain from creating an unnecessary fracas. It rapidly became apparent he bull headedly refused to learn from their unwilling silence continuing on to say what do you all say boys?, them coons is going to be right good enough to haul our luggage from the cabin, at that he turned and yelled at the Negros in a stentorian drill sergeant bellow to get their black asses shuffling raht smahtly, you all heah noo. Again the Negros chose to ignore his righteous braying, instead acting as if he didn't exist. His piggy eyes almost popping out of his head at their continuing to ignore his imperious commands while if at all possible his face taking on a ruddier glow. He had just begun another vicious tirade against them when my deciding it had gone far enough stepped in front of him to yell directly into his face to bloody well shut his blow hole before I did it for him, then inquiring in a hushed tone of voice if he entertained a death wish or was just plain nuts to even consider riling up them huge Negros as if they chose to any one of them could single handedly make very short work of him and not even come close to breaking into a sweat while doing so and that he best understand he could be rest assured he would receive no help what so ever from me if it came down to it, not to mention the fact it's quite obvious your buddies wisely prefer to remain out of it so show some common sense and decency toward your fellow man no matter what his color and shut your god dam face while you still have a head on your shoulders to do it with, do you understand?

Some what startled at the vehemence of my dictate he involuntarily stepped back a pace or two as if no longer sure of his ground, only muttering something about once having been a sergeant in the U. S. marines and not about to take any shit from a passel of coons much less from a poor boy white trash Canadian!

Well that cinched it, my brusquely informing him in no uncertain terms through clenched teeth that I didn't give a good god dam if he was the president of the U. S. A, as in case it had slipped his feeble mind he now stood on Canadian soil and would respect Canadian laws, plus the inalienable fact of my being the captain of the aircraft he intended to return to Pickle Lake on, at hearing that he began to protest and whine about my unfairly stomping on him. Ignoring his protest turned to the other five who made up the sergeants party, they immediately made it clear they wanted no trouble period. Once that had been settled to my satisfaction advised them to retrieve their gear from the cabin as we would be departing shortly adding they were to leave the sergeants as he would not be accompanying us as "racists" such as him were not welcomed aboard any aircraft I flew as this was Canada and not Little Rock Arkansas and we Canadians on the average abhorred racism, and he the sergeant appeared to be hard core.

While this exchange took place the group of Negros had quietly stood back enjoying my putting the boots to sergeant loud mouth with ill concealed mirth, one of them drawling out in his best Harlem manner that yeah man they shur nough could make reasonable use of a camp boy to see to the chores while they fished, and yes he had a nice chubby round ass, just what us low down black assed niggers likes the best, hain't that raht boys? the rest of them nodded their assent agreeing his being down right correct, but remembers boys we all rightly got to cut the cards to see who all gets to him first as shur nough none of us all that keen on a wet deck.

As the exchange concerning his future welfare took place as if he didn't exist the red neck sergeant could do little but stand there in perplexed and furious silence fists clenched, with raw fear beginning to replace the angry scowl that ran away from his face as what I had just stated concerning leaving him behind along with the threat of what the large negro had just said sunk in, looking around wildly as if seeking assistance from any quarter with his lips moving soundlessly finally able in a small voice tinged with the first touch of panic causing it to come out in a high falsetto squeaked out in a far less belligerent tone of voice if it was really my intention to abandon him to remaining with the Negros against his will?, most certainly was my cryptic reply, and as if in after thought adding and if by some misplaced hope might think you can force yourself aboard, well think twice about it for it so happens my having six very large very willing to offer assistance if required as you so fondly refer to them, "coons" that you took as your god given right to insult and demean without provocation, and what's more on Canadian soil yet, we Canadians react very badly to that form of undeserved and uncalled for racial harassment, so believe that they are more than willing to prevent your doing so if it gets down to that.

The others of his party having gotten caught up with the humor of his discomfiture were thoroughly enjoying watching him squirm, one sort of got the message in all probability during the course of a week they had long become weary of his overbearing loud mouthed personality, it must have in the sense of the word been a trial to endure.

On my encouraging them to do so they wasted little time in assisting the negro's to haul their gear to the cabin and being assisted in return while introducing themselves to each other and soon chatting away like old friends, that is except for the "sergeant" who thoroughly confused by it all just stood there in frozen silence uncertain as what to do or say next, his normally turkey red features slowly turning to a chalky gray as his eyes continued to flit wildly back and forth as he began to fully realize the implications of his plight, a satisfying revelation to observe that formerly loud mouthed overbearing hard core racist within a short space of time reverting to a badly frightened quivering chunk of protoplasm with tears of fear and frustration beginning to course down his cheeks to drip off his double chin, all the while his lips continuing to move soundlessly, actually I feared if pushed much further could possibly suffer a heart attack.

Somehow in spite of it all he managed to reach into a reservoir of misplaced confidence dredging up a new round of bravado babbling inanely about his by birth right, a white man by god and a citizen of the good ole U. S. A. and a marine sergeant to boot which constitutionally gave him the right to his remaining superior to a passel of low class Harlem coons and above all a poor boy white trash Canadian, good Christ it was almost inconceivable that dick head didn't have the capacity to learn when he was well off, I found it almost unbelievable that anyone in his precarious position would be that stupid or brash, he just didn't seem to get it obviously requiring an indelible lesson in humility and about to receive same in spades as no mouthy Yankee was about to get away with deriding a Canadian on Canadian soil and the captain of the very aircraft he planned on flying back to Pickle Lake on to boot.

Turning to the other five good ole boy's instructed them to place their gear on board the aircraft in preparation of our leaving momentarily, without question they're hauling ass right smartly in complying all the while grinning like shit house cats perched on an out house roof, they to a man easily guessed what was coming next while the compliment of huge Negros casually blocked the "sergeant" from attempting to join them while the largest of them commenting in his best corn shucking drawl, what's y'all hurry white trash, could it be y'all don't find our company to you all's liking?, well y'all got another week here with us black assed coons to learn some manners, yeah man ah shur nuff raring to have a go at y'all's chubby white ass, man ah's already some fierce anxious to give it a go, what y'all got to say to that white trash?.

At that point I must admit to feeling a slight tinge of conscience at instigating the poor beleaguered bugger's unenviable plight, but in truth he had brought on his own woes so remained adamant in forcing an indelible lesson upon him that would have the desired effect of teaching him just how difficult humble pie was to choke down. The large negro's dictating his probable fate must have finally hit home, the sergeants eyes suddenly becoming wild with fright as his voice began to crack uncontrollably upon beseeching me to relent and allow him to leave with us, my acid tinged reply there was no room on board my aircraft for hard core racists, obviously you must have overlooked the fact or conveniently forgotten or simply don't care you are presently standing on Canadian soil and may I remind you in case it has slipped your feeble mind we Canadians at no time tolerate racism in our country, not even way out here in our back yard!. At this he managed to choke off what was most likely intended to be a caustic reply, instead casting desperate glances between the implacable wall of huge Negros and the aircraft only to be met by a sea of grinning black faces. The largest and the meanest looking of them sensing they had him on the run commented in his best deep south field hand accent, boy's, ah recons we all made a deal to cut the cahds as to who gwine first go at white trash's chubby ass, but y' all knows and hopes y'all unerstands ah jes d'on fancy a wet deck be'in it offends my righteous sense of decency, ah mos s'ur hopes and prays y'all see's it mah way, upon hearing that the rest of them nodded their heads in assent saying they shur nuff reckons it all g'on down just fine with them as us black assed chillens have a whole week of playing with him ahead of us so noo problem!

Well the ringing silence that followed that statement seemed to crash around my ears before it was noticed a widening pool of urine had begun to puddle around the "sergeant's shoes while a tell tale spreading black splotch that formed around the crotch of his jump suit brought out howls of unrestrained laughter from the negroes and white people alike causing his already ruddy face to inflame anew in anger and embarrassment, my fearing his possibly experiencing a coronary being a prime concern as his breathing had become ragged and labored with his face once again losing it's normal turkey red hue and taking on the pasty shade of bread dough.

My deciding the charade had run it's course instructed the Negros to untie the ropes from the floats and to hang on to the wing until my having made my way into the pilot's seat cautioning them to make certain the "sergeant" didn't make a break for the aircraft as it would prove difficult to dislodge him if he ever managed to get in the door.

Upon hearing the finality of his being left behind he completely lost it screaming hoarsely while begging to be allowed to join us, allowing him to stew in his own juices for a spell while putting on a convincing act of hesitating momentarily as if weighing a great decision while looking down disdainfully at the pathetic bundle of misery groveling for mercy, my not at any time being one who enjoys creating or witnessing human misery decided to end it once and for all. In a deep and commanding tone of voice inquired of the contingent of Negros if they where willing to accept an apology from him for his rude and uncalled for racism, to a man they allowed that would go down all right with them providing he did so individually (oh man he sure as hell ain't going to like that).

Upon realizing the import of the judgment passed on to him his southern states roots manifested themselves in full force causing his eyes to flash with pure malice while swelling up like an over sized bull frog totally lost it near going ballistic screaming at me in a rage torn voice, you god dam Canadian poor white trash, do you really think you can get away with humiliating me to the uncalled for degree you have managed to so far and get away with it?, I'll sue you for all your worth,(That wasn't much at the time)blah blah and further more, feeling more amused then angered by his tirade allowed him to rant on for a time as his eyes hunted desperately for a way out between the security of the aircraft and the unyielding wall of large Negros who with narrowed eyes appeared to be sizing him up for further degradation. Then acting as if enough was more then enough swung down to plunk myself into my seat while loudly proclaiming, well sarge, do have a great time of it, see you next week.

That's all it took, that final statement served to break down any further resistance on his part, now totally convinced of his being abandoned to endure what ever atrocities the Negros cared to extend him caved in screaming he would apologize, just don't leave me, oh please don't leave me he sobbed, taking him at his word allowed to choke out an apology to each of the six Negros though definitely leaving one the impression he would have sooner fondled a snake visibly shuddering in revulsion with each hand shake, this state of affairs not going unnoticed by the contingent of grinning Negros with each holding his hand in a painful grip for much longer then necessary thoroughly enjoying his discomfiture.

Once that ordeal of a ceremony completed to my satisfaction he was allowed to place his gear and himself aboard the aircraft which he accomplished with great alacrity amidst much hooting and hollering of where sure nuff going to miss y'all white trash coming from the negroes leaving him thoroughly humiliated and quivering in a black rage shaking like a dog pissing razor blades with the following cat calls and peals of unrestricted laughter to speed him on his way. Sticking my nose into the cabin exhorted his cohorts to keep him in line as if he where to create any sort of a ruckus during the duration of the flight I would land immediately and throw him out bodily on some remote lake for the flies to finish off . The men being astute enough to realize it to be an empty threat sported huge grins as they nodded in affirmation as they too hugely enjoying the sarg`s well deserved come uppance and humiliation much to his chagrin but there was little he could do about it but quietly fume and sulk about his present lot as he plotted my demise.

Once on our way with a last fond wave to the still laughing negroes who no doubt would remember that fishing trip for some time to come the humiliating of the red neck sergeant remaining one of their favorite topics for some time when getting together for a beer not to mention I must have definitely left them with a favorable impression of Canadian bush pilots and Canadian hospitality in general.

The flight going smoothly and without incident until we had landed and the floats nudged up against the dock with our barely coming to a full stop before the sergeant bounded out of the cabin door with the alacrity of a frightened gazelle, truly an amazing feat for such a portly man to instantly make a bee line for the office with thoughts of revenge foremost in his heart. As he waddled up the slight incline with his buttocks seeming to taking on a life of their own as he crested the hill and sailed majestically into the flight office to not long after confronting the bewildered dispatcher to whom he spilled out his tale of woe imperiously demanding my being instantly beheaded and drawn and quartered immediately with his cohorts who had followed him into the office to listen with rapt attention to his vehement outburst breaking out in raucous peals of unrestrained laughter as his violent screams and threats to sue began to filter clearly out of the dispatch office`s open windows for all to hear and wonder about, they're racous laughter eventually subsidoffice's few snorts and sniggers as they wiped the tears out of their eyes allowing it to be shur nuff best goldang fishing trip they had ever had, each of them thanking me and shaking my hand they left the dock having great difficulty in concealing the huge grins that couldn't be held back for any appreciative length of time.

As was their wont the more experienced dock hands as usual paid very little attention to what had recently transpired their being long accustomed and inured to the wide range of emotions that commonly took place with each party of fishermen who flew with me, but one could still in all good consciences sympathize with the plight of the recent and very green replacement dispatcher who only being on the job for less then two weeks hardly knew which way was up never mind begin to understand the individual personalities of cynical case hardened wayward pilots who to a man possessed what could be only construed as a retaining a weird sense of humor, his had proved to be an onerous task from day one coming within an ace of going around the bend in frustration within a short time when attempting to deal in a logical manner with what could be construed as normal day to day problems, it soon becoming apparent the sergeant wasn't about to make his day any easier.

Knowing the badly rattled dispatcher would more then have his hands full with the sergeant's incomprehensible railings about something he couldn't begin to comprehend the ramifications of decided it best to stay out of it and leave him to handle the situation as he saw fit, justifying my decision on the grounds he had to learn how to handle people like the sarge if he intended to remain on the job for any length of time vowing to remain clear until the shit hit the fan of which was a certainty sooner or later took off for the hotel with a fellow pilot who had witnessed the initial exchange between the red neck sergeant and the dispatcher, asked me in a droll tone of voice who's dick did you step on besides your own this time around hart?

Once having related the story to him in detail it was all he could do to hold a glass of beer to his lips as each time he attempted to do so a loud snicker would burst out of his lips spraying beer all over the place, and when finally able to stop laughing and choking on his beer long enough to comment between labored deep breaths, Jesus hart I just don't understand how you do it, half the people who fly with you vow to your immediate destruction while the other half venerate you like you were some kind of a tin god or walked on water, what could I say, my being of shy and retiring nature tended toward remaining out of the lime light as much as possible, but we both enjoyed a hell of a good laugh over his all too astute observation.

Returning to the office a good half hour or so later found the red neck sergeant still deeply involved in seeking justice or in plain English "stirring up the shit" demanding that nothing less then my being immediately executed would go far in assuaging his mortification. The well harried and flustered dispatcher not knowing where to turn next had given up in confusion, throwing up his hands in despair unable to make sense out of the ravings the sergeant directed at him having failed in his attempts to calm down the irate red neck who now in full cry appeared to be on the verge of apoplexy as he screamed he wasn't about to pay for being unjustly subjected to uncalled for personal abuse from a poor boy white trash nigger loving bush pilot, at that the dispatcher who having witnessed my silent arrival cast a beseeching look of despair as if in a plea for assistance in seeking a way out of his present dilemma staring at his adversary in absolute perplexity. Oh Christ here we go again my realizing that stepping in to resolve the impasse he had no part in creating would without a doubt stir up quite the furor before it was satisfactorily resolved to the satisfaction of all concerned, deftly reached over behind the dispatchers shoulder to remove the red neck's tagged car keys.

Wisely for one with so little experience with the manifold vagaries of air travelers the dispatcher had refused to turn the key's over against the red necks imperious commands he do so as he had yet to settle up on his portion of the charges, the other five men had already quietly done so against his vehement protests. Dangling the keys in front of him coldly advised he had a choice, either pay his bill without further ado or begin the long trek back to red neck land by whatever means he could it was his call to make, upon hearing that dictum pronounced against him he demanded the use of the phone to call the police only to be advised it was for company use only forcing his having to waddle over to the hotel to make use of the pay phone.

The local police officer being a good friend to all at the base had long become inured to the machinations and ongoing intrigue that existed in the world of aviation. Having received the call for assistance from the red neck he called the base to inquire as to the nature of the problem to be assured it was nothing out of the ordinary just the usual B. S. and to not put himself out, this he allowed to be quite reasonable on our part having just sat down for his evening meal when the red neck had disturbed him, at that he yawned over the phone saying he had just completed a long day and planned on a long nap after finishing his meal.

Well that was right up our alley with my joining a few other pilots for supper at the hotel. It must have been over an hour before returning to the office to find the red neck sergeant pacing back and forth in righteous indignation agitated to the very core of his soul at the tardiness of the police officer muttering terrible threats under his breath without any one to heed him as the dispatcher had wisely chosen to take the opportunity to remove himself elsewhere.

Upon our trooping noisily back into the office he went silent only casting uncertain glances at the motley collection of rugged stone faced pilots who stared arrogantly back at him with amusement written all over their faces having seen it all many times before with their up yours attitude difficult if not impossible to ignore. The sergeant having being informed of this fact beforehand knew all too well he trod on Canadian soil in a very remote part of the country and his options if any remained few and far between. At one point we inquired of his cohorts who where not at all pleased about the continuing delay brought on by the red neck sergeant's stubbornness in refusing to settle up his charges until having had a chance to pour out his woes to the tardy police officer as to why they had tolerated such an obvious asshole in the first place, they answered it should have never happened as they were from long time acquaintance quite aware of his overbearing confrontational personality, but one of them being married to his daughter they had reluctantly and against their better judgment agreed to allow his accompanying them in order to keep peace in the family and as it had turned out much to their everlasting regret though admitting outside of the red neck sergeants sometimes unsettling presence they had thoroughly enjoyed their week long fishing trip greatly admiring beauty of our northlands and the remarkable capabilities of the Canadian bush pilots!

Well as it went Don the local cop eventually deigned to make an unhurried appearance with a humorous glint showing in his eyes having seen and heard it all many times before and being quite adept at defusing acrimonious situations that popped up from time to time. No sooner had he pulled up to the parking area when the red neck sergeant came flying out of the door in full cry to pounce on him like a chicken on a grasshopper braying about the foul dealings on our part as he charged over to the cruiser demanding I be arrested immediately on charges of defamation of character, threatening him with exile amongst a passel of coons and unlawfully retaining possession of his vehicle keys etc etc. His demands being so loud and insistent Don was forced to shout him down warning him in no uncertain terms if he refused to forthwith comply with the demands to shut his face perhaps a liberal dose of night stick might convince him of the folly of his ways, in other words back off and quiet down or else.

Once the dust had settled somewhat with all the onlookers experiencing great difficulty suppressing huge grins Don was able to extract his much embellished tale of woe, also taking statements from the other five men individually before pronouncing his conclusions plainly stating at no time had anyone assaulted him verbally or otherwise or illegally posses any of your property, the airways retains the legal right to demand payment for services rendered, so shut up and pay up before I run you in for showing contempt toward a police officer.

Having no recourse but to do as the police officer demanded unwillingly complied by attempting to issue a personal cheque drawn on a bank in the U. S. A to no avail, our being far too astute concerning them type of transactions as accepting a cheque drawn on an American bank would prove in reality to be worthless as he could stop payment as soon as he crossed the border leaving the company out of hand. Upon being apprised of our outright refusal to accept a personal cheque he immediately set up a howl of protest with Don once more stepping in to remind him that was our right to do so, indignant and reluctant at failing to pull the wool over our eyes nevertheless forced to pay by traveler's cheques while uttering nonsense threats of we would be hearing from his lawyer etc etc, our reaction to that empty threat was to yawn in his face much to the amusement of the gathered onlookers.

As I well knew it wouldn't and of a certainty it didn't end at that, the bean counters at head office had set it up so each individual group was issued with a large manila envelope that contained all the pertinent details required by the dispatcher to collect the charges owing on completion of the fishing trip, while on one side of the envelope a blank printed questionnaire was to be filled in on the details of their trip and how the facilities and services rendered added up blah blah, etc etc and so forth. Much later one of the girls in head office who worked with these issues discreetly informed me of the red neck sergeants less than complimentary comments on my part, it seemed nothing short of my being beheaded then drawn and quartered would assuage his injured pride, and of course accompanied by the usual frosty demands from lofty places to justify my actions report which as a matter of course ignored, then again one could not help but to wonder how they received the glowing report from the remainder of the sergeant's party and of course the six Negros?..

Big John

AS OFTEN MENTIONED BEFOREHAND ONE can be absolutely certain while residing or working in the Northern parts of our great country one is bound to meet up with and often work along side of those who by their very nature possess a colorful and distinctive personality.

One such individual who some where along the way came into my life and to be called "friend", who all too soon departed the land of the living in a violent manner while deeply involved in doing what he wished to at the time.

"John" an amiable generally good-natured six foot six inch individual of independent nature who bowed to no one regardless of their status or position, toiling solely in his own interest as he saw fit be it legally or otherwise reasoning the ends justified the means.

His one failing was an unquenchable penchant for hard liquor and of course easy women, other than that a man that that did not lack confidence in his abilities, thoroughly enjoying his chosen life style to the fullest.

It will be noticed by the astute reader my having made it a point to not reveal his full name out of respect for his memory and remaining family, in lieu of doing so referring to him throughout the story as "Big John"

Having through perseverance and dint of much illegal activities as deemed by the lawmakers along with pulling himself up by his boot straps had worked his way up to being a full time free trader with a string of very successful trading posts located in the northern settlements in direct competition with the venerable Hudson's Bay Co. of which he serviced pretty much on his own initially through the extensive utilization of a decrepit Cessna 180 that did yeoman service for many years before upgrading to a De-Havilland beaver aircraft, gaining a notorious reputation for flying through the most atrocious of weather conditions with a seeming aplomb that left us less gifted mortals squirming uncomfortably at the mere thought. Not only did he push through weather severe enough to ground all but the most determined, but routinely did so severely while staggering along in a severely overloaded aircraft, it was no small wonder the wings stayed on as he staggered through the air hanging on the propeller while unconcernedly nipping away on a bottle of booze. It seems he could handle fiery spirits with little effect to his capabilities as no one had ever known him to becoming inebriated or rowdy.

His like many others utilized our facilities to service his aircraft while renting warehouse space to store his trade goods. It can be truthfully stated his on a regular basis driving himself and his machine unmercifully, none of us could ever remember him ceasing his labors long enough to have his aircraft inspected by an engineer, only taking the time when it becoming absolutely necessary to repair or replace an ailing component or perform a much needed oil change, outside of that somehow very rarely experiencing any noteworthy break downs considering the god awful abuse the aircraft tolerated on an ongoing basis, his being an accomplished mechanic normally performed his own repairs.

One cold miserable early fall morning with the weather picture not at all to our liking keeping us less motivated types grounded who but Big John came suddenly blasting out of the murk surprising all to hell and back, our having previously bet on the fact that as daring as he could be would not dare to venture out into such atrocious conditions, he certainly proved us wrong.

Upon meeting him at the dock once he had landed and taxied in, he appeared to be totally unconcerned about having fought his way through less than ideal conditions, shocking us further upon blandly stating his intention to gas and load up immediately and to leave as soon as he had consumed a few cups of well fortified coffee.

Once gassed to capacity and loaded with five drums of fuel topped off with several cases of oil the aircraft appeared to be on the verge of sinking at the dock that upon the advent of placing his ponderous bulk on the float in preparation of entering the cockpit, but for the ropes restraining it from doing so we were absolutely certain it would have done so. Waiting until he had settled into the cockpit and cranked up the engine did we dare to loosen off the ropes wondering as we did so if the aircraft would turn turtle before gaining forward speed with his waving a friendly farewell out of the cabin window soon lost to sight in the gray threatening murk, our only able to track his progress by a muffled roar as he applied full power for take off, it seeming to go on for some time as the considerably overloaded aircraft struggled to leave the water requiring a considerable run to do so before lifting off to in all probability barely clear the stunted trees at the end of the lake.

Our having long become long accustomed to his daring exploits gave little thought to what lay ahead of him, if he chose to push inclement weather so be it.

Having little else to do we retired to the hotel to imbibe a hot cup of coffee and trade lies with each other. At the most only half an hour or so had passed when our being absolutely shocked to hear an aircraft flying over the hotel at a very low altitude with our as a matter of course making a mad scramble back to the dock to see who was the idiot that would dare to buck such terrible conditions some surprised to see the mystery aircraft that suddenly hove into view to be none other than Big John's, well his returning for any reason come hell or high water a new one on us, that was until able to clearly take note of the copious amount of oil that dripped from the belly of the aircraft completely coating the tops and sides of the floats obvious to all the engine had sprung a major leak spraying hot oil into the slipstream resulting in it's being widely distributed by the propeller blast to swirl around the engine cowling coating the entire windshield and forward part of the fuselage with black oil.

We could only stare and wonder as to how in the hell had he managed to find his way back in such poor visibility much less land that grossly overloaded aircraft safely considering he had somehow accomplished that feat with almost zero forward visibility available to him, that boy was awful damn good or lucky, perhaps a bit of both, not one of us could help but to quail inwardly at the mere thought of the extreme dangers he had recently endured.

On his unconcernedly clambering down from the cockpit it was noticed to be still clutching a half full bottle of booze wearing a vacuous grin on his moon face to state in a matter of fact tone to reckon to have developed a minor problem while not indicating the least vestige of uncertainty or shakiness resulting from his ordeal, if nothing else that boy sure didn't lack confidence seeming to accept taking such terrible risks in his stride. We to a man knew what he must have felt when first experiencing difficulty under such onerous conditions. I for one if having succeeded in pulling off what he recently had without accident would have by now found myself on my knees kissing the ground while exhorting hail Mary's by the score seriously considering becoming an all out snot dripping mumbling idiot of a drunk or a bible thumper exhorting meaningless passages to all and sundry from the highest hill.

As it stood his cavalier attitude left all and sundry shaking their collective heads in wonder and awe. Now that the excitement was over for the day once more retreated to the hotel to mull over that madman's latest escapades over another cup of coffee some happy to remain in a safe warm and dry environment.

On the average our being well experienced case hardened cynical lot, jaded to the nth degree as could be found under any stone, as motley a collection of proud to be who we were bush pilots viewing our accomplishments with the inordinate pride of those who with enduring persistence had survived immeasurable hardships in order to arrive at the peak of our chosen professions.

Pickle Lake being as close to an out of the way conventional back water town as one could possibly care to get, but at least it still offered one the opportunity to maintain their freedom to a degree few places allowed, a bastion of free thinkers and free enterprise sorts that entertained a laissez faire' attitude of live and let live.

Being well aware of our generation of bush pilots in all probability the last of a breed viewed ourselves as being the absolute crème de crème with every intention of remaining so to the end.

Yes without a doubt we of a matter of course often took chances that in certain incidences bordered on near madness, in some instances having done the unthinkable to somehow make it through, the aftermath often leaving us shaken to our very core, but all the wiser for having survived. Regardless of our seeming bombast and bravado Big John's daring simply left us in his dust as none possessed the rare qualities it took to hold a candle up to his hair raising exploits or when it came to pushing our luck in the weather conditions he routinely flew in as a matter of course.

Regardless of his bravado we knew with the deep certainty of them who being more than aware of just how hard he pushed it, sooner or later the odds where bound to catch up with him!. How prophetic our thoughts turned out to be, but still none among us remotely suspected for a moment his demise was to come about that very day or the unexpectedly strange circumstances in which it took place.

As was usual with us when forced to remain idle spent a great deal of time in the hotel coffee shop trading lies or in general just kibitzing around some what taken aback when Big John who had remained behind in order to locate the source of the oil leak suddenly made an astonishing appearance looking for all the world like a drowned rat to regale us with his having slipped off the oil slicked float ending up flat on his back in the shallow near freezing water during his attempts to remove a ruptured oil cooler from the aircraft, a formidable task at any time on that type of aircraft that would sorely test the patience of even the most benign in a warm well equipped hanger, difficult enough to accomplish while on skis or wheels, but an unimaginable proposition on floats with the added difficulty of being forced to work around and between float struts and brace wires that constantly thwarted ones progress, that alone sufficient to try the patience of the hardiest, but being required to do so in them less than ideal conditions required a far more determined man then me.

Big Johns surprising appearance in the hotel coffee shop bare foot and clad only in a pair of wet shorts leaving a trail of foot prints as he made his way across the room couldn't have stood there any more then thirty seconds or so staring uncertainly around as if not being sure of his welcome in his scanty attire with our staring at him in credulous wonder before his being suddenly pounced on by an obviously incensed diminutive English lady who owned and ran the hotel with an iron hand, woe unto them who for whatever reason raised her ire.

We to a man respected her intensely, walking and talking softly while in her presence. She scarcely could have reached a height of five foot nothing or weighed more then ninety pounds, still no one we ever knew of who had inadvertently or otherwise trampled on her toes ever failed to regret having done so or if the infraction worthy of note ever again allowed to return to her domicile, no matter who they were or what their social standing.

We of course found this altercation to be extremely hilarious with her standing her ground directly barring John from moving further into the room the top of her head barely coming up to his arm pits with her hands on her hips glaring malovently into his eyes while tapping her foot in righteous anger, a classical case of David and goliath, but to a man we would have placed our money on David. If so inclined he could have effortlessly swept her away with his little finger, but only seeming to noticeably shrink under her piercing gaze curling up his toes in embarrassment while stammering out near incomprehensible apologies as she hissed at him to remove himself at once or she would not hesitate to bodily throwing him out and not to even consider coming back until suitably attired.

It remained exceedingly difficult to not break into hysterical laughter at the woebegone wet dog look that came over his face upon having the riot act read out to him in front of us, retreating as quickly as possible casting concerned glances over his shoulder as if half expecting her to jump on him.

Having done her righteous duty that tiny power house sailed grandly back into her kitchen giving us a smug look of satisfaction as she passed, wisely we all maintained a stone face with no one as much as cracking a smile or even breathing hard just sitting there like a bunch of Easter island statues. One could have heard a pin drop for the next while before daring to resume a desultory conversation in a very guarded manner, no one desired to give that formidable little lady any excuse to boot us out by our becoming over loud or to allow our suppressed mirth at big john's come up pence to become too obvious.

A short time later big john made another discreet appearance casting furtive glances around the room as if half expecting to be apprehended at any second, the ill fitting coveralls he had somehow managed to scrape up appeared to be a few sizes too small for him but no one foolish enough to comment on the fact. Once having assured himself all appeared to be well sat down with a heavy sigh of palpable relief to drink at least six cups of scalding hot coffee in rapid succession liberally laced from the bottle of booze he barely managed to keep out of sight in one of his pockets, our finding it highly amusing in watching him surreptitiously pour a slug into each cup while keeping a wary eye on the entrance to the kitchen in the event the mistress of the hotel should suddenly appear and accost him with predictable results.

Once having dosed himself with many cups of well-fortified coffee the color slowly began to return to his moon face. In truth we had wondered at his seeming lack of discomfort from having suffered an unexpected baptism in near freezing water, his teeth never chattering or any signs what so ever of shivering, Christ it gave me goose bumps to even think about it, that big dude sure was some tough.

Having sufficiently composed himself hopefully inquired about the possibility of outright purchasing the re-conditioned oil cooler that was always kept on hand at the base maintenance shack, his being informed the powers that be in Thunder Bay would have to be consulted as it being out of our jurisdiction to make that decision. This carried out with his promptly making a phone call, once the chief engineer having been apprised of big johns situation readily agreed to selling the cooler for cash exchange. Big john never as much blinked, just returning to his aircraft to retrieve his well-soaked wallet from which he counted out the exact amount from a hefty wad of soggy large denomination bills.

having successfully transacted the purchase of a replacement oil cooler got right back to the mind bending job of removing the damaged cooler and replacing the new using my tools as required. One had to give him credit for staying power as he fell to it with determined vengeance. My being all too aware of what lay ahead of him cautioned the crew to remain a goodly distance away. I'm certain the ambient temperature surrounding him must have shot up at least ten degrees such was the heat of his passionate cursing accompanied on the occasion by a heart felt scream of despair emanating from his place of frustrating labors. Fearing for our health wisely removed ourselves to greener pastures until he either succeeded or set the aircraft on fire, at that very moment an even bet which would occur first.

Taking advantage of the inclement weather caught up with some long overdue paper work as the short fall day sped by keeping tuned in to the muffled oaths and violent curses as Big John labored on. The cold miserably wet day fast coming to a close when an oil smeared Big John emerged triumphantly from his labors happily exhorting the fucken thing is finally done and ready to go, now to say the least that left me somewhat impressed, his perseverance and tenacity in successfully completing such a difficult job in such a relatively short space of time left me wondering how he had managed it.

Once completing replacing the tools and support equipment surprised us by removing the ill fitting coveralls to stand bare footed and clad only in a pair of still wet shorts not seeming to notice the well chilled air, further surprising us with his unexpectedly announcing his intentions to leave once having topped up his fuel and oil tanks.

At first it took a while for it to sink in he actually intended to leave at that late hour, non of us being able to comprehend why anyone in their right state of mind would even remotely consider venturing out into questionable weather conditions that even now presented a light snow fall that came near to blotting out the remaining day light that was now fast fading. Once having accomplished servicing the aircraft he left us to gaze in wonder and trepidation upon leaving the dock to taxi almost instantly move out of sight in the deepening gloom.

Christ on a crutch, even standing safe and secure on the dock a pang of fear coursed through me at the thought of what lay ahead of him with our silently watching his circling in the bay as he warmed up the engine prior to taking off the aircraft at times appearing ghostly in the falling snow and rapidly lowering visibility.

Upon hearing the audible clunk of the water rudders being raised we then knew for a certainty he meant to continue on, once having applied full power we immediately lost any sight we may have had of him as the spray of water blasted back from the propeller blotting out his presence, only being able to track his progress by listening raptly to the ever decreasing roar of the engine as he moved further away from us until fading away completely, only then realizing to have as did many others holding my breath.

One could only marvel at his seeming ability to coax that grossly overloaded aircraft off the water and somehow well beyond our understanding keep it in the air. With mixed feelings of relief and apprehension we called it a day not giving it much further thought assuming anyone who could carry on doing what he did on a regular basis faced little problem in getting to where he was going, bad weather or not.

Two days later we received an anxious inquiry from his post manager if we by chance knew big john's where abouts?, that call giving us the first inkling that maybe things had not gone as well as first presumed, our still not having moved since the day of his departure due to continuing inclement weather conditions accompanied by many heavy snow falls that completely blotted out the landscape. If he had been forced down either by mechanical problems or weather even he couldn't handle, it could be assumed him to be safe and holding for weather, if that not being the case then we could only as a matter of course expect the worst, his having gone into the trees, a bad situation at any time but far worse this time of the year with the advent of the heavy snow falls we had recently experienced blanketing the landscape offered little if any hope of quickly locating him if at all. One could only hope in the remote chance of his surviving to not being badly injured or trapped in the wreckage unable to help himself, the very thought of that occurring at all gave me a bad case of the willies.

Four days and three nights having passed since our last sight of him left us in grave doubt as to his probable survival, without his being quickly located the lateness of the season made it extremely unlikely his being found until the following spring. To a man we all dreaded late fall flying as the cards where stacked against one at such a time, but regardless of the fears that pervaded one's very being and haunted our senses none would refuse in searching for him whenever possible as one never could be certain when by chance or bad karma their turn could well come about.

As it stood we could do little in the way of setting up an initial search due to the continuing inclement fall weather. During the odd break we could sometimes carry out short trips and as luck would have it one of our pilots who had been forced to detour around a severe snow storm barring his way scraped across a prominent ridge at bare tree top level suddenly spotting a trail of what appeared to be freshly broken tree tops, well that was hardly an unusual phenomena in that part of the country due to the sometimes fierce wind storms that often tore through the area creating massive destruction, but that rarely if ever occurred in a straight line as did these, appearing to follow the very top contours of the ridge. The momentary glimpse offered hardly gave him time to accurately place his position but not daring to circle back for another look in order to confirm his unexpected discovery wisely continuing on to Pickle Lake to land barely ahead of another storm moving into the area. Upon landing and his revealing his startling discovery we more or less zeroed in on the area where he had crossed the ridge.

As fate would decree it the temperature unexpectedly rose to slightly above the freezing level creating formidable icing conditions and increased snow fall that blotted out all visibility for the next week creating a real nail biter, being all too aware once the warmer air mass moved out of the area true winter conditions would prevail, in essence shutting down all further flying activity for the season. Tempers flared as everyone's patience became increasingly frayed while being forced to accept the endless waiting. Understandably all wanted to call it quits, but no one dared to back out with the possibility of the weather improving at any time holding us in thrall, as remote a possibility as it seemed we could only wait and hope, badly strung out from enduring endless hours of nerve twanging tension for far too long, too much coffee and worst of all not knowing big john's ultimate fate.

Being as no one could be absolutely certain when a break in the weather could suddenly occur allowing us to make cursory search, as nerve straining as it was all we could do but wait and hope.

Often the remote possibility that Big John still hopefully survived discussed endlessly with our feverently hoping he did, but more certain each passing day that at best fast becoming more wishful thinking on our part then a reality. With that disturbing possibility haunting our thoughts throughout each passing day we where more than ready when a much needed break in the weather finally came about allowing us to make a quick perusal of the suspect area using a de-Havilland beaver as it had the capability of flying slowly and also offered good visibility for the eyes of the volunteer observers in our search for broken tree tops that would hopeful lead us to the suspected crash site.

Having spent a fair amount of time cruising up and down the ridge to no avail almost on the verge of giving it up as the weather had once more become threatening until one of the sharp eyed observers suddenly spotted a trail of broken tree tops, turning sharply we followed the ridge in a more or less northerly direction amazed and disconcerted to observe an increasing trail of broken off tree tops appearing at random intervals directly in our flight path completely disappearing at times but generally becoming more apparent as we flew further along, it soon became increasingly obvious to us that for what ever reason the aircraft if that what it was that had broken off the tree tops had slowly descended randomly breaking off tree tops as it flew along, for the life of us no one could begin to imagine why such a highly experienced and capable pilot as Big John would allow that to take place unless totally incapacitated and no longer in control.

That possible scenario flashed all too vividly through our minds when vividly recalling the vast amount of booze consumed all through his travails, the numbing effects of his unplanned baptism in the icy cold water plus the delayed effects of the alcohol consumed together with exhaustion conspiring with the heat in the cockpit could have well combined to cause his passing out, but still one did not want to be too judgmental as the all too real possibility of a carbon dioxide leak from the aircraft's exhaust heater could have also contributed to his problem, and when one considers the poor to none existent maintenance the aircraft received in general that happening could not be ruled out.

Following the trail of broken tree tops as best we could considering the poor visibility eventually spotting his aircraft lying in a more or less upright condition in a dense grove of trees with one of the wings completely torn off the fuselage, circling the wreck for some time failed to detect any signs of life, with little to be done the approximate position of the wrecked aircraft marked on the map as no suitable lakes lay close by for us to land on and to make our way to the wreck not to mention the state of the weather dictated our returning to base as quickly as possible if we where to return at all.

Well we had done our part, now it was up to the dictates of the powers that be, we could well conclude our part in the search with a clear conscience.

Having informed the base of our discovery we made our hairy return to pickle lake barely ahead of a weather front closing in on us that shortly after our timely arrival once more canceled out any further flying for the next while with our remaining heavy of heart at our gruesome discovery, but at the same time vastly relieved to have at least located him against all odds, Big John had been a good friend to all for some time and would be sorely missed.

Our having endured an excruciatingly long wait before learning of his certain fate, now knew with an absolute certainty he would not ever be seen alive again, yes we to a man saddened by the strange turn of events that had ultimately cost john his life, but at the same time vastly relieved it was over.

Search and rescue having been notified of John going missing prior to our having located the wreck the fun began, the absolutely brain dead line of reasoning that followed our report of having successfully located the wreck led to our being subjected to a query that appeared to cast doubts on our initial radio call verifying our success in locating the crash site, the tone of voice used in questioning us made one almost certain to their resenting our having done so.

The public in general remains unaware and the incompetent government officials we are plagued with are determined to keep it that way, it is bush pilots that are largely responsible for locating a good percentage of missing aircraft, but the federally controlled search and rescue teams who wield a much larger club and not at all loath to use it undeservedly get all the media credits along with the posturing and hoopla that seems to be part of it. By and large the motley collection of bush pilots who being considered rather insignificant and make for poor media interest in direct comparison to the search and rescue organization to the point of being almost none existence, their accomplishments on the most part rudely brushed aside as they simply do not generate good press.

Once Big John's remains where retrieved by helicopter and returned to Pickle

Lake for furtherance we where stunned to be flatly refused access to bid our fond farewells to a one time friend, even the local policeman disgusted at their unfeeling callousness toward us heard to murmur quietly, Christ on a crutch, what's the big deal, how many bodies have you guys flown in throughout the years without having to face this beauracratic B. S? In truth it really not being anything remarkable for us on the occasion to pick up and transport a dead body, simply all in a day's work.

We where collectively relieved to see the last of the search and rescue team as none of us could abide their arrogance. The fact that we had spent two terrible weeks risking life and limb in hope of finding Big John alive went totally ignored by the media though in the end it was us that physically led the search and rescue helicopter to the crash site as they continuously failed to locate it even though being given the coordinates on the map, this slap on the kisser only served to further harden our already legendary disdain to any and all government controlled agencies. It must require a certain type of self-serving individuals to be devoid of shame to knowingly bask in false glory, in doing so it indicates a sad lack of character on their part.

Only much later where we to learn through an undisclosed source the two Para medics who had initially jumped into the crash site where to have found Big John still strapped in his seat and dead at the controls, immediately crushed to death by the five forty gallon drums of fuel on board at impact still maintained a death grip on a bottle of booze.

As if on cue the weather began to clear but turning icy cold creating shell ice along the shorelines, high time to call it a season and ferry the aircraft to various bases for change over to skis. One never knew just what fate held in store for them or what lay in the future, but knew with absolute certainty the coming winter season offered many a challenge for us, and to a man we looked forward to it as we lived for what we did best.

White Loon Lake Incident

AT ONE POINT IN MY career took a position with Green Air of Red Lake Ontario. One of their aircraft being the venerable "Stinson Gull Wing", a truly beautiful classic air craft I had hungered to fly for some time jumping at the chance to be checked out by Bill Green himself a pilot of exceptional pilot skills I had long admired, the one hour long check ride proved the Stinson and I where made for each other, god dam how I loved that haughty high strung air craft, it's demanding the most in delicate handling and woe unto them that let their guard down even momentarily, for if one foolish enough to allow it to happen she would with out warning or hesitation bite one on the ass.

In truth it was a delightful aircraft for an experienced pilot to fly, the beautifully sculptured gull wings a true masterpiece of elegant styling that gave it sensitive handling characteristics along with a fairly high cruise speed. Aside from that one soon became abundantly aware of they're offering poor if almost non existent power off low speed glide capabilities that dictated stuffing the nose down at fairly steep angle upon reducing power and applying full down flaps, in the event of power loss or out right engine failure the optimum glide angle quickly being reached upon one finding themselves to be sliding forward off the seat while bracing one's self on the rudder pedals. I have always claimed and stand by that assertion to this day if one where quick about throwing a greased anvil out of the window at the exact moment of catastrophic engine failure one would easily pass it on the way down .

Well I lived to fly that beast and when one loves that haughty lady as much as I did there was no hands on the clock. To go back in time when as a young man with stars in my eyes had the dubious opportunity to observe another

Stinson SR-9 Gull wing landing on ski gear and taxiing in to the water front of Red Lake where I immediately deported myself to admire it's sleek out lines, while doing so it was noticed a tongue of flame had began to visibly flicker from out of the lower cowling, as the pilot and owner Larry Roluf had made a bee line to the Lakeview Bakery for coffee shortly after arriving there was no one but me to attempt to snuff out the flames with my feeble efforts of throwing snow into the lower cowling proving to be impotent at best soon finding my efforts to be no consequence, made a mad dash to the cafe to alert the pilot who took off pell mell toward the burning aircraft in an understandable panic, but by the time he or any one else was able to arrive with a fire extinguisher it sadly proved to be far too late to save the aircraft from complete destruction by fire. I never did learn the cause of the fire or of it's ultimate fate when being disassembled and trucked away to where?, it was never revealed.

Strangely enough the Stinson SR-9 Gull Wing CF-BGN of which I had such a shameless love affair with was to eventually suffer the same fate when also being destroyed by fire one night by sick minded vandals during winter lay up, god dam that all but crushed me to see her fire stripped air frame reduced to heart breaking skeletal work of art, to have to witness my naughty lady reduced to a charred hulk tore at my heart strings like no other had before or since.

If my latest information is correct, Western Canada Aircraft Museum in Winnipeg Manitoba has since taken her over for static rebuild and display. She may be gone from my life but still lives in my heart.

Within day's of my being checked out dispatched on a month long charter that would just about cover the entire North East section clean to the formidable shores of Hudson's Bay East, and as far North as Churchill Manitoba taking us over some of the most daunting and forbidding

territory one could wish to traverse. Actually trembling inwardly with excitement at the chance to re-visit much of the same area I had not so long ago spent almost an entire winter criss crossing from one end to the other, but this time my doing so without the ever present threat of being accosted by the minions of the law.(See "Shadow's On The Wind), now I was to be given the chance to view much of the same area again but this time during the summer season and a side benefit being a chance to renew my friendships with many of the trappers we had dealt with during the time spent purchasing their furs.

The filming crew that were to accompany me were suitably impressed with my Bush Pilot credentials and my extensive knowledge of the North in general.

The extensive logistics required had been painfully outlined and planned by the crew chief (a dyed in the wool city boy)down to the last minute, but he stood warned that his exacting itinerary would soon prove worse than useless, there being far too many vagaries known and unknown to be contended with during the course of the trip that would in all probability trash his carefully planned itinerary of photographing on a tight schedule the life styles of the local natives we would be visiting, my blandly informing him that while traveling throughout the North country they would soon learn that Indian time is anytime, being as they are not slaves to the hands on the clock as is the white man who has willingly sold his very soul to economic slavery in senseless and blind pursuit of the useless and often needless material gain.

Before departure they where advised they would soon be entering a world totally foreign to them and their concepts, a world that up till recently had not kept pace with the so called modern trend and that most of the local inhabitants they would meet had not advanced too far from the life style they and their ancestors had been born into, for them it would almost seem as if they had stepped back in time a hundred years or more so great would be the cultural difference. Once on our way we made stop over's at certain selected native settlements, the crew quickly becoming impressed with my easy familiarity with the native population that met us each time we arrived at a settlement, their treating me like a long time gone relative with my speaking to them in their native tongue of which through the years of working with and along side of had become quite fluent at with they're in turn treating the crew with admiration and respect taking great interest in their camera equipment and strange mannerisms.

By this time the crew chief had finally recognized the folly of attempting to adhere to the dictates of the methodically constructed itinerary he had spent so many long painful hours creating, finally tearing it up in frustration and bowing to the inevitable, his pre-conceived plans as to how he had initially visualized it taking place and no doubt would have liked it to go vaporizing like the early morning mists, but to his ever lasting credit gradually adjusting to Indian time and customs albeit some reluctantly until the crew finding to their delight to be enjoying their new found sense of absolute freedom once shedding the mantle of present day conventions and allowing the irresistible lure of the north to totally inundate them.

As for me I fitted right in not being known throughout the North as the "White Indian" for nothing!

Over a period of time we traversed many a mile of featureless terrain that to the unpracticed eye seemed to be bare of any sort of life form, human habitation being noticeably sparse outside of the remote scattered settlements we visited with the crew soon becoming appreciative of the vastness and solitude as much as I did with my little by little enlightening them of the awesome wonders of the north as they could have never began to imagine it, beginning to see it through my eyes in experiencing people and places they had never before known or realized up till then existed and thrived in the remotest of areas, it proving to be quite the revelation for them!

Once they had gotten past their initial shyness and reluctance to converse one on one with the native people it didn't take too long before they're being inducted into their life style and customs and to have the ancient legends that had passed on down through hundreds of years over a smoky camp fire related to them to the accompaniment of many skin drums that pounded out their mesmerizing rhythm that soon entranced them. It never ceased to amaze me how the elderly natives when given the opportunity or occasion to do so proudly paraded their traditional finery to be demonstrated along with ancient ceremony and dances, some of which even I had never seen performed before, it seeming each settlement we visited attempting to out do the previous one keeping the camera crew tripping over each other in taking shots from every conceivable angle.

During a lay over at one settlement due to inclement weather the crew chief during the course of a lengthy conversation admitted to initially harboring second thoughts of my being the pilot they would trust their well being uncertain as to what they where letting themselves in for judging by my casual appearance that hardly fitted in with their pre-conceived notions of how a bush pilot should appear as for certain I hardly resembled or portrayed in any respect the outlandish role of a Hollywood version they no doubt entertained.

Only through the assurance from bill green of my being a totally competent pilot that knew the way's of the North country to a degree few white pilots had ever attained did they grudgingly acquiesce to my services, but by the time they had informed me of their earlier reluctance we had become close friends, their putting absolute trust and faith in my skills and having come to adore the Stinson referring to it as there "Bird". Eventually after many detours while making our way to the large settlement of Big Trout Lake a sizeable settlement that boasted many modern conveniences and amenities such as a weather station, nursing station, modern school and of course the ubiquitous Hudson's Bay Co. where I still dared not to show my face or they would have with a certainty had me shot on sight and or refuse to sell us much needed supplies and fuel, my cautioning the crew chief piquing his curiosity as to why no end when advised to remain as discreet about my being their pilot as possible while in the presence of the Bay manager during their shopping forays as the memories of my last winters unwelcome intrusion into his world and getting away with it must have still rankled. Something as outlandishly brazen as what we had successfully pulled off while avoiding the long arm of the law must have marred their image of being impregnable to a marked degree that would take some time to live down, so it considered politic on my part to keep as low a profile as possible during our time in the settlement even though realizing some of the locals faithful to the Hudson Bay would make my unwelcome presence known soon enough!

That night with my having regaled them in partial detail concerning my escapade involving the Hudson's Bay Co., they urged me on to relate the story of the great adventure from start to finish leaving nothing out.

They're of course having already heard the Bay's side of our so called unlawful depredations, but most certainly not of their shameless and questionable practices of literally enslaving the native populations to their will enjoyed the telling no end, but they as big city dwellers with a totally foreign concept of life could not begin to comprehend much less conceive of any one choosing to live in such a demandingly harsh environment at any time much less conceive of two white pilots surviving against great odds in such a remote area while daring to fly over it's width and breadth on a regular basis in the dead of winter. At the conclusion of the story their respect for my abilities as a bush pilot went up a notch or two but it remaining readily apparent to me they're not being totally convinced or certain of the validity of my story as such effrontery actually having taken place in such a remote and harsh environment far beyond their capability to absorb much less understand.

My being pretty much well known by the local native population wherever we went throughout the North with it posing very little problem for us to locate suitable digs in any of the settlements we visited. The crew chief had initially been stunned upon learning the high cost of staples purchased from the Bay, but the staggering cost of aircraft fuel really rocked him back on his heels, but as nothing could be done to alleviate it soon adopted a what the hell attitude, it was well he did for we had no other source of obtaining precious fuel.

While wandering through the settlement visiting old acquaintances decided to check out the name of the pilot who flew for some small outfit based out of there to be some surprised at finding it to be a long time acquaintance I had not seen or heard of for many years by the name of "Bob Sheppard", a one time notorious member of the Ontario provincial police.(see medicine man). As it had initially gone his for obscure reasons only known to him at the time had suddenly resigned from the ranks of the O. P. P. and abandoning his family to take up the life style of a trapper and to eventually become a bush pilot, a goal he had coveted for many years. As our relationship went quite a few years back to my early times as a budding bush pilot flying an old fashioned tiger moth bi-plane. One can only place his one time confrontational attitude to-ward me at the time as envy and jealousness, giving me a bad time of it at every possible opportunity to do so concerning my flying activities often threatening to charge me with flying illegal charters with only the timely intervention of the owner of Chukuni Airways who I worked along side of saving me from eventually having to shift my operation to a less hostile environment.

As it stood with my being well aware of his unsavory past and still continuing to have very little use for him even after my unexpectedly being part of saving his life from exposure. As it stood with our sudden and unexpected meeting again he appeared so pleased to see me being more than willing to assist us in any way he could with my relenting on old animosities to thaw out toward him enough to let down my guard, more than happy to let bygones be just that. Actually my change of heart to-ward him allowed us a very pleasant visit for the duration of our stay with his generously selling us some of his precious fuel thus saving us from facing the depredation's of the Bay. How he envied my flying the Stinson gull wing crawling over it from one end to the other studying every detail and taking great pleasure in sitting in the pilot's seat with naked longing mirrored in his eyes, he would have gladly and without hesitation sold his soul to the devil to be able to fly it !.

Once our tour had been completed we bid him adieu moving on to the picturesque settlement of "Fawn River". There we had a great time catching and releasing chunky speckled trout at just about every cast ,

my but they sure where delicious eating , such times are to be treasured. The crew simply couldn't believe the bounty of fish fur and game available to the native people in that seemingly desolate part of the country, but as they became more accustomed to the life style of the inhabitants of that vast and fascinating land their respect for them grew proportional to their ever growing knowledge of their customs for at first the seemingly empty vastness had at first intimidated them but it wasn't too much longer before their casting off the so called mantle of a modern society, virtually going native while enjoying their once in a life time chance to be completely free of the dictates of city living, slowly finding their able to interact with the way's and customs of the native people.

The original itinerary being long abandoned they soon adapted to the sway and rhythm of the land living every day as it came without further adherence to the rigorous schedules that they first thought must be strictly adhered to, instead allowing events to unfold whenever and however they would.

By now their having gained absolute trust in my piloting abilities and knowledge of the land we flew over left it up to me to take them to places deemed worthy of a visit with my making certain they got to experience a cross section of northern life styles they could have never begun to imagine, our crossing many a mile of seemingly barren of life areas that they had by now to a greater degree learned to understand and appreciate when combined with their new found knowledge of the lore and beauty of the north .

Having eventually made our way in a circuitous manner to the forbidding shores of Hudson's Bay with my taking the time and effort to point out places of interest and whenever able to do so the huge grounded barges to be found randomly cast up high and dry onto the rugged forbidding coast line, the tug crews that regularly plied the treacherous waters of the bay through the years on the occasion forced by dire necessity to deliberately slip the tow cable leaving the barge at the mercy of nature when caught up in a violent storm that on the occasion found them in the middle of the bay fighting for their lives while battling higher than normal wind and wave action that ultimately threatened to drag both tug and barge to destruction on to the shallow boulder strewn shores by the above were they would remain for all time, the heavily loaded barges eventually becoming so securely grounded they would prove impossible to salvage much less re float them

On one occasion when being invited to partake of a ceremonial feast with chief of the band and his large family that by chance boasted of many comely doe eyed daughters that where exceptionally attractive doing much to pique the interest of some of the younger members of the crew.(Me Too!). Noticing they seemed some what apprehensive at first about accepting the invite not being at all certain of what to expect cautioned them to out right refuse the chief's offer of hospitality would be considered an unpardonable slight and poor politics at any time.

Naturally they remained somewhat apprehensive, endlessly mulling it over between them but my admonition not to refuse along with common decency and curiosity eventually won them over. The normal state of affairs when dining with native people once the traditional (long winded) ceremony has been transacted the meal served it being more or less communal in nature with each person taking up a tin bowl or plate to then proceed to help themselves from a large pot of stew simmering away on the wood stove or open fire, then breaking off a large chunk of bannock (flat bread) usually made in a frying pan then taking up any convenient corner of the room to sit with your back against the wall to eat your meal. A few of the more timid members of the crew approached the proffered stew with cautious trepidation curiously querying me of it's contents obviously remaining suspicious of it's nature though it certainly smelled aromatic as it wafted off an appetizing odor.

Inquiring of it's contents, with my blandly stating it consisted largely of meat (Though failing to mention the source) and dried roots of certain plants and to get them off the track advised them to add salt to taste as native people didn't normally require it's use, this ploy seemed to assuage their fears some what though continuing to remaining somewhat hesitant to begin eating until I had helped myself to a generous portion being careful not to stir up the small skulls and whatever long experience had taught me certain be lying on the bottom of the pot. The native people and I covertly observed their actions in concealed amusement as they ladled a portion of the stew into their bowls with great care, almost as if half expecting something to suddenly jump out of the pot and bite them on the ass. For some odd reason that defied the odds the first three that helped themselves to the stew some how by the greatest of chance failed to stir up a tiny skull or two most likely due to the fact they had carefully ladled their stew from the middle to top portion without inadvertently stirring up the contents, the fourth member being some what emboldened by the first three not coming up with out any unpleasant surprises pitched in with gusto lifting up a ladle full of well stirred stew suddenly gave off a high pitched shriek like a fair maiden being de-flowered sending ladle and stew flying only catching himself upon realizing what he had done to look sheepishly around the room to be greeted by the sight of many grinning faces, but one had to give him credit for not being a quitter with his bravely retrieving the bowl and ladle to once more dip into the pot again with a visible shudder, but this time remaining circumspect about how he went about it being extremely careful to not dip too deeply this time to with trembling hands bravely set about sopping up the stew with a large chunk of bannock obviously feeling a bit foolish about having demonstrated his queasiness when first spotting the tiny skulls that grinned mockingly back at him.

My having long gotten accustomed to native fare throughout the years, skull stew made up of squirrel, rabbit and beaver and god only knows what else hardly gave it a thought when making it a point to deliberately fish half a dozen or so out of the pot to suck noisily on them in plain view for all to see, two of the more delicate stomached of the crew immediately bolting for the door almost trampling each other in their haste to clear the dwelling before losing their lunch while the other two bravely remained where they where with sickly grins plastered all over their faces that deepened noticeably when informing them matter of factly it was considered de rigueur to demonstrate one's appreciation of the fare set out before them, to suck noisily on the skulls with obvious relish as in doing so indicate done's enjoyment of the food, but to a man they politely declined to do so. Desert consisted of stewed dried apples and prunes without the benefit of sugar topped off with native style tea out of a well blackened kettle that had obviously been on the go for many a year being as black inside as it was on the out side from the constant presence of tannic acid from the tea leaves which are never completely cleaned out only removing a portion of the well steeped leaves and what ever else may have accumulated within over a period of time in order to make room for another handful of fresh tea leaves and an infusion of fresh water where upon it is placed at the very back of the stove to steep twenty four hours a day every day.

Naturally this time tried process produces a mighty potent brew that instantly coats one's teeth at the first cautious sip while coming near to paralyzing one's tongue and vocal cords, the crew to a man gamely choked and coughed as they slowly strangled after taking their first sip of that potent brew gasping for breath with tears forming in their eyes, one of them upon regaining the use of his tongue and vocal cords equated it to drinking battery acid, again my being long inured to native ways suffered no surprises or ill effects but still one had to give them credit for staying power only being able to finish their tea by lacing it with powdered milk and sugar to bravely drink it up though not one going back for seconds. The meal in all respects turned out to be a success, the native people in general enjoying the impromptu show to a high degree displaying much laughter and joking at the crew's expense, but all being said and done they had passed their initiation rites with flying colors and justifiably proud to have done so thus making it much easier for them to accept the way's of the north and it's inhabitants at face value beginning to relax and to accept the totally new life style they had so recently embraced much to their surprise to find it suited them well if only for a short time.

Their by now having become accustomed to the native's method of sleeping on pine boughs laid in any convenient corner of the one room cabin they took it in their stride to place their air mattresses in any unoccupied spot that suited them. The lack of hygienic facilities at first had thrown their sense of modesty for a loop finding placing of one's backside over a pole conveniently placed between two close set tree to answer a call of nature (sans privacy) didn't much appeal to their sense of decorum, but nature must have it's way and when the first of them forced to give in to dire need to move their bowels reluctantly gave it a go with my laughingly cautioning him to remember to lean forward at all times as not to lose his balance and end up toppling backwards as that could well prove to be an undesirable and unsettling experience and above all to keep his heels well spaced or suffer the consequences. Be as it may this time tried method which has prevailed for many a century is beneficial to the land as there is never a pile up of excrement to create a noxious odor or attract flies as the roving half starved packs of dogs to be found in every settlement quite efficiently see to the clean up duties.

Once having accustomed themselves to the native way of life very little of what took place no longer appeared to faze them to the degree it once had, taking each new experience as it presented itself in good spirits, filming every aspect of the native's life styles and customs reveling in each new adventure soon beginning to treasure the absolute freedom of mind and body that they discovered to be so overwhelmingly different from all previously known convention, to within a relatively short space of time casting off as much as they could the surly bonds of a strict demanding society they had as a matter of course endured for so long becoming as ratty and unkempt in appearance as me to the point they hardly recognized themselves. The camera crew's burgeoning respect for the native people's life styles, tradition's etc, set the tone for the remainder of the tour.

Some where along the way they had picked up on the mysterious workings of the "moccasin telegraph", openly scoffing at the possibility of such a far fetched state of communication existing much less function, but experiencing it's workings first hand would in time make true believers of them.

As we in turn bid each settlement goodbye their was always a lot of long faces among the native people who had adopted them and now visibly distressed to have them leave never to return, the crew had in the short space of time allotted them with each family gathering had within a brief period become immensely popular with their reciprocating in turn.

Shortly before leaving they where fore warned the moccasin telegraph would be in full swing just as soon as we lifted off the water informing all within their boundaries where we where headed for next and the people at the other end would be waiting expectantly for our arrival, well that certainly earned me a few snorts of derision, a few hearty chuckles and knowing grins, but having been long familiar with that unexplained phenomena ignored their humorous jibes knowing all too well the last laugh would be mine having seen it in action many times before.

On our arrival at our next fair sized settlement known as "Webequi" the docks and adjacent shore line where already lined with native people along with a few curious white faces mixed in awaiting our impending arrival, they're knowing almost to the minute when we would arrive. Radio communication being more or less in it's infancy not widely in use as yet except for government financed institutions such as the nursing station and of course the venerable Hudson Bay Co, but none of the smaller settlements up to that time having experienced as much as a tantalizing sniff of that modern day wonder so their was no way outside of the workings of the moccasin telegraph to communicate between settlements. On first viewing the large crowd of native people awaiting our arrival it left the crew perplexed bewildered and uncertain of what to make of it all as no one outside of ourselves knew our plans of flying to webiqui next except for the natives of the last settlement we had just left and they certainly did not have the use or convenience of a radio. As there was very little I could tell them of it's workings even though having been aware of it's existence ever since beginning my career as a bush pilot, always remaining a total mystery to me. Initially they had remained doubtful of it's authenticity but in good time they began to accept it as a given fact to fully embrace it's unexplained mystery with out question as I did.

Once again we went through the now familiar hoopla that went with filming the settlement and it's colorful inhabitants in full traditional costume. The settlement being fairly large boasted a nursing station that visibly appeared to be more modern and up to date then some of the ones I had on the occasion visited in our so called white man's modern day society. The nurses glad to see new faces welcomed us to stay with them in their residence, certainly a welcome change for us our being able to enjoy the luxury of a hot shower good food and a soft bed to sleep on, as it ultimately turned out the beds being far too soft in fact, our having become accustomed to sleeping on a thin air mattress spread out on a wood floor of some native's cabin found the bed's impossible to sleep on with our finally giving in to the inevitable and rolling out our sleeping bags onto the floor to sleep soundly.

We where treated royally by the resident nurses who being bored to near tears by their every day hum drum existence on a native reserve wholly welcomed our presence glad for the change of pace and new people to discuss current world affairs and of course our purpose for being there. The change of diet went especially well with us as Indian fare no matter how well presented still becomes old hat very quickly.

It has been many years now since having the chance or occasion to visit the far flung settlements again, but sad to say it has become my understanding that the open and generous hospitality once proffered to all itinerant travelers has now been severely curtailed or outright restricted to government drones and their hacks, anyone else including pilots are now left up to their own resources (usually in the cramped uncomfortable space of their aircraft) even when on government business. What branch of brain dead government introduced that poorly thought out policy never revealed to the public, also it became increasingly apparent the rotating replacement staff becoming clinical and aloof to-ward non natives. What had once been a close working relationship between pilots and nurses has since been regulated out of existence by self-serving control crazy civil servants or as they are now referred to as(Snivel Serpents).

The remainder of our tour more or less a repeat of the same hokum until we found ourselves heading up the coast to Fort Severn making it a point to while traversing that forbidding coast line making a slight jog over to Cape Henrietta Maria to see if we could locate the huge barge that recently had to be abandoned to it's fate in a violent storm by the tug which was forced to slip it's tow line before it's ultimately being dragged into shallow waters that would have instantly destroyed it's twin propellers and inevitably dooming the crew to a terrible fate. The barge having been abandoned long after I had left that part of the country, therefore it's actual position on that most forbidding of coast lines unknown to me at the time until one of the sharp eyed men spotted a mustard colored smudge further up on the boulder strewn shore line then one could believe possible given that the average depth of the water along the coast line is extremely shallow and boulder studded, it must have been one hell of a storm along with a monstrously high tide to have been able to drive such a huge heavily loaded steel barge so far up on shore. The sight of the grounded barge coldly reminded one the Cape not a good spot to experience engine failure at any time even during the summer months for even if by some remote chance one did survive a forced landing, it remained doubtful one would continue to do so for unless rescued within a reasonably short space of time for once the clouds of voracious black flies and mosquitoes found you it would soon be game over in an altogether unpleasant fashion the very thought causing my grip on the control wheel to involuntarily become a little tighter considering it best to not exacerbate my already uneasy passenger's state of minds any further as they stared in mesmerized awe at the mighty grey beard rollers that rolled in unchecked to crash with awesome intensity over the volks wagon sized boulders creating great curtains of ragged wind blown foam, a sight guaranteed to make the most staunch quail in fear, they had plenty to think about as it was.

To say we where some happy to have arrived safely at Fort Severn would be a gross understatement, my knowing from past experience the viscous tides combined with the mighty volume of turbulent water that rushed down the Severn River can and often does create monstrous tides up to sixteen feet or better depending on the wind wisely heeling the aircraft up onto the muddy banks as far as possible securing it with ropes to convenient boulders .

On inquiring pleasantly surprised to find the resident school teacher and his wife still remained and taught in the community their gladly welcoming all of us into their home even though it strained their facilities to bursting.

The camera crew wasted little time in setting up to do their thing leaving me free to wander through the settlement to re-new old acquaintances, some who where some surprised to have me re-appear so soon, but it soon becoming

378

painfully obvious the dour Hudson's Bay manager who had been apprised of my unwelcome presence within minutes by a company faithful made it apparent of not in the least appreciating my presence within his store ordering me out within minutes of my brazenly daring to enter his domain, nor would he consent to sell much needed supplies to the crew chief once discovering they had flown in with me. That small minded act on his part genuinely pissed us off though in itself presenting little problem as the school teacher had volunteered to help out in purchasing our supplies if we ran into difficulty with the manager who they were well aware from past experience continued to retain a lasting grudge against me for making him look bad when we had set up shop in the area to buy fur from the local trappers, but still we faced a dilemma it being a dead certainty he was not about to sell us any fuel from his stock at any price. Until we could somehow weasel our way past that we weren't about to be going any where soon unless carrying full tanks as alternate refueling points non existent except for our next stop in Churchill with the terrain in between considered to be far too formidable to even consider risking it with what fuel remained in our tanks, and I for one not about to take any unnecessary or foolish chances in that forbidding part of the country having had my fill of previously doing so.

Fortunately the teacher alleviated our growing concern by informing us the twice-weekly DC-3 shed. was due within the next few days, a radio call to pickle lake via big trout lake assured a delivery of three drums of fuel and a five gallon pail of oil.

As promised the fuel and oil arrived on schedule relieving us of a lot of anxiety but the head man of the crew being less than impressed when presented with the horrendous freight charges.(welcome to the great but prohibitively expensive north), but for what it was worth little to be done but accept what was. Rolling the drums from the airport to the river bank and laboriously transferring the gas bucket by bucket into the tanks a real mind bender of a job taking us three back breaking hours to accomplish finally fuelling the aircraft to capacity. The camera crew having completed their itinerary to their satisfaction left us in good shape and ready to move on to our next destination weather providing.

Our being up and ready to leave as soon as the tide rose to it's full height making it a simple matter to power the aircraft off the muddy bank once having completed our thanks and good bye's free to continue on our way to Churchill Manitoba, pretty much a case of following the extremely formidable coast line to that furthest of northern sea ports in Canada.

Cruising along fat dumb and happy parrelling the coast line the crew chief who rightfully remained in an unsettled state of mind upon first viewing the formidable coast line continuing to cast anxious glances out of the windows to observe with growing trepidation the awesomely fantastic sight of the huge grey beard rollers that would have easily crested out at twenty feet or better, their immensity and force had for better or worse caught his attention as they crashed on and over boulders the size of a small house that randomly studded the bleak shore line shooting up immense columns of water the shrieking wind instantly tore into sheets of wind borne vapor, no doubt it presented a beautiful but oh so deadly awe inspiring sight that left no question as to one's ultimate fate should they be forced down amongst them.

At one point while fidgeting nervously turning to me to inquire if there was any way possible of our making a safe landing in the event of engine failure, at that I had to rain on his parade by succinctly informing him we would not stand the chance of a snowball in hell if that where to unfortunately occur and he would only have enough time to stick his head between his legs and kiss his ass good bye before it was all over, upon hearing this less than assuring news turned a few shades paler while continuing to stare fixedly out of the windshield for the remainder of the trip most likely praying feverently for the trip to end. I may have sounded trite and unconcerned to him but I too shared a sense of unease. As for the other crew members they slept the sleep of innocents, not in the least concerned by the what if scenario that so devilishly tormented their fearful leader, continuing to sleep soundly through it all until our gratefully spotting the grain elevators looming on the sky line. Once having arrived circled button bay to give them a good look at the well rusted out stranded tramp steamer that a huge storm had driven up on the shore many years ago (So it was said) before touching down onto the welcome crystal clear waters of landing lake securely tying up the aircraft and hitch hiking into town.

If there is any one place I enjoy it has to be the town of Churchill, it's frontier spirit has always appealed to me as did the raw free spaciousness surrounding it. As I made the most of drifting around the town renewing old acquaintances and while doing so making new ones, the camera crew spent three very long days filming the town, grain elevators, the huge Northern Transportation tugs and huge steel barges that were used to supply all the coastal settlements during the summer months and lastly the long abandoned U. S. A. F. bomber command base that functioned during the nineteen fifties. One must give the Corp. Of Engineer's credit for their enduring ability to carve out such a huge air base in such a terrible climate within the time period they had, the job could have not been less than formidable demanding of man and machine not to mention extremely costly logistics wise as all the man power had to be flown in or most likely having arrived in Churchill on the rickety rail road fondly referred to by all as the "Muskeg Express" as did a lot of their materials but it is my understanding most of the hundreds of thousands of tons of building materials had arrived via sea going freighters that could only make it through the ice choked narrows leading into Hudson's Bay to make use of the deep water port for only a few months of the year, one can only begin to imagine what a logistical night mare that must have created.

Once the camera crew having completed their lengthy filming sequence they where worn down to a shadow of their former gung ho selves, rapidly tiring of our gypsy like existence and more than prepared to return to the welcoming comforts of modern civilization, god dam how I hated to leave, thoroughly enjoying my time out from under the crushing responsibilities of being pilot in command, a burden that often times weighed heavily on me. Having re-fuelled the aircraft from the local shell dealers truck and checked everything out we where on our way to big sandy lake with interim stops at various settlements in between for rest and fuel plus or whatever places of interest they chose to visit.

By this time we had accomplished all that, the end of the extensive and demanding tour had come close to it's end and just as well as we where all visibly beginning to show signs of wear having flown over many formidable stretches of forbidding terrain that by it's very nature totally intolerant of the slightest error, especially when running into inclement weather that in some cases stretched our fuel reserves and my nerves to the utmost limit placing a heavy demand on me and the machine not to mention one could so easily disappear somewhere over that trackless waste never to be found as that huge expanse of sere muskeg and numerous shallow lakes does not give up it's secrets easily, having accomplished what we had so far without incident being truly a rarity by escaping on the most part the usual and expected severe weather patterns normally associated with that part of the country.

One can only ponder at how strangely fate works when considering our having crossed many miles of forbidding landscape without a hitch, the last one hundred and forty four miles we had yet to cover upon leaving sandy lake giving us the worst fright of the entire trip with our unexpectedly coming within a hair of being wiped out by a freak storm.

On our eventual arrival at Big Sandy Lake the crew was amazed at the sheer size and complexity of the settlement with all it's modern day conveniences, but being road weary we only stayed a few days before leaving on our final leg of the trip to Red Lake late on a bright sunny afternoon, but as it often does in that area we soon ran into an extensive band of marginal weather stretching across our path consisting of heavy rain showers and imbedded thunder bumpers along with gusty winds that made flying the aircraft tiresomely difficult while producing a very rough ride for all being constantly pummeled by severe gusts that could have easily torn us out of our seats if not for the fact of being tightly restrained by the safety harness. For some strange reason that couldn't be fathomed at the time began to feel unreasonably threatened by what I didn't yet know causing my squirming restlessly in my seat. Normally high winds and heavy rain showers bothered me very little only being accepted as part of the game, but this time my instincts screamed at me to give it up and land safely while still able to do so safely.

Having learned the hard way through the years by trial and error had made it a concrete point (Well mostly) to never ignore my better instincts especially when feeling unreasonably threatened such as was the case at the moment by noticeably electrical charged air that gave off the faint but unmistakable odor of ozone potentially promising unpleasant surprises that could well prove to be life threatening, what ever it was it left me in an uneasy state of mind prompting me to without further ado give in to better judgment immediately landing on a beautiful lake I had long been familiar with, it's offering the security of a long point of heavily treed land with an easily accessible beach that boasted fairly deep water almost up to it's edge.(It also provided excellent fishing)Almost immediately after my securely nosing the fronts of the floats as high as they would go up onto the beach using a good blast of power to do so, our more or less just getting settled in to wait out a band of bad weather I had noticed rapidly bearing down on us as we landed, no sooner having driven the fronts of the floats up onto the beach when a violent wind storm that seemed to suddenly appear as if out of nowhere overtook us blustering wildly about blowing heavy sheets of rain that immediately oliberated all visibility outside of the aircraft, wailing like a banshee as it raged around us for what seemed to be some time doing it's finest in keeping all on edge as the aircraft on the occasion rocking and shuddering violently from the effects of a series of turbulent gusts pummeling us before the fast moving storm front gradually began to clear off to once more reveal impeccably blue sky, but still the eerie silence that continued to hang over the area like a heavy veil inexplicably bothered me even though all appeared to be normal with the wind having died down to a mere whisper leaving the waters of the lake to almost appear like a huge mirror reflecting the few clouds that moved by overhead in a stately fashion, but strangely enough not a loon or duck or any other sign of aquatic life that usually populated the lake in great numbers to come out of hiding once the storm passed could be seen anywhere further unsettling my already badly disturbed peace of mind. The unusually calm conditions and lack of water birds should have been sufficient warning that all not to be well, but with the crew becoming increasingly antsy by the minute and my also having contracted a bad case of get home It's foolishly ignored all the warning signals against my better judgment shoved the aircraft off the safety of the sheltered beach to taxi out around the end of the point and while involved doing so taking instant notice the heavily charged air still retained a disturbing trace of electrically charged atmosphere that we had initially experienced shortly before landing, but if at all possible more so. Nervously scanning the far western shore line gave me the jolt of my life upon observing an ominous gray green roll cloud charging toward us directly over the tree tops at the far end of the lake that was at the most only a scant mile or less away bearing down with express train speed, Initially shocked at the immensity and violence of the spectacle before us hesitated momentarily before fully realizing what it was and the imminent life threatening danger it portended as by this time the roll cloud had descended over the water whipping what could be seen of the trees on the edge of the lake into a frenzy with tortured water furiously twisting and dancing before it. Finally waking up to the fact we faced imminent and certain destruction without quickly finding some form of shelter as the hurricane force winds found in what was certain to be a line squall could easily top over a hundred miles an hour or better, never in my entire career had I ever reverted to using full power to viciously horse an aircraft on floats around in a tight half circle barely getting it behind the shelter of the point and ramming the floats up on the beach before all hell broke loose as the full fury of the squall descended on us totally wiping out all forward visibility in seconds, our tiny world quickly compressing into a nerve shattering crescendo of shrieking wind amplified by the tattoo of heavy rain and branches being violently flung back through the arc of the wildly spinning propeller to ricochet off the windshield while the incessant nerve wracking wail of the hurricane force wind all but drowned out the roar of the engine while I desperately maintained forward pressure the control wheel in an attempt to keep the floats of the wildly bucking aircraft pinned onto the beach knowing all too well the consequences of allowing the wind to get a hold of us, if that where to occur we would ultimately end up cart wheeling backwards to destruction. My arms had begun to feel leaden and numb from the constant pressure required to keep the control wheel pinned full forward it seeming to have taken on a life of it's own as the wind beat unmercifully on the control surfaces. After what seemed to be an eternity to us badly frightened mortals though most likely of a short duration the worst of it gradually passing over with the eerie shriek of the wind slowly winding down to a mournful wail finally subsiding to a low moan before daring to shut down the engine .

Surprisingly enough a cursory inspection of the aircraft revealed very little damage outside of the many branches sticking out of the fabric surfaces giving it the impression of growing hair. Removing what could be reached and cleaning out a good pile of well chewed branches mixed in with some still smoldering well scorched ones that had gotten jammed up against the hot cylinders from out of the front of the engine cowlings. Once having accomplished that to my satisfaction we began the onerous job of digging out the floats from the grip of the sand that had piled up around them due to the rocking motion induced by the wind and engine power having combined to firmly entrench them. Re-floating that god dam aircraft pure torture as the hot sun and high humidity brought out hordes of black flies that soon had all of cursing violently while impotently attempting to brush them off to no avail only ending up itching and bleeding copiously from the myriad of black fly bites, as one of the crew bitterly commented, the little bastards don't as much bite as chew of a good sized chunk of flesh and fly up onto a tree to eat it, truly a sage observation!. But one must give them little monster's credit for giving us the much needed impetus in freeing the floats from the sand, our eventually succeeding after applying super human effort that left us ending up in a near state of exhaustion and bleeding so badly the blood drying on our shirts felt like we where wearing cardboard. It was hard for one to believe them murderous tormenting little bastards could have possibly survived such a terrible wind force as the point of land we had so fortuitously sheltered behind having been almost completely denuded along it's entire width and length, but the fact they had all too plain by the sight of our bleeding bodies.

The crew chief deciding we had all the excitement we needed for one day informed us we would be cutting out the next two scheduled stops and instead flying directly to Red Lake in order to return to a semblance of modern life style, so there and then we bid White Loon Lake where we had come as close to meeting our end as we had the entire trip.

Eventually arriving safely and gratefully in Red Lake, glad to be back but during the process of taxiing into the dock already beginning to miss the gypsy like existence that had taken us over a great expanse of the North. After the crew chief had settled up with the airways and many hand shakes later we parted company as they began their long journey back to from where they had first come, but I did wonder would they still be the same people who had originally left a familiar life style to receive a lasting taste of a far different one that offered far less in one way but so much in another, no doubt they faced a difficult transition.

It may be the reader is not familiar with the term "line squall", my often having observed their capacity for total destruction of all they pass over had wisely kept my distance from them, how and why they are formed I must plead ignorance but some type of metrological disturbance must be required to create them, the one we encountered at White Loon Lake that came so near to causing our destruction gave me much to think about Once experiencing it's unbelievable power and fury and lived through it now had a new found respect for it's immense capacity to wreak destruction on any one or anything that got in it's way, one could say that was an experience I would not care to repeat. As it happened some years previous to our incident a long time friend of mine also a renegade pilot by the name of Ivan Cattleman had mysteriously disappeared on a lake very close to where we almost bought it with only a wing tip float and a seat cushion from his "Sea Bee" aircraft ever found. To this very day it remains my educated guess he had been caught flat footed in the open with no way to retreat from it's fury by a line squall that tore his aircraft to pieces, it would seem we where the lucky ones, poor Ivan it seems his luck just plain ran out that fateful day, well for what it's worth that's the risks of the flying world one takes their chances and hopes for the best.

Big Al-Politician Pilot

IT HAS BEEN OFT SAID, AND from my extensive experience living and working in the most remote corners of the North finding it to be an incontrovertible fact that for a variety of reasons attracts the most unlikely and diverse individuals one could care to meet with many of them in spite of being city born and bred and once having arrived and immersed themselves into the life style finding it very much to their liking remaining in the area for an extended period of time and in some cases never leaving eventually blending in with the local populace as part of the scenery, but they are the exception most choosing to leave after a short period of time unable or unwilling to come to grips with the remoteness and silent vastness of the North.

Bush flying outfits in particular abounded with wayward restless individuals who for the most part only choosing to stay for a season or two before moving on, often leaving the company desperately short of experienced pilots, it remained difficult at any time to attract suitable replacements being that most of them who chose to move on having done their stint in the bush and desired to take up residence in a more populous areas that offered a greater chance of upgrading their chances of moving ahead than could be found in a remote settlement often forcing the company to out of pure necessity to accept the less then suitable types, those that on the average lacked what it took or the experience required to find suitable work in the more populated areas.

As it turned out one day the most unlikely of replacement pilots showed up unannounced at the Pickle Lake air base, it being quite obvious to all upon being introduced his education and general demeanor indicating his not being the usual run of the mill down at the heels would be bush pilot type, but rather an obviously well heeled city slicker silver tongue sort that definitely gave one the impression of his having once been a used car or real estate salesman that most definitely knew his way around.

No longer holding the unenviable position of being the check pilot could have cared less what his qualifications where, that was some one else's problem now, but if I had read him right and certain to have done so he seemed to be the type that was more at home promoting salesmanship and time would prove my initial assessment correct, we where to soon discover his being an astute politician with a glib tongue never really twisting the truth out of manageable or unbelievable proportion, but by the astute use of omission not straying too far away from it, being able to at all times to maintain a fine line of the unthinkable mixed adroitly with the unbelievable and some how make it all seem sensible, easily and without conscious effort swaying the most jaded with a well presented application of smoothly applied silver tongued persuasive dialog, in short he would have triumphed as a politician if having chosen to do so drawing no lines in his relentless drive to get his way be it hand kissing, baby kissing or ass kissing or what ever else it took to succeed.

Time proved his methods bore fruit not taking more then three months to work his way into the good graces of those who could be instrumental in fast tracking his career.

By no means an accomplished pilot, only considered marginally capable at best never the less within an abbreviated space of time graduating to larger and more sophisticated aircraft, doing so in far less time than it normally took, on the occasion by passing those in line for advancement understandably creating deep rifts and an undercurrent of hard feelings from those who had been short changed. But that minor upset fazed Big Al not in the least, blithely forging on as if it was his god given right to do so.

Not one of us really figured out just how he ever managed to pull it off, but by dint of much back room maneuvering, a skill he soon proved himself to be a past master at had one way or the other successfully circumvented what was normally a sequence of mandatory check rides along with ignoring the completion of mounds of required paper work that kept head office and the government drones appeased, the rest of us lacking such sophisticated talent had little choice but to endure. Again his ongoing machination in making himself appear indispensable created a lot of acrimony and ruffled feathers but relentlessly boring on regardless of upsetting the apple cart in pursuit of his personal goals blithely ignoring and dismissing as childish the burgeoning hard feelings directed toward him.

Once having figured out his modus operandi and getting to know him better and to ignore his political bent, one found him to possess a genuinely likeable personality with his soon becoming a friend and a regular visitor to my home where in no time at all captivating my wife who simply adored his seeming big city sophistication falling all over herself every time he appeared at the door and in no time bringing my young and impressionable pre-teen aged daughters who soon fell under his spell perceiving him as a cut above the rest. My not being involved in company politics or caring less who was it mattered not to me how he conducted his personal state of affairs only calling him "friend", and that's how it stood between us.

Eventually working his way up to the Otter, the one aircraft I totally despised and refused to fly and in my way of thinking he was more then welcome to it beginning his stint flying on skis about the time we began to experienced an unprecedented mining exploration boom that took up every available aircraft to haul great greasy unmanageable god dam chunks of diamond drill equipment to various locations. The mind and back breaking job called for great perseverance and brute force to load into a beech craft, but as bad as that could prove to be loading the otter a far worse ordeal for the ground crew it's being capable of carrying the largest heaviest and awkward pieces due to the cavernous cargo door that allowed far larger units to be loaded, often our only being able to accomplish only a few trips during the short winter days due the extensive amount of time required to load and unload.

Out of sheer necessity everyone wore heavy work coveralls to protect our clothes from the ravages of grease covered machinery along with wearing heavy leather gloves to guard our hands against sharp edges and frayed cables which where to be found in abundance, our being forced by absolute necessity to every three or four days to wash them out in a pail of aviation fuel there having become so stiff from constant applications of foul smelling rod grease they could no longer be endured. That of course only applied to the ground crew and us pilots, the diamond drill crews regularly being coated from head to toe with sticky foul smelling grease on a twenty four hour a day basis appeared to pay little heed, only removing their grease coated coveralls to enter the cook shack or when going to bed (I'm not absolutely certain about that).

It so came about one day Big Al and I arrived at the same drill camp site only minutes apart with Big Al preceding me to the off loading area. As I pulled in behind him to await my turn noticed Al busily chatting up the drill foreman who appeared in all respects to be somewhat awed by his silver tongued line of shit as if he was some kind of newly arrived tin god. But what really threw me was when noticing for the first time Al's immaculate custom tailored flight suit that sported a myriad of zippers and flap pockets festooned with gold tipped pens and not what have you with not a crease out of place or a speck of grease to be seen anywhere, Christ he could have been posing for vogue fashions, one couldn't help but to compare their torn and grease coated coveralls with his and not wonder where they had gone wrong.

After a brief period of consultation they casually sauntered up to the cook shack for coffee and cake once the foreman had instructed his crew of French workers to begin to off load the otter. It took some time for the cursing and sweating men to wrestle them recalcitrant chunks of heavy ungainly finger and toe mashing grease coated drill equipment out of the otter, finally accomplishing their grimy task with great difficulty only to leave me gaping in absolute astonishment as they then commenced to re- load the otter with empty fuel oil drums and propane bottles. One could do naught but to shake their head in wonder and unconcealed admiration at Al's seeming ability to bend others to his will. As for me no such luck, remaining smeared from head to toe with sticky grease for if I as much as dared to think about refusing to pitch in and assist with the unloading and loading of my aircraft the crew also refusing to do so leaving me with little choice but to unwillingly work along side of them while smarting at the inequities of life.

How he managed as well as he did remained an ongoing source of wonder to us as he could put in a full days work flogging the otter back and forth hauling the much despised diamond drill equipment that was normally grueling back breaking toil for the rest of us lesser mortals, but he at no time to my recollection ever as much as got a smudge of grease on his immaculately pressed flight suit never mind his tanned to perfection deer skin gloves while the rest of us would fitfully straggle in to the office after a cruel days toil red eyed and foul tempered, almost cross eyed with fatigue and filthy beyond description wanting only to discard our soiled coveralls and to revel in a long hot shower in order to once more feel human.

God dam how we dreaded each day of the seemingly endless drill move praying it would soon come to an end. Eventually it would all wind down but we knew with a dread certainty that night mare of a job would in due course begin all over again in the not too distant future as the crews completed their drill programs with all their god dam back breaking greasy equipment having to be laboriously loaded to be flown to a new site or back in to Pickle Lake again.

At the end of the season all of us excepting Big Al appeared to be the most ragged ass sorriest lot of stoop shouldered hollow eyed collection of burnt out cantankerous bush pilots ever to mindlessly huddle in one place, creeping in and out of our aircraft like so many ancient pensioners. Of course Al who had only to fly his aircraft while not unnecessarily having as much as lifted a well manicured finger of a certainty remained well rested and buoyant much to the collective disgust of the other pilots who had been forced to labor like indentured galley slaves day in and day out for so long, but what really took the cake was he managed to fly the most hours and miles of anyone in a far slower aircraft yet and of course it follows earned the most mileage pay while putting out far less effort in doing so. But in the end it all rolled off him like water off a ducks back, it wasn't only that he was not forced to labor as mightily as we did, no one had ever known him to engage in hauling a load of fish or any other potentially

389

disagreeable cargo, that being relegated to us less gifted mortals. One can be absolutely certain that Big Al's seemingly stellar performance did not escape the notice of the brass comfortably ensconced in their ivory towers who eventually began to question the fact that a much slower aircraft carrying a much larger load could accomplish so much more within a given period of time than a much faster beech craft, wisely we to a man avoided being dragged into that one. But oh man he sure had all the government agency drones who often came our way clamoring for his services, there one must in all rights give him credit for elevating the esoteric art of ass kissing to heretofore unknown heights in cultivating their respect, he may have been venerated by the government drones, but absolutely reviled by the native population throughout the settlements, there sneeringly referring to him as the "big wind" or "words in the wind."

But as always all the hard feelings and recriminations directed against him all rolled off him like water off a ducks back, Al on top of everything else proved to be thick skinned. It wasn't only that his not having to labor mightily on a regular basis as we did, no one had ever known him during his tenure with the company to ever engage in hauling a load of fish or any other potentially disagreeable cargo, that being left up to us less gifted mortals but oh man he sure had all the government agency drones clamoring for his services, there one must in all rights concede in giving him credit for elevating the arcane art of ass kissing to heretofore unknown heights, he may have been venerated by the government drones, but soundly reviled by the native populations throughout the settlements, they're referring to him as the big wind or words in the wind.

Not exactly a resounding acclamation in any ones estimation, and of course failing miserably in bringing them under his spell despised them for making light of his saccharine attempts to win them over eventually giving up generally avoiding them as much as possible.

In time it became glaringly obvious to all he had some how worked his way into being more in charge of the day to day flight operations then our present dispatcher that normally passed on our marching orders, as for Big Al's dictates we as a matter of course ignored him. One day having reached the end of his patience with the whole affair the dispatcher suddenly threw up his hands in absolute frustration and despair to walk out in unconcealed disgust never to return.

Now this situation once again left us without a full time dispatcher as Al had his flight duties to attend to keeping him away from the base for long periods of time, but Al being who he was somehow within an abbreviated space of time managed to recruit a new gung ho would be dispatcher, from where and how and under what authority he had done so totally evaded us not that any one really cared.

Under Al's patient coaching the new recruit soon found his place bustling about sweeping clean all that came before him as all new brooms are first inclined to do with the unvarnished dedication of a true believer entrusted with the well being of the company. Closely observing his dedicated fervor in carrying out his job most of us could not help but to reflect on days long past when we too had felt impassioned with a burning desire to do the job well, but that was far into the past our having become permanently disillusioned and cynical, long having become hardened to all but stark reality. In all fairness we case hardened veterans decided it to be in our favor to co-operate with him as much as possible for he had an unobvious job to perform, all too soon he would discover his new found mantle would do little to prepare him to deal with the demands that lay before him, eventually reducing him to tears of hopeless frustration as it was obvious his being in the long run not cut out to face the whimsical pack of unruly headstrong cynical to a fault bush pilots along with by it's very nature the often heavy responsibilities that came with the job.

As it went Big Al met his match one fine day when seemingly out of the blue the company hired a lady pilot, as an amiable out going type one could not ask for a better person, not at all hung up by the usual burning desire to prove her worth at any cost, a fault that generally appeared to plague a good many of her sex when working alongside men, but only asking to be given a fair and equitable chance to do her job with her right from the start co-operating with and getting on with all, that is except for Big Al who took umbrage at having a lady pilot in the crew, regarding her presence as a personal affront to what he considered a man's world.

One had to give that little gal credit for moxie, once finding herself immediately getting off on the wrong foot with him despite all, finally lost her patience with his male chauvinist attitude making it quite plain she resented the demeaning and authorative manner he showed to-ward her, in short she took no shit from any one including big Al. Once being checked out on the aircraft she was to fly never shirking her job, no matter how difficult or dirty and gladly pitching in to help where ever and whenever she could.

Having taken a liking to her indomitable spirit allowed her on the occasion to accompany me in the beech craft gradually teaching her the intricacies of handling a beech craft, never had I trained a more astute willing to listen and learn pilot such as her. This as matter of course pissed off Big Al no end, it soon coming about with her finally losing patience with his smug overbearing attitude outright challenged his authority, well that totally unexpected confrontation momentarily took the wind out of his sails, but only momentarily with his adroitly changing his tactics using every conceivable wile he could dream up in a futile silver tongued effort to win her over which in the end only proving that transparent ruse to be non productive with her maddeningly ignoring his every entreaty. His not being one to graciously accept defeat from any quarter, especially from a mere female changed tact in a sly underhanded attempt to belittle and embarrass her by surreptitiously insinuating having used sex in order to advance herself.

Well that proved to be a major error on his part with her tearing into him with the unmatched ferocity and venom of a scorned woman, scathingly dressing him down with a sharp tongue dripping of sarcasm that would have caused a lesser man to flee while quivering in humiliation.

But not Big Al, his blithely shrugging off her passionate tirade with an all knowing twisted grin smeared all over his face knowing with a certainty it would only serve to goad her further, we who happened to be present at the time of confrontation just stood there in delicious awe at the heated intensity of the verbal exchange before it finally reaching a point where neither had any intention of backing off with the all too certain possibility of some one getting hurt forcing us to intercede in breaking up the argument.

In time it all blew over with their coldly ignoring each other with that tense state of affairs often proving difficult to tolerate in the close confines of our tiny flight office, but in spite of it all the truce held against all odds much to our collective relief.

Big Al as previously mentioned a bold pilot if not an exceptionally talented one while often foolishly choosing to push weather conditions so atrocious as to keep the rest of us grounded, he didn't appear to have any common sense or fear of risky weather conditions until it came about one day while enrooted to Pickle Lake from Sioux Lookout with an Indian affairs agent on board as a sole passenger while flying a Cessna 180, the weather picture becoming so threatening as to finally force him into following the rail road to Savant lake and then picking up the highway from there barely remaining at tree top level during the duration of the flight and as it turned out fortunately for Al the low level they maintained keeping the Indian affairs agent who being the veteran of many the hairy flight on his toes peering nervously ahead into the lowering gloom. Al being totally wrapped up in attempting to keep the road in sight and being so taken up in doing so completely forgot about the looming presence of the huge micro wave tower that stood in their line of flight until it suddenly and unexpectedly materialized out of the gloom directly in front of them, only the frightened scream of the Indian agent who had spotted the tower at the last possible second alerted Al who somehow in just the nick of time violently rolled the aircraft to the left barely managing to avoid piling directly into the tower structure with predictable results, but by the dammdest stroke of luck only snagging one of the profusion of guy wires with the outer section of wing tip shearing it clean off, the sudden jolt that badly twisted the outer panel of the wing almost causing a severe loss of control with Big Al barely managing to more by chance than skill regain level flight mere seconds before crashing into the trees.

Needless to say it was a badly frightened and well subdued Al that managed to finally limp in to the safety of Pickle Lake in a badly damaged aircraft that from all accounts flew raggedly threatening to depart from controlled flight at any given second.

It was with unconcealed wonder and awe we inspected the damaged wing arriving at the conclusion it remained nothing short of a miracle the aircraft had ever managed to remain airborne, there remained little doubt it's flying days were over until the wing being completely re-built.

As it went no one the least aware at the time of Big Al's close call until they had landed safely and had negotiated the hill from the dock to the flight office ashen faced and tottering along on rubbery legs that almost refused to function to in a noticeably quivering voice reveal his near mishap to a for once hushed audience.

Once the near mishap had run the gauntlet of officialdom, Big Al resigned from the company, either by choice or otherwise never revealed to us stating to have had his fill of commercial aviation. Of course no one believed that for a minute knowing that fast talking bugger always had an iron or two in the fire.

Sure enough and not to anyone's surprise within a period of two weeks came flying triumphantly back to Pickle Lake in a pristine Cessna 180 that belonged to an independent diamond drill contractor who was presently engaged in setting up a permanent base of operation in the immediate area.

It eventually came out that Big Al had sweet-talked the owner into purchasing his own personal aircraft with him as pilot to better service his numerous drill sites scattered throughout the north.

For a good period of time Big Al worked hard to subdue his natural enthusiasm managing to keep it on a tight rein until in time regaining a full measure of confidence along with developing an annoying habit of "hot shotting", This maneuver consisted of landing as close to the shore line as possible then driving the aircraft on the float step to as close to the dock as he dared only shutting off the power at the last possible second to fall off the step and to coast into the dock with a grand flourish. Our knowing that sooner or later he was bound to screw up with predictable results had the riot act read out to him to either cease and desist his cowboy tactics immediately or find some other facility to use, naturally he didn't take kindly to this ultimatum but having little choice but to do otherwise grudgingly obeyed the dictum though to a man our recognizing him for being the person he was we all remained well aware his overriding penchant for showmanship and never passing up an opportunity to strut his stuff bound to screw up royally sooner or later when undoubtedly making a bad judgment call and ultimately coming to grief. Our prophecy was to eventually come about in the strangest manner that anyone with even the most fertile of minds could have never begin to imagine.

Some how be it skill or just plain luck he managed to make it through the busy summer months without any minor or major mishaps or bending any metal. As it always has the seasons irrevocably ground on with us dismally facing the prospects of enduring another cold hard grueling winter of taking on natures worst while flying on skis. Al true to form and delighted with the nimble performance of the 180 on skis simply couldn't resist low fly by's and making fighter pilot type landing approaches that often had the hardiest of us holding our breath, then when taxiing to the revetment charging in to the hard packed loading area to at the least possible second blasting the engine while kicking in full left rudder forcing the aircraft turn in a half circle switching off the magnetos half way through, horridly sliding his seat back and exiting the aircraft with a flourish as it continued to coast to a stop to jauntily make his way up to the office. This showmanship went on for most of the winter without serious mishap. Then as the warm spring weather began to melt the snow surface during the day to once again freeze rock hard during the night leaving an extremely slick surface which all pilots treated with great respect when landing within a restricted area or toward the shoreline while exercising great caution when taxiing in to the parking area during early mornings, but of course that would have asked too much of Big Al to consider such a minor problem, he just never seemed to learn, the numerous near misses with one thing or another hardly fazing his confidence, but that was all to change one clear crisp early spring morning with the hard packed area remaining as slick as a greased weasel swimming in a barrel of snot, sure enough true to form one beautiful clear crisp morning Big Al came charging in as always with our standing at the top of the hill in gleeful anticipation of what we knew was certain to take place, not in the least disappointed when observing his attempting to blast the aircraft into it's usual half circle, but this time as anticipated the tail ski keel failing to grip the slick icy surface leaving the aircraft instead of turning as anticipated gaining forward speed to barrel straight ahead through an area littered with support equipment, fuel drums and not what have you with Al's eyes bugging out in surprise upon realizing the all too real possibility of ploughing into something or other immediately writing off his propeller in the process frantically shut off the engine to no avail having left it too late could only impotently hang on and hope for the best. We simply couldn't believe it, somehow in a manner that could only be termed as pure chance he managed to charge erratically through that minefield of obstructions only knocking over a few empty fuel drums in the process with the wing struts, that in itself nothing short of a miracle with the aircraft finally rocketing half way up the bank before coming to a shuddering halt with one very subdued and sheepish looking Al slowly slithering out of the door to face our riotous laughter and knowing smirks followed by a round of appreciative hand clapping. Being the indomitable personality he was quickly recovered his aplomb to bow graciously all around while offering to buy the coffee if we would assist him in returning the aircraft to it's rightful parking spot.

Of a matter of course we all pitched in willingly being there was none among us that hadn't screwed up at one time or another. That near miss only served to cool off his natural enthusiasm for a short spell before misplaced exuberance once more asserted it's self, but the next mistake he would make would lead to far more serious consequences, but that happening still lay in the future.

Al not being one to remain disparaged for any length of time soon resumed his cowboy tactics but wisely displaying a bit more caution while doing so then he had in the past not wanting to have to live down another embarrassing performance or worse yet chancing damaging his aircraft discreetly maintained his habit of blasting the aircraft around in his best cowboy fashion out of sight of our prying eyes at one or the other of the drill camps he serviced.

The one thing all pilots shared in common during the coldest of the winter months was the ongoing advent of frozen batteries that often proved to be useless for starting the engines leaving us to hand crank the engines in order to fire them up, an easy proposition with a beech craft on skis as the wasp junior engines started so easily, but still one had best exercise great caution at all times when doing so in setting up the engine controls correctly before attempting a hand start, As it happened that fateful day, Big Al having experienced battery failure forcing him to hand crank the engine for the last while in order to start it while awaiting the arrival of a replacement, this is normally no big deal with a Cessna 180 as they too hand started easily, but as mentioned previously one had to be certain at all times in exercising care to correctly set up the engine controls before attempting a hand start if one wished to avoid potential disaster.

That very morning my having occasion to arrive at the drill site with a load of fuel oil and spare parts where it just so happened Big Al had spent the night, once unloaded joined Al at the cook shack for a delicious breakfast, food never tastes as good as it does at a remote drill camp. Having satisfied our appetites we casually sauntered back to our respective aircraft where Al immediately busied himself with readying his aircraft for the first flight of the day declining my offer of help to get it started. Not being in any special rush to get back decided to wait until he was ready to go and return to Pickle Lake together.

Al's starting up of his aircraft went forward in a manner neither of us could have possibly envisioned as naturally it failed to occur to me that Al always being the consummate cowboy had made his usual arrival at the parking spot for the night and as always had blasted the aircraft in it's usual half circle and shutting down the engine by switching off the magnetos and then shoving the throttle in to the stop to prevent back firing of the engine.

That very same morning the unthinkable was about to take place with Al being his usual boisterous self as usual talking a mile a minute and as always in a great all fired rush to be gone. It all started to go badly for him while initially preparing the cold engine for starting by hand cranking, and in the process of doing so his overriding haste to get going causing him to screw up very badly by neglecting to set the engine controls beforehand, only priming the engine and switching on the magnetos but absent mindedly failing to pull the throttle back to idle position thus setting the stage for imminent disaster that came within a hair's breadth of ending his life in a very messy manner.

Positioning himself directly in front of the engine commenced to hand swing the propeller, after about the sixth attempt became impatient with the balky engine swinging the propeller violently in frustration to fortunately for him suddenly slipping sideways on a patch of clear ice just as the engine fired up with the propeller blades narrowly missing decapitating with his only just managing to scramble out of the way of the whirling blades, the engine initially spluttered hesitantly for a few heart beats before suddenly roaring fully to life at full throttle with the still cold engine backfiring and hesitating momentarily before settling down to running fairly smooth. Meanwhile Big Al fully occupied at the time in attempting to get clear of the aircraft before it ran him over only partly succeeding in doing so as the aircraft suddenly lunged forward as the engine reached full power with the ski colliding with and painfully flopping him to one side like a rag doll making me think for a terrible minute or two he had been struck and badly injured by the propeller, but as it turned out his having only been rudely pushed to one side and when attempting to rise taking a glancing blow to his shoulder from the horizontal stabilizer as it sped on by again rolling him over and over like a rag doll.

The scenario had occurred so rapidly one could only stare helplessly in awe and disbelief as the unthinkable unfolded before my very eyes.

Big Al having risen shakily to his feet took a few quick steps as if in hope of catching the aircraft before it's gaining headway before realizing the futility of his actions, the hopelessness of the situation mirrored in his eyes as he stood there helplessly muttering oh Jesus oh Jesus over and over again in an impotent litany eventually resorting to hobbling in confused circles with his face the color of bread dough, only able to watch helplessly as the runaway aircraft rapidly gained flying speed. From my viewpoint on top of the beech craft roof it appeared to momentarily lift off within a very short space of time to at first remain in wobbly level flight as it gained forward speed before the nose began to rise continuing to climb steeply until attaining a position slightly past the vertical before slowly falling over on it's back almost in slow motion before rapidly descending toward the ice surface with the engine appearing to cut out momentarily before roaring back into life slowly pulling the aircraft out of it's dive until almost reaching a level position with the wings miraculously remaining near level as it pulled through the bottom half of a loop just managing to do so before the skis contacted the ice surface so heavily I could have sworn to the spring steel landing gear splaying sideways until almost contacting the wing struts with a clearly audible clang before once more re-bounding shakily into the air to wobble along unsteadily for another good half mile before crashing into the heavy growth of trees that lined the lake shore with a distinctive crunching noise that made me wince, clearly carrying across the intervening distance creating almost the same sound one would hear upon stepping on a plastic bottle with the engine roar ceasing immediately.

Both of us having unwillingly watched the impromptu air show to it's conclusion in stunned silence at first had nothing to say to each other.

Big Al who had taken a few uncertain steps before realizing the hopelessness of it all when the aircraft had first gotten away from him once more began to wander in confused circles while muttering the now familiar litany of oh Jesus oh Jesus over and over again in a helpless despair while rubbing the shoulder where the horizontal stabilizer had clipped him. He appeared to be in such a terrible state of shock with his face the color of bread dough at first feared he was experiencing a coronary.

After calming him down somewhat convinced him to accompany me to the scene of the accident which he eventually agreed to do albeit somewhat reluctantly, an understandable state of mind when taking into consideration his unenviable circumstances.

Firing up the beech craft we taxied the intervening distance to the scene of the wreck, we didn't have to venture too far away from the shoreline before coming up on the remains of what had once been a pristine aircraft, now reduced to a pile of mangled twisted and bent metal. The tail section appeared to be completely unscathed but both wings had been neatly sheared off near their roots, somehow the rapidly moving aircraft had by the merest of chance managed to fly directly between two large widely spaced pine trees. They must have been solidly rooted to withstand the immense impact suddenly imposed on them with the only apparent damage to them being a lot of pine needles shaken loose and a limited amount of bark missing

where the leading edges of the wings had initially impacted. What really got our notice was the amazing sight of the engine and propeller which had obviously torn loose on impact traveling another six hundred yards or so before bouncing to a full stop in the deep snow. It was hard to comprehend how anything could have survived such rough treatment but both engine and propeller seemed to be in fair shape considering their ordeal, suffering little obvious damage on first viewing them. Christ, one could only wonder at the dynamics involved while chewing it's way through yards of thick brush and still remain intact with tendrils of steam rising into the frigid air from the still hot engine giving one the eerie sensation of it's being alive and breathing.

In stony silence Big Al retrieved his five star sleeping bag from the baggage compartment along with his map case and personals with our making our way back to the camp where he would use the radio to relay the bad news to the owner and to all and sundry who might have been tuned into that frequency.

My heart went out to that poor depressed wretched well-meaning bugger, he had screwed up big time and must now pay the price for having done so. His present dilemma nothing new to any of us engaged in the thankless job of aviation, simply said it was something we accepted and lived with every day of our careers, as long as one never screwed up you remained one of the boys accepted in the inner circle, screw up and one soon found themselves on the outside looking in with those you once worked with and called friend suddenly distancing themselves from you as if having suddenly contracted a dread disease.

Upon our return to Pickle Lake Big Al made himself scarce as possible for the first while, only visiting at my house whenever feeling a deep need for friendship and understanding, only remaining within the vicinity long enough for the accident investigation drones to conclude their findings before once more returning to eastern Ontario from whence he first came, through the intervening years we occasionally bumped into each other but the last ever heard from him he was captain of a courier jet, guess you just can't keep a good man down.

Surprisingly enough once he had gone we missed his loud extroverted overbearing personality, for if he was anywhere within sight or sound one was sure to be aware of it, the place seemed dead after he had moved on, I consider it an honor to have known and worked with him as his kind where the ones who made the north country a unique place to live and work, to this very day I still refer to him as "friend".

Mad Trapper

ONE OF THE MORE INTERESTING and memorable forays into the sometimes esoteric world of commercial aviation came about when one fine winters day being contacted by the local free trader located on McKenzie Island a short ways north of the town of Red Lake to return one of his customers to their trap line, one of many of a fairly large contingent of trappers who chose to deal exclusively with him be it a white man or a native as he had always dealt fairly with all of them, but the native trappers greatly outnumbering the whites making his request to fly out a white trapper to his remote trap line rather an unusual state of affairs for me as white trappers had pretty much faded out to the point of being almost none existent, but business was business.

Upon flying the tiger moth the short distance to McKenzie Island where the local free trader had located and set up a trading post within a short time after arriving in the area immediately introduced me to the white trapper who went by the name of Fred Rodman.

I never did find out how he had arrived there and after one look declined to inquire as he sized me up with the hardest unblinking blue eyes I had ever seen, his unwavering stare making me feel distinctly uncomfortable, one felt it would be like attempting to stare down a snake.

As it turned out my being informed much later on he had for reasons best known to him taken up the solitary life of a trapper, seeming to have chosen to go it alone, not appearing to for months on end desiring the company of any others than his sled dogs, only venturing away from his trap grounds twice a year to barter his accumulated furs and to stock up on the necessities of life.

Eventually it was learned the native trappers that occasionally crossed trails with him went out of their way to avoid doing so if at all possible, though discreet inquiry revealing that at no time did he transgress their trap grounds or in any manner make himself objectionable to them, he plain and simply gave off a black and foreboding presence that spooked them as it did me upon our first meeting.

Perhaps his being a loner had conditioned him to be a man of few words as when he did speak doing so sparingly, the words seeming to come from down deep inside with an accented rumble that made his speech difficult to understand.

The same morning we first met it became apparent his not being in an amiable state of mind, it turning out his being in the initial stages of recovering from a week long binge that understandably left him in a sorry state of affairs and hardly in the mood to exchange pleasantries, this is not an unusual state of affairs for men of his ilk, their self imposed exile with no one to share their time or thoughts with except their dogs, only having contact with others during their twice yearly trip to town to transact their business and to within a limited amount of time strike up or renew old friendships if any that inevitably led to a knock em down, drag out the dead snot dripping bender that lasted as long as their money and stamina held out, as a matter of course the usual unsavory retinue of hanger owner's who could sniff out an easy mark at any time present to exacerbate the flow of the trappers hard earned money and booze. A few of the hard core individuals could keep it up until eventually falling prey to a severe dose of delirium tremens or in other words a terminal case of the "snakes" or the DT's. Once reaching that point it soon brought their debauchery to a screeching halt, their totally futile efforts of attempting to swatting and flailing away at a host of imaginary creepy crawlers that their deranged minds told them to be plaguing and tormenting them while lurching down the street long haired and wild eyed drooling copiously into their heavily whiskered chins, pathetic wrecks of human despair with no were left to go being broke and out of booze, now unwelcome at their usual haunts.

Usually at this juncture the local constabulary stepped in to lead them bleary eyed thoroughly washed up trembling uncontrollably wrecks of human jetsam to sleep it off in the safety of the local hoosegow instead of leaving them in their helpless state to take their chances with whatever harm that could possibly befall them if left on their own or if in the colder days the all too real risk of passing out to sleep the sleep that never ends.

This to me constituted an act of kindness and good will toward a human desperately in need of aid and understanding even though confining them up to a jail cell with no hope of being able to access booze that would ease their agonies doomed them to enduring a living hell during the height of their withdrawal from the debilitating effects of alcohol poisoning, at first passing out in a coma like sleep for extended periods of time interspersed by periods of lunatic fringe ravings as they wrestled with re-occurring bouts of the "snakes" till finally purging the poisons from their sadly abused bodies eventually emerging sick and sorry stinking to high heaven disheveled caricature of a once proud human being, only wanting to quit the source of their despair and return to the security of their trap cabin to recuperate.

Once released from their cell it was common practice to take a taxi to the free traders place of business where their pre purchased necessities of life and a ticket home awaited them, the free trader being more than aware of their tendencies to indiscriminately blow their hard earned money on booze and what ever had as a matter of course upon the sale of their furs held back a sufficient amount of money to cover the cost of their supplies and air fare. Once all had been settled and done they were unceremoniously bundled into the waiting aircraft to be gratefully whisked back to their trap line.

Such was more or less the state of affairs Freddy Rodman found himself in, he couldn't have picked a finer morning to fly, the clear crisp cold air hovered at a balmy minus ten degrees below, one of them days when one felt so vibrantly alive.

That is until my euphoria took an instant nose dive upon confronting Freddie's malovent personality head on, leaving me wondering at just what in hell I had let myself in for this time around, but for better or worse irrevocably committed to seeing it through to it's conclusion as to refuse to do so would damage my relationship with the free trader who utilized my services on many occasions, it just wouldn't do to raise his ire.

Upon completing the difficult task of wedging Freddy and his supplies into the narrow confines of the front cockpit it barely left enough leeway for him to occasionally take a hefty snort from a bottle of whiskey he had concealed some were in the voluminous folds of his parka.

That of a certainty did not sit well with me, but consoled my self that he could not create too much of a ruckus being so tightly ensconced, on this he soon proved my being in error.

Once completing strapping his snowshoes and other various chunks of bulky paraphernalia onto the wing struts we were on our way to Uchi Lake, a one time vibrant gold mining community that had once boasted of a highly populous center with all the modern conveniences of the era including a hotel and two highly successful cat houses guaranteeing the miners female entertainment among other things.

The towns curtain call came about when the smaller mining operations were first pinched out by the insatiable demands of world war two that gradually choked out available man power, equipment and mining supplies gradually forcing the permanent closure of the Uchi mine.

Only upon taking up flying for a living did I become aware of the existence of what was now a ghost town, now the sole domain of Freddy Rodman.

Droning sedately across the snow covered terrain on a direct route to Uchi Lake, a harsh commanding growl that could be clearly heard over the engine noises rudely woke me out of my reverie coming near to causing me to piss my pants in fright, Freddy could have made himself heard over a thunder storm), His strident demand instantly caused me to rivet my attention onto the intervening space that separated the two cockpits finding to my distress to be staring into the business end of a very large caliber revolver being held in a very large hairy hand that shook noticeably while being pointed directly between my horns, Christ all mighty, in my shock and fear could have sworn to the muzzle resembling a young stove pipe

Once over my initial shock it came clear to me that Freddy demanding in a deep gruff voice as to where in hell did I think to be taking him?, at first my near paralyzed with fright vocal cords refused to function, but with an all out effort aimed at not antagonizing him further just managed to chirp out in a high falsetto that almost ended in a screech, to uchi lake of course, (I almost added "Sir"), at that he rumbled out in a menacing tone that I had best be god dam sure of it or it would go hard with me.

Well that not so subtle warning sure had me keeping track of our progress with my no time wandering more than a foot over either side of the line drawn on the map.

Fortunately for my well rattled and upset state of mind Freddy dropped off into a deep sleep, the audible rumble of his snoring keeping pace in volume with the engine noises.

Much to my everlasting dismay Freddy having some how failed to remove the menacing sight of the gun barrel which had drooped slightly upon his relaxing his grip in sleep to no longer pointing between my horns but still remaining a potent threat as he could involuntarily pull on his trigger finger while fast asleep doing me in, Christ I just about shit every time his hairy fist twitched with my impotently attempting to cringe away from the menacing sight of that gun barrel soon discovering it mattered not which way one leaned in the cramped confines of the cockpit it seemed to follow.

The remainder of the flight with my remaining near transfixed with fright seemed to take forever my squirming uncomfortably in the confines of that narrow cockpit while futilely attempting to move away from the omnipresent threat of the gun pointed at me.

One can be certain of my making the most gentle of landings in the bay hoping we wouldn't bounce over any unseen drifts or concealed snow shoe trails, breathing a sigh of relief when finally sliding to a stop in front of his cabin and shutting down the engine, the ensuing silence broken only by a series of loud stat taco snores emitting from the front cockpit as Freddy slept on, how he had ever managed to twist his huge bulk within the confines of that cramped space totally confounded me, but he somehow had leaving me stuck to stare in helpless fear at the menacing revolver pointed in my space, my just about experiencing a coronary every time his big hairy fist twitched in his sleep.

After a short period of soul searching decided to get it over with one way or the other unlocked the canopy latch that released with what sounded like an over loud snap instantly causing the muzzle of the revolver to once more point unwaveringly between my horns causing my near freezing up in paralyzing fear, holding my breath until the menacing gun barrel once more slowly sank down leaving me weak with relief to ever so cautiously slide back the canopy without creating too much noise for the cold air seeping into the cockpit reminding me the "Mexican" stand off had to end and god dam soon or we would both die of exposure, not to mention the engine becoming too cold soaked to re -start, something had to give pronto.

Having successfully slid back the canopy without disturbing Freddy slowly and cautiously levered my well chilled body out of the cockpit shaking like a dog pissing razor blades while maintaining a fixed focus on the gun barrel half expecting to be blown away at any second, much relieved to observe it's not wavering a hair as freed snored on totally oblivious to his surroundings.

Once having more or less gotten over my fright shakily went about covering up the engine to keep it warm, to then begin the time consuming job of removing the supplies packed around Freddy, having dredged up the nerve to do so cautiously pried the revolver from his unresisting hairy fist, and upon successfully doing so with great difficulty coaxing him into a state of semi wakefulness to have him clamber shakily out of the cockpit to once sliding off the wing immediately falling onto his face in the snow and resuming his loud snoring, it taking a determined and prolonged effort on my part to shake him awake by dint of much yanking and shouting to get him mobile to the point of his being able to get up on his feet and shakily stagger up to his cabin where he immediately crashed heavily onto his foul smelling bunk, my covering him up boots, parka and all with an equally smelly sleeping bag, as pissed off with him a I was for threatening me with his revolver, common decency dictated my offering assistance toward a fellow man in need, to leave him in his helpless state there remained a possibility of his freezing to death took the time to fire up his ancient but still serviceable wood burning heater in order to begin taking the chill from the cabin.

Ensuring all to be well with freed who lay contentedly snoring away turned my attention to his team of long neglected sled dogs who had immediately set up a disconcerting dirge upon our arrival. They may have been an immensely tough breed of dogs, but they too had their limits being near starved to death, not having eaten for at least a week their general condition appearing gaunt and shrunken with ratty fur and humped backs, upon observing their poor condition my heart went out to the poor devils with my diligently searching out the cache of dog food and frozen fish, cooked up a good portion of a mixture consisting of coarse oatmeal and tallow on my plumbers pot (blow pot), feeding them individually taking great care to remain out of the boundaries of their chains being quite aware of their half wild state and their propensity to only remaining amenable toward their master utilizing a long handled shovel to place each dog's portion to within easy reach were they immediately devoured it with mindless abandon, then tossing each of them two large frozen fish, awed by the immense power of their jaws as they rended the rock hard fish with the ease one would expend on a fresh loaf of bread, satisfied with having done what needed doing except for laboriously hauling Freddie's supplies into the cabin while the tiger moth's engine warmed up.

Before taking my leave made one more final check on Freddy, finding him in better condition then he had been in on arrival, his color returning to normal and sleeping soundly. Filling the wood stove to capacity and setting the dampers bid freed a silent adieu before departing on my return trip to Red Lake.

During the interim as we droned along reflected on the vagaries of life and the recent course of events that had taken up most of my day, arriving at the obvious conclusion it not being a very profitable one.

Early the next morning visited the free trader Fergus McDougal, a larger than life bluff outspoken Scotsman who minced words with no one, having known him for a number of years respected his straightforward honesty. On confronting him I immediately began to whine about the raw treatment received at the hands of one Freddy Rodman, at the conclusion of my heart felt revelation he almost doubled over in uproarious laughter that brought tears to his eyes, some what taken aback by his unexpectedly failing to commiserate with my sad story felt righteously pissed off at his cavalier attitude.

Once able to collect himself and wipe the tears of mirth from his eyes between bouts of ill concealed snickering matter of factly informing me this was Freddie's idea of a joke (a rather sick one as far as I was concerned) he enjoyed pulling off on unsuspecting pilots, but unknown to any of us at the time the gun was never loaded, that revelation in itself failed miserably in mollifying my bruised ego, only leaving me feeling more like a fool than ever, little wonder then my ending up flying him back to his trap line in the cramped uncomfortable cockpit of the tiger moth. For some reason that could never be rationally explained in time and further acquaintance found that strange taciturn man to be an enigma, my desiring to get to know him better volunteering my services in transporting him back and forth twice a year for a number of years, admittedly he took some getting used to with our eventually becoming close friends once becoming more or less accustomed to his normally taciturn demeanor, his gradually loosening up while in my presence but always remaining guarded and aloof while in the company of strangers, some one or something in his murky past had badly twisted his trust toward people, what ever upset had taken place it only served to cause his shunning the way's of society to take up a life style of loneliness and obscurity.

There remained little doubt of his being well educated being articulate of speech while eagerly devouring all the books, magazines and newspapers I could possibly garner from cover to cover on top of having a battery powered radio of which he kept up to the latest world events with. His seeming unquenchable thirst for knowledge continued to baffle me, one could only arrive at the unmistakable

conclusion there was a lot more to him than met the eye.

During the course of one of the trips he requested I stay a while as he had something he wished to show me, my readily agreeing to do so having become quite fond of him and he appeared to in all respects reciprocate in kind.

While we sat over a cup of foul tasting coffee that could only be described as being first cousin to crank case oil brewed in a filth encrusted pot that hadn't seen a decent scrubbing since Christ was in short pants, not to mention the grime encrusted cups that one could only hope the scalding hot coffee had sterilized or outright destroyed any potential undesirables that may have taken up residence on the rim.

At one point his reaching under his odiferous bunk to retrieve a small leather suitcase and placing it on the table. Upon opening it

the unexpected sight of bills of every known denomination tightly

crammed within left me staring open mouthed and totally speechless. It was quite obvious he got a real charge out of my initial reaction, smiling broadly as he stated he did not trust banks or government (who does?)choosing instead to stash the proceeds from his fur sales in a secret place, I was never to be informed as to the exact amount of money packed away in the suitcase, but in all respects it had to be quite substantial, as if to emphasize his ownership suddenly brandished his dreaded and now familiar nickel plated revolver stating it to be his insurance against any would be thieves, that possibility ever taking place an extremely long shot as very few had any reason to come his way, but then again who can say?. Upon closing and locking the suit case it was immediately replaced in it's present hiding place, he gestured for me to follow him outside to a patch of sandy soil adjacent to his cabin where he picked up a rusty well worn shovel that had seen better days, immediately commencing to dig until reaching an approximate depth of one foot before contacting a metal object, brushing away the remaining soil revealed it to be a ten gallon fuel drum with it's top cut off with a water proof cover replacing it, once the cover removed one could plainly see it to be packed so tightly with beaver pelts as to almost resemble an over sized cigar, other drums were also tightly packed with various species of fur, all perfectly preserved by the ice cold sand. Once satisfied with revealing their presence to me, the watertight coverings carefully replaced and the excavation once more filled in and smoothed over with a pine bough, if he hadn't for reasons best known to him revealed their presence, no one including me would ever have been the wiser.

Perhaps the reader may wonder why he went to all the trouble to preserve and conceal his furs, the simple fact is that many successful trappers employ this method when at the close of the season they find themselves with more than their legal quota of furs that can not be marketed that year, thus the above mentioned method of preserving them keeps them in good order to be sold the following year. Needless to say he did not bother to caution me to keep his secret, he knew his man.

On the very last trip I was to make with him, he surprised the free trader and me by only remaining in town long enough to transact his business while completely refraining from imbibing any booze what so ever anxiously returning to his trap line within three days. During his tenure in town the free trader and I both took note of his seeming preoccupation, not at all acting like his usual self, not knowing what to make of it put it down to personal affairs.

On returning as scheduled to pick him up, on arrival some surprised not to see him packed up and impatient to be gone, not at all certain as to what to make out of his absence, with no little trepidation conducted a through search of his cabin, it quickly becoming apparent he had not been there for some time, to further confound my dilemma no trace of his dogs could be found, this highly unusual and unexplained state of affairs just plain gave me a bad case of the "willies". Gathering up my remaining courage cautiously peeked under his odiferous bunk, not in the least surprised to find the suitcase gone, though while doing so coming near to jumping out of my skin at every creak and groan the cabin produced half expecting a pissed off Freddy Rodman to suddenly come crashing through the door brandishing the much feared nickel plated revolver, thankfully that never occurred as I am most certain if he had I would have died of fright.

Having had more than enough intrigue for the moment, felt far too spooked by the strangeness of it all to remain any longer electing to forego checking up on the cache of furs to see if it had been emptied, instead hastily returning to the security of my trusty steed, only when safely ensconced within the snug confines of the cockpit and on my way back to Red Lake did the frightening mystery of his unexplained absence and the corrosive pressure of Freddie's malignant presence abate.

Once back in town immediately took steps to inform the free trader of Freddie's strange disappearance where upon he queried my findings at great length, at the conclusion deciding to have me fly him to Uchi lake, if the absolute truth be known I harbored very little desire to do so but had little choice but to comply with his wishes. On arrival the hair on the back of my neck once more rose up like the bristles on a brush and I couldn't explain why for the life of me.

As expected the free trader made a through and meticulous inspection of the cabin from one end to the other taking a good look under the bed during the process, my never having mentioned a word to anyone about the suitcase full of money wondered why, perhaps there was a hell of a lot more involved than first met one's eye, being all too aware that Freddy didn't trust too many people doubted very much the free trader was privy to his secret cache of money.

Deciding it best to so informed the free trader about the buried cache of furs that earned me a quizzical hard eyed look, leading him to it's location were he immediately dug it up, for some unexplained reason found myself sorely disappointed to find the cache of furs intact, the trader upon retrieving the bundles of fur almost unintelligibly muttered something about freed leaving behind a hefty debt, as sincerely doubting that fact as much as I did wisely kept my thoughts to myself not wanting to be involved in the removal of the furs as for some obscure reason lost to me at the time felt an overriding pang of guilt at having some way or another betrayed Freddie's trust, but some strange sense informed me he would never be seen by either of us ever again.

On our loading up the furs and making our somber way back to Red Lake we discussed frees strange disappearance, the trader offering the opinion it was most likely his having broken through the spring ice dogs and all while making his final rounds for the season, for if he had met up with misfortune while on the trail the dogs would have chewed through their harness and have returned to the cabin. Well for what it was worth his theory to be as valid as anyone's, but my personal opinion which I kept to myself differed greatly, my not for a minute believing his having perished some where along the way, only convinced it having been time for him to move on deliberately revealing the location of the cache of furs for me to recover at will before doing so.

In all fairness the free trader saw fit to compensate me for both trips plus a substantial bonus leaving me with little to complain about, where ever freed had gotten to one could only wish that lonely taciturn man well in his new life, he was once considered a good friend and will always remain so in my thoughts and memory.

Occupational Hazards

AS CAN BE FOUND IN all occupations that extensively involves the transporting of goods and people, one can be certain of experiencing a plethora of pitfalls and associated hazards that one often has little choice but to contend with as part and parcel of the job, as bush pilots we as a matter of course transporting at one time or another just about every conceivable commodity possible.

Of a certainty we often faced manifold hazards while involved in doing so, weather being our biggest stumbling block, but poor maintenance practices on the aircraft coupled with large percentage of the companies one flew for that whole heartedly endorsed the "Simon Legree" attitude toward their work force.

Actually one of the worst scenarios one could wish to encounter usually occurred curing the height of the terrorist (tourists) season when the weather closed in on us preventing any further flying as if the god's of weather took great pleasure in humbling our efforts to be quit of the crowds of loud mouthed overbearing antsy fishermen who inevitably harangued us at every opportunity to near distraction often coming on with ill concealed derision and cutting remarks directed toward our being nothing less than a gathering of panty waist bush pilots at our adamant refusal to push weather just to satisfy their demands.

It has never ceased to confound me that those who knew absolutely less than nothing concerning bush flying or it's inherent hazards always the first to judge, it never entering their thick heads we hadn't survived as long as we had by taking unnecessary or foolish chances.

As upsetting the situation could be it often times became much worse when the god's of weather (mother nature) as if becoming bored with their lot required a bit of entertainment by creating what is known in pilot jargon as a "sucker hole", this consists of a patch of pristinely clear weather momentarily moving through the area with it's siren call luring the unwary or uninformed to foolishly venture out, often to their regret as within a short period of time the inclement weather would close in again usually far worse than before creating untenable flying conditions.

We as experienced pilots all too aware of this phenomena dug in our heels refusing to be pressured in to taking unnecessary chances just to please some one. Ultimately the ongoing whining and unrelenting harping directed toward our refusal to load up and go would eventually become unbearable to the degree of removing ourselves before the situation became over heated to the sanctuary of the hotel coffee shop if for no other reason but to preserve one's sanity or some one went too far as some of the hotter tempered pilots after a time being pushed to the bare edge of their tolerance could all too easily blow their cool resulting in more than a harsh words being exchanged.

On the occasion when involved in straight freight hauls during bad weather days with the dispatcher keeping up a relentless tirade of bitching and whining we would if the local weather picture allowed take off and gather at a pre selected "sanctuary" lake that offered an ideal sand beach to park the aircraft safely and far enough away the roar of the departing aircraft engines faded beyond hearing.

If it so happened the weather co-operated allowing our safely remaining where we were with no one wishing to chance pushing it any further we would build a huge fire and boil up our coffee pots, always being certain to have brought fresh and canned foods with us along with ample cooking utensils.

My being the inveterate fisherman made it a practice to always carry my fold up fishing rod with me to supply us with fresh caught fish that abounded in the lake, oh man were they some delicious served with fried potatoes with a side dish of pork and beans topped off with freshly brewed coffee while surrounded by the natural settings of a pristine landscape, what more could any man ask, it simply couldn't get better than that. To this very day them memorable times haunt my memories, often have I wondered why the good times are so fleeting, while the less than sylvan ones persist in bedeviling one, perhaps that concept is to found only in one's mind, but some how I don't really think so.

As the day wore on we kept a wary vigil on the local weather picture as we lazed about enjoying the camaradie that only those engaged in a common cause know in solid comfort free of all the normal pressures normally endured back at the base.

It was only natural the dispatcher would attempt to raise us on the radio, our foreseeing this possibility on the occasion transmitted a false message over one of our radios to side track him while pretending to not receiving his queries concerning our present position, if at any time he suspected anything we never heard.

Once having decided the day too far gone to risk being pushed out again or the weather becoming threatening would straggle away from our chunk of paradise to return to the vagaries of so called civilization, timing our individual take off from our lake to be certain of staggering our arrivals in order to land ten to fifteen minutes apart while chattering aimlessly over the radio. The dock boys as always greeting us with huge grins plastered all over their faces knowing to a man what had transpired, all of them at one time or another having participated. No doubt of our being consummate actors, not one of us at one time or another could have put the best of Hollywood to shame

On one occasion experienced the fright of my life upon allowing myself much against my better judgment to be bullied into flying a boat slung on a special rack bolted onto the float struts beneath the belly of the aircraft while loading two hefty fishermen and a fair amount of gear, up to that near fateful day had never flown a boat on a beech craft remaining totally ignorant of the consequences involved.

Not having any idea of what I was letting myself in for not prepared for what took place next. During take off it became immediately apparent the usual rapid rate of acceleration appearing to be somewhat on the sluggish side, the aircraft seemingly reluctant to leave the water when finally able to coax it to do so it's refusing to build the airspeed much past ninety miles per hour and that was at full throttle, the truth is we barely hung above the stall as a beech craft ceases to remain airborne once reaching eighty seven miles per hour leaving me with a mighty fine line to tread, as it stood a single hiccup from either engine guaranteed instant disaster.

Being so intent on the airspeed indication, momentarily forgetting about the distance remaining before reaching the far shore line, upon realizing my having left it till too late to safely abort the take having run out of sufficient space to touch down and bring the aircraft to a halt before running up on shore, leaving me with little choice but to keep on forging straight ahead as any attempt to make a turn at that low airspeed guaranteed one's instant demise, fortunately for all concerned the scrawny and well spaced pine trees that randomly poked out of swamp I was committed to dragging my ass over fortunately for all concerned offered me a way out, taking advantage of the situation desperately fire walled the engines into the over boost mode, an absolute no except in the case of a dire emergency, considering the situation had gotten as dire as it could possibly get with our buzz sawing our way through the top third of the trees that got in our way spraying branches and pine needles everywhere, fortunately again the neck of land being relatively narrow soon revealed the mouth of the shallow rock strewn crow river giving a much needed breathing space, but still it remained terribly dicey with our wings barely clearing the trees on either side of the river course calling for some fancy footwork on the rudder pedals to avoid contacting some of them.

As we continued to delicately thread our way the three seemingly endless miles before arriving at crow lake, we had just slid precariously around a wide bend to unexpectedly come up on and to frighten the living Jesus out of two canoeists who it appeared up till the time of our noisy and totally unexpected arrival had been enjoying nature's solitude, as we thundered on by a bare ten feet or less over their heads and as we did so my wondering if our slipstream had perhaps capsized them betting at the same time to their for certain requiring a change of shorts.

Not any too soon the most welcome sight of the river entering the confluence of crow lake as the cylinder head temperatures had climbed well into the never exceed zone, my immediately touching down on the welcome waters of crow lake without retarding the throttles a hair, once safely on the water the engines were allowed to idle for some time in order to bring the temperatures down, only then did the idea of checking my own shorts came to mind.

Upon finally able to shut down the engines found myself to be shaking like a dog pissing razor blades, furious with myself forever allowing the situation to deteriorate to the life threatening degree it had, once more proffered thanks to the deity that watches over brain dead bush pilots.

It took a fair amount of time of sitting on the roof of the aircraft to settle my ragged nerves while the slight breeze that blew the length of the lake slowly dried my sweat soaked body curiously watching the two obviously well pissed off canoeists paddling furiously as they bore down on us, on arrival a cute pug nosed red head immediately took it upon herself to climb up one side of me and down the other as she chewed my ass out to the quick, my being unable to suppress a wide grin at her flashing green eyes and the spirit of the righteous sermon she laid on me with righteous wrath, also the sight of her well endowed physique soon had my thoughts dwelling elsewhere, some how I don't think she reciprocated in kind.

Meanwhile my two passengers who had absolutely no idea of what had recently transpired, continued to stare mutely at me with bulging eyes that reflected total confusion almost causing me to break into restrained laughter.

Once having more or less gotten my self together dropped the offending boat into the water then tying it to an available snag that protruded from the bottom of the lake. Lacking the necessary tools to remove the offending boat rack it had to remain where it was until returning to base, just as well considering the foul mood I was in at the time it could have well ended up in the bottom of crow lake.

It was found during the return trip the aircraft still refused to handle normally due to the disturbed air flow created by the rack, upon landing back at base the offending rack was immediately removed to mysteriously disappear, my some what subdued passengers completing their trip in a more sedate fashion in the otter.

Well if that hair raising incident cold be construed as a lesson well learned, then it basically boils down to one has to first survive such an experience to derive the full benefit, yes one could truthfully say I definitely did but almost at a great cost to myself and two innocent passengers, from here on nothing external would be allowed on any beech craft I flew.

Sometimes later one of my fellow pilots met with disaster because of a canoe tied to the inside of the right hand float struts of the beech craft he was flying upon experiencing catastrophic engine failure on the right hand side shortly after clearing the shore line of a small narrow lake during take off, unable to reach the next lake to attempt an emergency landing in due to the fact the aircraft had become near uncontrollable barely hanging on the ragged edge of a fatal stall had little choice but to drive it on to the surrounding muskeg totaling the aircraft, fortunately neither him or his terrified passenger suffered nothing more than a violent shaking up, spending an endlessly long night battling off voracious hordes of mosquito's that were as he succinctly described it thicker than all the regrets in hell, one can bet they were more than grateful to be rescued by helicopter the following day.

One could never be certain when they would run into a situation far beyond one's control, one long remembered took place when being dispatched to retrieve an American hunter and his teen aged son, this being rather routine gave it little thought until arriving at the remote lake to be first met at the makeshift dock by the hunter's son, my being in somewhat of a foul mood from having spent the better part of the day involved in the muscle mangling back breaking job of wrestling on board great chunks of stinking moose meat plus having to suffer the indignities of pretending to be awed by how they had brought down an innocent animal using a scope sighted rifle of sufficient muzzle power to bring a Patton tank to a grinding halt, on top of it all while making a circling approach prior to landing spotted no less than three carcasses floating in the shallow water of a nearby river and being fed on by numerous ravens, at the time it must be admitted to my feeling a pang of unreasoning apprehension while taxiing into the shore line.

No sooner having climbed out of the cockpit before the hunter's son who without preamble launched into a horror story of how his dad had cold bloodedly gunned down the three moose floating in the river

for no other reason than he could, as if that wasn't enough to set me off proudly continuing on to inform me of his personally shooting no less than twenty six Canada jays (whiskey jacks) popping them off with a twenty two caliber rifle as they came in to feed on moose offal satisfying a blood thirsty desire to do so.

Already weary of it all and now further sickened and disgusted by the unnecessary carnage that had recently taken place unwisely shot off my mouth without taking into consideration the possible consequences of doing so when stating it to be highly illegal to kill more than one moose per one's license requirements, thus they could well be facing a world of trouble for having done so plus the fact that Canada jays were a protected species, the next thing I knew I suddenly found the business end of a gun muzzle pointed directly between my horns, I am not the least ashamed to admit the shock caused me to lose control of my bladder.

Up till then having faced many potential life threatening situations that more often than not came with the territory, but normally one more or less retained a degree of control over them, now it was a far different story with some one else having complete control over my fate.

As shocked as I was at the unexpected turn of events some how dredged up the courage to inform him if he was to do me in he irrevocably doomed himself to remain where they were until a search aircraft came looking for me. My already shaky knees threatened to buckle with relief upon noticing the madness glittering in his steely gray eyes slowly giving way to reason, perhaps it was his white faced son frantically tugging on his fathers arm while desperately entreating him not to hurt me that turned the tables, not for the rest of my days would I ever be able to wipe out the memory of that menacing gun barrel that had not once wavered a hair as he kept it pointed at me, never have I been certain if it was his intent to simply frighten me into silence or his finely balancing between sanity or insanity, to this very day it remains my absolutely firm belief it was his son tugging on his arm while begging him not to harm me that tipped the scales in my favor.

Once that most upsetting of situations had some what settled down with my attempting to bring about a sense of normalcy by insisting we load up and leave as soon as possible as I still had a busy day ahead of me, keeping up as much as possible a normal conversation between us fearing to act otherwise not being at all certain he wouldn't snap at any time, the time span spent loading and eventually finding ourselves on our way seemed to be the longest of my life, once getting back into the air immediately experiencing the most profound sense of relief at having survived and to have safely departed that place of horror. It took an act of intense concentration on my part to fly the aircraft in a normal manner while fighting extremely taught nerves that caused my control inputs to be jerky and uncoordinated.

Once having attained sufficient height a special frequency selected on the radio that would alert the person monitoring the frequency to have upon request a game warden and police officer on the dock to meet our arrival. The hunter who occupied the front seat along side of me warily demanded to know who I was communicating with, the hard eyed look that still retained a vestige of madness and the fact of his holding a still loaded rifle between his knees warned me to be extremely cautious, my matter of factly replying to be checking in at our main base as our usual protocol required, upon being informed appeared to somewhat relax, the saving grace for me at the time was my wearing a recently acquired set of modern head phones that boasted an attached boom mike that allowed one to speak into without being overheard.

The relatively short flight appeared to take forever, my overstretched nerves as tight as an over wound clock spring from the almost unbearable tension of the nerve unsettling fact his eyes never once ceased darting nervously from side to side as if half suspecting latent treachery.

Once arriving at our destination and carrying out what could be best described as more of a controlled crash than a normal landing with nerves all a jangle unconcernedly as possible taxied into the dock with his as I well knew he would be staring suspiciously out of the window for any sign of authorities in the form of game wardens or policemen, obviously to my everlasting relief finding nothing out of the ordinary concerning the bustling activity taking place on the dock.

The game warden and police officer in plain clothes had done it all many times over, therefore well practiced in the art of discreetly apprehending fish and game law breakers at the appropriate time. Sliding off the wing onto the dock unconcernedly walked up to the flight office on legs so weak and shaky it was all I could do to force them to function while as much as possible keeping my exposed back between the hunter and other people until gratefully able to duck out of sight within the office.

Discreetly observing the hunter out of the office window as he impatiently waited for his gear and meat to be unloaded, once that had been accomplished to his satisfaction and though remaining wary of those surrounding him found nothing to unduly alarm him nervously retrieved his vehicle and back it down to the dock, once they began to load up in preparation for departure the two law officers moved in on them flashing their badges, the police officer quickly seizing the still loaded rifle.

The hunter initially stunned by the totally unexpected turn of events quickly recovered unthinkingly attempting to retrieve his rifle by the use of force to overcome the police officer with the game warden joining in to the melee to quickly overcome and handcuff the desperately maddened hunter.

Upon being subdued and none too gently being hoisted to his feet he at my sudden appearance rounded on me with spittle spraying from his lips screaming I knew it was a mistake to not have blown your god dam head off while I had the chance you Canadian asshole, only the police officer restraining me from doing so spared him from receiving a well placed kick in the nuts or worse.

Once they had been taken away to be placed in custody with the police officer informing me of requiring a written statement in order to lay charges the long delayed re-action to the mind bending stress recently endured hit me full force leaving me violently sick to the stomach and almost too shaky to walk more than a few feet at a time, it had become readily apparent to all there would be no more flying done by me that day.

While resting in the security of my home did the worst of shock to my system begin to abate allowing my dwelling on the past traumatic hours, slowly beginning to realize my good fortune in having survived the all too real threat of death at the hands of a complete stranger obviously not completely in control of his mental faculties.

It not being unusual for us pilots to at one time or another to clash with what is loosely referred to as an American sportsman who often repelled and sickened us with their profligate attitude toward our resources openly flaunting our fish and game laws, out rightly acting as if it was their god given right to do so, for the most part encouraged by viciously money hungry camp owners (usually American owned) who saw it to be in their best interest to look the other way, it is no small wonder they are universally despised the world over as the "Ugly American".

Yes it was not an uncommon happening to be taken to task by an irate customer, but never in my wildest dreams ever conceive of any one outright threatening my very existence.

It took the better part of two days to return to a state of being more or less normal, now I had first hand experience of the meaning of "post traumatic depression" and how debilitating it could be.

As fate would have it another pick up of two moose hunters scheduled with me doing the flying, upon being advised a cold chill of apprehension ran down my spine with my coming within a hair of refusing to make the trip, suddenly realizing to keep on running away from reality would eventually cripple me permanently compromised by having one of our younger pilots accompany me. Upon arriving at the site marked on the map we could not locate hide nor hair of them eventually being forced to break off the search and return to base.

While enrooted I pondered the where abouts of the missing hunters and sometimes fishermen who had never been found, their fate remaining a mystery, many and varied are the tragedies that lay in wait for the inexperienced or unwary city type green horns when placed in a hostile environment they neither understand or worse yet underestimated it's dangers, many was the time I had been witness to tragedy in the form of gun shot wounds or the skeletal remains of a hunter or a fisherman who had wandered too far afield to eventually become hopelessly lost and to eventually perish from exposure, our on the occasion finding on arrival an overturned boat and an empty camp to bear silent witness to tragedy.

The most common by far being the advent of overturned or swamped boats and canoes due to inexperience or carelessness on someone's part.

_____ In one instance on returning as scheduled to pick up three moose hunters and while flying low over the lake they camped on some startled at spotting what appeared to be the bow section of an aluminum boat sticking out of the water, no one had to tell me a tragedy had occurred having witnessed it all many times before, just to be certain that no survivors remained at their camp, on arrival not at all surprised to find it empty and without question it had been some

time since anyone had been there. Circling the shallow sandy-shored lake in a vain effort to spot a possible

survivor or a body washed up, but only able to spot two bright red gas cans and some other unidentified objects washed up on a beach, during my final pass over the far end of the lake the furtive movement of either an animal or survivor moving through the thin undergrowth a short ways back from the shore line caught my attention, further investigation proved it to be the father of the two missing hunters who in spite of being without shelter of any kind had miraculously survived five days and nights of frosty late fall weather, subsisting on the offal from the moose they had killed on the first day of their hunt.

Upon landing and taxiing into shore he surprisingly enough when approaching him, his instead of falling all over me with relief at being found instead totally ignored my presence and initial attempts to speak with him with my being unable to make sense out of the litany of incomprehensible words he repeated endlessly as he drifted back and forth along a well defined path worn into the soft earth, the results of his endless pacing, only ceasing at spaced intervals to peer hopefully over the wide expanse of lake before once resuming his endless pacing. During one of his forays I managed to catch a few words as he drifted on by not seeming to take note of my presence at all, as close as one could tell they were the same ones repeated endlessly "the boys should be on their way back to get me any time now", his wide open unblinking eyes informed me beyond a doubt of his having slipped into a world of his own.

One didn't have to be overly astute to arrive at the conclusion of what had led up to the tragedy, two large men, a heavy load of moose meat, inexperience in handling an overloaded fourteen foot boat during passage to their camp through a following sea, a guaranteed recipe for disaster upon an overly large wave washing over the stern instantly swamping them, the icy water quickly dooming them to a fear filled death, upon the bodies eventually being recovered the following spring it became apparent that neither had worn life jackets, not that the wearing of them would have saved them, only prolonging the agony not to mention the cold hard fact their heavy parkas and boots would have eventually overcome the buoyancy of the life jackets dragging them down.

One can never be absolutely certain of the father having witnessed the tragedy, but I for one firmly believe his having done so, the mind numbing shock and helpless despair of watching his two sons drown too much for him to accept eventually allowing his escape into a world of his own.

Goddamit, how my heart went out to the old man, but there was no reasoning with him, his only blankly avoiding entreaties to return with me, but that in itself left me in a quandary, it would not be a wise move on my part to have a mentally unbalanced passenger in the cockpit with me, one could never be absolutely certain were that could lead to. With the bitterly cold short fall day rapidly coming to a close informing me of having to leave soon if wishing to land back at base before night fall.

As much as a difficult and detestable decision it was for me to make, it left me with no choice but to abandon the old man to the rigors of another frosty night without shelter. The overriding sense of guilt and shame that swept over me at having to do so tore at my sense of decency long after my departure, futilely attempting to justify my actions by consoling myself he had managed against all odds to have survived thus far, hopefully another night would not make an appreciable difference.

But still the very thought of an unpredictable late fall storm possibly moving into the area during the night left me in a terribly upset state of mind, for if that were to occur it would without fail seal his fate, in retrospect one wondered would that be such a terrible fate, for upon being rescued in all probability would have little else to look forward to but a cramped cell in a mental institution. Briefly considering not reporting finding him to the authorities, soon abandoned that line of reasoning as common decency forbade abandoning a helpless old man to death by exposure, besides that who was I to play "God".

Having managed to raise the base on the radio requested the local constable meet me at the dock upon arrival.

As requested the constable met me, but there being far too many curious bystanders hovering about we ended up in the privacy of his cruiser were he immediately began to tape my testimony on a portable recorder, at the conclusion it shocked me speechless upon being informed that considering the circumstances surrounding my testimony if further investigation proved it to be true I could be charged with abandonment, or depending on the state the police officer found the old man upon our eventual return possibly charged with involuntary manslaughter,(put that in your pipe and smoke it).

At the conclusion of my report the police officers statement it found me in a confused state of mind at the gravity of the veiled threats and feverently wishing to have gone about reporting the tragedy in a far different manner arranged an early morning departure to pick up the old man.

As it went the long night hours also finding me pacing restlessly with the haunting memory of the old man all alone to face another bitterly cold long night, that and the not so subtle threat from the police officer hanging around my neck did little in the way of insuring one's peace of mind, try getting some sleep with all that thrashing around in one's mind, goddamit how helpless I felt, it seemed every time one dealt with the minions of the law one invariably ended up with one problem or another.

As the excruciatingly long night dragged on with my coming near to wearing my own path to the door when every ten minutes or so anxiously checking the weather, finally giving in to overwhelming anxiety returned to the base arriving just as the first streaks of gray dawn stained the horizon with a faint blush of pink portending the arrival of inclement weather within twelve hours or less chilling me to the bone, at that time of the year the weather picture was never certain causing my anxiety to soar to new heights. Having readied the aircraft for immediate flight upon the police officers arrival our departing immediately. It soon became obvious the police officer did not welcome an early morning flight appearing to be withdrawn with an ill concealed air of hostility directed toward me, but for what it was worth I could have cared less. Once established at our cruising altitude sat back and reflected on the manifold reasons the average person remains on the most part extremely reluctant to communicate one on one with police officers in general if it could be at all avoided, being it mattered not how well intentioned or honorable one conducted themselves toward them, they unintentionally or otherwise never failing to leave one feeling sullied, perhaps it was their holier than thou power trip attitude that turned one off, the female officers generally being the very worst, they're mistakenly thinking they had something to prove.

The what if's that continued to race through my overtaxed mind as if following a closed loop, came near to driving me around the bend as the seemingly endless miles crawled on by with my becoming so agitated as to almost bounce in my seat.

On finally arriving at our destination my black mood left little room for niceties, my on the spur of the moment deciding to give the sulky police officer something to think about by performing one of my run away elevator landing approaches, well one can be certain that sure got his undivided attention, his eyes reflecting absolute terror, bracing his hands against the seat arms as he helplessly stared at the rippled surface of the lake rushing up at him as we descended at what it must have seemed to the uninitiated an impossibly steep angle with my flaring out at the last possible second to make a perfect touch down.

Normally reserving that type of landing when alone, it never being my policy at any time to deliberately frighten innocent passengers, but the police officer's generally sour demeanor throughout the whole ordeal finally deciding my handing out some of my own

While taxiing in anxiously scanned the shoreline for a glimpse of the old man near collapsing with relief to see him stumbling weakly along his well worn path. At first the police officer only able to sit and stare in complete disbelief at the sight of the old man making his endless rounds, that's when it dawned on me his at no time believing a single word I had said, that explained his hostile attitude toward me.

A sudden unreasoning anger and resentment of the shabby treatment received at his hands earlier on swept over me prompting my throwing decorum to the winds and snarling at him to get off his fat ass and do his god dam duty, his marked hesitation informing me his having no idea what to do next, it remained his call with my remaining clear unless officially requested to intercede.

The police officer to his credit initially attempted to reason with the demented old man to no avail, his only ignoring the police officer only continuing to maintain his endless vigil as if we didn't exist. The threatening weather picture that presented ominously dark snow clouds on the far eastern horizon that were fast moving in prompted me to inform the police officer our remaining time to deal with the old man becoming critically short with the leaden gray skies portending severe blizzard conditions in the near future, as if to verify my tense observation a few random snow flakes began to drift gently downwards a precursor of worse to come.

The alarming prospect of possibly being caught by bad weather seemed to break the officers indecision, his adroitly tripping the old man as he drifted on by, immediately pouncing on him to pinion his arms and handcuff him. As much as it bothered me to see the tactics used against the helpless old man who flopped aimlessly about while uttering heart felt appeals to please leave him there as his boys would soon be coming to get him, god dam how his pleas to be left alone ate at me, but the law is the law and shall not be trifled with regardless of not at times making much sense but still must at all costs be observed as after all the learned law makers having in their infinite wisdom surly covered all and any eventuality when it came down to protecting one's self from one's self.

Often have I questioned to no avail the illegality of the laws that removed the right of an individual to die as they saw fit where, when and how they chose, after all it is their life.

Well be as it may, it had become imperative we depart that place of misery and heart break and soon if we hoped to leave ahead of the rapidly approaching storm. Fortunately the old man remained docile offering no resistance upon being placed into the aircraft to be ignominiously cuffed and strapped in to his seat while copious tears of grief coursed freely down his weather beaten cheeks.

Some how it appeared to me even in his seeming dementia well aware of being forced against his will to leaving his two sons behind, god dam how my heart went out to him, an innocent victim of a terrible tragedy, perhaps he was not as far gone as first surmised.

The police officer insisted we first make a brief stop over at their camp about five miles further down the lake to as he subtly put it retrieve their personal possessions, this request going against my better judgment leaving me reluctant to do so, but upon realizing my failing to comply with his official request risked my coming under suspicion for any number of reasons, reluctantly complied.

It took the threat of leaving him behind if we didn't leave forth with as the snow flakes had begun to swirl about in Ernest on the rapidly rising wind, what it was he so intently sought I didn't know and cared less, only wanting to be gone. As it went we barely scraped our way home with a full blown screaming blizzard nipping at our tail the whole way, once moving into the area continued to rage insensately for three days and nights freezing over all but the largest deepest lakes in effect putting an end to our float flying season much to every ones relief.

They took the old man away, where to I never knew, but often one wondered how it would have gone with me if we had not by the narrowest of margins saved the old man from a certain fate?, perhaps it's best one didn't know the law being as convoluted as it is. The following spring the bodies of the two missing hunters recovered after five intensive days of dragging the lake bottom, finally bringing on closure to a grief stricken family. One annual event we all had learned the hard way to remain wary about concerned the return of the native fire fighters to their respective reserves at the

conclusion of the fire fighting season. Flush with accumulated back pay without fail cleaned out the stores of any and all video related items that the veteran store manager being well aware of this annual occurrence had the shelves overflowing with every known electronic gadget or gizmo available, and of course a virtual landslide of batteries to power them along side of mountains of various foodstuffs not normally available on the reserves, of a certainty this resulted in a considerable build up of excess weight, but that minor problem easily resolved as the tax paying public absorbed the added expense of chartering additional aircraft. The most interesting part of it all took place when the "cast iron" suit cases they had previously purchased were tightly packed with as many bottles of booze as could be stuffed in, they're gurgling a merry tune in concert with the heated curses of the dock hands as they heroically wrestled the coffin sized suit cases into the waiting aircraft.

Actually if the truth be known it was a big joke all around as by law we were forbidden to transport booze into any reserve, as it stood every one concerned up to the local law enforcement well aware of what took place, legally we were not allowed or authorized to check the contents of personal baggage.

But as the scheme of things went we were inevitably subjected to a backlash that more or less remained in lock step with the charade, for we never landed within sight of the reserve, only meeting up with a bevy of pre arranged boats far out of sight of the reserve that awaited us to spirit away the illegitimate cargo and it's owners of course, this act of a certainty construed by the RCMP as smuggling.

Eventually as we knew it would the event of a knock em down drag em out snot dripping barn burner of a drunken set to that rocked the reserve back on it's collective heels with the non drinkers taking to the hills or canoes to escape the inevitable carnage. The shamefull fact that those in charge of the reserve that should have at least demonstrated a vestige of leadership in most cases whole heartedly joining in, of course they were usually the ones when all has been said and done to create the loudest protests.

At times things might have gone too far with someone on the reserve being outright murdered or badly injured creating a god awful ruckus with the law inevitably jumping on our backs about transporting booze, but lacking concrete evidence of our deliberately committing a misdemeanor there was little to be done about any of it, outside of our receiving the usual veiled threats the matter quietly dropped. What has been written up till now can be construed as being only the tip of the ice berg when taking into consideration that manifold hazards that existed at any given time in our line of work.

Cold weather operations being by far the most demanding and dangerous times for us, inclement weather topping the list or sub zero temperatures that often did strange things to machinery, bad ice conditions, heavy snow and slush conditions to contend with, huge rock hard drifts that if landing on could all too easily damage an aircraft, this is only a partial list of the hazards that could trap the unwary.

We more experienced pilots went to great lengths to insure our well being knowing the price of carelessness could exact a very high price.

Suitable survival equipment could spell the difference between bare survivals or a modicum of comfort if by circumstances beyond one's control being forced down in sub zero temperatures.

It had always been a firm policy of mine to carry an ample supply of home grown "fire starters", these consisted of using a one pound tobacco tins stuffed with a full roll of toilet paper, then saturated to capacity with a fifty mixture of eusol and alcohol then tightly replacing the lid and sealing it with duct tape.

If and when it became an absolute necessity to as quickly as possible build a life saving fire, it was a simple matter of chopping a large gash through the lid of the "fire starter tin" employing an axe or knife to do so, then dropping in a lighted match to instantly produce a blue white extremely hot flame, one only has to add small pieces of twigs and correspondingly larger chunks of wood until obtaining a large warmth producing fire, the importance of being able to quickly create a life giving fire during sub zero temperatures can not be adequately stressed.

Considerable experience when forced by circumstances beyond one's control to have to force land and stay the night pretty much taught me to adhere to a strict order of first building a good sized fire then one turned their attentions to constructing an adequate shelter, it being a usual practice of mine to set up a small lean to facing the fire using a fairly large tarpaulin, then setting about cutting sufficient pine tree branches to serve as a comfortable mattress under my five star sleeping bag, only then taking the time and effort to pack one's tea pail with snow while keeping a sharp eye peeled for rabbit turds or yellow snow (the rabbit turds make the tea taste bitter), while waiting for the water to come to a boil one during the interim busies themselves retrieving their survival gear from the aircraft and preparing the aircraft for the night. Only then does one feel relaxed enough to sit back and imbibe in a nervous cup of tea

Establishing a sufficient supply of wood to last the night usually takes precedence, but can be done at one's leisure time allowing.

I can't speak for any other but doing so well before darkness sets in as it would be extremely difficult if not next to impossible for me to venture outside the glow of the fire light, even though there is nothing to fear, the only valid explanation for harboring that unreasonable state of mind could be the emergence of our ancestral past.

We may feel that in this day and age we are far too sophisticated and informed to think that way, but in truth it is really not that great a space of time since we swung down from the trees. Upon inquiry it came as quite the revelation to discover that a large number of trappers, both native and white shared the very same hang-up, it would appear our ancestral past still lives within our physic, strangely enough this unexplained phenomenon rarely if ever manifests itself during the summer months.

But then again our lives are full of small mysteries and unexplained events, they may only show with a subtlety only hinting to us of the unknown, and so we often place them in the margin of our lives, and within days or weeks we tend to forget they ever took place, other events are less easy to ignore and when we sift through the unadorned facts of their existence we are usually left confused as they do not conform to the world we know and like to believe we understand.

Of the many and varied types of aircraft flown at one time or another, the Beech-18 also known as the "Wichita Wonder", a twin engine aircraft of remarkable abilities when flown on ski or float gear. Having flown every available model in excess of seven thousand hours finding it to be my very favorite aircraft.

The only mechanical down side to an otherwise excellent in all respects aircraft was it's often troublesome electrical system that included the battery charging circuit and the starting motor system.

If one happened to be in a wheels or ski configuration, then starting motor or solenoid failure posed little problem as one could easily start the engines without the use of mechanical aid by what is known in pilot jargon as "hand cranking or bombing", this potentially dangerous method called for extremes of caution, but on floats it presented a very unpleasant aspect when required to do so, if a dock being available to stand on it made the situation all the easier, but in bush flying that is not always the case, I wish to make it clear that as many times I had been forced by circumstances far beyond my control to perform that most precarious procedure, at no time ever feeling at ease while doing so.

As it went the first year of flying a beech one found themselves involved in a steep learning curve, one of the first times the necessity to hand crank the left hand engine occurred upon finding myself as far away from any form of assistance as one could get having dropped off a group of six commercial fishermen on a far northern lake. Having ever so cautiously eased the aircraft into a rocky shore line that offered the all to real possibility of damage to the floats if a on shore wind should unexpectedly gust up, the interim between docking and completing the off loading kept me in a jumpy and agitated state of mind until finally able to fire up the right hand engine to gratefully taxi away from the threat. One can only imagine my surprise confusion and finally deep dismay upon punching the starter button for the left hand engine with nothing happening, at first my mind unable to accept this unexpected turn of events, my trying everything possible to no avail until the cold hard fact of my being totally screwed with no dock to return to and no where to turn for assistance, like it or not it was totally up to me to bail myself out of a bad position.

Taxiing in ever widening circles frozen with indecision as what steps to take next in order to alleviate the thorny problem, it finally dawned on me the only way out was to hand crank the engine, but how could that be safely accomplished without a dock?, never had I ever heard of it being done, when one thought about it how did one avoid the spinning propeller blades once starting the engine, there was simply no way.

To this very day it is not clear to me how the answer eventually arrived at, but as far out a gut wrenching solution as it well might be there remained no alternative even though the thought of physically doing so caused my breaking into a cold sweat.

Shaking violently from fear and anticipation began laying out one of my long ropes to insure it's conforming to the full length of the float plus an extra five feet to allow for sufficient slack then idling back the right engine to it's slowest idle locked the throttles of both engines after setting up the left hand engine for starting.

My next move was to shed all my clothes to instantly bring on an onset of violent trembling knowing all too well what unpleasantness was to come next, easing my way down the fixed ladder to stand bare assed on the ice cold float with the cold wind exacerbating my trembling almost to the point of being unable to proceed, my resolve coming within a hair of failing me contemplated giving it up before logic reminded me there was no other alternative but to continue on as best as one could.

Bracing myself by clenching my teeth against the cold wind carefully secured one end of the rope to the ladder, then double looping and securing the other end around my waist to in a state of pure unadulterated terror get down on my knees to crawl along the top of the float through the tangle of float struts until emerging in front of the engine.

Having at one time or another hand cranked every aircraft flown, beginning with my old tiger moth no stranger to the risks involved, but never in such a potentially dangerous position, standing there half frozen from cold and mind numbing fear staring at the formidable propeller, my shaky resolve totally abandoning me upon taking into consideration the all too real possibility of losing one's balance with no way of restraining one's self while heaving on the propeller blade with predictable results once the engine started, it simply couldn't be risked.

Torturously making my way back through the tangle of cold greasy float struts the rough surface of the float making further inroads on my already painfully raw knees crawled back into the cabin to procure a short length of rope to take back to the front of the float with me.

Gritting my teeth against the fiery agony of my now raw and bloody knees, once more determinedly crawled my way back to the front of the engine to face the mind numbing task of securing the looped rope over the front float bollard, carefully adjusting it's length to conform with my requirements that allowed me sufficient reach to swing the propeller.

Being so taken up with the formidable task facing me, completely forgot about group of fishermen who had watched my bare assed antics with wonder and undisguised curiosity, not having a boat as yet unable to come out to inquire if perhaps I had lost my mind.

But what really shook them up them was the advent of my bodily throwing myself sideways into the icy water upon the engine starting leaving them wondering if perhaps I had flipped my lid.

Being dragged at the end of the rope in that icy water until with far greater difficulty than first thought with pure undiluted fear of drowning goading me on till finally with a great effort managed to force my well stiffened limbs to co-operate, barely being able to pull myself up along side and to with considerable effort manage to crawl up onto the rear of the float, the entire sequence of events not something one would care to repeat too often.

Once retrieving the long rope shakily crawled into the security of the cabin weak with relief to have that most trying of ordeals done with .

Once having donned my clothes wasted no time taking off for Lynn Lake in a satisfied state of mind at overcoming such a formidable problem setting the cabin heaters to full hot in an attempt to alleviate my violent trembling.

Now having the time to reflect on past events, the sobering realization it could have all too easily gone the other way, upon initially giving the propeller a mighty snap it much to my surprise resulted in the engine suddenly and unexpectedly starting up momentarily stunning me for a few long seconds before being able to get my act together and throw myself sideways into the icy water to be almost instantly jerked painfully up against the side of the float to have a fair portion of skin peeled off my right arm as the aircraft taxied past, the shock of being suddenly immersed in the cold water instantly took my breath away leaving me to gasp and strangle until by sheer effort of will power manage to haul my near frozen body out of the freezing water losing a little more hide in the process while braving the icy blast of air from the propeller but all in all most happy to be there.

On arrival back at Lynn Lake and repairing the electrical fault returned to the lake to be met by a vastly relieved crew of fishermen, one could be absolutely certain of their having something of interest to relate to friends and family.

To a man, we all dreaded late fall float flying season with the low temperatures turning the spray from the propeller blast into ice that coated the floats and undersides of the aircraft gradually causing the aircraft to become logy and unresponsive, the extensive use of grease coating the exposed surfaces somewhat alleviated logy problem but not entirely. To make it doubly difficult the rudder cable system and the sheaves they rode in even though heavily coated with grease still froze up creating steering problems on the water that caused much concern and related difficulty while attempting to dock. Venturing out onto the slippery ice coated float in an attempt to free the cables or kick down the rudders which often froze in the retracted position an extremely risky proposition at any time requiring great caution on the pilot's part to avoid ending up in the icy water, climbing up and down the ice coated ladder rungs frightened me the most, an inadvertent slip guaranteed to inflict severe injury if not worse

In some cases the icing problem became so severe as to freeze up the elevator controls markedly restricting movement making any regime of flight extremely dicey, sometimes forcing the pilot to using only trim and engine power to retain a semblance of control, usually when it got to that stage further flight considered to be too risky curtailing the season with our breathing a collective sigh of relief at doing so.

Flying over mostly ice-covered lakes with only the largest and deepest of them still remaining relatively ice-free did little for one's peace of mind. On one occasion while checking out a newly hired Otter pilot on the basic rudiments of tying on and flying a boat, doing so much against my better judgment as if there was ever an aircraft despised by me it had to be an Otter.

In this case ending up in an unforeseen life and death struggle with my coming within a hair of losing the fight.

Once arriving at our pick up point indicated on the map we found it much to our dismay to be a poorly selected shallow rock studded shoreline calling for extreme caution on our part in approaching.

As it went we from the very beginning experiencing a very difficult time of it with one or the other taking turns standing in the shallow water preventing the shoreward float from grinding against a jagged rocky ledge as the slight on shore wind created a swell that tended to force the aircraft side ways while the other labored mightily while sweating copiously to load the seeming mountain of sometimes heavy and bulky camp gear that awaited us.

The conditions we labored under proving to be so difficult it taking far longer than it should have. We were definitely relieved to finally accomplish that difficult task, but there was no way in hell we were about to attempt to tie on the boat in them conditions as it would require a maximum effort on both our parts to complete such a demanding job so it was wisely decided to tow it to a more suitable location.

While my continuing to hold the float from contacting the rocky ledge the young pilot hurriedly climbed back into the cockpit to start the engine, one can only begin to imagine my disbelief and dismay at observing the propeller only giving a couple of weak jerks before ceasing to rotate at all as the battery went completely flat. My first reaction being absolute dismay, the next total confusion as what to do next, then a burning anger taking over while wondering just what that young peckerhead had at such an inappropriate time screwed up.

Finding myself so pissed off at the totally unexpected turn of events completely forgot about being immersed in ice cold water, only standing there while great confusion ruled the moment, just then he stuck his head out of the cockpit door eyes protruding like over sized golf balls to inform me of the obvious fact that for what ever reason we had lost battery power, his intent stare beseeching me to create a miracle, well for what it was worth he was out of luck, it not being my thing to walk on water or perform miracles, but still what to do? that thorniest of questions hanging over us like a black cloud.

At first totally confused by it all floundered miserably with our for the first while continuing to stare vacantly at each other as if waiting on divine intervention.

Being as we were totally screwed literally finding ourselves between a rock and a hard place with no obvious way out, as fate would decree it the wind began to freshen the gradual pitching motion building up to the point of making it increasingly difficult for me to avoid being caught between the float and the rock ledge, it being a certainty to remain where I was guaranteed severe injury, having got the message in spades but barely having done so when a larger than normal swell all but washed the float over me with my coming within a hair of being knocked over with my once recovering wasting little time scrambling out of there to safety, to hell with the god dam float, my continuing state of good health far more important to me than a pile of aluminum scrap.

Predictably once allowed to do so the shoreward float immediately began to grind and crash against the rock ledge, each nerve wracking contact causing the entire airframe to shudder in protest, one didn't require being a rocket scientist to arrive at the conclusion it to be a very brief matter of time before the float becoming severely damaged irrevocably dooming the aircraft and stranding us for the duration, something had to be done to and god dam quick to bring to an end the terrible pounding the float was receiving and it best we be bloody quick about it if certain disaster to be avoided. As is normal for me, once getting past the indecision mode usually able to think clearly allowing my mind during a period of high stress to reason my way out of most any emergency as we did in this case by employing near man killing effort to place the aluminum boat between the float and the rock ledge

The demands of placing the boat where it would do the most good left us near exhausted taking the time to catch our breath while viewing with some alarm the vicious pounding the boat was receiving, oh well I reasoned, better the boat then the float, but regardless of the fact we had come up with a temporary fix to one of our problems we still faced insoluble problems as the situation could not and would not remain in our favor for too much longer.

Again something had to be done if we had any hope of salvation, once again an idea that as far fetched as it first appeared to be with only a remote chance of succeeding was to if at all possible hand crank the engine, attempting to do so considering our less than favorable circumstances a long shot at best but what alternative did we have?

Upon informing the young pilot of my intentions, he at first stared open mouthed at me as if having taken leave of my senses, in a way his questioning my intentions understandable, an otter an easy enough aircraft to hand crank on wheels or skis, but extremely difficult if not impossible on floats, but again what choice did we have but if at all possible it would be attempted.

My heart sank to my toes upon viewing in helpless indecision the formidable task that lay before me, how could anyone unless happening to be seven feet tall or built like an ape or sasquatch swing that huge propeller while standing up to their ass in the water, well be as it may the lord hates a coward, but then again even lowly cowards are sometimes capable of performing great deeds.

The nerve wracking sounds of the boat gradually being pulverized goaded me into action, our taking the chance of wrestling that ungainly beast of an aircraft with no little risk to our selves further ahead to meet with another rocky outcrop that jutted a fair ways out into the lake.

With the nose of the aircraft pointed at a slight angle out toward the open water, the outcrop offered me near sufficient height to swing the propeller. Having clearly instructed the young pilot on the correct sequence for hand starting, pulled the propeller through while desperately hanging on to the wildly heaving float bollard in an attempt to steady myself until finding what is referred to in pilot jargon as 'Bounce" this in effect tells the person swinging the propeller the piston is on the compression stroke and most likely the first to fire, after many futile attempts at swinging the propeller that failed to start the engine leaving me near exhausted from the demanding effort, on top of being confused and perplexed as to why it refused to fire up as normally radial engines started easily, breathlessly yelling at the young pilot to switch the magnetos to the "off" position to allow my once more rotating the propeller to locate a bouncy cylinder, his totally unexpected answer leaving me stunned upon blandly informing me they had been in the "off" position all along as I as yet had not instructed him to switch them to the "on" position, god dam his bone headed unthinking stupidity, one would have thought he would have known better.

It took all the will power I could muster to prevent myself from swarming up into the cockpit and to bodily heave him into the lake, all that saved him from that ignominious happening was the fact of his being required in handling the engine controls if and when the engine started, otherwise there was little doubt of my having hesitated for a second in doing so, but as I was to soon find almost to my lasting regret he wasn't quite done making life difficult for me yet.

Standing up to my ass in the freezing cold waters reflected on what a hell of a position to find oneself in, my lower extremities having lost   all   sensation from the waist down (call me numb nuts) while my top half soaked with sweat from the man killing exertions required to swing that huge propeller. The cold water aided immensely in assisting to by degrees subvert the black rage that still threatened to boil over at any time, calling on my remaining patience clearly instructed the dick head of a pilot in a voice choked with emotion to be certain to place the "god dam" magneto switches into the "on" position and to if he valued his life to remember to press the "magneto booster button", once having verified he understood my instructions took a deep breath before giving the propeller a mighty heave, just about falling flat on my ass from fright upon the engine suddenly roaring into life at a far higher throttle setting than normally called for, it then became glaringly apparent to me that god dam bone head of a young pilot had gone into the panic mode, as the aircraft attempted to surge ahead, the right hand float swinging viciously toward me barely allowing enough time to duck under the spreader bar that had come within a whisker of mowing me down as the float partially climbed the side of the outcrop to then slide off sideways with a resounding crash and a welter of spray to continue bumping and grinding over the boulders until reaching deeper water with my at the last possible second making a desperate grab for the retracted float rudder desperately hanging on against the drag of the fast moving water knowing that to lose my grip guaranteed certain death by drowning, Christ that god dam water was cold, so god dam cold it all but paralyzed me. The overriding certainty of eventually losing my grip if not removing myself from the water post haste spurred me on to by the dint of sheer will power enhanced by a pure unadulterated desire to survive greatly aided my efforts in finally managing if barely so to drag myself clear of the water onto the rear float top removing a goodly amount of hide from my shins and knees in the process.

As if my unwelcome and unplanned baptism in the icy waters not enough for one day now forced to endure a virtual hurricane blast of icy air from the propeller as the bone headed young pilot in his panicked headword rush to place a goodly distance from the threatening shoreline had as yet to slow down while not for a second taking into consideration of what had become of me.

Desperately hanging on to the rudder cables while slowly and painfully inching my way to the rear cabin door all the while finding it unbelievable how stupid and unthinking the pilot was, his never for a moment considering slowing down and turning back to check on my welfare, at that point the horrifying specter of his being in the panicked state of mind he was could at any time unthinkingly decide to take off with me still clinging desperately to the float dooming me to a terrible death, that revelation struck me like a bolt of lightning.

If I had been near frightened out of my wits from the results of the past events it seemed as nothing in comparison with the horrifying thought of such an event taking place all but immobilizing further action on my part, fortunately good old fashioned debilitating mind paralyzing fear took over spurring me on with my determinedly crawling up to and clinging desperately to the steel ladder leading up to the rear cargo door requiring brute force reinforced by cold numbing determination to barely be able to pry it open against the propeller blast, but sheer desperation aided greatly in allowing my eventually squeezing through with great difficulty leaving a fair amount of precious skin behind before gratefully gaining the safety of the cabin, oh man not having the strength to do anything else for the first while but to lie panting on the cabin floor hurting something god awful, my poor bruised and beaten knees and shins having received brutal punishment now covered with drying blood not to mention the skin scraped off my back and ribs from my desperate efforts to squeeze through the door that guaranteed hurt city for some time to come, on top of it all shivering violently like a dog pissing razor blades, but as far as that went a little pain considered a small price to pay, all in all it could have turned out much worse, the suffering yet to come would of a matter of course be dealt with, it was great feeling to still be alive and well consoling myself with the thought if one's a hurting they ain't a dead.

Lying on the cabin floor in a state of near exhaustion attempted to marshal my thoughts while contemplating how close I had come to being wiped out of existence solely by the unthinking stupidity of another. After a brief spell of recovery it was time to deal harshly with that dick headed young pilot who mindlessly continued to bore on never at any time slacking his panicked charge leaving me wondering if he had taken leave of his senses, seconds before my coming up behind him it must have suddenly occurred to him of my being left behind, his just beginning to turn to go back were it had all begun, by the greatest of chance and determination had managed to survive solely on my own, it was well I had otherwise my chances of survival if having had to depend on him to return and pick me up before succumbing to the cold water nil to none.

What I had to say to him is at best unprintable, the long trip home the last one he would ever make for the company, his kind not required or welcome amongst our ranks.

As for the boat it was left behind to it's fate, we never knew much less cared what become of it.

Many and varied are the hazards a bush pilot faced during the course of their career, the one that profoundly sticks out in my mind through the years occurred one winters day while flying in questionable weather conditions that at one point found me over a huge stretch of muskeg dominated terrain while on a return trip to Pickle Lake, the weather picture having gone from bad to terrible within a short space of time, the reduced visibility barely offering sufficient forward visibility to maintain tree top height over the few scraggly trees that sporadically existed in the area with my after a time becoming uncertain of my exact ground position.

After flying along for another half hour or so had become totally confused and uncertain as to my ground position only able to spot the course of the odd river as it meandered through the featureless muskeg.

As if the situation not alarming enough it became that much worse when the heavy snowflakes began to stick and build up on the wing surfaces, now that was bad news for me as if it continued to do so the aircraft would gradually become too iced up to maintain flight, I had to get down and soon.

After a period of white knuckling it, as if in answer to my desperate plight what appeared to be a lake suddenly materialized out of the gloom directly in front of me with my immediately throttling back to slow down for a landing, upon touching down it was instantly noticed the aircraft appeared to be decelerating far quicker than normal, thinking my having inadvertently encountered deep snow and slush instantly rammed on full power to direct the aircraft toward the low lying muskeg shore line, not stopping until having driven it up high and dry.

Breathing a sigh of relief at my deliverance immediately set about seeing to the aircraft, not at all surprised to find the skis piled high with slush which was immediately removed before it could freeze solid, then jacking up each ski and placing lengths of scraggly pine trees under them to prevent their freezing to the muskeg surface.

Not being certain as to how long the bad weather would persist set about building a good sized fire and dragging in an ample supply of wood to last the night if it came down to that.

A brief foray out onto the ice soon informed me of the absolute necessity of packing down a runway before night fall if one wished to leave as the depth of slush and snow found to be the deepest I had ever encountered in the area, also something about the depth of the slush bothered me, but for the life of Christ could not ascertain at the time just what it was, only giving in to the inevitable and strapping on my snowshoes to begin laboriously packing a runway. For some reason not clear to me at the time kept the course of packed runway as close to the low lying shoreline as possible.

The short winters day fast coming to a close before completing packing the runway to my satisfaction, barely leaving me sufficient time to set up a camp for the night, it was with great relief I finally found time to boil up water for a cup of tea and thaw out my supper before calling it a day and turning in for a well deserved rest.

My intentions to have a good nights rest went for naught, something intangible incessantly gnawed at me disturbing my sleep, but try as I might failed to come to grips with what ever it was leaving me in an agitated state of mind that only allowed short periods of sleep before jerking wide awake, this unenviable and unwelcome state affairs lasting through out that longest of nights with my on the occasion giving it up and sitting next to the fire gazing uncomprehendingly out in to the stygian darkness beyond the circle of fire light.

Morning couldn't come soon enough, my impatiently awaiting the dawn so as to get an idea of the weather picture, it having continued to snow all night long somewhat relieved to at the first hour of a gray overcast morning to take note the pall of snow appearing to be coming lighter and hopefully to lift completely within the next hour or so as to allow my leaving.

While awaiting the weather to improve, busied myself in cleaning residual snow and ice off the wings and tail surfaces, noting with relieve and satisfaction the weather to be improving steadily took down my shelter in preparation for departure at the first opportunity. At about mid morning the snow fall ceased so suddenly it was as if someone had lifted a veil, my solely by chance happening to be looking toward the far end of what I had at first assumed to be a long narrow lake shocked speechless upon noting what appeared to be a fair sized cloud of water vapor rising up in the still air as if out of nowhere, a quick look at the other end of the long stretch of what I now knew to be a river indelibly informed me of what I already knew, I had in error landed in a stretch of river that had only formed a thin skim of ice and snow directly between two sets of fair sized rapids and by the dammdest stroke of fate had against all odds survived, the blood chilling thought that had I been flying any less powerful and low winged aircraft then a beech craft, there remained little doubt of my immediately breaking through the shell ice never to be seen or heard from again.

Near paralyzed with fright and indecision it took a concentrated effort on my part to start the engines and warm them up prior to taking off on an improvised runway packed down on ice, one could not be certain of, but what choice did one have? it came down to all or nothing, once satisfied the engines to be sufficiently warmed up and checked, set the flaps into the full down position, then steeling myself for whatever came next rammed on full throttle, never had I known that certain aircraft to take to the air after such a short run as it did that morning, using up less than half of the packed runway, sure enough upon getting safely into the air an extended circle over the area verified what was already certain, but what really choked me up was the total absence of ski tracks where I had landed and taxied in at a high rate of speed, the only sign of my ever being there was the packed runway and of course were I had driven the aircraft up onto the muskeg, leaving that place that had come so close to claiming my life a pleasure to never return to rated highly on my things to do and some glad to be able to return to Pickle Lake.

Some time later while in an introspective state of mind got to pondering the why's and wherefores of certain incidents that had at one time or another befallen me, the one that through the years that remained poignant was the exceedingly brief take off run from that threatening stretch of frozen river, often I have stated that a machine such as an aircraft is only that if one thinks of them that way, I for one have always thought of an aircraft or as far as that goes any machine as a living entity having an individual personality and not simply a soulless unfeeling mechanical contrivance. Ask any deep-sea sailor about the personality of the ships they sail on, you may receive some strange and unexpected answers.

This may earn me a fair share of disbelief and derision, but truthfully it is my firm conviction the aircraft sensed my fear and indecision and reacted accordingly.

This is only a brief and minor description of the hazards of the hazards routinely experienced by Bush Pilots and unsung engineers who unstintingly gave their all toward the profession.

In time as one became older and correspondingly wiser, it not being uncommon to begin to question our seemingly blind dedication to the aviation industry that for the most part not only offering deplorable working conditions along side of miserly wage compensation.

But one was not forced to remain in the industry against their will, one did so a matter of choice it not only being a means to the end but also a life style for a good many of us.

But as in any industry, everything has it's breaking point and upon us older thoroughly dedicated professionals began to be taken over and replaced by an emerging work force of college trained highly technical whizz kids that came armed with a virtual armory of superior intellect concerning the new generation of modern aircraft technology it became obvious it now time for my generation to bid the industry adieu.

Yes one can truthfully say the many years spent as a Bush Pilot and Aircraft Engineer were truly rewarding, but one can overstay their welcome with my reluctantly removing myself from the only world I ever knew and never returning.

In summation I have stated it many times before and most likely to repeat it many times more before time erases my memory.

If one is not living on the edge, then they are only taking up space
Hartley A. Weston Former Bush Pilot and Aircraft Engineer

438

A Pilot's View Point
On Flying A Beech-18

WHAT DEFINES THE CHARACTER OF a story, adventure far removed from the ordinary, risks taken to accomplish a difficult undertaking, the excitement of living on the edge, the fulfillment of doing what one wishes to do?, actually all the preceding, but rarely if ever is it stated or has it ever become common knowledge the difficult choices and sacrifices often demanded of those choose to follow their dreams. If by some remote chance a true to life realistic life style of a hard core dedicated 'Bush Pilot" ever produced, it would in it's entirety contain a greater amount of far out drama than the movie "

"Casablanca"while portraying a greater amount of edge of your seat excitement than any "off the wall" Hollywood screenwriter could ever begin to imagine .

Of all the various aircraft flown at one time or another, my all time favorite had to be the twin engine "Beech 18", be it configured with a set of floats, ski gear or wheels they all in their own way offered a unique challenge throughout the changing seasons.

To begin with the twin beech series is and always has been from inception one of the aerial wonders of aviation, it's sturdy construction and sleek outlines contributing greatly to the advancement of modern day aircraft. As a child growing up in a remote mining town known as Red Lake, located in the wilds of North Western Ontario where few roads outside of the bush trails used by the cat swings existed at the time the area depending heavily on the aviation industry to supply it's needs, we were always treated summer or winter to a virtual wonderland of early type aircraft including fokkers, junkers, bellancas, fairchilds, norseman, stinsons etc. not to mention a colorful variety of contraptions of doubtful origin that on the occasion graced the local skies, no matter who their manufacturer or their pedigreed I was totally fascinated by them all while they in turn all stirred up a strange not yet fully understood

longing within me.

As it went one fine day the most beautiful of aircraft I had ever seen up till then suddenly appeared at the dock, "CF-BGY" the first beech -18 I had ever seen haughtily standing 'out like a pea cock among common chickens, resplendent in her sleekness and sky blue livery, a virtual fairy queen amongst a motley appearing entourage of vintage winged wonders.

Right there and then it could only be construed as a naked longing to be captain of such a marvelous aircraft, though not deluding myself for a minute that in order to accomplish such a lofty goal would require unswerving devotion on my part for a good many years.

CF-BGY as found out later belonged to Starret Airways of Hudson Ontario and having the distinction of being among the first of it's type to be placed on a set of Edo floats and a set of unique appearing skis that enabled it's being placed in service during winter operations.

Unfortunately CF-BGY was to have a relatively short service life, ending up in a fatal crash enrooted from Red Lake to Hudson Ontario, the cause being ultimately traced to a carbon monoxide leak in the cabin heating system. Many years later after by dint of sheer perseverance in overcoming the myriad of difficulties eventually obtaining my pilot's license after completing a demanding often discouraging climb from the humblest of beginnings found me with reams of experience on many and varied types of aircraft, but I had as yet to realize my goal of captaining a Beech Craft as at the time they were not as yet that widely in use by most operators, and what there was almost called for a an act of parliament or one had to be far better connected than I was at the

time to even think of ever flying one. Well in time fate saw fit to decree it so, it so coming about my being advised

of a fish producing company wishing to expand the scope of their operations had recently acquired a Beech-18 from the War Assets Corp. and having a set of brand new floats installed at Bristol Aerospace in Winnipeg Manitoba and actively seeking a well-qualified pilot to fly it on floats and skis.

Having nothing to lose by applying for the position even though lacking a minutes flying time on a Beech Craft, but a fair amount of time on Anson's (Bamboo Bombers) and a light twin designated as a T-50 Crane once used as training aircraft by the armed forces managed to BS my way into being considered for the job, fortunately for me not too many pilots desired to make a full time career of lugging fish in a beech craft leaving the field fairly wide open.

Having applied for the job during the winter months leaving the remote possibility of being considered very much up for grabs as the season did not begin till late April or early May it proved to be some very long months of nail biting anxiety while awaiting for word from the company, never did time drag by more slowly but eventually much to my relief the long awaited phone call came requesting my presence in Winnipeg to complete the required paper work etc, I strongly suspected once they had short listed the prospective applicant had chosen me not only for my flying time qualifications but also taking into consideration my holding an Aircraft Maintenance Engineers certificate, thus killing two birds with one stone for the price of one.

Upon arrival at Riverton the owner and I saw to the placing of the aircraft into the water, once ready he placed himself into the right hand seat to observe my non existent skills as a beech craft driver, my not in the least lacking confidence in my abilities played out the role of god's gift to the world of aviation fired up the engines in what I thought of as in a very crisp and professional manner, then continuing to play "Joe Cool" quickly accomplished all the pre-flight checks, finally yanking up the water rudders once lined up with brisk breeze that blew straight down the pike to then advance the throttles to the take off power settings.

My gawd, the rapid sequence of events that took place next all but left me stunned as my mental state still lay firmly entrenched in the doggy Norseman take off mode, to this very day would swear to that marvelous beast of an aircraft being empty and light on fuel blasting off the water so rapidly we left our shadow behind with our almost immediately entering a fairly steep climb out, Christ if it so happened we had crashed shortly after leaving the water, I remain certain of my mentally remaining back at our initial take off point distractedly observing it's taking place.

It took a heart beat or two before my being able to catch up with the aircraft to ease off on the climb out attitude and reduce power while establishing a more normal state of affairs, all the while feeling some foolish about the cowboy style take off and at the same time feverently hoping to not having blown it, much to my surprise and great relief the owner of the aircraft instead of censuring me for displaying such blatant showmanship gave me an appreciative slap on the back enthusiastically stating I sure as hell knew my stuff when flying a beech craft and informing me I was hired.

Man if he had ever tumbled to the fact that high performance beast of an aircraft had initially left me in it's dust when unexpectedly sizzling off the water with my for the first few seconds grimly hanging on and going along for the ride, he might have reconsidered.

As it went my spending three years flying that marvelous aircraft through out the provinces before the cessation of all northern commercial fishing operations controlled by private fish companies came about, subverted by brain dead politicians who didn't know the first thing about the commercial fishing world desiring the industry be a totally government controlled enterprise, needless to say in the end like all government controlled entities the fish marketing corporation due to incompetence on the part of the government hacks that oversaw the day to day operation eventually brought on it's downfall predictably wasting millions of dollars of tax payers money, but the damage was done, to this day very few commercial fishing operations exist. Having flown a Beech Craft in every known configuration for the last three years had no problem at all in finding employment with an outfit known as Severn Enterprises who's stable of aircraft included a good many of them.

The fact that they're being located a good many miles off the beaten track in a tiny hamlet known as "Pickle Lake" made for difficulties in attracting qualified personnel, usually ending up with the washed up dregs of aviation who had pretty much reached the end of their careers.

Moving my family to that remote hamlet quite an experience in it's self, terrifying my wife half to death as we pounded our way north hour after endless hour once leaving the town of Savant Lake, the last of what passed for a semblance of civilization before resuming our journey on what appeared to be an endless stretch of teeth rattling vehicle destroying gravel surfaced road the endlessly long hours of driving causing one to question just what had they let themselves in for this time. Personally once we arrived and more or less settled in we soon became entranced with the anything goes life style as did my three children. Five years later when it came time to leave we all had tears of regret in our eyes.

The terrain surrounding the area soon discovered to consist of matchless beauty, my finding the extremely diversified landscape to be so unique, only the far northern areas of the province of Saskatchewan could begin to rival in offering a seemingly endless plethora of beautiful lakes and rivers, to the east stretched what to a new comer appeared to be miles of low lying muskeg that stretched clean to the shores of Hudson's Bay, an area that within a relatively short space of time I would become as familiar with as my back yard. Flying a Beech Craft on floats or skis had always seemed less of a job than a passion, flying sedately along on a pleasant sunny day could only be compared to having a ring side seat while observing a National Geographic presentation slowly unfolding in front of one while comfortably ensconced in your favorite chair. But regardless of the fact of being a great aircraft to fly it had its times to be reckoned with. On one memorable occasion while returning from a long trip with eight passengers aboard who had long since slipped into a deep sleep, my flying west directly into the sun that along with the mesmerizing drone of the perfectly synchronized engines had lulled me into a near comatose state of relaxation eventually falling asleep at the wheel.

Fortunately for all of us the twin beech is an exceptionally stable aircraft, trim it for level flight and employing rudder trim if required once setting the desired directional reference referring to your gyro compass, then one can with complete confidence remove one's feet from the rudder pedals, slide the seat back and relax, the aircraft will do the rest maintaining the selected heading and altitude until the pilot desires otherwise or the fuel tanks run dry.

As it went we eventually overflew our destination continuing to drone on in a westerly direction much to the consternation of the dock hands who observing my passage overhead informed the dispatcher who's incessant demands crackling in my head phones as to where in the hell was I going that finally roused me.

Fortunately all the passengers remained in a deep sleep, once having become fully aware of my predicament and cleared away the cobwebs of sleep humiliated and angry at performing such a brain dead act quickly oriented myself while discreetly performing an oh so gentle one hundred and eighty degree turn all the while cursing my stupidity, oh man I was in for it for some time to come. Once having established my heading to return to base soberly reflected on the last thirty-five minutes or so spent fast asleep, giving thanks the twin beech was as stable as it was.

The passengers to the best of my knowledge remained fast asleep until landing at Pickle Lake and far as I knew never the wiser.

Eventually it turned out my having amassed so much twin time arbitrarily selected by the mandarins of the company as a check pilot. It seemed a marked deficiency concerning correct single engine procedures existed within the ranks resulting in a far above normal rash of accidents attributable to incompetent pilot age during in-flight emergencies.

A short course by an accredited Dept. Of Transport airworthiness inspector gave me the required training within specified guide lines to check out existing and aspiring twin engine pilots in order to bring them up to standards.

A few of the pilots initially checked out absolutely shocked me at their demonstrating a near negligible knowledge of performing correct in flight emergency procedures, in some instances coming near to scaring the hell out of me while attempting to do so during a training session leaving me to wonder as just what in the hell was I doing there?

One certainly did not expect to be looked upon favorably during the period of time it took to satisfactorily bring the twin engine pilots up to standard, the satisfactory completion of the training syllabus reflected heavily upon me, so no mercy or exceptions granted to any one, once completing their training to my satisfaction a mandatory check ride that required a satisfactory passing grade by an accredited airworthiness inspector an absolute requirement if one wished to remain with the company Strangely enough while acting as a check pilot much to my and every one else's surprise failed a check ride due to the fact of my shutting down an engine and feathering the propeller so quickly it caught the ex air force airworthiness inspector completely by surprise with his screaming at me about my stupidity was going to kill both of us and demanding my immediately firing up the engine post haste. Totally confused by it all complied with his panicked request immediately, once the engine was back on line he coldly informed me of failing my ride and to return to base.

Much later it was revealed that the Canadian air force does not train their twin-engine pilots to shut down an engine and feather the propeller during flight as I made it a common practice to do, only simulating it.

Well one can be absolutely certain that got the attention of the brass, some high level string pulling must have taken place from the ivory tower forthwith as within days another airworthiness inspector appeared on the scene, this time a far more reasonable amiable type I had met before and held a warm respect for.

His first words upon greeting me was that he had found it difficult to believe my having failed a check ride on such a flimsy excuse, stating for Christ sake, how can any desk bound civil servant, ex air force or not who spends eight hours a day five days a week shuffling mostly meaningless paper work back and forth in a climate controlled office while you guys labor under the most intense demanding environment imaginable on an ongoing basis begin to pass judgment on how well you perform your duties as a bush pilot, something you guys do every single day, seven days a week, it simply does not add up in my mind, sometimes this beauracratic BS is almost more than I can tolerate, know any good fishing holes?, well I most certainly did with our going fishing in grand style once advising the dispatcher of our planning to be gone at least three hours.

The airworthiness inspector treated to three intense hours of the finest fishing he had ever experienced leaving him totally wrung out and a cooler full of fillets to take home with him, once we returned to base the appropriate paper work completed to the satisfaction of all with my being reinstated as twin engine check pilot. Some times there are strange things done beneath the noonday sun.

If the truth be known, check rides are only part of the equation and do not at any time guarantee compliance with the rules as set out by one's training for as in all things familiarity breeds contempt, two of the pilots I had initially experienced great difficulty in training to standards, they're at best only reaching a marginal level of competence no longer cast shadows.

For whatever reason their premature demise brought on by gross failure to observe iron clad rules that inexorably applied during single engine flight, of course in the end the aircraft was blamed for being unstable during a critical flight regime.

At no time could I ever take credit for not at one time or another grossly screwing up, to do so would see me as lying outrageously, one does not gain valuable experience that goes far toward ensuring one's ongoing survival without making gross errors and surviving them, if one is wise then one learns from their mistakes as I did when unexpectedly being confronted with near disaster.

During the first hundred hours or so of flying a twin beech my confidence in my abilities kept pace with my ego setting me up for a fall. In one instance experiencing a nerve shattering close call while landing with a heavy load of fish, having become some what arrogant and over confident regarding my expertise at making power off (dead stick) short landings with a full load aboard, in this instance foolishly allowing the air speed to degrade dangerously during the round out phase of the landing.

Having made a steep approach and just beginning to pull the control column back to level off the aircraft, having no sooner done so when the tail section began to hammer violently with the control column taking on a life of it's own rapidly shaking back and forth scaring the hell out of me, at such times one does not have the luxury of protracted analysis, one either reacts within a split second to hopefully alleviate the problem or it's game over, my without thinking instantly ramming on full throttle just barely doing so in time to prevent stalling on to the water in a tail low position to in all likelihood destroying the aircraft and possibly fatally injuring myself, as it was the near uncontrolled descent and following contact with the surface of the lake severe enough to create a spectacular bounce causing me to cringe in shame and fear. Once having more or less collected my wits slowly taxied in to the dock to give myself the required time for my feet to partially cease dancing all over the rudder pedals and my sweat soaked body to dry out some what, to say the least flirting with disaster unintentionally or not certainly gave one something to think about, not to mention it certainly took the wind out of my sails for some time to come.

What ever had gone so wrong that near fateful day haunted my thoughts incessantly. Having had the living Jesus scared out of me, not about to go about discovering what had taken place while flying a heavily loaded aircraft, once was enough thank you, I might not be so fortunate to escape disaster next time.

It took awhile before realizing the chance to climb an empty aircraft to eight thousand feet plus and to perform a series of slow flight tests that conclusively proved it to be virtually impossible to stall the wings in slow and level flight, but soon discovering the tail section another matter, it's instantly hammering violently as it approached an insipient stall when pulling back on the control column at too low an airspeed, at the conclusion of my experiments I knew what I had done wrong that day and eternally grateful for having survived it, thus becoming a much better and wiser twin beech pilot.

As we are all aware, no matter who we are or what our vocation we all retain the capacity to learn and profit from past mistakes, but however diligently one attempts to shape their destiny, one simply gets caught up in often unplanned or

unforeseen sequence of events as the following outlines. In time I came to the inescapable conclusion that the average bush pilot (I

never viewed myself as being average) to be a compromise between the fool hardy and the nervous with guts and common sense enough to tackle a dangerous or risky situation, but sense enough not to do it if any way out presented itself, yes without question a little scare now and then went a long way toward keeping a pilot on his toes, but god dam it man like me and so many others we had so many of them throughout the years we could have been centipedes

One near miss that occurred during a period when we were busily engaged hauling humungous chunks of back breaking finger mashing muscle straining pieces of greasy diamond drill equipment into a site located within the end of a blind bay parallel to a fast moving river, no pilot deliberately chooses to land in the restricted confines of a blind bay but the treacherous ice surfaces of the river dictated the choice.

As long as the weather remained cold the ski bottoms met with little resistance on the frozen ice surface one had to exercise great caution during their landing approach as to not come in at too great a speed and running out of available space ending up on the shoreline, taking off the other way while empty normally created no problems, that is until one fine day when the temperatures had risen sharply softening up the surface of the packed runway causing the snow to stick to the bottoms of the skis increasing drag, not giving it too much thought as once unloaded blasting off for Pickle Lake.

Unknowingly at the time I had stepped into a trap of my own making, only becoming aware of that fact upon the tail of the aircraft immediately lifting into the flying position much sooner than normal once full take off power had been applied with my soon discovering that pulling back the control column to it's limit failed to force the tail down while much to my dismay discovering that any attempt to reduce the power settings only exacerbated the problem when coming within a hair of stubbing my toes and digging both propellers into the runway surface.

Quickly recognizing the problem but remaining totally at a loss as to what to do about it, but something had to be done and god dam quick like as the available runway shortening up rapidly.

Man, this time around I sure as hell found myself between a rock and a hard place, unable to gain sufficient flying speed to break free of the clinging snow while at the same time unable to cut the power as to do so guaranteed standing the aircraft on it's nose inflicting a great amount of damage.

One can never say for certain why one does what they do at such stress filled times, but for some unexplained reason I could never reasonably explain made a wild grab at the flap control handle yanking it into the full down position, at that the aircraft literally exploded straight upwards and to immediately assume a horrendously nose low position along with an as yet low airspeed causing the wings to wobble alarmingly from side to side like the cheeks of a fat lady's ass while climbing a set of stairs with my frantically dancing on the rudder pedals in a near vain attempt to keep them level until sufficient flying speed built up and not a second too soon with my barely scraping over the trees that lined the bottom of the bay, once again it was shaken in boots time having avoided potential disaster by the narrowest of margins, the nerve rattling experience leaving me in such an agitated state of mind my feet continued to dance all over the rudder pedals for some time to come.

During the interim it gave me time to reflect on what had gone so terribly wrong, another hard lesson learned in the school of hard knocks that would not be soon forgotten, but Still one knew with a certainty there would be many more to come before the rug was pulled out from beneath me.

One of the strangest non-life threatening incidents to occur during my career took place while checking out a recently acquired twin beech.

Having taken along one of our aspiring young pilots for company decided on giving him some twin engine training after wringing out the aircraft to my satisfaction demonstrated a full engine out procedure with the engine shut down and the propeller feathered, after completing a series of single engine flight procedures fired up the engine again, when satisfied it to be performing satisfactorily began the shut down procedures on the other engine as always performing the required moves in a smoothly co-ordinate manner, once the engine had almost ceased turning pulled the propeller pitch control lever back into full coarse pitch position while simultaneously punching the feathering button, at that very moment the still rotating propeller entered a series of violent convulsions to such a frightening degree surging and vibrating to the point of threatening to tear the engine off it's mounts, it's unexplained gyrations all but causing me to piss my pants.

Up to a point nothing I attempted appeared to dampen the severe gyrations until in sheer desperation slowing the aircraft down considerably where upon the propeller rotated through one last shuddering revolution before ceasing it's gyrations, but not before having attained a half feathered position that created a terrible drag.

Having had more than enough and not willing to take any further chances elected to make an emergency landing on a near by lake.

Once safely on the water made an attempt to check out the propeller feathering function to no avail only meeting with failure no matter what, then it suddenly occurred to me the high pitched protesting whine of the high pressure oil pump that usually emitted from the wheel well when activated to be conspicuously absent.

Well that completely threw me, having previously checked the pump breakers finding them in the set position leaving me wondering were to turn next, as it stood unless coming up with some form of a solution to our problem it was glaringly obvious we were going no where, not knowing were to turn next taxied into a nearby sand beach to think it over.

Not having tools of any sort aboard much less having any great desire to delve into the mechanical functioning of the system decided to resort to a low tech method of twisting the propeller blades back into their normal fine pitch position.

Cutting down two sturdy poles with my axe and flattening one side of each about a foot in length at the approximately half way mark, tying a rope loosely around each end of the flattened areas, then sliding the two poles over one of the propeller blades approximately a third of the way along it's length and then the two of us applying a twisting motion to the blade until slowly forcing it against the fine position stop.

Satisfied all to be well we cast off from the beach to restart the engine and return to base to report the mechanical dysfunction to the base engineer who to his credit got right to it in tracking down the problem, shortly after doing so called me back to the dock to point out the problem, a close perusal inside the wheel well showed the complete feathering pump assembly had been removed and the oil lines that were usually attached to the unit capped off, Christ, one could have swept me away with a feather at seeing that, the base engineer initially tending toward dismissing my claim of the propeller partially feathering claiming it to be mechanically impossible, if by chance I had been alone at the time there would have been no way in god's green earth of my convincing him otherwise, only the young pilot's testifying to have witnessed it happen more or less convinced him it's having actually taken place.

Later on the base engineer and I discussed at great length how such an unlikely malfunction could have possibly taken place, our in the end arriving at the conclusion no clear cut reason existed why the propeller had reacted as it did, putting it down to a combination of a high forward speed coupled with my rapidly placing the pitch control lever into the full coarse position.

The subsequent installation of a feathering pump along with replacing the propeller which had begun to indicate signs of internal distress resulted in a fine performing aircraft I ultimately selected as my personal steed. The one thing a large majority of us twin engine pilots held in common was a tendency to wring the most out of our aircraft, often pushing it well beyond it's certificated parameters often scaring ourselves skinny during the process, no one I ever was aware of pushed it to the point of inviting certain disaster, but one can

be certain some god-awful close calls occurred from time to time. Due to the beech crafts requiring high take off and landing speeds one studiously avoided taking off or landing in rough water conditions as the aircraft did not come equipped with spreader bars between the floats thus one could all too easily impose excessive torsional stress on the airframe. Also it was a good practice to never if at all possible to attempt a down wind

landing or in a stiff cross wind if it could be at all avoided, during landing in either condition the twin beech on floats retained a nasty tendency to viciously swing down wind just as one is slowing prior to falling off the float step, at this juncture directional control quickly becomes minimal at best possibly placing one in hurt city.

As to be expected we often faced excessively rough water conditions we were expected to land on, the normal practice at such times was to choose a relatively calm area such as behind an island or a sheltered bay, then to slowly taxi through the area of rough water into our intended destination, but the catch being a suitable protected area not always available or of short length with one invariably overshooting their available landing area to end up jolting to a stop in an impressive amount of spray in the very same swells we had so conscientiously attempted to avoid. The hairy times could arise while attempting to turn the aircraft around and taxi down wind, the beech craft retained the ability to turn around in any wind condition, but one risked having a gust of wind picking up a wing halfway through a turn creating a frightening scenario as the float crashed back on to the water with a severe jolt that often vibrated the entire airframe, but worse yet was to experience a severe gust of wind suddenly getting under one's tail section to elevate it to an alarming degree leaving one staring fixedly at nothing but frothing water as the fronts of the floats buried themselves causing the propellers to pick up and fling back sheets of foaming water over the wings and windshield as one involuntarily leaned as far back in their seat as possible in a vain and utterly useless attempt to place their weight further rearward, only relaxing one's ridged posture upon the front of the floats once more breaking clear, it was always with great relief when one finally reached calmer waters. At times we were forced to delay our departure until the wind and waves subsided sufficiently to allow a take off without subjecting the aircraft to severe abuse.

Having faced the above dilemma far too often, decided enough to be enough one day when a rogue wave unexpectedly curled in behind me coming within a hair of broaching the aircraft, as it was quick action on my part only just prevented that occurrence but both engines came close to being drowned out as we dove into a trough, It is today as it was then a mystery to me how they managed to keep running after ingesting so much water, if they had both quit it is anyone's guess what would have taken place next, and if the truth be known I really didn't care to find out.

Well that hairy experience decided me, it was either find a solution to my problem when faced with less than ideal landing conditions, one way or the other it became imperative to come up with a sure fire method of reducing the amount of space required, either by making a much slower approach which was not always possible, or devising a method of drastically slowing down one's forward speed upon touch down or just plain give up on chancing it. Reflecting back on the days of flying the venerable "Norseman" brought back with instant clarity of a moments inattention during the landing phase when unthinkingly allowing the front of the floats to dig in decelerating the aircraft so rapidly water sprayed all over the windshield scaring me skinny.

Well that definitely gave one food for thought, but not in the least certain as to how an aircraft that landed as fast as a twin beech would react under such adverse circumstances, approached the experimentation phase very cautiously, gradually increasing the pressure on the front of the floats at each landing over a period of time until discovering one could safely apply full forward pressure on the control column immediately upon planting the full weight of the aircraft on to the water without it's indicating any tendency what so ever to swerve to one side or the other or to attempt to bite it's ass as did the Norseman, further experiment conclusively proved that when fully loaded the aircraft reacted somewhat differently then when empty shuddering to almost a full stop in a third of the distance normally require.

But one soon learned through trial and error the procedure not totally free of inherent risk for if one were a bit tardy in releasing the forward pressure on the control wheel as the slipstream over the elevator rapidly bled off to the degree of not generating sufficient force to hold back the natural buoyancy of the floats against the water pressure creating an imbalance of one force against another with the floats suddenly and unexpectedly popping out of the water with great force to violently slam the tail down into the backwash. in some instances the aircraft could well jump clear of the water potentially placing one in harm's way, this phenomena often happens to careless or unthinking flying boat pilots and is referred to in pilot lingo as "porpoising".

One soon learned the hard way that upon the aircraft decelerating to a certain forward speed it was imperative to release the forward pressure at exactly the right moment and to place the control column in the neutral position and above all hang on tight with both hands.

The absolute necessity to hang on tight cruelly demonstrated during the first time a full "Weston's short stop" method attempted, as was usual the controls placed in the neutral position holding on to the wheel with one hand with the other holding the throttles, the next thing I knew the control wheel viciously slamming against my chest not only surprising the hell out of me but also experiencing being painfully winded as the control column whipped backwards from the force of the backwash hitting the elevator as the aircraft settled off the step, one could say it was a lesson well learned. In time and continuous practice eventually became quite adept at performing unbelievably short landing, one can be certain this hard won learning experience came at a cost frightening myself but good on more than one occasion.

The remaining pilots who on the occasion had viewed my antics with great trepidation to a man refused to even entertain the thought of learning from me how it was done, collectively viewing me as a certified nut case who had never recognized his limits, perhaps they had a good point, but then again that's who I am. Of all the far out of the ordinary experiences to cross my path the most outlandish of them began upon being selected by the insurance company to test fly rebuilt aircraft, of course these duties being insufficient to keep me occupied the company saw me as a likely candidate to fly aircraft that had been changed over to floats off of a "dolly", a sturdy four wheeled cart with two fixed large rear wheels and two much smaller full costarring double wheels in the front on which an aircraft that had been changed over to floats was placed in order to take off

from a standard runway. I wish to make it plain that no form of prior training or check out methods

existed at the time, one just referred to long years of experience coupled with caution and common sense, but even at that it had its days.

Once the aircraft had been placed on the dolly, a light cord was attached to the float of the aircraft and then to a spring loaded brake handle located on the dolly braking mechanism, once the aircraft lifted off the dolly the light cord yanked up the brake handle actuating the braking unit before snapping off, this procedure normally brought the dolly to a screeching halt within a very short space, that is if all went according to plan, but that was not always a guaranteed happening, on the occasion something going awry with the dolly continuing to wobble wildly all over hell's half acre sheering off multiple runway lights on both sides off the runway before gradually slowing to a halt, in some instances losing it's equilibrium and tipping over to cartwheel end over end before eventually coming to rest in an impressive cloud of dust, strange as it may sound, it's being constructed so sturdily that rarely did any telling damage occur.

The normal procedure as follows consisted of towing the dolly out to the runway, once the tow bar removed and the dolly given one last check for serviceability, the pilot once receiving the all clear left to his devices.

As long as all went according to plan flying a twin beech off a dolly a normally straight forward matter, being so powerful it accelerated very quickly to effortlessly lift off the dolly within a short space of time, a slight cross wind was no cause for concern as one could employ asymmetric steering by leading with the upwind engine.

One of the never to be forgotten incidents that came within a hair of rubbing me out took place one beautiful sunny afternoon while flying a twin beech off the dolly, at such times sequences of events occur very rapidly demanding intense concentration and if one is wise they do not allow their attention to wander even for a split second.

Up to a certain point all seeming to be going well after applying full take off power with the aircraft accelerating smoothly with my keeping an eye on the airspeed indicator which had just reached the sixty five mile per hour mark when suddenly feeling a faint shudder course through the airframe for a split second before finding myself staring at bare runway at a very unusual nose low tail high attitude, at such times one does not have the luxury of protracted analysis, one either responds to the emergency on the very instant relying on long years experience with my instantly slamming both throttles wide open while simultaneously yanking back on the control column with the aircraft barely assuming level flight just as the floats made heavy contact with the hard surfaced runway with a resounding crunching noise causing the aircraft to immediately ricochet back into the air vibrating like an oversized tuning fork, to this very day I can still retain a clear and vivid impression of the instrument panel gauges suddenly begin to blur before my very eyes as did the wingtips.

Only the fact of my inadvertently having lowered the flaps to their full down position prior to take off along with instantly ramming on full emergency power and being a low winged aircraft utilizing ground effect kept me airborne if only barely so for the next few seconds with everything hanging in balance until the forward speed increased to a safe degree allowing my cautiously retracting the flaps a little at a time until the airspeed built up.

Up to that point being so taken up with handling the emergency, still hadn't fully realized what had so unexpectedly and without warning taken place, it was only upon gaining a safe height and the confusion that wracked my mind had some what settled down and upon circling back over the runway shocked to see the dolly to sitting in the middle of the runway no where near as far along as it should have been, then it came clear what had recently transpired to prematurely catapult me off the dolly leaving me facing imminent disaster precious seconds before reaching a safe lift off speed, the realization bringing on a violent shudder that coursed clean through me, for what ever reason it was apparent the braking unit had malfunctioned almost instantly bringing the dolly to a tire burning halt and pitching me off the dolly. How much closer one could have come to certain disaster and somehow survive I couldn't say and if the truth to be known did not care to find out, as it was if the brake unit had activated when my airspeed was much slower there was no way in hell that anyone no matter how experienced could have possibly maintained flight once bouncing off the runway, one would have simply stalled out and crashed with predictable results.

Having through the course of my career survived many a hairy experience well aware that what ever happens, does so for a reason, well so be it, but that tid bit of knowledge did little in the way   of ensuring my peace of mind, it still remained for me to land safely while not knowing if any structural damage had been incurred to the airframe during the severe impact with the runway.

As the aircraft appeared to fly normally made a few low and slow as I dared fly by's in order to allow the ground crew to asses the damage as best they could, the blood chilling information relayed over the radio gave me the expected but blood curdling report that both float bottoms to be severely damaged plus the rear float struts also appeared to be damaged, well that for certain ruled out landing on the water leaving me with no choice but to land on the grass strip.

Normally that was no big deal having landed a twin beech on floats onto a grass strip many times before, but this time around the fact the float bottoms being damaged and certain to create big time drag on touch down left me between a rock and a hard place.

It took some time for me to dredge up sufficient courage to attempt a landing, but the longer I delayed the twangier my nerves became, finally convincing myself the sooner I got it over with the better, as it was my already being soaked with sweat from good old fashioned fear and shaking like a dog pissing razor blades

Steeled myself for what ever lay ahead began to make a long slow as possible approach dragging it on with full flap and carrying a lot of power, the initial touch down immediately followed by severe deceleration, but no were near as first feared, but that's not saying it didn't have is moments as it certainly turned out once the full weight of the aircraft settled on to the grass the nose pitched violently down and forward while I impotently rammed on full power while pulling full back on the control column to eventually come to a grinding halt in very short order amidst an impressive cloud of dust and chunks of flying turf.

Deciding that was enough excitement for one day popped the top hatch to climb out of my seat soaked with sweat and to slide gratefully out on the wing with legs so shaky they almost refused to function, standing there watching the crowd of gawkers who had observed my spectacular landing come charging out to view the aircraft, they reminded me of a flock of vultures descending on a carcass in order to pick it over.

Not wishing to answer the sure to come questions of those the incident didn't concern in the least discreetly slipped off the wing to make my way to the hanger, and while there to visit the lavatory to check my shorts in private.

Once the aircraft had been removed to the hanger, an in depth inspection surprisingly revealed only minor damage to the airframe considering the terrible abuse visited upon it, the two rear float struts required replacement and the two rear attach points on the main structure severely buckled requiring repair, other than the floats which had taken the brunt of the impact with the hard surfaced runway receiving extensive damage requiring a major overhaul, upon completing the inspection the overall damage to the integrity of the airframe considered slight, one had to admit them beech craft sure were tough buggers. It is and will always remain so my honest opinion the Twin Beech is the one of the most

454

versatile aircraft ever to be placed in service as a "Bush Plane", without question it retained as all aircraft do inherent weaknesses, but they on the average

few and far between. The float mounting structure by it's very design lacked the robustness found

on the average bush plane calling for the pilot to exercise due diligence during operations in severe conditions, other wise they were an absolute pleasure to fly on floats.

When placed on skis they were an unparallel marvel to fly, fast, efficient and reliable in all conditions, if any weaknesses surfaced while mounted on ski gear I was never aware of it during the many years of flying them. In summation, I wish to point out that any short sighted detractors who found fault with the Twin Beech, they in my opinion to be sadly wanting, as the old saw goes a good carpenter does not blame his tools, neither then should any one worth there salt and willing to learn and to master the considerable intricacies of flying such a high performance aircraft that can and often does demand the utmost from a pilot, those who failed to do so of course blamed the

aircraft for their shortcomings. I for one will be first to admit it is definitely a "pilots" airplane that demands

respect during all regimes of flight, for it inherently retains vicious characteristics that could all too quickly bite an unwary or careless pilot on the ass, but for them that listened and learned to appreciate it's sterling qualities respected and enjoyed flying it.

Passing The Flame

IT HAD ALWAYS BEEN MY PRACTICE to encourage aspiring pilots and engineers alike, allowing them to accompany me on short runs. Like me at that age, they were eager to learn, hanging around the docks and airways, doing odd jobs and running errands; just happy to be involved in anyway and just to be near those beautiful, powerful bush planes.

I never forgot how enraptured I had been when, as a young boy, hearing those powerful beasts starting up. Coughing, spluttering and finally, in a very loud roar, catching; music to my ears. How I dreamed of one day going with those 'Gods' who flew them. What wonderful, exotic places were they going to see? I always made myself available when a plane landed, helping unload what ever, whether it be packages or fish. I was just happy to be involved. My pay was a fish in each pocket of my parka. A growing boy is always hungry.

As I grew older, by now being well known among the 'Old Timers' as a willing lad always eager to give a hand, they allowed me to scrub the belly of those beauties. Later came waxing and polishing. I now had my hands on those wonderful machines, and then one day, the joy of joys, I was given the privilege of washing and waxing the wings.

Much later I was permitted to sit in the co-pilots seat and watch while the pilot ran through the pre-flight checklists. Checking gauges and dials as I sat there mesmerized and totally enthralled.

Finally the day came when I was instructed on the start up procedures. When walking home later I don't think my feet touched the ground. I was walking on air! This started to happen regularly when one day a pilot tossed me his keys saying, "Okay Hart, start her up for me". I tried to look confident but all the while I was thinking, What? Me? God, what did he do? What did he say? I sat there in the Pilots' seat, momentarily blank, inwardly shaking, trying so hard to look like I knew what I was doing. I ran through the start up procedure, checked everything twice, set the throttle and turned the key.

I was so proud to be sitting there majestically, hoping some of my schoolmates were seeing my moment of glory in control of this powerful beast. I was truly 'king of the world'! My everlasting gratitude goes to all those 'Old Timers'. May they never be forgotten.

Looking at this young, aspiring lad had brought all these memories flooding back. Time to pass it on.

Hugh Carlson had been a close neighbour, ten years my junior but still a good friend. He was eager to help and passionate about aircraft. At 16 he was already taller than me, standing at 6 foot 6 inches. Later he would fill out to his true Viking heritage, a husky lad and just the person to help me load a huge fridge onto the Norseman. I was flying CFJDG that day and no matter what we tried we couldn't make that thing fit inside. It had to go somehow. Eventually we loaded that huge, heavy, propane fridge by tying back the rear door and allowing the fridge to stick out a good 18 inches. It was higher than the Norseman was wide and too big to turn so that was the only way.

The day was overcast with a promise of snow later, maybe. October was one of those months where any kind of weather could suddenly blow up. Our destination was the mining camp of Copper Lode Mining Co. on Fredalt Lake about 40 miles east of Red Lake. The miners were getting restless without fresh food. What looked like an easy run turned out as anything but. No sooner had we left Red Lake than the ceiling started lowering, the wind picked up gusting light snow, and the drag of the fridge sticking out didn't help. This was keeping me on my toes, literally dancing on the rudder pedals; the ceiling was getting lower by the minute. We were about 500 feet above the trees when, suddenly, the engine quit. Momentarily stunned, I couldn't think of why, and then I knew. I had been so involved with keeping the aircraft level I had forgotten the fuel gauge. I had estimated we had sufficient fuel for the trip there and back so I didn't give it another thought. I just had to switch tanks and while pumping furiously on the hand pump I realized we were now clipping the treetops as the Norseman has the glide characteristics of a greased anvil.

Glancing at Hugh I saw a white faced, bug eyed, young lad half way up the back of his seat while still firmly strapped in. Seeing me glance at him he finally managed to ask, shakily, "What ya gonna do, Hart?" Just then the fuel got through and the propeller roared to life. I had forgotten to slow the damned thing down and it took off with a scream. Smoke was seeping into the cabin with the smell of burning pine needles almost choking me while I was fighting to bring the prop under control. Hugh was now shouting above all the noise of the engine, prop and the thunder of breaking branches, "Do something Hart, quick!" Suddenly the trees ended at last giving us a clear space to pull the nose up but still we were only half way there. By this time the snow was so thick the visibility was almost zero. Regaining a little height we were able to avoid any further corpses. Gradually everything settled down to a mild scream and I only hoped there had been no damage done to the floats, as we needed them to land on the lake. Thinking back I had not heard any big bangs and felt no sudden pulls to the right or left as we banged through those treetops. And no fire; that was a close one. Now it was time to relax the pucker power, carefully plotting the rest of the way. We were still flying low when we finally reached our destination. Circling the lake we spotted the camp and the most welcome sight of a ready crew waiting on the dock to receive their much-needed refrigerator. Many hands made light of the work hauling the prize up to the cook shack where Hugh and I enjoyed a wonderful meal with many cups of strong coffee. We relaxed in the warmth with our new friends.

All too soon we had to leave. The storm had moved off allowing us a window to take off and return to Red Lake and the welcoming sight of the Green Airways dock. On the return trip Hugh had turned to me saying, "I can't believe how cool you were with all that was going on." Little did he know that I had been too busy to panic.

This experience did not dampen Hugh's eagerness, which was a great relief, as I did not want to frighten him away from flying. After that he flew with me quite often, usually quite uneventfully, apart from the usual ups and downs.